Luvvie Ajayi Jones is an award-winning author, podcast host, and sought-after speaker who thrives at the intersection of comedy, justice, and professional troublemaking. She is the author of the *New York Times* bestseller *I'm Judging You: The Do-Better Manual*, and her site, AwesomelyLuvvie.com, is where she covers all things culture with a critical yet humorous lens. She runs her own social platform and app, LuvvNation, which is a safe space in a dumpster fire world.

Luvvie.org

 @Luvvie

@Luvvie

# THE FEAR-FIGHTER MANUAL

*Lessons from a*

# PROFESSIONAL TROUBLEMAKER

## LUVVIE AJAYI JONES

**Author of the New York Times bestseller *I'm Judging You***

Quercus

First published in Great Britain in 2021 by

Quercus Editions Ltd
Carmelite House
50 Victoria Embankment
London EC4Y 0DZ

An Hachette UK company

A CIP catalogue record for this book is available
from the British Library

HB ISBN 978 1 52940 901 7
TPB ISBN 978 1 52940 902 4

10 9 8 7 6 5 4 3 2

Printed and bound in Great Britain by Clays Ltd, Elcograf S.p.A.

Papers used by Quercus Editions Ltd are from well-managed forests
and other responsible sources.

Dedicated to my warrior, my matron saint,
my grandmother, Olúfúnmiláyò Juliana Fáloyin.

# Contents

INTRODUCTION     xi

## BE

1. Know Yourself     3
2. Be Too Much     21
3. Dream Audaciously     43
4. Own Your Dopeness     59
5. Trust Where You Are     69

## SAY

6. Speak the Truth     85
7. Fail Loudly     107
8. Ask for More     123
9. Get Your Money     137
10. Draw Your Lines     161

# DO

11. Grow Wildly             183

12. Fire Yourself           199

13. Take No Shit           217

14. Build a Squad        229

15. Get a Nigerian Friend   245

16. Fuck Fear             265


EPILOGUE: COURAGE IN
THE TIME OF FEAR     273

*Acknowledgments*     281

# <sup>THE</sup> FEAR-FIGHTER MANUAL

# Introduction

I am a professional troublemaker.

What is a professional troublemaker, you ask?

A professional troublemaker is not the person who brings chaos into the midst of any room they are in. That person is a troll. A professional troublemaker is not someone who insists on speaking to hurt feelings. That person is a hater. A professional troublemaker is not someone who wants to disagree with people just because they wanna play devil's advocate. That person is a contrarian, and Satan never told anyone he needed a supervisor, so I'm not sure why so many people volunteer for the position.

A professional troublemaker is someone who critiques the world, the shoddy systems, and the people who refuse to do better. As a writer, a speaker, and a shady Nigerian, I am the person who is giving the side-eye to folks for doing trash things. I am the person who is unable to be quiet when I feel cheated. I am the person who says what you are thinking and feeling but dare not say because you have a job to protect, or you're afraid of how it will land. I even wrote a whole book called *I'm Judging You: The Do-Better Manual.* A book that I TRUST you've read by now. If you haven't, well, I'm judging you. *Clears throat.*

While a professional troublemaker isn't someone who manufactures chaos or crises, they do understand that chaos can come from being honest and authentic and going against the tide. Because in a world that insists on our cooperation even in the face of perpetual turmoil, not standing for it makes you a rebel. Professional troublemakers deal with it because they have a cause. They are often sharp tongued and misunderstood but always golden hearted. A professional troublemaker is committed to speaking the truth and showing up always as themselves, and is almost unable to bow in the face of a world that demands it.

People often ask me how I am confident in who I am, and how I have the nerve to say what I say. I've always shrugged and said I don't remember not being this person. Whenever I got in trouble when I was little, it was usually for my mouth. Being a Naija gal, I come from a culture that prioritizes age when it comes to giving respect, but that never sat well with me. Which is why Little Luvvie got punished usually for telling someone older that she didn't like what they were saying or doing.

But it's also because I come from a long line of professional troublemakers. My grandmother, Olúfúnmiláyọ̀ Fáloyin,* was the one I got to see as I was growing up. When I really give it thought, I realize I got a generation's worth of courage from Grandma.

---

*Pronounced Oh-LOO-foon-me-LAH-yaw FAH-low-YEEN.

My grandma was the chairlady of the board of directors of Team No Chill Enterprises. As an elder Nigerian stateswoman, she was the epitome of Giver of No Dambs.* She was too old to be checked. She knew how to take up the space she was given, and in the times she wasn't given space, she took it. She did all of this with a smile and charm that made her magnetic. She wasn't rude but she was direct. She wasn't hateful, but you would hear her speak her mind. She was open-hearted and open-handed and she prayed with the same fervor that she'd use to lambast you. She could not stand to see people cheated or treated poorly. In her honesty and given the fact that she approached everything with so much heart, she was deeply loved by so many.

This is the crux of what it means to be a professional trouble-maker.

## WHEN TROUBLEMAKING MEETS FEAR

My first book, *I'm Judging You: The Do-Better Manual,* asks us all to commit to leaving this world better than we found it. I wrote *Professional Troublemaker: The Fear-Fighter Manual* because in order to do better and be a professional troublemaker, you gotta do some scary shit. This book is the *HOW* to *I'm Judging You's WHAT.* How do we make sure we aren't leaving this third rock from the sun in worse shape than when we showed up? How do we make sure this rotating water sphere doesn't up and quit us? (Well, that answer, I don't know.

---

*Damb: Because it's more fun than "damn." Get used to this.

Mother Earth shoulda definitely kicked us clean off it by now because we've been such dreadful beings.)

There is a lot to fear in this world. In November 2017, I opened the TEDWomen conference with a talk called "Get Comfortable with Being Uncomfortable," which addressed this very subject. When the talk was posted, it was watched more than one million times in a month. At this point, it has received over five million views and continues to climb. Every single day, I get messages from people from all over the world talking about how much impact it had on them. The response lets me know that this idea of living through fear is a major pain point for people. We are afraid of simply showing up in the world, and it affects everything around us as a result.

But here's the thing: We're human. Fear is God's way of making sure we're not being utterly stupid and jumping off mountains without parachutes. God is like, "Let me put something in these beings I'm creating so they aren't constantly coming back here before their time. Because I know their goof-asses need limits." However, the same tool that keeps us from putting our hand in an open fire and leaving it there is the same one keeping us from telling our boss we cannot pay our bills because of how low our pay is, and that we need a raise to be able to live properly.

One of the things I've learned in my journey is how much fear could have stopped me at any moment from doing the thing that changed my life. Or doing that thing that led to me meeting the right person. Or doing the thing that allowed someone else to do the thing that changed their life. We talk about "living our best lives," but how are we gonna do it when we have fear holding our ankles down like some dad sneakers? (I will never understand why them

UGLASS* dad sneakers are a thing. Your feet look like they're embedded in some rocks as you drag those bulky things around all day. Why are people against nice things? Anyway, I digress.)

I don't think we can overcome fear. It's a constant fight and we will get endless opportunities to do scary shit. I'm not going to sit up here and say, "These are the tactics to do away with fear." Some degree of fear will always remain. But even though we're constantly afraid of being burned, not everything is a volcano with molten lava to avoid. Instead, we need to stop expecting fearlessness and acknowledge that we're anxious but we aren't letting fear be our deciding factor.

We have to learn to fight fear like we'd fight the hairstylist who messed up our haircut after we told them we only wanted them to cut two inches for a bob but they went on a trim spree and you ended up with a bowl cut. We gotta fight fear like it called our mama a "bald-headed, trifling bitch." We must fight fear like it drank the last glass of orange juice but left a swig and then put it back in the fridge. Rude AF.

Folks like me, who are committed to speaking truth to power, aren't doing it without fear. We aren't doing it because we are unafraid of consequences or sacrifices we are making because of it. We are doing it because we have to. We know we must still charge forward regardless. We must listen to the wisdom of mother Maya Angelou when she said: "Courage is the most important of all the virtues, because without courage you can't practice any other virtue

_____

*Uglass: Ugly + ass. Uglass.

consistently. You can practice any virtue erratically, but nothing consistently without courage."

For the professional troublemaker, the truth, of ourselves and of the things around us, is more important than the fear that stops us from pursuing it. The things we must do are more significant than the things we are afraid to do. It doesn't mean we don't realize there are consequences. It means we acknowledge that they may come but we insist on keeping on.

Professional troublemakers recognize that fear is real, and that it's an everlasting hater, but it must be tackled.

This book is a middle finger up to fear.

Now, I say all this acknowledging that there are systems that make saying "Fuck fear" riskier for some of us. Our marginalized identities compound the effect of wanting to step out of and over our comfort zones. I know that it can be a privilege to be in the position where you feel like you have the choice to be a professional troublemaker. That is why I'm hoping that this book, written by a Black woman, an immigrant who was poor at some point (but didn't know it), somehow allows you to have the gumption to be a troublemaker for yourself.

I think it is important that we know what our problems are, and that we create the solutions for them. We need to create the world we prefer to live in.

That being said, everything I ask of you in this book I ask of myself first, and I ask of myself always. This book is my excuse to tell *ME* to continue to make trouble in the best ways. It is me giving myself permission to not be fearless, because fearlessness doesn't exist. I think the fear will always be there, but what's important is that

I go forward anyway. This isn't a life of sine metu (Latin for "without fear"). It is a life of "I might be afraid but I won't let it stop me."

What I'm sharing in this book is what I would have loved to tell ten-year-old me so that she could always find the confidence to be different. Along with: Don't let them glue that weave in your hair for that college dorm fashion show. It's gonna pull out your hair and sabotage your edges for a couple months. It ain't worth it.

This is also the book I needed when:

- I knew I really didn't want to become a doctor but since it was the dream I'd tied myself to since I was little, I was afraid of choosing something else.

- I didn't call myself a writer even though I'd been writing four times a week for nine years, and my words were reaching people in ways I'd never imagined.

- I was asked to do the biggest talk of my career and I turned it down two times before saying yes because I didn't think I was ready, and I was afraid I'd bomb onstage.

This is also a book I need now, in the times when I'm not feeling so bold. It's a book from me to me that I'm letting other people read. Because even now, I still need the prompts I've put here. Even now, I still need to remind myself to do the scary shit I'm compelled to do and deal with how it falls. Even now, I still stop myself from time to time. This book is for me: the me from yesterday, the me from today, and the me in the future who will need the extra push. It is the book I want to give to my kids one day to embolden them to move through this world unburdened.

In the BE section, I'll be talking about the things we must get right within us before we can do the things that scare us. Because half the battle is with our own self, our own insecurities, and our own baggage. We gotta Harlem Shake it off. (Did I just age myself? I'm fine with it.)

In the SAY section, I'll be pushing us to use our voices for our own greater good, and therefore everyone else's. We're so afraid to say the things that are necessary, and it is part of the reason why we find ourselves constantly fighting a world that doesn't honor us. We've gotta say what is difficult even when our voices shake.

In the DO section, I'll be encouraging us to start putting movement to that voice we're unsilencing. A Ralph Waldo Emerson quote I love is "What you do speaks so loudly that I cannot hear what you say." It is time for our actions to start proving the truth of our words.

Throughout this book, I'm also going to share stories of my grandmother, because her life is truly my biggest lesson on living beyond your fears.

My hope is that the next time you want to do something that takes your breath away as you think about it, you'll find words in this book that tell you, "Yo. You got this. Even if it fails, you will be okay."

So . . . let's get to it.

*Me telling on someone to my grandma at her sixtieth birthday party, and her making it seem like what I had to say was the most important thing in the world. One professional troublemaker to another.*

# BE

We have to make some internal shifts if we wanna fight fear, because what we think is possible is a major part of how far we can go. In the BE section, we're going to talk through the work we gotta do within us, so that even when we're afraid, we're forward-moving.

"FEAR: HALF THE BATTLE IS WITH OUR OWN SELF, OUR OWN INSECURITIES, AND OUR OWN BAGGAGE."

—Luvvie Ajayi Jones

# 1

# KNOW YOURSELF

**We fear our full selves.**

 We are afraid of who we are, in all our glory (and grit). We're constantly searching for that person. Or forgetting that person. Or repressing that person. Instead of standing strong in who that person is.

Being FULLY ourselves is necessary for us because it serves as a grounding force. I find that's the case for me. There is a lot to be afraid of in this world, because, in general, things can be a wreck out there. And none of us need to be afraid of who we are in our whole personhood, because who has the time?

This standing in your full self isn't about being an immovable person whose beliefs are stuck in a rock. It's not that can't nobody tell you shit, or that you're not able to admit when you're wrong. Instead, it's about having a strong sense of identity. It's about knowing you belong in this world just as much as anyone else. It's about taking up the space you earned simply by being born.

One of my favorite poems is "Desiderata," written by Max Ehrmann. My favorite part is: "You are a child of the universe / no less than the trees and the stars; you have a right to be here. . . ."

"YOU HAVE A RIGHT TO BE HERE." You sure in the hell do.

Oddly enough, knowing this fullness of who you are doesn't make you more stubborn. Instead, it makes you more likely to grow, since you know you have a solid foundation that doesn't change even as you learn new things and new perspectives. This is a step you need to be a professional troublemaker. Because you will GET IN TROUBLE. Guaranteed. What makes you realize it's worth it? This process of knowing the fullness of who you are.

A lot of fear fighting and professional troublemaking is confronting things that will knock us off our square. Things that will slap us into dizziness and make us forget everything we know is real. We need solid feet, rooted in something strong, to continue to stand. Knowing ourselves is important because it provides that foundation for us. It doesn't allow anyone or anything to tell us who we are. Because when people tell us how amazing we are, that's good to absorb. But what about when someone tells us we aren't worthy? Or we don't have value? Or we don't deserve kindness and love? Or that we deserve paper cuts? To know thyself is to not take all the praise to head or take all the shaming to heart. To know ourselves is to write our values in cement even if our goals are in sand.

To know thyself is to know your core, and for me, to know my core is to feel rooted in something outside myself. It is to know not only *who* I am but *whose* I am.

# WHOSE WE ARE

Whose I am is not about belonging to someone or being beholden to people. It is about the community you are tied to that holds you accountable. It is about knowing you are part of a tribe that is greater than yourself. It is about feeling deeply connected to someone, and knowing that no matter where you go, you have a base. If we're phones, knowing whose we are is our charging station.

I learned the importance of WHOSE you are growing up. As a Yorùbá girl, I am part of a tribe that prioritizes our people sometimes as much as it prioritizes an individual. Collectivism comes alive for us through the traditional oríkì (OH-ree-kee).

What's an oríkì? It is a Yorùbá word that combines two words to mean "praising your head/mind." *Orí* is "head" and *kì* is "to greet or praise." An oríkì is a greeting that praises you through praising your kinship and speaking life to your destiny. It is your personal hype mantra, and can be spoken or sung.

The original attempts to tell you who you are make up your oríkì. It's used to remind you of your roots and your history. It might include the city your father's from, and where his father is from. It might include the things that make your family name special. It brags on your people. It lets people know who you WERE, who you ARE, and who you WILL BE. It reminds you of those who came before you and blesses those who will come after. It might even include some shade.

Oríkìs are often sung at birthdays and celebrations. They are also sung to see you off into the next life. An oríkì connects you to your ancestors, and it will move even the most stoic to cry because you feel it in your chest. Your tear ducts just give up the ghost and let the water go.

I am the granddaughter of a woman named Olúfúnmiláyọ̀ Juliana Fáloyin, and she's the one who serves as my compass. When Grandma would say her own name, she'd always say it with a smile. Which makes sense, because her name literally means "God gave me joy." It was like her very self and presence brought her joy. When they sang my grandmother's oríkì at her funeral, I got emotional because it was a poetic affirmation of her presence on this earth and a send-off. It was a standing ovation for her spirit.

This is part of my grandma's oríkì:


Ọmọ Ògbóni Modù lorè, mẹ̀rẹ̀ ní àkún
Ọmọ Fulani Ìjẹ̀ṣà a múni má parò oko ọni
Ọmọ a fi ọṣẹ fọṣọ kí ómọ Ẹlòmíràn fi eérú fọ ti ẹ̀
Ọmọ arúgbìnrin owó bọ̀dìdẹ̀
Ọmọ Olúmoṣe atìkùn àyà fọhùn
Ògbóni gbà mí, Ọ̀dọ̀fin gbà mí
Ẹ níí tó níí gbà lẹ̀ gbani


What it loosely means (because there are some Yorùbá words that don't exist in English, and it is really tough to give exact meaning) is:

The child of royalty . . .

The child of the Ìjẹ̀ṣà Fulani who dominates one and
   dominates one's property
The child who brings out soap to wash his/her own
   clothes while someone else's child brings out ashes to
   wash his/hers
The child that springs up money (wealth) in multiples
The child who beats his chest as he speaks (speaks with
   confidence)
Ògbóni, save me. Ọ̀dọ̀fin, save me
It is the one that is prominent enough to save you that
   steps up to do it

It ties her back to those who came before her and gasses her up.


I don't know my oríkì. Many of us don't. Like a lot of traditions, oríkìs have been de-prioritized as generations pass. I'm out here oríkì-less AF. But it's okay. I'm fine, really. I'm not mad at all that by the time I came along, folks were more blasé about it (clearly I'm low-key salty, but I'll deal with that with my therapist).

However, a lot of what we already do is derivative of oríkìs and we don't even realize it. The tradition of the oríkì isn't just in Yorùbáland; it's gone on through the diaspora. You can see it in the way people rap about themselves. It's in the way people praise God. It's in the way we say who we are in the moments we feel most proud.

When Christians praise God, we say: King of kings. Lord of lords. Alpha and Omega. The beginning and the end. The I am. The Waymaker. That's an oríkì if I ever heard one.

When we think about how people are introduced in something as made-up as the TV show *Game of Thrones*, it tracks. "Daenerys Stormborn of the House Targaryen. First of Her Name. The Unburnt. Queen of the Andals and the First Men. Khaleesi of the Great Grass Sea. Breaker of Chains. Mother of Dragons." THAT IS SUCH AN ORÍKÌ! Didn't you feel gassed up on her behalf anytime they introduced her? I know I did. That's what it is for!

I tend to write ones for people I admire to gas them up as I please. I've done a few in the past.

For Michelle Obama: Michelle LaVaughn of House Obama. First of Her Name. Dame of Dignity. Melanin Magnificence. Chic Chicagoan. Boss Lady of Brilliance. Owner of the Arms of Your Envy. Forever First Lady.

For President Barack Obama: Barack Hussein of House Obama. Second of His Name. Swagnificence in the West Wing. He Who Speaks in Complete Sentences. Shea-Butter-Skinned Leader of the World. Michelle's Boo. 44 for Life.

For Beyoncé: Beyoncé Giselle of House Carter. First of Her Name. Snatcher of Edges. Killer of Stages. Citizen of Creole Wonderland. Legendary Black Girl. Wakandan Council President.

For Oprah: Oprah Gail of House Winfrey. First of Her Name. Changer of the World. Protector of the Realm of Noirpublic. Creator of Paths. Breaker of Chains and Limits.

For Toni Morrison: Toni of House Morrison. First of Her Name. Architect of Words. Acclaimed Author. Shifter of

Culture. Netter of Nobel Prize. Writing Domino. Legendary
Laureate.

For Aretha Franklin: Aretha Louise of House Franklin. First
of Her Name. Dame of Detroit. Empress of Elevated Sound.
Reverberation Royalty. Vocal Victor. Sovereign of Soul.
Aural Authority.

For Janelle Monáe: Janelle of House Monáe. First of Her Name.
Citizen of the Future. Walker of Tight Ropes. Sprinkler of
#NoirPixieDust. Rocker of the Baddest Suits. Giver of No
Intergalactic Fucks. Head Android of Wondaland.

So, how do you write a simple *Game of Thrones*–style oríkì for
yourself? Here's the formula, and how I come up with the intros.

*First Name and Middle Name of House Last Name. Number of*
*Her/His/Their Name (i.e., Juniors are "Second of Their Name").*

That's the easy part.

The next part: Throw humility away. The point of this is to give
yourself all the credit. I want you to acknowledge the things that
make you proud and the things you have accomplished. They don't
have to just be professional, but they can be things that feel like your
superpower. Feel free to use royal titles for yourself (Queen, King,
Earl, Duchess), because why not? (If anyone from the monarchy is
reading this, sorry but not sorry for the appropriation.) Get creative
with your descriptors if you want. I am also a fan of throwing some
alliteration in there for extra pizzazz.

*Noun (occupation or descriptor) of Noun (thing).*

*Luvvie of House Jones. First of Her Name. Assassin of the Alphabet. Bestseller of Books. Conqueror of Copy. Dame of Diction. Critic of Culture. Sorceress of Side-eyes. Eater of Jollof Rice. Rocker of Fierce Shoes. Queen of the Jones Kingdom. Taker of Stages. Nigerian Noble and Chi-Town Creator.*

I could keep going, but I'll stop here. You need one of your own and I want you to write it. Now if you have the time. If not, come back to it.

I know you might be thinking, "But those people Luvvie mentioned are famous and extraordinary and hugely dope. I can't even measure up to that." And to that, I say, "Slap yourself." Right now, slap yourself. I want you to leave that kinda talk behind. Because yes, those are some AMAZING people, and they have achieved a lot.

But so have you. By being here on this earth, you have done enough. (We'll deal with impostor syndrome in a few chapters.)

What if you have a complicated relationship with your family members? Or you don't have any familial ties? Or you were adopted so you don't know your biological family history?

For those who might not have blood ties to the people they love most, you are still part of a people who cherish you, adore you, and are glad that you are here on this earth in this space and time. To you, I send love. Not knowing the binds that tie you by blood does not preclude you from belonging to a people or a community or a tribe.

If you are someone who can truly say you don't have an answer to

WHOSE you are, and this book has made it to you and these words are being heard or read by you, then you are truly someone who should laugh at fear. Cackle at it, even. Having no one is not a cause for shame here but one for pride, because it means you have moved through the world, drop-kicking these obstacles by yourself. You are a warrior. Your oríkì can start with ARMY OF ONE. You have battled life by yourself, and even though it might have bruised you and maybe almost drowned you, YOU MADE IT TO LAND! You are still here. High-five yourself. Army of One. Solo Soldier. Fierce Warrior. Rock of Gibraltar has nothing on you.

You might be reading this and saying, "I'm a stay-at-home mom. I don't have professional things to put in my oríkì." Well, being a mom is a whole job that you don't ever retire from, and you are constantly working overtime without pay. TRUST that there are a lot of accomplishments there.

*Raiser of Future Leaders. Keeper of Everyone's Shit Together. Master of Calendar. Expert of Efficiency. Queen of the Last Name Dynasty.*

Everybody needs an oríkì.

I need you to spend this time bragging on yourself. Type this up, write it up, put it somewhere you will remember. Laminate it, even. You will need this one day—in the moments when you see the worst of yourself or you fall flat on your face. You will need this when you feel like you have failed.

You know those times when you're talking and between every word, you're clapping your disbelief because someone talked to you like you're some useless nonentity? Yeah, those too. In those times, you can read your oríkì and remind yourself who you be (yes, who you be). After you calm down, or to even help you calm down, I want you to have this thing handy, to bring you back to the reality of how dope you are.

Cool? Cool.

## WHO WE ARE

Beyond knowing WHOSE we are, there's knowing WHO we are. Outside of our connections to anyone else, we have to know what is important. People often talk about searching for themselves and my simple ass be like, "Where did you go?" But that's me being basic. I know that all too often, we swallow back our impulses, needs, and wants so much that we forget what they tasted like. We lose the appetite to be ourselves because it's been insulted, beaten, trampled, punished, abused, and made fun of out of us. We look up one day and realize we've been performing who we are for so long that we have lost the map.

This uphill battle is no fault of our own. And it is by design that we swallow who we are to fit in. I am always taken aback when people ask me how I am so confident. I am confident because I am constantly doing work to ensure that I do not lose sight of me, so I never have to go looking for me.

When we are sure-footed in who we are, we always have something to come back to. When we know what defines us is not any job or thing we own or professional title we carry, it makes us less likely to lose our way if we lose any of those things.

If I feel like I might wanna lose sight of me or fade, I ask myself the following questions, and then I write the answers down. My fairy godmentor (she doesn't know I've claimed her) Oprah often talks about what we know to be true. Well, these questions have given me clarity to figure that out.

## What do you hold dear?

This is what is important to you. Is it family? Is it friends? Is it not losing your edges even though they're weak and wearing a knitted cap that isn't properly lined in the winter might cause your hairline to fall one inch backward?

## What are your core values?

Our core values are what we stand for and what guide us. Mine are:

*Honesty:* This is one of my top values, partly because I'm a bad liar and have a terrible poker face. But mostly because I want to feel trusted by those who know me. It's important that I am one less person others need to doubt.

*Authenticity:* I am who I am, no matter where I am or who I'm with. Authenticity is close to the honesty core value because it insists that I be honest about myself and how I show up. It doesn't mean I am the same all the time, but it means if I'm quiet, it's because I am allowing myself to observe in the moment. If I'm partying and being the life of the party, in that time I am feeling boisterous.

*Benevolence:* I think it's important to be kind, and being generous with the things we have is a major part of that, whether it's knowledge or time or money or energy. It means we are less selfish about our lives and think about what we can constantly give to the collective for the greater good.

*Shea butter:* Yes, shea butter is a core value because I think we'd all be better if we were more moisturized. Get some good body butter in your life and watch your life change. You wake up without rustling your sheets with your extreme ash.

## What brings you joy?

What makes your heart smile? Helping people by telling them what I know brings me joy. Having people tell me something I did or said made an impact on them melts my heart. Yes, there's a Captain Save-a-Planet complex there, but I'm working that out with my therapist.

## Even on your worst day, what makes you amazing?

At a time when you aren't in the mood to be the best you, what still makes you incredible, just as you are?

## What is worth fighting for, even if your arms are too short to box with God?

Let's say you know your uppercut is weak and your jab is rubbish. What will make you lace up your gloves anyway? What do you think you will make the "no violence" exception for? I know I can't fight worth a damb, so I gotta be clear on what will push me to fight if necessary. For me, it's seeing someone who doesn't deserve it be abused or rendered defenseless or voiceless.

## What do you want them to say when they're lowering you into the ground?

When it is my time to leave this earth, I want people to say, "The world was better because she was here." I also wanna make sure whoever tries to act like they wanna jump in with me because they're auditioning for Best Mourner of the World, y'all tell them to sit their ass down because this ain't the time for them to be attention whores. I'll be giving them a fierce side-eye from beyond.

All of these questions are things I ask and continue to ask myself, because when I've written the answers down and I go over them, they are the best memento of me. They are my life mission statement. They are my atlas when I find myself off course after a tough encounter or meeting or date or DAY. I look at it when I realize that I, and everyone else, seem to have forgotten who the hell I am (I sure felt it multiple times during wedding planning).

## YOUR LIFE MISSION STATEMENT

Write your own life mission statement, your compass. Here's the template. Fill this out.

What's your name?

Who are you proud to be related to?

Even on your worst day, what makes you amazing?

What/who do you hold dear? What do you cherish?

What are your core values? What do they mean?

What brings you joy?

What is worth fighting for, even if your arms are too short to box with God?

What do you want them to say when they're lowering you into the ground?

*Download this worksheet and other professional troublemaking resources at FearFighterKit.com.*

Here is mine:

*I am Ìfẹ́olúwa Luvvie Àjàyí Jones. I am the granddaughter of Fúnmiláyọ̀ Fáloyin and the daughter of Yẹ̀misí Àjàyí.* I am the wife of Carnell Jones. Even on my worst day, I can look in the mirror and be proud of the woman I've become. I have no regrets. My family, both blood and chosen, are who I hold dear. What I cherish is my life, lived happy, whole, and healthy. My core values are honesty, authenticity, benevolence, and shea butter. This means I tell the truth, I'm real to myself and others, I'm generous, and I refuse to be ashy because I should always prioritize being moisturized.*

*It brings me joy when I'm able to make someone else's life easier. Also, seeing my enemies upset. Because: petty. I didn't say Jesus was done working on me yet. What I fight for are people who feel like they are powerless or voiceless. When I'm no longer here, I want people so say, "The world was better because she was here."*

---

*Yorùbá is a beautiful tonal language whose alphabet uses accents to reflect the sounds. You'll see those accents on the Yorùbá words I have used throughout this book. My name, my grandmother's name, and my mother's name are written here fully accented to honor the traditional language. Moving forward, the accents won't be present on me and my mom's names because we don't use these accents in our everyday lives.

Colloquially and in the world, Yorùbá words, especially names, are often written without accents. When I write my own name, I don't include the accents, and I wanna honor myself in that. I went back and forth about this decision of whether to include them in our names throughout the book, and then I asked my mom for her opinion. She said, "I don't think it's necessary. We are who we are, with or without the accents."

I honor tradition as I honor self.

You can show it to others but you don't need anyone else to read it but you. Above all, it is for you.

This exercise not only lets you know who you are on paper, it also shows you who you aren't. We are often weighed down by other people's projections, preconceptions, and the patterns they expect from us. We are frequently defined by systems, stereotypes, and structures that are larger than us. To know who we are is to insist on knowing we are not what others put on us. We are not the names people call us. We are not our worst moments. So when people try to impose all this agony and trauma on us, we can say, "Nah. That's not my problem." Once you know who you are, it's easier to refute who you aren't.

Do you know who you are? Do you know how much fight it took for you to be wherever you are today? Do you know how many things could have gone wrong to keep you from even being born? Do you know that none of the people you are scared of and none of the situations you're afraid of are bigger than any of that? Do you understand how dope you are, because there are battles you have fought and mountains you have climbed that almost took you out? But they didn't. They did not. You are here now and one thousand motherfuckers shouldn't be able to tell you shit that makes you feel like you don't deserve good things.

Don't let people who can't spell your name right tell you about who you are. Don't let folks who only have courage behind a keyboard define your goodness or your worth as a person. Do not let people who are already rooting for you to falter insist on your value, because they will steer you wrong.

When you are tempted to believe someone's tainted version of you, or believe their projection of who they think you are, reread your mission statement. Remind yourself of who the hell you are before trying to remind anyone else. Because, ultimately, the world will continue to misunderstand us and call us patchy-headed scally-wags with lice. We can't control that. What we can control is our own image of ourselves, and how surely we are worth loving, defending, and redeeming. In all of our messed-up, scared glory.

Your professional troublemaking depends on it.

I hope you feel sufficiently gassed up. I hope this is a chapter you are able to come back to time and time again. I hope in future chapters when I ask you to do things that might be tough, you feel encouraged to know that you are okay. And that you are reminded that you are a legacy of a lot of things going right (even if a lot has gone wrong on the way to this point).

# 2

## BE TOO MUCH

**We fear being judged for being different.**

 When we talk about people being their full selves and how a lot of people are afraid of it, it's not that people don't want to show up as themselves. It's that they know that when they show up in their full splendor, they will be judged for it. Being ordinary and unremarkable is hardly a life goal, but we are often scared into being that way.

Even though people like to act fake-offended at the idea that they're being judged, we know good and well that we are all judging each other. We just happen to critique each other on the wrong things, like what we look like, who we love, what deity we worship, if any. Instead, we should assess each other on how kind we are, how we're showing up for other humans, and how we're contributing to the world's problems, large or small. (I also like to judge people on whether they drink kombucha, because I don't understand how anyone can appreciate something that tastes like moldy beer, toenail clippings, and bad decisions.)

We judge each other and are judged every single day on who we are and how we are. And oftentimes, people bang their internal gavel on us and decide that we are too much.

*TOO (adverb): "to an excessive extent or degree; beyond what is desirable, fitting, or right." (Dictionary.com)*

To be TOO something is to do or be something to a level that folks find to be uncouth. It's to be different.

Many of us have been called too loud. Or too aggressive. Or too passionate. Or too intimidating. Or even too quiet. Or too sensitive. Or too tall. Or too short. Or too Black. And when people say we are TOO something, they aren't making a casual observation. They are requesting that we change this thing, that we turn the volume down. Then we feel self-conscious or embarrassed, and turn inwardly to fix something about ourselves that someone else has defined as a problem.

The problem: What we've been told is too much is usually something that is core to who we are, or how we appear, and often it's something we cannot change.

How is someone too tall? Should they hunch over to come down to your level? How is someone too Black? Should they peel their skin off their body to have less melanin? I don't understand the gall that leads people to make some of these judgments. Unfortunately, we internalize these critiques and it leads to us worrying about being different in any way.

As a Black woman who is opinionated, straightforward, and unapologetic about it, I am secretary of Team Too Much. I even bring the kettle corn to our monthly meetings. I've been considered aggressive or loud or angry for simply being direct. Black women are often on the receiving end of the "too loud," "too brash," "too aggressive" notions, because our very being has become synonymous with too much. I'm convinced it's because people see the divine in us and it is too bright for them to deal with. Meanwhile, they better put their shades on and deal with all this Noir Pixie Dust.*

I especially balk at "too aggressive." When someone says that, did they see us randomly walk up to someone on the street and punch them in the mouth? Did we push someone into a wall for no reason? Did we cuss a nun out? Or is it that we didn't put enough eager exclamation points or emojis in the emails we sent a colleague? Did we ask for what we wanted in straightforward terms? How are we being aggressive? What have we done to earn that title? At least let me earn whatever you accuse me of.

Being accused of TOO MUCHness is to be told to take up less space. Being TOO much is to be excessive. How do you combat that? By being less than you are. And that concept feels like nothing other than self-betrayal. The inverse of too much is too little. I'd rather be too big than too small any day.

Can you imagine if someone walked up to you and said to your face, "I need you to be less"? You'd clutch your pearls and be

---

*Noir Pixie Dust® is what I consider to be the magic of Black people, especially Black women. Yes, I trademarked it. You know people like to steal from us.

offended. But THAT is what they're saying when they say you're too much—they're just saying it in a less accusing and more shaming manner, so you take it to heart. You internalize and absorb it and commit to changing yourself.

All for what? For the whims of people who are more fickle than a ripening avocado. (Seriously, how are avocados okay when you go to bed, and then you wake up to something that looks like a kiwi? Wonders shall never cease.)

Who we are should not be beholden to the moods of the people we are around, their insecurities, or their projections. Because when someone says you are too much, it is more of a statement on them than it is on you.

You ARE too Black for that white-ass person. Your melanatedness is blinding to the caucasity.

You ARE too tall for that short-ass person. Your height makes their neck hurt, but what's that gotta do with you?

You ARE too aggressive for that complacent-ass person. Your passion irritates their inactivity.

You ARE too quiet for that disruptive-ass person. Your calm makes them agitated.

You ARE too big for that small-ass space. Your vastness chokes their insignificance.

In all of these, your job is not to stop being this person you are accused of being. You aren't supposed to constantly shape-shift to make those around you feel better about their own insecurities or failures. Your job is not to chameleon your way through life to the point where you forget what your true colors are.

If you are too big, then it's a reflection that the place you're in is too small for you. It isn't your job to get smaller to fit there, but to find a place that is bigger than you so you can take up all the space you want and grow infinitely. Anyplace that demands you shrink is a place that will suffocate your spirit and leave you gasping for air. Who wins? Not you. Not anyone, really, because the version of you that they will get is the diet, fake-sugar, stevia version that probably has a bad aftertaste. They might THINK that's a great version because you're so dope that even you at half capacity is more on point than you expect. BUT they don't get the you who is free to show up and be your best, because you are spending time trying to be representative of whatever they think is palatable. And that constant shrinking and dwindling is how giants get locked in cages. You don't belong in a cage simply because it's where others want you to be.

My grandmother was the Queen Mother of Team Too Much International Association of Extra People. Being too much was woven into her spirit. She was too bossy, too confident, too aggressive, too brash, too headstrong, too assertive, too feisty, too strong, too dramatic. Mama Fáloyin, as so many people called her, was the definition of boisterous. Everything she did was big, and I don't think it occurred to her to ever shrink herself.

Let's talk about her theatrics. As an older Nigerian woman, being too dramatic was an obligation of sorts, a set of cultural mores to follow. It was destiny fulfillment. In fact, her entire existence demanded that after she got to a certain age, she had to be melodramatic; otherwise she wasn't doing it right. It made her a joy to be around even when she was upset, because it was often super amusing.

Grandma used to come to the United States once a year and stay with us for a couple of months at a time. She had a tendency to do the most, so of course she and my mom would clash from time to time. One day in particular, they had a major argument and Grandma, in all her feistiness, got extra upset.

This lady suddenly went in her room, threw a few things in a trash bag, put on her shoes, and came into the living room. She had on her house scarf, socks, and sandals. She threw on her coat and grabbed her purse. She looked ridiculous cuz nothing matched or went together, but that was part of the act. We asked her where she was going and she replied with, "I'm leaving. I'm going to go sit at the bus stop and wait for the people who pick up old people to come and get me." I didn't know when the laugh escaped my mouth, but it was too late to catch it. I cackled! She looked at me, all serious, almost offended.

ME: Grandma, who will pick you up?

GRANDMA: I don't know. Someone will take pity on me and come get me.

I wanted to be like, "Lady, stahp it." But I couldn't because I was not about to be the target of her wrath, so I had to fake-beg her to stay. You know she wasn't going anywhere. The trash bag made no sense, because this woman had perfectly good luggage, but she had to do her one-woman show. Also, is there some sort of random old-people pickup service that I haven't heard about? Like a dogcatcher for elders? Like a free Uber service for hysterical geriatrics? Whew! It was hilarious. You might say it was too dramatic, but at least it was amusing.

And TOO EXTRA? Well, she was a pro at that. When my grandmother turned sixty years old in 1991, she decided to do a seven-day celebration to commemorate her life. It was in Ìbàdàn, Nigeria, where she lived and where I grew up. She rented three massive tents and closed off three blocks in front of and surrounding her house for the festivities. No one had to RSVP because everyone was invited. I don't think folks counted, but there had to be about a thousand people who came each day. A cow was killed every day and served in delicious stew for everyone to partake in. The jollof rice was endless. Grandma hired Ebenezer Obey, who was Nigeria's top musician at the time, to come sing and perform from evening to sunup. Literally. He got off the stage at 6 a.m. She threw three major parties in those seven days, and her church choir performed. Come on, holy concert! They showed what an anointed turnup really is. We members of her family wore aṣọ ẹbí* the whole time. Mama Fáloyin herself wore the heaviest of laces, and gold chains so big she'd make

*Aṣọ ẹbí (pronounced asho-ehBEE) is Yorùbá for "clothes of kin." It's matching fabric we wear for special occasions, and it signifies to people that those in it are close family and friends of whoever is celebrating.

some rappers jealous. She had two cakes for each day. I especially remember the one that was in the shape of a Bible, because: super Christian. The whole celebration was A LOT. Some might even say it was too much. But why not? How many times do you turn sixty? Once! Do it big, ma'am!

Whether you thought my grandma was TOO anything, you didn't wanna miss that party. This same woman who people thought was too loud was the one people came to, to help them raise a ruckus when they were being treated unfairly or had a problem with some figure of authority. She was loud not only for herself but for people who she thought didn't have a voice to be loud for themselves. I remember plenty of times when we'd get visitors who were looking to her to mediate a conflict they were having with someone who was trying to cheat them. One phone call from her and it would be resolved. Her loudness was not just in service of herself, and people didn't consider her TOO loud when it was in their favor. It is also why she was deeply honored.


I am a proud Nigerian woman. But when I was nine, I moved from Nigeria to the United States and started at a new school, and my confidence in myself was shaken for the first time ever. It was one of the only periods in my life when I felt like I needed to shrink myself because I was too much. I was too different.

(Let the record also show that I didn't know we were moving. I thought we were going on vacation, like we had in the past. Nobody consults the baby or tells them the decisions, I guess. SMDH. What tipped me off that we had moved? When my mom enrolled me in school. I was like, "Wait. We're staying here? But it's cold." We had the nerve to move from balmy-all-year-round Ìbàdàn, Nigeria, to Chicago, USA, where the air makes tears run down your face for eight months out of the year.)

Anyhoo, the first day of school when I walked into my classroom, the teacher asked me to stand in front of all these strange faces and introduce myself. I immediately knew I was different, and I felt self-conscious in a way I never had before. Who I was and where I was from were too off path from what the people in that room were used to. It was my first time walking into a room where not everyone looked like me.

I was sure of nothing. Even the question "What's your name?" felt like a trap. The answer was Ifeoluwa Ajayi,* but right then and there, nine-year-old me knew that the kids (and the teacher herself) wouldn't pronounce it properly, and they'd make it heavy on their tongues, like it was a burden. My name felt like it was too much. It was too foreign. It was too Nigerian. It was too strange. And it wouldn't do.

I wasn't ashamed, because I am truly proud of my name and love it. But I felt like I needed to protect what is a sacred part of me. So in the three seconds after I was asked, I decided to introduce myself as Lovette instead. It was a nickname that one of my aunts would call me from time to time, because Ifeoluwa means "God's Love." (Lovette became Luvvie in college.) Every time afterward, when teachers looked at my original first name on their roll call list and frowned or said, "Whew, okay this one is hard," my decision was

_____

*Ifeoluwa Ajayi is pronounced as ee-FEH-oh-LOO-wah ah-jah-YEE, but please don't call me by my first name. It's reserved for the people closest to me. Luvvie will do. (Gotta draw that line. We'll talk more about boundaries in chapter ten.)

affirmed. (They also butchered AJAYI, which is not even a tongue twister but is often turned into one.) The message I kept getting was "This thing about you makes us uncomfortable."

As a Naija girl, I knew the way I spoke was also too strange. The fact that I called a pen "Biro" and cookies "biscuits" weren't my only clues; the first time someone called me an "African booty scratcher" because of how I spoke, I said to myself, "Oh chick. We gotta lose this accent quick, fast, and in a hurry." So I talked less and listened more to how my classmates spoke. By the time I started high school, I had lost most of the telltale sign that I was new: my Nigerian accent.

The one thing I didn't let go of was my food. I still brought jollof rice for lunch. I had briefly tried sandwiches, but I'd be craving spices by the end of lunchtime. So there were times I'd sit in the corner as far from my classmates as possible, to avoid the questions of "What is that smell?" and "What are you eating?" Abeg, face your front and let me enjoy my food in peace.

My heritage, my name, and my mother tongue made me feel too different. And as teenagers, being too distinct from your peers was not cool, so I did my best to not be TOO Nigerian.

Then I got to college, where the best learnings are outside the classroom. It was at the University of Illinois where I reclaimed my Naijaness. It was there that I met others with stories like mine, who also went by new names to keep theirs from being butchered. It was there that I realized that my perspective, which is very much informed by my culture, was one of my superpowers. It was there that I started the blog that led to the life I live now. It is where I stopped hiding the fact that I love switching back and forth between my mother tongue and English, even in a room full of non-Yorùbás.

Who I am in the world today is an unapologetically Nigerian American, Chicagoan, Black woman. As I inhabit all these identities and seamlessly move through them, that thing that was TOO MUCH about me is a major factor in my success. My humor and writing style are tied to all these parts of me.

I hope that a young Black girl or an immigrant who finds themselves in strange lands can see me and know they are not TOO much of who they are. I hope they know they too can let their tongue take them back to their roots without shame. I hope they know their name isn't too distinct. I hope they know they can thrive and build a life that they want, being exactly who they are at their core, even as they come to school smelling like stock fish.

I do not want us to allow people to squelch our TOO MUCHness.

Beyoncé is someone who people frequently say is too much. Her Sasha Fierceness. Her love of glittery onesies. Her out-of-this-world performances. Sometimes people get offended at how she dares to be so BIG, but it's clear she knows that ain't her business. Her job is to take up ALL the space she wants when she wants, and it has made her a living icon. It pays off because that is what has allowed her to be the greatest entertainer alive. After her historic Coachella performance, she cemented that title. She then STAMPED it after her incredible visual album *Black Is King*. LIVING ICON. If you disagree, argue with your step-niece. (This is my book and it's the truth. Bloop.)

I think about how Oprah Winfrey is constantly accused of being TOO MUCH for appearing on the cover of *O, The Oprah Magazine* every single month for twenty years. To run a successful magazine is no small feat, but to do it for two decades is the stuff of legends. Thank God she hasn't let people talk her out of what she's known to work.

Michelle Obama's book tour for *Becoming* was in arenas. People thought that was TOO MUCH too. Meanwhile, our Forever FLOTUS was making a whole documentary in those sold-out appearances. The book became a worldwide bestseller. The vision. The boldness. The guts. I'm so here for all of it.

Imagine if any of these women allowed people to convince them that what they wanted or who they were was TOO MUCH. The brilliance we would all be cheated out of would create a vacuum.

Shout-out to those of us who've been told we are TOO TALKATIVE. Or TOO MOUTHY. Some of us are now able to get paid good money for that as professional speakers. Some of us put the words we have in our heads on paper and write books that allow us to help our parents retire. AMEN! Our TOO MUCHness can really be beneficial. All it takes is time, opportunity, and prowess.

Whatever it is that people think we are TOO much of comes in handy when it benefits others. However, when it stops being of service to folks' lives and starts making them uncomfortable, that is when it becomes something we should stop. This reaction tells me our TOO MUCHness is clearly useful. That thing that we are too much of is our superpower, and we should wield it with pride.

The person who is considered TOO sensitive is probably someone with a high emotional IQ. They're in tune with how people are feeling, allowing them to detect when a situation will have emotional consequences. They're often really thoughtful about how they speak to other people, and they are the calm in storms. On trips, they're the ones who help mediate fights when everyone gets on each other's nerves.

The person who is TOO uptight is probably the one who is great at organizing the group trip. They'll make sure when everyone lands, they'll have transportation to the hotel. They will also make sure the itinerary is set and ready to go. That type A–ness is extra useful for a project manager.

The person who is TOO turnt is the one you end up on adventures with on the trip. Their spontaneous spirit means you will be sure to get into some fun shenanigans that you will never forget. We'll just hope you all don't get arrested while in a foreign country.

You might be wondering, "What if people are right if they say I am TOO something? How do I know I'm not ignoring valid critique?" Good questions.

I ask myself a few questions when it comes to determining what we should consider credible and what we should consider compost.

Is this thing hindering my personal growth?

Is this thing harming someone else?

Is this critique coming from someone who loves and respects me?

If the answer to all three is no, then wipe your shoulders off, pick your head up, and keep it moving. Otherwise, let's dig deeper on those questions.

## IS THIS THING HINDERING MY PERSONAL GROWTH?

The thing that people are saying you are TOO much of—does it hinder your personal growth? When the thing actively makes us behave in ways that are contrary to our core values and incongruent with the person we wrote about in our mission statements, it is worth taking seriously. I cannot say I hold benevolence in high regard and then be stingy with my money and time on a regular basis. If I have $100 in my pocket, see someone who is experiencing homelessness and asking for money, and all I reach for are three pennies I find at the bottom of my purse, then I am not honoring who I said I was. THEN I am probably being TOO stingy.

Am I being TOO brash and stern and rigid? Well, do I refuse to evolve my thoughts and ideas because I maintain that my way is the only right way? That can be an obstacle to getting better at humaning. This probably also means people think of me as an immovable person, which means I'm likely to end up with fewer challengers and more YES people. That is how people become unchecked terrors.

Maybe I'm TOO loud, therefore not encouraging others to be heard in a room I'm in, ensuring my voice is the only one that is being amplified, and not allowing a diversity of ideas to be represented. In those moments, we don't need to stop ourselves or think our ideas aren't necessary. But we can remind ourselves to step back. We can be intentional in knowing when to prioritize the collective voice instead of our individual one.

## IS THIS THING HARMING SOMEONE ELSE?

Is the thing that I am being critiqued about emotionally, mentally, or physically detrimental to someone else? If so, then yes, I should chill and go work on myself. The person who is called too aggressive might need to get their lives right if it comes with them being abusive to those around them. There absolutely are people who will put hands on other people, even those they say they love. Being physically aggressive mostly comes in handy if you're a professional boxer or an MMA fighter. But a regular human being who is known for constantly throwing 'bows? That is certainly not who I want to be, and that is not someone I want to be close with. Am I enabling their abuse? Will I feel safe around them? Will I be the object of their physical aggression?

Are you being too loud when you visit someone who has a newborn, therefore waking them up? Please take the time to shut up, because you deserve a cuss-out for being inconsiderate. That new mom or new dad has the right to drop-kick you out their house. Relax yourself. You can also definitely be too loud if you're in a movie theater or a library and you need to use your inside voice. (Lord knows I don't have any inside voice. I got an external articulation with my Nigerian ass. I whisper at 50 decibels, but God ain't done working on me yet.)

Does your sensitivity mean you cry anytime you are challenged, therefore using your tears to manipulate others into always giving you your way? There are people who weaponize their tears to avoid accountability. That's not sensitivity but manipulation, and it can breed a lot of resentment in your relationships, both platonic and romantic, because people feel like you invalidate their feelings. That's harmful because it says that they do not matter.

Frankly, sometimes when white women cry, it can literally put Black people in jeopardy. Picture it: A white woman feels challenged or uncomfortable about something a Black person said or did. Instead of using her words, she cries. Instantly, no matter what the initial catalyst of the situation is, she ends up being appeased, pacified, and pampered. We've seen literal white-woman tears shut down conversations, even if she was the instigator of the conflict. The other person? Ends up being scolded. Or fired. Or arrested. Or killed. When Lorelei cries, heads roll.

So yes, times like those can lead to someone else's harm. That is when you check yourself and do better.

Otherwise, we need to be clear about when we are being TOO to a fault.

If whatever you are being accused of is not somehow infringing on somebody else's rights or silencing somebody who has less social access than you, then what is the real accusation? We've all been in rooms with really loud dudes who won't use the shutthefuckup coupon code, and what they do is create disarray with no purpose. But when people accuse you of being loud, is it in the moment when you are trying to make the room better? Is it in the times when you are speaking for somebody who doesn't have a voice? Is it at the times when people would prefer that you not shake the table? In those instances, you aren't being too loud. What you are being is too inconvenient for that room. You've made that room uncomfortable.

## IS THIS CRITIQUE COMING FROM SOMEONE WHO LOVES AND RESPECTS ME?

If the "too much" is coming from someone you aren't sure has your best interests at heart or who has been hypercritical of you in the past, then it might not be something you should internalize. I surround myself with people I trust and love and who aren't afraid to pull my card. When THEY, my life's board of directors, call me in and tell me I am being TOO something (like stubborn, stern, thoughtless), I reflect, process what they say, and then figure out how I can do better and show up better next time.

If it's coming from someone who is a troll or a known hater or even someone who might be going through their own trauma in the moment, I have to take it with a grain of salt. This is especially useful in the age of social media, where thousands of people can make judgments on who we are at any given point. Imagine a tweet that goes viral, that has people you will never know and who don't give a shit about you coming at you. As they are telling you you're TOO something, you will need someone close to you to vouch for that thing to be given credence.

But here's the thing. Sometimes the people who tell us we are TOO something are those who love us dearly and want the best for us. They can be people who are closest to us (parents, friends, spouses) and really do adore the ground we walk on. They mean us well, but sometimes we hear "You are TOO _____" from them. It is possible that they are trying to protect us by making that judgment, but they can be projecting their own insecurities, anxieties, and fears onto us in the process.

You have a mother who is more of a quiet type? She might have told you she thinks you need to be more calm or to stop being so brash all the time. We've had family members tell us we're too skinny in an attempt to make sure we are eating as we should be, but it comes across as shaming of our bodies. And shout-out to all the aunties who have greeted someone with "You're putting on too much weight" or "You're getting too fat." They mean well, but the road to hell is paved with good intentions.

Many a kinfolk have created inferiority complexes in people they love with their declarations that we're TOO something. And instead of rejecting their callousness and letting their lack of chill slide off our backs, we take it to heart, blamelessly. Because the people with the ability to hurt us the most are those we love the most.

This third question should not be considered without the first two, because if we do take on what our family and friends say about us ALWAYS, even though the thing they critique does not hinder our personal growth or hurt anyone, we'll be walking replicas of them. Or we'll spend our lives trying to measure up to the person they THINK we should be. We'll be in constant pursuit of their validation, as opposed to constant pursuit of our own growth. And chile, that is exhausting.

Someone called you too tall? Do they not understand that it means they are less likely to need a step stool when you're around? Don't they realize that you can always see above folks at the concert so you can help narrate what's happening onstage? Plus, you probably take amazing group selfies because your arm has reach. Who needs a selfie stick? Not you!

Someone thinks you're too bold? It means you get anyone's attention, and that comes in handy in a crowded room. It means you aren't easy to forget, and that is charisma.

Someone thinks you're too emotional? It means when you're about to get a traffic ticket, you can probably cry on cue and make the cop feel guilty enough to give you a warning.

I'm kidding. Sort of.

So what should you do? BE TOO MUCH. And do not apologize for it. If your TOO MUCHness is not obstructing your personal evolution or actually hurting someone else, stand in it.

Notice I said PERSONAL evolution. Professionally, there is A LOT hanging on us being as un-different from what is expected as possible. We enroll in courses and workshops that teach us how to interview exactly like someone else. We pose for LinkedIn pictures in white button-downs so we can look very standard. If you like leopard as a neutral, you're told not to walk into an office wearing that because it's too odd for a business environment. You like red suits? Nah, we want gray or blue because red is too bold. You want to show your enthusiasm and take charge? You're told to chill, so you can be more of a team player.

We are taught that being TOO different is not welcome, so basing ourselves and our barometer, on our worthiness in our professional worlds, will lead us astray time and time again.

At work, we encounter a lot of people with a lot of feelings. Oftentimes, you are doing your job AND the job of babysitting other adults' feelings, without getting paid overtime for the emotional labor. That in itself is how a great deal of people get convinced that they are TOO MUCH. They are showing up to work in full Technicolor when the business model is all gray scale.

If we base whether we are TOO MUCH on our jobs, we will forever be too much. I wanna take the time to give kudos to those of you who are working and thriving in corporate environments. Those of you who have to go to work and talk to your coworkers in compliment sandwiches so they don't feel like you're being too aggressive. Those of you who learned to bite your tongue even when you wanted to tell that douchebag in the cubicle next to you to go straight to hell. Shout-out to the ones who know their boss is incompetent, yet manage to get work done in spite of them. You have to do your job and theirs, AND perform the politics. I see you. I salute you. I pay my respects to you.

I think about the Black women who have to show up to work after busting their ass to do amazing work, in spite of coworkers with fragile egos who reported them to HR for being "too _____." I see you, woman who knows she's smarter than everyone in that meeting but has to nod and smile so she isn't considered aggressive. I see you, person who shows up with straightened hair so she won't be considered too Black for a place that says they value diversity but the only other person of color is the admin at the front desk. You might have to do what you gotta do to keep these checks coming (until you can find a place where you don't have to wear these types of masks), and I got nothing but respect for it.

To everyone who has been told they are too much, that they are excessive in some way and made to feel like their extraness means they aren't enough, I see you. I feel you. I am you. So what do I do? I insist on being me. The totality of me. And then I add some extra me-ness.

Sometimes I add some extra ME seasoning on myself when I step into a room, because I want people to get used to looking at someone walking in, maybe not in a package they expect, doing good work, and being excellent.

I am often invited to speak at conferences or internally at Fortune 100s, and when I ask what the dress code is, I'm usually told business casual is safest. And check it. I LOVE blazers and oxfords and wing tips. Forty percent of the time, I dress like an old white man from Maine who owns a yacht. My closet is full of the finest in preppy clothes. However, there are times when I will shirk the dress code and defy it on purpose for the sake of being too different. Why? So people know that we belong, in all our forms, in whatever uniform we show up in.

Once, when I arrived at a tech conference I was hosting, the room was full of Chads and Everetts (white nerdy dudes). I was one of two Black people in the room. I showed up the next day wearing a shirt that had Lionel Richie on it, with the words "Hello, is it me you're looking for?" Because the MC they expected probably wasn't me, but there I was anyway. Take that, take that, take that.

I acknowledge that not everyone has the social or professional privilege to always be a rebel with a cause. And I am not here to make you feel some type of way about doing your best. Rather, I want you to keep your head above water in a world that might feel like it is trying to drown you. Do what you can when and where you can. Don't beat yourself up. Lord knows you got enough trees to cut down. You don't need to be your own personal thorn.

I am, however, here to let you know that you aren't alone in being told you are TOO MUCH. And there isn't anything wrong with you. I am encouraging you to examine the times you have downplayed yourself for the comfort of others. I want you to reflect on the times you have been made to feel like you do not belong or you do not measure up or your presence is somehow a nuisance because you are a highlighter in a sea of pencils.

You will always be too much for somebody. You wanna be smaller? Sure, you can try. Some people will still consider your attempt not good enough. You turned your ten down to an eight when they were looking for a four. Why even try? Just give them the full ten. We can bend ourselves till we break trying to conform. And I promise you there will still be someone who is not satisfied.

Your TOO MUCHness is a superpower, and haters don't wanna see you don your cape. So what do you do? Be so much. Be the full totality of you. Add some extra to the you-ness. Be TOO MUCH because no matter what you do and how hard you try, someone somewhere will still think you are TOO something. You #minuswell (might as well) give them real reason to think so. Be the Youest You That Ever Youed.

# 3

# DREAM AUDACIOUSLY

**We fear having too much hope.**

 We live in a world that often feels like the headquarters of Mayhem Enterprises, breaking our hearts into pieces every single day with chaos and madness. It is too willing to disappoint us with tragedies, horrific news, and bad hair hats. And we have to live in constant suspense, not knowing when these things will happen to us. Pandora's box is forever opening.

So I get why we fear dreaming. It's hard for us to get our hopes up that things will go the way we want them to. Yet, and still, we need to put this worry as far away from our psyches as possible. You might call it madness, but I call it necessary.

When we are afraid of having too much hope, we're actually afraid of being disappointed. We are anxious about expecting the world to gift us and show us grace, because what if we end up on our asses? So we dream small or not at all. Because if we expect nothing or expect something small, we cannot be disappointed when the big things don't happen. We think it's a great defense mechanism, but what it really is is a liability on our lives, because we are constantly bracing for impact. When we are afraid of thinking things can be too good, it can become a self-fulfilling prophecy. We think life, in all its summabitchery, is waiting to punch us in the neck and go, "OH YOU THOUGHT I WAS GONNA BE GOOD TO YOU?" so we don't dream because we don't even wanna give it the satisfaction of pulling the rug from under us.

This shows up in real life when we don't go after jobs we want because we already expect the answer to be no. We might not apply to the school we wanna go to because we think we have no chance in hell of being admitted. But what if we would have met a life helper or the love of our life there, or landed that perfect internship that would have led to the job of our dreams? Basically, we end up living the colorless versions of the lives we truly want, which then confirms that life is shitty.

Here's the thing. Life can absolutely be a filth bucket, even for people who TRY and STRIVE and DREAM. The difference is that those people can go to sleep at night and wake up in the morning knowing that they at least tried. They can take some small solace that they did what they could. Life's shenanigans can be off-the-chart levels for them. But they blame life, not themselves.

Many of us have lost our ability to dream, or we were never allowed to have it in the first place, since we live in a world that makes it really hard if you're not white, male, straight, Christian, able-bodied, and cisgender. We've been bound by oppressive systems that are designed to not give us an inch, even when we earn a mile. We have been shunned and disrespected and erased from the things we are entitled to. We are constantly living in default survival mode, so dreaming is a privilege and an allowance we haven't been able to afford. Imagination is also a benefit that has been yanked from us, because shit ain't fair. Glass ceilings have shown us that all we'll do by wanting more is continue to hit our heads on limits. So we wake up one day having been stripped of the very hope we need if we're gonna have a fighting chance at anything resembling equity in this world.

I want to dream like white men who have never been told there are ceilings for them, let alone caps. I think about the story of Summit and Powder Mountain.* What's Summit, you might ask? It's an invite-only social organization that has its headquarters on the mountain it owns (Powder Mountain). Let me repeat: An organization has property on a mountain that it has spent money on. DID YOU KNOW MOUNTAINS ARE UP FOR SALE??? Because I surely didn't.

Nah, let's talk about THAT. I'll give you the tl;dr (too long; didn't read), simplified version of the story. Summit started because a group of white guys who wanted to change the world for good would invite their friends for weekends in cabins on a mountain they liked in Utah. Then they started going to this mountain more frequently. So

---

*Alyson Shontell, "It's Official: 4 Young Founders Just Bought a $40 Million Mountain to Party On," *Business Insider*, May 7, 2013, https://www.businessinsider.com /what-summit-series-is-and-why-it-bought-40-million-powder-mountain-for -summit-eden-2013-5.

they thought, "Wait, since we're here so often, why don't we buy the mountain and invite more of our friends? Let's make this a thing." And they did just that, buying Powder Mountain for $40 million and getting others to invest in their dream.

I have a few questions that I'd love to ask them:

- How did the conversation about buying the mountain even go?

- Did anyone laugh at the first person who brought up the idea?

- Were they all high, and on what?

- When they reached "Okay let's buy the mountain" consensus, were they afraid of this idea?

- Who do you call when you're looking to buy a mountain? I know there's no yellow pages listing for that. (Meanwhile, I know I just dated myself with that reference.)

The audacity of unshackled white men is massive. The only way I wish to be more like them is by having the lack of oppression that gives me the freedom, gumption, and unmitigated gall to think it's even possible to own a mountain. I want that dauntlessness. The system that white men created, designed, and profit from, that makes the rest of us afraid of our own shadow while they step on our backs, is well done, ain't it? It works so well.

This must be said: It's not that the men of Summit are smarter or even braver than anyone else for thinking about buying a mountain. No. I mean, they are smart, but they (like millions of white men) benefit from being constantly centered, elevated, and catered to, so they have not been programmed to expect less from the world, like the rest of us have. Why would they not think of owning a mountain?

We need the nerve and rashness to dare to think these things are possible too, even when we know that we might need to be four times as good, three times as qualified, and twice as professional to get what they will have handed to them when they walk into a room in their cargo shorts, half asleep. So I say with this caveat and without naïveté: Dreaming big is in itself a privilege. However, I'm asking us to trick ourselves into thinking we have the privilege of dreaming big.

B eing audacious enough to dream means discovering the courage to think your life can be bigger than you can even imagine. But often, we don't get there because we are afraid of what happens when hope doesn't pan out. We fear how disappointed or heartbroken we will be.

That is why we have to take the risk and think that what we want to happen is even possible in the first place. Dreaming is a gesture of courage in itself, because to envision our highest timeline is to be bold enough to think someway and somehow, it could come to pass.

On my journey as an accidental writer, author, and speaker, there have been a lot of times I was afraid to dream too big, lest I be let down. But other times, when something happened, I realized it was because I had actually spoken that hope out loud, even if only to myself. Take how my life has changed after writing a vision statement more than ten years ago. In fact, let's rewind to even earlier than that.

Growing up, I knew exactly what I wanted to be: Dr. Luvvie was the dream, because I was bookish and I wanted to help people—you know, the hope of immigrant and first-gen kids everywhere. When we moved to the United States from Nigeria, that dream was one of the few things I brought with me.

Throughout my academic career, I didn't have to try hard to get A's. I would write all my papers the night before they were due or the morning of and get A's. But when I started college at the University of Illinois as a Psychology premed major, Chemistry 101 happened to me.

I attended that class every day and went to office hours with my professor and teacher's aide, but it was an utter struggle. At the end of the semester, I got my grade: a solid D. D for Don't. It was the first of my academic career, and I definitely sobbed like someone had burned my pot of rice.

After having a come-to-Jesus moment with myself—like, "Sis, you don't even like hospitals. You'd be the worst doctor ever!"—I went to my adviser and dropped premed, deciding I'd probably do better pursuing my psychology degree and getting my master's in industrial/organizational psych. I could still help people that way. YAY ME!

(Fun fact: I didn't tell my mom that I had dropped the premed part of my major, so three and a half years later when she came to graduation, she was like, "Okay, so where's the premed graduation?" Me: "See, what had happened was . . . I got this D in chemistry. I dropped that dream very quickly. But hey, I finished college in four years! YAY ME!" I'm an everlasting vagabond. Chei. I think at that point, she was basically thinking since I got out of college and ain't nobody call her about me getting in trouble or acting a complete fool, it was my life. She trusted me with me, which was a gift, because that could have turned out badly. HEY YOUNG PEOPLE READING THIS, DON'T TELL THIS LIE OF OMISSION TO YOUR PARENTS. I will not be held liable for it. Cool? Cool.)

As my doctor dream was ending, another was beginning. My friends peer-pressured me into starting a "weblog." And by "peer-pressured" I'm pretty sure I only needed one suggestion and I was into it. I started my first blog in early 2003; it was titled something emo like *Consider This the Letter I Never Wrote*. In it, I documented my whole college career, writing about exams I wasn't studying for, the D I got, roommate problems. The blog used Comic Sans font, so you know it was a mess. But I loved this new hobby, and my psychology classes too. I did a few marketing internships and realized I was good at marketing too.

When I graduated in 2006, I deleted that undergrad blog and started what is now AwesomelyLuvvie.com. New life, new blog! I'd work my nine-to-five job in marketing, but when I came home, I'd blog. As I wrote about the world and how I saw it, word of my blog spread, and in 2009, I won my first award: Best Humor Blog in the now defunct Black Weblog Awards. I was geeked because here I was getting recognition for my hobby.

Hobby. Yeah, okay.

Get this. I was afraid to call myself a writer. WRITER? WHERE? I was afraid of that title and all the dreams that could come from it that I would be unable to fulfill. Toni Morrison and Maya Angelou and Zora Neale Hurston. Those were writers. I was just a girl who put up blog posts talking about whatever was on my spirit. Writer? "Bish, bye. You can't measure up to that title." That's what I told myself.

I liked my job as a marketing coordinator for a nonprofit that trained organizations in telling their stories in digital media. I was making enough to pay my bills, which weren't many. I was fine. Except I wasn't. I was bored with the job, and I felt restless. But I wasn't going to quit. Nah, son. We don't do that. We will just swallow down the discomfort and keep clocking in every day.

What I should have remembered is that whole honesty-as-my-core-value thing. When I refuse to be honest with myself, the lies I try to tell, even to myself, don't go well. My work ethic is one of my strongest traits, but I started being a shitty employee. I would show up to work and give my some, not my all. I'd update my blog at my desk. And one day, I fell asleep at a staff meeting. Like, full-on eyes closed, head dropped. In a staff meeting of nine people. BRUHHHH. As an employee, I was being increasingly trash.

In April 2010, I was suddenly laid off. They said it was due to budget cuts. I had the nerve to be surprised, y'all. The gall to feel like I'd been blindsided. Sis, you've been a rubbish employee for months! In fact, they did me a favor by laying me off, when they would have been justified in firing me.

That layoff/firing was God and the universe pushing me to take a leap of faith to stand in this writer dream I was too scared to have. But I'm a stubborn goat, so I didn't see it as that. Instead, I was on

Monster.com sending résumés left and right because I needed my biweekly paychecks and insurance! This shoe habit was not going to keep itself up, after all.

Throughout this period, there were times I'd wonder if I needed to stop putting so much time into my blog, but I couldn't quit. Something wouldn't let me. I still didn't consider it anything but my part-time hobby, when all signs were pointing to the fact that my purpose was to use my written words to make people laugh and think critically, and to make the world better.

I was a writer. But I was afraid, because there was no real blueprint for me to follow, and I didn't feel like it was a tangible-enough profession. To make money as I job-hunted, I designed websites and consulted with small businesses and other bloggers to teach them how to tell their stories using social media (my specialty).

After a year and some change of looking for a traditional job (and still blogging), I finally got hired for a full-time position as the social media manager for a global food brand. I went into the office on that first day, decked out in my "I'm serious" business-casual slacks and a button-down. My first task was to create a deck for a campaign, and I was in there knocking it out! Then came 1 p.m. and the walls of that building started closing in on me. Isweartogawd I wanted to slide off my nice ergonomic chair onto the floor and lie there. My spirit was not gelling with this new job. That night, I wrote an email to my new boss. I thanked them for the job and notified them that it was my first day AND my last. Bless it, but I couldn't do it.

In the meantime, other opportunities continued to pour in, all related to my writing. I finally started wondering why I was so afraid of being a writer.

A few months later, I was credentialed to do press coverage on the red carpet and backstage at the Academy Awards (February 2012). I was chosen because a producer who loved my blog thought I should be there. There I was, in my role as Awesomely Luvvie, backstage at the Oscars, eating Wolfgang Puck's shrimp and chocolates, next to journalists from the BBC, CNN, *Entertainment Tonight!* Me. A whole me! WOW.

That experience shifted my world: I was in that room and breathing that air because of my gift, because of my words. How was I NOT a writer? I might not be Toni or Maya, but I was Luvvie, and the fear of the writer title had kept me from truly honoring my purpose. Fear can very concretely keep us from doing and saying the things that are our purpose. But when I made the decision that I was not going to let fear rule my life or dictate what I do, my wildest dreams started coming true.

After college, I had two big dreams that I put down on paper numerous times, through vision statements I'd written or random "life bucket lists" I'd made over the years. One was to write a *New York Times* bestselling book. The other was to help my mom retire one day. As a single mother, Yemi Ajayi has always been one of my prime motivations to soar in this world. The sacrifices she made—moving us to the United States and leaving everything behind, somehow managing to make a dollar out of ten cents—allowed me to dare to dream. And she did it with such grace that I didn't even know that we were one paycheck away from being out on the streets.

I've wanted to make her proud with my life, and I've wanted her last decades on this earth to be as worry-free as possible.

When I turned thirty in 2015, I decided it was going to be my year of "Afraid? Do it anyway." I was going to pursue anything that scared me or that I wouldn't typically do, like Shonda Rhimes's *Year of Yes*. That was the year I went skydiving, when I traveled solo to five countries, and when I wrote my first book. I climbed that personal mountain and poured out seventy-five thousand words that became *I'm Judging You: The Do-Better Manual*. I finally could write that book because I overcame my fear of calling myself a writer. The courage I needed didn't come from a special class I took or some diploma I got. It was literally a shift in how I saw the thing. The monster didn't stop being so big. I just decided to fight it.

The book was published on September 13, 2016, and on September 21, 2016, I got the phone call that it had hit the *New York Times* bestseller list at number five. I was officially in a club that came with special privileges and my life instantly changed. My fees doubled and doors opened for me that I didn't even know existed, which led to my other major dream being realized.

A month later, I called my mother and told her she could stop working because I could now handle the bills for BOTH of us. It was the biggest pleasure of my life to be able to show her that all her work and sacrifices were not in vain. My book hitting the *New York Times* bestseller list allowed me to tell my mom to retire. And that dream led me to the opportunity to write this second book, dedicated to Yẹmí's mother, my grandmother, Fúnmiláyọ̀.

It all began with a blog from a girl who thought she wanted to be a doctor but was really a writer. But she was afraid of that title, and what failing at it could look like. Then God was like, "My hard-headed child, I got plans for you. Trust me. Rest in it." And after my stubborn ass ran out of excuses and dared to use the title that scared me, things began to fall into place in a way that felt divine.

I was afraid because I couldn't find an example of a writer like me, but I became that example for myself. And because of that, I am now that example for other people. We are prone to thinking that if we haven't seen what we want, in the exact form we imagine it in, then it isn't possible. There's a Black girl somewhere who can tell her parents, "I want to be a writer, and I can do it because look at Luvvie." Oftentimes, when we want something that doesn't come with a manual, we are afraid of it, because we could lose our way since there's no map. Well, maybe WE are supposed to draw the map, so someone who comes behind us won't get lost. Create the map you didn't have. That's what I did. We must give ourselves permission to be who we want to be, even if we don't have the blueprint yet, and that starts with dreaming.

It is truly a blessing to be able to speak my dreams, even if only to myself, and see how they have been realized. I know there's no magical dream fairy that grants wishes. And I don't necessarily claim luck in this either. I think I've seen some of my wildest dreams come true because I've put in a lot of hard work. I also give credit to God's grace, because I know there are people more talented than me or people who work harder than me, whose names we will never know.

But I am always hopeful. While we may voice our wants, we may not always get what we dreamed of, in the exact form we dreamed of it. However, it is important to continue to dream, even in the midst of disappointment, because it opens up our minds and lets us see things bigger.

To many, dreaming is living in a fantasy world where all things are possible and therefore nothing is possible. It's child's play. It's a futile exercise. To some that's inspiring, and to others it's frightening. But when anything is possible and there are no parameters, it actually means more than we know can happen.

The lives we live are full of people's dreams realized. The things we use every day are born from the audacity of someone who thought it was possible. There are many times when I'm traveling and I'm in awe of the fact that I'm in a tin can in the sky. When I'm eye level with clouds and think, "Bruhhhh, whose great-great-great-great-grandparent would have thought this was possible?" that shit feels magical. Science is made up of imaginations that ran wild and dreamed magical things that actually became achievable.

So why don't we operate our lives in this way?

I often think about all that my grandmother overcame to become the fierce woman I ended up knowing, like being orphaned at seventeen and having to start life over. That woman, born in 1931, ended up doing things and creating beings that led to me. Through dreaming that her life could be what she wanted, I am here today, standing on her shoulders. Her existence convinces and coerces me to let my imagination run wild. So I owe it to Fúnmiláyọ̀ Fáloyin to think of pies in the sky with my name on them.

She dreamed of raising children who would be God-fearing and good as people. She dreamed of having a family that would never know the suffering she went through. She dreamed of more than what she had in front of her, as a young girl from Lagos, making a way in a world that thought it owned her. Her ferocious spirit knelt for no one, and even as a wife, she maintained her independence. She saw the world and lived loudly.

I've written this book knowing that if she were alive to read it, she would go to everyone she knew and tell them that her granddaughter was a published author, that her name will be known by people far and wide and never forgotten, in a book written by the baby girl of her third child. It would make her do that grin of hers where she'd show every tooth. She'd circle every mention of herself and show each one to everyone she encountered. I think about how proud she would be to be in the center of a book that I am claiming now, in print, will sell millions of copies and inspire people to live their best lives (let's DREAM). She would take cabs and make the drivers stop and read my book with her, as she paid for her fare. She would tell them to buy eight copies for them and their children. She would be the best marketer EVER for this book and anything else I did. I am my grand-mother's wildest dream and, honestly, it is the pride of my life. If I accomplish nothing else, I can know I've done that.

When we dream, we're giving others permission to do the same.

When our dreams are big, we're telling the folks who know us that they don't have to be small either.

When our dreams come true, we're expanding the worlds of others because now they know theirs can too.

We must dream and dream boldly and unapologetically.

Sometimes we must dream so big that we make people uncomfortable. That is actually when you know you're doing what you should—when you mention something to someone and they gasp. YES! LOSE YOUR BREATH ON MY BEHALF.

You might be saying, "Wait. I gotta tell people my dreams? What if they jinx it?" No, you don't have to tell everyone all your dreams. I think it's most important that you tell yourself first. Others do not have to know. Not everyone is entitled to your deepest desires. Some people don't deserve the insight into our goals. Our lives aren't about those people. Our dreams can't be stopped by them either.

BUT . . . but . . . keeping our dreams to ourselves doesn't necessarily mean we're on the right track either. There are many times when I mention my goals to someone and they go, "Wait. I think I know someone who could help." There are times when my dreams have been spurred forward by someone I met at the right place when I decided to be bold in my words.

In 2018, I was burned out from traveling so much and working so hard, and I decided that I would take the month of July off. I had the privilege of being able to make that choice, and I recognize that. I made a declaration to myself and even posted it on Instagram, saying, "I'm not going anywhere or getting on any planes unless Beyoncé or Oprah call."

So what happened? I got a call from Yvette Noel-Schure, Beyoncé's longtime publicist, inviting me to the queen's first North America stop of her On the Run II tour. CAN I COME? YES I CAN COME!!! And I hung up and laughed and laughed because my life is weird and I keep saying these weird things out loud and they keep happening.

I've learned that the audacity to speak my dreams out loud, even if only to myself, has taken me far. I marvel at how many times the things I have dared to say have come true. The things I have let myself dream about. I ask, not with entitlement, but with hope, and magical things have happened.

Have the audacity to dream and ask. Sometimes the universe/ God amplifies the ask to bigger levels, and that is the best surprise. You have everything to gain, as they add suya seasoning and Maggi cubes to your desires.

If we do not give ourselves permission to dream, how do we give ourselves permission to thrive? So give yourself the allowance to think about that thing that feels too big and too far to touch.

Life's adventures never promised a straight path, and that's often what stops us. But we must dream. All we have, even in the worst moments, are the dreams of better things to come.

# 4

## OWN YOUR DOPENESS

**We fear being perceived as arrogant.**

 We spend our lives trying to be humble and modest, because we've been told that to do otherwise is to think we're superior to others. We dedicate a lot of time to ensuring that nobody can accuse us of being too proud. A part of me is all, "Yes, let's keep perspective and stay grounded." Another part of me is like, HUMILITY CAN GO TO HELL. LET THESE HOES HAVE IT.

Sometimes you gotta show up, show out, and let people know that you have arrived, so they gotta make room.

There is an oft-posted quote that says, "Carry yourself with the confidence of a mediocre white man." In the previous chapter, I talk about having some of their gumption, but I don't wanna carry myself in the way they do it cuz that confidence is bland AF. It might be ballsy, but it doesn't come with much swag. Instead, I want us to carry ourselves with the confidence of an older West African woman who has been through some things, come through on the other side, and doesn't look like what she's been through. A thousand useless goats can't tell them nothing.

My grandma was the queen of Smell the Roses While Here. What does that mean? It means that woman was not shy about accepting any and all love sent her way. Growing up with her, I saw what it was like to be unapologetic about how awesome you are. It wasn't that she was arrogant or went around to people declaring how amazing she was. Nah. She didn't have to. But others made sure they told her how incredible she was. And not only did she say thank you, she also sat in the compliment and let it fill her heart up. She didn't run from it, make excuses for it, or diminish herself in an attempt to seem as humble as she was supposed to be.

Mama Fáloyin loved the Lord with all her heart. And like many Black grandmas around the diaspora, she had a main line directly to Jesus and His Holy Posse. So, on Sundays, where would you find her? In church, of course. She was a staunch Christian, and specifically a member of a denomination called Cherubim and Seraphim (C&S). Actually, correction: She was a prophetess at the church. No no. I'm not giving her all the glory yet. Her official title was the Most Senior Mother-in-Israel Prophetess Fáloyin. I want you to read that again. My grandma had a certificate from the church crowning her as THE MOST Senior Mother-in-Israel Prophetess Fáloyin. I laugh about how things and people do the most, but she literally WAS the most. I don't even know what that whole title actually means, but if there's one thing Nigerians love, it is grand titles. The longer, the better. The more grandiose, the better.

Members of the C&S church wore white gowns, prioritized praise and worship, and therefore spent five hours at each church service. My grandma herself contributed to making each service at least thirty minutes longer. Lemme tell you why.

Service started at 10 a.m. Praise and worship went on for about thirty minutes. Then Grandma would show up at around 10:30. (Because why should she be on time? A WHOLE her.) When the pastor and choir learned that she was outside and ready to come in, EVERY-THING stopped. I'm talking record scratch. Stop the presses, and stop the singing. Her presence was then announced to the church as the doors opened, and a whole welcome committee met her by the doors to usher her in.

Then, music started playing and my grandma, like the perpetual holy bride of Christ that she was, made her way down the aisle dancing. As if that wasn't extra enough, Grandma would dance five steps forward but stop to take two steps back, for true peppering and scattering! BRUH! She took her sweet time, and the mini-carnival lasted all the way down the massive church till she took her place at the pew in the first row, at the seat only she could occupy. If doing the most was a sport, that lady was a Hall of Famer. Entrance theme music? Welcome committee? Interruption of services? Dancing for your life? CHECK CHECK CHECK CHECK.

The church insisted on doing this regularly, and Granny, not being shy, protested minimally. She reveled in it. And that in itself is revolutionary behavior, in a world where you are not encouraged to celebrate yourself.

We do not all get a weekly celebration of our very presence via song and dance, but there is something to be said for how we would handle it if it ever came. Many of us don't even know how to accept compliments. Someone tells us our shoes are cute and we're quick to go, "These? Please. I just pulled them out the back of the closet," when a simple "Thank you" could go a long way. People might tell us, "You look amazing," and we go, "Nah, you." There is, of course, nothing wrong with exchanging compliments, but how often do we do it because we are uncomfortable with being praised? How often do WE praise ourselves after doing something great? How often do we sit in the good vibes of someone SEEING us, acknowledging it, and sending some words to prove it? We don't get a gift for being the most self-deprecating in a room. Or being the one who can make fun of ourselves best. We have mastered that. Now I want us to master the art of owning our dopeness.

What I learned from my grandmother is how to allow myself to be truly celebrated. Women, especially, have been told that humility is a required character trait. And somehow, that humility has been turned into perpetual self-deprecation. We've been convinced that the more we downplay our awesomeness, the better the world is. As if knowing we're the shit is somehow a threat to the climate. As if accepting celebration of our wondrous ways makes gas prices go up. As if knowing we wake up and piss excellence is a cause of world hunger.

This permeates everything we do and how we move through the world. When you are not used to owning your dopeness, odds are you're actually covering up how amazing you are. We're not gassing up ourselves like we should, and how does that show up? It means we end up selling ourselves short.

Some of us struggle with telling our friends and family our accomplishments and good news because it seems like we're bragging. But your achievements are factual things. Not speaking about them doesn't mean they didn't happen. And you know what? If speaking about them makes someone feel like you're bragging, so what? AND SO?

You post or send a text about something you've done well. And the person who sees it on social or receives it rolls their eyes at you BECAUSE YOU DID WELL. Or they unfollow you. Or they delete your number. Is that someone you actually want in your life? Is that the person you want to sit next to you every day? Is that the person you want to invite to your home? No? Okay then, why do they matter? Why do their thoughts about you actually make a difference? And then, what if this is someone you actually do not know at all and have never met, and they are mad and call you arrogant because you keep winning? What does this person have to do with you? Should this stranger be the reason you now keep your leveling up to yourself? Is this person the one who will stop you from celebrating yourself?

NO.

Do not let people make you feel bad for being successful, and for being you, and for being amazing, and for being accomplished. If people get upset at you for announcing something you did, those people are not your people. Those people do not deserve your dopeness. And those people serve no important role in your life. Anyone who is upset that I'm doing well is an enemy of progress, and I don't need them around me.

Let's be real. Standing unapologetically in how good you are and how worthy you are will have some people not liking you. Because sometimes we reflect other people's shortcomings. We are a mirror of their failures. And because of that, we will be the target of disdain because people want that confidence and resent it in us. That is perfectly okay. Thankfully, I'm not motivated by others' hate, but if I were, I'd have a trophy shelf where I've collected my naysayers' tears into bottles of various sizes.

Owning your dopeness is not about being liked by others. It's really about being liked by you first. One of my favorite proverbs is "When there is no enemy within, the enemy outside can do you no harm." If you are strong in yourself, the actions of everyone else are less likely to move you.

There are really terrible people who think they're amazing. And people believe them strictly because they've convinced others that they're the shit. Knowing that there are subpar and mediocre-ass people out there who think they deserve all the good in the world and want heaps of praise, when your EXCEPTIONAL ass is questioning yourself at every corner, makes me fight the air. Trust and believe that there are people with far fewer skills than you who cannot be swayed from thinking that a party should be thrown in their honor every day. People who cannot hold a torch to you are out here crowning themselves. Never underestimate the effect of confidence. If you believe you're the dopest thing walking, you might convince people of the same, just because you're so headstrong about it as a fact.

It's time to accept we're incredible specimens. You do not have to wear a T-shirt saying, "I'm the greatest of all time." I'm not saying be arrogant, but I am saying we err on the side of humility to our detriment. Do. Not. Shrink. We've had so much practice shrinking ourselves and trying to make ourselves smaller that when it's time for us to take up space, we don't even know how. Even when we are called, we run. Even when we are celebrated, we tell people it's too much. Even when we're told to speak, we use a whisper. Why? Who are we helping by being muted versions of ourselves?

Some of us not only make ourselves smaller, but we apologize for our very being. We actually say sorry for our presence, as if we exist as some sort of transgression to others. We say sorry when someone passes us on a sidewalk, as if both of us don't have a right to be there at once. We even say sorry for our FACES. I've seen people write on social media about a picture they posted, "Sorry that my face looks like it does." Wait. You are asking people for forgiveness for your visage? HOW? WHY? What did your face do to them?

But I get it. A lot of it is tied to our past traumas, low self-esteem brought on by years of criticism, and other layers of baggage. The world has thrown enough daggers at us that holes remain. This isn't the book that will help you break through those (because that is a book in and of itself). I simply ask that you stop apologizing for your existence and for the things attached to your body. Even if you feel like you should, I am here to tell you that you should not.

And if you don't want to do it for you, do it for the young child in your life who is seeing you apologize for your vitality. Stop saying sorry for yourself, so that the young person can know that they are also not supposed to apologize for who they are. That their existence does not warrant apology but warrants celebration. That the world is better off for them being here.

It makes me so sad that we do this, especially women.

Somewhere along the way, they told us our glitter was ashes. They told us that what we touched turned to dust, not gold. They convinced us that we bled as punishment, not purpose fulfillment. Somewhere along the way, our magic was minimized. They said we were ordinary, not walking proof of miracles. And we started believing them. We did. We let the world tell us we had to apologize for ourselves. We had to be polite but stern, sexy but not too sexual, bosses but not bossy, confident but not cocky, motherly but not matronly. We had to hide the rough edges they created in us and be soft but not fluffy.

And Black women? Well, we've been told we're the mule when we are the mother of all of this. We are jewels. We are the reason for poems to be written, sappy love notes with metaphors that seem hyperbolic but are more grounded in truth than you know.

Somewhere along the way, we were told we weren't enough when we are truly EVERYTHING. We are literally LIFE everlasting. We are God's vessel. Science can't explain us. We are magic. Don't let nobody tell you shit. You're made of pixie dust. They just don't know what to do with it.

N ot owning my dopeness almost had me missing out on a major blessing and honor. Lemme tell you that story.

In the beginning of 2016, I was getting ready for the year of *I'm Judging You*. My first book was going to be released in September, so at the top of the year I was focused on that.

In March, I got an email from the OWN team, congratulating me for being chosen as part of Oprah Winfrey's inaugural SuperSoul 100 list. It was a list of one hundred people who Oprah thought were "elevating humanity." I read the email and basically laughed because I just knew it had to be spam. This must be from the same Nigerian prince who said he had $342 million inheritance for me. LMAO. Good one.

Then I got a text from someone who works at an agency that works with the OWN team to tell me to check my email for something important. I was like, "Wait. Was that email real??" I had to go into my spam folder to retrieve it. Sure enough, it was legit. I had been chosen as one of a hundred people who Oprah thought was doing some dope things in this world. BRUHHHHHHHH lemme just lie here in disbelief.

After I managed to close my mouth and call a few people I love while squealing, I finally read the email and saw I was invited to a SuperSoul 100 brunch, just for those who Lady O had chosen.

When I showed up, I was sitting at a table with Sophia Bush. I looked over at the next table and saw Ava DuVernay and Arianna Huffington. Then I looked across the room, which was on the OWN lot, and saw Janet Mock and Zendaya. I was truly floored. In my head, I kept yelling, "How did I get here amongst these giants? HOOOWWWWWW? Was a mistake made?"

No mistake was made. You're dope. You're in the room. Own it. OWN it. Tuck in the impostor syndrome and charge forward. Allow yourself to be celebrated, even among luminaries. You belong.

That is how I finally met Oprah, after being in many rooms with her over the years but never having the courage to introduce myself.

On three previous occasions, I actually said that when I finally met her, she'd have already heard and known my name. Well, this time she chose me to be in the room with her. And I was still shocked by it.

All of it is related, and when you aren't standing in your greatness and you're questioning the grace you find, it is impostor syndrome at work. How often do we let that lack of trust in our amazingness block our blessings? We'll tackle that in the next chapter.

M y grandmother always celebrated herself. I still think about how she smiled with her whole face whenever she told us what she was up to or a new thing she'd done. She was earnest in her pride in herself, without diminishing herself or others in the process. And she would not allow others to speak for her. I remember going to a doctor's appointment with her, and the doctor, seeing this older Nigerian woman, assumed she couldn't understand English. He turned to me and said, "What is her birthdate?" Grandma, not missing a beat and smiling widely, said, "Ask me. I was born July 31, 1931." And I sat there like, "You heard the lady."

I want to be like her. If arrogance is the worst thing about me, then I'll be really winning. If thinking highly of myself and being self-affirming is a fault, I want to be the walls of the Grand Canyon.

Speak of yourself and your work with exclamation points, not question marks. When someone asks you who you are and what you do, speak definitively. "I write." Not "Well, I kinda write, sometimes?" If you don't know, they don't know. We must honor ourselves in a world that doesn't want us to, and we will wait for nobody's permission.

And above all, do not question the grace.

# 5

# TRUST WHERE YOU ARE

**We fear success.**

 What would happen if we showed up as the best version of who we are? How many excuses would we run out of? How would our lives change? Who around us would change? What would change day to day?

We often talk about fear of failure, but fear of success is just as real, if not more so. A lot of times, we know we have exactly what it takes to get what we want or to see our dreams realized, but it scares us to think of how limitless our lives can really be. Maybe we're scared by the possibility of living up to whatever excellence we achieve. Maybe we're unsure that if we taste success, we'll be able to sustain it. Or maybe we worry we can't handle what comes with it. What would it mean for us?

My fear of success is certainly real, because I know that new levels bring new devils. Oftentimes, that's what I'm truly afraid of, even more than the failure part.

A lot of this worry comes from impostor syndrome: questioning whether we deserve whatever the opportunities are, which leads us to talking ourselves out of winning before we even get into the race. Why are we so afraid of what could be that we never give ourselves a chance to soar?

My grandmother didn't finish high school, because when she was eighteen, her parents died and she had to make a way for herself and her little sister. She never got any major degrees, but you couldn't tell that woman she didn't belong in any room she found herself in, whether it was a room where the president of a country was or a room full of taxi drivers. She didn't waste time questioning herself.

That TED Talk I mentioned, which changed my life and has millions of views? I wrote that talk early in the morning, in a taxi on the way to the airport for one of my work trips, because I wanted them to reject it so I wouldn't have to do it. That's how afraid I was of it. That is how afraid I was of what could happen—not if I failed but if I was really good at it.

Back in July 2017, I was invited to speak at TEDWomen by curator Pat Mitchell, the legendary journalist and correspondent. I wanted to say YES because I had wanted to do an official TED Talk for a while! I'd done two TEDx Talks before, but this was an invite to do a talk on the official TED stage. I was already booked for a different conference in a different city that day, so I hit a *wall slide* and declined. These are champagne problems, I'm aware. Still.

Two weeks before TEDWomen (which was happening November 1), I got the schedule for the other conference, and it turned out that the only thing happening the first day was an optional VIP party. I was like, "Wait. Maybe I can drop by TEDWomen in New

Orleans for a day to cheer on my friends and then head to New York." So I hit them up and let them know I'd like to have a day pass to the conference. Upon which they were like, "Why don't you come speak?" And I was like "WAIT WHAT?!?" Pat Mitchell wanted me to take the stage while I was there.

And this is where I panicked and did the thing that is a surefire way to hustle backward: I let fear dictate my decision making.

Here's the thing: TED is really picky about speakers and preparation. People get coaches, talks are vetted, and when you take that stage, you have been prepped extensively for it. Those talks don't soar for no reason. There is a lot of work behind them! So, here I am, two weeks before a TED event, being asked to take the stage. I'm in my head like, WHAT ABOUT MY COACHES? I DON'T EVEN HAVE A TALK YET. OMG TWO WEEKS IS NOTHING.

I did not want to take that stage and bomb. I was not gonna embarrass myself and shame my family name on that big stage. Who did I think I was, to be jumping in last minute? NAWL. So I decided that I was gonna decline (again) and tell Pat I'd be in the audience cheering. I wrote out a three-paragraph email expressing my regret about how I wished I could make it work, but I could not. I was tired after a really full fall of city-hopping for the Together Live tour, and I did not want to bring less than 100 percent to their stage. I was afraid I would fail with drowning colors. Right before I hit Send on the email, I decided to call my girl Eunique Jones Gibson.

ME: Sis. They asked me to do a TED Talk and it's in, like, a week and a half and I think I'll decline because I'm not ready. Everyone else has had months to practice and coaches and here I am sliding in at the eleventh hour.

EUNIQUE: Well, you ain't everybody.

ME: Well, shit.

EUNIQUE: You've been on a stage twice a week for the last six weeks. You've been speaking professionally for almost a decade. Everything you've done up until now has been your coach. Everything has prepared you for this. You're ready.

ME: Whoa.

EUNIQUE: And if they didn't think you could do it, they wouldn't have asked you. You are doing it.

ME: Gahtdamb. Drag me, then! My edges. Here, take them.

EUNIQUE: Aight, get off my phone and go prepare for your TED Talk. Kill it. *Hangs up.*

Bruh, she got me SO TOGETHER. I went in my email and deleted the draft I was going to send Pat. But a part of me was still shook.

The next day, I wrote my talk. While I was in an Uber. On the way to the airport. My one-hour trip to the airport was spent crafting this talk, and I hit Send on it as the car pulled up to O'Hare airport.

I was expecting the TED team to be like, "Luvvie, what is this nonsense? No, never mind. We made a mistake." And I woulda shrugged and said, "Y'all sure did. Whew." I would have been fine because I was looking for any reason to chicken out. But they loved this talk! HOWWW???

Then they told me I needed to be in New Orleans two days before the conference so I could practice, which was required of speakers. I couldn't be in NOLA until the morning of November 1 because I was getting an award in Chicago the day before (brag on yourself, folks!). Again, champagne problems. I was like, "Well, here's the part where they kick me out, which is fine." But instead they were like, "Ah. Well, let's do video rehearsal, then."

Oh and the conference was starting at 6 p.m. on November 1. To make my other conference, I had to take the last flight out, which was at 8 p.m. I let them know, thinking, "Okay, this is the last straw." Pat replied by telling me it was no problem, and they would make sure I was the opening speaker at TEDWomen so I could make that flight.

Every time I thought they'd be like, "This ain't gon' work. Thanks but no thanks," they found a work-around to another one of my (valid) excuses.

At this point, the punk in me wanted to lie out on the ground. I was fresh the hell out of excuses and I REALLY had to do it. I was going on first, after the intro.

I MEAN. Talk about votes of confidence.

The night before the talk, I was at home rehearsing to an audience of one: my husband, Carnell. He was like, "This is pretty good, but I think it's missing something." So I sat down at my computer and read it over and over again, and started changing things. Before I knew it, I'd changed half of the talk, because I wanted it to be the best it possibly could. The new version was one that infused more of my story. It was better. Much better. And over the next two hours, I rehearsed it more times and prayed to God that I would get on that stage and not fail.

The next morning, I hopped on the flight to New Orleans, exhausted because I'd gotten so little sleep from reworking my talk and from being the last-minute packer that I am. I was on that flight looking downtrodden, with tote bags under my eyes. But instead of sleeping, I put my head against the window and repeated my talk to myself over and over again because I had decided to do it from memory, and I still didn't have it memorized.

When I arrived, I kept reading my talk script, and going through it over and over in my head, because I wasn't using any prompts besides the slides that would run behind me. There was no confidence monitor or teleprompter that would help me. I was spooked because this wasn't a talk I had given before.

I don't get too nervous when I'm about to give talks, but for this? I WAS NERVOUS AF. And I was going to be the first speaker! The one thing I wanted to guarantee was that, at least, I'd look good. My yellow blazer, with black blouse, and black jeans, paired with hand-beaded Italian slippers, were my version of a security blanket. Even if I sucked, I wanted folks to be like, "Her speech was trash, but she looked GOODER DINNAMUG." I had my signature red lip, and some drippage in the form of diamond jewelry on. Let's do it!

The time for my talk arrived quicker than I realized it would, since time conspires to embarrass you sometimes. Pat announced me and I walked on the stage, onto the red TED circle, and saw the audience. But before I could say the first word, my mic pack fell off the back of my pants.

*Ha!* Way to start. So I had to stand on the stage in front of all these people as the sound guy came out to adjust it. Oddly enough, this calmed me *a lot* because hey, shit happens. I took the opportunity to be all "HEY Y'ALL!! How you doing?" It worked some nerves off, because one of the things that were bad that could happen had happened. And I didn't die. It actually wasn't even a big deal.

And then I started my talk. In ten minutes, I dropped more than seventeen hundred words, challenging people to be truth-tellers committed to doing and saying what was difficult because that is necessary for us to move forward. I used myself as the example, how my life changed when I decided to stop being led by fear. I used the idea of being a domino, because the first one to fall causes others to do the same.

Ten minutes and fifty-four seconds straight through. No stops. The TED Talk I gave is the one you can see now.* There is no editing magic. I never paused because I forgot a line. I didn't run backstage to go check my script because I lost my way. My voice did not shake. It poured out of me like I had been doing that very talk for years.

I said my last sentences: "It is our job, it is our obligation, it is our duty to speak truth to power. To be the domino, not just when it's difficult—especially when it's difficult. Thank you."

---

*View the TED Talk at http://go.ted.com/luvvieajayi.

I immediately ran off the stage because I had not forgotten that I had a plane to catch (it was 6:25 p.m. at that point). But before I could leave, the stage manager turned me around and said, "I need you to go back out there and see the standing ovation you're getting right now." And I walked back and saw people on their feet cheering for me.

I was overwhelmed in the best way. I coulda cried, but I didn't have time! I took a bow and ran right back off the stage.

I jumped in the car and made it to the airport by 7:10 p.m. I ran through the airport and made that 8 p.m. flight with thirty minutes to spare. On the flight, I was exhausted but geeked. I was geeked, y'all. I knew I'd killed it. I had done something to be proud of.

A week later, I got an email saying they would like to feature my talk on TED's home page on December 1. I coulda fallen off my chair, because TED doesn't guarantee when talks go up. Some don't see the light of day for six months after they happen, and mine was picked to go up in less than a month.

And surely, when that day came, "Get Comfortable with Being Uncomfortable" was front and center on the TED home page. Within a month, the talk had received one million views. And now, millions have watched it and the number is still growing. Most important, the messages I've been getting from people all over the world who let me know how my talk spurred them to take an action they might not otherwise have taken, have stuck with me.

This talk. This thing I did. In it, I talked about being more conscious of not letting fear lead my decisions, but sometimes I need my own reminder. I let fear of not being ready almost keep me from doing this very thing. Doing the talk was being my own domino, because I thought I wasn't ready. I was proving my own point, even in the process of getting to that stage. It wasn't that I wasn't fearless, it's that I did it anyway. And when we are honoring our gifts, we have to stand in them.

Impostor syndrome is the cousin of fear. Both are boundless bastards.

Impostor syndrome is the feeling of wearing a mask and playing a role that you don't feel at home in. It is present in those moments when you feel like you or your work are a fluke, and that you're a dwarf among giants. Many of us have experienced this, especially when we're in some sort of creative industry. Why? Because we are our own worst enemies and we do not give ourselves enough credit.

I let impostor syndrome trick me into thinking I didn't belong on that TED stage, just like I had when I questioned how Oprah could have chosen me for the SuperSoul 100 list. Let me repeat this. I let impostor syndrome tell me that I was not worthy of where I was being placed and the opportunity that was presented to me. But impostor syndrome lies.

How many times have we let impostor syndrome convince us that we should say NO to YES questions? How many times have we dropped the key to the door we should be opening because we didn't think we were ready? How often have we allowed fear to talk us out of that room that could be life-changing?

How many times has impostor syndrome told us not to write the book, not to audition for that play, not to apply for that job that we are qualified for? How many times have we let impostor syndrome keep us from doing the work we're supposed to do?

We let the voices in our heads spin tales of inadequacy, and we believe them. We look in the mirror and wonder if anyone else realizes that we're just faking it. That voice that is throwing hateration in our confidence dancerie has been allowed to take over, and we sit there thinking we're playing a part we aren't qualified for. We let it convince us that we are not good enough.

Impostor syndrome tells us that we need to be perfect; otherwise we are failing. We need to realize that perfection is the enemy of progress and it does not exist. If you're constantly striving for perfection, you'll be so afraid of failing that you won't create that thing because you'll think it's not good enough. So then you don't let it into the world. Then nobody gets the value of your work, because we never see it because you're too busy constantly trying to perfect it. Take the pressure off.

Impostor syndrome convinces us that what makes us different reduces our worth, when it is truly the opposite. As I said in chapter two, our difference is often our superpower. As a professional speaker who has taken stages all over the world, I find myself in rooms where I am often the ONLY Black woman, and I happen to be the keynote. Instead of letting it OTHER me, I use it to affirm how necessary my work and my voice are.

My Blackness, on those occasions, is an anchor for me. When I walk out of the room, those in it will not forget who I am. You might not remember Scott and Tim, but you're going to remember Luvvie, who came in her fedora, her red lip, and sometimes a pair of crispy

Jordans or wing tips. I must remember that I'm not in there because anyone is doing me a favor. I am there because I bring value to any space I'm in. My opportunities are not from people taking pity on me, but are a result of consistent hard work over a sustained period. To deny that fact is to betray myself and the work I've put in. Impostor syndrome be damned.

My job while in the room is to give value and then try to figure out how I can ensure I am not the ONLY next time. I must recognize my privilege and figure out how to use it so I can leave the door open behind me for someone who looks like me. Because the next time I'm in that room, I don't want to be the ONLY (Black person, woman, person with rhythm, etc.).

Why should I feel out of place? Because I'm not like everyone else in there? Sure. But I am not any less than they are. How did the other folks make it? It's not necessarily because they're smarter. It's not automatically that they know more than I do. It's not because they're more clever. It's that they found the cheat codes or knew somebody who knew somebody.

Impostor syndrome tells us that everyone else is better than us, because they seem to be further ahead or have their shit together more than we do. It tells us that we deserve less than we're worth, because we are replaceable. Impostor syndrome will have us questioning what people say about us that's good. We will ignore the fact that they say we're smart, talented, and gifted, and that the work we do is necessary. But the moment someone tells us something opposite, we take that on as fact. We will, very quickly, believe somebody's negative ideas about us but question five people telling us something positive.

What would happen if we actually took on the positive things people are saying about us, instead of internalizing all the negative? Maybe impostor syndrome wouldn't have such a strong hold on us. Maybe we could use the logic of those numbers to boost us up when we think we aren't ready for a big moment presented to us, or ready to start that business or ask for that promotion.

It lies to us. Impostor syndrome is a liar, and too many of us have accepted it as truth. How do we fight it? How do we kick it out of our heads, or at least turn the volume down?

I remind myself that:

**I am not the best. I don't have to be. I am enough.** The idea of "best" is temporary. The person who wins a race won it once. The next race, they might no longer be the best. Are they at least in the top three? Did they beat their own time from the last race? We can reach for being the best, but thinking we've lost just because we didn't win is the quickest way to psych ourselves out.

**I've worked my ass off.** At minimum, that hard work has earned me a ticket in. Even if I am not the best, the fact that I KNOW that I work hard is enough to grant me admittance to that room. My grind got my foot in the door. I can at least give myself that.

**Even if I happen to be in the room by accident and by no doing of my own, I AM IN THAT ROOM. It is no longer an accident. Once I'm in there, I am already worthy.** How

do I make it intentional and purposeful? What is my assignment while I'm breathing in that air? I take the opportunity
to learn from the best. I walk away from that room inspired,
with a resolve to be a superior version of myself. So next time
I AM in the room, I feel at home in it.

I've ended up in spaces with the people I admire most, and each
time, I question how I ended up there. EVERY SINGLE TIME. But
after I reflect, I go back to some of those reminders. I worked hard
for this. I don't have to be the best. I am enough. Since I am here,
then it is no accident. I walk away knowing that I need to keep doing
what got me in that room, and I need to keep doing it well.

Impostor syndrome does have some redeeming value. It keeps us
humble. It keeps us curious. Doubt has purpose sometimes. If
we don't think our work is good enough, we strive to do better and
be better. Which then makes us greater because practice does just
that. It turns us into lifelong climbers who DO end up belonging
in any room we end up in, because we've continued to work at our
craft.

The folks who are unequivocally confident in their abilities are
the ones who do not become better at their craft. They think they're
so good that they just need to show up. They are the ones who don't
grow, because they're too busy singing their own praises and patting
their own backs without the compulsion of evolution.

Practice makes you get better. People who are great at things have
committed to something long-term, and done it repeatedly.

M e, in my yellow blazer, black shirt, and red lipstick—I stood on that TED stage and was exactly who I am. I was reminded that my journey was unfolding exactly as it should.

And to think, I almost said NO. When the YES I said changed my life in the best way possible. And what I had to do was trust where I was, and trust that I was ready for it all.

# SAY

We need to use our voices. In this section, I ask us to speak up about what we want and need, because our silence doesn't serve anyone. Being quiet about our lives, stories, problems, and lessons does us no favors. When we want to say something and our voice shakes, we should take that to spur us forward, because that is when it is most necessary. Let your voice tremble, but say it anyway.

"WE'VE GOTTA SAY WHAT'S DIFFICULT EVEN WHEN OUR VOICES SHAKE."

—Luvvie Ajayi Jones

# 6

# SPEAK THE TRUTH

### We fear the power of honesty.

 We are afraid of the truth. Point-blank period. We don't like hearing it, sharing it, or seeing it. The truth can be the boogeyman. What's wild is that the truth is essential in a well-functioning society, so how are we doing when it isn't welcome, let alone prioritized? We're doing terribly.

We fear honesty because it exposes the rawness of life and our flaws, which we are too willing to ignore. It calls us to the carpet, because once you know, you can't unsee the ugliness of what was exposed. You might even have to do something about it. The truth challenges us to change and be better, and those are all tall orders.

We are also afraid of rocking the boat, which often comes with speaking the truth. We don't want to disrupt harmony in our spaces, and that tends to happen when we challenge what feels comfortable or expected. This is why I believe that one of the biggest forms of courage is being radically honest and transparent.

One of my favorite quotes is "A lie can travel halfway around the world while the truth is putting on its shoes." (Google never knows exactly who said it, as it's attributed to, like, five different dead old white guys, but it's a whole fact!) There was a study done by the University of Massachusetts* that found that in a single ten-minute conversation, most people lied at least once. It's what we do, and we're so used to comfort and harmony that we put those above all else. It's not that we're all lying for the sake of it; we are doing it for self-preservation and to be liked. But oftentimes, it bites us in the ass. It is part of why we are in constant disorder.

Do I lie? For sure. Everyone does. I'm not gonna sit up here and tell you I don't because that would be a lie. But I try really hard not to spew falsities, and I've been that way since I was young. I've known for a long time that I don't know how to lie well because I don't have a poker face at all. My face is a visual outside voice and all my thoughts are loudly written on it. When I'm lying, you can tell.

Growing up, I wasn't the kid who was getting in trouble for climbing trees or touching fire. I was a very self-assured child, so when I got in trouble, it was because of my mouth. I was always defending myself or somebody else. "That's not fair" was one of my favorite phrases as a mini-human. In fact, I'd often get in trouble for saying something that was so direct that it would come across as

---

*University of Massachusetts at Amherst, "UMass Researcher Finds Most People Lie in Everyday Conversation," *Eurekalert!*, https://www.eurekalert.org/pub_releas es/2002-06/uoma-urf061002.php.

rude, then I'd get in further trouble when I'd try to justify what I said. And when I was punished, I didn't understand why I was in trouble for telling the truth.

My very Nigerian mom probably wanted to wring my mouth a few times. I'm actually sure she did. And when she did punish me, I'd tell her that I felt offended and that she owed me an apology. I would write her letters expressing my disappointment in her disappointment and how I felt like I got the short end of the stick. Bruh, I really tried it. Petite and bold.

Even though I'd take whatever punishment came my way, I've known for a long time that truths make people deeply uncomfortable. What did I do, as the professional troublemaker that I am? Made a career out of it. But that was a true accidental happening.


I started my first blog in 2003, as a freshman in college. It was before Facebook, Twitter, Instagram, all of that, back when Myspace was on its last legs. I enjoyed talking about my undergrad life and all the ensuing shenanigans. Writing my thoughts online was a gift to myself, because it allowed me to write in the way that felt most authentic, most real, most truthful.

Blogging was not a career for me then, because it was still considered "playing on the internet." But because I didn't consider it a career, I couldn't fail at it—that was a gift. Since I had no expectations, I didn't doubt my writing or my voice. And when you are writing like nobody's reading, it's going to come out in the truest way possible because there's no agenda. That lack of pretense allowed me to write the things that sometimes made people feel uncomfortable. And as people began to see me as the person writing what they were thinking but didn't dare to say, I gained an audience.

As my blog got bigger and bigger and I got my first awards for it, I realized that people thought my work was extraordinary. I was confused, and not even on some fake-humble shit. Seriously, I was like, "Why? All I'm doing is writing what I think about the world and telling what I see is truth." Then I wondered what everyone else was doing. Were they bullshitting? Were they in these streets not coming correct? It was years before I realized that what made me stand out was the simple act of being straightforward and authentic. I wrote without deceit.

Collectively, we aren't used to truthfulness. It's not because we are bad people, but we shirk honesty so often, even in small instances, that when the big moments come, we don't have the language or capacity for them. If we lie in casual conversations, what happens when we're confronted with important things that really matter or make an impact? We don't have the practice.

I'll give you an example of a small moment. Your friend walks up to you and says, "So I got this new haircut from a new stylist. Do you like it?" You look at your friend and somehow their bangs are cut crooked and this stylist has sabotaged their hair. It's not really curling all the way over.

Your instinct is to instantly say, "Yes, of course I love it." Because right then, you don't want to hurt your friend's feelings or rock the friendship boat. I understand. But then your friend takes a selfie and drops it on Instagram. Now they have a different angle of this haircut and they're like, "Aw hell. That was not what I wanted. This looks really janky!" They come back to you and say, "I just posted my picture on Instagram. Why didn't you tell me my bangs were busted? I asked you if you liked my haircut, and you said you did."

Your friend knows you lied to them. You didn't love their haircut. I know you wanted to make sure you didn't hurt their feelings, but now your friend has a reason to doubt your word. The next time they ask for your opinion, they might be wondering if you're telling them the truth or giving them an answer that appeases, without candor.

In a world that is overflowing with things to side-eye and question, let us not be the type of people who others feel the constant need to distrust. Instead, I want us to be the friends or village members who others count on not only to please them, but to see them at their best. In that way, honesty is a love language. Affirm me with facts. I cannot say I am my sister's or brother's keeper if I'm expected to lie to you constantly. How can I care for you when I can't be open and honest with you?

So how would I deal with that small moment of the haircut gone wrong? Well, two ways. If it's completely messed up AND your dye job is weak, I might have to tell you since you asked me. If it's simply not MY taste, I might reply with something like "What matters is that you like it. If you like it, I'm good with it." Smoothhh. You can't accuse me of lying. Of course I also believe in "Friends don't let friends be raggedy without telling them."

But what about the times when somebody asks us something big or drops a problem at our feet and says, "What do you think?" What about when we are faced with injustice that makes us feel less than, or someone else is doing something that harms us and we have the opportunity to address it? Because we don't want to bring tension, we might let the truth go by the wayside.

I see meetings as a microcosm of the world and how we move through it. You can test out life in a meeting, and *Lord of the Flies* can happen. How many of us have been in meetings where somebody drops an idea that is at worst terrible and at best ill-thought-out? All of us. The answer is all of us. When it happens, often the room goes silent as people try to decide whether they should say something and challenge it. Oftentimes, no challenges ever come. Whenever I see public backlash from a company or brand for airing an insensitive commercial or tone-deaf campaign, I always wonder who was in the room. Who did not tell the truth about the wackness of whatever it was? There is always at least one person there who knows the shit ain't gon' land well. I always wonder, "Why didn't that person speak up?"

Person 1: They're tired of always being the one to speak up, so they're taking a break.

Person 2: They felt it wasn't their department or charge, so it has nothing to do with them.

Person 3: They felt like it wouldn't be welcome in that room.

Person 4: They felt like they would get punished for challenging it.

All of these are valid reasons.

If you are person 1, I feel you on a spiritual level. You've earned a break, and you are really hoping someone else picks up the trash. I am not even mad at you.

Person 2, I also get it that you want to mind your business. Unfortunately, this is your business. It can affect you if the results of the campaign hit the brand hard and they have to make cuts as a result. It can quickly become your business. We are too willing to absolve ourselves of responsibility about the things that happen in our midst under the guise of minding our business, and it is to all of our detriments. If our neighbor's house is on fire, we cannot take comfort in the fact that it isn't our fire because that smoke can reach our houses next. It is in our best interest to help them put out the fire before it becomes ours, because everyone's well-being should be community business.

Person 3 has detected that the atmosphere is probably one of gaslighting, and they don't feel empowered to speak up. Person 4 has probably seen someone suffer for speaking the truth. Persons 3 and 4, I feel you on a visceral level. You want to preserve self because you've seen others somehow get negative responses. You have all the right to not wield your authenticity because it might very well be weaponized against you. While many people can say they experience this, Black women in particular are put into these situations on a regular basis.

Black women show up to work every day having no room for error and no defenders, especially in crucial moments. In my life, I know I'm SUPPOSED to work for myself. Why? Because after hearing the stories (daily) about what Black people deal with when it comes to their white coworkers who can't handle anything remotely close to the truth, I realize I don't have the tools to work within a corporate environment. They gotta do their jobs AND make sure they are not offending the tender sensibilities of Chad and Becky. It's a lot.

If I worked in an office, I would absolutely get an annual review saying that I was "aggressive," and I would eventually get fired. I know this because I don't have the tools.

I firmly believe that Black women are the adults in the room of the world. We're so often in the role of chaperone, not because we want to be but because we have no other choice. We're thrust to the front of the class because we realize that the whole place will go down in flames if we aren't there. I believe Black women are the moral center of the universe, and can't nobody tell me different. In spite of the fact that we have our heads stepped on, are disrespected constantly, and are treated like we are disposable, we show up. We speak up, show out, and stand up for everyone, even those who don't deserve it. We catch hell for it.

But folks don't listen to us like they should. Things would be so much calmer if the world honored our voices more. There'd be less chaos, more equity, and less suffering if folks understood that Black women got the answers. We're basically part of the largest group project ever, and unfortunately our grade depends on everyone else. We're the ones who refuse to get an F, so we do all the work and everyone benefits from the A that we, and only we, earned.

For us, the compulsion to preserve self is beyond earned, and I salute sistas who are navigating in the best way they know how. I salute those of you who have to deal with the microaggressions, the microappreciations, and the megaprejudice every day. I see you. You are superheroes. So when you still decide to speak up in spite of all this, I know it's a gift. One that we cannot take for granted. Now we need everyone else to step up and speak out.

I won't lie to you and say, "Follow your heart, speak the truth, and nothing bad happens." NAH! Shit can get real and there can be consequences. There is certainly risk to speaking up. However, I would rather risk that than risk regretting my inaction or my silence. I think a lot about the poet Audre Lorde asking, "What are the words you do not yet have? What do you need to say? What are the tyrannies you swallow day by day and attempt to make your own, until you will sicken and die of them, still in silence?" I don't want to hold on to these tyrannies. My disappointment in myself is a much greater consequence to me than other people's disappointment in me.

So how do you find the courage to speak up knowing that there can be fallout? When we are afraid of telling the truth or making a room uncomfortable, the first thing we need to do is figure out the consequence we are afraid of. What is that thing? And then what is the worst-case scenario that comes from that thing? Maybe you'll get written up by human resources (HR), or maybe your client will drop you if you challenge their idea. Or is it that you might get fired if you speak up? What is it that scares you most about telling the truth in this moment?

Now, IF that thing happens, can you figure it out? If you'll be fired and you need that money to eat, by all means, file your nails in that meeting and watch it go to hell. Most Americans are living paycheck to paycheck, so a disruption to their pockets doesn't bode well for how they can live.

My challenge here, however, is to those who are financially secure and not acutely afraid of not having a home if they can't work for two months. On Maslow's hierarchy of needs, if you have the physiological and safety needs handled? This is for you. You have the room to take some risks. Yes, you. We're often so afraid of the consequences that come with speaking up and making rooms uncomfortable that we don't think about the best-case scenario that could happen if we actually do this thing.

If the consequence is you get fired, is that an actual place you want to work? If you can get fired for challenging one idea in one meeting, is that company worth your time and energy? If the consequence is not that you'll be fired or written up, then what is actually on the line if you speak up? Is it that you won't be liked by whoever you challenged?

I've made a career out of being a straight shooter. Not because I walk out the house saying, "YAY TIME TO MAKE PEOPLE UNCOMFORTABLE TODAY," but because I understand that if I'm supposed to show up in the best way possible, I can't be quiet if what's going on around me is not okay. I feel like I have no choice but to be the challenger.

Being a truth-teller is no walk in the park. It is exhausting always feeling like you have to be the adult in the room. It is tiring to be the challenger with no backup. But I also think rooms are elevated when we're in them. If people know you are in the room, then they might be less inclined to bring rubbish in with them because they know you'll throw it out. It means they know they better come as correct as they can so they don't hear your mouth.

Similarly, if you're in the room with the person who's going to ask the questions that matter, the person who's going to say, "Is this idea as fully thought out and as thoughtful as it could be?" you will not present half-baked ideas. If we all exist in a world where we know that everybody's expecting the best of us, that is what we're going to bring into the room.

Challenging people or systems is not easy, even if you've been doing it all your life. It is an intentional decision folks make.

When I turned thirty, I went skydiving because one of my friends asked me to go with him. When he asked, I said YES so quickly that I couldn't take it back. It was such a strong yes that even I was shocked. Being a woman of my word, I stuck to it. So we traveled to some out-of-the-way place on Long Island and signed all types of documents basically saying if we went splat, no one was liable. We got on the plane and went up something like fifteen thousand feet. I was strapped to the professional guy who was jumping with me, and as we were getting closer, he strapped me so tight that I was off my seat. My whole weight was on him, and that actually gave me comfort because I was like, "Well, now you have skin in the game because if I die, you die too. Great, let's do this."

That momentary piece of courage instantly disappeared when we were sitting at the edge of the plane and I was seeing the earth beneath me. I was like, "Oh, this is a bad idea. I've done some stupid things. This is one of them. Why am I doing this on purpose? I'm paying somebody to fall out of a perfectly good plane." Talk about first-world problems.

The moment when we fell out of the plane, I actually forgot how to breathe for three seconds. It was as if my body's reflexes were like, "Nope, nope, we're not good at this. No." Then my body was like, "Remember? Okay, do that using-your-lungs thing." I took a deep breath at some point as we were free falling, and the parachute popped open and we started floating in the sky as my jumper gave me an aerial tour of the New York area. It was stunning, and I was so glad I did this nutty thing! When we landed, I even landed on my feet!

When I want to say something that might feel uncomfortable or difficult or bigger than me, I go back to that time when I jumped out of the plane and lost my breath for three seconds. I think about how when I caught my breath and was able to look at the earth, in wonderment, all I saw was beauty. It was the best thing I could have done. It felt right, even as it was still petrifying.

Even though I've had practice being the truth-teller and the challenger all my life, telling the truth feels scary each time. I say this because a lot of times people believe that being honest comes easy for challengers. They think, "Oh, you've been doing this for a while. You're used to it. You're fine." No, it's never really fine. You just get used to the practice of telling this truth in spite of the fact that it's scary.

If you think about those challengers, the people who constantly make others uncomfortable with their truths, or who show up in the best way they can no matter what room they're in, and you think, "I wish I could do that," I'm here to say you can.

H ow do you decide when to speak up or challenge?

Being a professional troublemaker is not for the sake of making people uncomfortable, or being a contrarian, or making a room tense. Challenging is about expecting the best of everybody and making sure that they're seeing their blind spots. How do you do this?

Be human. Every single day we have to walk with empathy in the rooms that we're in. We have to see people from where they're at, and we have to recognize their actual humanity. Sometimes when it's really tough to challenge somebody, I say, "Okay, as your fellow global citizen, I feel the obligation to challenge you in this way."

Questions are also a really great way of challenging people. This is what happens in therapy. Your therapist is really asking you a whole bunch of questions, without telling you much, letting you lead yourself to the solution. So sometimes being the challenger is simply asking really good questions. The terrible meeting idea? Reply with "Have you thought about this deeper? What other angles might we look at this from? What are the challenges that might come up if we take this action?" The racist joke someone tells? Ask them, "Can you explain it to me?" so they have to now put words to their prejudice.

We've all met (or been) somebody who's tactless in telling the truth. That's who we conjure up when we think of someone who is a challenger or professional troublemaker. We're thinking about the person who keeps it real in the wrongest way. Don't be that person who is loud and contrarian or cruel for no reason. Be the person who's thoughtful as you do it.

Now, I'm not saying you will not ruffle feathers even if you want to be thoughtful. But if you attempt to be as well informed as possible, you are at least minimizing the risk. That's all you can do. I ask myself three questions before I say something that might shake the table.

**Do you mean it?** Is this thing something I actually believe?

**Can you defend it?** Being the challenger, I also have to be okay with being questioned and prodded. My ideas need to be explored deeper. Can I stand in it and justify it? Do I have receipts?

**Can you say it thoughtfully or with love?** Is my intention good here? I might think I am righteous in my indignation or in my questioning, but am I saying it thoughtfully or with love? No matter how righteous it feels, no matter how true it might feel, if I say this thing in a way that's hateful or that makes people feel demeaned or less than, the message will not land.

*Do you mean it? Can you defend it? Can you say it with love?* If the answer is yes to all three, I say it and I let the chips fall. Whether I need to present a challenge in a meeting, or to a friend, or to my mom, I run this checklist to keep myself from being completely tactless. It holds me accountable to what I'm really saying and keeps me in check with myself.

It's not a foolproof method, and there are still times I make mistakes or say something I shouldn't. But these questions help you keep your intentions good. Mind you, good intentions might still make for bad impact, but they give you a place to start. Be as thoughtful as you can be. How the challenge lands isn't in your control. Once you have thought about it, you're not being impulsive, you're not being hateful; you're being your solid self, you've done your best.

Each of these questions serves a purpose in ensuring that I stay on solid ground. They are my checkpoints. They are my way of ensuring that even when I'm angry or emotional, I can pause and say, "Wait a minute, is this thing worth saying? Is this the way you want to show up?" It gives me courage to say YES, this is how.

The other thing we need to be aware of when we want to speak the truth is the power we walk with. In my first book, I talked about doing the privilege walk in college. It's an exercise where participants stand in a straight line horizontally in a room. People's hands are resting on the shoulders of the people next to them. The moderator then reads a series of questions, prompting them to either step forward or to step back. For example: "Step forward if you can easily find a Band-Aid in your skin tone in stores." "Step back if your name is frequently mispronounced." "Step forward if you attending college was a foregone conclusion." As you move farther apart, you actually have to break apart from your neighbor. At the end of it, everyone is in different positions. It is a physical representation of power and privilege, and it is incredibly compelling.

Because of my privilege as a straight, Christian, cisgender woman who comes from educated parents, I ended up in the middle. When

I looked back and saw some of my classmates behind me, I remember feeling this visceral sense of responsibility because I wanted them right next to me. The fact that I had to break with them made me feel guilty. I realized then that one of my purposes is to make sure that I don't have to see people behind me. If there are people behind me, I need to find a way to get them by my side.

This is important because when I walk into rooms, I have to recognize the power that I'm walking in with. That realization drives my voice and lets me know that I should say that tough thing. If we leave our power behind, or don't even recognize that we have it, we risk thinking we can't do things that are difficult.

As a professional speaker, I know that when I am onstage in any room, I am the most influential person right then. Why? Because I'm the one with the mic. I can step off the stage and that can instantly change, but in the fifty-five minutes when I hold the mic, I lead. My job is to disrupt what's happening and to use that clout to make sure somebody else who has less authority feels just as significant and seen. Or that someone who doesn't have the mic still feels heard. I am not in the room to make the executives comfortable. I'm there to speak for the intern who couldn't get a word in at the meeting.

One of my friends (who happens to be a brilliant activist and teacher), Brittany Packnett Cunningham, introduced me to the phrase "Spend your privilege." She got it from disability rights advocate Rebecca Cokley. It is the concept that the privilege we have in this world is endless. It doesn't run out. You don't use your voice today and have to re-up the next day. Power is limitless, and using ours for other people does not diminish it. We have to utilize our influence, capabilities, and MONEY for the greater good.

I don't ask people to do the things that I don't ask of myself first. Oftentimes, we need to see somebody else try something risky before we think we can do it. And my career has been a lot of risky moments, but I always use myself as an example. I'm this Black woman who has ended up in some grand rooms, in spite of often being a loudmouth.

I'm not asking the most marginalized people among us to be the ones taking this mantle on. I'm challenging those who are rich, white, straight, and cisgender to do the work. Stop waiting on the rest of the world. And if you decide to wait, make yourself useful.

Let's go back to the meetings. If you are not the truth-teller in the room, you can at least be backup for them. If you aren't going to be the first domino, be the second. If I am typically the person who starts off and asks us to rethink whatever the idea is, having someone chime in with their affirmation of my challenge is refreshing and incredibly helpful. If you believe in the challenge, back it up, because there is strength in numbers. No one wants to be on an island, standing by themselves.

That being said, there are times when I don't always want to be the truth-teller. There are times when I sit and think today's going to be the day when I do not say anything. I'm not challenging. I'm not asking the questions.

We're so often passing the baton to other people, thinking it's their job to tell the truth, but what happens when the challenger decides to take a break? We can't take for granted the person who usually challenges, because it is not just one person's job, it is everyone's jobs. We all need to be the challenger, but everyone is waiting on Superman, when they have red capes too.

For women, this strength in numbers is especially important because we're in spaces where we're constantly being interrupted. Or somebody else will say the exact same thing we just said and get credit for our idea. It's easy to ignore one and it's hard to ignore two. You can't erase three. Strength in troublemaking numbers is necessary!

Instead, many of us are too willing to be quiet when it's needed and dole out empty microappreciations. If after the meeting you walk up to the challenger and say, "OMG I'm so glad you said that," then you're trolling in microappreciation. You're telling me when nobody's listening. The currency I needed is not even usable, and nobody's here to see it. If you cannot back me up in the actual meeting, what is the point? Let's do less of that, and make sure that in the room, we're proverbially taking a stand, not waiting till it's all cleared out. Actually stand next to that person. Use your words to affirm people out loud and give them more credence.

So many people have to deal with that every single day, and I want that to happen less. And that's why I say kudos to people in corporate environments, who have to work with people who are not being courageous or are being silently courageous to them after the fact, which is not courage.

I know I would've been fired a couple of times by now, because if I were on the receiving end of microappreciation, I would've been like, "You know what, keep that." And then somebody would have reported me to HR and then here we are. Because I focus less on the niceties of it all. I want to be kind to you by making sure that I'm showing up for you, by making sure that I'm speaking up when you're afraid to. But what about the moments when I don't want to speak up? Who speaks up for me? Who speaks up for the person who is the challenger?

A lot of people wonder why they are surrounded by people who lie to them. It's because they've proven themselves to be people who cannot be trusted with honesty, lest they weaponize it. If you have an environment where people will be punished for speaking up, then you gotta deal with the consequences of shitty work. If you're the friend who hangs up on their friends anytime they try to tell you about your wack-ass choices, then they'll probably keep quiet as you continue to be secretary of Team Bad Decisions. It's the bed you made, so lie in it.

You want more honesty around you? Ask for it. We have to create spaces that welcome people to feel comfortable to speak and challenge. If there's someone who is usually quiet, seek them out. "Hey, I would love to hear what you have to say. I'd love to hear your feedback and questions. I know a lot of us have been dominating this conversation, but your voice is important. So can you tell us what you think?"

Speak the truth, not only to your Facebook friends, but to your family. What is the use of yelling about racism or homophobia or transphobia or patriarchy to the randoms who hit a button to get our content if we aren't challenging those we know in real life? We sometimes think we're doing work by being loud online, but then we'll be quiet in the rooms we're in, quiet around the people we can touch, quiet in front of the real circle of influence we have. Speak truth to those closest to you, not just the random behind the screen.

A lot of people think they have no platform. You do. Your platform is your kin, squad, colleagues. Do the work close to home so you can have far-reaching consequences. We are most easily moved by the words that come out of the mouths of our loved ones.

I think a lot about the moment when I almost didn't say something because I was told there could be negative consequences. I think about when I was deeply uncomfortable because I could have lost a lot of my livelihood when I spoke out against a conference that was engaging in pay inequality. And I think about the anxiety that I walked into those moments with. But if I only tell the truth when it's easy, what's the point of whatever power or privilege I have? Truth-telling has to be done in the moments when it's really hard. That's when it actually makes the most difference.

And yes, we're afraid of the worst-case scenario happening, but what if the best-case scenario happens? What if we change systems in the rooms that we're in or we change the people we come across because we dare to be people who decided to show up and use our necessary voices?

I say this as a Black woman who is constantly speaking truth to power, who is trying to do it in the most real way she knows how, who sometimes missteps. The greater version of ourselves is the version that is willing to be courageous in the very tough moments. Because those are typically when we need to be most courageous. When it's that scary, when you want to go hide under a blanket, when somebody is telling you that you should be more quiet, do not be more quiet. If you're compelled to do or say this thing, then you're probably supposed to do or say it.

We need to prioritize the truth, because the world is full of things to point out, injustices to fight, systems to dismantle. If we're not starting with honesty, how do we know the problems we need to tackle? You don't fix something you don't know is broken. You don't lie your way to an equitable world or coddle your way to equity. We gotta find our individual integrity and our collective candor for the greater good, and we start by being honest, in whatever space we're in.

A lot of us are risking smaller things than we realize when we choose speaking truth. REAL truth-tellers are the freedom fighters who have been literally beat up, jailed, or killed for daring to challenge the status quo. The Black Panthers we are not, as we sit in glass spaces afraid to simply tell someone, "That's not a good idea." What we are putting on the line is usually not our lives or our freedom.

No one said this would be easy, but the things worth doing are usually not easy. You knew that, though. Truth-telling is a muscle, and like all muscles, it needs practice and exercise to be built. I hate working out, and anyone who says it's fun is a liar and a cheat. Yet I do it because if I don't, it is to my own detriment. I will suffer most for it. Being a gatekeeper of truth takes practice.

When I first started doing public speaking, my voice would shake for the first five to ten minutes I was onstage. I'm not sure if anybody else detected it, but I sure did. And I kept talking, and eventually my voice stopped shaking. I don't know when it happened, but one day I got onstage and I realized my voice wasn't shaking anymore.

I reflect on the words of the world-changing GOOD trouble-maker John Lewis: "When you see something that is not right, not fair, not just, you have a moral obligation to do something, to say something, and not be quiet." We have a moral obligation to tell the truth. Tell the truth, even when our voices shake. Tell the truth even when it might rock the boat. Tell the truth, even when there might be consequences. Because that in itself, makes us more courageous than most people in the world.

Use the three questions, know your voice is necessary, and speak truth to power. Even a whisper of truth makes a difference in an echo chamber of lies.

# 7

## FAIL LOUDLY

**We fear failing.**

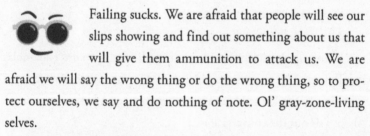 Failing sucks. We are afraid that people will see our slips showing and find out something about us that will give them ammunition to attack us. We are afraid we will say the wrong thing or do the wrong thing, so to protect ourselves, we say and do nothing of note. Ol' gray-zone-living selves.

If you're living a life of color, of impact, of note, you will make mistakes. You will fuck up. You will show you are an everlasting fool who constantly needs to get their shit together. And that's okay. Because failure is necessary. It's essential for us to live loudly. It is painful, it is usually unexpected, and it can knock us on our asses.

I have failed a lot, and I have failed out loud. It is a rite of passage for your greater good, and we must learn from it.

n 2018, on the day Aretha Franklin died and we all collectively mourned her, the conversation turned to who would do her tribute. What artists could live up to Ms. Franklin's legacy to memorialize her in song? Names were being thrown around online, and someone suggested the name of a beloved R&B artist who was big in the early 1990s.

In my occasional impulsiveness, having not heard the person's name in a long time or noticed them release any new music in at least fifteen years, I tweeted, "Under what rock did they pull that name from?" A few people were like, "That's actually a good suggestion." A lot more people were like, "Yeah I wouldn't have thought of them first in this tribute lineup." The conversation continued as more names were thrown in the pot.

All was well. Or so I thought.

I woke up the next morning to my replies being in utter shambles on Twitter. The conversation had shifted to the fact that since I was not born in the United States, and therefore not African American, I should sit out the conversation.

Thus started the biggest public fail I've ever had.

My friends started hitting me up as they began seeing it all over their own timelines, and I asked them for advice. Should I reply to this? Should I let it ride? Should I speak up for myself? Should I act like I don't see it and tweet other random things?

I chose the "sit this out" route for hours until someone tweeted something that I felt was derogatory about me. That's when my ego took charge and I replied. I responded by saying something about how I noticed that they were trying to other me. I also threw in something about them being so pressed by what I considered to be a simple tweet inquiring about how someone pulled up that particular musician's name.

That was me throwing gasoline on the fire, which caused it to now rage.

And rage it did. My name ended up trending on Twitter. I was the number eight most tweeted-about subject in all of the United States for about an hour. Half the people were calling me everything but a child of God and the other half were wondering why this word *Luvvie* was all up in their timeline. The one who was usually doing the judging was being judged. And very, very loudly.

I logged off. I knew it was bad because I kept getting all types of texts from people checking in on me. "You good? I see what's happening. I'm sorry. Lemme know if you need me."

People were saying I was an entitled Nigerian who didn't know what the hell she was talking about. Folks dug deeper into my tweets, looking for ways to show that I was anti-American and anti–Black American, and anything that could be deemed offensive. Think pieces were written about me, and my name was plastered everywhere, it felt like. Anything I ever said about being Black in America was up for scrutiny. I was dragged.

I felt beat up on and lied about. So I wrote a response in a blog post, explaining myself and talking about how much I was not the person I was being accused of being. Long story short, I didn't approach it well because nowhere in it did I say sorry.

That blog post started a fresh firestorm, with some people becoming deeply invested in my fail and fall. One person went on

Facebook and posted a status about me, saying, "I want to destroy her career." Someone made an anonymous email account where they sent anyone who was a brand partner or any upcoming speaking engagement a message suggesting that clients disassociate from me. One popular anti-Black misogynist sent his audience to target me, bringing a lot of "go back to Africa" and "bitch die" comments onto my platform.

I was in shambles. Whatever tough skin or self-assurance I thought I had? This pierced straight through it. I felt like I was in the Battle of the Bastards, as the troops came at Jon Snow with all sorts of ammunition, and he just looked at them hoping for the best. I was Jon Snow if Jon Snow was lying on his couch crying and hating himself.

I couldn't eat. I refused to eat. My boo even took me to a crab boil, which is one of my faves, and I sat there staring at the delicious goodness of perfectly seasoned seafood and barely touched it. Just like how they say God gets mad if you pass by the color purple without acknowledging it, I bet God is pissed every time you waste a good crab boil. I lost eight pounds in a week. I, who am 120 pounds soaking wet on a gluttonous day when I drink a lot of water, lost eight pounds. So you know I was looking ghastly AF.

And it was my fault. All of it was my fault. I was beating myself up more than anyone else could. It's one thing to disappoint others. That shit sucks. But to disappoint myself was the tougher thing. I felt shame in a way I never have. I was so upset at myself because I made a mistake and said something I shouldn't have. I should have known better. I should have done better. I should have been better.

People went looking for things to be mad at me about, but it was MY fault for giving them things to find. It was my fault that they could say I'd been insensitive. Or said tone-deaf things. Or sometimes was just stupid. Had I not given them anything, they wouldn't have found anything to use to drag me through the mud.

I knew I was wrong. I wasn't a victim of people's meanness as much as I was a victim of my own big-ass mouth, which sometimes isn't as thoughtful as it should be, or maybe makes a joke that isn't a joke because it demeans. My two feet, which were always anchored to the floor, rooted in really liking who I was, felt shaky. I had faced backlash before but not to this level, and not for this long. It felt unrelenting.

So I went dark online. My friends called me to check in, and at the worst moments to remind me of who I really am. They gave me stern talking-tos in the middle of assurance, and they kept me from going deeper into the rabbit hole of shame. My partner said, "You let people steal your light."

I made an appointment with my therapist, because SOS! I was not okay! A few days later when I went in, she told me I was exhibiting symptoms of post-traumatic stress disorder: disrupted sleep, lack of appetite, and an acute sense of being in danger even in innocuous moments.

The incident had knocked me off my square in such a major way. I was drop-kicked off my game and I ran away and hid. I was afraid I would never recover from this thing, and my name was taking an irreparable hit. I legit wanted to quit everything and move to a small town somewhere and be a librarian. Because: dramatic.

The worst part? It made me afraid of my voice. I questioned my judgment. Up until then, I had walked through life rarely doubting my confidence in my voice, the biggest gift God had given me. But after facing this very public backlash, born from using my voice in a careless way, I began second-guessing my gift. I was scared of my own bold shadow: "Shit, if I say this thing, will people get mad?" I felt flutters in the pit of my stomach whenever I'd want to say something, truly afraid and taken right back to the moment when I saw my name on Twitter's trending list. I stopped writing. I stopped speaking up. I hid.

For a year, I didn't write anything on my website besides the TV recaps I was commissioned to write. On Twitter, I was extra cautious about posting anything too strong, lest I ruffle the wrong feathers and start trending again. On other social media, I'd still post about what was on my mind, but I did it with extra "You sure you wanna say this?"

I justified not using my voice as, "Well, maybe I need to evolve out of blogging. Maybe my work needs to look different. Hey, I'm still saying what I need in other ways, through my podcast and whatever."

I was still feeling bruised by the humiliation of it all, so I wanted to leave it behind. That was my ego talking. That was the failure talking. It was fear talking.

My book agent was asking me, "So what's book two gonna be about?" I told her I was still thinking about it. What would I even write about? What did I have to say?

Almost a year to the date, another legendary death rocked the world: Toni Morrison passed away on August 5, 2019. The writer who I quoted on page two of *I'm Judging You: The Do-Better Manual*: "If there's a book that you want to read, but it hasn't been written yet, you must write it." Ms. Toni told us that, and who was I not to listen? Her words had literally been life's instructions for me. She was the woman who made me too shy to call myself a writer because I felt like her words were too great for me to be in the same category with her.

But that woman had left this world, and her death convicted me. I'd never met her, but her permanent absence jolted my spirit awake. It wagged a finger at me because I was choosing to lie down instead of doing what I was put here to do.

I was reminded that writers don't stop because people critique them, no matter how harsh they think it is. They don't abandon their craft because they feel misunderstood or their feelings get hurt. They don't leave their purpose behind because they have loud detractors. They take the mistakes they made and let them spur them to make even better art. God said weapons would form. You do not let them prosper by letting them stop you from using your gift.

The first thing I wrote was a tribute to Toni and what she meant to me, as the favorite teacher I never met. After that, I got the idea for this book. I had spent a year afraid of myself, of my voice and my gift. I could no longer let fear dictate my life.

My journey is truly one of fighting fear constantly.

I failed very loudly, very publicly. But how could I use that for something greater? That sense of defeat was for the greater good of me, and the only way it would be for naught is if I didn't become a better version of me because of it. I asked myself: Why did it happen as it did? How do I move forward? What am I supposed to learn?

So many lessons.

When it comes to failing, we come up with stories about who we are because of it. That is where the shame came in for me. I felt like I got caught with my pants down and my ass all out in the open. I felt exposed and raw, and thought everything I'd achieved was clearly a sham because it was about to get taken away. As people pointed out whatever old problematic thing they didn't like from my raving dumbass twenty-four-year-old self on Twitter, I felt embarrassed.

The lessons were plenty.

## THE OLD ME WAS NECESSARY

With therapy, I began to realize the girl from then was necessary because she became the woman from now. And I had to thank her for the work she did and the person she was, because she led me here. Then I had to thank the me now, in her thirties, who is more aware of herself, the strength of her voice, and the world. I couldn't be me without her, so my shame was not needed. I needed to give myself grace and forgive myself for my mistakes.

I had to be kind to that girl from then, the one who was afraid to call herself a writer because she didn't think she could measure up to the title. That girl could've never written this book, could have never confidently showed up in these rooms that I've been in and done her best work. The person who used to talk before she'd think could not be the person with the platform that I have now because I wouldn't use it as responsibly as I do now. I think about how the person who made thirty-five thousand a year could not be the same person who signed a six-figure book deal. I wouldn't even know how to handle the taxes, let alone what to do with the cash.

But that girl had to exist so I could write about her and her mistakes and the things she had to learn through the fire. Luvvie 1.0 had to be here so she could grow into Luvvie 3.0, who could write this book.

## NONE OF US BELONG ON PEDESTALS

Not one of us. We are flawed people whose jobs make us seem grander than we are. I know I can be trash and have garbage ways. I am not infallible or smarter than someone just because I have the platform. Nah. I got kicked off my pedestal and I hope people didn't put me back on it, because I don't deserve it. Leave me down here, because I can't live up to the standards folks often ascribe to personalities they follow. I will disappoint you. I will let you down. I will fuck up. But I will hopefully never stop learning how to show up in the best way I know how. I will not stop growing. I will not stop holding myself accountable to who I say I am.

## WHEN THESE MOMENTS OF RECKONING HAPPEN, WE NEED TO NOT WASTE THEM

Another lesson for me? The judge will be judged. I often challenge people to do better. This also means I will be challenged to do the same. I will be in the court of public opinion too, because I'm bound to make mistakes. What matters is how I handle it and move forward. That is what I will truly be judged on, and on this, I was held in contempt.

I should have apologized without defending or explaining myself. People want to feel seen and heard when we have done harm. I needed to atone, take accountability, and promise to show up differently next time. I did harm, and I should have copped to it early.

A proper apology woulda been something like:

*Hey everyone, today has been distressing, and to see my name in the lights in this way is something I am not proud of. I fucked up and I'm sorry. My words made people upset. My intention, whether good or not, doesn't matter, because we all know intention is not synonymous with impact. I should know better and should be better. I need to make sure that I am being even more thoughtful with how I show up in the world. I have a major platform and with that comes higher expectations. I won't always meet them. In fact, I expect to fall short again. But at least I can aspire to be better than I am. I'm sorry.*

That humility could have saved me a lot of trouble, because I was wrong. Not just because of what I said, but how I acted at being challenged. I should have taken the knee and moved forward.

After all this, it also became clear to me that my name was bigger than I realized. I'm not just some random Chicago girl by way of Nigeria, tweeting and cracking jokes with her friends. I am Brand Luvvie, with more than one million total followers on social media. I am representing Company Awe Luv. No matter how much I think of myself as some girl who started writing one day and cool things happened, I am at the helm of massive reach, and it is clear that my responsibilities are greater. My voice carries. My platform is large. I owe the best of me to an audience that's larger than ever before and bigger than I ever imagined. I have to act accordingly.

This doesn't mean I change my voice, but it does mean I have to move slightly differently. I used to be David but now I'm Goliath, and that's a tough pill to swallow. I'm no longer the underdog who can throw bones, but the big dog who gets bones thrown at me. That, for me, is frightening. It means who or what I speak about now has to be different, because my platform is larger.

The whole incident felt like God was grabbing my face and telling me, "You're at new levels. I need you to move different and be more responsible." I mean, did He have to make it so painful? Probably. My stubborn ass probably needed that jolt of reality. Message received, Holiness. I hear You, okay?

I was reminded I should always punch UP, not down. ("Punching up" is when you challenge someone with more power than you. "Punching down" is when you go at someone with less.) Yes, I need to punch up, but who that includes has shifted because I now wield more influence and weight. I can find myself punching down if I'm not cognizant of this dynamic and my stacking privilege. This is why humor is dynamic, and why comedians have to change their routines over the years. The legendary comedian who is doing $50 million Netflix specials can't do the same jokes he did when he was a struggling stand-up comic.

I also learned that I can be proud of my work, but I can't tie my worth to it, because it can be fleeting. While we should own our dopeness, we can't let all the outside praise we get go to our heads. People will love us one day and HATE us the next.

This experience made me more kind, because being at the end of hateful arrows feels harrowing. I've been scathing in the past in my critiques of others, and it was a necessary heart check to chill on that. Growing up looks like being kinder.

Being in the midst of that storm reminded me I need to help other Black women when they find themselves in similar positions. To be a visible Black woman, especially, is to commit to being abused over and over again in hopes that it doesn't pierce your heart too much. I now make it a point to check in on the prominent ladies I know when it becomes their turn in the fire. Hearing from caring voices, even if they aren't super close to you, is helpful.

It also made me wanna vigorously defend Black women who find themselves called out for mistakes that aren't hate-filled. This platform and this voice ain't just for the comfortable times. If people come for me because I've defended someone, I'll deal. I am loved and valued. I deserve to be defended and protected even on my worst days, and so do others.

It takes a lot to be a prominent Black woman. I admire Beyoncé, Serena, and Oprah for more than their work. I deeply respect the grace they show under constant pressure. They're photographed when their expression could be translated to shady and they trend for days, as all types of people make up whole storybooks about their frame of mind. And they keep quiet through it. That is what I don't have yet and I'm trying to learn: the art of shutting the fuck up even as people try to come for you.

One of my mistakes in all this was responding at all to some of the people who were coming for me. I'm the person who usually tells my friends to chill when something similar happens to them. I didn't take my own advice and it blew up spectacularly in my face. I fanned the flame. Yes, I felt hurt, but we ain't gotta attend every fight we're invited to. Next time, I need to ask, "What would Beyoncé do?" Sis wouldn't even act like she saw it. Instead, she'd be somewhere creating amazing art as people talk about her recklessly. It's why I had to start paying my Beyhive memberships. That woman deserves us stanning.

## MY PRAYERS NEED TO CHANGE

As I grow and my career grows, I need to say stronger prayers. There's nothing I can really do besides try to always be thoughtful and learn from my mistakes, but I can't say I will never make a mistake again. So if I make the next mistake, does that mean I am now going to be knocked off my square for the next year, because all these arrows decided to point at me?

I'm also going to pray to be fortified in the instances when people call me what I'm not, because it's not going to stop. I can say the sky is blue tomorrow and somebody might be offended by it. Right? If they chose to be offended by it, they will be offended by it.

I have to be fortified, because when the weapons form, may they not prosper. I can't not fulfill God's assignment for me because some people don't like me. I need to learn and get fortified and pray that my armor is stronger than ever, that it gets stronger by the day, that my feet are more solid and planted than ever. I need to pray that as a leader, I'm showing what it looks like to fail and move past it.

I think of my grandmother, whose prayers I know cover me every single day. Those three-hour middle-of-the-night prayers gotta be responsible for some of my success, because I've made it here in spite of and because of myself.

I am a recovering asshole who will use every face-plant as a step stool to be better, smarter, tougher, kinder, and more gracious. I'm thankful for that D I got in chemistry. I'm so glad I got fired/laid off from my marketing job. And trending on Twitter for being reckless with my words was a blessing. Each time I fall on my face, it's a cosmic reboot and redirection that sets me on the path I'm actually supposed to be on. It is a recalibration of my life's GPS. Failure always gets me to higher ground.

I have nothing to regret cuz the falls are necessary for me to learn the things I do not know (and they are plenty). We can fall flat on our faces and rise up in the ashes of our old selves, better than before.

I sleep well at night because I'm at peace with myself and my soul. I wake up in the morning and look at myself in the mirror and really love the woman who looks back at me. She's flawed AF but knows without question that she is better than who she used to be. And she knows her mistakes do not define her; her lessons do.

Similarly, you are not your worst moment or worst mistake. You know who you are (go back to chapter one—that exercise comes in handy when you're in the middle of firestorms). In the midst of your mistakes, it might feel like the world is collapsing or you won't ever recover. But everything, even your worst moments, is temporary. Humiliation is temporary. The acute pain is temporary.

Know that grace and accountability can coexist. Grace makes you forgive yourself for your mistakes and accountability lets you know that the lesson learned must be remembered and those mistakes can't be frequent. It's a dance you must do.

Failure is life's greatest teacher, and the only way we truly fail is to learn nothing from the valleys we experience.

# 8

# ASK FOR MORE

**We fear disappointment.**

 One of my favorite mantras, which I heard a long time ago and still hold dear, is "It's better to live a life of 'Oh well' than a life of 'What if?'" Many of us are living the what-if life because we do not know how to ask for what we want, what we need, and what we would like. We are constantly leaving things on the table that could be for us because we are afraid of the nos that may come. We don't want to deal with the blow that comes from putting ourselves out there and possibly getting rejected, so we end up being people who never ask.

I wonder what would happen if we were given the permission to constantly ASK FOR MORE, from life and the universe, from relationships, from bosses and colleagues. What might happen when we realize that NO won't kill us but YES could change our lives?

I love this sentiment by the brilliant Paulo Coelho, author of one of my fave books, *The Alchemist*: "The mere possibility of getting what we want fills the soul of the ordinary person with guilt. We look around at all those who have failed to get what they want and feel that we do not deserve to get what we want either. We forget about all the obstacles we overcame, all the suffering we endured, all the things we had to give up in order to get this far."

Our inability to ask for things comes from a lifetime of learning that to ASK is often to be disappointed. It's a well-earned fear. At no point do I think we wake up one day and all of a sudden find ourselves mute when it comes to asking for what we want. Instead, I think we've all had experiences that tell us it is risky to ask people for things. We are Team I Will Figure It Out Myself or Team I Got It, Don't Worry About Me. Why? For a few reasons.

Some of us became these people by necessity. We might have had to raise ourselves because our parents weren't there, physically or emotionally. Or growing up, we didn't have friends to count on. Maybe no one ever provided for us, so we've had to figure out how to do it ourselves. Maybe the only person there for us was us. Perhaps we've had to be this person because no one else has proven loyal, reliable, or stable enough to show up in the way we need.

Or maybe we became this person because we had some painful experiences the times we did ask for something. Maybe it blew up in our face one time too many and now we're afraid of asking. Maybe someone threw something they did for us in our face during a moment of strife, and we've carried that experience around with us as more reason to never ask people for anything.

Whatever your reason is, it's valid and I don't blame you. As someone who has had more than a few "What the hell was that?"

experiences related to me asking for help, I get it. I feel you on a spiritual level. We go together like kettle and corn. That is why I'm here to tell you to ASK FOR MORE anyway.

Unfortunately, the reason doesn't make not asking any less harmful or stunting to your life. When we don't know how to ask for things, for more, we aren't getting everything life can offer us. Does life owe us something? Not really. But life has a whole treasure trove of things we can tap into, which if we don't ask for, we don't get. Like in James 4:2: ". . . we have not, because we ask not." I know it's not as black and white as that, but I still repeat that passage to myself because it is an affirmation of what I'm supposed to be doing and what is in my capacity. I'm less attached to the result knowing that I at least did my part: the asking. Anything else is a bonus.

It took me going to therapy to really understand that I was somebody, in all my boldness, who was afraid to ask for more. Lemme tell you how my therapist, who is a kind middle-aged Black woman (who could be anywhere from thirty-five to sixty-five but I can't tell, because we tend to be ageless and our Black refuses to snap, crackle, or pop), told me about my whole life.

I like going to therapy because I enjoy paying for someone to read me for filth. During certain sessions, I end up word-vomiting about feeling stressed out. I pride myself on being Team I Get Shit Done no matter what, both professionally and personally, and I handle pressure well, but even Atlas shrugged after a while, didn't he?

One day, I was particularly stressed out about work plus home stuff, and my therapist said, "Have you asked your partner for help?"

ME: No, I got it handled. He got things going on too. This is mine to handle.

HER: Why? Don't you think he would want to help you as much as he can?

ME: He would. He's actually asked me what he can help with.

HER: Why don't you tell him to take some things off your plate?

ME: Well, I figured that because I said I got it, I want to stick to my word.

HER: I see why you're stressed out. Your husband sees it too and has asked to help but you aren't letting him help. What do you think that does?

ME: Frustrate me because I need the help and frustrate him because he wants to . . . oh you just tried to get me with my own wisdom!

HER: [Blank stare]

ME: You're right. I'm tripping.

HER: Do you not think you deserve to be helped?

And that is when my head blew off my neck. Do I not think I deserve to be helped? AUNTIE, READ MEEEEE. DRAG MEEEE. SLAYYY ME!

This is how we ended up exploring how I put boulders on my back while other people carry rocks because I would rather shoulder the burden. This is partly because I trust me more to handle it, and partly because I don't think I deserve the help because I tell myself that others need help much more than me. Meanwhile, my back is breaking, all so I can feel like I'm helping others not break theirs.

Did I just read you your life? Yes, I did. Welcome to Club I Got It Even to My Own Detriment. Our meetings are every other Tuesday. Please bring snacks that won't cause heartburn.

Let me break me down for you. I have always been the Responsible One and I feel a deep sense of responsibility for myself, my path, and my actions. I was the seven-year-old who never had to be told to study or do her homework because she was already doing it. I got straight A's and condemned myself for the B's before anyone else could.

I don't want people to worry about me. The world is enough of an unpredictable junkyard. I have never wanted to give those I love or those who I am around another reason to be anxious, upset, or stressed out. If I were a superhero, I'd be SuperIndependent. I don't need anything from anybody. I haven't even asked anyone, my mom included, for money since I was seventeen years old. And I've worn this as a badge of honor for a long time.

As the Responsible One, that same insistence on not being a burden on anyone also came with the self-imposed duty to ensure the people around me were doing okay. Since I was fine, I felt obligated to make sure they were too. This turned me into the Giver Who Never Asks, and that is a problem.

Shout-out to those of us who are GIVERS. We define ourselves by how much we give to others. Our benevolence as a core value is something we are very proud of. (Remember chapter one? Yeah, Auntie Generous over here.) However, GIVERS are usually bad at being TAKERS, which is a liability.

There are so many people who will give you the shirts off their backs but don't know how to receive something as simple as a compliment without feeling like they have to hand it back somehow. I'm a recovering giver, meaning I used to be unable to ask for help or receive gifts without feeling like I owed someone.

We gotta check our motives when all we do is give without knowing how to receive. How can we allow people to fully show us love if we don't allow them to be generous to us? We love the feeling that we get when we're like, "Hey, I just did this thing for somebody." So then why don't we allow others to get the same feeling when they give something to us, whether it's a compliment, a gift, or their time?

When you are only handing out without receiving, you might be unknowingly leading with your ego. Maybe deep down, you love being thanked. Maybe subconsciously, it feeds your ego to always be Captain Here You Go. We love how good it feels to give. Generosity also helps us hide our vulnerability. Always handing out help but never asking for it is ensuring we aren't seen as weak. Or maybe we don't think we deserve moments of service ourselves. We don't want people to think we're taking advantage of them. We don't want to show up as somebody who needs somebody else. It's a problem because we are not being fully honest with ourselves and the people in our lives.

A lot of us will find ourselves in crisis before we say, "I need help." And in those moments of overwhelm, odds are we do not have anything to give, because we're already exerting ourselves to the limit. If we need help, it shouldn't depend on what we can give right back. You don't have to be drowning before you raise your hand and ask for help.

When I began to learn I can receive without being indebted to someone, I began to get freer. I'm still a work in progress on that front. But I now say thank you and mean it. Now I commit myself to giving to someone else, knowing that they don't owe me either.

I have my family and my friends and my village to thank for forcing me to become somebody who got okay with asking for and receiving help. The way the people I love show up for me, give me so much of their time, money, energy, advice, and presence, forced me into TAKING from them. They used love as action to disarm me and to give me help before I could even ask. Their love taught me that when I need something from them, I can ASK.

My village also taught me that there are some acts that are so meaningful that no matter how much I could try to "repay" them, there is no tit for tat because each act of benevolence stands on its own. There's no one thing you can do that's going to feel like an even exchange. Shoot, if someone gives you their kidney, you can't turn around and give them your lungs. That's not how it works.

I have received some large gifts in my life that have stunned me into silence, driving this lesson home. Take, for example, my bachelorette party. Nine of my girlfriends flew me to Anguilla (first class). They bride-napped me and took me on a six-day trip to paradise, taking care of everything. There were no details left untouched. They even made a website to commemorate the trip, and we used the hashtag #BridalLuvv.

The trip was loud, flashy, and expensive AF (we stayed at the Four Seasons villas). Me that just got nice things yesterday. I still remembered, in the past, sharing a bed with friends on trips we insisted on taking, even though we could barely pay our bills. I remembered when the Four Seasons was in my vision statement. Now we were here and it was real life, and I had friends who insisted on giving me this experience.

On that trip, I felt deep gratitude because nine people thought I was deserving of so much of their time, their money, their energy, and their love. I thought back to my therapist saying, "Do you not think you deserve this?" I spent those entire six days in awe because I was like, "Wow, I'm worthy of this?" It made me realize that a lot of the times when we don't know how to receive without feeling like we owe somebody, it is because we might not think we are worthy of that gift, or we might not think we can live up to it.

I couldn't begin to repay it, so I just had to take it all in and be thankful. It was game changing because no one is obligated to do things for us, small or large. But sometimes you will receive gifts and love strictly because you are you, no other reason. When people do that and give to you, receive it. Try not to question it so much. Try not to be like, "Why me?" Why *not* you?

What you can do is continue to be kind and generous. In the process, do not be so quick to turn down help or gifts. Know that you are deserving of the favor because you are here.

In times of frustration, I've lamented how I've ALWAYS done everything myself and this is why I don't need anyone to do anything for me. Meanwhile, I've gone to the ends of the earth for people, even when they didn't ask.

One day, my husband basically channeled my therapist and read the scrolls of my life to me. He said, "You being so openhanded seems to be a function of you not wanting to exert the same pain point on somebody else. I'm going to challenge you to stop saying how much you don't need from someone. I want you to stop saying how much you don't ask for things from people and how much you take care of everything yourself. You say it out loud so often. I ask that of you because what I hear when you say that is you're wearing it as a badge and accomplishment. If this was the Struggle Olympics, that may be okay, but it's not."

You should see the way my edges instantly retracted into my scalp. DID YOU JUST READ ME SO ACCURATELY WITH MY OWN WORDS? You know when someone says something that is so on point that you have no comeback because your brain is doing the "But They're Right" Running Man? That's what happened when he said that to me. The realization that I had come to define myself as someone who did not need anyone. What cookie did I think I was gonna get by running myself into the ground? What martyrdom did I think I was aiming for?

What is the win when we insist on being self-sufficient even in the moments of drowning, when all we need is a hand as we flail in water? Are you saying there's no Lived a Low-Maintenance Life and Needed No One cookie? Well damb. I think about the Brené Brown quote: "I've learned that gasping for air while volunteering to give others CPR is not heroic. It's suffocation by resentment." A WHOLE SERMON.

We are so used to being called strong, especially Black women, that some of us consider it a weakness to need the support of the people we consider community. We cannot base who we are on how little help we need, or how much we are helpful to other people. Because what if there comes a time when we have nothing to GIVE? Does that render us terrible people? Do we lose our compass? Do we feel less than because of it?

When we don't ask, or we don't receive well, we might be blocking our blessings. This goes beyond the times we need help. When we do not know how to ask for what we need or ask for more, we end up receiving less than we should. The truth is, people will give you the absolute minimum if you let them. Sometimes we aren't even "letting" them. We are afraid of being TOO difficult or demanding (hey, chapter two), so we accept the first thing they offer us.

I come from a long line of hagglers, and my grandmother was definitely one. Haggling is an exercise in asking for more until you are satisfied. So why did I come to America and forget my haggling ancestry? I should have been treating job negotiation like a Nigerian market, where the motto is "Always ask for what you want." The first no isn't what they mean. Keep asking, and even if you don't get exactly what you want, you are as close to it as you can get. "At least you tried" is a way of life.

When Mama Fáloyin would come to the United States, she'd ask me to take her to her favorite flea market in Chicago. By me taking her, she meant she needed me to come to be extra hands to hold the plethora of stuff she would be buying. Also, to push the second cart.

My freshman year of high school, K-Swiss shoes were all the rage. My mom, being the coolness blocker that she was (see also: single mother who couldn't afford to buy $75 shoes), wasn't getting me a pair. And since my allowance was, like, $5 a week, the save-up for them would take months.

So me and Grandma went to this large warehouse that honestly instantly overwhelmed me. I had insta-regret the moment we stepped in there because ten thousand square feet of disorganized bins of stuff you have to rummage through is my idea of hell on earth. (That and having to take a Spirit Airlines flight.) I was ready to drop all my sins for sainthood because if real hell was this, I SURELY wasn't tryna go.

After about ninety minutes of rummage fest, I somehow stumbled upon a pair of all-white K-Swisses. They were mid-length, with the five stripes and the white laces. WHAT?!?!? Look at my luck and God! Those shoes were the apple of my eye instantly. (Teenage Luvvie was tacky, doe, so she didn't know them shoes were some UGLASS things and that is why they ended up in a bin in a random warehouse, not in a store on a shelf. All I knew was: OH SNAP I CAN HAVE NAME-BRAND SHOES.) I didn't care that they basically looked like high-top socks with rubber at the bottom or that someone had done a bad job of gluing rubber under some dingy socks (because, mind you, they were white fabric, not even leather).

Grandma saw my excitement (cuz I was probably looking like Eeyore before this) and told me to put them in the cart. I was trying to not get my hopes up, because I knew they weren't gonna make it home with me. They were gonna be too expensive. I just KNEWED it. So we get up to the cashier and the shoes ring up as $25. I'm like, "Well, there goes that. She's gonna drop these." Instead, Grandma goes, "My friend. These are for my granddaughter. Please. Can I have them for ten?" I'm in my head thinking, "This lady is nuts," while also silently mourning the shoes I almost had.

Y'all. When I tell you my grandma somehow got them to agree to selling these shoes to her for $8? WHAT VOODOO SHE DO? And they threw in a mug she saw by the register for free. I was like, "THIS IS ANOINTING." Just bold and manifesting clearances. Gaht-damb superwoman. Ask and you shall receive indeed. Ask boldly, believing the answer is already yes.

I wore those K-Swisses OUT! Those five stripes were probably down to two by the time I was done with them. But the audacity to ask. It was everything. Ask for what you want. The universe might surprise you and say YES.

Lemme drop a quick scripture on you right quick. Matthew 7:7: "Ask and it will be given to you; seek and you will find; knock and the door will be opened to you."

What would happen if we all had the sense of entitlement of a Stewart who couldn't even hold a candle to us in a game of Scrabble?

What would happen if we all asked for things with the confidence of a Connor who we'd beat in an IQ test by at least twenty-five points? Can you imagine the game-changing wave of us good, smart, thoughtful people having the nerve of a Garrett who didn't have the sense God gave a goat? My goodness. We might get somewhere!

Or what if we all had the boldness of an older Nigerian woman who believed she can get what she wants through kindness and that smile of hers? Mountains could move!

Do not force yourself to want less to appease other people. Do not dumb down your needs so you won't want to ask for more. You want what you want. Ask for it. A NO will not kill you.

Ask for more, because if the fear of disappointment stops you from going for what you want, then you are choosing failure in advance. It's a self-fulfilling prophecy. If we don't think that we should ask for the thing we want, whether it's a promotion from our boss, or more acts of service from our partner, or more attention from our friends, then we are opting for the NO, instead of trying for a YES. If we get the NO, we are still in the same place we are, losing nothing. But what if we got the YES, which would lead us closer to where we want to be?

When you choose to let fear keep you in your comfort zone, you might think that you're avoiding disappointment when what you're really doing is choosing that path, because you will know that you aren't getting what you want and need. The NO will not kill you, but the YES could save you.

My life changed when I got the courage to ASK for what I want. The courage to ASK people to stop doing things I don't like. The courage to ASK people I work with for what I thought I deserved.

The courage to ASK my partner for what I needed to feel loved. The courage to ASK my friends for their shoulders when I needed to cry. The courage to ASK the universe/God for things I thought were far-fetched.

I know we've heard "Closed mouths don't get fed." It is cliché. But it is true. We close our mouths as people do things to disrespect us. We close our mouths because we do not think we are in the position to ask. We close our mouths because we're afraid of NO. When I learned to open my mouth, my life transformed.

I didn't get smarter or cuter or less loud or less quiet or more interesting. But I was no longer so afraid to be vulnerable and say when I needed help. I was no longer tied to the thing of "I'm the one people don't worry about." I humbled myself and realized that life is not about taking on more than we can stand so someone else can soar on our backs.

You know what happened when I started asking for more? Magic happened. By magic, I mean people gave me more. The love I hoped people felt from me came back infinitely. I felt stronger, knowing that in this world, I didn't walk alone. I felt more loved, because I gave people a chance to show up for me, and to feel just as good as I did when I was leading by giving. And I felt more confident, because things I've dreamt, and some things I never even fathomed, started happening for me.

# 9

# GET YOUR MONEY

### We fear being considered greedy.

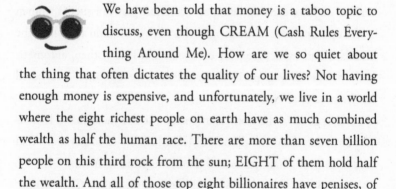 We have been told that money is a taboo topic to discuss, even though CREAM (Cash Rules Everything Around Me). How are we so quiet about the thing that often dictates the quality of our lives? Not having enough money is expensive, and unfortunately, we live in a world where the eight richest people on earth have as much combined wealth as half the human race. There are more than seven billion people on this third rock from the sun; EIGHT of them hold half the wealth. And all of those top eight billionaires have penises, of course.

There is nothing fair about capitalism, and we're all just pawns in it. Butttt I wonder if the pawns can have a little bit more money while we're on the board.

Women are especially discouraged from caring too much about money, because we are supposed to be constantly service-minded, even as others plot how to stack their coins. People assume we want to be in service, and we're pressured to feel obligated to serve. That's why more women over-index in working in nonprofits. According to a project done by the Bayer Center for Nonprofit Management, women make up 74 percent of the nonprofit workforce and are often paid 74 percent or less to do the same job as a man.* We are half of the population but represent three-quarters of those who work in an industry that is all about the greater good. And because nonprofits have fewer resources, historically underpay for labor (because: broke), and are then considered women's work, this love of service we have ends up being an economic justice issue. If women make up 74 percent of the people who work in an industry where the standard and expectation for compensation is low, then, automatically, there is no wage parity for us. Already, we're going to be cheated by the state of affairs.

Doing good in the world is important. It also sucks that it is completely undervalued and debased. Meanwhile, major corporations that lead with profit first, not social good, are printing money! PRINTING! Apple has more than $245 billion in cash. If their CEO went to the ATM, he'd get a receipt that reads $245,000,000,000. CVS receipts everywhere would be jealous. (BTW, why the hell are they so

---

*Peggy Outon, "Women in Nonprofits: Then & Now," *GuideStar*, https://trust .guidestar.org/blog/2015/11/20/women-in-nonprofits-then-now/.

damb long? CVS itself gotta be killing the trees in the Amazon for constantly printing the Dead Sea Scrolls when all you went in there to buy was a pack of Mentos.)

Meanwhile your local nonprofit, which is trying to feed kids from low-income households, has to lie prostrate at the feet of funders, begging like Keith Sweat to fund their $30,000 program. They gotta write two-hundred-page proposals with promises to spend every dollar on the program, not on staff, as if PEOPLE aren't the ones who run the programs. And then IF they are blessed by receiving HALF of what they need to run said program, they gotta send back a hundred-page report that no one got paid to write, because the money can't go to labor. Make it make sense, Fatha Gawd!

Women do that work, with long hours and low pay. In a capitalist society, philanthropy is a burden only we bear, and that has real consequences.

Society does not put the pressure of service on men, so they are able to be capitalists without guilt. You know what pays people a lot? Being an executive in the private sector. Eighty-six percent of Fortune 500 executives are dudes.* Meanwhile, women are made to feel guilty when we want to make adequate (or a lot of) money. Our capitalism comes with a hefty dollop of contrition, because we're afraid to collect our coins, even when the means are clean. We worry that if we care a lot about money or talk about it too much (levels that are super subjective), we are being covetous. Even though we

---

*Kristen Joiner, "Like the Vacuuming, Nonprofit Work Is Women's Work," *Stanford Social Innovation Review*, June 12, 2015, https://ssir.org/articles/entry/like_the_vacuuming_nonprofit_work_is_womens_work.

HAVE to care about money to survive. Everything we get to do is tied to our financial wellness.

This fear is why I feel like women are the ones most likely to do fundraisers ON OUR BIRTHDAYS, asking people to donate money to someone in need. You know those fundraisers on Facebook, where someone's birthday happens and they're asking their friends to give a certain amount to a cause they chose? I *LOOOOVE* our selflessness, but at what cost are we being so giving? It seems like the times we finally do ask for help are solely when it's for someone else's benefit.

I often wonder if the people who are doing fundraisers on their birthdays are behind on their own bills. Are you raising money for breast cancer when you don't know where your rent is coming from, because the job you work so hard at isn't paying you an adequate living wage? Are you selling merchandise from your side hustle and donating proceeds to a local nonprofit when your car note couldn't be paid because you had to choose between that and your child's asthma medication? Sis, you deserve all those coins so you can stand up straight. You do not have to donate anything if you are currently not sure where your next five meals will come from.

Women create and work in nonprofits because, as the nurturers, we say, "We want to help the world." No, help yourself first, sis. And then help the world. Put your mask on first and all that jazz. I preach the gospel of us leaving the world better than we found it, but we also have to be able to leave ourselves better for it, not worse.

We've been told that our goodness in this world is directly tied to how much of ourselves we sacrifice for other people. The pressure to sacrifice ANYTHING is only placed on women. It is OUR jobs to do these fundraisers and to give in excess. To the woman who is making thirty thousand and doing her best but is still struggling to make ends meet, I want you to know that your number one priority is not to save someone else, when you yourself need saving in the moment. But hey, person who is single, has no loans, makes a hundred thousand, maybe you can give more so she won't feel like she has to.

This extends into business especially. We get cheated, particularly as women or as marginalized people. We have been told that people do us a favor by wanting to hire us. All our lives, we have received the jacked-up message that we are less significant and more disposable, and we should yield for everyone else's convenience. So then we internalize it all and wire our mouths shut to protect ourselves.

I do not blame us one bit. The world really has done the job of convincing us that we are liabilities instead of assets, and it's utter bullshit. Some of the fight has been abused out of us, so we are getting deceived left and right, underpaid, overworked, and underappreciated.

The systems of oppression stacked against us devalue us and render us at their mercy. I am VERY clear on that. White men are the measuring stick of it all because they've created it and run it like the unfair well-oiled machine it is.

It is why a white woman makes 79 cents for every dollar Biff makes.

- Latinas make 54 cents for every dollar Chad brings in.

- Native American women make 58 cents for every dollar Trent gets.

- Black women get 62 cents for every dollar Brock takes home.

- Asian women make 90 cents for every dollar Logan secures.

We are systemically hustling backward and it's not okay.

I've talked about how the last time I worked full time for someone else was as the marketing coordinator of a nonprofit that taught other nonprofits how to tell their stories well. At the time, it was my dream job. I remember applying, crossing my fingers, and hoping I'd be so lucky to get an interview. Well, I got the interview and aced it. In September 2008, I received my offer. "Your starting salary will be $35,000." Dang, I'd hoped I could get $40,000, but who was I to be greedy? I instantly replied back to the email and accepted.

I didn't negotiate one thing. Not even the two weeks of paid vacation. Not the 5 percent salary increase I *might* get after a year. I know. Nonprofits are notoriously not gonna pay a lot, but now I know that there is usually more money on the table. Because Me Now knows more. I should have asked for more money.

If you don't take anything else from this book, please absorb this:

ALWAYS NEGOTIATE YOUR JOB OFFERS. It doesn't matter how good the offer is! Always ask for more. A few reasons:

1. Nobody is doing you a favor by hiring you. NOBODY. You are hired to do a job because you have the skill. They need you to do this thing.

b. You are supposed to negotiate. In fact, when you don't negotiate, you are going against standard practice. It's part of the steps of the game of business. You have the right to ALWAYS ask for what you think you are worth. The answer is less your business (you can't control that), but the ASK itself is FULLY your business (you control that). DO IT ALL THE TIME.

iii. The first offer is not the best offer. As in, people always have more money than they first bring to you. The first number thrown at you is NEVER the highest number someone can pay you. They offer you $40,000? Odds are that they have $45,000 in the budget for you. Ask for $7,000 more and they might meet you in the middle. Too many of us opt out because we are afraid. Which leads me to:

4d. You asking for more money (or vacay time or benefits) does not mean they will take back the offer for employment. Just because you say, "I want more," doesn't mean they'll say, "We don't want you anymore." I know it is a major anxiety we have that if we negotiate, they will somehow be offended and take everything off the table. Listen here: Headhunting and hiring and team building are EXPENSIVE for companies! If you are afraid that an offer will be taken off the table the moment you throw a number out, go back to number 1. They are not doing you a favor by offering you a job: They need you too. And HR knows searching for someone else can get expensive and time-consuming. Folks don't want to go back to square one. When they find you, their perfect candidate, they don't want you to walk away. They need you. THEY NEED YOU. So remove the fear that asking for more will mean you lose the job. You won't.

V. Women and people of color haven't been told to negotiate. I've talked to so many HR folks and they always tell me that this makes them face-palm. One of my friends sent a job offer to a candidate. The person accepted immediately. She was like, "SHIT. WHY DIDN'T SHE ASK ME FOR MORE?? I had $15,000 more for her." And before you say, "Why don't people just pay us everything they have? Isn't that what's fair?" Eh. If only business was about fairness. It's not. You have to play the part of the game where you tell them, "This isn't enough. I want more." And then they come back with, "FINE, we found more." I was never given permission or told to ask for more at a job. I found out somewhere along the way.

The number we accept in the beginning of our careers follows us. That $35,000 I accepted without question could have affected every other number I received from that point from that company. A 5 percent raise for $35,000 is $1,750. Sooo that brought me to $36,750 after a year. Imagine if I had negotiated to start at $40,000. Five percent of that is $2,000, which would bring me to $42,000. The same position at the same company could have gotten me over $5,000 MORE in one year if I had simply asked. Not asking for more literally costs us money. It is expensive to be quiet sometimes, and this is one of those instances. We have to ask for more money.

I need us to negotiate ALWAYS. Need. I want us to stop leaving money on the table.

So, my salary of $35,000 from the last full-time job I had? That is now something I've made in one weekend or through one hour of work, and it is WILD to say. How did I get to this point? Well, I built a massive platform, spent ten years building my name, wrote a *New York Times* bestselling book, and proved over and over again that excellence was something I hold dear.

And that number is large. I went from not being able to ask to be paid more than that for a year to asking for it for one event. Let me tell you how I learned to ask: I researched, practiced, and asked for it in spite of the alarms in my head that tried to convince me I was out of line. In spite of the impostor syndrome that gets me from time to time to say, "Who are you to ask for this?" In spite of the guilt of knowing that I've made more in one year than my mother made in one decade of work.

I have negotiated my way to numbers that make me laugh from the discomfort of their enormity.

There are entire books on how to negotiate. Consider picking one of them up. In the meantime, here's my CliffsNotes version:

1. Research the industry. How much are your peers making? How much do people get compensated for comparable work? Know this because it arms you with leverage when you walk into a room. That knowledge is power you can use.

b. Know that you are not being greedy for asking for what you're worth, or asking for more money.

iii. Say the number with an exclamation point, not a question mark, and shut up. What I mean by exclamation point is when you are asked what you want, say, "I'd like $50,000!" Don't say, "Umm . . . I'd like $50,000???" ending with your voice becoming high-pitched so it sounds like you're asking a question. If you're asking the question and not telling, it sounds like you're not sure you're worth the money, so why should they be sure? Say your number with confidence and then say nothing else. Sit there and wait for their response. It is not your time to say more because it will look like you're overexplaining. Before the number comes up, you've already talked about the value you bring, so now is the time for you to kick the ball into their court and wait for them to pick it up.

I've had friends in HR tell me how they have encountered people who said the number they wanted and went silent. And then after five seconds of waiting for the other party to respond, the person jumped back in: "No, it's fine. I can go lower too." NOOOOOOO!!!! Don't do that! I know silence from the other side can be uncomfortable, but do not retract your want! It is valid. The other person is probably processing and doing calculations. Fear kicked in, which is why we sometimes take back what we said we want.

In addition to negotiating for more, we should not stake claims on being cheap hires. Being known as a low-cost hire should not be our value proposition. You are not the Dollar Store and you shouldn't be. I will never be the least expensive option or use that as a rallying cry for someone to want to work with me. Why? Because you get what you pay for, and I know what I bring to the table.

Your value is not how low budget your work is, but how good it is. And people need to be willing to pay for your service. If they cannot afford you, then either they save their money to the point where they can or they go to someone whose services or products are less expensive—but that person doesn't have to be you.

You might have heard of the concept of FAST. GOOD. CHEAP. Pick two out of three when you're looking for a service. You cannot have all three.

If they're FAST and CHEAP, they probably aren't that GOOD. If they're GOOD and CHEAP, they aren't FAST. If they're FAST and GOOD, they are not going to be CHEAP.

People expect all three and I be like, HOW, DOE?? Often, people will pick CHEAP over GOOD. That's how folks end up with

Microsoft clip art logos. If someone is all three, they've undervalued their work, because if they're fast and good, they should not be cheap.

We're often willing to accept less than we want because we're afraid of leaving money on the table. "I cost $100 but they have $20. I should take the $20 because at least $20 is more than $0." Nope. Because now you're saying $20 is the price for you, and next time they want you, they will remember paying the $20 so they probably won't come prepared to pay that $100.

You can, of course, donate your services for causes that are important, or accept lower fees on a case-by-case basis. But as a habit and mantra, success, especially as an entrepreneur, often lies in getting paid what you ask, for the work you do. The people who pay you well for your work give you the freedom to now donate your time to a nonprofit doing good work, or to kids who need what you have to offer. (How often are men expected to donate their time, energy, and services for others? And when they refuse to, who guilts them for it or calls them selfish? How often are men expected to be paid in exposure? Which . . . let me go there . . .)

People LOVE offering us exposure for payment. But exposure is not currency I can use to pay my mortgage or support my shoe habit. I be wanting to say "Expose deez nuts" sometimes. I know I don't have nuts, but the sentiment stands. As someone who started my entrepreneur life as a blogger, I know what it's like to be offered exposure as a serious form of payment from people who didn't know they were being useless.

Every day, a brand that throws millions of dollars to whatever agency creates their simple-ass sans serif logo that conveys "minimalism," even though it's literally their name spelled out in Helvetica font, emails an influencer asking them to do a campaign for "exposure." And every day, an angel loses a string in her harp.

Are they going to make money off this campaign? Odds are, they are. They want us to work for free even though we're making them money, placing them in front of our audience, and doing work that will take us hours (and sometimes days) to complete on their behalf. But they want to pay us with exposure? *Naija accent* Thunda fire you!

Exposure hustling is writing for one of the biggest news outlets on the web and them offering to pay me by tweeting my username on their account so I can get more followers. My mind is always blown by the unmitigated gall. You know what? They can ask, but my answer can always be HELL NO.

I think about a Nicki Minaj story that changed my life and how I look at asking for what I'm worth and my coins. It's all about pickle juice and why we should refuse to drink it.

Why pickle juice? Well, Nicki Minaj was booked for a photo shoot. When she showed up on set, none of the amenities she had asked for were there. She went to catering, and instead of food, there was only a jar of pickles on the table. The clothing options were awful. The whole booking was terrible, so she walked away. Her agent tried to stop her, but she wouldn't accept the situation. She wasn't going to allow pickle juice to be an anchor in future negotiations.

As she said in the MTV documentary *My Time Now*, "I put quality in what I do. . . . So if I turn up to a photo shoot and you got a

$50 clothes budget and some sliced pickles on a motherfuckin' board, you know what? No. I am gonna leave. Is that wrong? Wanting more for myself? Wanting people to treat me with respect? You know what? Next time, they know better. But had I accepted the pickle juice, I would be drinking pickle juice right now."*

It's a great lesson in knowing your worth, standing in it, and demanding it, even in the face of people telling you you're supposed to accept less. She knew her value. DO. NOT. ACCEPT. PICKLE. JUICE. Because again, people will do and give us the minimum that we accept. We'd love to think they will be virtuous, but people are selfish.

T he pay gap is so real for women, and it makes me want to fight the air everlasting.

I got an email asking me to speak at a tech conference in Europe, and my lecture agent replied. For every speaking engagement, we ask for my fee, as well as my flight and hotel to be covered. They replied saying they don't really pay speakers and don't pay for travel but "The exposure would be great for you." I remember thinking, "Well, clearly I'm exposed because you found me. Y'all came to me!" And it was a big tech conference that was super dude-bro heavy, so I really doubted that they weren't paying anyone.

I'm part of a group of 250 influential women in business, technology, and media. It's called TheLi.st. We talk to each other about everything from business to personal questions. One thread might

---

*"Nicki Minaj Doesn't Want Your Pickle Juice," *Rap-Up*, https://www.rap-up.com /2010/11/26/nicki-minaj-doesnt-want-your-pickle-juice/.

be about searching for a good investment app, another might be about looking for a nanny for the babies, another might ask who has leads on a chief marketing officer job. It runs the gamut. Every day people are talking and sharing and deepening connections. So I go on TheLi.st and I say, "Hey everyone, I was invited to speak at this conference, which makes more than 15 million euros a year. They're saying that they don't pay anybody."

Within fifteen minutes, women on TheLi.st were like, "Oh, no. One of my guy friends spoke there last year. He was paid, and his books were covered, and his travel was covered." Someone else said they spoke there and their travel was covered.

Because TheLi.st is really diverse, with women of all ethnic backgrounds, I was able to get a useful sense of hierarchy and pattern when it came to how this conference paid people. White men who went to speak were paid, and if it wasn't in cash, the conference bought quantities of their books. Plus their travel was covered. White women typically had their travel paid for. A few Black women who were asked to speak at this conference were told exposure was their compensation.

If NO ONE was paid and it was a policy across the board, then I could make the decision on whether donating my time was worth it. Knowing everyone was treated equally would be okay. But that wasn't the case.

In that moment, I realized I had to be the person who faced her fears head-on and still chugged through. I had to show that I am the person I say I am.

I told my agents that this pattern of pay was not okay and I had a major problem with it. I said I wanted to speak about it publicly. My agents know me well and know I am a truth girl, but they low-key freaked out. They made great points that if I spoke out about it, I might have a harder time booking other engagements from conferences who saw my public pushback and thought I might do the same to them. This could hit my pockets. They were rightfully afraid for me. And honestly, I was afraid for myself.

So I went through my three questions (see chapter six).

I checked in with myself and them: "Okay, I've been speaking for almost a decade; I'm in some pretty influential rooms. I've been on some prestigious stages, and I have a lot of access. I command a pretty big fee. If I can't be the one to speak up about this, who can? Am I expecting the person who just started speaking yesterday? The person who has never gotten paid for a speaking engagement? Am I expecting the person who just got their first speaking engagement last week to now be the one to challenge pay inequality in tech, which is a major industry that is run by dudes who don't look like me? Who am I expecting to do this work, if not me?"

I knew I had the ability to speak up, but I also knew that I was very likely to be punished for using that power. All of those fears were tied to money, being afraid of being greedy and being afraid of the consequences that could come when I, a Black woman, asked loudly to be compensated fairly for work I was expected to do.

Then I thought of my worst-case scenarios: that I would get fewer speaking engagements or none at all. People would stop requesting me, and a big revenue generator for my work would come to a screeching halt. Well, then I'd have to switch up my business model to take on more individual clients. I can always go back to doing consulting focused on marketing. I can always help other small business owners create massive platforms for themselves, like I did for myself. I wouldn't become homeless if I actually made this point and it ruined my speaking career, because if I ran out of my savings, of which I had six months' worth of expenses, I could go lie on my mama's couch till I got back on my feet. I thought through the catastrophic consequences that could happen from speaking out, and even from there, I realized I would still be okay.

After going through all three questions, and the worst-case scenarios, I knew the answers were YES, so I decided to go on Twitter to talk about the situation. It began an hours-long conversation, with others also sharing their stories and frustrations about moments when they were being offered toenail clippings as payment for their work. One woman talked about how she and her brother had been separately invited to speak at a conference in China. They told her they had no budget for speakers. They told him they'd pay him $20,000 and fly him on a private jet to the conference. HER OWN BROTHER. Same work, completely different payments.

Whew shit. Then a *Forbes* writer, Christina Wallace, who also happens to be on TheLi.st, asked me if I'd like to go on record about the situation. Of course, being the glutton for punishment that I am, I said yes. Christina wrote about it with the title "It's Time to End the Pay Gap for Speakers at Tech Conferences."* The caucacious guy who ran the conference ended up sending me and Christina an email full of fucked-up feelings. Because you know what Boris (his actual name) doesn't like? Being challenged and called out. This goat said,

---

*Christina Wallace, "It's Time to End the Pay Gap for Speakers at Tech Conferences," *Forbes*, March 13, 2017, https://www.forbes.com/sites/christinawallace/2017/03/13/pay-gap-for-speakers-at-tech-conferences/.

"When we reply saying 'we don't have a budget for speakers,' the whole unpleasant truth is that we need to prioritize whom we spend our limited budget on, and in this case it's speakers that are perhaps more relevant for our audience, more sought-after. That is far from saying we think Luvvie Ajayi isn't worth paying—we're absolutely sure that for the right audience and in the right city, she easily commands her fee."

*Flava Flav voice* WOWWWWW the audacity of caucasity is alive and well. The dog whistle, basically saying they're not paying me since Amsterdam ain't Atlanta. Ain't that some shit?? I was facing my front* when y'all came to ME to speak.

Boris blessed us, though, because the piece got updated with his response, further proving my point. He doubled down on the point that the article was making: that they can see me and all my expertise, and the fact that I'm good at what I do, and still not want to pay me what I'm worth, strictly because they don't think I fit the demographic. Basically, I'm too Black to be paid.

The fear I had—that I would lose money after people saw me speaking up against this conference—didn't happen. Quite the opposite, actually. That *Forbes* piece got a lot of attention and ended up getting me more invitations to come speak. That is also the year I did my TED Talk. So, all these really cool things happened from that piece. If I had never spoken up because of fear of repercussions, then the rewards might have never come.

If you're asking me to donate my time, that's one thing. But don't insult my intelligence by telling me the exposure will be worth it.

---

*Facing my front = minding my business.

"We don't have a budget for this campaign, but we will promote you. This will be great exposure."

We're so afraid of charging what we're really worth because we fear that people will walk away. I say good riddance to bad rubbish. People who want to pay us pickle juice for champagne work have to get used to hearing no. Don't come to undergrad with elementary expectations. Don't come to this rice party with a kale dish. I've bent over backward for the opportunity to work with some companies before. I've charged what I knew was less than my value just to "build relationships," and in the end all I felt was cheated. And THAT is the greatest suck of all. When you realize that you were taken advantage of and you let it happen, that's also when you decide you don't want it to happen again.

firmly believe that people have gotten us to be silent about money in order to take advantage. Our silence is being weaponized against us. We've learned for such a long time that you don't talk money, but it's part of the reason why we get cheated over and over again.

I realize the privilege I have by having a network like TheLi.st, where I can go and ask for radical transparency. I'm able to call a friend and say, "Hey, they want me to do this thing. Here's the fee." Friend will be like, "No. They have double that. Go back and ask for double." I'll hang up. "Yeah, so I'll need this." "Okay." "Sweet." It was that easy? I just had to know y'all had double? Because nobody told me. The value of sharing this type of information cannot be underestimated.

When we think about money, we think about me-me-me. The

worst part is we are doing ourselves a disservice. If I'm walking into any room, I'm not cheap. The problem is, if I don't tell you what my price is, and you tell the same person what your price is and your price is a tenth of mine, that doesn't do me any favors. Why? Because they hear my number and they think, "Oh, she's expensive." I'm not expensive, but I am valuable and I'm asking for what I'm worth. None of us win in this scenario when our work is similar but you're undercutting my prices. The win comes when we can be open and honest and we are both paid fairly.

None of us win when I am up here and you're down here. When we're quiet about our numbers, we're actually cheating each other. But when we share numbers, other people also get used to hearing these big numbers coming from women. "Oh, you don't have enough for my fee in the budget? It's cool. I can't come. Oh, you found it. Thank you."

I want us to stop feeling guilty for dropping a number that we are actually going to earn. Getting paid is not getting a favor. You're gifting them with your work, with the service, with the thing that you studied, the thing that you've put hours into. That is the thing that they're paying for, and they should pay every dime. Do not feel guilty about being a capitalist who wants to do good in the world.

There's a reason why something like 95 percent of billionaires in the world are men. It's not because they're smarter than us or work harder than us. It's more that they have no guilt attached to making buckets of money, and the systems prop them up to allow them to do so. They have no guilt for wanting to be financially prosperous.

You have a right to demand what you're worth. And just because your color might be darker and/or you're a woman does not mean somebody should pay you less. WE have $1 trillion in spending power. So when you show up on our doorstep saying you only have a tiny amount of money to work with, you're insulting me and my skinfolk. Your diversity budget has nothing to do with me.

In the words of Professional Troublemaking Prophetess-at-Large Robyn Rihanna Fenty, "Bitch better have my money."*

My grandma did not play about her money. My aunt told me a story of back in the day when my grandmother was a wigmaker. She learned to make wigs to make ends meet, to supplement my grandfather's income. They did have six kids to raise, after all.

Anyhoo, word of Grandma's wigmaking skills had traveled, and she was hired by the wife of a governor. When Mama Fáloyin delivered the wig to the lady's house, she wasn't there at the time. Grandma realized the lady was trying to shaft her money. NO MA'AM. NO SIR. That's what you're not going to do. So Granny refused to leave until she got her money. At first, they told her the lady wasn't home, so Mama Fáloyin said that was fine, she'd wait for her. And wait she did. After a few hours passed and they realized she wasn't leaving till she got her money, someone finally came outside and handed her what she was owed. THAT'S RIGHT.

Do not be afraid to insist on someone running you your coins. Do not feel like you're being a shark for sending reminder emails on an overdue invoice. Understand that sometimes, you do have to take off your earrings via email and let someone know that the consequence of not paying you means extra fees on top of what they already owe. Collect your coins, without guilt!

---

We are afraid of talking about money, of admitting that we want more of it, and of insisting that people give us what we have earned. We fear people walking away from us. We fear losing opportunities. We fear getting the reputation of being close-fisted. All valid, but if one of the things people use to disparage me is that I'm serious about being paid, then let it be. In fact, put it on my epitaph: "She came. She saw. She didn't play about her coins."

There are systems in place that are actively working against us in every way. The world is unfair to everyone who is not a straight Christian white dude. It is set up for their triumph, their comfort, their wealth-building. It is designed for the rest of us to be born poor, live poor, and die poor. It is also designed to gaslight us, by teaching us to be afraid of what happens when we want the piece of the pie that belongs to us, but they've hoarded.

I'm not asking for you to ignore the system, nor am I saying it is your job to dismantle that machine. We're disenfranchised in a lot of it. But I am asking you to ask the world for more and get your money.

What happens after we ask is out of our control. We might ask for more money and they still tell us no. But it's important for us to ask so we have a chance to get it. Because not asking is a guaranteed NO, unless we find a saint who says, "I know you didn't ask but here's extra." That doesn't come too often. By asking, we increase our chances of getting something more, even if all we get is 20 cents more. It is still more than we had. It's still more than we were gonna get.

When we ask for more money, we're not breaking up systems or fixing everything, but we are putting ourselves a little bit closer to something that resembles parity. And if we don't do it for ourselves, who is going to do it? I want to think that the world is benevolent and people are really kind and would go out of their way constantly to ensure justice and equity, but it's not how it goes. A lot of this will fall on us; we have to roll massive boulders uphill because we don't have any other choice.

So ask for more, get your money, and do it without guilt. And then when you get money and you have abundance, pass some of that on to someone else, and we can have a circle of giving. But we cannot be of service to others if we can't be of service to ourselves first.

# 10

# DRAW YOUR LINES

## We fear not being considered nice.

 People can be some no-personal-space-respecting goats, all up in our faces and spaces when we don't want them. That's why it's so important for us to be serious about boundaries. And as I get older and my grays disrespect my edges more, one of the facts of life that I hold dear is knowing that we have to teach people what we expect from them and how we want to be treated. If we do not, we'll constantly have people getting on our nerves, and life is too short for side-eye-induced high blood pressure.

Boundaries are some of my favorite things to draw. They became so when I realized that I had an obligation to let people know when they do something I don't like. As the professional cantankerous auntie that I've been since I could talk, I am not the most patient person at times. That's because I have some firm lines I don't want people to cross, and when they do, it instantly grinds my gears. Since

I have zero poker face, my annoyance is usually written all over it, because as I mentioned earlier, my face is basically an outside voice.

For me, drawing boundaries is a matter of social grace. If I don't, I'm probably looking like someone stole my last cookie, and no one wants that. We must create and vocalize our boundaries, no matter how much it might be jarring to others.

Having boundaries and drawing our lines is not about playing keep-away with people, and it isn't about preventing people from getting close to us (well, sometimes physically it is). It is about establishing the standards and the treatment we expect and deserve.

People often feel entitled to our lives, energy, time, space, and platforms. Usually, it's not from malice but from habit, and we are not used to creating and standing in boundaries. We tend to move freely. We touch, kiss, and move other people's bodies. We manage other people's time. We infringe upon other people's platforms. It is how we operate as a society. What's wild is MOST people are annoyed by someone crossing their boundaries.

So why are boundaries so difficult to establish? Why do we have such a hard time telling people to stop that thing we don't like them doing when it pertains to us? Because we are concerned about ostracizing people and making them feel uncomfortable. We fear disrupting harmony, hurting feelings, and seeming difficult.

As I'm moving through the world, of course I must consider other people (I'm not a sociopath). But like the flight attendants tell us as we post our last Facebook message before takeoff, we must put our oxygen masks on first before we do it for others. I need to feel as comfortable and as assured as I can. I am not obligated to use my time, body, space, or energy in ways that don't suit me.

However, while everyone else isn't necessarily responsible for my comfort, they also might be culpable in my discomfort. Lemme explain. When I walk into a room, the people in it do not have to make sure I'm feeling tended to and perfectly at home. HOWEVER, if the folks in the room start throwing insults my way, then they are liable for my uneasiness. That being said, my boundaries are my responsibility to voice, because what happens when people don't realize I've drawn lines in invisible ink? They're not culpable if they don't know. We often get mad at someone crossing boundaries we didn't establish, and we have to ask ourselves how the person could have known to do better by us or to do something different.

Yes, there are some universal boundaries we should all honor, like consent should come before sex. A person should be able to walk down the street butt-nekkid wearing nothing but socks and a smile, and no one should touch them, unless they have a sign that says, "Touch me freely." Even then, I might still ask.

Besides those, we cannot assume anything else of anyone. Do we realize how much we go through life letting people talk to us any kinda way and doing things to us that we don't like? What do we do about it? A lot of times, we roll our eyes. Or we deep-sigh. Or we hope they magically stop doing that thing we don't like. But people will bring trash to you if you are a willing receptacle.

We cannot assume everyone is operating from the same understanding. We do not operate from the same mind frame. This is why we have to be intentional about speaking our boundaries out loud. We gotta speak up about the things or space we need from people. That is our responsibility. Whether or not people honor it is theirs.

Personal, professional, emotional, and physical boundaries are all important. We think we can't afford to tell people our boundaries for fear of ostracizing them. But really, we cannot afford NOT to tell people our boundaries, because when we are silent, we betray ourselves. And we must betray ourselves less.

One of my grandmother's biggest boundaries was being spoken to in a loud voice in the middle of conflict. Here's the thing: Nigerians do not have an inside voice at all. Come around my family during the holidays and it sounds like a hundred people are in the room, even if it's only twenty. Yelling as we speak to each other is a love language. Even now, when we get on the phone, we act like 5G cell phone service is not a thing, and that our phones are tin cans connected by string. We are SO LOUD. We use whatever the "unnecessarily loud" decibel measurement is. I remember when I used to make fun of my elders for doing it. Now I'm an elder and I do it.

Even with those cultural mores, Mama Fáloyin did not suffer fools when it came to how she wanted to be respected at all times. Yes, you might yell her name in glee when you saw her and to hype her up (in church and anywhere else). But if she was talking to you sternly and you raised your voice? There was hell to pay. By hell, I mean dramatics.

GRANDMA: Did you finish your homework?

YOU, slightly frustrated and with a slight tilt up in your voice: Grandma, yes. I said I finished it thirty minutes ago.

GRANDMA: Ehh so you're yelling. Óyá come and beat me.

Sis, how did it escalate so quickly? How did my slight annoyance become "In fact, go get a belt and beat me"? It was hilarious when you weren't the person on the other end of it. I swear, she would sometimes respond to situations as if she were in her own personal *All My Children* episode. (Which was her favorite soap opera, by the way. That was her shit! Maybe it's because the theatrics were right up her alley. When Susan Lucci kept getting nominated for a Daytime Emmy but not winning, I think Grandma went to Jesus to intervene. Next thing you know, Susan is standing on that stage holding her award. Amen, saints.)

So Grandma would also pull the "Your own mother wouldn't talk to me like that," which would instantly shame you for the unearned brazenness you showed. Your ego would be knocked down to size.

This line that my grandma drew was known by adults and kids alike. What you not gon' do in the presence of Fúnmi Fáloyin is raise your voice at her in discontent. She'd straight up ask you, "You and who?" It's a question with no real answer, because it's one of those "Lemme make sure you know who you're dealing with" things. And I saw it over and over again, how the most blunt and surly people honored that line of hers. I saw how Nigerian police, who often give no fucks about decorum, would yell at someone in one sentence and speak to my grandmother with such deference and warm tones the next.

It let me know that people are capable of acting like they have sense. They just wield that based on who is in front of them, and what that person has allowed them to get away with. Although it is not our fault when people abuse or disrespect us, how others treat us can be a reflection of our allowances.

At the core of setting boundaries is trying to minimize self-betrayal as we exist in this world. The person who I need to make sure is okay at the end of the day/life is me, because I'm the one I have to answer to and I'm a critical child of God. Whew! I'm tough, more so on myself than anyone else. And if I gotta tell ME that I somehow bent myself out of shape for someone else, I'ma be mad as hell at myself. I've been mad as hell at me plenty of times before, and I find it really hard to forgive myself. That alone has made me insist on getting better and better about being clear to others about my limits.

I'm usually leery of people who don't have any clear boundaries. Why? Because their lack of boundaries means they are less likely to understand the paint-thick lines that I draw. They might have a hard time with me speaking my limits, seeing it as an act of hostility instead of an act of self-preservation. Plus, they might take my strong boundaries as lack of transparency and vulnerability. They will have a hard time honoring mine. There is an African proverb that says, "Be careful when a naked person offers you a shirt." My structure will make your free-willingness look like austerity.

One of my biggest boundaries is that I don't like hugging people

I don't know. I'm not anti-hugs, because I don't mind waist-bumping folks I know (who also like to be hugged by folks they know)! What I am not a huge fan of is squeezing the body of someone whose name I am not familiar with. This is a tough boundary to have. Why? Because people love to hug! It is a sign of kinship, friendliness, and sometimes kindness. And I, as someone who has a book and is somewhat visible and relatively approachable (when I don't have Resting Side-Eye Face), look pretty huggable. So the fact that I don't really like hugs from non-friends and -family can make me seem aloof when people meet me and I decline. And because of that, I find myself letting strangers hug me way more often than I'd like, and then feeling some type of way after.

How it happens: Someone sees me in public (like in the airport) and they're excited and I'm honored! They go, "I'm a hugger!" I wanna respond with "I'm a Capricorn!" since we're shouting out random attributes. I see their smiles and it makes it that much more difficult to say, "I'd prefer to fist bump." (After COVID-19 and learning how few people wash their hands, I don't even wanna shake hands anymore.) But a lot of times, I'm not even given the choice in the hug. My reflexes are slower than I'd like, and before I can say anything, I'm face-deep in the bosom of a woman who loves my work. I'm both honored and slightly taken aback. I walk away feeling a bit surly.

In that case, when meeting someone who really likes me, I'm afraid to disappoint them or hurt their feelings. The easier choice is to accept the hug. But easier for who? Not me. If it's a day when I'm at a conference speaking, I could be doing that two hundred more times. One paper cut isn't bad, but two hundred might hurt like hell. I'm not comparing hugs from strangers to paper cuts. OR AM I?

Hugs feel very personal to me. This is why I'm not giving them to everyone I meet. This is also why they're such a tough boundary. People take it personally because it probably feels like a personal rejection. I fully understand how someone could feel slighted by being told that their gesture isn't welcome. However, it's one of those "it's not you, it's me" situations. As an experienced introvert, I find my energy sapped by people. Peopling makes me tired and I usually have to recharge after doing it a lot. Hugs are Super Saiyan levels of peopling when they go into the hundreds. Protect your space and energy in the decent ways you know how.

I've asked people what the best way to decline a hug is. A large number have advised me to say, "Oh, I have a cold." Or "I'm not feeling well." Soooo the answer to telling people about what I want is to lie? Nah. Why do we need to betray ourselves in that way, by creating a false moment in order to receive the response? Who does it serve? The person who wants the hug? Okay. Meanwhile, now you're having to fake sniffles. All for what? To prevent the discomfort of someone who feels like they should receive a body squeeze from you. I don't even think the means justifies the end.

Others have advised me to make sure I'm holding something in both hands. Or that I do a quick *Matrix* backbend to avoid people's grasps. So I gotta be flexible, doing yoga and training with Mr. Miyagi at home to practice and get quicker reflexes to avoid folks' arms around me. Won't it be easier to be able to say, "Hey, I'd prefer not to do that, person whose name I don't know"?

Even the hugging expectation is super gendered. Men's personal space is often respected. Women are supposed to be the nurturers and our bodies seem to be community property, so we're expected to wanna hug folks at will. NAWL.

Many of us were not allowed to draw our boundaries growing up, especially with family. We've all seen it, or had it done to us, when we were little: A family member would visit and we'd be forced to hug them. In those moments, we learned that being related dominates our agency and we started thinking that we do not have the right to make choices for our comfort. These small moments have far-reaching impact on how we move through the world.

We normalize constant betrayal of our needs and ourselves and others around us when we do not take boundaries seriously. We say that everyone has access that is irrevocable, no matter how terribly they treat us or show up. It is not necessarily our fault, but it is our problem.

While drawing strong lines in person can be hard, even electronically we are very hesitant to create the boundaries we need. Because again, we prioritize everyone else's harmony over justice.

Social media is the land of crossed boundaries, because there is something about being behind a keyboard that makes people forget all their home training. Folks stay acting out on there.

Since boundaries are my favorite things, right under wing tip shoes and red velvet cupcakes, I have a lot of them regarding how people should interact with me online. And I very quickly realized that in order for me to not have my entire nerves be tapped on by people and their good intent, it was important for me to make loud PSAs about what my lines were.

There are a few things that really grind my gears and cross my virtual boundaries.

- When people tag me in photos I'm not in to get my attention—this is the virtual version of cold-calling me to tell me about your event.

- When people tag me in photos I'm not in to get my audience's attention—this taps on the shoulders of those who follow me. It's like putting a billboard on my lawn.

- When people direct message (DM) me to ask for a favor when they've never messaged me before—this is like walking up to a random stranger on the street and asking them to buy the T-shirt you're selling. Can you at least say hi first and introduce yourself? It always feels like some sort of invasion when the ask is money. I've had someone ask me to pay for their tuition before, and it felt like someone reached directly into my pocket rummaging for cash.

All of this is not to say don't talk to me. Rather, it is to say treat me like a person you want to build a relationship with, not someone to take advantage of. Asking for help or a favor is not the problem. The problem is doing it without regard for creating real rapport.

What happens on social media is both a gift and a curse. Because we are all now two degrees separated at most, we feel like everyone is accessible. At its best, this allows us to forge deep connections with people we might never have known otherwise. At its worst, it makes us forget that behind the names and profile pictures are real people. If we kept in mind that we are not entitled to anyone's space, time, or energy, we'd act like we have broughtupsy.

As an early adopter of social platforms, I've been cognizant of the importance of curating the space I want for years, because our experience on these mediums is wholly dependent on who we let into our eHouses. The people we friend, follow, and like determine the quality of the time we spend scrolling. You might look up one day and find that logging into Facebook stresses you out, because half your timeline is touting janky-ass conspiracy theories and the other half are pro-troglodytes. If your eyes bulge out your face and you want to drop-kick everyone in the face, you should know that it is time to make a purge.

Facebook, for example, allows you to have five thousand friends. Just because that is the maximum doesn't mean that is the number you should have. Just because your house can safely fit one hundred people in it doesn't mean that is the number you should invite for dinner today. We don't control a lot in life, but we can manage who we let into our physical and virtual spaces.

So you know I got rules for how I accept social media connections.

## FACEBOOK

Treat this as the summer picnic of social media. Ask yourself: Have I met you in real life? Do I actually know you by face, and if I see you walking and a road is between us, will I make it a point to cross the street to come greet you, or will I duck behind cars so you won't see me? Why is this important? Well, if I don't want to cheerfully acknowledge you in person and would rather do calisthenics to avoid you, then why do I need to see your posts in my timeline? A lot of people blanket-friend everyone they went to high school and college with. That is how they end up getting upset that the dude who was the first-string quarterback is now a raving Tea Party guy who you think is also running a local cult. UNFRIEND, SIS. No one needs that energy.

## TWITTER

Twitter is the equivalent of a happy hour on social media. Ask yourself: Would I maintain more than a five-minute conversation with you if we met at a mixer? At this place, where everyone is talking and I'm moving from conversation to conversation, would I sustain a conversation with you because I find you fascinating? This is relevant, as it's a space where we're sharing thoughts, opinions, news. I want my timeline to be useful, funny, timely, and interesting. This is also where you might wanna avoid the person who believes the world is flat.

## LINKEDIN

Treat LinkedIn like it's a professional conference. Ask yourself: Does our work overlap in some way career-wise? Would we end up at the same professional event? As we all put on our white button-downs and show up as the most industry versions of ourselves, will your posts be relevant to me in business? Can we actually network? This is where I must avoid the multilevel marketing schemers. No, I don't wanna promote your weight-loss tea, and I certainly don't wanna sell your fake-ass Lisa Frank leggings.

## INSTAGRAM

Instagram is the house party of social media. Ask yourself: Would I sit through a slideshow of your last vacation pictures? I'm on Instagram to let my hair down, be a little bit more open about my day-to-day, and share the highlights of my world and thoughts. Sometimes the highlights include lowlights too. It's a platform that allows us to be both professional and personal. The folks I wanna follow there have to be intriguing to me on some level.

There are people I know in real life who I would not add on LinkedIn. There are people I don't even know and have never met who I follow on Instagram. There are folks who I wouldn't necessarily break bread with whose tweets are my must-reads. Our social media choices can be personal, even when we say they aren't. I can like you as a person but hide you in my feed if your work tires me out or saps my energy.

Across the board, I don't typically follow or friend complete strangers. In the times when I do hit "Follow" on someone I've never met, it's because I feel connected to them in some way. I saw their work, and I liked it. Or they left a comment or two that made me laugh. We often say there are no strangers in the world. I agree when people make themselves organically familiar. This doesn't include the trolls who comment under every picture you post saying, "Follow me." You already know I ain't for that. Block block block.

With the strong criteria I have for how I let folks into my eLife, you might be saying, "Wait, but won't that create an echo chamber?" It absolutely can if the only people I follow are thirty-five-year-old Nigerian Americans with short hair who grew up exactly as I did. But somehow, I still don't think all I have are people who think exactly like me! We can disagree, but what everyone who I let in has in common is that they care about humankind and on a basic level are decent human beings. I find them to be mostly kind, smart, and funny.

The people who are racist, sexist homophobes who are transphobic aren't the ones I allow in. And when they slip through, I fix that quickly by removing our connection. If, in an attempt to not create an echo chamber, we let these folks live in our electronic villages, we're almost vouching for their fuckshit.

I also do not let hate or slurs fly in my eSpaces. One of the things I'm most proud of is my audience (shout-out to LuvvNation) and the energy of my platforms. While the rest of the internet can often be a dumpster fire, my comments section and my blog are the opposite. It is something that I speak about often, because the people who read my work tout it. The community I've built over the years of writing online knows that if my name is attached to a space, I expect you to show up correct. That means being thoughtful and not a hateful shrew. People say half the fun of my work is my words, and the other half is the comments in response.

In the moments when something I write goes viral, and it's shared on troll pages and I see my space overrun by the type of people who make you lose faith in humans, my audience handles it before I even have a chance. Seeing how protective they are of the safety of the space lets me know I've done something right.

This is also why I am not shy about deleting foolishness that people bring to my space online. My social media is a dictatorship, not a democracy. I block, report as spam, and mute as needed. I am not obligated to receive or consume debris that someone drops at my feet. I take it out the back and throw it in the ether. I'm not the United States government, so speech that I deem daft does not have freedom to live on my platforms.

We spend a lot of our time, online and in real life, having our boundaries crossed. And we say nothing. Why not? Because we might think we're making a big deal out of nothing. Or we question whether we're being crotchety. Or we wonder if it will make us less likable since we will be asking someone to do something different.

Well, if it's getting on your nerves, why shouldn't you say it? It is for the betterment of you and whoever is on the other end. When someone crosses my boundaries the first time, I assume it's because they didn't know. So then I tell them. If they do it over and over again after they have been told, I assume they don't care. At that point, my action to remove them from my life is blameless. I done told you, but you ain't listen. When people don't respect your boundaries after you've told them, block them without guilt. They don't get access to you anymore.

People will not like it when you start establishing and enforcing your drawn lines. They will feel like you built a gate to keep THEM out, instead of seeing it as a gate to keep anything that doesn't serve you out. They might take it personally, and there's gonna be very little you can do about that.

I remember receiving a note from someone who was mad that she couldn't comment on my Facebook personal page. She felt like I was "keeping people at bay." I replied back with "I have a public fan page, a Twitter account, an Instagram account. And I cannot keep some semblance of privacy on my personal page? That is a lot of access. Can't help that you feel that way. It is what it is."

These things aren't only online occurrences. I was at a friend's personal event, stuffing my face with food, when someone came up to me to ask for a hug and a selfie. And I said I'd do it once I finished eating. She got offended and let a mutual friend know that I wasn't nice. Maybe I should have dapped her up and kept it moving, but I thought I was being "nice" by saying I'd do it after I finished chewing food. But nah, she still got upset. That lesson is: Don't be afraid of not being nice, because people will take from an interaction whatever they want. It is out of your control, good intentions and all.

When you draw boundaries, people might say you've changed and you think you're somehow better than them. They might say you are not nice. Let them. In fact, they will be saying it from afar because it won't be to your face since your drawn lines are so good, they won't be able to reach you. Preserve your sanity, because even if you try to bend yourself backward for folks, they'll still say you didn't do enough. You don't OWE anyone your time, energy, or platform. Do not feel guilty about being protective of any of those things.

Before I got married, my VERY strong boundary was not to speak about my relationship or whether I was even in one. As a result, folks who were nosy created stories about my love life, my sexual orientation, and whatever else they wanted to fill in the gap on. All I asked of folks was that whoever they thought I was dating (he/she/them) be a bad bitch, and I would be satisfied. PLEASE start a rumor that I had an affair with Rihanna. That'd be lit!

When I got engaged, I posted a picture of me and my boo (now husband) on social. The post went up five days after it happened, because I wanted to take my time and not rush breaking boundaries I wasn't even fully comfortable with. Before I posted, I asked myself, "Shit. Now do people have to know?" But I said yes because my ring was gonna tell on me so lemme tell on myself. When the post went up, it got SO MUCH ATTENTION. I got 54,000 likes and 8,800 comments. I have done a lot in my life and accomplished a lot. The engagement post is the one that garnered the most likes and comments EVER for me. It was overwhelming. I remember people being like, "OMG I didn't even know she was dating someone." It's possible to be visible and still keep some of our spaces to ourselves.

Don't be out here clocking my womb. I've already had people be like, "OMG you posted a random piece about babies. You tryna tell us something?" I'm still a tithing member of Real G's Move in Silence like Gnomes Church. Just cuz you know I'm married doesn't mean I'm gonna be live-posting everything. Ain't gon' be no peeing on a stick on Instagram Live happening.

I've found weddings are the event of the world where people will most test your boundaries. If you are not used to drawing lines, you might not be ready to have a wedding. Consider going to a court-house and calling it a day, because people will TRY YOU during weddings. I don't know what it is about folks and that day. All types of randoms allasudden feel entitled to everything in your life. From the folks asking if they're invited (if you have to ask, odds are the answer is a swift NOPE) to the kinfolk who wanna bring plus-four. You got plus-four money? WHO IS PAYING FOR ALL THEM PLATES?!?

(Low-key, I know if my grandmother were alive when I got married, she'd have wanted to bring a whole posse of the village plus ten. And I'd have given it to her. I thought about her on my wedding day. She would have had an amazing time. She would have had her own entrance moment, like her church one. She would have worn ALL GOLD EVERYTHING with matching shoes and bag and dripping in at least five gold chains. She would have loved the man I married.)

Remember: Your life is not a carnival and not everyone should get a ticket to it. I see my own life as a highly exclusive club (where there are beds and the rice flows and no one has to wear heels or uncomfortable clothes), and the ones who come in are on the guest list. They are the people I know are a good time and won't start a fight. The cool thing is, if someone rowdy comes in, I can kick 'em out at anytime. Remember: Not everyone gets a ticket to your life. This is YOUR club, so you have the right to have whoever you want in there.

Draw lines, even if the person is family. Honestly, it's especially important to know you can have boundaries with the people you love. These are the folks we feel most obligated to bend till we break for. These are the ones who can manipulate us to erase the boundaries that are most important to our well-being. These are the ones who early on teach us that our feelings aren't worth protecting because we are erroneously obligated through blood connection.

Do not get to the point where you give everyone everything you have, in terms of energy and time and brain power and money and even your presence. Because what will happen is you will be left with nothing and they will still have everything that you gave them.

Know that you have the right to have your preferences, your borders, your boundaries. Tell people outright that you prefer another type of behavior. Wear a T-shirt. Make PSAs. Use a hashtag. Feel no guilt about it. Prevent riffraffery and the enemies of progress from constantly piercing your territory. Build a wall to keep tomfoolery out.

Draw your lines without guilt.

# DO

We can't be all talk with no action. In this DO section, let's start doing the things that might seem scary.

"GROW ANYWAY.

DO WHAT'S HARD ANYWAY.

CHANGE ANYWAY."

—Luvvie Ajayi Jones

# 11

## GROW WILDLY

**We fear change.**

 Change is scary because we fear the unknown and the new territories it takes us into. We like what is familiar because that is what is comfortable and what we know intimately.

I come to you, as Change Averse Club president, because I love control and I love knowing things. The mystery that comes with future things is my kryptonite. You'd think a lifetime of not being psychic would have gotten me used to it by now. But I've been forced to deal with it because I have the nerve to want better things, and I realize how old habits, old ways, and old thoughts won't get me those things.

Let's face it: I am a mess. I mean that in the most self-aware, not-put-downy way possible. Like how Forky from *Toy Story 4* declared, "I am trash!" because he knew it was fact, since he was made up of literal garbage. As humans, by default, we are walking compost heaps who are constantly trying God's patience and daring Him/Her/Them to activate another flood. As a species, we're lazy, selfish, self-serving, money-obsessed, climate-killing atomic fragments. The fact that Jesus hasn't come to get us yet, dragging us by our soiled hoodies, is a testimony of praise.

And I am a fool who has put her foot in her mouth more than a couple of times, with a stubborn streak and a perfectionism problem that sometimes requires me to be told to go occupy a seat because I'm doing too much. I'm a piece of work in progress. Can't nobody tell me my flaws because I'll read that tome of a list to you in a hot second.

Humans are sentient sewage sometimes. It is what it is. What we can do is attempt to not be as scummy as we used to be. If we at least try, we can be better and assure ourselves that we're not complete litter. It's the least we can do, honestly. This is why one of my life's goals is to not be the same type of trash I was last decade, last year, or last week. I'm probably the same fool I was yesterday and that's okay. I'll give myself that grace. But tomorrow? I should be better.

What happens when you commit to not being as terrible as you used to be? It means you are going to change. It means you are constantly going to be different from who you used to be, even if only in small ways. It means the only thing that will stay the same is your perpetual evolution. It's that quote from an old dead Greek dude, Heraclitus of Ephesus, come to life: "Change is the only constant in life." Nobody has proven this wrong yet.

What I know is that who we are right this moment is not who we're going to end up being. Not only should we want to change, it is our duty to change. It is our duty to constantly look to be better than we are. And you know what that is? Growth. Growth is an obligation, and we gotta give ourselves permission to grow wildly, like my cuticles after a month of neglect.

Permission is one thing; execution is another.

Once you know you gotta get doper and better, now comes the part where the ground you stand on will be shaken up. When folks talk about "growing pains," they mean it literally. Change is not fun. Growth is not sunshine and rainbows, because it means our comfort zones are going to be pulled away from us. It means what's convenient is not going to be what prevails. Shit is hard, and that's why it is scary.

This is also why change often happens by force, not by choice. We don't wake up one day and say, "I feel really comfortable and things are great. I should make a change." That's not typically how it happens. Usually there's a catalyst that coerces us into shifting.

Sometimes it's something external, like losing our job unexpectedly or getting sick outta nowhere or finding out we're pregnant or losing someone we love. OR GETTING MARRIED *coughs*

Other times, the force is internal—not a major external moment but our conscience, our spirit. We're feeling bored or we're feeling like we're not in the right place. Or we're feeling unexcited to wake up in the morning because we have to clock in somewhere we don't want to go. Or we're feeling like we are gasping our way through life. Whatever the impetus, internal or external, change can throw us off our feet.

n my life, the moments I've been called to change have been very clear, like moving to the United States when I was nine and having to become the new girl for the first time ever in my life.

Or like the time I got to college, took Chemistry 101, and got the first D of my academic career (see chapter three). That was when I dropped my premed major and my lifelong dream of being a doctor, and through a series of domino moments became a writer, which led me to this book.

There's the moment when I received major backlash online and learned that I needed to be better as a thinker, as a human, as an intellectual, as somebody with a platform (see chapter seven).

There's me getting married and realizing that I have to be less selfish and less me-me-me, and that I also have to work through my own trauma to make sure I'm not passing it on and projecting it onto my partner.

Each one of these cataclysmic moments was deeply uncomfortable, agonizing, with tears (snot bubbles included), and shrouded by struggle. They had me doubting everything I knew to be true. I could feel my emotional bones stretching, and the growing pains felt physical at times.

But each one of these incidents also led me to becoming the person that I am now. Even if I didn't understand it in the moment, change always leads me to something greater. My life is a testimony to the instances when I've been forced to change, and the lessons that I've learned have always been greater than anything I could have imagined. And those lessons were stairs to the person I am now, and who I am now is another step to the person I'm going to be.

There's an Igbo proverb that goes, "A palm nut that wants to become palm oil must pass through fire." "Diamonds are formed under pressure" is another good reminder. YES. To become who you must be, you gotta go through some things!

Growing wildly is sometimes not a choice but a need, because life will give you no other slot. In these moments, we have to know change is as much a part of life as breathing is.

I think about my grandmother. Mama Fáloyin might have once been a chill, patient, soft-spoken person, but I wouldn't know. There's no point in even speculating, because her life was filled with so many abrupt occasions that insisted she change from moment to moment. All of that contributed to the woman who I knew to be tough, fierce, take-no-shit, and loving with all her heart.

Fúnmiláyọ̀ Fáloyin was born in Lagos as Fúnmiláyọ̀ Láṣọ̀rè, to David and Celina Láṣọ̀rè. David was an educated man, a teacher by trade, while Celina kept the home running. They had five children, and Fúnmi was kid number three. Fọlọ́unṣọ́* followed her. Their last-born died at a young age.

When my grandma was about sixteen or seventeen years old, her life changed completely. Her paternal grandmother was next in line to rule Ọrún Èkìtì,† a town in Èkìtì state, Nigeria. Their lineage had come up in the succession of the throne, and because her grandmother was a woman, she couldn't become king. She thought about her son,

---

*Pronounced Faw-LAW-oon-SHAW
†Pronounced Ay-Kee-Tee

David, and chose him to take her place, since he had the knowledge and the preferred gender of royalty in a patriarchy (yup). Often you are left with very little choice when strong traditions like this call, so my grandmother's parents uprooted their family from the hustle and bustle of Lagos to the rurality of the rituals of Ọrún Èkìtì.

I cannot even imagine what such a disruption to your life would feel like. Overnight, Fúnmiláyọ̀ became a princess, along with her younger sister, Fọlọ́unshọ́. At that point, she was the oldest child still at home, because her two older brothers were out in the world.

Within a year of ascending the throne, my grandmother's father, David, died suddenly. Because life can be a summabitch sometimes, her mother, Celina, passed away not long after that.

In less than eighteen months, my grandmother's life turned upside down. She went from being a city girl, in a household with both of her parents, to moving to a town and becoming royalty, to becoming an orphan. She had to grow up very quickly from that point because LIFE DOESN'T OFTEN WARN US THAT IT'S ABOUT TO DROPKICK US IN THE FACE.

As the oldest heir who was traceable, my grandmother was made a regent of Ọrún Èkìtì. A regent is someone who is appointed to rule in the interim as they find a king. She stayed regent for a few months, until they finally found a new king. Can you imagine how an eighteen-year-old who had lost the people most important to her might feel, and then to be told to handle the business of a city? Bruh!

After that, she was moved to Iléṣà, under the charge of her uncle, her dad's younger brother, who happened to be a cartoon villain. His legend precedes him as a man who wasn't only tough but was also cruel. This uncle then sold all of her father's property and heirlooms, because nothing enables greed as much as death. Instead of these things coming to my grandma and the remaining siblings, it all went to him. Plus, he set fire to David's house. It's why we don't have any pictures of the Láṣórès. So much burned down with that house.

So Fúnmiláyọ̀, at eighteen, takes on parenting her younger sibling, thirteen-year-old Fọlọ́unshọ́, while under the control of a man who stole everything that she was entitled to.

Going from having a family of four to only two of you remaining in so little time had to feel like heartbreak whiplash. How could she have even grieved? Did she smile at all in those days? Did she ever think hope was a useless emotion? Did she ever want to give up on everything and wither away? Did she feel equipped to carry on when so much of what and who she knew as her grounding was gone?

She didn't seem to be the giving-up type, because after all those curveballs, her uncle decided to throw her another one: an arranged marriage. Fúnmiláyọ̀ was informed that she was being betrothed to some older man, so at eighteen, she would be forced to start a family with some stranger.

Since she wasn't given any other option, she created one herself: to run away.

My grandmother took her only remaining sibling and fled Iléṣà to Ìbàdàn, two hours away, to start life over, rather than be tied to a man she never knew by a man she probably wished she didn't know. She chose the road that felt freer: Start with nothing. This was 1950, a time when women were still supposed to be YESSIR-ing men who claimed authority over their lives. This teenager, who had been to hell on earth and could have stayed there, decided to trade that hell for another in a city where she didn't really have roots.

In Ìbàdàn, she met my grandfather, Emmanuel Ọládiípọ̀ Fáloyin. It is there that she started the legacy I hail from. It is there that she birthed my mom, Olúyẹmisí (her third child). It is there that I was born. It is in the family house that she and my grandfather built where I learned that family was my safe harbor. It is there where I became the first version of myself.

Mama Fáloyin's life was full of moments when the old her wouldn't serve her or keep her safe. Her life was full of times when she had to choose to change where she physically was. Her early life was tumultuous enough that she might never even have survived long enough to give birth to the woman who would give me life and allow me to be here.

She HAD to change. Fúnmiláyọ̀ at fifteen, living in Lagos, was not the same person at seventeen in Ọrún Èkìtì. That person at eighteen in Iléṣà was not the same person who then showed up in Ìbàdàn. She wouldn't have survived in Ìbàdàn, so she had to be done away with. But all of those people had to exist to become the sixty-year-old who threw a seven-day party to celebrate six decades of not breaking even when life tried to snap her in half. Her joy was in knowing what she had to weather to get to where she was. Like Miss Sofia from *The Color Purple*, all her life she had to fight. But she was always victorious.

I think about another set of wise words from Miss Angelou: "You may not control all the events that happen to you, but you can decide not to be reduced by them."* Change sometimes shocks us into learning maturity, resilience, and discernment. These are all things we need, but sometimes the reason we're afraid of change is because we're scared of what other people will say. Imagine if my grandma had stayed in Iléṣà because of what people would say about her if she

---

from *Letter to My Daughter* by Maya Angelou.

didn't become Random Old Man's wife? Chile, we must DO it anyway. My grandmother was not reduced by those struggles, even as they changed her.

As we are going through life, and people who know one version of us see us grow, we might hear them say, "You've changed." Sometimes, it will hurt our feelings to hear, because that's the intention behind the statement. They're saying that we are no longer the old us and that they don't recognize who we are. But what they're really saying is THEY haven't changed. They might be thinking we aren't on the same level as them anymore and are projecting that onto us. And yeah, it's really easy to be offended by it. We might be tempted to make somebody else feel better and say, "No, I haven't changed. I'm still the same person." We are wrong. We did change. We tried something new. We got new results. We changed our worlds. Maybe we're not on the same level anymore, and that's okay. It doesn't mean I'm better than you. It only means I'm different.

Not changing is a detriment. What if we are supposed to spur positive change in everyone else? What if we are supposed to push everyone else out of their box?

Instead of taking affront to the notion that we've changed, we should simply say, "Thank you for noticing. I've been working hard at being better." Because to change is to adapt to challenges we've faced. It means we are adjusting to what life has thrown us and doing things differently. If the change they see is us being more cruel, hateful, and thoughtless, then maybe we can say, "Hmmm . . . I should adjust." Otherwise, NAH.

They see that you are not exactly like you used to be, but why is that an insult? Why would you want to be exactly who you used to be? That means you aren't doing your job as a person. It means you're not doing what's necessary. Change is necessary. To be the same person you were last year or last decade means you've learned nothing new and you're doing things the same way and at the same level you used to. It means that you're not growing, and what's not growing is dying. To be the same person you used to be means you're not getting new tools to handle what life throws at you. It means you're insisting on talking the same way, thinking the same way. It means you're not pushing back on what you think is true. Things are constantly changing around you, so why would you stay the same?

I can't stop growing just because it's going to make somebody more comfortable. My job in the world is not to make other people comfortable. And if they somehow take my evolution, my adjustments, my choices as an affront to their lack of evolution, then I guess I am doing it right. We should all want to change. We should all want to be better. We should all feel like we're more prepared to handle some of the curveballs that are thrown our way. And to be quite honest, a lot of times the things that we have to do, the people we have to be, the places that we have to go will require us to change. We can't be sorry about it.

Your change and your choices aren't about anyone else. They are about you. What is best for you might offend other people because once you start making choices that are truly yours, others might project their failure to do the same on you and resent you for it. That is not your fault, nor is it your business. Grow anyway. Do what's hard anyway. Change anyway.

magine this: You and another person both start on the first floor in a climb to the top. You are taking big steps and quickly find yourself on the seventh floor. But when you look down, the other person is only on floor three. Sure, it warrants comparison because you started at the same place. The distance is more clear. The thing is, though, we don't go up the stairs at the same pace. Our journeys are different. The dragons we each have to slay are different. Instead of comparing, our job should be to cheer each other on and tell each other to keep going. Maybe we even warn them of the dragons that await and share how we beat ours. But instead we take other people's growth as an affront.

When someone calls you "funny acting," it might mean they aren't used to the new you, whatever they perceive that to be. You're someone who is known to be quiet and now you've been using your voice more? Funny acting. You used to go to all the parties and now refuse to be at the club? Funny acting.

You used to be the go-to for "I need to borrow some money," but now you've insisted the bank is closed? Funny acting. You used to constantly be the organizer of events, parties, and friend get-togethers, but you stopped because you need to focus more on building your dreams? Funny acting.

You know what I say? BE FUNNY ACTING THEN! If me looking like I'm trying to get my life together is me being funny acting, then call me a clown if you want!

People might think you've changed because they would change if they were in your position. But what's actually changed is their behavior toward you. Often, it is completely outside us. It happens.

What people see as you changing is really you doing what is necessary to meet your goals. It is you doing what is needed to honor your own boundaries. It is actually you trying to ensure that you aren't placing everyone's needs over your own like you used to.

As you evolve, you should not let people weaponize the old you against the new you. There are those who will hate your growth so much that they will remind you of your past in an attempt to piss on your future.

When people want to judge you from four versions of you ago, there's not much you can do. You just gotta keep being this version and accept that they never received the software update cuz their device can't handle the tech upgrade (iPhone 2S faces). You can't come and break your neck trying to get people to see you now when they don't want to.

I'm telling you, people will try it. "Remember when you used to . . . ?"

"Sis, remember when your eyebrows looked like sperm over your eyes, with the super thin tail? Whew, 1998 was rough for you. But look at you now! You changed that shape. Why can't I change?"

Every auntie in life is good for this. "OMG I remember when you used to pee in the bed." Ma'am, that was literally thirty years ago and I was four. Can you not?

When people remind you of your past selves, tell them yes, you remember her/him/them and you're glad they existed, because who you are now is so much better and you're thankful for it. Further pepper them by saying how proud you are that you, with all your flaws, keep doing the work to make sure you are never that person again. Then smile widely and tell them you wish they'd grow up too. (Okay, maybe don't add that part. I'm still petty. I ain't grown out of that yet.)

We fear change and then attach the guilt of what we could lose to it, further making it harder to welcome with open arms. I want us to give ourselves permission to grow and change, without guilt.

When my first book came out and instantly hit the *New York Times* bestseller list, my life changed immediately. I went from being a girl who blogs to being an author in an elite club. I was already traveling a lot, but my inquiries tripled and my fees doubled. I basically lived on planes, in between speaking engagements.

What that meant was I stopped being able to write three times a week like I had been doing. As the side-eye sorceress of pop culture happenings, reacting to what was happening in the world with my commentary was what had built my career, and suddenly I didn't have time for it. Why? Because I barely knew what city I was in at any moment from the rapid pace I was on. And I carried a lot of guilt about it. As my audience asked, "Ooo I wonder what Luvvie will say about this," on news that was happening, I'd be running (late) to catch another flight, and I'd feel these pangs of fault, not being able to do my job.

What I didn't realize was my job had changed, and that was okay. My job was no longer to be the person sitting at home every day in her pajamas, reacting to the news of the day. My job now was to take stages, telling people about my lessons, my mistakes, and my triumphs. My job was to make sure the book I had written, a manifesto of my thoughts about life, had the furthest reach it could have. My job was to ensure that a Black woman like myself could also get these doors opened for her.

It was change I didn't readily accept, because I was stuck in a cycle of guilt and fear that my audience would think I'd left them behind. That thing that got me to where I was? Turns out it needed to be left behind to get me to where I needed to go.

What I didn't realize is that the people who were upset that I'd "changed" and didn't blog anymore weren't the people I should have been speaking to. The ones who saw my posts on Facebook, Instagram, and Twitter and cheered these new adventures on were the ones who mattered. The ones who said, "I miss your blog posts but I LOVE this new season in your life" were the ones who fed my spirit.

I was no longer the girl with the blog updating every day. I had evolved into the bestselling author, the international keynote speaker, the CEO of a media company. I had grown, and that was exactly what was needed, because it allowed my work to have more impact. It also ushered in more attention and scrutiny on my words, and even though that sometimes led to egg on my face, it also led me to being so much more thoughtful than I was.

What happens when we're given permission early enough to change, to grow? When we are told, "Listen, I already know you're going to have to be different from who you are today and that's okay. Don't feel guilty about it." How much does that free us, when we know that this isn't something to run away from, but to look forward to? When the people in our lives can say, "I know you have a book tour coming and you'll be MIA. I'll be here when you get back. Because the new life that you're leading is calling for you to be gone more often and I support you"? Whewww! The freedom.

As I've leveled up in my career, I've had to be less accessible at certain points in time to people I love. Sometimes I'm so useless that I need my assistant to be the one booking brunch time with my friends. I could have been hit with the "Oh, now I gotta go through someone to see you?" And I have been. But the friends I am closest to are the ones who go, "I've already asked your team about your availability. See you in a week." Same goes for when I was writing this book and my husband said, "You're on deadline. Let me know if you need to disappear somewhere for a week to get it done."

Imagine waking up in the morning and not feeling shame because your friend knows change looks like us not having the same time we used to have on the phone together, or it means we might have to schedule the next time we see each other. Imagine not being worried about who we are offending with the change that is required of us. It gives us wings. We can now do the best work of our lives. We can be the best people possible without constantly being afraid of what we're leaving behind, who we're leaving behind, or who's feeling small as we're trying to be big. When the changes that I need to make aren't met with eye rolls of inconvenience but are met with affirmations of understanding, I have the room to stretch as I need.

We have to learn how to change and how to grow without guilt. Once we do that, we'll be freer in general for it because the fear of change will start to go away a little bit. We begin to learn it's a part of life and something we have to do. We know it might be uncomfortable, but we realize the most uncomfortable things are usually the most necessary things. It can be good to be in our comfort zones, but sometimes the comfort zones insulate us and keep us from doing what we're actually supposed to do.

Give yourself permission to grow wildly. To transform. To change your opinions. To change your surroundings. To change three times a day while on vacation because you've had all these outfits just waiting to see the sun. You ALWAYS have a right to be different from how or who you were, if that is what is in your heart. You have a right to change your mind about your beliefs. You have a right to change political parties after learning more. You have a right to change the color of the bathroom, so don't let that be the reason you don't buy that house (*side-eyes all the shoppers on HGTV's House Hunters*).

Change: It's not optional. It's life's necessary and perpetual go-to that can break our hearts, make us scream, thrill us. It will challenge us and sometimes make us wonder if we can make it past the pains of it all. I think about young Fúnmiláyọ̀ and how many times life stretched her till she almost snapped. I wonder how she made it through constant change, and how many times she was afraid of taking the road less traveled but did it anyway. I think about one of her favorite scriptures, Psalm 61: "When my heart is overwhelmed: lead me to the rock that is higher than I." That is what I chant to myself in the times I'm called to grow beyond what feels feasible. I always end up on those high rocks, and I'm thankful.

# 12

# FIRE YOURSELF

**We fear losing control.**

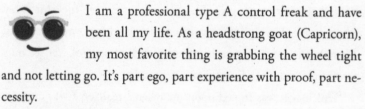 I am a professional type A control freak and have been all my life. As a headstrong goat (Capricorn), my most favorite thing is grabbing the wheel tight and not letting go. It's part ego, part experience with proof, part necessity.

As I've mentioned, my kryptonite is feeling like I am not in charge of situations, and that outcomes could depend on someone else's whims. It makes me uneasy.

Needless to say, this is not ideal when you live in a world with other people. Life is one giant group project, and our grade is largely dependent on other people's actions, since we're trapped in this giant web of other beings with two legs, two arms, and a brain. So I double down by insisting on driving every single thing I think I can. I bear-hug my responsibilities, afraid to be loose and lose. Kahlil Gibran said, "Our anxiety does not come from thinking about the future but from wanting to control it." A WHOLE WORD.

The fear of not being in control is real and normal. It's also a liability, truly. I got to that conclusion when I realized that I was adding to my own suffering by not accepting the fact that I am truly not in control of a lot of things. None of us are. It is a tough Achilles' heel to have, because life is a series of things that happen that we didn't see coming. God is the ultimate organizer, humans have free will, and even when we do our personal best, things can still go to hell in a handbasket.

As you know, people can be abominable. Pure walking compost. We can be shallow, fickle, and trifling. We give fellow humans plenty of reasons to not trust us. And if you are already someone who is cynical or prone to give side-eyes, when you see fuckshit everywhere you look, you tighten your grip on the things you care about. There is a lot of reason to be afraid of lack of control. Yet we must try to fight that fear. Because it is necessary.

This lesson was forced upon me when I realized I was doing so much that I constantly operated in a mode of exhaustion. But it wasn't a lesson I learned and then absorbed and stuck to. I've had to fire myself. I have to fire myself. I will have to fire myself. It is a constant struggle, like many of the lessons in this book.

There are three people I trust above all else in this world: me, myself, and I. I've spent a lifetime depending on myself, getting things done no matter what, and making the impossible seem easy. And it ain't just my story. You're probably reading this right now and nodding your head. I see you. I get you. I am you. I know that if something is in my hands, it will get handled. Olivia Pope is my mentor. Black women are my lucky charms and guiding lights. WE DOES THIS. That trust I have in myself has led to so many wins that my faith in myself is massive. It's why I'm harder on me than anyone else can ever be. It's why I think I could climb mountains if I really focused. It's why I wrote this book. I trust me so hard. That's ego.

But it can be a detriment. Self-reliance, just like anything else, can be a problem when there's too much of it. What we call independence and self-sufficiency is often us operating from a place of fearing chaos. What happens when we depend on other people and they let us down? What happens if we put something in someone else's hands and they drop the ball? What happens when we lose something because we trusted it to someone else? We run that scenario over and over again and find ourselves doing everything ourselves. But what is the consequence? What do we lose as we hold and juggle ten balls at once?

We can lose a lot. When we take on too much because we trust and depend on ourselves for a lot, we get overextended. We look at our plate and it looks tall. We look at our to-do lists and they look endless. We look at our lives and feel overwhelmed. Being a card-carrying member of Team Everything Falls on Me is exhausting. EGG-ZOS-TEEN.

You wake up one day and realize the dark circles under your eyes have claimed eminent domain, and that headache you used to get sometimes is now knocking all the time. You're stressed out, burned out, and tapped out. And you're cussing out the people closest to you for doing the smallest thing because every gahtdamb person is tap-dancing on your very last nerves. Oh just me? Fine.

But really. What are the consequences of us living life carrying responsibilities purely on our backs? Plainly, we tire ourselves out. The truly bad part is when being tired is so much our default that we no longer think of it as a negative thing. We think it just is. We deal because exhaustion in the rat-race world is normalized!

In our everyday lives, trying to control everything not only guarantees that we will ABSOLUTELY miss some things, but it can actually cost us more. We cannot do it all by ourselves, no matter how many planners we have or time-management apps we use. When we take on too much, no one thing can receive our full attention and things are bound to fall through the cracks, cracks we might not even know exist. We're running constant checklists in our heads and it's keeping our shoulders by our necks.

On occasions like these, life can sometimes force us to fire ourselves through circumstances beyond our control (yup), like aging, or accidents, or health issues. What happens then? We, Team I Do It All, find ourselves in a place that feels so foreign it might as well be Mars. A place where we are unable to do for ourselves. A place where we HAVE to depend on others, even for the most basic things.

I think about my grandmother. Mama Fáloyin was as self-reliant as they come. Fire herself? NEVER. Who? A whole her. No. She even used to tell my grandfather that she didn't need him, to remind him that she could handle whatever with or without his help. Grandpa was a man of few words, so he'd just blank-stare her till she tired herself out from ranting.

My grandmother became a widow in December 1991, four months after that epic sixtieth birthday bash. Life can be an insufferable bastard sometimes. As she got older, she began to rely more and more on her kids and grandkids. She got diagnosed with diabetes when she turned sixty-four, and had to start taking medication for the first time. The years went by and age made her shrink a bit physically, and she couldn't move around freely like she used to. A few years later, she had a stroke, and one of my aunts had to go to Nigeria to bring her to the United States to get treatment. The woman who used to hop on a plane to head anywhere, whenever she wanted, was now unable to even speak, let alone travel unaccompanied.

I remember visiting her in the hospital one day and being taken aback by how helpless and fragile she seemed. The fierce dynamo I was so accustomed to couldn't even feed herself. The tears came before I could stop them.

The doctor told us that she might never talk again, and I think my grandma took it as a dare. A couple months later, her speech was back to 100 percent. The stroke she wasn't supposed to recover from seemed like an extended hiccup. She walked a bit slower, but other than that, she was okay. But after that, my grandmother started letting people do things for her in a way she hadn't previously. It must have been a jarring thing for her to experience.

After she recovered here for a year, she wanted to be back at her own house doing her thing, so she returned to Nigeria. She had house help staying there with her, had other people running errands for her, and seemed less intense about controlling day-to-day things. My mom would call her and ask her what she was eating and if she was taking her meds. Before, Grandma might have been annoyed about being fussed over in that way, but by then, she realized it was a show of love.

It was another twelve years before we lost her. But whenever Mama Fáloyin was in the United States, she'd come and stay with us, even though we lived in a small apartment. My mom would regulate her food, meal planning for her to make sure she wasn't snacking as she liked—her sugar intake had to be leveled. Grandma couldn't go on her random shopping trips for hours like she used to (this was before everyone had cell phones, so we didn't want anything to happen and she couldn't reach us). When she got cataracts in both her eyes and couldn't get surgery on them until they matured, she needed my mom to help her arrange her pillbox.

I remember one day, she came to me and said, "Tell your mom I said thank you. She takes really good care of me. God will continue to bless her." It was with so much appreciation. I'm a useless somebody, though. I'm not sure I relayed the message. But my mother knew her mother's gratitude, because she heard it herself. This lifelong soldier had dropped the reins and allowed herself to be fully in the hands of someone else. It was a show of strength, in her moment of weakness, to surrender herself to someone she knew would not let her fall.

If love is a verb, is there a greater show of love than to abdicate your very being to the person you raised well enough to hold you up? What is pride when we can have love shown to us instead?

I hope that one day we are surrounded by people who we trust enough that we can let go of our control. I pray that I'll have lived a life that's so good, I'll be blessed with people who are a reflection of it. And those people, if needed, can be entrusted with my very life. I aspire to live in a way that I attract that favor.

On the professional side, we say we're chasing success when what we're really doing is chasing money. On the personal side, we think we're chasing happiness when what we're really doing is trying to fulfill other people's happiness, not ours. I had to redefine success for myself. A successful life is one lived on my own terms, not one where I end every day more tired than the last. And if everyone else around me is happy but I'm empty, then I have betrayed myself.

Empires of one do not exist, in business or in our intimate lives. Businesses aren't built with just one person. A family doesn't exist if only one person is in it. We cannot do any of this life thing alone, so we gotta learn how to let go quicker than we realize.

For years, I was a solo entrepreneur. (The only people I was paying on a regular basis were the IRS, and they came for 30 percent of my little coins every year without fail.) I was blogging on my site, freelance-writing for outlets, doing social media consulting, brand ambassadorships, event hosting. I was my own assistant, manager, publicist, accounts payable/receivable, editor, graphic designer, social media manager, chief operating officer. And of course I was CEO. "Tired" was my middle name but I called myself "grinding."

Then in 2015, I went on a vacation to Kenya with a group of my friends. Seven days of gallivanting with my girls was the plan, but I still managed to throw some work in the mix. I had a meetup with the Bloggers Association of Kenya one of the days and it was incredible. It was a sold-out event where I got to meet and talk to one hundred of my longtime readers in Nairobi.

The other piece of work I had to do was to write a recap of the TV show *Scandal* for *Vulture*. Around that time, my *Scandal* recaps were hugely popular, because my three-thousand-word synopses of each episode filled you in on everything you needed to know about the show, even if you didn't watch it. They were one of the most thorough on these interwebs, which is why they got much praise, even from Shonda Rhimes herself.

I told my editor that I would make it happen come hell or high water (heh). At 5 a.m. Kenya time, as everyone else slept, I was watching a feed of *Scandal* as it aired live in the United States. I needed to make my deadline.

At 8 a.m. as my crew woke up to get ready to go to the elephant orphanage, I told them they might have to go without me. My recaps took an average of three hours to write, and I was only halfway through at that point.

My friends decided to wait for me, even though the elephant orphanage closed at noon and I got my work done by 9:30 a.m. (*\*fist pumps\**). After getting dressed and commuting, we got there at 11 a.m. I still hadn't slept BUT ELEPHANTS! However, I was exhausted. I was on vacation but I still couldn't afford to relax, because if I wasn't working, I wasn't making money. Being solo got old right then and there. I was almost too tired to enjoy this thing that I was so excited to do in a country I was seeing for the first time, because I had gotten no sleep. I knew I had to change things up.

That night when I watched my friends sleeping soundly, I was like, "Daaaang I'm jealous." Work-life balance is already a scam, but

I had none. It was all work cuz I was motivated by the ability to pay bills and buy shoes. The only way I could do that was to be on the clock, even while on the other side of the world.

One of the consequences of being a one-woman team? The inability to relax when it is needed. We can't be fully present at any moment because we're running checklists of things undone and remembering emails we didn't answer and projects we haven't pitched.

So what do we need to do? We need to fire ourselves from being the Responsible One. Firing yourself isn't about letting go of everything you do and letting everyone run through wildly. After all, you know I'm a fan of boundaries. Firing yourself is about finding people who you can rely on to do what they need to do.

So how do you do it?

## CREATE SYSTEMS THAT CAN, AT LEAST, SIFT OUT THE OVERTLY BOGUS PEOPLE

When you fire yourself, learning to ask people for help when you need it is a good start (see chapter eight). But more important, know who to ask by paying attention to the people who show up for you over and over again. See who asks nothing much of you. Who offers to help you when you need it, not looking for payback? Who doesn't care whether you're Jenny from the Block or J.Lo?

There are people who have earned our trust and deserve to be allowed to show us love by doing acts of service for us. They are around us, waiting to be tapped in. But we're often so busy trying to get things done that we don't see them.

Professionally, have a hiring process that tries to sift out incompetence and laziness. Hiring is not a science but an art, and it is hard as shit. People have learned to interview well, so some folks will talk a good game. But focus on finding people who are passionate about the work you're doing, are willing to work hard, take initiative, and are forever students.

This part is tough if you're new to this, so . . .

## BE OKAY WITH SUCKING AT THIS

I don't like not being good at things I do. And as much as I trust myself, I'm not good at everything, which really annoys me and my ego. So firing myself was hard and messy and is hard and messy and I'm still learning how to do it better.

One of the first things I did was get an assistant to handle emails for me. She was with me for four years and then she moved on. And then I went through five assistants in a year. Why? Because I still wasn't that good at delegating. My previous assistant was really good at finding things to do and filling the gaps I needed filled. But when it came time for me to have someone who wasn't so self-starting or intuitive, I bombed. I SUCKED at being a boss who gave expectations, deadlines, and whatnot. So I kept having people fail at their jobs, since I still was in "It's easier if I do it myself" mode. It was so frustrating.

We can all fall into the trap of "It's easier for me to do it than to teach someone else." Buuuut you can spend one hour a day doing something (accounting for five hours of your week every week) or you can spend five hours (one time) teaching someone what you need done, and now you have saved twenty hours' of work per month.

Accept that handing the reins over is not going to be easy. You might even feel like you're shirking your responsibility. "I should be the one doing this." Why should you? Is it only YOU who has the skills to do it? Check your ego. Unless the task is literally requiring your brain, someone else can do it, so it doesn't HAVE to be your responsibility.

As you let go, you will probably get on folks' nerves micromanaging, since you have an EXACT way you want it done. You might still try to exert control by dictating everything to a T, since that fear doesn't automatically go away just because you're doing something about it.

Do you want it done or do you want it perfect? Also, what is perfect anyway?

Note here: I am LITERALLY reading myself for filth right now. This whole section is for ME to reread because I gotta get my shit together regarding this. I'm a work in progress. Let's work on this together.

## ACCEPT THAT PEOPLE WILL DROP THE BALL

The other thing you have to do is accept that people will disappoint you and mess up in some way. Your husband might forget to pick up the dry cleaning. Your assistant might spell someone's name wrong in an email. Your kid might not wash the dishes squeaky clean. People WILL do janky things on your behalf. This is inevitable and there's very little you can do to avoid it. Why? Because you do not control anyone else, even if you pay them or birthed them or decided to marry them. Even if your instructions were impeccable. It's probably gonna drive you up the wall when it happens.

Your job is not to automatically take the reins back when this occurs. You either decide to give grace because this person is otherwise reliable and this was a solitary mistake, or you reassign the task or job to someone else. If people make mistakes over and over again on your behalf, then yes, fire them from that thing. But instead of being the one to replace them at the helm, find someone else. Has this person made a massive mistake before? Is this a pattern or an exceptional moment that isn't common?

## FORGIVE. RETRAIN. FIRE.

Those are your options. None of them are "Just do it yourself." On deadline? Sure, do it yourself this time. But after that, don't take it on! You don't have time! Let someone do it even if they won't do it as well as you would. Maybe doing it long enough gives them practice. Basically, give people a chance to fail instead of failing them before giving them that chance.

Besides, every mistake is not catastrophic. Every mistake is not going to erase all you've worked for. Every mistake does not hold equal weight. When they drop the ball, what was the real consequence? Did you lose money? An amazing opportunity? A chance to do terribly nasty and amazing things with Idris Elba? What did you lose?

Ask yourself if you can recover from it or if the damage was irreparable. And then determine if the person is holding themselves accountable and taking it seriously. Are they learning the lesson they need to learn so it doesn't happen again?

## REMOVE THE GUILT

One of the hardest things to do is overcome the guilt we might feel when we realize we cannot do it all. We feel guilty because sometimes we make judgments about who we are and what we are worth based on what we can do for folks. But we're not being fair to ourselves when we do this. Yes, you need help. That's okay. No, you shouldn't be able to do it yourself. Yes, you are still supermom in whatever shape you find yourself today. You don't have to be the person with five arms who can vacuum, cook dinner, help with homework, and entertain all at once. Oh your mom was? Well, ask her how many times she wanted to jump out of a first-floor window onto soft grass and just lie there. That doesn't have to be your story.

Yes, you are still a boss if you aren't the person doing ALL the day-to-day work of operating the company. Actually, I think you are even more of a boss if you have a functional team.

Also, someone else's failure or lack of success or even lack of action should not lead to instant admonishment of ourselves. They messed up. Okay, was there a part we played in it? Did we not give the right instructions? Did we not prioritize it correctly? It doesn't matter. We gotta learn to let go of the need for control by understanding we don't control outcomes, even if we give the best training, the best love, the best cheat codes.

I think about the times when I've trusted someone to do something and they didn't. It's served as positive reinforcement of the habit of doing it all myself. "SEE?? I gave someone the chance and they let me down. I should have done it myself." Then I'll beat myself up because I shouldn't have even been in the situation. Then I get mad at me that I should have done it myself and stopped being lazy. When how the hell can I even think I'm lazy? Sis, who do you think you are, Storm? You're not an X-Man. You're not being lazy. You happen to have a lot of things to do, ma'am. Guilt will have you stuck on what you should have done instead of how to move forward, and it's not worth it.

## TRUST THE COSMIC DESIGN

Above all, trust life. Yes, it's a raving douchecanoe at times. But trust the universe/God. Sometimes I think half my reason for believing in a deity is so I don't lose hope and think life is a random mixture of arbitrary instances and none of it has any structure. That might drive me mad. I choose to believe in a higher being as an anchor and a grounding. I don't think I have a choice but to have a deep belief that it will work out. It lets me get out of bed even when I'm feeling low.

If control is a mirage, trust that God will order your steps. Have faith that Allah will place the right people in your path: the helpers.

One of my favorite prayers when I'm about to walk into a new room is: "Please let my helper find me. Let me not miss the right connection I am supposed to make. Let me not miss the reason I am here."

Trust that the mistakes or hiccups or learnings are all to prepare you for the path you're walking. I believe that even when I've made hiring decisions that didn't work out, they were for the best. Each time made me look within and ask myself, "How can I be a better leader for the next person?" As a result, I'm a much more astute boss. Falling on my face over and over again in a revolving door of folks who didn't work out as I tried to fire myself was a mirror. I realized that I hadn't had the practice at this, but to build the empire I want and the impactful company I desire, I would have to develop skill sets I didn't have before.

ANNND if you're bad at firing yourself, hire someone who can help you do just that. There are all types of consultants who specialize in this. Fire yourself from firing yourself!

You can do all of this and it might still be hard. You might still wanna do it yourself. People will still disappoint you. You might trust the wrong person. None of this means you have to do it yourself. Get off that hamster wheel. Keep looking for the right person. They exist. The person who can assist you without fucking up basic calendar details is out there. The accountant who can file your taxes without getting you audited exists. The housekeeper who can come and clean, even if your apartment is just one bedroom, and leave your space so perfectly tidy that you wanna buy her a short set and matching bucket hat is in the world. The partner who will let you nap and take care of the kids so they don't destroy the house is somewhere. The babysitter who could tutor them in math, because common core is clearly an alien language, exists.

Firing ourselves doesn't mean we hand over our keys to the next random person we find and let them drive us into a wall. It means we move over, find people who are better suited to do what we need them to do, and we let them do it. Because right now, we're on hour thirty-two of the road trip, and we're still driving all by ourselves. We might have only stopped once to pee but dassit. Meanwhile, our eyes are bloodshot and our shoulders are by our necks and our stomachs are grumbling because we haven't had time to eat.

When we fire ourselves, it means we've pulled over to the parking lot of someone who is a really good and safe driver. We scoot over to the passenger's side as they get in. They drive and we catch up on sleep for a bit. We wake up, all is well, and our job is to keep the snacks coming and the music bopping. We end up at the place we wanted to go, well rested and ready for adventures. Plus, we enjoyed the journey and the open road and were able to appreciate all we took in.

Fire yourself. Move over. Let the wheel go.


One of the things that has gotten me to this point in my career has been my consistency and my grind. I have pushed through and delivered time and time again with my writing, especially on my main website. But now? I'm clear that I can't do that anymore. I can't put life on pause to meet certain deadlines anymore. I'm pulling my

OG card and firing myself from the expectation of always being on call. I have paid my dues and now I am building a team of folks around me to help manage it all. This empire of ONE is done, personally and professionally.

I need help. And that's okay. You need help? That's okay. You don't think you need help? Get help anyway.

Maybe you have to be a team of one by necessity. Maybe it's because every dime you make, you try to magically stretch it to a dollar to live, pay your necessary bills, and maybe have some left over to buy a pair of shoes every six months or something. Maybe you want to fire yourself but don't have the means. I see you and I was you. And I hope one day, in this unfair capitalist nightmare we find ourselves in, you happen to make enough to get you the help you need. In the meantime, I hope you shed the guilt of not being able to get everything done all the time. I hope you are gentle on yourself when you drop a ball. I hope you give yourself grace when you cannot handle everything facing you.

Fire yourself from the expectation that you should be Superwoman or Thor.

Fire yourself from the mom guilt that says you have to somehow create magic every day for your little broke best friends.

Fire yourself from the scolding you usually give yourself when you look at your bank account and see it isn't where you want it to be.

I see the quote that folks use to "inspire" others to do more: "Beyoncé has the same 24 hours a day as you." No, she doesn't. Even Beyoncé wouldn't tell you that. She might have 240 hours in her day because she has ten people doing various things for her life to run smoothly.

Do not let social media highlight reels make you feel bad for being a tired and fed-up team of one. Don't let folks guilt you for not getting to items 3 to 10 on your to-do list because you spent the day juggling allthethings and ran out of time. Do not think your job is to become more productive in a world that makes it really hard to get things done if you aren't part of the 1 percent.

I've been writing online and professionally for almost twenty years. I've been working for myself full-time for eleven years. The time I spent being a team of one has taught me a lot, made sure I can juggle seven balls at once, AND has been my proof that I CAN do this. But there can no longer be just me. I need to sleep more. The "sleep when I die" mantra is not cute. No, I need to sleep NOW.

We have to be vulnerable and know that we are always risking being heartbroken or burned. Yet and still, we must charge forward. We have a finite amount of time in our days and lives. We simply need more people. We have to drop the ball and give other people the chance to gift us with their time and services.

FIRE YOURSELF. Outsource some of your life. Because you know what won't be cute on a tombstone? "Her grind was impeccable and she did it all by herself." We have no one to prove anything to. Especially those of us who have established ourselves for over a decade. What other receipts do we need to show? We have to fire ourselves from being all things to all people today so we can have room to become the kickass future people we gotta be.

It is time. Build your team. Find your helpers. Get some more sleep.

# 13

# TAKE NO SHIT

## We fear ruffling feathers.

 We are afraid of being ostracized in any way by the people around us, and we fear coming across as difficult, because at our core, we want community. We want to be liked and we want people to think we are nice. Whether we're kids or full grown, acceptance by other humans is a need, because it is how we are hardwired. So we try our best to do what others will consider palatable or cordial or amiable.

As a result, we swallow our words and our feelings down while plastering a smile on our face, even when we want to scream. We acquiesce to people and then spend our lives being constantly devalued and disrespected. In our need for acceptance, forced niceness ends up doing us a major disservice, as we prioritize others' wants above ours.

When I wrote *I'm Judging You*, some people said: "You wrote a book admitting that you're judging people?" And I said, "Yes, because I am." We're all actually judging each other. The problem is we're judging each other on the things that make no sense: what we look like, who we love, the religion we practice, the color of our skin, the gender we say we are.

Instead, we should be judging on other things: Are we showing up in the world in the best way possible? Are we being kind? Are we making sure that we're holding ourselves accountable for other people too? When I say I'm judging you, I'm not judging you because of what you look like; I'm judging you by who you actually are.

I think that we are often wasting our time trying to be nice. Why? Because humans are fickle beings. People are consistently inconsistent about what they want, so when we base our actions on the end goal, which is to be considered nice or anything else, it can be for naught. There is no way you can guarantee that somebody will like you. In the words of Elyana Rausa, "You are not required to set yourself on fire to keep other people warm." So what's the point of trying so hard?

When we go out of our way to people-please, it feels like a trauma response. It's as if we are placing our value on being as agreeable as we can be in order to be loved or accepted. It is often self-betrayal.

There is nothing wrong with wanting to be "nice," but I don't think that should be our goal. Granted, I'm not saying walk around with the intent of being an asshole. Nah. But being seen as cordial should not be the main motivator of our behavior.

Instead, I think we should aspire to be kind. To be kind is to be generous, fair, honest, helpful, altruistic, gracious, tolerant, understanding, humble, giving, vulnerable, magnanimous, service-driven. To be nice is to smile a lot and be chatty with random strangers. Nice is talking about the weather. Kind is caring about whether someone has an umbrella in case it rains.

People have niceness and kindness mixed up. Niceness might mean saying positive things. But kindness is doing positive things: being thoughtful and considerate, prioritizing people's humanity over everything else.

I don't exist in this world for someone to describe me only as "nice" when I'm not in the room. Nice can be empty and shallow and passive. Nice tells me nothing about someone when that is the only thing that is used to describe them. If I ask someone about you and their strongest statement is "She's nice," then I'll assume you're a walking doormat. Or you're someone who is always smiling, even in the moments of strife, which feels dishonest. It says to me that I might need to question you more on how you're really feeling. It tells me nothing of note. Nice is the saltine cracker of adjectives; it's bland.

When we're always trying to be nice, we take a lot of shit and deal with a lot of people's awful behavior, and we don't hold them accountable. We end up being at the other end of unjust things more than we should, because in our politeness, we relegate our own feelings to the bottom of the barrel.

We don't have to do any of that to be loved. We don't have to bend ourselves backward to have the people who matter see us and cherish us. Even if you're cantankerous, you can still find folks who will stan you!

Mama Fáloyin was one of the kindest people I've ever met. She was also super feisty and took no shit, and people knew that. If anyone tried her, she'd get all Queen Bee on them and sting. But her

heart was huge and to her, everyone was a neighbor she was responsible for. If people were in a bind, they'd knock on her door, and she
would listen to them, help if she could, and send them off with a
Tupperware of food and a truly meant prayer of "God bless you, ọmọ
mi" (my child).

When she died, she died loved by droves of people. There were all
sorts of dignitaries and people who had known her closely for decades paying their respects. Granny was Team No Chill, and she was
adored. She wasn't a woman who felt the need to placate others if
that wasn't her real thought in the moment.

Some of the stories I've heard about her are legendary, especially
from when she was younger, before I was even born. When my mom
was in elementary school, her teacher took some scissors to her hair,
as punishment for her not having her homework done. My grandma
flipped out! The next day, she took my mom to school herself, while
holding scissors. She got there and asked for the teacher. Why was
Grandma there with scissors? Because she said since the lady cut her
child's hair, she was there to cut the teacher's hair too. She was dead-
ass serious. It took ten people kneeling down in front of Grandma,
begging her and invoking God's mercy, for her to abandon the mission and go back home. That teacher never tried anything else with
any of the Fáloyin kids again.

My grandma could have let it slide, but you know what would
have happened if she had? The teacher would have thought it was
okay to keep doing extreme things like this. This is why I push back
against the constant encouragement to take the high road when we
are harmed. I think some high roads need to stay under construction.

Let's talk about taking the high road, because it is definitely a thing people tell us we should do to somehow be the better person. You know the one time I disagreed with my fave Michelle Obama was when she said, "When they go low, we go high." Honestly, when people go low, sometimes we have to meet them there. If you go low, I might go gutter.

I am not a fan of asking folks to turn the other cheek in situations where they shouldn't feel obligated to do so. On certain occasions, the insistence on taking the high road is actually harming us more than it's helping. Putting harmony over justice and civility over amends is a harmful practice if we are telling people to constantly bypass defending themselves or standing against what is awry. I'm not for the kumbaya of it all. People read that Jesus told us to turn the other cheek and love our neighbors, but that is the SAME person who also flipped tables in a temple when folks did too much.

The need for niceness permeates how we move through the world, address those in our daily lives, and even combat systems that don't serve us. We are always trying to be "civil" above all else.

In June 2018, America's forty-fifth president (and the first walking Cheeto in the White House) signed an executive order that led to the separation of migrant children and their parents at the United States border. The people's champ and forever truth-teller, Maxine Waters, was very vocal in her rightful critique about it, saying: "We don't know what damage has been done to these children. All that we know is they're in cages. They're in prisons. They're in jails. I don't care what they call it, that's where they are and Mr. President, we will see you every day, every hour of the day, everywhere that we are to let you know you cannot get away with this."* NO LIES TOLD. The next day, her own party called her comments "divisive." If the truth is divisive, then what it is pointing out must be what is especially repugnant. Chuck Schumer said, "We all have to remember to treat our fellow Americans, all of our fellow Americans, with the kind of civility and respect we expect will be afforded to us." Sir, those kids in cages aren't being treated with ANY type of civility, so please have a fucking seat.

When will people realize that niceness and taking the high road are not going to save us? You don't make change by being civil to the people who are not looking at other people as full humans. Being nicer about how you're talking about Trump is not doing anything. There's a thin line between being nice and enabling bullshit.

If we can't put justice over niceness, what are we doing as a people? Where are we going to end up if we continue to turn the other cheek when somebody harms us? The people who harm us are not being told to be civil or nice or to take the high road. It's always the person who's been victimized in some way who is told to make that choice. Does that serve us? We're going to be civil and we're going to nice our way into bondage.

Here's the thing about villains and people who harm us. Usually when somebody does something to you that is not just disrespectful but harmful to you as a person, you're already past the point of civility. This person isn't looking at you as a full human being. You can't change their behavior or affect the outcome by being really nice

---

*Jamie Ehrlich, "Maxine Waters Encourages Supporters to Harass Trump Administration Officials," CNN, June 25, 2018, https://www.cnn.com/2018/06/25/politics/maxine-waters-trump-officials/index.html.

about it. This is why people who insist on politeness miss the point. All this "We should be nicer" gets us nowhere, because if people wanna take offense to our words, they will find a reason. Nah, I'm not nice. Yes, I will challenge your bullshit.

Why do people prioritize civility over justice? Justice does not come just because you're begging for it. Justice does not come because you're being nice about the other person who's not giving you justice. So I don't understand the insistence on this high road.

When you are in a fight for your life, when you're in a fight for the world, when you're in a fight against something like white supremacy, how sweet your tone is won't be a factor in getting basic rights. You don't civil your way to justice.

And when we talk about folks protesting in the streets, people get mad because "Well it's not orderly how people protest." When half of the country is wishing for immigrants to be separated from their family members and we're being told to be civil about it, what is civility doing for us? What is this niceness doing? We're prioritizing the wrong thing.

Someone (some thing, some system, some power structure) convinced us that if we were more civil or respectable or dressed nicer, we'd be more worthy of justice or love or good things. We are worthy of all those things TODAY. Now. Even when we cuss and swear and we don't form our sentences perfectly. Even if we aren't buttoned up. Even if we mess up sometimes.

I want us to push past the idea that civility or niceness is the key. Fights are not about politeness. I'm not saying we have to be assholes to everybody. I'm not saying we have to walk around being angry. I'm saying that when it's time for us to challenge systems and people, how we say it should not nullify the message. We can still be kind, but we do not have to be nice. And our needs and wants are valid even if we don't express them neatly.

We need to TAKE NO SHIT, and if you need permission to do that, consider this that.

This doesn't mean you address everyone who brings trash to you or says something about you. You don't have that kind of time. It also doesn't mean you accept every invitation to fight. Nah. It means in the times when it's called for, and you will know those times, do not feel bad for meeting someone in the basement. This doesn't mean you're a bad person or you're immature. It means you made a decision to engage with someone as they asked for it. Sometimes a good "BITCH WHO DO YOU THINK YOU'RE TALKING TO?" is warranted. Sometimes you gotta remind people that messing with you comes with a cost. It be like that, and folks gotta deal. And sometimes, taking no shit might even look like silence to the person who is trying to force you to pay attention to them.

We've spent so much time telling people to be nice and civil that we feel like we have no room to defend ourselves in a world that's constantly at war with us. You don't owe anyone civility if they have traumatized you. Nor do you owe them a hello, even in person. They can take this full side-eye.

I am calling on us to challenge ourselves to be more truthful, to be more outspoken. Be kinder, speak louder. Use your voice and don't let people silence you or make you feel bad because they don't see what you're doing as civil or nice. Fight for people who are not you. Insist on being uncomfortable and taking yourself outside your usual space to fight for other people who might not have the right to fight, or the voice, or the money, or the stature, or the positioning. That's kindness.

I aspire to be kind, and I hope my actions are kind. I hope when I'm gone, someone somewhere describes me as such, because my life is a journey in giving as much as I've received. Kind is compassionate. And we can be kind and generous, but we need to take no shit. The first person we need to be kind to is ourselves.

Grandma was Team Take No Shit. When she was younger, there was a time when she was taking a seminar at her church to go up in the ranks. She was the first woman allowed to even take it, so it was a big deal! When she completed all the requirements for it and called the church to say she was coming for her plaque, the pastor said he wasn't going to give it to her. The moment Grandma heard that, she hulked up, put on some pants, and rode to that church. See, Mama Fáloyin didn't wear pants often. She was usually in a dress or caftan. She only wore pants for two reasons: Because she was cold. Or because she needed to fight.

Well, when she showed up at the church in her fighting pants, the pastor didn't want the smoke, so he went into his office and locked the door. Who born him to say NO to her getting what she had earned?

What did Mama Fáloyin do? She stood in front of his office door and refused to leave. "You can be in there all day but I'll be out here waiting. I'm not going anywhere until he gives me my certificate."

My grandfather, who was usually the peacekeeper, backed her up and said, "You better give it to her. She will be here all day and I will be right here behind her." I STAN a supportive bae! Long story short, she walked out of that church with what she came for. The pastor, who wasn't used to any of that, learned on that day that Fúnmiláyọ̀ Ọmọ Láṣọ́rè is not one to trifle with.

They cherished her at that church. If she was missing from church for too many weeks in a row, they'd send a contingent to go visit her to see if she was doing okay or check on whether they'd somehow offended her. But really, they loved her dearly.

When my grandmother died in 2011 in Nigeria, the high-ranking women in her church insisted on being the ones to dress her, instead of the morticians. They wanted her to have the utmost care as she was prepared. They wanted to send her off with love.

We traveled to Nigeria as a family to give her a proper send-off. I was in the room as Mama Fáloyin got her last bath. I remember trying to take in everything that was happening, because I didn't want to miss anything about it. I was acutely aware of the fact that I was bearing witness to a sacred space and ritual. Even as the chemicals in the room made it hard to breathe, I dared not move. The tears that streamed down my face weren't just from the formaldehyde—they were also my grief and gratitude.

I remember staring at the body of the person who was the prototype of womanhood for me. As they dressed her, they prayed over her. It was done with such care, too, putting her in one of the white gowns she wore for church (a sutana) that my aunt picked out. They draped one of her favorite purple sashes over her with sanctity. My heart throbbed because it was the utmost display of love. My goodness. To be cherished and respected like that, having lived openly, freely, totally. I was affirmed by it because it was the pinnacle of a life well lived.

She did it on her own terms, even when she was painted into corners. She did it joyfully and genuinely, fiery and full of moxie.

A life well lived is not one where you made sure the rooms you were in didn't have friction. A life well lived isn't about plastering a fake smile on your face. A life well lived is not about how many people you did not upset. A life well lived is one where you commit to being kind. Where you connect your humanity to that of others, and it shows in the way you move through the world. And that's what we gotta do.

We will ruffle feathers. We might be the villains in a few people's stories. We might even blow up a few bridges. But our worth is not based on how much we acquiesced to the people we knew. The goal is to betray ourselves less.

So, be kind but take no shit.

# 14

# BUILD A SQUAD

### We fear betrayal.

 Although we spend our lives looking for the approval of others, we are also afraid of building community outside of our families. I have come across a lot of people who hail the fact that they are movements of one and don't roll with a squad. We know those people. Sometimes, we ARE those people.

But the thing is, we NEED people.

Humans are not meant to do life alone. Even the most introverted and crotchety of us are not meant to be recluses, living life away from everyone with no one to turn to. When people are imprisoned, there is a reason why the biggest punishment is solitary confinement. To lock a person away from all human contact is to torture them.

We need people to cheer for us, encourage us, challenge us, scold us, love us, be there for us. But we are afraid to need people. We are afraid of community. What are we afraid of when we don't embrace this need?

We are afraid of being deceived or double-crossed. We do not want to be betrayed, and the fear of that hurt often keeps us from squadding up in the way we need to. We are also afraid of being rejected, and that's a form of betrayal, ain't it? We are afraid of giving people the power to punch us in the proverbial chest because we've let them get close. Some of us have parents who have beat it into our heads to "trust no one." We carry their traumas as ours. We wear their fears as ours before we can even understand the world in its most basic ways.

To squad up is to form community with people who aren't our blood. It is to create bonds and friendships and acquaintanceships with others, allowing them access to us. That access is tied by nothing but free will, and it can be revoked at will. THAT scares us. Our family? Well, they're kinda obligated to stick around through our bullshit, but no one else is. That means we're beholden to the whims of other humans who we've grown attached to.

Like a lot of our other fears, this one is valid and earned. Humans can be dishonest, selfish, self-centered, and all that other jazz. They give us many reasons to wanna lock ourselves in dark rooms and say nothing to anyone ever again. So I totally understand why someone could be of the team "no new friends." Or "no friends at all." Sometimes the drama that people bring into our lives tempts us into thinking, "Fuck everyone. I'ma just be by myself." I get it.

Yet, we can't surrender to this temptation. We absolutely need to squad up, and we need to do it outside our bloodlines. It's a crapshoot, and some of us luck out while others end up with the worst guides ever. Since we don't get to choose our original kin, those we choose to become our family are key guides in this life journey.

The communities we belong to are an important part of our identity. They TEACH us what is acceptable, respectable, or tolerable, from the way we dress to the music we listen to, to the things we consider our core beliefs. None of your friends smoke? Well, you'll be less likely to. None of your friends have a master's degree? Where do you even start if you want to get yours? All your friends dress like members of the Addams Family? Then your seersucker shorts will probably seem out of place.

Our lives are one big group decision, try as we may to seem utterly unmoved by others' whims. It's a chicken or the egg syndrome. Do we select who we hang out with based on who we are, or do we become who we are based on who our friends are? Although it might be scary to think about others having this much control over us, I say we accept it and use it to our benefit.

My grandma was an alpha woman in every way. She got married by choice, and didn't lose herself in the identity of "wife of Emmanuel." In a period when women being hit by their husbands wasn't just okay but the norm, that wasn't her experience. I don't think my grandfather was that dude, but if he had any temptation to be that dude, I'm sure he was out of it. Grandma could BOX. She came from a family of fighters. She was Nigerian Miss Sofia, and according to stories I've heard, my grandpa used to shake his head and say he just got out of her way when she was upset.

Once in Nigeria, she was in the car as my uncle drove and one of my aunts was in the front seat. They got cut off by a driver, and instead of him being apologetic, he started cussing at them. My uncle pulled over and got out. You'd think my grandmother would have been the peacekeeper. NOPE. This woman jumped out the car herself, grabbed the driver by his shirt, and threatened to slap him and the person who was in the car with him. At the end of it all, the driver and his passenger ended up prostrating themselves at her feet to apologize for disrespecting her.

How did she become this chick? Well, having to fend for herself since the age of eighteen probably made her grow some seriously tough skin. And somewhere along the way, she curated a squad of other tough-ass, take-no-shit Nigerian women. Married or not, these women LIVED. They didn't discourage her from taking up space. In fact, her crew of fellow professional troublemakers hyped her up and affirmed her in the times when she had to put on pants and let someone have it! At her sixtieth birthday, they were right next to her, in their own specific fabric, looking like the proud, territorial friends we all want. I think they all coordinated their "sunglasses even though it's nighttime" look.

Bold women rock with other bold women because we create space for each other and affirm identities society is usually so quick to denounce. We normalize each other's bravado, which allows us to step into the world with confidence. It's almost to the point where if you don't stand up with your head tall, you'll feel slightly out of place. The badassery of my friends usually reminds me who the hell I am and why I need to keep my chin square, and that is a gift I've gratefully received and will continue to.

The people we are surrounded by really do affirm our lives and our decisions. They can peer-pressure us into being and doing better, because seeing them up close can inspire us to know what's possible.

I hate working out because it feels like trash during and especially after, and, like I said earlier, anyone who says it feels good is a liar and a cheat. Even with that core belief, sometimes I work out strictly because my friends are working out. Sure, I could do it because it is good for my heart health and yada yada, but sometimes I don't want to be left out and that's what gets me to do those thousand jump ropes.

You also need a strong village to hold you up in the times when you can't. If people demean you or make you feel like you aren't worth loving or defending, your squad will remind you of who you are. If you doubt everything you know about you, they bring you back to what you stand for. The real ones don't go running after you fall on your ass. Who is there taking your hand and pulling you back on your feet? Remember them.

My accomplishments might be half because of my drive and the other half because I don't come from half-stepping people. The people who I love do amazing shit, so that's also my job. If they were slackers, maybe I'd feel less pressure to always GO. Without competition or envy, we can compare ourselves to them with the lens of "Well if it's possible for her, it's possible for me." My crew normalizes winning.

As I discussed in chapter one, it is integral that we know whose we are. Who do we come from? Who do we claim? Who do we belong to? This WHO isn't just about the last names we carry or the legacy of our lineage. I firmly affirm the fact that I belong to a crew of dope-ass friends too.

Entrepreneur Jim Rohn made popular the idea of "You are the

sum of the five closest people to you." This rings true to me. Even if that number isn't five, I am the sum of the villages of people who have surrounded me throughout my life. How far I've been able to go has been directly tied to those people. How smooth or rocky my journey has been is because of those people. How big I dream has been because of their confidence.

Even beyond the gassing up of each other, I find so much value in how my friends are my greatest challengers. We take "my sister's keeper" and "my brother's keeper" literally. Part of the reason is because we are representations of the people we claim. We represent WHOSE we are.

We challenge each other because if I'm your keeper, your under-skirt can't be showing on my watch. Your mistake can't go un-checked; otherwise I'm leaving your back wide-open, when I said I got it. It's about holding each other accountable and calling each other in (not out) when we fall on our faces. If you're making piss-poor decisions, your friends should be able to pull you by your collar and tell you to get your shit together. A friend group that does that is a gift, and will always ensure that we are being the version of our-selves that we'll be proud of. Otherwise, we'll have to answer to them, and we don't want that smoke.

There are so many rewards to building a proper village that the accompanying fear isn't worth it. Throughout my life, I've felt be-trayed and abandoned and rejected by people who I let into my life. We've all felt it. It's knocked me on my ass a few times. But I also think about what others have done for me or said to me that has lifted me up or pushed me forward. Those moments beat any of the betray-als. Those times attest to the need to never harden myself completely.

When I say "build a squad," I don't mean "make everyone your best friend." We can have multiple squads, all with different purposes and proximity. I have multiple groups of friends who I've met in different times of my life, in different spaces, who serve different purposes. Some people might exist in multiple squads. That's okay too.

Part of the reason why people struggle with friendships (and relationships, for that matter) is that they expect everyone in their lives to fulfill all their needs. We expect friends to mentor us, play hard with us, challenge us, be our shoulders to cry on. Yes, our friends are supposed to do that, but no one or two people can do or be all of that for you. You have to spread that responsibility around.

We are less likely to experience the deep betrayals and the rejections if we understand that people serve certain purposes and not everyone can be in the same role with the same expectations.

I think there are five types of squads that we all need.

## 1. THE DAY ONES

The Day Ones are the friends you've had since you were younger, before the glow up or whatever it is that people know you for now. They are the ones who can pull out embarrassing pics of you at any time, since they have ample. They remember when you had the snaggleteeth and can humble you in a hot second. Remember when you had chicken pox in the eighth grade? They do! They have the proof. They also might call you by a nickname that no one else knows now. Y'all went to elementary or high school together or grew up in the same neighborhood. These are the people who knew you when none of you had agendas and when all of you were a mess, and they couldn't care less what you do now.

Why is it important to have these people? Because they're a mirror of who you were. They give you perspective, and as you're going to conferences or meeting new people or getting promotions, they are a reminder of how far you've come, and of the person you used to be when you were still dreaming of who you are today. No matter how successful your Day Ones get, the fact that you can reminisce and tell old stories that make you all laugh till you snort is clutch. Having the people who knew you when you had nothing or still wore jersey dresses is important because it's a grounding force.

## 2. THE PROFESSIONAL CREW

These are the people you've met along the way who you've bonded with in a professional setting. Work husbands and work wives fall under this category. Y'all might have met at an internship or at a job or some industry cohort group. Y'all grab coffee together or go to the bar after work. They might cover for you when you miss an important meeting or give you a heads-up about a project the company is working on that could lead to an advancement for you. These people met you in a place where you were looking to level up or get those checks and go.

Your shared experience makes these friends important, because they can look out for you on the business front. And all that time spent together means you can vent to them about work things that you might not want to bore anyone else with. They can be a key part of growth because they'll have access to insights no other groups of your friends would. That alone makes them essential.

## 3. THE MENTORS

Mentors are the business version of "not your little friends." They are essential because even though they aren't your peers, they can be life rafts. Mentors might take the form of a college professor who became your favorite thought leader, an old boss who championed your work and made sure you got your next position, or someone you met at a conference, had great conversation with, and now have access to. Because mentors care about your life even outside of the business (because your personal life absolutely affects your career), you confide in them. They're friends as well as guides.

Mentors are incredible, because they can unlock doors in our lives. They can make our dreams more tangible, because they are invested in our success. We need a new job? Well, they might be able to make a phone call to someone who then makes a phone call to get us the interview we need to be considered. They actively ask, "How can I help?" without necessarily expecting anything.

The domino effect mentors have is amazing. It was a mentor of mine (Barbara Allen) who nominated me for the Chicago inaugural chapter of New Leaders Council, which I got accepted for. It was there that I wrote a vision statement, three months before I got fired/ laid off from my job, that allowed me to see my dreams on paper.

And many of those dreams have been realized. Barbara nominated me simply because she thought it would be good for me to have that cohort experience. My mentors have brought up my name in rooms and gotten me opportunities I wouldn't be able to get myself. They have opened locked doors.

## 4. THE PLAY GROUP

Your Play Group is the squad that you travel with, party with, kick it with. Y'all hang out to turn up, relieve stress, and have adventures. A lot of times, you meet this crew in college, where the union parties are plentiful, and when sweating your hair out in a too-hot club was your idea of a great night. They might have held your arms at one point as you grinded into some off-balance dude.

The Play Group is a part of your self-care routine, because they remind you that life is fun. Maybe now you're doing less weekend barhopping and more getting drunk at someone's house on a Wednesday. Still, these are the people who allow you to blow off steam without judgment. They are important, because they balance everything else.

## 5. THE TRUE BLUES

We've all heard that if you end up with two or three people in this category, consider yourself blessed, which is a word. The besties are an important subgroup and everyone ain't that.

The True Blues are the people who know where all the bodies are buried, because they were probably right there with the shovel next to us. We can be our truest selves with them, without pretense or angst. They've seen us at our worst but hold space for us to make it back to our best selves. They will fight for us, even without our permission. They will come to our house and open our fridge like they live there. Your mom probably asks you how they're doing once a month, and sometimes she doesn't because they've called her already. The inside jokes are aplenty, and they've seen you in the morning when you still had eye crusties.

Our True Blues aren't automatically people we've known the longest. They are people who showed up somehow, at some point, and barreled their way into our hearts. We don't know how to NOT trust them, because they've shown us over and over again that they are here to stay. Sometimes they'll disappoint us and upset us, because we are all flawed. But friendship isn't about perfection.

Each of these groups is essential to having a well-rounded village and is fundamental to our well-being. And these groups are dynamic. Just because someone started in one box doesn't mean that is where they will remain. I have a few friends I met professionally who became True Blues over time.

Also, each group plays different roles and fills a different gap. Maybe the Professional Crew isn't the one we tell about our frustration with our partners. Maybe the Play Group isn't who you want to pour on about why you want to quit your job. Maybe the True Blues don't wanna go out partying all the time. But there are people we have who fall into one or more (or all) of these categories, and if so, that is TRULY amazing. A Day One who you ended up working with who loves to kick it as much as you AND happens to be slightly older and more accomplished? What are the odds? Tiny.

You have to be okay putting people in boxes and not stressing them out to be anything but who they are. Not everyone is equally invested in our lives and well-being, even if they are our friends. If one group can't understand, another one of those groups will.

Conflicts will arise, but friendship doesn't mean zero discord. Commitment through thick and thin doesn't just apply to marriage but to friendships too. You will drop the ball and disappear from time to time because life happens to you, but one mistake or missed birthday does not mean you are disposable. Similarly, your friends will do the same. But when things arise that don't work, talk through them, even if it means a tough conversation. Sometimes you can move forward, and other times you might not be able to.

Do I have Day Ones I no longer speak to? For sure. Have I had professional friends become public enemies? A few. Do I have mentors who sometimes disappear after they feel like I've climbed higher than they can help? Absolutely. From each, I try to inspect myself for my part in the breakdown, as nothing is ever truly one-sided. And I try to figure out how I can be better the next time. It is always tempting to wanna take my friendship ball, lock the park, and go home. But if I had done that in 2006 when a close friend sent me an email to end our friendship, I wouldn't have been emotionally available to meet the friend who would later become a True Blue, who moved mountains for me at a time when I truly needed it.

That being said, there will be times when you need to let go of someone completely. How do you know who to cut loose? When the thought of this person stresses you out, it might be time to cut them off. And if this person makes you feel bad about who you are, they might need to get kicked out the community. This is different from the person who's challenging you and telling you to fix mistakes. But if they make you feel bad about who you are and they're mean to you, let them go. If you can't depend on this person in a time of crisis, you might have to step back from them, and that's okay.

I'm super loyal, so it's hard for me to cut people off. But when I have to do it, it's because I realized this person no longer wishes me well, or there's something about this person that I double-guess, which makes it hard for me to be straightforward and open. Or maybe we naturally drifted apart.

Everyone ain't gonna to come on this life journey with us, and the friends we have today will not necessarily be the friends we have tomorrow. As we get older, our friendships change. We leave some people behind.

When we fear squadding, we fear betrayal, and it's real. Do not trust EVERYONE. Sure. But "trust no one" is the quickest way to build titanium walls that no one can break through. Either we learn to let the moat down for those who are allies, or we keep the wall up, protecting ourselves from both the ones who want to see us fall, and the ones who will fight for us to keep us standing. Sure, walls keep the villains out, but they also keep the heroes out. In the process of being vigilant against the sheisters, we keep ourselves from connecting with the best people. So I take the risk. I am cautiously open, choosing to trust people until proven otherwise.

Even with all that, the friends lost, the feelings of betrayal, I am where I am today because of the FRAMILY I've been able to have. As I've risen in my career, it sometimes feels like I'm in rarefied air. It can feel lonely to step into spaces where I am the ONLY or one of two. But I walk in there on the backs of my sisters and it is an invisible security blanket.

The best-case scenario is to find friends to cleave to and rise with together. Compare notes, be sounding boards and sometimes jumping boards. If or when you fall, be buffers for each other. People can be everlasting buffoons at their worst, but at their best, they are the soft place for us to land.

So how do you do this? How do you build this community of people?

Be intentional with building a squad that will ride for you, challenge you, hold you accountable, and pick you up in the valley moments. Let the record show this doesn't mean stalking people. Please don't go out here saying Luvvie told you "be intentional," which translated to "bug people until they are tired and finally say yes to you." I didn't say that! Okay great, I've clarified.

Friendship isn't about keeping score for who is a better friend to who, or who has done the other more favors. It's about showing up as needed, to the best of your ability and capacity. It's about the action of it all. Friendship by word alone is empty and pointless. Simply be willing to show up, especially in times of need.

In order to be the friend you would want, you also need to be willing to be vulnerable. That fear we have of betrayal is legitimate, but we cannot let it keep everyone around us at arm's length. If we do, they won't know who we are, what we need, and how dope we can be. Without opening up, how can we show and receive the love we need to and from our comrades? Knowing it's a risk shouldn't stop us from being our full selves. If our friendships end, at least we know it's not because we didn't do our part.

I also believe in quality over quantity. I know they say if you have two good friends, you're lucky. Well, I feel really lucky because I definitely have more than two, but I think it's because over the years I've been able to also do work on myself to make myself a good friend. When we talk about friendship, it has to be reciprocal, right? You can't just be expecting good friendships when you're not a good friend yourself.

To be a member of a valuable squad, you gotta ditch your spirit of competition. There is a not-so-thin line between being inspired by our friends' success and being jealous of it. Are you the friend who isn't threatened by someone else's win? Are you the person who can cheer loudly because you're genuinely happy for your friend's success? If you aren't, then worry less about how to get a dope squad and more about becoming that person. Do that work.

And to have the powerhouse squad of your dreams, make sure you are leveling up yourself. I've been asked a lot how I have made such powerful friends, and folks have asked me what I did to get them. I leveled up on myself and my work and started ending up in dope rooms and getting dope opportunities that led me to meeting dope people. The key is *I* leveled up. I got better. Got more grown. Got doper. You attract who you are. I didn't force friendships.

You also have to make sure you are vouchable. What's that? Well, make it easy for your squad to be your walking Yelp. Don't make it difficult for people to recommend your presence in the room. When people say "it costs nothing" to speak someone's name up, I low-key disagree. If I'm speaking you up, it's an explicit recommendation. If you're someone who will drop the professional ball I passed to you, now my name and my judgment get tainted. My friends know they can recommend me for a paid gig and I will show up and kill! Similarly, when I speak them up in their absence, it is with confidence that they will deliver spectacularly. You are my friend, and you're not necessarily entitled to my platform, but if you're doing dope stuff, I'm going to talk about it. I'm going to use that platform because I know you won't embarrass me for putting my stamp on you. When building your friendship dream team, look for the people who believe in your work but do the work themselves too.

Our friends are part of the fabric of our lives. Pick the best people you know and hold on to them. Curate a crew of people who cheer you on, challenge you, check on you, and are committed to creating an awesome life with you. Recognize the people who are great at gassing you up, not watering you down.

Find your people. Hold them close. And know you belong somewhere. While you do that, rise together.

# 15

# GET A NIGERIAN FRIEND

### We fear the savagery.

 Nigerians are world-renowned loudmouths who happen to exist in every place on earth, roll deep, and have a reputation for cleverness. We are legion, so hear us roar.

I think everyone needs a Nigerian friend, play cousin, or auntie in their lives. They really do. In a world where fear rules our lives and we get used to cowering, we need to surround ourselves with some rowdy energy that takes up space unapologetically. That's where Nigerians come in. Not saying others aren't this, but there is a certain je ne sais quoi that allows it to be found in Naijas. We are the parliamentarians of Team No Chill. We will add color to your life. We will loan you bravado if you ever need it.

Why will your life be better for having a Nigerian who you can call friend or framily? Let me break down the reasons.

We are amazing verbal fighters. We don't even have to know how to physically fight, because the way our tongues can beat anyone down. Our opponents won't have the will to box us because we will have already destroyed them with our words. You want word soldiers and prodigious pepperers on your team, because we can take up arms for you without ever picking up a weapon or throwing a punch.

If you know enough Nigerians outside of a professional setting, you probably already know that insults are our love language and favorite pastime. It's not in wickedness either (most times), but it's because we relish the loving humbling we get to do when we slap each other with words.

You see, from childhood onward, our parents and family members have rained insults down upon us with reckless abandon. And when they weren't slandering us, they were directing their disrespect to others, so many of us learned how to assassinate people with our words very early. Plus, we learned that you can disgrace both those close to you and strangers, enough for them to clutch their pearls. This is what makes us undefeated in the art of verbal shaming. We are truly unfuckwitable.

Many of us can recall some of the tongue-lashings we got, and still remember the way they stung then. Have you ever been insulted so badly that you can't even respond? Instead, a single tear just rolls down your face, in mourning of your previously intact psyche.

Here's the thing. I'm of the Yorùbá people, and our language is deeply metaphorical. It's a highly descriptive tongue, with words for many things other languages might not have. This allows our insults to cut different. It's a sweet tongue with a spicy execution, and some of that sweetness is diluted as we attempt to translate to English. All

I know is, Yorùbá people gotta be the pioneers of the put-downs, with tongues that are Weapons of Ego Destruction.

There are two types of insults: the ones we use toward people we love and would fight for but need to humble from time to time, even in jest. And the other is for people we see as our opponents. You might clutch your pearls at these but trust me, they're our ways of greeting.

Before lunch, you might have heard that you're a useless goat, or you're daft and senseless. The one I used to hear *a lot* when I was little, with my sharp tongue: "Ẹ́lẹ́ẹ̀kẹ́ èébú ni ẹ́." That means "cheeks full of insults." It's not my fault. It was preparation for who I am today.

But some other insults meet us in moments when we make bad decisions and they want to let us know how much they disapprove. Such as:

- "Big for nothing ijot (idiot)." All this height you have but you have no sense to match it. You're big, for no reason.

- "See your head like a four corner cabin biscuit." SpongeBob SquarePants has nothing on you.

- "Your head is so big with its five cardinal points corners. N, S, E, W, and D for Dummy point!" Because why not insult me using geography so I can learn something?

- "Ó wú bi búrẹ́dì to já sí omi." Translation: "You are swollen like bread soaked in water." This one is especially harsh if they use it to insult you AFTER you got mad from an original insult. This might cause tears.

- "If I slap you, you'll see heaven." Sooo you just wanna slap someone into other dimensions. Why do we gotta go there? The slap might not come, but the threat is enough to make me reassess my life.

We're forever roasting each other and other people's heads and mouths. Some of the insults we use make no sense, yet they still hurt like hell when you receive them. The diasporic tradition of dirty dozens is our favorite game, and we don't play fair—we play to hurt souls. Some of us are still recovering and in therapy to unlearn these insults and the hurt feelings that came with them. Chei.

The one thing that does help? When you see you're not the only one getting pepper-sprayed with slanderous words. Everyone gets it in equal measure, so you take it less personally than if you were the sole object of disgrace. It ain't just you. Silver linings, right?

It's even worse if the person we're facing is someone who has actually done something to us and we don't feel loyal to them or know them at all. Here are five of the most savage insults I've heard directed toward opponents:

- "The thunder that will strike you down is still doing push-ups." Not only do I want thunder to strike you down, but I'm also letting you know that the thunder itself is working out so it's at its strongest when it does it. SHEESH!

- "If I want to kill myself, I will climb to your level of stupidity and jump to your IQ." Fatha God! So you're just highly foolish with low levels of sense. Look at life.

- "They didn't born you or your forefathers well." Why must we go to the ancestors? What did they have to do with this? But sometimes you wanna play dirty. This is how.

- "Walking around like the unflushable toilet you are." You're full of shit and there's nothing you can do about it but offend us all.

- "You're an article with no commercial value." Chisos (Jesus) is Lord. How did we get here? Nobody's supposed to be here!

You might actually wanna learn how to fight if you have us as friends, because the way we will flout and flog people on your behalf, we might be challenged to a duel from the pure offending of it all. If the person we're beefing with hears me call them a "standard bastard" or "swaggerless buffoon," they might wanna square up, understandably.

Our insults bring different smoke to you. If reading folks for filth were an Olympic sport, Nigerians would be Hall of Famers. As your friends, we will increase your slander vocabulary, to be used sparingly, in the moments when someone has done the most with the least. We call those people aláṣejù (pronounced: ah-lah-SHAY-joo). *Aláṣejù* is a Yorùbá word that translates to "doer of too much."

You don't have to wield this weapon every day, but when you do, it will be potent clapbackery. I filter myself from my natural savagery of it all, so when people think I'm letting folks have it, they should know I am holding back, cuz I could be way worse.

Here's the thing, your Nigerian friend might insult you for sport, but no one else can. We're deeply loyal and stan those in our inner circles. You have nothing (read: everything) to fear but our mouths.

A lot of times, Nigerian group chats look like this:

PERSON 1: Good morning, useless people.

PERSON 2: You're foolish. How ah you?

PERSON 3: Head Goat in Charge, I'm fine.

PERSON 4: I saw you on Instagram looking sezzy.

PERSON 5: Eh so it's just them looking fine. Wharrabout me?

PERSON 4: Face your front. I wasn't talking to you. Big mouth.

It's all love! Can't you tell? Ha! But no one else can call us foolish or useless, because we'd squad up real quick because we took offense. Which in itself is a conundrum. How are we both unbothered and easily offended? Ask our parents. They're the royalty of incongruence. They'll hurl insults at you, but if you even LOOK like you're somehow upset, then they get upset. Similarly, they get very easily offended by the actions of others. Insults might be one love language, but taking offense is another. Remember the person who saw them at a party in 1977 but didn't greet them? They're still upset about it today, in a new millennium.

We somehow straddle the line of not taking anything personally and taking everything personally. We have learned to get words thrown at us and have them slide off our shoulders, while also taking offense to everything being done to us.

You can tell your Nigerian friend, "You ain't shit," and they might laugh because they know for sure they are from royalty (even though they might not be), and your words will do nothing to affect their elevated sense of self. But similarly, come to their house and decline their offer of food and see them feel attacked that you dared to show up in their abode without being hungry, therefore not needing the delectable goodness that is Nigerian jollof. HOW DARE YOU??

That brings me to . . . we are great because we won't let you carry your grudges by yourself. We will help. In fact, we are so good at holding a grudge that even after you drop it, we're still behind you, holding on strong. We remember who did what to you and when, even if you forgot, and we will be sucking our teeth anytime we hear their name. "Oh, so you and Jane are cool again? Did she beg you? Oh okay. Mtchew." And then we continue to side-eye. You might call us petty, but our response might be "And so?" We are Petty Wap for sure, and we know it.

That's another reason why you should get a Nigerian in your life. We've grown Teflon skin after decades of facing verbal dropkicks. We are thick-skinned and often unbothered by what others have to say about us. When you hear that you're an olódo (dummy) for breakfast, what else are people in the world gonna say to you or about you that will damage your spirit? You tell me I can't accomplish something because I'll never amount to anything? Well, it's my job to show you wrong.

On top of all of that, getchu a Nigerian friend to get the ego boost that comes with it. Why? We balance out the insults we might throw your way with ultimate cheerleading and hypeman-dom. Can't nobody gas you up like a Naija pesin, because we keep the same energy across the board. The way we celebrate you will make your head swell five times its size. At which point we will then say, "See your head like water balloon." Because: balance.

Imagine walking into a room where your friends are, and you're dressed up. And you hear "Blood of Gideon! Look at Luvvie of life. Finest of all fine babes! In fact, another one is a counterfeit because no other copies will do!" Or "Everlasting God on the throne! So you want to kill us today with beauty, àbí? You just want to scatter us and leave us nothing because you decided to bring yourself looking like the Queen of Sheba. It's not your fault, but the anointing." And sometimes, a long drawn out "WAWUUUUU" (because a simple "wow" just won't do) as they put their arms on their head for an extra measure of disbelief does the trick. You get that type of reception and I dare you to not instantly feel unfuckwitable.

My grandmother was a pro at making people feel like they walked on money. She had a friend who she would hail every time she saw her as a greeting. "AH! Ọ̀rẹ́ mí àtàtà, MARIAMU ỌMỌ BÀBÁ GOD." Translation: "My important friend, Mariam, God's child." Imagine someone greeting you by reminding you that you are heir to the Alpha and Omega. Me too, my head swells in return.

We won't let you feel humble. HUMBLE! Which kind? For what??

There is power in the gassing up that goes beyond the looks. It is an exercise in infusing confidence and courage in each other. It is a braveness drill, to get you to understand how dope you look and are, and how unstoppable you truly are. This comes in handy in the moments when you face scary things and wonder if you can make something big happen.

When you bring fear to the people who insist on making you feel like you just slayed everyone's spirits, they throw it out for you. They make the big things feel like foregone conclusions, and it's amazing to have and hear. The only thing Nigerians fear is God, Ghana jollof, and our parents' disappointment. Everything else? We can tackle it.

Growing up, our parents' expectations of us could either crush us with pressure or push us forward. A lot of us chose to be pushed forward, and that's because excellence was normalized. Doing big things in your life was the assumption, and you had no reason to do otherwise. To the point where if you got a B on the homework, they'd ask you if someone got an A. You'd of course reply with yes. And then they'd wonder what made that person different from you. What made them do better? They'd inquire with the shady "Did that person have two heads?" You'd say no and they'd sit there looking at you like the foolish person you were in the moment. Was that person better than you? *No.* So why not you?

As a seven-year-old, you might have been like, "But wait." But as an adult, I see the benefits in the train of thought. A lot of us carry that lesson with us, and we've become grown-ups who do the same, in different form, to our friends.

I have a crew of friends who are all from West Africa. If I go to that squad crew and tell them about an amazing opportunity I got in disbelief or with a hint of impostor syndrome creeping through ("OMG I can't believe it"), they set me straight: "Why not you? A whole you like this! Who else would it be? In fact, we're upset they didn't call you before this."

Why not you? That role you want to audition for. That doctorate you want to earn. That book you want to write. That stage you want to take. Why not you? Are the people who are able to do it not born on days that end with *y*? They are.

We all need the reminder that the people who have the opportunities are not somehow inherently better than us. They might have more privilege (which pushes them forward), but if the opportunity came to you and you ended up in the same room as the person with the trust fund, you gotta be doubly proud of yourself. YOU DID THAT. A whole unstoppable you!

Friends are quick to remind you of it and it is sweet. That bravado that we carry and pass out to people around us is a gift. It can be misused and become a superiority complex, but I think about how relentless Nigerians can be, and how we wear pride like a coat. It might be a coping mechanism because we come from a country where there are more than two hundred million people and everybody wants to be somebody. We say, "Naija no dey carry last" as a creed and affirmation and insistence.

Nigerians wake up and cough adversity.

You go to the market in Nigeria and the woman carrying water on her head, selling it for 500 naira ($1.30), will wonder why you dare to stand in her way as she needs to walk. She might even shame you a little for being in the wrong spot. Her head is held up high. Apologize for what? She might not have a kobo to her name, but she will also not think twice about taking up space.

Sure, our rudeness and aggression can be too much and often in the place of efficiency and good service. Like how going to a Nigerian embassy is an exercise in futility. IsweaterGawd, if you want your blood pressure to go up, go to any Nigerian embassy in hopes of getting a passport or visa in a timely (or courteous) manner. There, you will face the type of shenanigans that make you lose your hard-earned home training and any semblance of kindness.

There was a time when the Nigerian consulate in New York ended up on the news because they hadn't processed new passports in more than ten days because the air-conditioning unit had stopped working, so their equipment was overworked. But they hadn't notified anyone, so people who traveled from out of town with appointments showed up to locked doors at the Nigerian embassy.

I don't know how we dabble in excellence as a cultural value on one hand and then offer the most piss-poor of standards when it comes to receiving and giving services. Like I said, we're a complicated and convoluted people. We really do add flavor (or confusion) to your life.

Nigerians are extra AF. To be Nigerian is to be a lifelong aláṣejù, and we're not sorry about it. Our weddings are proof because Nigerians use holy matrimony as an occasion to do the utter most with the most. We have costume changes, money dances, and all the pomp and circumstance one can imagine could be part of such a moment. I swore I was not going to engage in all of that.

I was wrong.

I did all of it. In fact, I did it twice. I had two weddings in one day. The first was in the morning, from 9 a.m. to 12 p.m. That was our traditional Yorùbá wedding. In the Yorùbá traditional ceremony, the groom asks (begs) the family of his bride for her hand in marriage and he has to prove how bad he wants to marry her. He makes a promise to not just his family but hers that she will be number one in his life. His family also brings gifts to show they want to welcome her into their fold.

For our Yorùbá wedding, the clothes we wore were handmade aṣọ òkè (a.k.a. top cloth), and mine had thousands of stones sewn on it by hand. It took months to make. We had fifty people in our collective aṣọ ẹbi squad, which is the group of people who wear matching fabric and gèlè (head ties) on that day. Their fabric tells guests that they are our tribe.

Our Western ceremony was from 6 p.m. to 1 a.m. Two hundred fifty people joined us that day to celebrate our love, eat great food, and have their knees go out because of dancing too much.

My mom made sure to bring her own extra too. Part of the reason why I initially wasn't going to have a wedding carnival is that I happen to have a Nigerian mom who never asked me, "So where is your husband?" or pressured me on what I should do for a living. My mother has always trusted me with my own life, which is the ultimate compliment from a parent. She's low-key, doesn't roll with a big crew of people, and is perfectly fine in her own company. She doesn't even like going to parties. So much so that when people invite her to parties, she sometimes gets offended. "Have they seen me come to stuff like this? No. So why are they calling me?" Meanwhile, she'd probably get offended if they didn't invite her. It makes sense.

Anyhoo, when I got engaged, she was the first person we called, and she was so excited! She already knew it was happening because my boo had gone to her to ask for my hand in marriage. But the call to her made her show all of her teeth. Fast-forward six months later, and we're deep into planning the wedding. The only responsibility my mom had was picking her clothes for both weddings. All I did was give her colors to coordinate with, and all she had to do was pick the fabric her clothes would be made with. The morning colors for my family: all gold everything. Evening: She could wear whatever color she wanted. This lady ended up picking twelve different fabrics before landing on the final ones. That wasn't her most extra part, though.

A few months before the wedding, my sister turned forty and one of her friends surprised her at home with a saxophonist to play her

"Happy Birthday." We all also surprised her by showing up, so when sis came home from the spa, there were TWO surprises: Mom and saxophonist. Well, after she got the surprise of her life, she went to change because we had planned a dinner for her. The saxophonist stayed playing and my mom had her own private jam session, dancing along. She became instantly fond of him and by the time he left, he was like, "Thank you, Mommy!" How did you dance and end up with a son? I laughed so hard because it was exactly something Mama Fáloyin would have done.

A few months before my wedding, my mom comes to me and Mr. Jones.

MOM: So I want to have the saxophonist at the wedding.

ME AND BAE: *Exchange looks.*

ME: What would he do? We already have our musicians.

MOM: Well, I like him. He can sing me in when I'm introduced at the Trad [traditional wedding ceremony].

ME: Hmmm, let's talk to Akeshi about it, since she's the planner.

I didn't get a chance to talk to Akeshi because my mom had called her and let her know that she'd bought the guy's ticket from Houston. I got the call and I cackled! You know what? She hadn't asked for much else in the wedding-planning process. He could sax her and the fam in as they danced. And he could play at the cocktail hour. Why not? It would be so chill and relaxed.

The wedding day came and saxophonist did his thing at the Trad. Then he started playing Nigerian gospel turn-up songs during the cocktail hour, and it was a WRAP! The cool vibe? Who needed it? LET'S DANCE! It got so LIVE that at one point he was having a dance battle with one of my girls, Ayọ̀délé, where he spun and hip-thrusted. BRUH!!! People started throwing money up in the air.

There's a video from our cocktail of someone's mom (*coughs*) dropping it low to the ground as someone else's mom (*coughs*) stuffed the front of her dress with dollars while someone else stood behind them pouring money on their heads. Reception hadn't even started yet.

Long story long, my mom's extra-ness really contributed to the day and led to an overall amazing time, before the REAL turn-up happened at the reception. It was good times. The moral of the story is that I think everyone should go to a Nigerian wedding at least once in your life. It's a beautifully colorful spectacle, a feast for your eyes (and stomach), and a treat for your day. But most important, know you are worthy of being celebrated with live music even at an event that is about your daughter, like my mom.

We Nigerian people are a passionate lot, and we love us some Jesus (well, those who are Christians do). You haven't heard prayer until you've heard a Naija person pray and give God the glory. We cover everything with the blood of Jesus and we often take it above and beyond.

We take praise and worship very seriously because Christ is our bestie. This is why sometimes you don't even wanna tell your parents that something is wrong because you don't wanna be subjected to fifteen minutes of revival when you're in your Uber. All you wanna do is commute and you're on the phone tryna whisper, "AMEN." But then you hear "I DON'T HEAR YOUR AMEN!" so you shift in your seat and try not to disturb anyone within earshot.

Nigerian aunties are the prayer professionals, and they seem to have a mainline to God. If you tell someone you're cold, the prayer you might get could go like this: "May the God of holy fire SET ABLAZE any manner of snow, ice, frozen precipitation, subzero moisture in the matchless name of Jesus!" LMAO! And AMEN O! I receive it in His mighty name!

The prayers in my texts and emails and voice mails are enough to destroy a country of enemies. You just know when you say AMEN, your haters are somewhere expeditiously getting paper cuts. The prayers can get so intense that they're borderline curses.

Having Nigerians pray for you, especially in times of crisis, might have you feeling bad for whoever wronged you. I've heard someone say, "And may your enemies never prosper," and I've been like, "Wait. Should I affirm that?" Sometimes Nigerians pray so hard that you're pretty sure they've started cussing. "May your helper never sleep until they've done what they needed in your life." Ummm . . . amen? In fact, who borned you and dared you not to say a loud AMEN?!? You must want to be your own enemy of progress, blocking your own blessings.

We do Old Testament flood-the-earth appeals to Christ. There's even a Yorùbá song called "Mommy O" that praises moms and prays for their longevity on this Earth. All is well, until the line in it that prays that anyone who wishes your mom a short life will be run over by a trailer. It escalates so quickly!

We pray heaven DOWN! Even in worship, we're intense. When a church is called Mountain of Fire, you should know they ain't there to play bald-headed games about their supplication. They're the ones who might pray something like "The same way a bird flies and doesn't collide with anything, may your destiny's airplane never collide with anything." Wow, what a vision!

If you're reading this, maybe you already have a Nigerian friend. Or maybe you don't. Maybe you're thinking: "I mean I did go to school with some Nigerians, are we friends?" To that I ask, has their mom cooked for you? No? Then you're probably not friends. It's okay. It's not too late for you.

How do you make Nigerian friends? How do you find a shady and bold Naija to squad up with in this scary world, so y'all can take it on with sharp tongue in tow? I have a few tips.


## GO TO A COLLEGE LIBRARY

If you go to any school library, you are sure to find at least one Nigerian there, nose buried in books. They're studying to be a nurse, doctor, lawyer, engineer, whether they like it or not. You hear "Go and face your books" all your life and you do just that when you get to undergrad, cuz you don't want the lambasting that will come if you don't. It's as simple as that.

## GO WHERE AFROBEATS IS BEING PLAYED

If you're walking by somewhere and you hear some Afrobeats booming, there is a West African there, especially a Nigerian. The drumbeat, the ample opportunity for lyrics, the vibes—we're all about it. Dip in there and join us as we drop it low and let our bodies move to the beat. And when you join us, we'll gas you up and the story can go from there. In fact, seek out the Afrobeats Night at any club and you're good. But that's easy. You knew that, right?

Also, you can buy a pair of white loafers. I feel like 83 percent of the white shoes that exist in the world are owned by African men. Facts only (by facts, I mean I completely made that up). You will not meet a Nigerian man who does not own a pair of white loafers of some sort. I don't know why they had a meeting and agreed this was their uniform. Bless it.

## DECLARE ALLEGIANCE TO
## NIGERIAN JOLLOF

Jollof is a tomato-based rice dish that is the West African version of basically every yellow rice. And because we love to center ourselves, let's compare it to other dishes. Paella is Spanish jollof. Fried rice is

Chinese jollof. Jambalaya is Creole jollof. You get me. It is a necessity in the Nigerian diet, in all its spicy and flavorful goodness.

Jollof was not created in Nigeria; the Senegalese were the pioneers. But we are deeply passionate about the fact that we think our jollof is the best. Because: Nigerians. We are in a never-ending jollof war with our Gold Coast cousins, the Ghanaians, and we know the truth: Naija jollof carries first. (I love that even if you wanna argue with me right now, I've already put it in this book, so you can argue with your reflection.)

Anyway, to get a Nigerian friend for life, a shortcut is to denounce Ghana jollof. You must talk about how it doesn't have enough peppeh and how it doesn't measure up. It doesn't matter whether you mean it or not. Them the rules. I don't make them; I pass them along. You can't be neutral in this war. You gotta pick a team.

I know you know a Nigerian (we're everywhere). Cultivate a real relationship with them. Get a Naija auntie who can pray the Holy Trinity down. Get a Naija friend who will gas you up, insult you, and then have a dance battle with you at the same time.

Your life will never be the same.

# 16

# FUCK FEAR

## We fear FEAR.

Fear is a hater. Fear will have you sitting down when you should be standing up. Fear will have you not saying that thing that is necessary when you need to. Fear will talk you out of your purpose so quick that your destiny gets whiplash.

Fear is real, primitive, and innate. It's one of the most natural emotions. To not have any fear is actually a physiological disorder called Urbach-Wiethe disease, and it happens when the brain's amygdala is damaged. True story.

We are not supposed to be walking around fearlessly. Our angst is a biological necessity because it keeps us safe from doing dumbass things without safety nets.

To be afraid is to be human. But I think that's assuring: It's really cool to know that we're all out here walking around with varying levels of "WTF is this?" happening at any given time. Some of us have learned to hide it better or handle it so it doesn't overtake us. Some people make choices to move past their doubts, knowing it might not work out, but they will try anyway, while others can point to pivotal moments when they have let fear be their main decision factor. But we all feel it.

I wrote this book because I want to always be the type of person who overcomes her doubts. But in my life, I have been the type of person who let fear dictate her decisions more times than I can count. My journey to where I am today was longer than it could have been because I let fear stop me from owning my purpose and my passion and my profession for a long time. And it wasn't until I made the decision to push past those scary moments that I started seeing my life move forward in ways that blew my mind.

The choice to fight fear is not like joining some lifelong club that once you're in, you can't get out. Nah. It's a moment-by-moment, day-by-day decision. The biggest scaredy-cat in the world can decide to do something brave at any moment. It might be as small as ordering a doughnut they've never had. Or as big as proposing to the love of their life. Or as audacious as going skydiving because their friend asked them.

We are all fighting battles with the world, systems, ourselves. Battles that are easy to lose. It's so much easier to keep doing what feels comfortable. What feels safe. But then we might look up one day and realize that we've safety-netted ourselves into lives that feel like cages. Cages can get comfortable, but comfort is overrated. Being quiet is comfortable. Keeping things the way they've been is comfortable. But all comfort does is maintain the status quo.

What forces us to live comfortable lives that might not serve us?

What forces the people in our lives to shrink? It is partly caused by our fears and other people's angst layered on top of each other.

Do we realize how often we pass on our fears to other people? Do we realize how much we impose the things we are afraid of on the people we love and care about every single day? I know exactly why people are afraid of choosing the path that is unfamiliar, of experiencing things and being free. We are constantly telling people to be scared.

I took a trip to Mexico one year and posted on social media, casually, about loving how I was getting the opportunity to eat mangoes every single day, because they are my favorite fruit. I got so many comments from people who were warning me that I would end up lying prostrate to the toilet throne, because when they ate mangoes, they had the runs. Meanwhile, it was day six and I was perfectly okay, and continued to be. The same thing happened when before the trip I told people I was going to another country and was told to "watch out for kidnappers." Or when I said I was sitting outside and someone warned me about how the mosquitoes were going to make a meal out of me. Mind you, at no point was I asking people for advice. I was simply sharing what I was doing, and I was instantly met with tales of misfortune.

I get it. The world is scary. Shit happens. But we lead our lives with so much fear. We're so busy bracing for constant impact that we stay right where we are, too afraid to move, because that monster we think is around the corner will jump out.

Sometimes this anxiety comes from our loved ones. The generational curses we talk about breaking can be limitations that those we love have habitually placed on us. The weapons that have formed might actually be from our families and friends, who meant well but ended up using ammunition of apprehension on us. Breaking cycles can mean unlearning what those closest to us have taught us.

How free would we be if we weren't being tethered down by other people's anxieties, doubts, and insecurities? How high could we fly if people weren't pulling at our ankles to keep us grounded to earth because that's where they are?

You deserve to be free of other people's weight. You deserve to be unbuckled from other people's doubts. You carry enough of your own. We all deserve to walk light.

When people try to drop their bags of fears at our feet, let us drop-kick the bag back to them. We don't want it. I'm not holding your doubts. I'm not making space in MY life for YOUR angst. I will not sleep under a blanket of your dread. It's not mine to carry. No thank you.


Sure, we can live lives where we are minimally afraid because we've covered ourselves in bubble wrap and don't take any risks, but THAT life is boring. That life is wasted. That life is a version of fluorescent beige. Your gravestone will be all, "They were here." Dassit. Dassall. You'll get to heaven and God will roll His/Her/Their eyes at you. All this breath, all this movement, all this BEING. And you wasted it being the person version of a flavorless rice cake. What will you have done that you were proud of?

When I'm dead and gone, I want to have left a mark. It's like in the movie *Coco*. We only truly die when our names no longer pass off someone's tongue. I want to be missed. I want my absence felt. I want my contributions to be bigger than my small stature. I want this world to be better because I was here. And if I'm moving with fear and doubt and anxiety first, I'm standing in no gaps, writing in fluff, speaking in whispers.

I am not fearless. But I've learned to start pushing past fear because oftentimes, the fear itself is scarier than whatever is on the other side. It's like being afraid to walk through a dark hallway. If you close your eyes and run through it, you'll be okay. And you'll look back and say, "That wasn't that bad."

For me, fighting fear is facing freedom. We owe it to ourselves to say FUCK FEAR, and we owe it to the people who look up to us, or surround us, or love us.

We owe it to ourselves to lighten our load and drop dead weight. Drop it all. The friends who don't really have your back. The partner who makes you feel worthless. The job that makes you tired of waking up. The trauma that makes you self-sabotage. The self-doubt that makes you think you're not good enough.

We owe it to ourselves to climb the mountain that feels too tall.

The world isn't going to get less scary. We might never get braver. I'm basically lowering my expectations. That's why I say we need to acknowledge that and get on with the shits. We must keep doing the things that scare us, knowing that what is right is often the opposite of what is easy.

Get on with it, and start by forgiving yourself for not having the courage to do something you wished you had in the past. Forgive yourself for not speaking up in moments that might have called for it. Forgive yourself for the mistakes you've made that now feel avoid-able. You did your best with the information you had and under-stood at the time.

Everyone who has done major things has started with one step. It wasn't that they looked up one day and it was all done for them. (Well, except for some white dudes. Because Daddy and nepotism are the best security blankets.) Most people who did major things or changed the world got the idea and one day decided to take one step, followed by another, followed by another. Rome wasn't built in a day, but the bricks they laid to build it had to begin on some day.

Those dreams we have the audacity to dream? They can't stay on the "wish list" pile forever. Well, they can, but then what was the point? We actually have to DO.

So, in case anyone needs encouragement to BE, SAY, DO, here it is, because really cool things can be waiting for you on the other side of fear. The big things we are so afraid of doing because they seem too ginormous for us, we must do. Even if we do them poorly. Ask that scary question. Write that book. Learn that language. Check off the bucket list. Travel to 150 countries. Start that major business. Purge your shoe closet (*looks at myself*). Run that marathon. (This is not my ministry and I still think marathons are conspiracies. Of who? I'm not sure.) Go on that audition. Make that move.

Do all that shit. Or do none of that, if that's what you're com-pelled to do. But that thing that you keep thinking about but you keep stopping because you're afraid? DO THAT THING.

In the moments when I want to run back to what's comfortable or I dare to cower in the face of doubt, I think about Olúfúnmiláyọ̀ Juliana Fáloyin, my guardian angel and my prototype of a professional troublemaker. That God-loving, favor-finding, whole-face-smiling unicorn of a woman. I think about her, as a teenager, starting her life from scratch by herself at the age of eighteen. I reflect on the woman who doctors told wouldn't speak again when she had a stroke. I can't help but muse on my muse who moved through the world boldly confident that God and her faith were bigger than any fear.

I carry and will continue to carry my grandmother with me everywhere I go. Every day, I look down at my right hand, at the gold filigree ring I never take off. It's the one Grandma gave me one day when I saw her wearing it and instantly squealed how much I loved it. Without hesitation, she took the ring off and handed it to me. It's funny that it adorns the middle finger of my dominant hand. It works.

A professional troublemaker is someone who is committed to being authentically themselves while speaking the truth and doing some scary shit. Here is to us, daring to live boldly. I owe it to Mama Fáloyin, my favorite troublemaker, to do this. When fear tries to stop me, I need to put on my pants, say a little prayer of strength, and dance for twenty minutes to celebrate my insistence to conquer doubt.

Fear is a hater, a liar, and a cheat. To be FEARLESS is to not commit to doing LESS because of our fears. We owe ourselves fearlessness, and we can start now.

# EPILOGUE

# COURAGE IN THE TIME OF FEAR

In the middle of writing this book, the coronavirus (COVID-19) pandemic began. It wasn't enough for me to be working on my most vulnerable piece of writing yet, which in itself scared me to pieces. Then the world had to throw other wrenches in the mix and gift us with a never-before-seen deadly virus that flipped everything upside down. There's also murder hornets and human-sized bats we gotta worry about. And any other animal that is native to Australia. This is a lot of scary shit to deal with.

To have to write this book about tackling fear, in the midst of this chaos, was a test for me to see if I can do and be who I say I am when it is especially difficult. Hundreds of thousands of people have died from this virus and there are still those who are thinking, "I'm not going to stop this from letting me live my life." They have somehow convinced themselves that there is nothing to fear, even as science and data and common sense grabs their face (from six feet away) with the warnings.

In this instance, I believe they are being wildly foolish. This is when fear serves its ORIGINAL purpose: to keep us from acutely endangering our lives and the lives of those in the world. When we are staring down the barrel of a gun whose bullets are a virus that is highly contagious and killing people at rates in multiples of the seasonal flu, fear is valid and necessary. This anxiety is based on facts. If we do not have it, we are likely to put the people in our community, even those we don't know, in jeopardy. We are likely to put ourselves in harm's way.

Now compare that dread with the uneasiness you get when you have to speak up in a meeting. Or the jitters you get when you have to tell your parents you don't actually want to be a lawyer but a photographer instead. Or the worry you have because you don't want to dream too big because of the potential disappointment. Those fears now seem trite, don't they? Probably not, because they are legitimate also. But next to any kind of physical or medical threat—whether it be a virus, a treacherous political climate where Satan's minion got the nuclear codes, or when you're stopped by the police and you're Black and you're not sure if the dude in blue is going to see your brown as a weapon—the trepidation we have in our everyday lives can feel silly.

If life has taught us anything, it's that it's full of uncertainty. And that's some scary shit. Right now, I don't know how this pandemic will unfold, how many lives it will ultimately steal, or how long we will be inside, unable to touch those we love (outside of those under our roofs). The only thing certain right now is that nothing is certain. The unknown is disquieting, and it's easy to give in to anxiety.

What we can do when we are in uncharted waters is to know we are doing our part. I might be indoors, but I'm not hiding from the world or the work that got me here. I am using my fear to put pen to paper, because writing a "Fear-Fighter Manual" during a time of rampant unease is almost poetic. It's like God sent me a dare and I'm being charged to rise to the occasion. It's meta AF.

Some people have needed to rest during what is happening. I couldn't, because book deadlines with advances are real. Plus my editor and agent are bold women who ain't afraid to call me to the carpet. But more important, in a global crisis, I felt helpless to do much more than the work I am purposed to do: WRITE. I'm staying home and staying out of the way of the essential workers. And I'm writing because that is my catharsis.

Times of crisis and chaos present us with the opportunity to do the best work of our lives. People use words that they pull from the depths of their spirits. People paint with strokes that they summon from their souls. People sing notes that come from the cosmos. People innovate. We must keep doing that.

Another thing we can do when we're in uncharted waters: Ask what we can learn from this. What is this experience trying to teach us? How are we supposed to change because of it?

Right now, I am hoping we learn to be kinder and more generous to each other. I hope we give each other a bit more grace.

I also hope that we begin to really understand that everybody's pain is our business. Because it can become our pain very quickly. You can't just be like, "That house is burning? Well, that ain't got nothing to do with me." Because the fire can spread to your house very quickly. We have to understand that if we can put out their smoke, then it doesn't become our fire. Let me repeat: The quicker we can put out their fire, the less likely it is to become ours.

Everybody's problem is our problem too. When we see people being discriminated against, and we keep quiet and think it has nothing to do with us, we're off base. You don't think you're next? I extrapolate situations to see how they can come and affect me very quickly. I know that if something bad happens to someone else, it can happen to me too.

These crisis moments call for us to elevate whoever we are. To change, grow, mature, evolve. If we do not, we're going to keep getting the same expensive and heart-wrenching lessons. We need to ask ourselves what we should be learning from all this.

What would my grandmother say right now if she were alive? How would she deal with these times? She would pray over Bible passages during her three-hour 3 a.m. vigils. She would tell me to pray. She would have called the whole family with the Bible passages she thought we should read for protection (Psalms 91 and 121 were her faves). Her assurance would calm my spirit, and even though she might not be in front of me, I'd see her smile. I would know that there was a prayer warrior advocating on my behalf in the middle of a worldwide storm. I would probably sleep better because Mama Fáloyin and Jesus had a conference call where my name came up.

In her absence, I'm trying to fill my own gap.

That being said, I still have to do my part and not let the idea of faith keep me from being fearful. Because to use my Christianity as armor would be to invalidate what is material. Toxic positivity is real, and some people hide behind religion to escape real life and real circumstances. And it's dangerous.

What's toxic positivity? It is the idea that you should always have a positive response to every situation, no matter how severe the circumstance is. The intent behind it is admirable: that we should find the good in everything, in an attempt to keep our eyes on happy. But the results can be harmful.

Sure, constantly wallowing in negativity is not healthy. However, what makes this positivity toxic is that it discredits feelings and makes people feel weak for not being able to plaster a smile on their faces at all times. It is a way to sidestep dealing properly with our lives. You know what toxic positivity often is? Denial. Avoidance. Evasion of reality. It is why we must acknowledge that fear is legit, and it is natural.

Everything does not have an immediate upswing or feel-good to it, and that's okay. Life can be a cruel hellcat sometimes and we can face shit that will knock the wind out of us. What we often do is pull our Jesus card and skip over the part where we actually deal with facts. What we should do is feel our feelings, take the time, and then move forward.

Christians are champs at toxic positivity. We excel at it because we have been taught that faith and fear cannot coexist. We've been Instagram-graphicked to pieces about how there is no way we can believe in God yet still be anxious. But it is an oversimplification of scripture and a flattening of what is normal human experience. Even people who aren't religious or spiritual have received the message that to be courageous is to be fearless. So add that to the God guilt that we tie to fear, and we have the perfect storm of people feeling inferior for daring to be apprehensive. It's an oppressive state of affairs and I'm judging us HARD.

People die and folks will retort, "Well, at least they're with God now." Or "Everything happens for a reason. It's part of the plan." Which, okay cool. Glad we believe that. But when we invoke those words when someone is feeling pain that is as physical as it is emotional, it says that whatever their feelings are should be soothed by the platitudes of looking at the upside. It isolates and others them in their pain.

I'm here to tell you that you can be a Christian or spiritual or a monk and still worry. You can be connected to a higher power and still be anxious. You are not doing spirituality wrong by still having the nerve to be worried. Worry is a part of life. The goal is that we don't let the doubt render us catatonic with defeat. You can be scared, but move forward and live. That's what matters.

There are times when we will be anxious because we have a valid reason to be.

Some of us are legit scared, if not for ourselves then for the people we love or for society at large. Listen, I'm afraid half the time. Fear is here. It is present. I acknowledge that I feel this thing, that it is scary and uncomfortable, and I go forward anyway.

This is why I'm writing this book. The goal isn't to not feel negative emotions; it's that we don't let them consume us. Whether you're a deacon or a heathen, I don't want you to feel you are failing at life because you are not always on Hashtag Gratitude mode. Worrying doesn't mean you don't trust God. It doesn't mean you're weak. It means you're human.

Fear is there and it is natural. It will always be present. And yet we must still keep going. We can't afford to let fear, whether big or small, legitimate or contrived, numb us.

Here I am, writing through it, writing to it, and writing from it. It shall be well. Someway.

All my love to
Fúnmiláyọ̀ Fáloyin

# Acknowledgments

---

TURN ALL THE WAY UP! When I finished my first book, *I'm Judging You*, I felt like I climbed a mountain. With this book, I feel like I did it again, with better shoes and a warmer coat. And almost got knocked off a couple times but pushed against the wind and got to the top anyway, making the view even sweeter.

Shout-out to meeee, cuz I DID THAT! Sometimes stopping to smell the roses looks like high-fiving yourself, and this book is something that feels revel worthy. Also, people write books and forget how to act. I am people.

My life truly is a testimony of God's grace, and this is yet another thing I've done that I hope makes Her/Him/Them proud. I am constantly shown that my steps are ordered by forces greater than me, and for that I am thankful.

Grandma, I know you're still working on my behalf and fighting for me from Beyond. Thank you. I hope you love this.

It took a village for this book to come together. Thanks to my agent,

Kristyn Keene Benton, who sent me a set of dominoes when it was time for me to start writing. She used my own words ("be the domino") to remind me of what my mission was, and her deep belief in my work pushed me forward. She also didn't side-eye me anytime I called her with some random idea.

Thanks to the team at Penguin Random House for believing in this book, this message, and my voice! Props to Meg Leder, my editor, who championed this book and made my words sing!

To the man I married, Carnell: thank you for playing many roles, as best friend, husband, and anchor. You see me in ways I'm sometimes not audacious enough to see myself. You don't let me have limits because you see stardust all over me. I remember when I finished this book and said, "Wow. This is the best thing I've ever written." You replied with, "I'm so proud of you, and it should be. You're the best YOU you've ever been." And my heart grinned like a Cheshire cat because words of affirmation are my top love language, and you get me. And I thanked God, once again, for blessing me with a life partner who affirms my very being. Mr. Jones, you're dope AF.

I am surrounded by love and people who prove that there is GREAT-NESS in the world, in the form of soft places to land. Shoutout to my family. I thank God for my mom. I am the daughter of Oluyemisi, who is the daughter of Fúnmiláyọ̀, who is the daughter of Celena. From her, I've learned generosity and the art of stunting when it is necessary. She is love in walking form.

I gotta shout-out my big sister, Kofo. You are the cheerleader of life, gist partner, dance partner, matron of honor, sometimes twin. Your heart is gold and you deserve all the good things life has to offer. Thanks for the grandma stories I forgot too. Whew, we got some of our funny from that lady.

So many thank-yous to my aunt, Bunmi B. She's the one I called over and over again to tell me more stories of Grandma and verify my facts, and she provided the oríkì. She's a quiet storm, a woman of integrity, and a joy bringer. Thank you for always picking up my calls, being the family historian, and for that laugh that brightens up a room.

Our family is a true tribe unto itself: Dele, Morayo, Rolake, Wonuola, Folarin. I'd fight for y'all but you already know this.

I surround myself with people who don't allow me to be raggedy, and for that I am thankful. I even pay someone to hold me accountable to being less trash. So I must thank my therapist, Dr. Patterson, who earns every dime she is paid as she blows my mind in our sessions by reading me for filth (so professionally) constantly. The mess I am today is half the mess I was years ago. Shout-out to Aliya S. King, my friend, mentor, and first person who read this entire manuscript in full and ran her editing comb through it. She is also great for snatching my eyebrows with truth, and her edits for this book elevated my words.

LOVE to my FRAMILY (friends who become family) for peer-pressuring me into greatness and being everlasting dream enablers. Boz, Justina, Yvonne, Cynthia, Tiffany, Eunique, Felicia, Jessica, Tahira, Myleik, Maaden, Seun. They're the ones I call when something feels BIG, almost too big, and they always remind me that "If not you, then who?" Y'all push me onward and upward, constantly loaning me power whenever I'm lacking. Thank you, and I love y'all!!!

ALL THE LOVE to the citizens of LuvvNation, the most thoughtful, funny, chill-deficient play cousins on the interwebs. Building a safe space in a dumpster-fire world is one of the best things I could have done, and when people tell me my audience is amazing, I grin. Why? Because if they're a reflection of me, then they are proof that there is ample goodness in this world. LuvvCousins are the best!

Thank YOU, dear reader, for taking the time with my work. You and I officially go together. To have people find value in my work is such an honor. For that, lemme bless you with some prayers. May you never stub your toe on the side of the bed in the middle of the night. May you always season your food perfectly. May your pot of rice be perfectly cooked always. Amen.

This section could be a tome in itself, and there are so many more people who are significant to me who are not named here. You are probably one. Abeg don't be upset if I didn't name you. I had a word count to adhere to (see how I'm just throwing my publisher under the bus—HA!). But for real, thank you to everyone who sees, reads, buys, shares, and takes in my work.

Thank YOU for seeing me.

*Luvvie*

# *Vittoria*

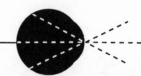

**This Large Print Book carries the
Seal of Approval of N.A.V.H.**

# *Vittoria*

## Robert Merle

### *Translated by Barbara Bray*

**Thorndike Press • Thorndike, Maine**

Library of Congress Cataloging in Publication Data:

Merle, Robert, 1908-
    Vittoria / Robert Merle : translated by Barbara Bray.
    p. cm.
    Translation of: L'idole.
    ISBN 1-56054-122-9 (alk. paper : lg. print)
    1. Large type books. I. Title.
    [PQ2625.E527813613       1991]               90-29258
    843'.914—dc20                                CIP

Thorndike Press Large Print edition published in 1991
by arrangement with Harcourt Brace Jovanovich, Inc.


Cover design by Carol Pringle.



The tree indicium is a trademark of Thorndike Press.



This book is printed on acid-free, high opacity paper. ∞

# LIST OF WITNESSES

*in the order in which they make their first deposition*

Monsignor Rossellino (Il Bello Muto)

Giulietta Accoramboni

His Eminence Cardinal Cherubi

Caterina Acquaviva

Marcello Accoramboni

Aziza the Wasp

Raimondo Orsini (Il Bruto)

Father Racasi

Lodovico Orsini,
*Count of Oppedo*

Prince Paolo Giordano Orsini,
*Duke of Bracciano*

Gian Battista della Pace,
*Bargello*

His Excellency Luigi Portici,
*Governor of Rome*

Domenico Acquaviva (Il Mancino)

Alfredo Colombani,
*Squire to Raimondo and Lodovico Orsini*

His Eminence Cardinal de' Medici

Father Luigi Palestrino,
*Theologian*

His Excellency Armando Veniero,
*Venetian Ambassador*

Giuseppe Giacobbe,
*Leader of the Roman Ghetto*

Giordano Baldoni,
*Majordomo to Prince Orsini*

Baldassare Tondini,
*Podesta of Padua*

# Preface

I made the acquaintance of Signora Vittoria Peretti forty years ago, when I was translating John Webster's brilliant but uneven play on the subject, which was written in a language that made Shakespeare's seem crystal clear.

It was only ten years later, while reading Stendhal's *Chroniques italiennes*, that I realized how horribly unfair Webster's account of Vittoria was. He may have been misinformed, but how, when the facts show her to have been a victim, could he have blackened her name to the point of calling her the White Devil? The suggestion is that in her the beauty of the flesh concealed a diabolical soul. Puritan misogyny! The poor woman is persecuted and imprisoned, and it is all her fault.

Stendhal's story consists of some thirty pages, but it is not the original work some say it is; rather, it is a literal translation of an old chronicle. It must have attracted him because of his predilection for strong passions and energetic characters.

In 1957, I wrote a short story based on the chronicle, but it left me dissatisfied. It took me some time, though, to realize why. Vittoria was good, intelligent, cultivated, and generous. It was not for these virtues, however, that she was idolized, but because female beauty was overvalued in a male-dominated society, and this was more dangerous for its object than for morality in general.

In our day, Vittoria would be a star, and the worst that would happen to her, though pathetic enough, would be that she would lose her admirers as she grew old. But in the sixteenth century, life was quite different. She was sold in marriage to a man she did not love. Her virtue was fiercely guarded. She was kept in seclusion twice, and even, for a few months, imprisoned in Castle Sant' Angelo. She was spied on, kept under surveillance, betrayed by her confessor. Her reputation was publicly tarnished. A pope annulled her second marriage.

In short, she was a woman alone against a whole society. For her fate to be comprehensible, the archaic, brutal, and vindictive setting of her life must be known. Precisely this seemed to me to be lacking in the story I wrote in 1957. It was too linear. It described what happened, but neglected the background necessary to explain why.

I thought at first I could simply rewrite my earlier attempt as a novel. But I soon saw I had to undo everything and start again, to revise and expand my research, and to give the story a much broader, more imaginative treatment: new or newly conceived protagonists, fuller background for other characters, and a narrative style that would bring out the extreme complexity of the situation with which Vittoria had to contend.

When my researches were complete, I went to Lake Garda, and was moved by the sight of the palace where Vittoria spent her last summer of happiness, in 1585. Its name is different now, but the four centuries that have passed over it since have done it no harm except to darken its stones. It is quite unlike a Venetian villa; it stands, rough and austere, beside the water. When I saw it, even the great magnolia trees on the jetty did nothing to lighten the atmosphere; their petals were falling, one by one, to the ripples of the misty lake. The air was balmy, but the place was melancholy.

Not a tile was missing from the palace. How sad to think that houses live so much longer than the men who build them. I would have preferred it to be the other way: to have found nothing but pillars strewn on the ground, and Vittoria herself sitting on the ruins amid her long tresses, rewarding me with a grateful look for having told her story fairly and with compassion.

# 1

## *Monsignor Rossellino (Il Bello Muto)*

Five years ago — to be precise, on December 5, 1572, at seven in the morning — as I was going up the steps leading to the Vatican, I tripped and fell; my neck struck the edge of a step, the blow crushed my larynx, and I would have died there and then of asphyxiation if a barber-surgeon, who happened to be nearby, had not opened my throat with a small pair of scissors. The wound healed, but the accident left me dumb.

In those days there were no more than ten barber-surgeons in Rome, and I concluded that if Providence had put one of the cleverest of them in my way so early in the morning it must have been because Providence deliberately intended the barely credible series of events that then affected my life: my fall, the crushing of my larynx, the barber's intervention, my dumbness, and my meeting with Cardinal Montalto.

I had been one of the most brilliant preachers in the Eternal City. The nobility of Rome flocked to my sermons, which brought me not only fame but also the favor of exalted ladies. They would often invite me to their palaces, set delicious dishes before me, and generally make much of me, asking nothing in return but that I speak to them, with my usual fire, of the pains of hell or the bliss of heaven. They derived great pleasure from whichever I depicted, and I was foolish enough to take pride in this.

I was then twenty-eight. According to the women in my family — and everyone knows how the visceral sex loves to chatter — I was quite good-looking. And although my behavior was virtuous, I did glory in my flesh, being conscious that the charms of my corporeal frame greatly enhanced those of my eloquence.

In the summer months, Countess V. liked to sit under an ancient tree in her garden, surrounded by her friends, and listen to me. I remember how, when I described — vividly but with proper restraint — the tortures of the damned, little drops of perspiration would break out on her lovely brow, gasps would escape from her parted lips, and her graceful neck would suddenly flush. It was as if she enjoyed the thought of yielding up her little body to the demons' cruelties. As I spun out my description, her agitation would increase, and this so affected me that I would embellish my account with further details — which I cannot now call to mind without shame.

After my throat had been carved up and my fine deep voice had fallen silent, I realized that a snake had been stretched out along one of the branches under which I used to preach, just waiting for the right moment to drop between the Countess and me like a dreadful bond.

It was a fig tree, and, though it bore leaves, it was barren.

I concluded that the same divine hand that had withered the fig tree in the Gospel had taken away my voice to prevent me from falling into sin. And the sin of my weak flesh was perhaps not the worst. So I was considering retiring into a monastery for the rest of my life. But then I received a terse note from Cardinal Montalto asking me to call on him.

I would guess Felice Peretti, who had received his cardinal's hat two years before, had chosen the name Montalto to reflect both the loftiness of his ambitions and the ruggedness of his character. I trembled as I drew near the terrible Cardinal's palace, though the building itself was modest. I knew that as grand inquisitor in Venice he had fallen upon the immorality of the clergy with fire and sword; his austerity had made him so universally hated that the priests had finally prevailed upon the Senate to expel him from the Most Serene Republic.

He now lived in such seclusion that I had never set eyes on him. And, to tell the truth, I was disappointed at first. At that time, Rome was full of magnificent prelates, of whom Pope Gregory XIII was undoubtedly the finest. He was then seventy years old but held himself very erect; agile and graceful in his movements, he could vault into the saddle like a youth.

Cardinal Montalto was of no more than medium height, and although he wasn't a hunchback, as some spiteful people claimed, he gave that impression, with his head sunk between massive shoulders. His head struck me as out of proportion to the rest of his body, and, as a former Franciscan, he wore his hair and beard long: both were disheveled and carelessly trimmed. This gave him a rough appearance that was very unusual in Rome, where most prelates looked like pebbles worn smooth and shiny by the tides.

A large nose, thin lips, protruding chin, bushy black eyebrows — in contrast to his pepper-and-salt hair and beard — and deep-set black eyes, very bright and piercing, added

14

to the strength, but scarcely to the attractiveness, of a countenance that, were it not for my profound respect for His Eminence, I might best describe as savage.

He was ill-favored, fallen from favor, and I expected no favors from him. Even so, I was surprised by the roughness of his manner and the imperious curtness of his words.

"Rossellino," he said, not replying to my dumb show of civilities, "sit down at that little table. Yes, there. In front of you are pen, ink, paper, a lighted candle, and a brass tray. Why the candle? To burn your answers as soon as you have written them. Why the tray? To hold the ashes. Now write. And no hypocrisy, please. Still less, clerical jargon! Just the truth, pure and simple — if the truth ever is pure. If you lie even once, I'll have you shown the door. Are you ready?"

This opening terrified me. I took the goose quill in my trembling hand, dipped it in the ink, and waited. The answers, which follow, were written on little squares of paper. As soon as I'd written what I had to say, the Cardinal, who was standing behind me, snatched it from my hand, glanced at it, and immediately burned it in the candle flame.

"Are you chaste?"

"Yes, Your Eminence."

"Leave out 'Your Eminence.' It slows down

15

the writing. Have you ever been tempted not to be?"

"Yes."

"Where, when, and with whom?"

"In Countess V.'s garden, before I fell down on the Vatican steps."

"Explain."

"I was describing the torments of the damned to the Countess. It disturbed her. Her agitation disturbed me."

"Have you seen the Countess again?"

"Not since my accident."

"How do you see your accident?"

"As a decree of Providence. My fall saved me from falling. I realized the vanity of the life I was leading and that my fine voice was just a snare. I was the first to be caught in it."

"Well said! What do you plan to do now?"

"Bury myself in a monastery."

"Ill reasoned! You are a secular priest. Stay in the world. Serve the church."

"Is that possible?"

"Of course. What do you consider the ills that beset the state?"

"Anarchy, corruption, contempt for the law, and the fact that bandits, titled or not, go unpunished."

"And the ills of the church?"

"Immorality, the craving for riches and dis-

16

play, simony, absenteeism among the bishops, and the use of excommunication for nonreligious purposes."

"Good, good. But complaining about abuses isn't enough. They must be remedied."

"Can I remedy them?"

"You cannot, but I can. Do you want to help me?"

"Is that possible, when I'm dumb?"

"Yes. For that very reason."

With his implacable black eyes riveted on mine, Montalto was silent long enough to convey all the implications of what he had said.

I wrote: "I offer my devotion, loyalty, and silence to Your Eminence *ad majorem gloriam Dei et Ecclesiae.*"

"Good. You shall be my chief secretary. But, Rossellino, I did not inherit a fortune; I do not buy and sell preferment; and, unlike a lot of other cardinals, I do not receive an allowance from Philip II of Spain for selling him my vote in the conclave. So you won't be paid much."

"That doesn't matter."

"Good. What do you think of the present pope?"

When I hesitated, Montalto glared at me and shouted: "Answer! Answer at once! Say what you think!"

I wrote: "It's a great sin for a priest to have

a natural child. For a pope it's a scandal. It's an even greater scandal when he makes his natural son the governor of Rome."

Montalto tore the square of paper out of my hand, burned it in the candle flame, and said curtly: "Go on."

"The Pope is indolent. He never lifts a finger to remedy abuses. All he cares about are the arts, the splendor of his court, and his collection of jewelry."

Montalto read the piece of paper and for once watched it burn on the brass tray. A half-smile played over his thin lips, though I noticed it did nothing to soften his countenance.

"Where do you live?"

I wrote: "With an elderly aunt on the Appian Way."

"I wager she spoils you outrageously."

"Yes, she does."

"Women have two ways of weakening a man: food and the flesh. You will come and live here, Rossellino. You will sleep in an unheated room. And you will eat with me and like me — poorly and scantily."

"I shall regard it as a very great honor, Your Eminence."

"No fine phrases. You may go. I will see you tomorrow."

And that was how I became chief secretary to Cardinal Montalto. When Gregory XIII

18

heard this, he joked about it for a week. "Il Bello Muto" — as he called me — "must have committed some very great sins when he still had his voice; otherwise he wouldn't have undertaken the awful penance of living in Montalto's hovel, sharing his meager rations, and putting up with his temper. As for Montalto, he's accomplished a typical monkish trick, and got himself a secretary who couldn't be more discreet."

## Giulietta Accoramboni

I was born in Gubbio, in Umbria, where my father and his brother, Bernardo, made and sold majolica plates and dishes. The glaze used on these was imported from Majorca by Arab craftsmen; it produces a very clear white base that takes colors well. The colors only retained their brightness, however, because of a luster invented by the painter Giorgio Andreoli, from whom, in his old age, the brothers bought his factory, which was also in Gubbio.

Majolica ware, famous not only in Italy but also in France, Austria, and all the rest of Europe, usually has a carefully painted head of a man or a woman in the middle, surrounded by a border illustrating an allegorical theme.

I remember one on a wall in my uncle Bernardo's house: it depicted the haughty profile of his wife, Tarquinia. The worthy folk of Gubbio called her La Superba, because of her physical attractions and also her overbearing character.

The allusion to the last king of ancient Rome did not displease my aunt. In her youth she had dreamed of marrying into the nobility, and sometimes, looking at the ducal palace opposite her house in Gubbio, she found herself regretting that she had become the wife of a rich merchant, when her beauty might have opened other doors.

The plate bearing her portrait met with a peculiar fate. One day, during a furious argument between Tarquinia and her son Marcello, he rushed toward her in a blind rage, his hands outstretched as if to strangle her. At the last moment, frightened by the enormity of the crime he was about to commit, he deflected his wrath to the majolica portrait, wrenched it from the wall, and smashed it to pieces on the floor.

I ought to explain why I was witness to this symbolical murder. In the summer of 1570, there were a few cases of plague in Gubbio, so Tarquinia decided to retire to her house in the country with her three children, her husband, and me. This was no proof of my aunt's affection for me, but, rather, of mine for her daughter, Vittoria. She and I were playmates, and, because I was three years her senior, I was also to some extent her mentor.

Uncle Bernardo had some scruples about leaving my father in charge of the factory at a time when to stay in Gubbio meant risking one's life. But having spent his whole life deferring to La Superba, out of a mixture of kindness and indolence, he could not bring himself to oppose her even when justice and brotherly love demanded it.

True, his cowardice saved his life. But at what cost! The plague that then ravaged Gubbio carried off my mother and father, my brothers and sisters, and most of the factory workers. Bernardo's sensitive nature began to succumb to the weight of his grief. The factory, too, was in a bad way. It was hard to replace the Spanish-Arab workmen who had died in the plague, and my uncle, though a good artist, lacked my father's business talent.

This was the moment Tarquinia decided to move to Rome, in order to marry of Vittoria in accordance with her own ambitions. I saw poor Bernardo begging and praying when he should have been giving orders. In the end, as usual, he gave in. He and his younger son, Flaminio, stayed in Gubbio and struggled to derive from majolica the money Tarquinia needed to rent a fine palace in Rome, in the Piazza dei Rusticucci, near St. Peter's. There she at once began to keep open house.

Marcello, who was not interested in majolica or, indeed, in any other kind of work, accompanied his mother to Rome, where he set himself up as a nobleman, wearing dagger and sword, learning to fence, and making high-ranking but shady friends, who doted on his equivocal good looks. He also cultivated the friendship of a rich widow old enough to be his mother. With her, as with his mother, he often quarreled, mainly about the money he borrowed. Strangely enough, no one in Rome ventured to doubt that he was a nobleman. Of course, he was exceedingly pugnacious, and a disagreeable look was enough for him to jerk his sword from its scabbard. Moreover, there was no shortage of pseudo-noblemen in the Eternal City.

This brief sketch is enough to show that my uncle Bernardo's family was divided equally between angels and devils. The angels worked in Gubbio. The devils spent money like water in Rome. To tell the truth, Vittoria was neither angel nor devil, but a bit of both. As for me, I didn't really count, and this didn't change when, just before he died, Bernardo adopted me. The reason La Superba didn't object to this was that it posed no threat to her children: Bernardo by then had nothing but debts.

Since I am about the only person in the family with an ounce of common sense, I think I can best describe Vittoria. I won't say I am without prejudice — because I love her — but I refuse to join in the idolatry that surrounds her on all sides. I have a rational love for her, even though she herself is so lacking in reason.

On the diabolical side, Vittoria inherited from La Superba her passionate temperament, her unyielding character, and, for those who know her well, her touchy pride. She also inherited Tarquinia's beauty; but in this respect she greatly surpasses her mother. For the goodness that came to her from her father, and from him alone, gives her eyes, her delicately curved lips, and her smooth features a most engaging sweetness. The inside has affected the outside. I predict that her face will age well, whereas time has made Tarquinia's grim and inhuman.

Vittoria is tall and imposing. Her big blue eyes are fringed by black lashes thick as leaves on a tree. And, incredible as it may sound, when she undoes her silky blond curls, she has only to tilt her head back and her hair touches the ground. In Gubbio, she could not appear in the street without everybody, young

and old, coming up to her and saying respectfully, "With your permission, signorina," and
reverently touching the golden fleece with the
tips of their fingers.

When she is naked she can hide her whole
body with her hair, but it takes so much care,
is so heavy, gives her so many headaches, and
so often makes her lose her balance if she turns
too quickly that she frequently talks of having
it cut off, at least to waist length. I am the
only one who finds this a sensible idea; it
plunges the rest of the Rusticucci palace, servants included, into such consternation, draws
such screeches from Tarquinia, and obviously
pains Bernardo when he brings the gold he
has managed to scrape together in Gubbio,
that out of sheer kindness Vittoria resigns herself to remaining a slave to her own beauty.

She was fully developed at eleven, and at
thirteen was almost what she is today: a
woman made to rule over the world and over
men. Whenever anyone from Rome strayed
as far as Gubbio and asked disdainfully what
there was to see in our little town, some would
say the ducal palace; others, the palace of the
Council; but the wisest answered, "Vittoria
Accoramboni." And if the visitor had the good
fortune to see her in the street, he would return to the city of the popes full of extravagant
praise for our Bellissima.

That was what we called her in Gubbio: the adjective *bellissima* was as inseparable from her name as *serenissima* was from that of the Venetian Republic.

Vittoria's hair was washed every week on Tuesday and Saturday. This rite involved our whole domestic staff: the men to keep up a good fire, bring buckets of hot water to fill a wooden bath, drain out the dirty water by means of a tap in the bottom of the tub, replenish the hot water, and so on; the women to apply to the long masses of hair special treatments. Meanwhile, Vittoria, sitting on a stool at one end of the bath, the back of her neck resting on a little cushion on the edge and the whole length of her tresses in the water, would read Petrarch's sonnets, sometimes aloud.

I think she got into the habit partly in order not to be deafened by the chatter of the maids crowding around her, and partly because she adored poetry. Tarquinia had seen to it that she received the education of a queen in all respects. She even knew Latin.

Since towels alone were not enough to dry such a long and luxuriant mane, they had to be supplemented by a fire or, if the weather was fine, by the sun. The latter, according to Tarquinia, had the additional advantage of heightening the golden tints. So on fine days

Vittoria would be conducted with some ceremony to a south-facing balcony and installed on a chair, two maids holding her hair like a train so it would not touch the ground on the way. As soon as their mistress was seated, they spread the great lengths of golden silk on a special rack, like choice fruit left to ripen.

This ritual occurred in the early afternoon, and, since the people of Gubbio knew about it, every idle stroller would make for my uncle Bernardo's house on the appointed days in the hope of catching a glimpse of Vittoria's hair absorbing gold from the sun.

The same custom continued after we moved to the Rusticucci palace, but Tarquinia now put more emphasis on decorum. So it was no longer carried out, magnanimously, in public, but, unseen, in an inner courtyard.

The open-house policy Tarquinia initiated at such expense on her arrival in Rome did not produce the expected result. A number of gentlemen, young and old, handsome and ugly, frequented the palace, but, although Vittoria attracted them, her father's indigence did not. It was all very well to marry a merchant's daughter and enter a family without connections, but in that case the merchant must be rich. In this case, he had nothing but debts, and these cast a shadow over Vittoria's

26

dazzling beauty. Moreover, the daughter was proud and educated, and did not suffer fools gladly. She would have been more popular if her mind had been more ordinary and her character less haughty.

For two years Tarquinia kept her daughter on display without receiving an offer, despite all the real or alleged suitors who swarmed around her like flies around a drop of honey. To tell the truth, the least alluring of the swains did make a few timid overtures, but Tarquinia, although not actually turning him down, did not encourage him, saying equivocally that her daughter, just turned sixteen, was still too young to marry. Although Francesco Peretti was the nephew and adopted son of a cardinal, La Superba considered his nobility too slight and his fortune too unremarkable. In her early days in Rome, nothing less than a prince would have satisfied her. But for some time now she would have made do with a marquis or a count. However, she found Peretti's offer somewhat comical and rash, and she considered it very good of herself to treat him so politely, merely meeting a semirequest with a semirefusal.

On April 15, 1573, an event occurred that Tarquinia might have expected if she had paid as much attention to other people as she did to her own ambitions: my uncle Bernardo died. He had never forgiven himself for leaving my father alone in Gubbio during the plague. The decline of the majolica factory, Tarquinia's move to Rome, the absence of his beloved daughter, her mother's unceasing demands for money and the debts incurred to meet them — all these had seemed to him a punishment from God. Instead of struggling against his misfortunes, he had only longed for them to crush him altogether.

The news was brought one day on the stroke of noon by Flaminio, who had ridden in haste from Gubbio without an escort. We were taking our midday meal when he appeared, covered with mud, still wearing his boots, his hair disheveled, his doublet undone, and tears streaming down his cheeks. As soon as he saw Tarquinia, he went toward her with outstretched arms, as if to seek refuge in her bosom, crying out in a voice of desperation: "Father is dead! We are ruined!"

Tarquinia stood up, white as chalk. But instead of taking him in her arms, she frowned, put her hand over his mouth, and whispered furiously into his ear: "Are you mad, saying we're ruined in front of the servants? Do you want the whole of Rome to know it by tomorrow?"

"Oh, Mother, Mother, Mother!" cried Vittoria, her voice rising as she spoke. Unable to say more, she left the table and ran from the room, her long hair streaming behind her.

"Giulietta," said Tarquinia, showing no expression, "go and see she doesn't play her usual trick of shutting herself in her room. I wish to see her this evening."

I rose, astonished at her coolness.

"My son," she went on, turning to Flaminio, "just look at you! Half undressed and covered with mud! Go and tidy yourself, and I'll see you in your room in about an hour. We have things to discuss."

To join Vittoria in her room I had to go through the whole house. Every corner was already loud with servants' laments. Of course, Bernardo had been a good master, and some of them might be afraid of losing their jobs if the household's style of living was cut back. But they also wept out of decorum, out of the common people's desire to show they shared our grief. The maids in particular mourned easily. They had made a specialty of births, marriages, and deaths and were always ready to join in with the appropriate emotion.

At the foot of the stairs I met Marcello, magnificently dressed in a doublet of pale yellow satin, with a dagger at his side. He caught me by the arm and said: "I've just arrived from Amalfi. What's the meaning of these tears? No one can speak to tell me what's the matter. Do you know?"

"Your father's dead."

"Oh!" he said.

But his large black eyes remained dry, and his handsome face was expressionless.

"Well," he said at last, "it was only to be expected. Why did he make himself a slave and beast of burden to that virago? Where's Vittoria?"

"In her room. I'm just going to her."

"Good," he said, his upper lip curling in an ironic smile. "Have a good cry together! There's pleasure in tears. As for me, I can't stand moaning and groaning, and I'm going to shut myself up in my room. I'll come out only to tell Tarquinia what I think she ought to do now that — largely thanks to her — our ruin is complete."

"Tell me now!" said Tarquinia haughtily, appearing beside us. "But do it in my room, away from other ears. Don't leave us, Giulietta. Your good sense will be useful."

As she spoke she took Marcello's arm as if to lead him away, but he threw her off violently.

"Don't touch me!" he hissed. "You know I hate being touched!"

"Even by Vittoria?" said Tarquinia harshly.

"Especially by her!" said Marcello, his

30

handsome face distorted in sudden fury. "I've known it for a long time: women are octopuses, nothing but tentacles and suckers. And Vittoria's no exception."

Tarquinia said nothing for as long as it took to open the door of her room and usher Marcello and me in. Then she shot the bolt, turned to Marcello, and said with spurious mildness as she fixed him with her cold blue eyes: "How strange, Marcello! I'd have thought Vittoria was an exception, that there was a soft spot for her in your heart of stone."

"The heart of stone I inherited from you!" said Marcello, with an angry glare. "Apparently the death of the man who sweated blood for you in Gubbio doesn't bring one tear to your beautiful bright eyes."

"Nor to yours!"

"Mother! Mother!" I said (for I was obliged to call her that whether I liked it or not). "Forgive me, but there's no point in my staying if you are going to quarrel."

"You're right, Giulietta," agreed Tarquinia, casting me a disdainful look nonetheless. "You're the only one here with any common sense! Well, Marcello, since you have an opinion on what's to be done, let's hear it!"

Marcello went and stood by the window with his hands on his hips, perhaps to put his face in shadow and make it less easy to

31

read. Or, since he had an instinctive sense of theater, perhaps to present an elegant silhouette against the outside light.

"I'd like to point out," he said, "that my advice is purely disinterested. Since I don't cost you a penny, Mother, I am not affected by our imminent ruin."

"Which shows that Margherita Sorghini's tentacles and suckers are good for something at least," said Tarquinia scornfully. "They keep you in food and clothing."

"Yes," said Marcello. "And now that you've spat your venom on the lady whose friend I am —"

"A very expensive friend," said Tarquinia.

"As I was saying, this is my advice: sell the factory in Gubbio as soon and as profitably as possible. That will pay your debts."

"Only some of them," said Tarquinia.

"Perhaps. You should know. Then marry off Vittoria as soon as you can profitably do so."

"Do you think I need you to reach those conclusions?"

"In that case," said Marcello with a sneer, "I wager you have a few fine suitors up your ample sleeves."

"Only one who has declared himself," said Tarquinia with a sigh. "Francesco Peretti."

"Peretti! Good Lord, that wretched fellow!

Minor nobility, little fortune, and less wit."

"But he's a cardinal's nephew, and the Cardinal has adopted him; he's given him his name and treats him like a son. He'll inherit the Cardinal's fortune."

"Some fortune!" said Marcello, throwing up his hands. "Montalto lives in the barest palace in Rome, his coach is a wreck, and his horses, which he feeds no better than he feeds himself, are so skinny they can scarcely walk. If they weren't held up by the shafts, they'd collapse. And Montalto's so absurdly virtuous that he's refused the allowance Philip II wanted to give him. A fine cardinal! And a fine heir!"

"I know, I know," answered Tarquinia, frowning. "But what can I do? I haven't had time to find anyone better."

"In other words," said Marcello wryly, "Bernardo died too soon for you."

He folded his arms theatrically over his chest. But Tarquinia saw neither the affectation nor the irony, any more than she realized the unseemliness of what she had just said. As for me, I was amazed by the blatant cynicism of both mother and son. But I couldn't help seeing that, though each was devilish enough, Marcello, for all his airs, was the shrewder and less insensitive.

"Well, what do you think, Giulietta?" asked Tarquinia condescendingly.

She looked down on me because of my position as a poor adopted niece and literally because of my small stature, but also because my mere prettiness could not compete with the majestic beauty of the women of her family. However, she did show me the kind of respect people like her reluctantly grant to those with virtues they themselves lack and take no trouble to acquire.

"What do I think about the marriage, or what do I think about Francesco Peretti?" I answered after a moment.

"Both."

"Well, I quite like Francesco. There's nothing brilliant about him, of course, but he's gentle and refined, and does have a certain courage and dignity."

"What about the marriage?" asked Marcello, looking at me intently.

"From what point of view?"

"Vittoria's."

"Francesco will do anything she wants, so she won't be unhappy."

"And what about Peretti himself?"

"He's too good a man to be happy living with an Accoramboni."

Marcello burst out laughing.

"But you're an Accoramboni yourself, Giulietta!" he said.

"So I know what I'm talking about."

34

At that he laughed more heartily still.

"Hush!" said Tarquinia, hissing like a dozen snakes. "Marcello, how can you roar with laughter on the day your father has died? What will the servants think if they hear you?"

"They'll think I'm crazy, and they'll be right. We're all crazy in this house. All except Giulietta. My father was a coward whose wife made him tremble. Flaminio is a prize idiot, the dupe of his own pious playacting. My mother's a gorgon —"

"And Marcello's a pimp!" said Tarquinia harshly.

Although the light was behind him, I saw, or thought I saw, Marcello turn pale.

"Madam," he said tonelessly, "if you were a man, I'd already have put two inches of steel in your chest."

Despite the melodramatic language, this was no pretense. His hand shook on the hilt of his dagger, and I got the distinct impression he was restraining a furious impulse to have done with his mother once and for all. I sprang forward and placed myself between them, as I'd done more than once since I'd entered this unruly family. They carried every passion to excess.

As I pushed Marcello back with both my hands against his chest, I could feel him trembling in the effort to stifle his fury. He didn't even see me. His black eyes seemed to dart thunderbolts at Tarquinia over my head.

"Marcello!" I cried. "Please!"

He saw me at last and relaxed, and the shadow of a smile — a genuine smile for once — appeared on his face. Perhaps he was remembering how, as a child, I had sometimes intervened between him and his mother and received blows meant for him.

"You're a good girl, Giulietta," he said. His voice was low and breathless, and he gripped my arms with both hands. Then, as if surprised at this gesture, he pushed me away.

"Since I see you both agree with me," said Tarquinia, without a trace of irony, and evidently blind to the danger she'd just been in, or unmoved by it, "I shall inform Vittoria at once of my plans concerning Peretti."

"At once?" I asked indignantly.

"You won't do anything of the kind, Mother!" cried Marcello. "I'll find a way to prevent you. I'll camp outside Vittoria's door if necessary. You can see her tomorrow. At least have the decency to give her a day and a night to weep."

He swiftly left the room, and when, soon afterward, I went to his sister's apartment on the upper floor, I found him in the little antechamber that sometimes served as

Caterina Acquaviva's bedroom.

He was lying full-length on a sofa bed where Caterina often spent the night to be within call. It was quite big enough for her, but so small for Marcello that his feet hung over the end. The daylight, entering through a little south window, fell on his saturnine face, and he was toying with his dagger — a childish but disturbing game, it seemed to me — trying to catch sunbeams on its naked blade.

Right after I entered the antechamber, Caterina came out of Vittoria's room. Closing the door carefully behind her, she told me Vittoria had been asking for me and had just sent her to look for me.

Caterina Acquaviva was as fresh and lively as her name — dark-haired and plump, with a wonderfully smooth olive complexion and large innocent eyes. When she saw Marcello lying on her bed, she blushed. Her brown bosom, left half uncovered by a square neckline, began to heave, and in a tender voice she couldn't keep from trembling she said: "Signor Marcello, you'd be more comfortable if I took off your boots."

"If you like," he answered indifferently; he did not apologize for occupying her bed or give her so much as a glance.

I found Vittoria sitting by the window, with her long tresses tossed over a high-backed chair, the ends reaching the floor. Her hands lay clasped in her lap. She wasn't weeping. She was just staring into space.

"Oh, Giulietta!" she said in a subdued voice. "I'm glad to see you. You at least loved our poor father. Oh, how badly we treated him!"

"You have nothing to reproach yourself with," I said after a moment's silence. "It wasn't you who decided to leave Gubbio and come to Rome."

"But it was because of me we came!" she cried. "And you know how much I've enjoyed living here. Poor Father, slaving away in Gubbio while we were amusing ourselves here."

I made no answer, for it was true. And it was true too that Vittoria had sometimes seemed to forget Bernardo even existed. I remember that it was at this precise moment I first asked myself whether Vittoria's dazzling beauty was as great a gift from heaven as everyone said.

To break the silence I asked: "Vittoria, tell me truthfully — would you rather be alone?"

"No. Stay. I thought I heard Marcello's voice outside. Is he back from Amalfi? What is he doing here?"

"Guarding you. He's sworn to stop Tarquinia from coming in."

She heaved a sigh and leaned her head to

one side. "Thank him for me. Tell him he can come in and see me if he likes."

I went into the little room outside, closing the door behind me before I spoke to Marcello. There was a heavy curtain over the door too. I didn't want Vittoria to hear; I knew only too well how Marcello would take his sister's disguised request.

He hadn't moved or sheathed his dagger. He'd put it down on the little table nearby and seemed to be sleeping. This allowed Caterina, sitting cross-legged on a cushion on the floor, with her back against the wall, to contemplate his features without fear of rebuff.

As soon as I appeared, she stood up guiltily, but I told her to sit down, Vittoria didn't need her for the moment. I spoke softly so as not to wake Marcello. Just then Flaminio glided into the room, as quietly as he did everything.

Flaminio was a smaller, paler replica of Vittoria. His short, fair curly hair grew in a halo around his head, and his pale-blue eyes lent a subtle look to his otherwise rather insipid countenance. In my opinion, he was so pious he ought to have joined a religious order long ago. Then he would have escaped both the family quarrels and the exhausting work at the majolica factory. Better still, he would, with time, have made a pretty little monsignor, adored by the ladies of his congregation as he already was by all the maids in the Rusticucci palace, with the exception of Caterina. She had other aspirations.

Flaminio, though he had made no more noise than a mouse, did not have time to open his lips. Marcello leaped up and had him by the throat in one bound. I realized then that he had only been pretending to sleep, to escape Caterina's dumb adoration. I did not intervene: Flaminio was in no danger. Because he never returned a blow, Marcello considered it beneath his dignity to strike him.

"What are you doing here?" said Marcello through clenched teeth, though his voice was low. "Who sent you? Answer! Who sent you? Tarquinia? What message did she send? Answer me, you envoy of the devil!"

"But I haven't any message," replied Flaminio in the gentle lilting voice that always surprised me. I never found it convincing, because it was not incompatible with pious falsehoods.

"Well, what are you here for?" said Marcello, without either relaxing his grip or raising his voice. He was probably afraid of attracting Vittoria's attention, knowing she always protected her younger brother.

"I want to see Vittoria," faltered Flaminio.

40

"She can't see anyone," growled Marcello, with a furtive glance at Vittoria's door, as if afraid she might open it and prove him a liar. "Not anyone," he repeated. "I'm here to keep everyone away. So be off before I throw you out!"

Still holding Flaminio by the throat, he opened the door to the gallery and shoved him through it. The palace was built around a square courtyard with cool trees and a pool in the middle. The open gallery on all four sides benefited from the sun or shade of the courtyard according to the time of day.

"Marcello," I said as soon as he'd shut the door, "what you said isn't quite true. Vittoria said to tell you, you can go in and see her if you wish."

Joy was so swiftly succeeded by coldness on his face that I doubted I'd really seen it. He threw himself down on Caterina's little bed, shut his eyes, and said: "No. I don't want to. I've no use for tears and sighs, upturned eyes, and all the other mumbo jumbo women go in for. Tell her I'm tired after my journey, and sleeping."

That night, after I had gone to my own room, I had a strange dream. I call it strange because dreams are usually vague and shapeless, whereas this one surprised me by its coherence and the clarity of the words uttered in it. So strongly did they imprint themselves on my mind that when I thought about them next day I could scarcely believe I had not really heard them.

I was alone in a magnificent large room with precious rugs covering the floor and the walls, which were lined with divans on all four sides. In the middle stood a low octagonal table of fragrant cedar, covered with fine oriental carving but bare except for a big shallow dish in which some strong but to me unfamiliar perfumes were burning. There were no other furnishings. The huge door, also of cedar, was studded with iron and had a barred spy hole in it. I knew, without trying it, that it was locked.

The room was well lit by a single window, opening like a door, that let in the morning sun. It was protected outside by a wrought-iron grille, through which I could see a beautiful garden full of flowers. In the middle of the garden stood a big golden cage full of brightly colored birds, singing. I wanted to go nearer, but the grille was bolted.

As I stood there looking at the cage, I saw that more birds, like those inside the cage, were fluttering around it, apparently as eager to get in as the others were to get out. Just like us, I thought: we long to be united with the one we love; yet after the bonds are forged, we come to find them too heavy.

Though this thought passed through my mind, it did not make me sad. I was a prisoner too, because I could not push aside the grille or open the heavy cedar door. As I watched the birds fluttering in the cage, I felt light and happy, as if I might at any moment do the same. And I really was light, for I wore neither stifling bodice nor heavy farthingale. I was naked beneath a long, loose saffron-yellow robe with a low neck, made of soft, clinging material that left my limbs delightfully free. Catching sight of myself in a long Venetian mirror on the wall, I went over, and was surprised to see I was taller and, what is more, prettier than I had been the day before. It seemed to me that any man who saw me must love me. I twirled around and danced on tiptoe about the room, my arms outstretched so that my wide sleeves were like wings. Everything felt like a caress: the folds of my gown, the warm breeze from the garden that I could feel through it, the perfumes burning in the bowl, the carpet deep and soft beneath my feet.

Suddenly, to my great displeasure, I found I was not, as I'd thought, alone in the room. Vittoria and Caterina were there, both dressed in long robes like mine but in different colors, Vittoria in pink and Caterina in purple. I noticed with annoyance that the colors suited them. But it was their attitude that increased the sudden dislike I felt for both of them.

Caterina was sitting on the carpet, her dark head resting on the edge of a divan. She had let the wide opening of her robe slip down, showing a plump shoulder and more than half revealing her dark and perfect breasts. Her black eyes, which looked huge and very bright, were fixed expectantly on the heavy nail-studded door.

As for Vittoria, sitting primly on a divan, I had at first no criticism to make of her demeanor. But when I looked more closely at her face, it seemed to me less beautiful than usual, and I saw on it an expression of duplicity I had never observed before. Her attitude soon confirmed it. Standing up, she said nonchalantly, as if to herself: "This gown is much too hot. Since we're alone, I'm going to take it off. My hair will be enough to cover me."

She took off her robe and stretched out on the divan, arranging her hair to conceal her bosom and belly. Then she gave a little sigh and shut her eyes, as if getting ready to go to sleep. But I wasn't taken in: I could see her lids were admitting a slit of light, and that she too was watching the door. I don't know which I hated most at that moment: Caterina's

44

immodesty or Vittoria's hypocritical propriety.

I resolved to be irreproachable and shame them both. I sat down on a divan with my legs close together, crossing my arms over my chest to hold the unseemly low neckline in place. After a while I noticed that the divan I had chosen quite at random was exactly opposite the door. I decided to make up for this by keeping my head turned resolutely to the right, as if I were looking out at the garden through the grille. After a moment I was pleased to notice that in this position I would be showing my better profile to any visitor entering through the door. I remember that, far from feeling guilty at having this involuntary advantage, I regarded it as a reward bestowed by Providence for my modesty.

Caterina let out a stifled cry, and by following the direction of her head I could see what had upset her. A face had appeared in the spy hole, though its features were not clearly visible because of the bars. Its black eyes, however, were quite plain, as were the dazzling looks it darted at each of us in turn, quite transfixing me.

I could see too that Vittoria, try as she might to seem impassive, was staring into space in such a way as to bring out the beauty of her glance. As for Caterina, with her breast heaving, her mouth half open, and her head rolling to and fro on the edge of the divan, she seemed to be seething in some infernal cauldron.

The nail-studded door swung ponderously open, and Marcello appeared. None of us showed the slightest surprise. He was wearing a long robe of Titian red, and his dagger hung from a golden belt around his waist. He locked the door behind him, removed the key, and held it up to us in a theatrical gesture. Then he strode over and threw it through the grille and into the garden. That done, he went back to the middle of the room, paced slowly around the low table, looked at us one after the other, and said, with an ironical curl of the lip: "Now you're in my power, my doves, and you won't escape me."

I rose from where I was so modestly seated, walked over to him boldly, and said: "But you're a prisoner too, Marcello — you've thrown away the key."

"Correct, Giulietta," he answered with a smile. "You might say I'm as much your prisoner as all of you are mine. But that's not really so. I am free. And here" — drawing his dagger — "is the instrument of my freedom."

Twisting and turning the dagger in his hands so the blade caught the light, he tried

46

to reflect it successively on Vittoria, Caterina, and me.

"Do you mean you intend to take your own life, Marcello?"

"Yes. But not without taking all yours first."

"Why?"

"What's the point of living," said Marcello, "when in the end we all die?"

Suddenly Vittoria opened her blue eyes wide, threw aside her hair (at the risk of revealing her breasts, or, more probably, intending to do so), propped herself on one elbow, and said: "Why me, Marcello?"

"Life," he answered in a low, weary voice, "is a deceitful and cruel game. Women are but fleshly snares. Whoever comes within reach of their tentacles succumbs and dies. I prefer to kill myself, and you with me."

I was furious with Vittoria for trying to attract Marcello's attention. To recapture it for myself, while at the same time showing him how docile I was, I went over close enough to touch him and put both hands on his chest, saying sweetly: "May it be as you wish, Marcello. Kill us if you must. Only, tell me which of us you're going to kill first."

"You, of course, Giulietta," said he, his eyes smiling, "because you're such a good girl."

Then I woke up. I don't know why, but

47

when I realized where and who I was, I began to think of my dead family. And my life seemed so horribly empty that I began to weep.

When I finally grew tired of weeping, I dried my eyes, struck the flint, and lit my candle. Then I went and looked at myself in the little Venetian mirror — a smaller version of the one in my dream. For some time I stood scrutinizing my reflection, as if it could tell me something about myself that I didn't already know. Strangely, I felt different, though I could not have said whether the change was for the better or the worse.

I felt uneasy. Why did my dream make Marcello into a kind of hero when in reality, despite my old affection for him, I regarded him as unscrupulous, lazy, violent, and corrupt? And why had the dream so unfairly depicted Vittoria as a monster of hypocrisy, even suggesting a sort of incestuous attraction for her brother of which I knew she was entirely innocent?

I went back to bed, blew out the candle, and lay for a long while with my eyes wide open in the dark. I didn't even try to sleep: I knew I wouldn't succeed. Although I was not responsible for the vagaries of my dream, I felt guilty at having harbored such ungenerous feelings about Vittoria, even in my sleep. I began to have doubts about myself. Was I really, after all, the good, "reasonable" Giulietta, the very embodiment of common sense, that everybody took me for?

# 2

## *His Eminence Cardinal Cherubi*

The year Gregory XIII came to the papal throne, I became vicar-general to His Eminence Cardinal Montalto. But the honor — if such it was — did not last long. A year later, in May 1573, to be exact, the Cardinal dismissed me from his employ with his customary discourtesy.

Since certain far from charitable rumors circulated in Rome about my fall from favor, I should like to explain — with the simplicity of heart that is, so to speak, *nutrimentum spiritus* — the reason it came about, a reason so trivial that in future it will be a subject of astonishment to all men of intelligence. The fact that a woman — Signorina Vittoria Accoramboni — was, if not the cause, at least the occasion of it can only add to their stupefaction.

I do not know that I can be suspected of bitterness or resentment on the subject, for my sudden dismissal, though so painful at the time, soon turned out to be a blessing in disguise.

As soon as His Holiness Pope Gregory XIII heard that His Eminence had put me back on the shelf — or "sent me back to my gondolas," to use the contemptuous expression the Cardinal himself did not shrink from employing — he spread his protective wing over me and, taking the Cardinal at his word, recommended me to the Patriarch of Venice. The Patriarch accepted me into his service the more readily because I was a Venetian, and also because the Pope dropped the hint that he intended one day to make me a cardinal.

This prospect particularly pleased the Patriarch, who cherished papal ambitions himself; though he thought that by taking me in he would be making a friend who might one day vote for him in the conclave, when the amiable soul of Gregory XIII was summoned home by its Creator. In fact, when the time came, he did not get my vote. Alas, there was nothing I could do about that. And some still remember with weeping and gnashing of teeth the man who *was* elected.

I now regard the time I spent with His Eminence Cardinal Montalto as a sort of earthly purgatory into which I was plunged for the expiation of my sins. For, although the Cardinal really was remarkable in point of intelligence and energy and for the austerity of his life, God forgive me for thinking it would have been better for those around him if he had had a bit less virtue and a bit more gentleness. This applies even to such utterly devoted servants as Il Bello Muto, his secretary, and to objects of his special affection, like his adopted son, Francesco Peretti.

But it cannot be denied that he did show some kindness to those two. He went to the trouble of inventing a sign language in which the former could communicate with his master more quickly than in writing. And he did his best, or thought he did, to ensure Francesco's happiness. But absolute submission to his tyrannical temper was the price both had to pay, and to pay a hundred times over, for his favors.

Certainly the Cardinal's virtue was without flaw or weakness. But there is such a thing as too much excellence. *Tutior est locus in terra quam turribus altis:* the earth is safer than the top of a tower. You do not have so far to fall. It may be that my virtues are small in the sight of God, and I'm not ashamed to admit that if Montalto's disfavor brought me the favor of His Holiness, it was less on account of my own merits than because of Gregory's hostility toward His Eminence.

In Rome, everything is known and nothing

is said. Since I wasn't a Roman, I might have remained ignorant forever of the reason for this aversion if Cardinal de' Medici had not mentioned it to me one day. His powerful and illustrious family made him so invulnerable he could afford to tell the truth from time to time, even in the Vatican.

According to Cardinal de' Medici — I'm transcribing his veiled allusions into plain language — His Holiness disliked Montalto, first, because he suspected him of wanting to succeed him; second, because the Cardinal was a Franciscan — and the Pope, like the people of Rome, regarded friars as hypocrites; and third, because the asceticism of the Cardinal's life seemed an implicit reproach to his own.

Be that as it may, from the first day Gregory XIII sat on the supreme throne he rigorously refused to include Montalto in his government, and, despite the great abilities even his enemies admitted the Cardinal possessed, never entrusted him with any post. Worse, he seemed to ignore his very existence.

As His Eminence's vicar-general — albeit of recent appointment — I was one of the first to notice a great change in his appearance. I cannot say whether he was grieved by his undeserved lack of favor or if his extreme austerity had undermined his robust health. He never complained. But suddenly he seemed

53

bowed with age, his bright black eyes grew dull, at least in public, and he started to move about on crutches, as if his crooked though strong legs had all at once refused to serve him. He rarely spoke, and as soon as he did open his mouth he was racked by a painful cough. He, who had been so quick-tempered, so haughty, so impatient of other people's opinions, was now regarded by the other cardinals as a paragon of humility.

Not by the Pope, however: his antipathy toward Montalto remained unchanged. His entourage even had the greatest difficulty in persuading him that out of respect for Montalto's crutches he ought to exempt him from kneeling when he approached the papal throne. When people praised the invalid's unfailing gentleness toward his peers, the Pope said dryly: "I've seen a lot of things in my long life, but I've never seen an eagle change into a dove."

And to tell the truth, once the Cardinal was back in his own palace, which he seldom left, I never saw his powerful talons or curved beak offer his familiars or servants the smallest vestige of an olive branch. His cough did not prevent him from scolding, nor did his crutches keep him from appearing wherever he was least expected. I do not know whether he was as moribund as he looked, but neither his suspicion nor his tyranny ever relaxed.

He gave further proof of these qualities when he learned that Francesco Peretti was aspiring to the hand of the beautiful Vittoria Accoramboni. From the very day he heard about it, he started to collect information about her and her family. He acquired — and I know how, though I don't know through whom — the services of a maid in the Rusticucci palace who, by a fortunate coincidence, came, like him, from Grottammare, in The Marches. The girl did not betray her mistress for money, but because the Cardinal was in a position to help her relations, who earned a precarious living by fishing. His Eminence also won over the Roman priest Racasi to his cause. Racasi was Vittoria's and her mother's confessor. I do not know the details of the inquiry, but I do know its result. The Cardinal called me in at the last minute to consult me because I had relations in Gubbio. But I could only confirm what he already knew: Vittoria had the reputation of being beautiful, kind, and virtuous; her brother Marcello was a good-for-nothing and her other brother an incompetent; her mother was an ambitious woman seeking a wealthy match for her daughter. The majolica factory in Gubbio was up for sale, and, worse, the family had not a penny left to bless themselves with.

"In short," said the Cardinal bluntly, "these people are living beyond their resources. The Rusticucci palace is just a hollow shell. That's not the kind of family I want Francesco to marry into."

At that moment poor Francesco, who was allowed to come and go freely in his adoptive father's apartments, entered the room. Hearing what had just been said, he was as petrified as if he had heard his own death warrant. He turned extremely pale, threw himself at the Cardinal's feet, and stammered, though not without some vehemence: "Father! Father! You crucify me. I can't live without Vittoria! She's a most exceptional woman, as distinguished for her virtues as for her charms. Of course I'm not blind to her origins. But is she to be condemned for the faults of her family, when she herself doesn't share them? Oh, Father, in fairness to me and to her, I implore you to see her and listen to her before you banish her from my life."

I must confess I was surprised by the force and skill of his plea. Like everyone else in Rome, I regarded Francesco Peretti as a naïve, amiable, but somewhat unintelligent and unambitious young man; in fact, rather spineless. I now saw that when driven by strong emotion he was capable not only of courage — and one needed that to confront the formidable

Montalto — but also of wit. He had appealed to the quality the Cardinal prized above all in others and in himself: the sense of fairness.

I could see that the Cardinal was as surprised as I was to find that the son he still regarded as a child might be a man. But at first he said nothing.

His Eminence was very calculating, and never made an unpremeditated answer. He dragged himself, on his crutches, over to the window looking out on the courtyard, and stood silent for some time, with his back to Francesco. It was then I noticed how the crutches added to his apparent deformity, making his neck sink deeper between his shoulders. Taking the unwieldiness of his body and the fierce and heavy countenance that seemed drawn downward by a large nose and a protruding jaw, one had to admit Montalto had little reason to glory in the flesh. Come to think of it, perhaps that was one of the reasons Gregory, who, though over seventy, was still a handsome man, disliked him so much.

There were four people in the room just then: the Cardinal, standing by the window with his back to the rest of us; Francesco, rising from his knees and gazing at his uncle as if his life depended on him; Il Bello Muto, silent and still as a cat; and me. I was curious, to tell the truth, about what His Eminence would decide to do, and uncertain whether his natural inflexibility or his love of justice would prevail.

However, when he turned around, he spoke not to Francesco but to Il Bello Muto.

"Rossellino," he grumbled, "I see there are some withered heads among the geraniums in the middle of the courtyard. That is not as it should be. Tell the gardener to cut off the dead ones."

By way of reply, Il Bello Muto raised his eyebrows and made a sign with his right hand, which I only understood because of Montalto's brusque answer: "Yes, now. Once a thing's decided upon it shouldn't be put off."

Then he looked at his son. "Go and bring Vittoria to me, Francesco."

"What?" said Francesco, dumbfounded. "Now?"

"Yes, now. It's only fair I should see and hear her."

Montalto, like all great politicians, had a talent for showmanship. (In my opinion, that may have accounted for his crutches: I occasionally wondered if he really needed them.) I could see that, while giving in to Francesco, he was trying at the same time, by this sudden summons, to preserve his reputation for inflexibility. The gesture was effective but superfluous. He could just as well have waited till next day to see Vittoria. But that would have been to procrastinate, and the master, magisterial even when he yielded, was giving us a lesson in morality: just as Il Bello Muto should fly to see to the dead geraniums, so Francesco should hasten to fetch Vittoria. It escaped no one that there was something regal about Montalto's impatience.

I have often thought that if, when Vittoria arrived, I had asked His Eminence for permission to retire, seeing that the interview was a family matter, I might have avoided my subsequent sudden fall from grace. But as I've said, I now have reason to bless the curiosity that made me stay, eyes and ears agog. Even though her beauty was famous all over Italy, Vittoria, being yet unmarried, went out rarely except to Mass, and then she wore a mask and a long cloak that concealed her figure. So I had never really seen, still less heard, her, and had no means of guessing how the maiden would stand up to the Minotaur.

Like St. Augustine, I weathered various storms in my youth, and they left me, like Gregory XIII, with a son. But after I rose to the purple, I put away such faults, and Providence decreed that age should come to the aid of my virtue. Not that I proclaim, with the poet Terence, *Deleo omnes dehinc ex anio mulieres:* Henceforth I banish all women from my mind. On the contrary: debarred from more intimate dealings, I delight still in their beauty. And, now moved merely by aesthetic considerations, I have become infinitely more exacting in my appraisal of their charms than when I was swept along on the surges of the blood.

That is why, when told in advance that some Roman lady is beautiful, I am often disappointed when I see her, and her imperfections leap to the eye. But this did not happen when Vittoria appeared in Montalto's dilapidated palace and absolutely lit up our ancient dwelling.

I was surprised by how tall she was, and how graceful too, as she showed by the way she knelt before the Cardinal's chair, her large skirts making a charming frame around her slim waist and her long hair falling down in a truly regal train. As she kissed His Eminence's hand she retained the modest, sober, yet proud air that had at once struck me. I could see only her profile from where I stood, so I moved noiselessly behind the Cardinal's chair to see her full-face. From any angle her features were perfect. And when, after touching Montalto's ring with her lips, she looked up, I was dazzled by the light of her great blue eyes. I say "light," not "brilliance," because, although they were brilliant too, I believe their radiance came as much from her beautiful soul as from themselves.

I could not say whether some rays of that beauty managed to pierce Montalto's thick skin — or perhaps I should say his armor. But when he spoke to her, his glance was less fierce and his voice less harsh than usual. "Please sit down, signorina," he said, almost courteously.

She did so, after sweeping her golden mane around in front of her. As she draped it over her knees, she inadvertently attracted the Cardinal's attention to this typically feminine adornment, which, as such, must have struck him as reprehensible.

He frowned and said with his customary bluntness: "Couldn't you put your hair up instead of displaying it like a flag?"

Vittoria, seeming not to notice his rudeness, answered calmly: "I've tried, but it's so heavy it makes me lose my balance."

"Cut it off then!" said Montalto, his black eyes suddenly flashing.

"I wish I could," said Vittoria with the same unfailing sweetness. "It's a great nuisance to me. But I cannot. My mother has categorically forbidden it."

"*Dos est magna parentium virtus,*" said Montalto sardonically, with a significant

61

glance at me. "The virtue of parents is a great dowry" was a reference to Tarquinia's reputation.

I was about to reply, with a faint smile, when I thought I saw Vittoria turn pale, and wondered whether she had understood the Cardinal's meaning even though he had shrouded it in Latin.

A silence ensued, disagreeable to everyone, including Francesco, who stood behind Vittoria's chair much less in control of himself than she was, blushing and paling alternately and fixing his pale eyes anxiously on his uncle. As for Il Bello Muto, back from his errand, he kept looking from his master to Vittoria in astonishment. Not insensible to feminine charm (it was said that before his accident he entertained the warmest possible sentiments for Countess V.), he was probably wondering why the Cardinal had begun by picking a quarrel with Vittoria. Perhaps, like me, he was remembering that Mary Magdalen had dried Christ's feet with her long hair, and that Our Lord, far from telling her to cut it off, had accepted her homage with gentleness.

There was not a trace of softness to be seen at that moment on Montalto's fearsome mask. After the slight relaxation at the start, when he had seemed surprised by Vittoria's beauty and dignity, his face had soured. The discussion about her hair seemed to have roused the latent misogyny so frequent in celibate priests that one wonders if they have been as deserving as they claim in remaining chaste.

Be that as it may, Vittoria's cause seemed lost before it was even pleaded, for Montalto turned to Il Bello Muto (perhaps he was vexed with me for not answering his quip about Tarquinia) and spoke again in Latin: "*In vero formosa est. Sed rara est adeo concordia formae atque pudicitiae*": She really is beautiful. But beauty and chastity rarely go together.

Il Bello Muto, who, in spite of his unbounded veneration for the Cardinal, didn't always agree with what he said, raised his eyebrows and looked at his master doubtfully, as if wondering whether his malicious quotation was really apt. He had a great advantage over all Montalto's servants: since he could express disagreement only in signs, it was easier for His Eminence to forgive him for it.

Though I was extremely shocked by the Cardinal's quotation from Juvenal — for in my view nothing about Vittoria's reputation or behavior justified it — I put on a neutral expression, not wishing to expose myself again to Montalto's displeasure. As for poor Francesco, who would have been furious had he understood Latin, he sensed that something was going on. His pale eyes darted like anxious little animals from one to another, as if begging for an explanation of Montalto's words and the silence that had followed them.

The silence was broken by Vittoria. Looking up with the reserved yet proud expression that had already impressed me, she fixed her luminous eyes on the Cardinal and said mildly: *"Reverendissime pater, Juvenalis errat. Mihi concordia est"*: Most Reverend Father, Juvenal is mistaken. In me they do go together.

"What?" cried Montalto in amazement. "Do you understand Latin, signorina?"

"Yes, Your Eminence," she said simply, without any attempt at showing pride or pleasure.

The Cardinal said nothing, and there was another silence, this time very different. Although his fearsome mask remained impenetrable, I thought he must be revising his opinion. It was hard for him now to conclude that, because Vittoria's hair was long, her ideas were short and her brain light.

But Montalto's austerity derived from the strictness of his principles and not from any barrenness in his nature. He loved beautiful gardens and fine sculpture, and his secular learning was as extensive as his religious scholarship. As for women, although he suspected that souls were in danger from their femininity — his misogyny had its origin in theology —

he was not insensitive to their beauty. But he would have preferred them to be like flowers: colorful but tethered to the ground and dumb. He would also have liked them to wither after a few days, so that one would not have time to get attached to them. At first, he seemed overwhelmed by the radiance of Vittoria's appearance, but then his principles reasserted themselves and he imagined the chaos that such incomparable beauty could bring upon the state. He was thinking of separating her from Francesco, but she proved to him that she was a human being worthy of respect: she could speak Latin and had read Juvenal.

I am reporting what I took to be the rapid evolution of the Cardinal's attitude toward Vittoria, but I do not blame him for being harsh with her at first. I deplore it, of course, but there was plenty of precedent. Our Holy Mother Church has not always been kind to the more charming half of the human race. Remember that it was not until the Council of Mâcon, in the ninth century — and then by only a small majority — that the bishops agreed the *gentil sesso* possesses a soul.

Montalto, forgetting the suspect length of her hair and the snakes that the devil had no doubt hidden in it, now saw that Vittoria possessed not only a soul but also a mind. He started questioning her in Latin, and was obviously pleased that she understood so quickly and replied so well.

"You must have had a good teacher, to have read Juvenal," he said.

"An excellent teacher, Your Eminence. He was kind, pious, and learned. He was a Franciscan friar."

Knowing the Cardinal belonged to the same order, she gave him a smile in which a touch of badinage mingled with truly filial benevolence.

I must confess that smile enchanted me as much by its subtlety as by the kindheartedness it revealed. I saw in a flash that Vittoria had already forgiven Montalto for his unkind remarks, and asked nothing better than to look on him as if he were the father she no longer had. I could tell His Eminence must have the same impression, for his fierce black eyes softened and he said more gently: "How was it this friar was so fond of Juvenal?"

"He despised the morals of our age and admired Juvenal because he criticized the morals of his."

"Did this friar introduce you to Italian literature too?"

"Yes, Your Eminence. He made me read Dante, Petrarch, Boccaccio, and Ariosto."

"And which did you like the best?"

"Dante, for his imagination, but most of

all Petrarch, for his sweetness."

"Not Boccaccio?"

"No, Your Eminence. I don't like Boccaccio at all."

Vittoria said this with some emphasis, and Montalto smiled.

"What has he done to you that you dislike him so much?"

"My tutor made me read his *Corbaccio*."

At this we all laughed heartily, except Francesco, whose learning was confined to a smattering of law. He merely smiled, not because he had read *Il Corbaccio*, but because he saw that ice had been succeeded by sunshine, giving life and warmth back to his love.

"So you don't care for Boccaccio's satire against women?" said Montalto.

"No, Your Eminence," Vittoria replied. "I think it is cruel and unfair."

"Well," said the Cardinal affably, "to get your revenge on your friar, you ought to have read Ariosto on the religious orders."

"I did," cried Vittoria. "My tutor recommended it."

Montalto clasped his hands together and started to laugh again.

"Splendid! A friar with a sense of fair play! And one who could make fun of himself. Vittoria, since you love Petrarch for his sweet-

67

ness, please recite the sonnet you find the most moving."

"Gladly, Your Eminence," said Vittoria.

Unfortunately, I cannot remember which sonnet it was, but I do remember the voice in which she recited it: a voice at once so soft and vibrant that I cannot do it justice by any comparison with birds or the most crystalline of bells. The voice, the diction, the play of her features, and the expression in her great blue eyes combined to create a unique moment; it delights me to think of it even now.

Montalto beckoned Il Bello Muto to him and with his help stood up, supported on his crutches. He looked at Vittoria for some time; then, with a gentleness I had never heard in his voice before, said: "Vittoria, when you are married —"

"What, Father?" cried Francesco, transported by happiness.

But Montalto waved him away as if he were a fly, and went on: "Vittoria, when you are married, I would be pleased if your domestic duties left you time to come and read to a sick old man now and then."

"Oh, Father, I'd be happy too!" cried Vittoria, throwing herself at his feet in an access of affection and good will.

And indeed, when she left the Cardinal's palace, Vittoria had several reasons to be glad.

She might have parodied Julius Caesar and said, "I came, I saw, I conquered." Yet I was not sure that her victory, one of whose effects was to save her family and herself from want, really pleased her in her heart. I had noticed that throughout the interview she had not looked at Francesco once.

True, she was very young, and it is possible that at that stage in her life she prized the marriage more highly than she did the mate.

But the most surprising thing about that encounter was what Montalto said afterward — words that were indirectly to have such an enormous influence on my life, for the worse at first, and later for the better.

As soon as Vittoria had left the room, seeming suddenly to empty it of warmth and light, His Eminence dragged himself over to the window. He stood there with his back to us watching Vittoria as, escorted by Francesco, she crossed the courtyard, passing the bed of geraniums he had ordered Il Bello Muto to have neatened. Then, turning painfully to face us — for it was difficult to maneuver that heavy frame on crutches — he shook his head several times and exclaimed: "How could anyone see her and not love her? Hear her and not adore her?"

"Just so, Your Eminence," I said. And I made some excuse to leave the room, so anxious was I that he not see how flabbergasted and — why not admit it? — amused I was by what he had said.

Now as ill luck — or, as it turned out, good luck — would have it, the following day I had to go see the Pope in the Vatican. I found His Holiness very morose, though he had no reason to be: he was in perfect health and living a life quite free from care. But about once a month Gregory would be overcome with melancholy. This black mood was dreaded by his entourage, because while it lasted he would often make decisions extremely detrimental to the state, and when he recovered he would refuse, with the quiet obstinacy of the weak, to rescind them.

Finding him thus depressed, with members of his court trying hard to distract him, I thought to cheer him up by telling him about the interview that had taken place between Montalto and Vittoria. At first he listened with rather a sour expression, but when I came to the memorable remark with which the scene had ended, he cried: "What? What? Cherubi, did you hear properly? Did Montalto really say that? Are you sure?"

"I could hardly believe my ears, Your Holiness, but, yes, he did say it."

"What?" cried Gregory, suddenly forgetting his hypochondria and roaring with laughter. "Montalto said, 'How could anyone see her and not love her? Hear her and not adore her?'? Oh, Cherubi, she must be a very beautiful girl to have struck a spark of humanity from that old wreck!"

He put his hands on his fat little belly and laughed till tears ran down his cheeks. He made jokes to his courtiers on the subject for the rest of that day.

And on the next day, Montalto sent me back to my gondolas.


## Caterina Acquaviva

Although I'm only a maid and of low birth — my father's a fisherman in Grottammare, and his only possession is his boat — I do know how to behave, and I'm not uneducated: I can read, and even write a little. And to whom do I owe it all but to Signora Vittoria Peretti? She had the infinite patience to teach me, though she was very young herself at the time. She was the same age as me — sixteen — when I entered her service. She never treated me as a chambermaid, but more like a companion and confidante, and she went to a lot of trouble to knock the rustic corners off me. As a result, when I go to see my family in Grottammare, my mother finds fault with me: "Just look at you now! A real signorina! Can't eat unless you use a fork. You even bring one with you from Rome, and keep it in a case, like a jewel. A fork! Holy Mother! It's only natural to use one to shift muck, because that stinks. But a fork to put a perfectly good piece of conger eel in your mouth, caught this morning by your own father, and cooked by your own mamma! I tell you, Caterina, you insult your father. You insult your mother. And you insult God. A fork, my God! An invention of the devil! The fingers God gave you aren't good enough for you, little fool that you are. And as if that cursed fork isn't enough, what's this I hear? You know how to read and write? And you're proud of it, shameless hussy. You're ruined! What man's going to want anything to do with you after this?"

She's quite right about men. The last time I went to see my parents in Grottammare, Giovanni looked very grumpy — and he had held me so close on my sixteenth birthday! I scare him, and he doesn't like it. After all, I'm only a woman, nothing. And when he plants a couple of smacking kisses on this mere woman's cheek, she can hardly bear the smell of him. I ask you, how could I ever live with a man who reeks of fish when in the Rusticucci palace I'm used to mixing with gentlemen with a sparkle to them, and who smell of perfume? Not to mention the handsomest of them all, whose name I can't bring myself to utter, so little has he any eyes for me. Even though I'm so pretty.

Of course, I'm not as tall and beautiful as Vittoria, but I'm not unattractive: dark, with black eyes and an olive complexion. And I don't mind saying that when it comes to bosoms, there's no one in petticoats who can rival mine for size, plumpness, firmness, and color. That's why I wear square low necks — to show it off, no matter what Giulietta Accoramboni says. She accuses me of immodesty and trying to lead men on by showing my bare skin. Jesus! She can afford to be a prude — she's got about as much tit as my elbow! She could show all she's got without attracting anyone. As far as I'm concerned, it doesn't make any difference whether I'm covered up or not. I don't go around with a bare arse, as far as I know, yet there isn't a man in the house whose eyes I can't feel on me like a warm shower when I wiggle past him. Oh, yes, there is one, alas! The only one I'd like to like me. The world is badly organized, as my father says when he comes home from the sea without a single fish. As for that fish of mine, I don't know what nets you'd need to catch him.

Anyway, the signora's always been so kind to me, so trusting and generous, that my heart is bound to hers with links of steel. To say I love her is putting it mildly. If you want to know the truth, I'd die for her if her life was in danger. I'd even — and may Our Lady forgive me for such impious words — I'd even kill for her. The fact is, my life with her is a paradise. I see her, hear her, serve her. And she, that lovely woman, forgets her rank and beauty and talks to me like a friend — to me, just a little worm beneath her feet!

The last time I went to Grottammare, I told my mother, and only her, how His Eminence Cardinal Montalto had got my confessor to have me report on Vittoria. My mother grabbed hold of me, called me wicked and ungrateful, and beat me. May God forgive the poor ignorant woman! It was only for her and Father that I agreed to do it. The little cottage they live in by the sea is rented to them for next to nothing by the parish priest. And how could a parish priest resist a powerful cardinal to whom he owes his living? Anyway, why all the fuss? Or, as my father, who's a Tuscan, would say, the stink? Vittoria's as virtuous as she is kind. What could I say of her but good?

Not that she dislikes men. She likes them as much as I do. But, unlike your humble servant, she's too proud not to be chaste. Before she married Signor Peretti, I was the only one who knew whom she liked and whom she disliked among the men who used to come to the palace. She was distant and dignified with all of them, and never showed the slightest partiality. How I wish I had such self-control! I, who can't see the object of my adoration without going red and white and all of a flutter! I'm like a volcano in eruption, sending out lava in all directions. Vittoria's as calm as a volcano that's extinct. But watch out: inside the crater it's still seething.

I take good care not to say anything like this in my reports for His Eminence. I tell only about actions, and they are blameless. As for thoughts, let Vittoria's confessor guess what they are and sort them out for himself. But it takes a clever man to see into a woman's heart; she can't always understand it herself.

It was six years ago that necessity forced Vittoria to marry Francesco Peretti, who, I know, has nothing in common with the sort of husband she'd dreamed of. Not that, like Tarquinia, she'd set her heart on a prince or a duke. No. What she'd have liked is a hero. If you ask me, she's stuffed her head too full of tales of chivalry. Signor Peretti is too sensitive and considerate to make it a bad marriage. But nobody could say it's a good one.

Vittoria still goes on dreaming, without realizing that what's permissible in a girl is not permissible in a wife. As for Signor Peretti, what do you think a husband must feel like when he's only occasionally tolerated in his wife's bedroom, and when after six years of marriage he still hasn't given her a child? But maybe that isn't even his fault. Who knows?

If you want my opinion, Signor Peretti is too timid and doesn't know how to show off his own good points. One evening in November, coming back from Vespers with his mother and me, he was set upon in a narrow alley by three bandits, who tried to rob him. He immediately drew his sword and faced them, wounding two of them, driving all three away, and getting a flesh wound in the arm. And what do you think he did when he got back to the palace? He made me swear on my medal of the Virgin Mary that I wouldn't mention the matter to Vittoria; he said he didn't want to worry her! That was a prize opportunity for him to cover himself with some glory in Vittoria's eyes, since she has such a high opinion of heroes. Poor Signor Peretti! He's so awkward I feel quite sorry for him. I don't like to speak ill of my own sex, but, if you ask me, it doesn't do to treat us too gently. Nor to implore us for the favor of spending a night with us.

But Signor Peretti is like his mother, Camilla — gentle and kind. When she came to live with us in the Rusticucci palace, I could tell just from looking at her delicate, sweet face which of the two old women was going to get the better of the other. Not that La Superba is horrible to Camilla. It's just that the Perettis aren't made of stern enough stuff to stand up to the Accorambonis. It's no accident that swifts win out over swallows: they've got bigger beaks, stronger and more sharply curved. I'm just telling you things as I see them, with my own natural common sense.

Still, Signor Peretti has been very kind to my family. He helped them a lot when my father damaged his boat on the rocks a couple of years back. And he's very lenient with my brother Domenico. I'm ashamed to tell you that Domenico is a bandit. But, as everyone knows, in this unfortunate country there's a scallywag in most families, even among the nobility. Unfortunately for me, the Accorambonis are no exception.

To get back to Domenico, he's ten years older than I am, and the only left-handed one among his brothers and sisters. When he was a boy, my father used to beat him to make him use his right hand "like a Christian." But it didn't do any good. Domenico even crosses himself in church with his left hand. This worried our parish priest, who thought it was a mark of the devil and used to warn my mother when she went to confession that if Domenico didn't mend his ways he had little chance of salvation.

But Domenico didn't mend his ways, and instead of calling him by his real name, which, after all, was that of a saint, people in Grottammare got into the habit of calling him Il Mancino, the left-handed one. Nicknames aren't unusual in Grottammare, but people didn't say Il Mancino in the same way as they said Il Zoppo, the lame one, and Il Cieco, the blind one. Everyone knew that to be blind was a misfortune, but to be left-handed was, as the priest said, a mark of the devil.

Because Domenico did everything with the wrong hand, it didn't surprise anyone that he turned out badly. He quarreled with our father when he was eighteen, and took to the road as a bandit. When he was broke or ill, however, he always took refuge at home in Grottammare. My father would never speak to or even look at him, but he didn't forbid my mother to feed and look after him. Everyone in Grottammare would know he was there, but no officer of the law would ever have been foolish enough to come to our place and arrest him. He'd have had to deal with my father and my four other brothers, and if the row went on long enough, with the other master fishermen.

Il Mancino was also banished from Rome for his bad deeds. But sometimes he slipped into the city at night, and then, at my earnest request, Signor Peretti would grant him his hospitality and protection. This was extremely good of him, for when the Bargello, the chief of the papal police, heard about it, he read him a lecture that ended as follows: "Signor Peretti, you are nursing a viper in your bosom, and someday it will bite you."

"It's in the nature of a snake to bite," said Peretti, smiling. "It can't help it."

"As you like," said the Bargello. "Don't say I didn't warn you."

But sometime later he himself rescinded my brother's banishment.

I confess I'm always glad to see Il Mancino, even if he is a bandit. I like him best of all my brothers.

When I was a little girl, it was a great honor and joy for me to sleep in the same bed with him. I remember how, after the candle had been blown out, he used to stroke me gently, and drop little kisses on my neck. These caresses sent delicious shivers down my spine. But when I got older, my mother wouldn't let me go on sleeping with each of my brothers in turn; she made me share a bed with my two older sisters. They were great sluts already, and didn't treat me nearly so nicely.

Il Mancino has black hair and a swarthy complexion. He's on the small side, but slim and wiry and very strong. He leans a bit to one side as he walks, and moves as silently as a cat. He speaks softly, and his black eyes are soft too, especially when they rest on me. But when he's angry his eyes grow suddenly harsh; one glance is enough to make me want to sink through the floor. I tremble with pleasure as well as fear. That's girls for you: all of them raving mad, and each as bad as the other. Rank has nothing to do with it. Signora Vittoria spends all her time dreaming of her heroes, and my head is full of bad boys — my brother and the other, whose name I won't say.

## Marcello Accoramboni

It was on July 15, 1580, at noon, that I stabbed Recanati, and I had good reason for doing so, even though others thought there was no need.

I'd made up my mind to kill him two and a half months before. But I hadn't looked for him, I hadn't lain in wait for him. I'd decided to leave it to chance. And if chance hadn't brought him so miraculously within reach of my dagger before July 30, I'd have given the whole thing up.

I had settled on July 30 as the last date for his execution. After that, I'd have let the chatterbox off. Why July 30? Just for fun. Since the only thing I had against him was words, I wanted chance to decide for me whether he deserved to live or die. In short, I wanted to give him a chance to save his miserable skin. In the same spirit, I sent him a message by Il Mancino to say, unless he wanted me to make him eat his words, he should keep out of my way. But the idiot only laughed! The saying is right: "Whom Fortune wishes to destroy she first makes mad."

I could have said that in Latin once, when I was learning Latin, with Vittoria, from a Franciscan friar. But I've forgotten it all by now. She, of course, remembers everything.

We're so different and yet so alike, she and I. I was born an hour after she was. I've been told the priest who baptized us took a very poor view of twins, especially when they weren't of the same sex. He thought it unwholesome for a boy and a girl to be close together in the same womb, and told Tarquinia one of us would probably be an idiot or die in infancy. Neither of us died, and no one has ever taken me for an idiot. But I've always thought, and still do, that Vittoria is the only one of us who's really intelligent. As for the soul, that's even more unevenly divided. There's only one soul between us, and she's got it. All I have are instincts.

Because I was very swarthy and Vittoria was famous all over Gubbio for her golden mane — twice a week our little town paid more or less public homage to it — I always thought, as a child, that I must be ugly. I was glad of it, and quite happy to live hidden at Vittoria's feet. But as I grew older I realized that women's eyes, all women's eyes, were always feasting on my face. When I got to be a man, it was worse: they started to cling to me like octopuses. Their eyes and smiles and cloying words all bothered me. I found them all the more horrifying because between Vittoria and me, though we were very fond of one another, there had always been the strictest reserve. We'd been as close as it's possible to be before we were born, but after, as if by common accord, we kept our bodies more utterly apart than any ordinary brother and sister — so much so that I can't remember ever kissing her, or even touching her with the tips of my fingers.

It would be foolish to conclude that I hate the female body. To put it bluntly, I quite like entering it, and get gratification from crushing its softness with my muscles and my weight. But that's not enough for the sex with tentacles. They have to love me, tell me about it, cling to me. I can't bear that devouring sort of love. To me it's an insult compared with the distant, noble, disembodied affection I feel for Vittoria.

As for Recanati, here's how the whole thing came about. On July 15, at midday, not far from Santa Maria della Corte, I caught sight of him riding alone in his carriage. He was lolling back on the cushions and glancing with great complacency at the passersby on either side, not so much to observe them as to make sure they observed him in all his luxury. And indeed the vehicle he was riding in was a splendid affair, beautifully carved and gilded, and drawn by four magnificent chestnuts, whose golden manes streamed in the wind as they sped along. I was daydreaming in the sun at the time, and had forgotten all about Recanati. But seeing him suddenly like that, so arrogant and sure of himself and so near — the street was a very narrow one — I felt a new surge of hatred for him. Our eyes met, though only for a few moments, because of the speed at which his carriage was traveling. I darted him a furious glance, to which the craven wretch replied with a scornful smile, confident in the speed of his horses. I trembled with rage, my hand on my dagger. It was only two short weeks till the end I'd set to my vendetta. For a moment, I thought of running after him, but apart from the fact that his carriage was moving so fast, it would have been beneath my dignity. I walked on, head bowed, knees trembling, gasping for breath, and stifling my impotent rage as best I could.

It was then that chance — I don't like to call it Providence — came to my aid. A heavy wagon drawn by six big horses, and, as I learned later, full of carved stone being delivered to the Vatican, suddenly got in the way of the carriage. Recanati's horses pulled up short, a collision was avoided, and the incident would have been over in a few seconds if the drivers, an irascible lot in general, hadn't started exchanging insults. These were followed by lashes with their whips, after which the two combatants dismounted and began to fight. Great din and confusion ensued, with passersby taking sides.

I was a little way off and, though my heart beat faster, deliberately walked on at the same steady pace, still leaving chance to decide whether the carriage would move forward or Recanati be left within my reach when I arrived at the spot.

It was as if the thing had been planned from

all eternity. The wagon was blocking the carriage's path, the chestnuts were whinnying and pawing the ground but couldn't move on, the crowd had eyes for nothing but the two brawling drivers. The way was clear.

Coolly, taking my time, I climbed on the carriage step. With my left hand I seized Recanati by the throat and with my right, not uttering a word, put the point of my dagger to his heart. He recognized me and turned pale. His eyes rolled in their sockets with terror. Sweat started out on his brow. He couldn't speak. He just shook his head several times, trying to say "no."

I felt great disgust then for what I was about to do. Not because it was murder, but because Recanati was a coward. The sweat was streaming down his cheeks now; my left hand was wet from it. I'm sure I wasn't gripping him so tightly he couldn't speak — it was just terror that silenced him and made him hang limp as a rag doll in my grasp. Worse still, his cowardice made him give off an unbearable smell, and I felt so nauseated I nearly gave up and spared the wretch's life. I hesitated a second or two, feeling more like an executioner than an avenger. But how could I abandon my vendetta without seeming a coward myself, in my own eyes? It was fear, really, that drove me on, fear of losing my self-respect.

I pressed on my dagger, and was amazed at how easily it sank into Recanati's body. There seemed to be no effort on my part: it was as if he were made of dough. I'd never have believed it was so easy to kill a man.

As for Recanati, he shuddered, grimaced, and gave a couple of gasps, as if desperately seeking air. That was all. Then he sank back on the cushions, his eyes staring. I pulled out my dagger, wiped it on his doublet, and put it back in its sheath. Then I jumped off the step and looked around. The drivers were still fighting, the crowd was still shouting encouragement, and it looked as if no one had noticed what had been happening in the carriage.

I strolled off without a backward glance and walked to Margherita Sorghini's house. I felt nothing but some slight difficulty in breathing, because of the heat, and also a kind of sad astonishment at how easily my sharp blade had pierced Recanati's heart.

The maid told me Margherita had just taken her midday bath and was resting on the "little terrace." It wasn't really little. It had a view over the whole of Rome, and an original feature in the form of a large tent in the middle — a sort of canopy with white linen curtains that could be drawn to keep out the wind or the sun. Margherita, naked, was lying inside on a huge couch, white to match the curtains.

When I came in, she propped herself on an elbow and looked at me inquiringly. She could see from my face that something unusual had happened.

I signed to her not to ask questions. Noticing the bath of cold water, in which she liked to cool herself in hot weather, I stripped off my clothes and plunged in it up to my neck. The clear water seemed to cleanse me of my crime. Through the white top of the tent, I could see the shadows of swifts as they swooped like arrows in all directions, uttering shrill cries. Although I believe in neither God nor the devil, I was sure I had committed a great sin. Yet what I felt at that moment, strangely mingled with the sense of well-being that came from the coolness of the water and the shadows of the swifts, was not remorse, but great disappointment. Recanati's murder meant nothing to me. For it to be satisfactory, he'd have had to know he was dead. I'd blown out a candle, and the candle wasn't even aware it had been extinguished. I felt Margherita's eyes on me and frowned. She at once looked away. As with all women — except Vittoria — there's something of the octopus about Margherita. But because she's twice my age and scared to death of losing me, I've managed to train her. Apart from lovemaking — and it's I who decide on that — she refrains from touching me or putting her arms around me, and from stifling me with all the thousand little wiles with which women usually try to ensnare men.

I got out of the bath, drew aside the curtain, and went into the harsh sunlight, blinking and breathing in the pleasant bitter smell of the geraniums around the edge of the roof. The tiles were so hot I had to hop from one foot to the other. When the last drop of water had evaporated, and my shoulders and the back of my neck were beginning to burn, I went back into the tent. Margherita, who must have been watching me through the gap in the curtains, shut her eyes just in time. Her jet-black tresses and olive complexion, the dark rings on her breasts and dark pubic hair all attract me. Little wrinkles score her eyelids, her breasts are heavy, and her ripening beauty looks already on the point of fading. But I love her in her decline and in the slavery I've reduced her to, though I suspect she still retains the upper hand.

I stood by the couch and looked at her: she didn't dare open her eyes. That's how I like her — defenseless, abandoned, docile. Without a word I fell on her and possessed her. After a while I felt her disobeying my rules and making surreptitious little movements with her hips in order to attain her own pleasure. But I was too far beyond words, too carried away by the inevitability of my orgasm. I came, and she let out one little cry. A swift seemed to answer her.

I slid off the couch to the mat that covered the floor of the tent, not wishing to prolong contact any more than necessary. I feel slightly guilty when I do this, because this is the rule Margherita finds it hardest to accept. Giulietta says that having made my mother an object of hatred and my sister an object of adoration, I don't know which way to turn when it comes to other women, that I'm really afraid of them. But I don't know if in this instance I should trust to her common sense. What experience has she of relations between men and women? Worse still, her judgment is clouded because she loves me too. And I hate the word "love."

Because Margherita provides me with clothes and food and lodging, everyone in Rome whispers that I fleece her. They'd say it aloud if they weren't afraid of my sword. This opinion — yet another one! — is so far from the truth that it hardly bothers me. If Recanati had said only that, I'd never have taken the trouble to kill him.

I don't ask anything of Margherita. She's the one who chooses to shower gifts on me, in the hope of binding her young lover to her. That's just where she makes a mistake: I'm already bound. Even if I found a young girl with the same charms, I wouldn't exchange my elderly mistress for her at any price.

Sitting on the mat, covered with sweat and gradually getting my breath back, I leaned against the couch, my neck resting on a cushion Margherita had slipped under it. If I'd turned my head, I could have seen her fingers an inch away from my hair, and I could feel she was restraining a longing to stroke it, as she does sometimes, very lightly, when I'm making love to her and she knows I'm too wrought up to stop her. I looked at her fingers. She wears many rings, and I sometimes put them on my own fingers and admire the stones. She'd give them to me if I asked her. I realized, then, that it was the hand, not the face, that gave away a person's age. Margherita's body was ten years younger than her face, and her face ten years younger than her hand. I leaned my head to the right and kissed it. I regretted it immediately, when I felt her trembling at the unaccustomed homage.

"Take your hand away," I said curtly. And went on almost at once: "I've just killed Recanati."

Margherita moved her hand away and sighed. When she spoke, her voice was subdued: "I thought as much."

But because she is always, at least apparently, punctiliously obedient, she didn't ask questions. I often wonder whether this acceptance of my rules isn't a game to her, a game she plays with the utmost skill; she'd be a coquette with a lover who wanted her to. She didn't really need to interrogate me: her silence was a question in itself. And she knew very well that at that moment I had a great need to confide in someone. So who is it who's governed by my rules?

"Do you want to know why?" I asked grumpily.

"Yes."

Nothing could be more correct or in accordance with my rules than that "Yes." And if it hadn't been for the suppressed quiver in her voice, I might almost have thought she was laughing at me. But no. I was sure she was calculating the difficulties — perhaps insurmountable ones — the murder was going to introduce into our relationship.

"Two and a half months ago, in La Monteverdi's salon," I said in a low voice, "some cliché-loving fool said Vittoria Peretti was beyond any doubt the most beautiful woman in Italy. Recanati was there — and you know what he's like: all show, all vanity and brag, with scarcely enough brain to tell his left hand from his right. Well, that imbecile was annoyed by the praise of Vittoria, and he said, in his pompous, conceited way: 'Yes, Vittoria's very beautiful. Too beautiful. So beautiful that one day she'll turn whore.' He hadn't seen me. I came from behind a palm and threw myself on him. But people separated us. The next day I sent him a challenge, but he answered that he came from too ancient and noble a family to fight me."

"What?" said Margherita. "Noble? Him?"

"He's no more noble than I am. He refused out of sheer cowardice. And it was that that cost him his life, at least as much as the stupid impertinence that made him think I wouldn't dare stab him. When I sent him a message by Il Mancino that I was going to, he pretended to laugh."

"What's going to happen now?" asked Margherita.

"I don't know. And I don't care. Don't ask questions. If Recanati had accepted my challenge, I'd only have wounded him in the arm. He deserved what he got for being such a fool."

They heard the door to the terrace opening, and Margherita asked, trembling: "Is that you, Maria?"

"Yes, signora. Il Mancino wants to see Signor Marcello. He says it's important. Very important."

"Already!" exclaimed Margherita. She

turned pale, shot me one look, then lapsed back into silence and immobility.

I felt perfectly calm, even jaunty, as if detached from my own existence. I got dressed and went down the spiral staircase to the inner courtyard, where Il Mancino was pacing back and forth as well as he could in the space available, but, as always, sideways, his eyes darting everywhere.

"What, do you want?"

"To tell you to leave her, signore, and go to the Rusticucci palace."

Il Mancino never looks you straight in the eye when he speaks to you. He gazes at your belt, at the place where your purse hangs, as if weighing it.

"Why?"

He sighed. He's a taciturn fellow, though he prides himself on speaking good Italian, not the patois of the fisherfolk of Grottammare. His lengthy dealings with the papal police, moreover, led him to the simple conclusion that the less you say the better it is for you.

"Signora Sorghini," he said with his customary politeness, "is a wealthy widow, but she lacks influential connections. So her house isn't immune from the police. Whereas your brother-in-law is a cardinal's son, and the Bargello would think twice before searching the Rusticucci palace."

"Do you think he might want to?"

"Certainly, signore, if you're in it."

"What do you mean?"

Il Mancino looked at my purse in silence. I began to undo the strings, and he suddenly became eloquent.

"This afternoon," he said, "the Bargello was questioning Maria Magdalena, the one they call La Sorda. But she's not really deaf; she only pretends to be because it helps her cheat her customers and make them pay more than the amount agreed in advance. Perhaps I should mention she's a whore," he added primly.

"Get to the point!" I said.

"We've got plenty of time. The Bargello has asked for an audience with the Governor about you, and there are lots of people waiting ahead of him."

"Cut it short anyway. To think I took you for a man of few words!"

"I am, signore, but in this instance, and with your permission, I'd like to give you your money's worth. While the Bargello was questioning La Sorda about some quarrel she'd had with a client, someone rushed in and told him he'd seen Recanati murdered, seen it with his own eyes, and knew who the murderer was. The Bargello looked very worried. He sent

94

La Sorda away, and she ran straight to the Mount of Olives."

"Is that where you meditate?"

"It's where I drink. It's a tavern."

"And I suppose this La Sorda is one of your friends?"

"For shame, signore!" said Il Mancino in a shocked tone. "I don't mix with such people. But La Sorda knows the vast esteem in which I hold you, signore."

"And she gave you this information?"

"She didn't give it to me, signore; she sold it to me for fifty piasters."

"I'll give you a hundred if you'll walk in front of me and spy out the land on the way to the palace."

"Thank you for your bounty, signore," said Il Mancino, "but I wasn't asking for anything. I was acting out of friendship."

"So was I."

There was no trap waiting for me at the gate of the palace, so the Bargello must still have been discussing my fate with the Governor. But so the gatekeeper wouldn't see me and have some tale to tell if he was questioned, I slipped in by a small back door to which I had the key. Il Mancino came in with me; it was one of his hiding places, because Francesco offered him protection.

The first person we met in the courtyard

was Il Mancino's sister. She paled and then flushed when she saw us, threw herself into her brother's arms, and jabbered at length in incomprehensible Grottammare patois, casting surreptitious but ardent looks at me all the while. I turned my head away, but it was no use: she could still see me in profile, and my cheek felt as if it was burning. Caterina Acquaviva is undoubtedly the worst octopus of the lot. Giulietta says she's "fresh and lively," like her surname, but I see her as a furnace, rather than a stream. And I don't like the way she exhibits her bosom.

I ordered her, curtly, to go and tell Vittoria I was here, and she swayed off in her usual manner. Amazing how proud the ugly little monkey is of her little body. I forced myself not to watch her. She'd have felt it.

I told Vittoria the whole story. She flushed when I recounted what Recanati had said about her, but that was her only reaction. When I finished, she hurried off to tell Francesco, who immediately had his horses harnessed and went and asked for an audience with the Pope, to whom, after all, he was third chamberlain.

Gregory XIII heard him out patiently. Although he hated Montalto, he loved the Cardinal's adopted son, perhaps because it was obvious he was no genius.

"Since time immemorial in this land," he said, "a brother has always considered himself as much insulted as a husband by anything that seems to call his sister's honor in question. So there is some excuse for this young man. Tell him to pray and repent. That does not mean he is pardoned. But if he does not commit another murder, the papal police will leave him alone."

Though it was much praised in Rome, the Pope's leniency did not impress me: there was nothing evangelical about it. Whenever Gregory didn't know what to do about something, he first tried to imagine what Montalto would do if he were pope. In this case, it was quite plain: Montalto would have had me arrested, tried, and hanged. Gregory did the opposite, and with a pleasure I would describe as malicious if I weren't talking about the sovereign pontiff.

# 3

## *Monsignor Rossellino*
## *(Il Bello Muto)*

Every morning and evening I thank Divine Providence, which caused me to fall on the steps of the Vatican and struck me dumb, thus snatching me away from my worldly successes and from earthly perils in order to engage me in the service of a master who sometimes is harsh (though not more so than he is to himself), but who works unremittingly for the glory of God and the church.

In my view, though, it is wrong to see Our Savior's hand in all the hazards of life, great and small. The devil is not so weak that he plays no part in the convergences and coincidences that put souls in danger, and that God in His omnipotence allows so that He may put his creatures' virtue to the test.

I will relate here, for the edification of the faithful, one of the most dramatic and baneful of these coincidences, because it led astray an entire family and was the origin, not only of abundant blood and tears, but also of great disturbance in the state.

When this story begins, six years had passed since Francesco Peretti married Vittoria Accoramboni, and in all that time hardly a day had gone by without the wife of the Cardinal's adopted son visiting His Eminence for at least the better part of an hour. In fact, the Cardinal saw her more often than he saw Francesco, who was often too busy at the papal court to see his father. I do not know exactly what Peretti's minor post was, though he was extremely well paid for it — if not as well as the Pope's son was for his. Even so, His Eminence would only have had to say the word for Francesco to run and throw himself at his feet. If the Cardinal did not say the word, it was because, although he greatly loved his adopted son, he was even more greatly bored by him.

"Francesco has all the virtues," Monsignor Cherubi used to say, before he was dismissed. "The only thing he lacks is charm. He hasn't read anything, seen anything, done anything, or learned anything." If His Eminence had heard this remark (which I took good care not to repeat), he would have replied that Monsignor Cherubi had all the charms required for a successful career but lacked certain virtues, including discretion.

His Eminence used to take his midday meal with extraordinary punctuality on the stroke of noon — and I can remember what a frugal repast it was too, for I shared it with him — and afterward walked for about half an hour in his garden. This involved some quite strenuous exercise because of his crutches, but it was also a relaxation, since the Cardinal took a close interest in his trees and shrubs and, in the summer, his flowers. So close indeed that for the head gardener, who accompanied him, it was the most dreaded moment of the day. Nothing escaped the Cardinal's eye: a weed, a clipped hedge out of true, an unhoed or unwatered flower bed, a rose bush with greenfly, a stake not driven in firmly enough. Such minor imperfections in the garden vexed His Eminence almost as much as the major abuses Gregory XIII's slackness had allowed to develop in the state.

When he had made his inspection, the Cardinal would limp back to the palace, but to go to his library he had to abandon his crutches and be carried upstairs on a chair borne by a couple of hefty footmen. Then he would dictate letters to me until he drew out his watch and said, with thinly disguised satisfaction: "Four o'clock. Vittoria will soon be here."

Sure enough, on the stroke of four, with a punctuality that I later learned greatly astonished everyone in the Rusticucci palace, his beloved niece, as he called her, would arrive, dressed in a high-necked gown, her radiant countenance framed by a lace collar, her only ornament a single row of pearls. This austerity was deliberate. Yet how can one speak of such simplicity except as a virtuous intention, when Vittoria's wonderful golden mane hung down over her shoulders like a truly regal train?

So many little jokes about these daily visits had spread through the court, encouraged by the malice of Gregory, that His Eminence decided, quite early, that they should always take place in my presence. I felt an intruder between uncle and niece; so I used to sit out of the way at a little desk and copy a letter, as quiet as a mouse. It was not enough to be dumb; I tried to be invisible as well.

When Vittoria took leave of His Eminence, however, she always summoned me back into the land of the living with the most ravishing smile of farewell. The first time she noticed my presence in this way, I was as amazed as if the Madonna in the picture on the Cardinal's right had stopped contemplating the infant Jesus for a moment to look at me. I trust no one will be offended by this comparison. What painter would not have been happy to have Vittoria as a model for a Virgin and Child? That is, if she could ever have agreed to pose for such a subject, for it would have been supremely painful for a woman who was never a mother.

When Vittoria had sat down facing her uncle, the conversation invariably began with the Cardinal questioning her closely about the physical and moral health of the inmates of the Rusticucci palace. Was Flaminio at last going to embrace his true vocation? Was Marcello at last going to get down to work? Why did he not marry the rich widow he was infatuated with, instead of flaunting the fact that they were living in sin? Would it not be wiser for Francesco to pack Il Mancino off to the farm he had inherited from his father in Grottammare, instead of letting him sponge on his hospitality in Rome, spending most of his time in a tavern with a blasphemous name and making money as a pimp? How was poor Camilla's ulcer? Would it not be better if she had her meals in her own room, instead of exposing herself to Tarquinia's constant sarcasm? Could Vittoria not use her influence with her mother to stop the two old ladies' fighting? Giulietta was twenty-five now: why was a marriage not arranged for her, since she was not pious enough to go into a convent? He had noticed Francesco was putting on weight. Should he not take up riding and fencing again? And he had heard that the gatekeeper drank. It was a bad habit in anyone, but worse in someone whose job it was to stay wide awake and alert. Why did they not dismiss him and get someone else?

And so His Eminence tried to set things right in the Rusticucci palace, just as he did in his garden every day, and as he dreamed of doing in the state. But here as elsewhere he showed his political astuteness: he was careful not to mention Caterina Acquaviva's loose morals, because she was a valuable source of information.

There was one other subject the Cardinal never mentioned, for fear of hurting his niece, and that was the barrenness of the marriage that meant so much to him. Heaven knows he worried enough about it! Although so secretive by nature, he even spoke about it to me.

"You know, Rossellino," he said one day, though without explicitly referring to Vittoria, "it's a very bad thing for a woman not to have children, especially if she has a lively imagination. Sooner or later she'll start thinking that perhaps some other man . . . ."

Whatever she may have thought about some of them, Vittoria answered her uncle's questions skillfully and with dignity, never showing the slightest impatience. She sat with her beautiful hands resting on her hair, which she draped over her lap to avoid sitting on it — the very attitude that had so annoyed the Cardinal at their first meeting.

She was too fond of His Eminence and had too much admiration for his intelligence not to acquiesce in his speaking as head of the family, even at Francesco's expense. But she accepted it only within certain limits.

Her answers were qualified. She agreed with his suggestions concerning Flaminio, Il Mancino, the gatekeeper, and Tarquinia's role in the "fight between the old women" (the Cardinal, as in the case of Cherubi's dismissal, sometimes expressed himself rather roughly). But Vittoria pleaded her "husband's authority" as an excuse not to make any decisions. She was more evasive about Giulietta. If Giulietta didn't favor either marriage or the cloister, there was no way of forcing her. When it came to her twin brother, Vittoria became frankly defensive. Whose fault was it if Marcello found in La Sorghini the affection so cruelly denied him by Tarquinia in his childhood? And wasn't it obvious that in this unfortunate affair he had been the victim rather than the seducer? The liaison was certainly a scandal, but would it be less scandalous if he married a woman old enough to be his mother, and married her for her money?

From anyone but Vittoria, His Eminence

would not have been able to tolerate such opposition to his own opinions. But I think he was fascinated by the combination in her of the gentle and the indomitable. I am sure that he, as a Franciscan of very austere morals, had never experienced the emotion of love, such as I myself had felt for Countess V. before my accident. He was all the more unable to call it by its proper name because at the time he first came to know it he was a bent old man, crippled and ailing, for whom it was a great effort to hoist himself out of a chair, and, on his crutches, walk a few steps around his garden. So how could he have given the name love to an inclination not accompanied by physical desire? Thus the Cardinal was able to love Vittoria in all innocence, and Vittoria was able to let him love her without fear, reassured by his cloth, his age, and his state of health. To a certain extent at least, she returned the exacting, jealous, uneasy, and imperious affection he lavished on her. How otherwise, with her proud nature, would she have put up with his screening so strictly, through her husband, the people the Perettis were allowed to socialize with? Especially because it resulted in such a contrast to the sort of life she had led before she was married, when the Rusticucci palace kept open house for whoever, respectable or otherwise, had enough spark to aspire to her hand. What sacrifices she must have made in the past six years for a marriage in which she had found neither the felicity of a deep attachment nor the happiness of motherhood!

Because of the restrictions imposed by the Cardinal, there were not twenty people in Rome who could claim the rare honor of visiting or being visited by Vittoria. It often struck me that the life of a sultan's wife was hardly more sequestered, and, though nothing would have induced me to say such a thing to the Cardinal, I did think all those precautions were in vain. There is no wall the devil cannot get through if he has friends within, as I know all too well.

On March 19, 1581 — a date I am not likely to forget, because on that day His Eminence got into the most furious and unjust rage with me — Vittoria, after replying to the Cardinal's questioning, was reading aloud in Latin from St. Augustine's *Confessions*. Her uncle was interrupting her on every page to demand some comment, exactly as he would have done with a priest, when a visitor arrived who was due at five o'clock.

I should explain that, because of his hatred of pomp and ceremony (a hatred that Gregory dismissed as a hypocritical affectation of simplicity), the people to whom the Cardinal had granted an audience presented themselves at the time arranged, without being preceded or announced by a majordomo; we had none. The only stipulation was that they must be absolutely punctual.

Cardinal Montalto had many visitors, including various eminent noblemen, Italian and foreign, attracted by his great reputation for wisdom and experience. To tell the truth, he used his audiences and his correspondence to win their support, and court gossip had it that he was gaining allies in case some great misfortune occurred. The question would be answered only "What misfortune?" with sealed lips, sanctimonious expressions, and evasive looks, or even shrugs at the foolishness of asking. Apart from a victory by the Huguenot heresy, there was only one great misfortune feared in the Vatican, and that was one never mentioned, though people thought about it all the time. It was the death of Gregory XIII.

This would be a greater misfortune because it would present the problem of who his successor would be. Seeing Cardinal Montalto cultivating the friendship of the mighty, who could fail to conclude that he was thinking of making a bid for it? True, when the cardinals gathered in conclave to choose a new pope, they were cut off from the outside world; so much so that their food was passed to them through a hatch, and the dishes were inspected to see that no messages were smuggled in. But even so, who was so naïve as to think that the princes had no influence on the vote? Everyone knew that in a previous election the imperious Philip II of Spain had ruled out sixty-five of the cardinals, leaving the conclave only five candidates to choose from.

Prince Paolo Giordano Orsini, Duke of Bracciano, who had an appointment with His Eminence at five o'clock on March 19, was far from being as powerful as the King of Spain, but he did belong to a leading Italian family. Moreover, through his wife, Isabella, he was related to the Grand Duke of Tuscany, Francesco de' Medici, whose brother was a cardinal with considerable influence. So, Bracciano was rich by birth and by marriage. He had also performed great feats of valor at the Battle of Lepanto, in which the Grand Turk's ships had been destroyed by the combined fleets of the Christian powers. Venice had afterward appointed Bracciano commander of its galleys, and for the last five years he had been winning renown hunting down Barbary pirates.

This great captain was also a man of taste and culture, open-minded, a lover of the arts, interested in everything. He was a protector of poets and sought the company of learned men, such as His Eminence. Physically he was of good stature, but did not appear tall because he was so broad. He had blue eyes, sandy hair, regular features, a strong neck, and a complexion weathered by his sea voyages. As a result of an arrow wound in the thigh received at Lepanto, he walked with a slight limp; as if to disguise this, he took long strides. But the resulting air of aggressiveness was belied by his mouth, which was soft and hungry-looking.

He was a happy man who had succeeded in everything except marriage. Isabella, tired of his long absences, had had an affair with a relative, Troilo Orsini. Troilo, horrified by his treachery, had run away to Paris, where he thought himself safe from the vendetta sworn against him by Isabella's brother and husband. A year later, he was located in the French capital by an arquebusier that Francesco de' Medici had hired to strike him down but not to kill him outright, so that its owner would have time, before finishing him off with his dagger, to tell him who had ordered his death.

Isabella's adultery had, to use the expression then current, "drawn a mask" over the faces of the Medicis and Bracciano, and it was necessary for her to die too. This unwritten law, barbarous though it might be, was accepted so naturally in Italy that when Gregory XIII was told of the execution of Troilo Orsini, he blandly asked: "And what have they done with the Duchess?"

It was surprising indeed that they had not done anything. She had been shut up for five years in her palace at Bracciano, waiting for death. But death had not come, because her husband could not bring himself to kill her. He had loved her. She had given him a son, Virginio. Moreover, although he was a warrior, he had no liking for blood, least of all the blood of a woman. He knew it would not add to his glory, even though custom excused, even demanded, the execution of an adulteress. Is it not strange that common people and princes have not paid more heed to what Our Savior said about such cases? "He that is without sin among you, let him first cast a stone at her." In our daily lives, do we really pay only lip service to Christianity?

To return to March 19: as soon as I saw by the clock on my little desk that it was five minutes to five, I wrote on a piece of paper, "Your Eminence, it is time to end the interview," and gave it into his hand. I emphasize that I put it into his hand, and not on his knee, as he maintained afterward. Then I went back to my seat, surprised that the Cardinal had not at once taken leave of his niece, as he usually did when I gave him a little reminder of that kind. I thought about reminding him again, but remembering that he had rebuked me the day before for what he called my "excess of zeal," I decided not to. And very sorry I was that I hadn't. At five o'clock exactly, unannounced, in walked Prince Orsini, Duke of Bracciano, with the long, swift stride that always made him look as if he were about to attack.

He was advancing into the room with his eyes fixed on the Cardinal, a courteous smile on his lips, when he suddenly caught sight of Vittoria. He stopped dead, as if thunderstruck, turned pale, and stood with his eyes riveted on her. The thick carpet covering the tiles of the study floor had muffled his steps, and Vittoria had not heard him come in. She went on reading from the *Confessions* in her clear, harmonious voice.

His Eminence, restraining his vexation with difficulty, said: "Leave us, please, Vittoria. I have to speak with Prince Orsini."

Vittoria looked up, saw Bracciano, and rose to her feet. The book fell from her hands to the floor. She glanced at it in dismay, but her eyes returned to Bracciano, and she said in a tremulous voice, still looking at the Prince, though her words were addressed to the Cardinal: "Forgive me for being so clumsy, Uncle."

"It's nothing! It's nothing!" exclaimed His Eminence, his dark eyes blazing. "Rossellino will pick it up! Rossellino, see Vittoria out."

Not knowing which of the two orders I was supposed to obey first, I hesitated.

The Cardinal glared at me. "Are you deaf as well as dumb? See Vittoria out!"

Vittoria seemed to emerge from her trance. She kissed his hand as if in a dream, walked by the still-motionless Prince with down-cast eyes, and went through the door I held open for her. As she descended the stairs, I noticed that the tips of her golden tresses touched each step. Her left hand, on the marble balustrade, was trembling. When I took leave of her at the door leading into the courtyard, and her maid came forward with her mask and the great cape with which she covered her hair, she forgot to give me the gracious smile with which she usually deigned to acknowledge my existence. The maid arranged the cape over her shoulders, and, before pulling up the hood, Vittoria put on her mask. It was black, with three little brilliants between the eyes. At first she placed it on her forehead, while she fastened the ribbon at the back of her neck. As she did so, she half closed her eyes, and I could see that her lovely countenance was pale and devoid of expression. When finally she pulled the strip of velvet down over her face, it was as if she were lowering a mask of fabric over a mask of flesh.

## Aziza the Wasp

I was born in Tunis. People in the part of the world I'm in now would describe my parents as Moorish. When I was ten years old, I was abducted in broad daylight from the medina by some brigands, who sold me to a pirate. No sooner was I aboard his ship than he set sail, intending, I later found out, to scour the shores of the Adriatic in search of plunder. His name was Abensur, and he'd bought me, not as merchandise for resale, but as something to beguile his idle hours during his dangerous expedition.

He was a believer, and conscientious according to his lights. When I told him I wasn't yet fully formed, he swore not to deflower me until I'd become a woman. And he gave me a little dagger, to defend myself against the advances of the crew. I was, and am still, as nimble and quick as a little monkey, and twice I used my dagger to sting a hand that tried to hold me too close. That was why they nicknamed me the Wasp.

The breezes of the Adriatic are even more unpredictable than those of the Mediterranean: they can be blowing like fury one minute and die away the next. One day, Venetian galleys appeared on the horizon. Abensur ordered his single-masted tartan to change tack, and it went bounding away over the waves before the wind. But after an hour, the wind dropped, the boat was becalmed, and the galleys were gaining on us. When it was clear we were going to be captured, Abensur, who knew there was a price on his head, buckled on his money belt and dived into the sea. The shores of a country called Albania were just visible in the distance. I found out afterward that the Albanians are a fierce people and they hate the Turks, who've been trying for centuries to make slaves of them. And they hate the foreigners who pillage their coasts even more. But who knows? Perhaps Abensur did manage to reach land and survive. God is great!

I liked Abensur. He was both tough and gentle, like all real men. I'd been longing to be a woman, so he could possess me.

The sailors on the Venetian galleys that captured us were free men, not slaves. And they soon proved it: those of our men who hadn't been killed in the boarding fight were put in chains, to be sold later in Venice. They diced for me, and I was won by the one I thought the worst of the lot — a fat, stinking, one-eyed fellow with a beard, who seemed to have some kind of authority. I tried to run, and when he tried to grab me, I pricked his arm with my little dagger. He let out a roar and called on the others to help him. Of course they caught me and took my dagger. The man with one eye, foaming with anger, tore off my clothes and tied me naked to the rail in the full glare of the sun. He said he was going to leave me there to cook until nightfall, and then hand me over to the appetites of the crew. After that he would indulge his own pleasure by stabbing me.

All this he ordered to be translated into Arabic for me by a young sailor who seemed to be given more kicks than kindness by the rest of the crew. He'd hardly finished his translation when all hands were needed on deck, and I was left alone in the blazing sun, the ropes cutting into my arms and legs. After some time, the sailor who spoke my language slipped through the rigging like an eel to bring me a drink. He whispered that his name was Folletto, and that he felt sorry for me, because he was often beaten too. He had big black eyes in a woman's face, gentle and attractive. I realized what use he must be put to on the ship. A boy on our tartan had served the same purpose. But our crew, unlike the Roumis from the galley, were grateful for his favors and did not repay him with blows and contempt.

All the time my suffering lasted, those brutes kept coming up one by one to look at me, prod me as though I were a sheep in the market, and sneer. I tried to be brave, but, in addition to getting terribly scorched by the sun, I was quaking inside, not so much at the thought of the final stroke of the dagger — I welcomed that — as at what I'd have to go through before I died. My stomach turned at the thought of those coarse, evil-smelling swine sprawling over me. More than once I was fleetingly sorry I hadn't given myself to Abensur.

But Folletto, effeminate though he might be, wasn't lacking courage. At the risk of his life — may the Almighty reward him! — he made his way to the stern of the galley and told the captain what I was going through. To get to the bottom of it, the captain came forward in person — something he usually never did, according to Folletto. I could tell from his lofty manner and magnificent clothes that he was not only the captain of the ship but also some great emir. I thought him very handsome, with his sky-blue eyes, hair like a gold coin, and shoulders wide as a door. He was so tall my head scarcely came up to the middle of his chest. With him came a tall thin man I supposed was the mate and Folletto, who translated his questions.

"What's your name?"

"Aziza the Wasp."

"Why the Wasp?"

"Because Abensur, my master, gave me a little dagger to stick in the sailors who tried to come near me."

"You were a virgin, then?"

"I still am. Abensur never touched me."

"Who tied you up?"

"The man with one eye. He won me, gambling. I stuck my dagger in him."

The fair-haired Emir seemed to be thinking. Then he spoke quietly for some time with the mate. According to what Folletto told me, the captain was from Rome, like him, and the crew were Venetian. The Emir knew Venetians too well to set them against him by acting hastily.

Finally he told Folletto to untie me, and sent the mate to find the man with one eye. My bonds had been so tight I could scarcely stand when Folletto released me. The Emir told him to give me something to drink and to help me get dressed. He kept his eyes on me all the time this was being done. I liked his eyes. Sometimes they were pale blue like the sky at dawn, sometimes — but only when he was angry — they were the blue of a steel blade.

When the man with one eye came, he swept off his cap to the Emir, bowed low, and called him "my lord." But he spoke like a man quite sure of himself. "Your lordship knows," he said, "that when a woman is captured aboard a prize she belongs to the crew. And this one is mine. I won her at dice."

"She's a wasp. She's stung you. And she'll sting you again."

"No, she won't. I'm going to squash her."

"She won't be any good to you if you do that. Sell her to me."

"With your permission, my lord," said the man with one eye, scowling at me. "I'd rather squash her."

"The fair-haired Emir turned to the mate and said: "Assemble the crew."

When all the sailors were gathered around us, the Emir spoke to them: "This girl is a wasp. She has stung the man with one eye, and the man with one eye wants first to let you loose on her and then to squash her. I want to buy her from him. If he agrees, I'll pay each one of you ten ducats in compensation."

When Folletto translated this to me later,

he explained that the Emir hadn't picked the sum of ten ducats by chance. It was the price of a well-known harlot in Venice, where the galley would, in three or four days' time, put in if the wind was favorable.

The sailors agreed to the proposal unanimously, and the man with one eye saw it was time for him to parlay. If he held out, he'd have both the Emir and his comrades against him.

"My lord," he said bowing again, "since you're so generous with my mates, I'll be generous with you. If you want the wasp, I'll let you have her for five hundred piasters."

"Five hundred! Deuce take it!" cried the Emir. "Your generosity costs me dear!" He seemed to weigh me, scraggly little cat that I was. "It's a heavy price," he said, "for such a light piece of goods."

The men all guffawed at this. All except the man with one eye. He meant to stick to his figure.

"My lord," he said, "the price of a thing depends on the pleasure the buyer expects to get from it."

"There's something in what you say, master," said the Emir. "You shall have your five hundred piasters. The mate will pay you right away."

Sure enough, the mate came back soon with

a big jute sack, sat down on a stool behind an upturned barrel, and paid out ten ducats to each of the crew and five hundred to the man with one eye.

I'd never seen so many gold coins in my life. I asked Folletto in a whisper why the Emir was giving away all that wealth.

"To buy you!" he said in Arabic.

"To buy me?" I answered in amazement. "Wouldn't it have been easier for him just to slit the one-eyed man's throat?"

"No, no!" Folletto laughed. "They don't do things in that way in Venice. In Venice people buy and sell."

Since the Emir needed Folletto as an interpreter, he gave him the job of looking after me, and the poor boy was no longer at the mercy of the lust and brutality of the crew. On the Emir's instructions, he started to teach me Italian — not the Italian of Venice, but the language as spoken in Rome, where he and the Emir came from. I made rapid progress, because I passionately longed to understand and make myself understood by my new master.

Folletto told me his own name was really a nickname; it meant elf or sprite. Nature must have made him a boy by mistake: apart from the sexual organs, his body was completely feminine.

The Prince — I now called him by his Italian name — told me, laughing, that he would be as decent a man as Abensur the pirate, and wouldn't make love to me until I was old enough. But he did ask me to share his siesta, and seemed pleased to see from the expression in my eyes that I was wild with pride and joy at his suggestion. It was very hot in his cabin, and he slept naked: I was dazzled by the huge proportions of his body and the whiteness of his skin, like marble. Later, in Italy, I saw a statue that's called the Farnese Hercules — it was just like him, and seemed to me to give off the same sense of power. God is indeed great to have put me in the bed of such a man!

Each of his thighs was as thick as my whole body, and when he stretched out his leg, the muscles were like steel. I gazed in wonder at the breadth of his shoulders and at his chest, curved like a shield and covered with a mass of short golden hair. When he slept, the strength didn't leave his body. Every so often some little muscles would contract and ripple beneath his skin like waves on a calm sea. I would lie propped on my elbow and look at him, longing to run my small hand over the vast expanses of his limbs. But my adoration was mingled with such respect I didn't dare. It was hot, but that wasn't the only reason my skin felt damp. The Adriatic swell made the ship move up and down, and it was as if my master were rocking me in his arms.

When he opened his eyes, he seemed surprised at first to see me there. Then he recognized me, smiled, and, seeing from my eyes what I was feeling, murmured some words in Italian that I didn't understand but that sounded as sweet and musical as bird song. He drew me toward him and started to caress me, and I was amazed at such gentleness and patience in one so strong. Tremors ran through my body, and I could feel myself vibrating like a viola. I was surprised to hear myself uttering little moans in time to the rhythm of his caresses. I'd never moaned or cried out when I'd stroked myself. But the pleasure my master was giving me now was infinitely stronger and more piercing. I lay with my head in the crook of his huge shoulder, passive as a doll in his large hands, and truly abandoned myself. The one notion in my head was the delightful thought that I repeated to myself with every groan: He is my master. I belong to him. He can do with me as he wills.

When it was over, seeing that his body hadn't remained indifferent to my emotion, I stretched out my hand toward his sex, but he caught my wrist and shook his head. "Not until I've possessed you," he said in Italian. I didn't understand; so he called Folletto — who was either asleep or pretending to be asleep in a little cubbyhole in the cabin — and asked him to translate. Then, smiling, he ran his great fingers through my tangle of black curls, turned his back to me, and went to sleep.

Later, when he'd dressed and gone on deck, I asked Folletto why my master had rejected my attempted caresses. He thought for a minute; because of his dual nature, he understood men as well as women, but he always needed a little time to sort out his own complications.

"You already feel you belong to him, with one caress," he said. "But he won't feel you're his until he's entered you. Men think it's very important that it be their sex that makes a woman belong to them. They don't understand that women always give themselves beforehand."

"That's true, Folletto! Quite true! How do you understand it so well?"

"Because I'm in love with the Prince too, Aziza. And when you moan in his arms, it's your place I'd like to be in, not his."

This embarrassed me, so I changed the subject. "What will he do with me when he gets back to Rome? Sell me? Put me in his harem?"

Folletto began to laugh.

"The Roumis don't have harems, Aziza," he said. "They have a lawful wife. And sometimes they take a concubine."

"What?" I said, astonished. "*A* concubine? Just one?"

"Sometimes they have several," he said, "but one after the other."

That made me sad, for I thought that when my master got tired of me he'd get rid of me. I told Folletto.

"No," he said. "He'll keep *you*."

"Why?"

"Because you belong to him without thinking he belongs to you. So with you he doesn't have to be afraid of screams and tears, or whims and fancies, or jealous scenes and endless demands for money. For him, you'll be the harbor where he can come and anchor after a storm."

When I think of it now, I don't know whether what he said was meant as a prediction or a piece of advice. But I followed the advice, though it wasn't always easy, and now the prediction has come true.

A month after that conversation, my body became mature, and when my period was over, my master took me one day during the siesta — but so slowly, after so much preparation, in so many stages, with so many pauses, that I hardly felt it at all, only the joy and pride of being a woman when his great penis so gently and delicately filled me.

Our fleet of galleys was still sweeping the Adriatic in search of Barbary pirates, but they grew fewer and fewer, frightened off by the Prince's reputation for invincibility. When my master saw I could understand Italian, he decided the time had come for him to convert me to his religion. After we put in at Venice, he had a priest come on board to instruct me.

Before this Roumi actually spoke, I was a little afraid of what he was going to teach me. But when he said God created heaven and earth and man, and was the master of human destiny, and that we did good when we obeyed and evil when we disobeyed Him, and that when they died good people went to paradise and wicked people were delivered over to the devil, I knew that Allah and God were one and the same deity, called by a different name according to whether you were born in Tunis or in Rome. And I had no more scruples about being baptized. I did wake up sometimes in the night, though, and say to myself: "Well, my poor Aziza, you're a Roumia now, and the concubine of a Roumi! What would they think of you in the medina? And what would your poor parents say if they knew?" Sometimes I'd cry, and sometimes I'd laugh. I cried when I thought of them, and laughed when I thought of myself.

Since we've been back in Rome, there have been other women in the Prince's life, but, as Folletto said, not all at once — only one after the other. But he's always kept me as his confidante and friend; he hasn't concealed anything from me about his love affairs.

That's not to say he doesn't want my caresses any more, or I his. Every so often he sends for me through Folletto, who says with a sigh, "Go. He's asking for you." I find the Prince not lying on the bed but sitting propped up with cushions, and without saying anything I lie down between his thighs. He strokes my curly head with both hands, and gradually his legs stiffen until they imprison my body as in a vise. I like that imperious way of gripping me as if I were his mare. And I like it when his hands press my head down harder and harder in a gallop, until he lets out the hoarse groan that seems to come from the depths of his body. I feel proud that I've given him his supreme moment at the same time as he belonged to me. He gasps to get his breath back and says, "Come up here," and I cuddle up with my head on his heart and say: "Listen to how hard it's beating! How strong it is! It'll never stop!" "Yes, it will," he says. "It will stop one day."

I sense a shadow in his voice. He's thinking of the wound in his thigh, which has never healed since the Battle of Lepanto. I say again it's because the Roumi doctors don't look after him properly. We've got two great doctors in Tunis, one an Arab and the other a Jew, and I'm sure their medicines would be better.

"But how can I go to Tunis," he asks with a shrug, "that den of pirates, when I've hanged so many of them?"

I listen to his heart, beating less rapidly, as I lie curled up beside him, my head in the crook of his left shoulder. He's so broad I can hardly reach over his full chest and touch the crook of his right shoulder.

I'm sixteen now. I get enough to eat, and I have a large appetite. But I haven't got taller or fatter, and I don't weigh any more than a feather. My breasts are no bigger than pomegranates, and I've got little hard round buttocks, like a boy. I really can't see what he finds to love in me, except perhaps the color of my skin, which is olive brown, and my curly hair, gazelle's eyes, little nose, and big mouth.

I lie with my nose against his skin, which smells nice — it always smells nice, even when he's been sweating. I say nothing and wait. Although I'm impatient too, the waiting is delicious. I'm absolutely sure what's going to happen. Paolo's a fair man. He won't send me away until I've been satisfied too. I shut my eyes and wait with all my being.

But sometimes we quarrel, always about the same thing. I usually know how to keep quiet, but on this subject I get so cross I can't hold my tongue. "You ought to have done it five years ago! She was unfaithful to you with one of your relations. What a disgrace! And all you've done is shut her up in your palace at Bracciano! And now she gives herself to the guards, to the grooms, to the muleteers, to the scullions! Every day she dishonors you more!"

His eyes go gray as steel and he shoves me from him. "Be quiet! Go away! You're just a barbarian! How can you, a woman, tell me to kill another woman? You're no more a Christian than Francesco de' Medici is, or his brother the Cardinal, or the Pope. Francesco exhorts me to deal with Isabella 'like a gentleman'! His brother exhorts me to behave 'like a Christian'! That's what he said — 'a Christian'! What a joke! And the Pope pretends in public to be surprised I haven't yet 'cleared matters up.' But listen to me, Aziza, once and for all: I'm a soldier, not an executioner."

I don't say anything. I just sit on the bed with my arms around my knees. I look at him sideways, like a little girl who's been scolded and beaten, though he's never raised his hand against me. It always touches and amuses him when I look at him like this. He's not taken in by it, but he's a man who loves everything about women, even their wiles. "Come here, you naughty girl," he says after a moment. And I throw myself into his arms and cuddle up against him. If only he'd suddenly want to take me now, how happy I'd be to be covered by his great body!

I'm not really bloodthirsty, and it doesn't matter to me whether he kills his wife or not. I'm Paolo's slave, not even his concubine. But it makes me furious that his wife should dishonor him. I hear what people say in various places, even in the street, and it makes me furious to hear them call such a hero a coward, even under their breath.

That last little quarrel took place before March 19. After that, of course, things changed.


### Raimondo Orsini (Il Bruto)

My brother Lodovico, Count of Oppedo, and I belong to the younger branch of the Orsini family. The head of the older branch — and thus of ours as well — is, as everyone knows, the great, the beautiful, and the brave Paolo Giordano Orsini, Duke of Bracciano. He reigns in splendor in four-towered Montegiordano palace, just across the Tiber from Castle Sant' Angelo. Lodovico and I have to make do with a much smaller palace with no towers and no right of asylum.

I find it intolerable. Why shouldn't we, Orsinis too, be able to give shelter and protection in our own house to anyone we like, even a bandit, without the Bargello breaking in, hauling our guest off, giving him a mere pretext of a trial, and hanging him? What true Orsini could swallow such an insult?

And Paolo Giordano has another advantage over us. Not only has he done well with his inheritance, but also he's acquired more wealth on top of it. The five years he spent in the service of Venice brought him enormous wealth, since he was allowed to keep half of all the prizes he took.

He's been a good kinsman to us, and not at all stingy with his piasters. But lately he's tightened the purse strings. Last January he said to me: "Raimondo, here are ten thousand piasters for Lodovico and you. Now listen: they're the last you'll get. You spend money like water, and trying to bail you out is like trying to fill the Danaides' barrel." At least, I think he said the Danaides. I don't know why on earth they tried to put wine in a barrel with holes in it.

The worst of it is, it got around that Paolo wasn't going to pay our debts any more. From that day on, we haven't been able to get any credit, not even from the Jews. So when the ten thousand piasters had gone up in smoke, we had to resort to extreme measures: we sent a couple of our men to waylay travelers in the Nora mountains. Unfortunately, the wretches are brutes and, not content with robbing, they often kill their victims, even when it isn't strictly necessary. It's true that in my youth I used to be called Il Bruto, because I was rather free with my fists and feet, and if an affair got complicated, I tended to use my dagger. But that's not fair either. My brother Lodovico is as quick on the draw as I am, but people have never called him Il Bruto, because he's got a pretty face and knows how to read and write.

I can sign my name, and that's enough for me. I believe the sword's more useful to a gentleman than the pen. Just the same, I've got more than my share of shrewdness, and that had better not be forgotten.

Paolo asked me to come see him in his palace on March 28, and he added a note saying, "Please be discreet. Don't bring twenty other people with you." I was much intrigued when

131

the secretary read that out to me.

"Ah, Raimondo!" Paolo said, welcoming me in his great hall with his usual warmth. "How are you? How's my great baby been managing since I weaned him?"

"Quite well."

"Quite well as far as cash is concerned, or quite well morally?"

I smiled and gave no answer, not being sure if he knew that the two bandits at large in the mountains were our men.

"You don't answer," he said. "You don't trust me, though I'm older than you and your kinsman. Do you take me for the Bargello? Well, never mind. Sit down and have a cup of this good wine. I want to ask you to do something for me."

I sat down, but he remained standing. He didn't drink either, but paced back and forth in silence. Suddenly I thought: Paolo, the great Paolo, usually so regal and sure of himself, is embarrassed.

"The thing is," he said at last, "I've decided to put an end to Isabella's scandalous existence."

"That's a change!" I said. "For five years you've been refusing to do it!"

"The reason is, Raimondo, that Isabella is sinking deeper and deeper into bad ways. Five years ago, she was only an adulteress. Now she's a veritable Messalina."

I frowned. "What are you talking about, Paolo? I can't understand you! To start with, who's this Messalina?"

"A woman with an insatiable appetite for men, who gave herself to anyone, day or night."

"And where's this marvelous creature to be found?"

"Raimondo! She's been dead for centuries! She was an empress in ancient Rome."

"What's the point of talking about her if she's dead?"

Paolo didn't answer; so I thought for a moment and said: "What it amounts to, Paolo, is that for five years you refused to kill your wife, and now you've made up your mind to do it. Well, that's your business."

"No, Raimondo," he answered, looking me straight in the eye. "It's yours. I want to entrust you with the execution."

"Me?"

"Yes, you. It goes without saying that I'll reward your devotion."

I was silent. It was the first time this idea had entered my head, and to tell the truth, I found it rather shocking.

"I thought it was the custom for the husband to kill an unfaithful wife himself," I said. "He's the one she's insulted."

"Never mind about custom. I want to go about it differently. I'll write you a note so that Isabella will know you're doing it for me."

"Yes," I said slowly. "Like that it would be all right, I suppose. But you're depriving yourself of a treat, not killing her yourself. She did give you horns."

I looked at him as I said that, and I thought he went white.

"I'm not depriving myself of any treat," he said quietly. "I loved her, remember."

After a moment, I went on: "You said something about a reward."

"Twenty thousand piasters."

"I'd have thought thirty thousand."

"If you like!" he answered angrily. Then he said it again. "If you like! We're not going to haggle. That would be too sordid."

"Listen," I said, annoyed by his tone. "It would be cheaper if you got one of your bandits to do it, one of those you shelter in your house."

"Certainly not!" he cried. "That would be unworthy of her and of me! If she doesn't die by my own hand, it must at least be by the hand of another Orsini."

I thought again and said: "Paolo, you've said she's a trollop. Would you let her be treated like one . . . beforehand?"

His eyes flashed with fury. "You haven't changed, Raimondo!" he said. "You really are a brute! Who else would think of that at a time like this?"

I stood up. "If I'm a brute," I said through clenched teeth, "the brute will take his leave."

He seized me by the arm. "No, Raimondo. Don't get angry — please! I need you."

He made me sit down again, took a few more paces around the room, and then went on: "Do what you like about Isabella. But I don't want her treated inhumanly."

"I didn't intend to. Even II Bruto can have a heart."

He took my hands. "Oh, Raimondo, I'm sorry. I've hurt your feelings."

"No, no," I said, hastily pulling my hands away.

After that, not wanting to part with ruffled feelings, we talked of other matters. But I still couldn't get over what he'd said. Once again I'd come up against the family view of me: that I'm a brute and a dullard. I didn't want to leave without demonstrating, even in veiled terms, that I wasn't as stupid as he supposed.

"Paolo," I said innocently, "you've lost your secretary, I believe."

"Lost is the word. He's become a priest."

"I have a suggestion, if you want to replace him."

"Who?"

"Marcello Accoramboni."

Paolo looked dumbfounded. He stood there speechless, blinking. I went on with a detached air: "He's educated. He even learned Latin once."

"How do you know this, Raimondo?" he asked, raising his eyebrows. "Have you met him?"

"No. But I know a girl who often sees him."

"Who?"

"Caterina Acquaviva."

"Who's she?"

"Vittoria Peretti's maid."

Then he really went white. To conceal his agitation, he turned his back on me and went over to look down at the huge inner courtyard. That didn't tell him anything he didn't know, I'll wager. The outlaws he gave asylum to camped there day and night, and he maintained them in the knowledge that he had only to arm them to match the power of the Pope himself.

"This girl — how well do you know her?" he asked, without turning around.

"I tumble her whenever I feel like it."

"Could you arrange for me to meet her?"

"I could. But I don't think it's a good idea."

He turned and looked at me. "Why not?"

"Her parents live in Grottammare. I suspect she's in the pay of Montalto."

"In that case," he said, "we'll say no more about it."

He took me by the arm and led me to the top of the stairs. I was glad to find him so polite after I'd wormed out his little secrets. As a matter of fact, I was quite touched. My affection for him revived, and I said: "I could introduce you to Marcello Accoramboni, though."

"What? You just said you didn't know him."

"I don't. But he fraternizes with Il Mancino."

"Who's Il Mancino?"

"A brigand turned pimp, and Caterina's brother. He haunts a tavern called the Mount of Olives. Some say he owns it."

"You mix with some strange people, Raimondo," said Paolo with a little smile.

"So do you," I answered, "judging by those I've seen in your courtyard."

We embraced and went our separate ways without coming to any decision about Marcello. Of course, Paolo didn't really need me to introduce him, now that I'd told him who Il Mancino was and where to find him.

As for Isabella, as soon as she saw me appear

outside the walls of Bracciano with my squire, Alfredo, and my heavy escort, she realized what I'd come for. I hardly needed to show her Paolo's note. But she received me with kindness, and with no trace of fear on her beautiful face. After asking me to sit down, she started to talk to me quite easily and with the utmost courtesy.

"Whatever you do, you must thank Paolo for having let me go on living for five years after my affair with Troilo. It's much more than I'd hoped for. Tell him I'm touched that he didn't have the heart to kill me himself. Naturally, Raimondo, you're not very keen on this kind of job either. You've always had a soft spot for me. Don't say you haven't. And I've always thought it unfair that they call you Il Bruto. Your eyes aren't the eyes of a brute. Nor are your lips."

She rose gracefully from her chair and came and kissed me on the mouth. Then she went and sat down again as if nothing had happened.

"How do you propose to do it?" she asked, quite naturally.

I gulped and mumbled: "By the legal method: with a red silk cord."

"Oh, no, Raimondo," she said, "not like that — please! Strangling makes people look so ugly! I don't want to look ugly after I'm

138

dead. No. A dagger, Raimondo, a dagger! Right in the heart!"

"Whatever you say," I murmured.

"And one more little request, Raimondo," she went on, quite conversationally, her head on one side. "I'd like you to give me another three days of life, please."

"To put your affairs in order?"

"Oh, no!" she answered with a carefree laugh. "My affairs have been in order for five years. . . . But I've noticed there are a lot of handsome fellows in your escort — starting with you. You always hankered after me, Raimondo. Don't deny it."

"I'm sorry, Isabella," I said, lowering my eyes. "It's all very well about me — I'm your cousin too, like Troilo. But the others? How could you have become such a . . ." I tried to remember the name Paolo had used, but I couldn't. So I said: ". . . such a lustful woman?"

She laughed again. How beautiful she was! Those teeth, that mouth, those eyes, that forest of black hair!

But then, serious again, she said: "When Paolo and I were together, we used to make love often, several times a day. He was an indefatigable lover. And he could do wonders with his mouth. I wanted to make love all the time, Raimondo, all the time. I adored

139

Paolo. In the intervals, I made do with thinking about him, dreaming he was making love to me. Then he went away. His absence was hell. So one evening I threw myself at Troilo, just because he looked like his cousin. Poor Troilo, he nearly died of fright, and soon he ran away. Then the whole world collapsed. Troilo was killed, my son was taken away from me, and I waited for death. While I was waiting . . . You see, Raimondo, some people make themselves drunk with wine; now you know what I make myself drunk with."

I spent the night with her, and the next morning at dawn, when I got back to my own room, I started to cry. I couldn't see why she had to die. She was so alive.

During the morning I went to see the chaplain, and after I'd made my confession I said: "Father, you know why I'm here."

"Yes," he answered.

"But I don't want to do it until she's confessed. I don't want her to die a sinner."

The chaplain was so old his face was almost fleshless — all you could see on the bones was his almost transparent skin. He was so much like a skeleton that I was almost surprised to find there were eyes in his hollow sockets, though when you looked at them you could see they too were dead.

"I haven't heard her confession for a very

long time," he said in a voice so faint it seemed about to fade away completely. "What would be the use? She doesn't repent! Her only idea is to sin again!"

"Will she be damned?" I asked.

"Who knows?" he cried, throwing up his bony hands.

"Father, hear her confession, I beg you. Hear it one last time!"

"No, no, no!" he answered, with a vigor that amazed me. "It would be a false confession. Yet another. Even when she's kneeling in front of me, with downcast eyes, reciting the list of her iniquities, I can see she's still reveling in them."

Wild with rage, I watched him go; if he hadn't been a priest I'd have run him through.

I had my midday meal alone with Isabella in her room.

"Give me the key, Isabella," I said, "so that I can come in whenever I wish."

She smiled. "Take it," she said. "It's in the lock. But you might not find me alone."

And with a bitter curl of the lip she added: "Thank God, I'm not often alone." But she continued at once, lightly: "How's Paolo? Has the wound in his thigh healed? Does he still have his little Moorish girl?"

"Yes."

"What is she like? Have you seen her?"

"Once, by accident. He keeps her out of the way. She's kind of a skinny little kitten, with big eyes and a big mouth."

Isabella started to laugh, God knows why, and then went on, quite gaily: "There have been others, I'll wager."

"Plenty."

She raised her glass to her lips, but didn't drink.

"Men are lucky, Raimondo. They can sleep with anybody and everybody, and people don't call them harlots. And when they commit adultery, no one kills them. Still, I wouldn't not be a woman for anything. Come on, Raimondo. Hurry up! What are you waiting for? If you're not careful, I'll start calling you Il Bruto!"

Her hand clutched mine, and she pulled me out of my chair, her eyes blazing. Her couch was low and twice as wide as an ordinary bed. Rugs, draperies, and cushions were the only other things in the room. The curtains were drawn across the window because of the sun.

When I got back to my room, I sent for Alfredo. He's actually my cousin, on my mother's side, and he's the one who ought to be called Il Bruto. He's as strong as a bull and ruthless as a wolf. You can tell just by looking at him: he has a muzzle rather than a face. But in his way he's devoted to me, and I'm quite fond of him. Lodovico says that's because I feel intelligent when I talk to him. But Lodovico's wrong: I never feel intelligent. I live in a sort of cloud, and I don't really understand what's going on. The mere fact of being alive puzzles me. One day I asked Paolo to explain it to me, but he only laughed.

"Alfredo," I said, "about Isabella: I'm going to do it today."

He opened his piggy eyes wide. "But this is only the second day. You promised her three."

"Exactly. And tomorrow morning she'd think, My last day has come, and, brave as she is, she'd be afraid. I don't want her to be afraid. I don't want her to suffer. I want to kill her without warning, so she doesn't even realize it."

Alfredo looked at me, curious. "You don't want her to be afraid," he repeated. "You don't want her to suffer. You want her to die without realizing it."

"Yes."

"Why?"

"Don't ask me. Just find out how it can be done. I'll wait for you here. I have the key to her room."

He nodded and went off, pleased that I was trusting him. I threw myself on my bed and tried to sleep, but couldn't. Alfredo came back as it was getting dark.

"Now's your chance," he said. "Amin is with her."

"Who's Amin?"

"The muleteer here. A gigantic black. She has him service her every evening."

Alfredo was holding a couple of stilettos with long thin blades.

I swallowed. "Why two?"

"One for me and one for you. When Amin's on top of her, I'll stab him behind the ear. That'll kill him stone dead. Then I'll pull him off her, and you can stab her in the heart. Stilettos make a small wound, and there won't be much blood."

I stood up, trembling in every limb, and downed a large glass of wine. "Come on then," I said.

"We'll have to take our shoes off first," said Alfredo.

I led the way into Isabella's room. My hands were clammy, and my heart was thumping so loudly against my ribs I was afraid everyone would hear it. In the dark, I could just make out the huge form of the black on the couch, but I couldn't see Isabella. She was underneath him, letting out childish little moans. I knew she was so far gone she wouldn't be able to hear

144

my heart beating, or anything else.

Alfredo moved forward, but I pulled him back. I wanted them to reach the height of their pleasure.

It was a long wait. Amin was panting like a bellows, sweat streaming down between his shoulder blades. I was fascinated by the incredible strength and speed his muscular buttocks showed as they moved back and forth. Isabella, invisible, groaned softly and mournfully, like an infant with a fever.

Then Amin let out a single hoarse, triumphant cry, and she uttered several cries too, in a shrill climax. When she stopped, I gave Alfredo a shove, he leaned forward, and everything happened as he'd said it would. Isabella's face gave one convulsive twitch, she blinked, and it was all over. The room was suddenly filled with silence. We two still living gazed down at the two corpses.

"At least they died happy," said Alfredo with a snigger.

I turned on him angrily. "Get him out of here. Throw the body anywhere you like. Leave me alone."

The black was so heavy Alfredo couldn't carry him and had to haul him out of the room by the shoulders. I locked the door behind him and went and knelt beside Isabella. I took one of her hands in both of mine. It was still warm and supple. Tears rolled down my cheeks, and I started to pray. But I felt gloomy and numb. Between repetitions of the Lord's Prayer, I wondered dimly why it was so wrong for Isabella to have done what she did. When her hand had grown cold and stiff in mine, I stood up and left her.

# 4

## *Marcello Accoramboni*

I began to ask myself a few questions after a sudden change came over the way of life in the Rusticucci palace: the exits and entrances were so closely guarded our peaceful home seemed more like a citadel under siege.

This had an effect on the mood of the people living there. Lips were sealed as well as doors closed. Everywhere, I met silence, tension, and anxious expectation. You'd have thought that, instead of being a stone's throw from St. Peter's, the palace had been transported into the heart of a brigand-infested forest, and an attack was expected from one night to the next.

Peretti, who seemed to be the source of these severe measures, never mentioned them. Though usually so affable and talkative, he now spoke very little and avoided people's eyes. Vittoria was pale and practically dumb. Camilla and Tarquinia had called a halt, at least for the moment, to their verbal jousting.

Flaminio spent all his time praying, and never left his room except to sit at meals with downcast eyes. I thought Giulietta would be the best person to approach in the circumstances, but she admitted she knew nothing, and seemed mortified that no one had informed her or asked her advice. The servants observed their masters and, like them, remained silent.

It seemed to me that even Tarquinia didn't know the reasons for the new regime. She kept darting inquiring looks at Vittoria, who seemed not to notice. Judging by her increasingly imperious manner, I suspected she wouldn't be able to restrain her curiosity much longer. And, sure enough, one night, about an hour after the evening meal, as Vittoria was going up to her room, La Superba also rose to her feet. From her determined air, I guessed it wouldn't be long before I stopped her. But I waited a few minutes, to let them actually cross swords before I intervened.

After a suitable interval, I went up the spiral staircase to the gallery around the courtyard, lighted that night by a splendid moon. I crept stealthily along to Vittoria's room.

There was no light in the antechamber. Thinking it was empty, I started to cross it, but I thought I heard the sound of breathing. I stopped and held my own breath. At first I could see nothing, but when I'd got used to the dark, I could make out Caterina, standing with her back to me, listening at Vittoria's door, listening to what mother and daughter were saying to each other. If anyone asks how I recognized Caterina when her back was turned, I can say plainly that I recognized her behind.

She was listening so intently that I got within reach without her noticing. Grabbing her by her hair with my left hand and clapping my right over her mouth to keep her from screaming, I pulled her back into my arms and dragged her out to the gallery. She struggled and lashed out in all directions, and tried to scratch me, like a cat. She even tried to bite the hand I'd put over her mouth. But as soon as we were in the gallery, with the moonlight on my face, she became as meek as a lamb; she gazed at me submissively and remained leaning against me. But I set her roughly on her feet, and, holding her at arm's length by the neck of her dress, I led her to my room, where I locked her in and told her to wait for me.

I then retraced my steps, and, without pausing to knock, went into Vittoria's room. She was sitting at her dressing table looking at herself in the mirror and languidly brushing her hair. Tarquinia stood behind her open-mouthed, interrupted in one of her charac-

149

teristic tirades. The only word I heard before she caught sight of me was "coach." From this I deduced that she was complaining about being treated like the fifth wheel of a coach, and not told anything. She'd protested about this more than once since Vittoria got married, and always employed the same comparison.

"Madam," I said, with a mocking bow, "there are two people who are superfluous in this room: you and I. If, like the rest of us, you are puzzled about the new order of things in this house, apply to the person responsible — Signor Peretti, your son-in-law. Vittoria is obviously neither able nor willing to answer your questions."

"I grant you she's not willing," said Tarquinia, raising her voice, "but I doubt very much that she's unable."

"Even so, have you the power to force her?"

"She owes me an answer!" cried Tarquinia. "I'm her mother!"

"Madam," I said, bowing again, "you must see that this exaggeration is ridiculous. The fact that you're her mother doesn't give you unlimited rights over her. In particular, it doesn't give you the right to force her confidence or prevent her from getting some sleep. Allow me to give you a piece of advice: Get out!"

"Who are you to give me advice?" she cried, giving me a look of the utmost contempt. "A murderer and a pimp!"

"Mother!" cried Vittoria. "You're only provoking him."

"Yes, and I'll provoke him again!" shouted Tarquinia in a fury. "A murderer and a pimp! As for you" — she whirled around on her daughter — "you can't say anything to me when I ask you a question, but you soon find your tongue to defend this ruffian."

"Madam," I said, "you shouldn't resort to insult so fast. Insult leads to violence, and if you don't leave this room immediately, this ruffian will be reluctantly obliged to throw you out."

"Scoundrel!" she cried, drawing herself up. "Would you use violence on your own mother?"

"With pleasure," I answered, grinning.

Tarquinia's eyes glittered, but she could see from mine that I meant what I said. She gathered up the folds of her huge skirt and swept haughtily out of the room. It struck me yet again that what really annoyed me about La Superba was not so much her obnoxious character as her love of dramatics. And she couldn't act.

"I'll leave you, Vittoria," I said. "Lock your door in the future if you want to avoid incursions from the fifth wheel of the coach."

Ordinarily, this little joke would have made her smile, but not now. I looked at her in the mirror. She seemed tired, and was brushing her hair without her usual energy. Her lovely face showed nothing, not even sadness.

"Remember, Vittoria," I said quietly, "what you want, whatever you want, that's what I want too."

I don't know why I said these words, which later proved prophetic. But I'm sure I was expressing my inmost feeling. I've never thought of Vittoria and myself as being really separate.

"Thank you, Marcello. For everything."

She looked at me in the mirror and I looked back at her. Her face was brightly lighted by the candelabras on either side; mine was in the shadow. So the difference in our coloring was less visible than usual, and the likeness of feature and expression infinitely more striking. My heart began to thump. It was as if the secret of my life was there, and I had only to decipher it.

"Thank you, Marcello," she said again.

And she shut her eyes for a moment. It was as if a curtain had fallen on a play that would go on being acted unseen. I left her to her thoughts and went out, closing the door softly.

Caterina hadn't moved from the low chair on which I'd planted her before locking her in my room. But I noticed right away that she'd undone a couple of buttons on her bodice; the square neck showed off more of her bosom. What a fleshly snare she was, this girl! But she was her own victim. It was plain that all she was conscious of was her femininity. From the roots of her luxuriant hair to her calves, which her short skirt more than half revealed, she was all lure, bait, line, and trap.

When I came in, she stood up, half frightened but still making play with her large eyes, parted lips, and supple body, all with an air of feigned embarrassment and false naïveté, but all too genuine willingness. If while showing me her beautiful bosom she could also have shown me her pretty behind, I'll wager she would have. Quite astonishing was that, though she was throwing all her sexuality in my face, she wasn't vulgar.

As she stood there, still and inviting, I realized she was expecting to be punished, and that I'd have to punish her myself if I didn't want to denounce her to Peretti. He'd have dismissed her at once, and I didn't want that: Vittoria was attached to her. She'd even taught her to read.

So I stepped forward and gave her two vigorous slaps. Then I held her by the shoulders and shook her.

"Who pays you to spy on Vittoria?" I yelled.

It was a purely rhetorical question. I didn't think she listened at the door for any reason but the curiosity typical of maids or the tendency they have to identify with their mistress.

Her answer left me speechless.

"Oh, but the Cardinal doesn't pay me," she said, tears welling up in her eyes. "He comes from Grottammare, and I'm afraid of harming my parents if I don't do as he says."

I turned my back to hide my stupefaction, and walked over to a little table with a five-branched candelabra on it. I stuck the flint and lighted the candles one by one. There was a stool by the table, and I sat Caterina on it. Strangely, this ceremonial seemed to impress her more than the two slaps.

"How do you get your reports to the Cardinal?"

"Through Father Racasi, the priest who hears my confession."

"Often?"

"Once a week. Twice, since March 19."

This was the first time I'd heard that date mentioned, but I showed no surprise.

"Tell me everything that happened that day," I said.

"Nothing much," she answered. "It just so

happened that on March 19, as my mistress was taking leave of the Cardinal, she met Prince Orsini. She was very affected by the encounter."

"How do you know?" I exclaimed. "Did she tell you?"

"No. That's just it," said Caterina brightly. "She didn't say anything. And usually she discusses everything with me. I can tell by what she's been like since."

"What has she been like?"

"Lost in dreams."

If that was Vittoria's state of mind, it was easy to imagine the effect the meeting might have had on the Prince. Everything was clear now, including the state of siege we were living in. The Cardinal must have been afraid Orsini would abduct Vittoria.

"Listen to me, Caterina," I went on after a few moments' silence. "From now on, when you make your confession to Father Racasi, you're not to say anything about Vittoria but what I tell you to say."

She answered without hesitation, her whole body leaning toward me: "Signor Accoramboni, I'll do anything you want."

"Do you tell Father Racasi about your sweethearts?"

"Of course," she answered, lowering her eyes. "I don't leave out my mortal sins.

I'm a good Catholic."

"Does he ask you their names?"

"No, never. Just the number of times I've committed the sin of the flesh with them."

"How many young men have you got?"

"Two," she said. I couldn't tell if her confusion was real or assumed.

"From now on, you'll have only one."

"Which have I got to give up?" she asked eagerly.

"Both."

She stared at me. She was only too delighted to do as I wished, but she didn't dare understand what I meant. I signed to her to stand up, stretched out my hand, and touched the two buttons she'd undone.

"Do you want to know," I said, "who's going to be your only sweetheart?"

"Yes," she answered, quivering from head to foot.

"You'll find out once you've finished what you started when I wasn't here."

Again she couldn't quite bring herself to understand, but having undone a third button without seeing any disapproval, she undressed with a grace that was natural and some little simperings that were not. Curiously, when she blushed, it wasn't her brow and cheeks that colored, but her neck and the upper part of her bosom.

As soon as she was naked, I took her hand and led her over to the bed, where I had her sit down. I stood there looking at her. She didn't say anything; she was still rather afraid of me, though her big black eyes were very eloquent. How strange women are! How incomprehensible that complete submission to their lovers that they call love! For my part, I'm both attracted and repelled by these curious animals. I don't know why, but I always feel a great impulse to punish them. Sometimes I think, You're out of your mind, Marcello. What does it mean? What do you want to punish them *for?*

The truth is I can never quite understand what I do. Certainly I decided to sleep with Caterina to get her out of the Cardinal's power and make her the agent of my own designs. But what were my designs? I still didn't know, except that they included what had always been my first priority: to protect Vittoria.

But Caterina wasn't only an instrument. As I was standing by the bed, I felt not only ardent desire, but also a kind of tenderness. However, although I couldn't conceal the former, I decided to hide the latter — at least, as long as I could. I don't trust octopus-women, the ones who cling to you.

Caterina soon recovered her usual boldness. Her breath came shorter and louder, and when she saw me undo my doublet the whole way, her hand didn't hesitate to run up my trunk hose in the opposite direction. Her fingers trembled a little as they undid the laces, but not from fear.

At evening Mass four days later, in the Rusticucci chapel, Caterina sat down behind me, in the back row. She leaned forward and whispered in my ear that Il Mancino wanted to see me. I slipped her the key to my rooms, which I keep on me so that La Superba can't poke her nose into my affairs.

"Lock him in my room and bring back the key," I whispered. "I'll see him in a quarter of an hour."

When I joined him, Il Mancino rose and bowed. He's short and wiry and upright, and his bows are both respectful and proud. I like them; they make you feel that the esteem he has for you is tempered by the esteem he has for himself. Like his sister, he's lost his Grottammare patois, and he knows how to express himself: he speaks correct, even elegant Italian. He's a subtle fellow, and his meticulous politeness is intended to convey that he expects as much in return. He's been treating me recently with a tinge of courteous familiarity. He knows that though I'm neither a bandit nor a pimp, I've used my dagger in Rome in broad daylight. He also knows I live on the generosity of Signora Sorghini.

"Sit down, Domenico," I said, returning his bow. "Would you like some wine?"

"Thank you, no, signore," he replied, bowing again. "I never drink between meals."

"And your health is all the better for it."

"Signore," he said, "if you'll allow me to come straight to the point, I have a message for you and some useful information. The message won't cost you anything, because I've already been indemnified by the person who sent it. On the other hand" — he lowered his eyes delicately — "the information will have to be paid for."

"Very well," I said. "Let's start with the message."

"Prince Orsini, Duke of Bracciano, would like to meet you tomorrow on the stroke of noon in a room at the Mount of Olives."

"Prince Orsini? At the Mount of Olives, in a room frequented by prostitutes?"

"It's a modest place, to be sure," said Il Mancino, "but easier to get into unnoticed than the Montegiordano palace. I know the tavern quite well. Plenty of respectable people just pull their hat down over their eyes and their cloak up over their nose when they go there. No one will spot the Prince."

"I'll be there. Now let's have the information."

"There are two pieces of information. Perhaps you already know the first — if it isn't public property by now, it soon will be. If it's not new to you, it's free. Otherwise, it will cost you twenty piasters. I rely on your word."

"And so you may."

"The Prince's adulterous wife, after so long a reprieve that people thought it would last forever, has been dispatched."

"When?"

"A week ago."

"You shall have your twenty piasters."

"Signore," said Il Mancino, "the second piece of information will cost you fifty."

"I'm listening."

"My sister Caterina, in obedience to some third person," he said with no expression, "has dismissed her two admirers. One of them was Raimondo Orsini. It's a pity you didn't think to ask my sister his name, signore — it would have saved you fifty piasters."

"It's a pity," I said dryly, "that Caterina didn't think to tell me. She's an affectionate sister, and takes care of her brother's interests."

"No, no, signore!" cried Il Mancino. "You mustn't think that! Caterina is absolutely uncalculating. She can't see farther than the end of her nipples."

His jest amused and convinced me. "What's the point of this information?" I asked.

"That's for you to judge," he answered with feline prudence.

"I'd like to know what you think."

"The Prince might have hoped to reach my sister through his cousins, and through her to get in touch with the signora, your sister. Now that possibility is gone."

"Well reasoned."

And on my part, unwittingly, well played. Little did I imagine when I told Caterina to dismiss her two lovers that one of them was an Orsini.

Next day, on the stroke of noon, with my cloak over my nose, as Il Mancino had suggested, I went to the Mount of Olives. I didn't recognize anyone in the press of people.

Il Mancino's sight must be keener than mine; before I saw him, he whispered in my ear: "Follow me, signore."

We went up a rickety wooden staircase, passing a scantily clad woman who shrieked as she ran down. She was pursued by a man brandishing a cutlass and also yelling. Il Mancino tripped and disarmed him as he fell. Then he seized him by the collar, shoved him against the wall, and said, with a smile on his lips but a harsh look in his eyes: "Signore, squabbles between lovers are settled peacefully here. Find a table and order a pitcher of wine in my name. I'll join you."

The man obeyed, now gentle as a suckling lamb. "He's one of La Sorda's customers," he explained. "I don't approve of her methods. I'm all for honesty — at least, as far as possible."

He pointed out a door on the landing. "That's the place," he said. "And if you don't mind my saying so, signore, don't be too haughty. The Orsinis are very hot-blooded."

"So am I."

I felt my sword in its scabbard, knocked once on the door, then entered abruptly, flinging the door against the wall in case anyone had had the idea of hiding behind it. I found two gentlemen, one standing, one seated, both wearing black masks. My noisy entrance had startled them. I shut the door behind me, taking care not to turn my back toward them. Then I made the briefest of bows and put my hat down on a stool, to have my hands free if there was trouble.

"Gentlemen," I said, "I am Marcello Accoramboni. Which of you is Prince Orsini?"

"I am," said the man who was standing.

The other one looked out the window as if he wasn't involved.

"I'd be obliged," I said, "if you'd speak to me with your face uncovered."

"I see no reason why I should take off my mask," said the gentleman curtly.

"The reason, signore, is that I'm not wearing a mask."

"Come, come, my friend," said the man at the table, "don't make it a point of honor. Take it off, since he asks you to."

"It's a strange request! And made in a curious tone."

"My tone," I said, "was dictated by yours."

"Please take it off," said the second gentleman. "It's I who am asking you this time."

The other obeyed, in a fury, and when the mask was off, his face struck me as very handsome except for an insufferable air of conceit. But what I noticed more strongly was his youth. I'd seen Prince Orsini since he returned from Venice, and the person I was looking at was a good twenty years younger.

"Signore," I said, "you have lied to me. You are not Prince Orsini."

"I am Lodovico Orsini, Count of Oppedo," he replied loudly, "and I can't allow the first rascal who comes along to call me a liar."

"Rascal?" said I, half drawing my sword.

"A quarrel here, gentlemen? In this low tavern?" said the other man.

He rose and put a powerful arm around Lodovico's shoulders. It was plain the gesture was an affectionate one, yet at the same time it paralyzed the Count. I slipped my blade back in the scabbard and waited. I seemed to remember that Lodovico was Raimondo's brother, and that they were a pair of robbers, despite their noble birth. Either this Lodovico was incredibly quarrelsome or he bore me a grudge for depriving his brother of Caterina's favors.

"Come now," went on the other gentleman, "calm yourself, please! Signor Accoramboni will think we've lured him into an ambush."

Taking him by the arm, he sat him down at the table by the window. Lodovico crouched forward with his hands clutching the edge, darting murderous looks at me, which I pretended not to see.

Then the second gentleman took off his mask and said: "I am Prince Orsini."

This time it really was he. Anyone who has ever seen him, even once, can never forget him. It's not that the Prince is especially tall; he's scarcely an inch taller than I am. But he's very powerfully built, broad-shouldered and barrel-chested, and his legs are very muscular. His face is handsome, with strong regular features, a voluptuous mouth, large bright eyes, and short reddish-gold curls, such as you see on Roman medals. His expression, while reflecting pride and authority, is also sensitive and courteous.

I would have been won over by his appearance if his subterfuge with Lodovico hadn't still irked me. Had he been trying to test me, to see if I was adaptable and obedient enough to do his will? If so, my reaction must certainly have undeceived him.

It didn't look like that, however. He gazed at me in silence, and the more his eyes scrutinized my face, the more reasons they seemed to find to like me. But, of course, I soon realized that it wasn't my person that attracted him, but my resemblance to Vittoria.

"Signor Accoramboni," said the Prince with studied courtesy, "I must beg you to forgive me for asking you to come here. But if it's agreeable to you, I have a proposition to make."

"My lord," I answered, bowing, "I shall listen with the greatest interest and respect to any honest proposition you choose to make."

He must have marvelous self-control, for he scarcely raised an eyebrow at the word "honest." Yet hadn't I made it plain that if his proposal was not, he couldn't count on me to cooperate?

"I'm told, Signor Accoramboni," he went on, "that you can read and write, and that you were taught Latin."

"As far as Latin is concerned, my lord, I forgot it faster than I learned it. But it's true

I can read and write, though I'm no scholar."

"I'm not looking for a scholar," said the Prince with a smile. "I used to have one as my secretary, but the wretch has left me to become a priest. Would you like to take his place?"

It took me a full second to answer, so taken aback was I by the suggestion, coming from so lofty a personage and made so graciously.

"It would indeed be a great honor, my lord," I said with a bow. "But there are difficulties."

"What difficulties?" said the Prince, a flash of impatience in his eyes.

"It seems to me that as Your Highness's secretary I would rank above all the other people in your household."

"Of course."

"But I've heard that many of them are allies and relations, belonging to the most ancient nobility."

"That is so."

"Well, I don't see these dashing gentlemen accepting someone like me, whose nobility is recent and controversial."

I said this proudly and sardonically, with my hand on my hip. Everybody in Rome knew I'd promoted myself when I arrived.

My words produced two quite opposite effects. Lodovico growled like a mastiff on a

166

chain, but the Prince's reaction was friendly. It both tickled him and earned his respect that I should make fun of my sham nobility at the same time as I insisted that his entourage must defer to it. He burst out laughing.

"Signor Accoramboni," he said good-humoredly, "once you're my secretary, no one in my house will dare make fun of you."

"Not even," I said, looking at Lodovico, "the Count of Oppedo?"

"Not even he," said the Prince.

"The Count of Oppedo," put in Lodovico offensively, "doesn't stab people without warning in a coach. He fights them fairly, in a duel."

"As I would have, Count," said I, "if Recanati had accepted my challenge."

"Come, *carissimo*," said the Prince, "you know that's how it happened. And Signor Accoramboni had good reason: Recanati had gravely insulted a member of his family in public."

"A member of his family" — how the Prince had enjoyed saying that! At the same time, the words disturbed him, and the image of Vittoria was superimposed upon mine. The emotion was too much for him: he clasped his hands behind his back and started to pace the little room, his eyes downcast.

"Well," he said at last, stopping in front

of me, "is that the only difficulty, Signor Accoramboni?"

"I can't foretell the future," I answered, "but for the moment I see no other."

"So you accept?"

"With deference and gratitude," I said, bowing.

Lodovico growled again, not because of my words, which were irreproachable, but because of the irony with which they were uttered. As for the Prince, he raised one eyebrow and gave me a quick inquiring glance. But I had foreseen it. My eyes were already lowered, and my bearing meeker than a girl's.

"As to the emolument —" began the Prince.

"Please, please, my lord!" I cried, looking up. "Let us not speak of that. I have made up my mind to accept no reward. The honor of serving Your Highness is enough for me."

Lodovico fumed again, and the Prince looked slightly ill at ease. If he didn't pay me, my dependence on him would be purely nominal. But he was too shrewd to press the point.

"Signor Accoramboni doesn't need the Orsinis' money," hissed Lodovico. "He has other resources."

"Yes indeed," I said calmly. "I am the lover of a rich widow. And I pray the Lord every day that I may retain her favor. I wouldn't like to have to turn brigand and rob defenseless travelers in the mountains."

At that, the Prince laughed openly. Lodovico, white as a sheet opened his mouth to reply, but his kinsman silenced him with a wave of the hand.

"Signor Accoramboni," he said, with the utmost courtesy, "I shall expect you at Montegiordano palace at ten o'clock on Monday. Please forgive me for asking you to meet me in this hovel. I wouldn't, in your own interest, have wanted you to be seen entering my house if you were going to reject my proposal. Now, of course, things are different."

I picked my hat up from the stool and made the Prince a deep bow. I made another one, curt, stiff, and meager, to Lodovico, who replied with a nod.

Then I went down the rickety wooden stairs, not touching the banister, which was black with dirt from countless hands.

I've advanced a pawn on the chessboard, but I don't know where the move will lead me. I've made three enemies: Raimondo Orsini, Lodovico Orsini, and, as soon as it's known that I'm working for the Prince, Cardinal Montalto. As for the one friend I've acquired, he obviously means to use me as a tool.

We'll see about that. I like the Prince well enough, but I know he was a mercenary in the service of Venice: he's half pirate and half condottiere. In a state as weak as this one, with a pope as spineless as the present incumbent, he must think he can do as he pleases. He'll be disappointed.

## Aziza the Wasp

Ever since March 19, my master hasn't eaten or slept or done much. He spends hours lying on a divan, dreaming, or wandering aimlessly around the palace. He hardly even goes riding. The wound in his thigh is bothering him again too, and his limp has become more pronounced. He still requires my caresses, but as soon as they're over, he lapses into melancholy, which is unlike him.

Naturally, I was jealous at first, but I managed to stifle it. I know exactly what my place is in my master's heart, in his house, and in his country. My place in his heart is quite important, though there's no chance of its ever being first. My place in his house is small. My place in his country is nonexistent: who would take notice of a little Moorish slave bought for five hundred ducats on a Venetian galley?

After March 19, I did my best to use the

feminine art of patience with Paolo. As soon as I realized he wanted to be alone, I left him, making sure that my departure was unobtrusive. When we were together and he wanted to be silent, I didn't utter a word. When he tried, unfairly, to pick a quarrel with me — with me, Aziza the Wasp — I let my tongue lie at rest in my mouth. And when he started praising the beauty of his beloved, he could read nothing but sympathy in the big black eyes looking into his.

And so I succeeded — not always easily — in remaining his confidante and the skinny little cat on whose head he puts his great hands when he wants me to be his.

On the evening of the day he asked Marcello Accoramboni to be his secretary, he related the interview to me in detail, and I listened in amazement to the torrent of words issuing at last from his lips. He was nearly within reach of his goal, he said. He was exultant.

I could scarcely believe my ears on hearing this great captain talk such childish nonsense.

"But, Paolo," I said, when his eloquence flagged, "if what you say is true, you haven't really won Marcello over to your cause. He's distanced himself from the gentlemen of your family: from Raimondo, from Lodovico, and even from you. He's insisted on having his sham nobility recognized just to show what a low opinion he has of yours. And by refusing any salary, he's emphasized how little importance he attaches to your wealth. You are in his debt, not he in yours. And you can't rely on him to help you abduct Vittoria and become her lover. Is it likely a man who stabbed Recanati to death for saying a word out of turn about his twin sister is going to help you turn her into an adulteress?"

My master's blue eyes turned grayer than the blade of his sword. He was beside himself.

"Go away, you Moorish devil!" he cried. "Go away and never let me see you again! Or I'll tell my majordomo to sell you!"

I was very sorry he was angry, but not at all intimidated by his threat. My patience, my submissiveness, and my love have tied so strong a bond between us that he'd find it very hard to break it. Besides, he is a just man. And he proved it two days later.

He sent Folletto to fetch me. As usual, after showing me into the Prince's bedroom, the boy curled up in a corner, quiet as a mouse, and prepared, all eyes and ears, to follow our frolics. Although my Italian was perfect now, and the Prince didn't really notice, Folletto continued to stay nearby, as he had on the galley. His presence did trouble me, for he'd told me he derived a kind of bitter pleasure from imagining himself in my place, giving and receiving the caresses that made me moan.

He must have been disappointed that day, though. All we did was talk.

"Aziza, my wasp," my master said, looking at me with his bright affectionate eyes, "there's really quite a large brain in that little head of yours. You were perfectly right about Marcello. Yesterday evening I wrote a long letter to Vittoria, and I asked him to give it to her. He turned pale, threw the letter on the table, and said, through clenched teeth: 'My lord, you insult me! Do you think I'm the sort of man to suborn my own sister?' And he drew his sword, his eyes blazing."

"Drew his sword on you? In your own house? What did you do?"

"I drew my sword too."

"Oh, master, you shouldn't have condescended. You, a prince! And he isn't even a nobleman!"

"Yes," said Paolo, "but he looked so handsome, and so like Vittoria. As I expected, the duel lasted only a minute. I just pricked him in the arm, and I called my barber to dress the wound. I was astounded that he'd had the audacity to face up to me. When the barber had gone, I picked the letter up and held it out to him.

" 'My intentions toward Vittoria are honorable,' I said. 'But I must find out how she feels.'

"Marcello was pale — he'd lost more blood than I'd intended — but his black eyes were as fierce as ever. He looked at me for some time, then said: 'If your intentions really are honorable, I'll do my best to further them, provided Vittoria returns your feelings.' Then he took the letter and left."

When Paolo paused, I stayed silent so long he grew impatient.

"Well, what do you think, my wasp?"

"I think you've promised to make Vittoria a duchess, but she's already married."

"I know that. What else?"

"Francesco Peretti is the son of an influential cardinal and a protégé of the present Pope. I think that if your plan is what I believe it is, you're setting out on a highly dangerous course."

"I know that too," he said curtly. And, naked as he was, he got up from his couch and started pacing up and down like a caged tiger.

## Caterina Acquaviva

After March 19 came a fortnight when for various reasons I was very happy. First, Vittoria didn't confide in me, as she had done before. This worried me all the more because I was afraid she might have found out I was sending reports about her to the Cardinal through Father Racasi. But, since after March 19 my reports didn't have anything in them, I gradually stopped fretting. As for her thoughts, no doubt they weren't the kind you tell anyone, not even another woman, not even a confessor. *I* didn't tell Father Racasi everything! Far from it.

Another thing was the sacking of the old gatekeeper at the Rusticucci palace. He was fond of wine and women, and a girl could easily get around him by allowing him a few minor liberties, pinches and so on. But he was replaced by a grim wretch who stuck to the letter of his instructions and wouldn't let anyone in or out, man or woman, except Marcello and Il Mancino.

I was particularly upset because I couldn't get out to visit my two sweethearts, Raimondo Orsini and Silla Savelli, who had together rented a room nearby to meet me in — turn and turn about or, as I preferred, both together. I'm ashamed to admit that, afraid it might make people think badly of me. But how can I change my nature? When I tell Father Racasi it's not my fault I'm made like that, he says it is a fault in me, and I must pray to God to correct me. So I pray and pray, but after a while, instead of thinking about what my lips are saying, I'm thinking about Raimondo and Silla.

After March 19, like everyone else here, I lived in complete seclusion. As far as I was concerned, in such painful chastity that I wondered whether in the long run I wouldn't dry up like Giulietta and lose all my curves.

Two long weeks went by in that sad situation, and then one evening Il Mancino smuggled me a letter from Raimondo, who suggested coming to see me in the palace. He asked me to draw a map to show him how to reach me. At first I really didn't know what to answer. I thought the whole thing was very risky. Still, I longed for his embraces so much I couldn't sleep, and I was about to do as he said when Marcello found me listening at Vittoria's door, gave me a couple of slaps that could have felled an ox, and them made love to me. I'd been dreaming of him ever since I entered Vittoria's service, so a few seconds in his arms left me in transports of happiness. I was walking on air! I had wings!

I told him all about my reports to the Cardinal and showed him Raimondo's letter.

"My dear Caterina, you're as stupid as the moon," he said. "It's more than time I took you in hand. Do you really think Raimondo wants a map of the palace to come and see you?" He laughed. "With your permission, I'll answer that letter, through your brother."

I agreed. Marcello had only to look at me for my whole being to say yes.

I don't know what answer he gave Raimondo, but it can't have been very agreeable, for two days later my brother brought me a furious note:

Caterina,
You must be the vilest trollop who ever crawled on the face of the earth to have dropped two well-born gentlemen like Silla and me for the arrogant scoundrel who dictated that reply to you. But just you wait! My dagger will make him answer for his insults with his heart's blood. As for you, if, when you're finally let out, I ever meet you in the street, be sure I'll make lace of your innards. So you'll

be punished, you whore, where you've sinned the most.

Raimondo

This threat filled me with fear. So as soon as I could slip into Marcello's room, I showed it to him, even before I undressed. He shook his head gravely.

"Caterina," he said, "did you ever take money or presents from those two?"

"Never!"

"Then they've no right to call you a whore. But the description fits them perfectly, since they live off Prince Orsini. It fits me too, of course, since I live on the generosity of Signora Sorghini. So there are three male whores on the one hand, and on the other a respectable girl who works for her living and who, far from selling her pretty little behind, gives it away just for pleasure."

I cocked my head. "Signor Marcello," I said, "do you really think my behind is pretty?"

"It's perfect," said Marcello seriously. "I'm sure there's not its equal in the whole of Rome. Now listen to me, Caterina, and don't worry. My heart's blood is in no danger from Raimondo's dagger. How could he dare kill his powerful cousin's secretary? As for your nice little innards, sticking a stiletto where he's no longer allowed to stick something else is just an angry dream. If he really meant to do it, he wouldn't have signed his name to the threat."

Marcello went on to say that Silla must really have written the note, because Raimondo can't read or write. My fears set at rest, I'd had enough talking and started to undress. I may be foolish, especially in the eyes of such an educated man as Marcello, but there's one thing everyone must admit I'm good at: I always know exactly what I want.

Three days later, as I was brushing Vittoria's golden hair while she sat at her mirror, Marcello came creeping in, his doublet thrown over his shoulders. When he reached up to keep it from falling off, I could see there was a bloodstained bandage on his left arm. Vittoria caught sight of it in the glass and gave a little cry, thus covering up mine.

"It's nothing," said Marcello. "A little accident. I was fencing with the Prince."

"Leave us, Caterina," said Vittoria.

"No, no," Marcello cried. "Let her stay. I trust her completely now. She deserves it."

He exchanged a look with me in the mirror, and a flood of warmth swept right through me. Our Lady knows I've always been full of reverence and gratitude for the signora. But imagine what my feelings for her were now that her brother had made me his own!

As I was trying not to step on Vittoria's hair, which hung down to the carpet, where it spread out in a long train that I'd carefully arranged in a coil, Marcello stood behind me, so near my back went hot and cold with little shivers.

In the glass I could see him feeling for something in a pocket of his doublet. He brought out a sealed letter and put it down beside a jewel box on the dressing table.

"What's this?" asked Vittoria, tonelessly.

"A letter that a great nobleman who's in love with you humbly begs you to read," said Marcello.

Vittoria turned pale and dropped the ring she had been polishing. It was a big uncut diamond set in gold, covered by a V in smaller stones. Although it was quite a handsome ring, she never wore it. According to Giulietta, that was because it was a present from Signora Tarquinia. If you ask me, it was because Signora Tarquinia had given it to her just before her father died.

The ring with her initial on it rolled around twice before coming to rest an inch from the saucer holding the sponge Vittoria had been using to clean her rings. Her hands gripped the edge of the dressing table so hard her fingers were white. When Marcello put the letter down in front of her, I stopped brushing her hair, but a few seconds later I went on, so as not to appear curious. But I was brushing more slowly, and listening to her breath coming in faint gasps. She was looking at the letter like a bird at a snake. Although her face was ashen, it betrayed nothing, and when I listened more carefully, her breathing seemed normal. The only real sign of emotion was the way her hands were clutching the dressing table.

I stole a glance at Marcello's face in the mirror; beneath his was mine (he's a head taller than I am), and beneath mine Vittoria's. How handsome he was! Even then I couldn't help noticing and being affected by it. His eyes were riveted on Vittoria, and he too seemed impassive. But I knew he was as anxious as his sister by the unconscious twitch of his lower lip that showed whenever he was nervous.

At the time, it seemed to take Vittoria an age to make up her mind, but when I thought about it later, I knew it couldn't have been more than a few seconds.

Frankly, when she finally seized the letter, broke the seal with trembling fingers, and read the contents not once but twice, I felt hurt and disappointed. I know I'm an incorrigible manhunter myself, and need the fingers of both hands to count my past lovers. But I haven't been married at the altar, so at least

I'm not an adulteress. If you ask me, since she knew what she was going to read, she was already being unfaithful to Signor Peretti.

While she was reading, Vittoria tossed her head impatiently. I realized that my brushing was annoying her, and stopped with brush in midair, holding my breath. I glanced again at Marcello in the mirror, but he'd moved away as if he'd lost interest, and, with only the dressing table lighted, I couldn't see him properly in the shadows. Looking back at Vittoria, I could guess how hard she was trying to remain expressionless. But she couldn't keep her face from flushing.

As soon as she'd read the letter the second time, she put it to the flame of one of the candles. Then, taking the sponge out of the saucer with her other hand, she set the letter in its place and watched it burn. Marcello came toward us again, but instead of standing behind me, he went and perched on the edge of the dressing table.

"What answer am I to give," he asked with an attempt at lightness, "to the nobleman who's written to you?"

"There is no answer," said Vittoria haughtily.

It seemed to me she was trying to have it both ways. She had allowed herself the pleasure of reading a love letter from the man she loved, and now she was allowing herself the pleasure of acting the virtuous wife. I must say I'm not so complicated as that: when I've decided to be naughty, I just go ahead. I don't try to have one foot in the camp of sin and the other in that of virtue.

Marcello gave a mocking little laugh. "Well then, Vittoria," he said, "I wish you good night and pleasant dreams."

As he spoke he bent over without touching or kissing her, but putting his right hand on the dressing table between the sponge and the ring. When he straightened up again, the ring was gone. It was so skillfully done, I could scarcely believe my eyes.

Before he left, he brushed against my hand, which meant he wanted to see me in his room when my duties were finished. I shuddered from head to foot, and felt a quiet rush of pleasure go up my legs and down my back. That may sound silly, but it's just what I felt.

I didn't lose my head, however. So Vittoria wouldn't suspect, I said: "Signora, Signor Marcello has taken your ring with the V on it."

"Yes," she said absently, "I know. I saw him. Let him keep it. It's a habit of his. When he was little, he used to steal my dolls."

Then she added: "Leave me, Caterina. I need to get some sleep."

183

I curtsied and went out. She didn't need sleep at all! What she needed was to be alone with her thoughts. She might be a lady, but I was better off than she was. My lover was only a few yards away from me. And, thank God, he wasn't a dream.

There was one thing that bothered me, and I decided to clear it up as soon as I set foot in Marcello's room. "Signor Marcello," I said, "what am I supposed to tell Father Racasi about all this?"

"Say I brought Vittoria a letter, and she burned it and said there wasn't any reply."

"So she didn't read it?"

"No."

"I'm sorry, but that's what Father Racasi calls a sin of omission."

"Have you told him the name of your new lover?"

"No."

"That's a sin of omission as well. So that makes two."

But why I found it easier to commit two than one I don't know.

## Marcello Accoramboni

It took me a couple of hours to disengage myself from my little octopus's tentacles. But I like Caterina, even though she *is* an octopus. She brings to the act a proletarian gaiety that Margherita lacks. And it's not true she's "as stupid as the moon." It's our Italian expression that's stupid. The moon is supposed to be foolish because it has such an innocent round face when it's full. But foolish it isn't, judging by the number of amorous exchanges it encourages, or even causes, in the summer by its very presence.

As a matter of fact, Caterina is quite shrewd. But — how shall I put it? — her shrewdness is limited. Il Mancino was right when he said she can't see farther than the end of her nipples. In her period of painful chastity, she so longed for Raimondo's embraces that it never occurred to her that the map he asked her for might be used to abduct Vittoria.

That evening, after she left me, my thoughts took a more serious turn. I hadn't blown out the candle, and I lay on my bed twisting the ring I'd stolen from Vittoria round and round on my little finger. "Stolen" is perhaps too strong a word. She never wore it. She disliked it, simply because it bore witness to Tarquinia's natural bad taste, and was indescribably ugly. But, because of the V in diamonds, it could serve my purposes.

I wasn't thinking in order to make up my

185

mind. That was already done. I was just trying to understand why I'd come to that decision. What a job! I've noticed that in a situation in which you're emotionally involved with other people, three things have to be dealt with, of increasing difficulty: to know what you think, to know what you feel, and to know what you want. In this case, the subject was not myself, but Vittoria, my other self.

Because our natures were so alike I'd always been able to tell, from certain signs, what was going on in Vittoria's heart. But on March 19 she severed the link between us, and I could find out what was troubling her only through Caterina, that insignificant but crucial witness. I had to rely on observation, instead of intuition. And it was now important to me to know what Vittoria felt and what she wanted, even if she was doing her best to blind herself to it.

From that point of view, what had just taken place in her room was extremely revealing. When I put the letter from a "great nobleman" who was in love with her down in front of her — an act highly offensive in itself, especially by a brother — what she ought to have done, without the slightest hesitation and without even touching the thing, was tell me contemptuously to take the infamous object back whence it came. But she did nothing of the sort. She did hesitate. But her hesitation was merely a pause to manipulate her conscience. From that moment, the outcome was not in doubt.

She opened the letter. Neither curiosity nor the pleasure of being flattered played any part in her decision. Vittoria, who was adored by everybody, was quite above such petty vanity. She opened the letter because she loved the Prince, because she wanted to be his, and because she couldn't resist his appeal. When she broke the wax seal — and how those lovely fingers trembled doing it! — and began to read — in front of two witnesses, what's more — she was already betraying Peretti.

When she'd read and burned it, she said haughtily, "There is no answer!" What a farce! I caught Caterina's eye in the mirror, and even she wasn't taken in. Yes, Vittoria, there was an answer to that letter, a very explicit one: the answer lay in having read it.

But the answer might not be as plain to the Prince as it was to me. So I decided to give it a shove in the right direction the following day.

Meanwhile, I saw that the goal I guessed at would be reached only through plenty of blood and plenty of mud. If only Peretti hadn't been the son of a cardinal, and if only Prince Orsini had been friendly toward Gregory XIII, it would have been easy for the Pope to issue a *precetto* irrevocably annulling the marriage between Vittoria and Peretti. How many times has the present Pope made use of this reprehensible procedure for completely nonreligious reasons? By this means an unfortunate adversary is "demarried" overnight from his lawful spouse — the couple live henceforward in mortal sin — and is excluded from the communion of the faithful. But here there could be no such solution. Anything that could be done would have to be done in spite of the Pope and Montalto. In other words, in the face of both the spiritual and the temporal power of Rome.

A terrifying prospect! Though for me, as I twisted Vittoria's ring around my finger in the candlelight, there was something exhilarating about it. I felt that with the tiny prod I meant to give events, just to bring Vittoria nearer to her heart's desire, I, the good-for-nothing, the scoundrel, Recanati's murderer, and La Sorghini's pimp, was going to make the whole state rock on its foundations.

Next morning, I presented myself at Montegiordano palace at the usual hour. The majordomo showed me straight into the Prince's private apartments, telling me confidentially that his master had gone out early with a few attendants for a gallop in the

Campagna. I guessed this was to beguile his impatience. Instead of waiting to hear the news I was expected to bring, he'd arranged for me to do the waiting. It was one of the little political wiles by which the great ones of this world try to make you think they're as great as they're supposed to be. I went to a sunlit window overlooking the huge courtyard, that chaotic encampment of all the people — outlaws, exiles, fugitives from papal prisons, bandits on the run — to whom Orsini gave asylum, board, and lodging in order to build up his power against the Pope.

Suddenly, the main gate opened, and the Prince, at the head of his suite, galloped without slackening his pace straight through the archway and across the whole courtyard. There was a terrific scramble, with the crowd first falling away on either side and then surging forward to hail him like a returning monarch. He dismounted at the foot of the tower from which I was looking down, and I heard him limping heavily but powerfully up the stone stairs.

The door was flung back hastily by a page, and the Prince advanced with the aggressive stride forced on him by his limp. The swing of his broad shoulders seemed to propel him forward even faster. His Roman head, covered with the red-gold curls that made him look like a living statue, came to rest in the sunlight flooding through the window.

His breath coming in gasps, his blue eyes gazing straight at me, he asked: "Well?"

Without a word, I pulled Vittoria's ring from my doublet pocket and held it out to him. He took it with a look of amazement, turned it around, and noticed the initial picked out in diamonds. At that, he turned so pale I thought he might faint. He stood there open-mouthed and speechless, his blue eyes glittering with all the joy welling up inside him.

Sensing a question he was unable to put into words, I told him, adding only one word to what Vittoria had said: "My lord, there is no other answer."

# 5

## *Father Racasi*

Every Friday, accompanied by my second curate, I used to go to the Rusticucci palace to confess Signora Camilla Peretti, Signora Tarquinia Accoramboni, Signora Vittoria Peretti, and the latter's maid, Caterina Acquaviva. My curate confesses the rest of the staff. Ever since Francesco Peretti, probably on the advice of the Cardinal, has kept his household strictly secluded, however, I also take my first curate, so that Francesco and Flaminio can make their confessions to him. As for Marcello, he's never there on Friday; according to his mother, he confesses to a mendicant friar at the widow Sorghini's house.

On Saturday, Cardinal Montalto, to whom I owe so much, does me the great honor of hearing my own confession, and I take the opportunity to lay before him the tricky problems I'm sometimes confronted with by the people to whom I act as spiritual adviser. His Eminence always listens carefully, and I admire the perspicacity and subtlety with which he manages to resolve my difficulties.

The Cardinal has a reputation for austerity and even harshness, but I must say that to me he's always shown the utmost indulgence. Although there is a confessional in the oratory adjoining his study, it would be hard for him to enter it, on crutches. So he remains sitting in his usual armchair, and I kneel at his feet. But with a consideration for which I'm very grateful, he always tells Il Bello Muto to put a cushion under my knees before he leaves us.

The Cardinal is also lenient toward the sins of which I accuse myself. True, the list has grown much shorter as the powers that led me into temptation have waned. The sin of the flesh is now as far from me in thought as it is in deed. As for the sin of greed that took its place, that has dwindled, together with the efficiency of my stomach. I sometimes think sadly that I'll attain the saintliness I dreamed of as a child only when age and illness have reduced me to a vegetable existence. But where will the merit be then?

"Peccadilloes, Racasi, mere peccadilloes!" the Cardinal said to me impatiently yesterday, shaking his terrible head. "Now let's hear your little problems."

"Oh, Your Eminence," I said, "I have had

one indeed since yesterday! But it isn't a small one. One of my female penitents was sent a love letter by devious means. And she read it."

"She read it!" said the Cardinal, his black eyes looking daggers from beneath his bushy eyebrows.

"It's really more complicated than that. She says she read it. But her maid, whom I confess also, says she didn't."

"It's not complicated at all," said the Cardinal shortly. "She might have read it when the maid wasn't there."

"Yes, but the maid says it all took place in front of her, and that her mistress burned the letter without opening it."

"Then the maid's lying," said the Cardinal, frowning. "Have you told her so, and rubbed her nose in it?"

"Your Eminence," I said, hanging my head, "I could hardly do that without betraying the secret of her mistress's confession."

"True! True!" exclaimed His Eminence angrily.

He mastered his wrath, though, and I went on: "But mistress and maid both say the same about the answer that was given to the messenger. The person it was addressed to burned it in a little saucer and told the messenger: 'There is no answer.'"

"But she had read it!" cried the Cardinal

indignantly. "Did you think to ask if she'd read it twice?"

"Yes, I did, Your Eminence," I said, secretly rather pleased with my zeal. "And unfortunately yes — she had read it twice."

"God in heaven!" said the Cardinal. After a moment he went on: "What did she feel as she was reading it? Did you ask her?"

"Yes, Your Eminence. The penitent spoke of being in great confusion."

"Be more precise."

"She said she felt shame and remorse, but at the same time she was disturbed. I might even say tempted."

"Did she say 'tempted'?"

"No, Your Eminence. She didn't actually say the word. But I deduced it from the fact that she was disturbed."

"Don't deduce things!" cried the Cardinal. "Stick to the facts! Did she strike you as truly repentant?"

"Your Eminence," I answered, "you know what women are. Even when they're weeping for their sins, they still manage to enjoy them."

"I know, I know!" said the Cardinal. "Spare me the obvious. Tell me the facts."

"Well," I told him after a moment, "my penitent thinks she repents! She sincerely believes so."

"Sincerely! And what about you, Racasi," he thundered. "Are you sincere? Or are you trying to reassure me?"

This question agitated me greatly. I was afraid that in his wrath the Cardinal might name the penitent, of whose identity he was supposed to be ignorant. Fortunately, he must have realized what a terrible situation that would put me in, for he pretended to have forgotten what he'd just asked me and went on more quietly: "Anyhow, no one's conscience is ever sincere. Which of us can deny it?"

I was flattered by that "us," to his appealing to my experience as well as his own. But as I couldn't indulge in vanity right in the middle of my confession. I just bowed my head in agreement.

"One last point, Racasi, and I'd like a straightforward answer, please. And now I'm appealing, beyond the facts, to your intuition. If the lover gained access to your penitent, could she, in your opinion, resist him?"

I shook my head and answered sadly, with downcast eyes: "I doubt it, Your Eminence."

"Help me up, Racasi," said the Cardinal roughly.

I rose to do so, but as soon as he'd fitted his crutches under his armpits, he waved me impatiently out of the way. Then he turned his back on me and went and stood in front of a picture of the Madonna and Child that hung on the wall. He stood looking at it for some time, but, if you ask me, without seeing it. He shook his head several times, and I heard him mutter brokenly: "Oh, my poor boy! They'll kill him."

I felt so uncomfortable at having overheard him that I didn't know what to do with myself. I couldn't leave the room without the Cardinal's permission, not to mention his absolution.

Perhaps he sensed my embarrassment, because he swung ponderously on his crutches, transfixed me with his terrible black eyes, and ordered: "Keep your lips sealed about all this, and leave me, please."

"But, Your Eminence," I stammered, "you haven't given me absolution."

If I didn't look up to the Cardinal with such gratitude and veneration, I'd say no penitent was ever granted the remission of his sins faster, more absentmindedly, or in more of a mumble than I was then. But His Eminence, for reasons of his own that were no business of mine, was too deeply disturbed for me to hold it against him.

Although I believe, as the church teaches, that when a priest pronounces absolution he really does speak in God's place, *"in loco Dei,"* and must be fully conscious of his extraordinary privilege in doing so, it is only too true that, through care, fatigue, anxiety, and human frailty in general, Christ's representative may sometimes deliver in a mechanical and routine manner the words that should each be considered and weighed with the utmost gravity. But it is very wrong for a priest to take such things lightly: confession, by allowing him to fathom the hearts and minds of the faithful, gives the church immense power in the city of men.

I say this in all humility, without sitting in judgment on anyone, least of all on those whom divine grace has placed far above me both in the state and in the hierarchy.

## Lodovico Orsini, Count of Oppedo

That Thursday evening, knowing how Paolo hates unpunctuality, I made a great effort to be at Montegiordano on the stroke of nine.

"Ah, here you are at last!" he cried, embracing me in his usual manner — that is, clutching me in his herculean arms and half crushing me to death on his vast chest.

"But I'm not late!" I said, disengaging myself.

"True enough," he exclaimed in surprise, glancing at a clock. "Forgive my impatience, dear cousin. And please stop casting those murderous looks at Marcello; you know how touchy he is. He even drew his sword on me — on me, Lodovico! — just for a word he took amiss. But enough of that! Marcello is my secretary and my friend. And I want you — do you hear, Lodovico? — I want you to be friends too. Give him your hand."

"What?" I cried. "Give my hand to that reptile?"

"Count," said Marcello, drawing himself up, "you need to revise your zoology. A reptile doesn't have hands. But," he added, putting his hand on the hilt of his sword, "it can bite."

"It won't!" cried Paolo. "Come now, Lodovico, your hand in his this instant, or I really will be angry with you."

I obeyed, and took Marcello's reluctant hand. It was cold and dry and didn't grip mine. The young buck was certainly bold enough, and held his life cheap.

"Sit down, Lodovico, and listen," Paolo went on. "I've never been so close to open war against the state. Montalto has closed his door to me, for one thing. Yes, Lodovico, he's actually done that. What an insult! Next, he's shut his niece up in the Rusticucci palace, pretending to believe I'm planning to abduct her!"

"You probably would," I said wryly.

"Certainly not!" snapped Paolo. "I've told Marcello, and now I tell you: my intentions are honorable."

There were a number of things I could have said on that score, but I didn't want to reveal my true feelings. As I saw the situation, Vittoria was an unscrupulous adventuress, and Marcello a pimp, twice over — in living off La Sorghini and in prostituting his sister in the hope of plucking a duchess's coronet for her out of the mud. As for Paolo, he'd fallen right into the hands of those sinister twins, those mere nobodies from a majolica factory in Gubbio! He, an Orsini Prince, was cherishing the senseless dream of taking that harlot to him for a second duchess, forgetting that if he did so, his son, Virginio — an Orsini through his father and a Medici through his mother — might find his heritage challenged by a creature born on the dunghill of the common people.

"Are you listening, Lodovico?" asked Paolo impatiently. "Or do I have to say the same thing a thousand times? Montalto, not content with sequestering his niece, is taking her under escort tomorrow morning at dawn to Santa Maria, and she and her family are going to be shut up in a castle there. And — listen to this, Lodovico — most of the escort will be papal troops. The Pope himself is trying to thwart me. It's an insult, a deliberate insult to me, an Orsini! But he's mistaken if he thinks I'm going to accept this."

"What do you mean to do?"

"Attack the escort."

"That's what he hopes you'll do," I said coolly. "Do you intend to attack on the way or at Santa Maria?"

"I don't know yet."

"Well, let me tell you, Paolo, neither is feasible. I know the area like the back of my hand. I went hunting there a couple of years ago."

"That's why I sent for you," said Paolo, smiling.

"The castle is really a fortress," I went on. "It's built on a cliff overlooking the sea, and the sea is very rough on that part of the coast. The place is surrounded by high walls, and the only way to get to it is along a road that leads to a huge cleft in the rocks, where there's a drawbridge. The countryside is bare and arid. And it all belongs to Montalto."

"I'll attack before they get there, then," said Paolo.

"That would be much worse. The road is narrow, and runs between the sea and rocky hills that are uninhabited and have no paths or tracks over them."

"Perfect!" said Paolo. "No line of retreat for the escort on either side when we attack them."

"And none for you either, Paolo."

"What do you mean?" said Paolo, with a start. "Do you mean I might be beaten? I have enough men at Montegiordano to attack the escort five to one."

"That's not the point. You couldn't deploy them. Remember the terrain: a narrow road between inaccessible hills and the sea. You're quite likely to be attacked yourself from the rear."

"By whom?"

"The papal army. You surely don't think you and a large body of men are going to set out from Montegiordano at dawn tomorrow without the Pope being informed immediately! He'll send some of his troops after you, to take you from the rear. The rest, in Rome, will seize your palace. And mine too, while they're at it.

There was a lengthy silence. Paolo strode back and forth, stooping forward, with his head on one side. I knew my arguments had convinced him; so I said no more, just let them sink in. That whore had driven him mad, but not to the point of engaging in open war with the Pope under adverse conditions and with his army dispersed. He still had a streak of reason left.

Suddenly he let out a kind of roar. "The sea, Lodovico! I'm a sailor. Why didn't I think of it before?"

"The sea?" I said. "That's a wild coast, unprotected from the open sea, with no creeks or bays. How could an army land there?"

"An army couldn't — no. But a boat could, launched from one of my galleys out at sea."

"The sea will be watched."

"By day, but not at night."

"At night? With all the reefs there are along that coast? Even if the boat escapes them, it'll be smashed against the cliffs."

"No, no!" cried Paolo. "There's no coast so inaccessible that you can't find a place somewhere to haul a boat out of the water."

"Suppose that's true: how do you think you'd persuade the Signora to escape with you by that route?"

"I won't even try! Do you think I'd expose her to such dangers? But at least I'll see her! And at least," he added softly, as if to himself, "I'll be able to make sure she returns my feelings."

I was dumbfounded. I'd been sure that, to be so taken with the creature, his dealings with her must have gone much farther than the first encounter at Montalto's house, which Raimondo had heard about from Caterina. So things were much worse than I'd thought. He really did love her. The devil was in the woman — she'd bewitched him!

"My lord," said Marcello suddenly, "my place is in that boat. I claim the honor of going with you."

"Oh, Marcello," said Paolo, putting his arm around the man and drawing him close, "you're a brave fellow. I knew it!"

I pretended to be looking out into the courtyard, so shocked was I by Paolo's familiarity with the wretch. Good God, he was treating him like a brother-in-law already. The world had turned upside down. And all because a scrap of skirt and a wisp of hair had struck this great Prince's fancy! A man who'd already had more women than an August night has stars. What did this female have that the others lacked? She was beautiful? A cow is beautiful, but I wouldn't let even my squire marry a cow!

I gradually recovered my composure, and, turning toward Paolo, even managed a smile.

"Well, *carissimo*, I see you're not to be persuaded against this crazy venture. May heaven protect you! I'll pray you aren't drowned. What an end that would be for a famous admiral!"

He laughed and embraced me before I left. I smiled again, but there was rage in my heart. I ran down the stairs, my hands clenched and my teeth set. Oh, Paolo, I thought, you don't deserve to live. You dishonor the Orsinis!

I couldn't believe his extraordinary frivolity. He'd summoned me just because he knew I was familiar with the country around Santa Maria. Apparently it hadn't occurred to him that I might be shocked by his plans concerning that loose woman. Worse still, before I dissuaded him, he'd been quite ready to engage in open war against the Pope, though that could only end in his ruin and mine as well, and of course that of our brother. How could anyone excuse, or even comprehend, such criminal blindness?

That night I had a dream. I can't call it a nightmare, because when I woke up and thought about it, I felt happy and peaceful and relieved of my fears. In my dream Paolo and the Peretti twins were at Santa Maria, being pursued by the papal army. It was night, and they were in a little boat trying to reach Paolo's galley, out at sea. But the boat struck a reef and started to fill with water. Marcello went under first. Vittoria's voluminous skirts held her up for a while, but she too gradually sank. Only Paolo survived, but a wave swept him onto a sharp rock, which cut off his penis. I was on board the galley when he was pulled out of the water. The ship's surgeon dressed his wound, and when he'd finished and I glanced at him inquiringly he said quietly, "He's only fainted. He'll live, but he's no longer a man." I looked at Raimondo, standing beside me, and said coldly, "Thank God." When I woke up, I went over the dream in my mind. After a while, I got up and wrote it down. I thought it might be prophetic, and I wanted to make a sort of appointment with the future.

## *Giulietta Accoramboni*

I now know the reason for our strict seclusion in the Rusticucci palace. And for the unbearable tension that resulted from it, for Vittoria's refusal to speak to her husband, and for our sudden departure for Santa Maria. What pains me is that instead of finding out from Vittoria, who seemed to have forgotten all the deep and time-honored bonds between us, I owe my enlightenment to Francesco Peretti. On the Cardinal's orders, he left his mother and mother-in-law behind in Rome (where no doubt the one will finally peck the other to death). At Santa Maria, since Vittoria still refused to speak to him, he's so isolated and desperate that he's forced to use me as a confidante.

So I know the story of the letter that was received, read, and burned — a story that takes on its full ominousness only when you know the sort of man Prince Orsini is, his power in the state, his reckless love of women, and his rash and rebellious character.

Francesco was reluctant to tell me everything. The Cardinal had made him promise never to reveal to his wife that he knew about the letter. No doubt His Eminence didn't want to give away his source of information, which was Father Racasi or Caterina Acquaviva, or perhaps both. Be that as it may, when Francesco told me about the infamous letter, he asked me to keep my lips sealed on the subject.

He made this request at the top of a watchtower we'd been exploring on the cliff. We looked down on a tiny inlet far below, where waves broke on rocks, producing masses of fleecy white foam. According to the majordomo at Santa Maria, it was in the privacy of this inlet that the bishop who owned the place before Montalto used to bathe. Sure enough, leaning out I could see, despite the spray, steps carved in the cliff for him to climb down to the little beach.

The watchtower must have been built in the days when this part of the coast, inhospitable though it is, used to fear incursions by Barbary pirates. This explanation was reinforced by the little stone sentry box in a corner of the platform where we were standing, whipped by a strong, chilly wind, although it was now May.

"My poor Francesco" — I spoke into his ear, for we were nearly deafened by the whistling of the wind and the crash of the waves — "I don't mind promising to keep it secret. It doesn't make any difference to me. But it was wrong of you to promise the Cardinal to do so. And it would be even more wrong of you to keep your word."

"Come out of the wind," he said, taking me by the hand. "I can hardly hear you."

He led me into the sentry box, where three small holes had been glassed over, and we were more sheltered. There was no door, however, so gusts swept in now and then.

I repeated what I'd said before, and Francesco listened, looking both anxious and puzzled. I felt sorry for him because Vittoria still wouldn't speak to him.

"Why shouldn't I have promised the Cardinal not to mention the letter?" he asked.

"Because when you speak to Vittoria, you

won't be able to mention the wrong she's done you either."

He looked at me. Kindness and sincerity and almost all other virtues were written over that honest face. All that was missing was strength.

"*Has* she done me any wrong?" he asked doubtfully.

I was amazed to see that not only was he still faithful to a wife no longer truly faithful to him, but also he wanted to think of her as being absolutely pure.

"Come now, dear friend," I said, holding him firmly by the arm, "it was you yourself who told me: she received a love letter sent by devious means and, knowing full well who'd written it and why, she opened it."

"But she burned it!" he cried, with so innocent a surge of hope that my heart felt a wrench.

"The fact of having burned it," I said, "doesn't alter the fact of having read it. And having enjoyed reading it, presumably, since she read it twice."

"But she confessed!" he said.

"To her priest. Not to you."

"She wouldn't have wanted to hurt me," he said, averting his eyes.

I was tired of seeing him cling to his illusions. It annoyed me, and I said, more roughly than I intended: "I suppose it's because she doesn't want to hurt you that, since March 19 she's closed her door to you."

He flinched, as if I'd struck him, blinked, disengaged his arm, and turned away, obviously ashamed to let me see his suffering. I reproached myself for having been so brutal, but I soon deflected these reproofs onto Vittoria. How could she, usually so magnanimous, be so cruel to him? But I knew my criticism didn't ring true. I'd just been harsh to Francesco myself. It was awful to be harsh to a man who was so kind. But he wasn't merely kind — he was soft, and it was the softness in his character that called forth that kind of response from a wife. Moreover, how could you blame a wife for not being sensitive to her husband's feelings when she was married to him against her will and didn't love him?

Francesco went and leaned against the wall and said flatly: "Wouldn't it be indelicate of me to show Vittoria I know something she's chosen to conceal from me?"

For a moment I was speechless. Poor Francesco! Such scruples! And how little he knew about women! Delicacy is a virtue they value highly in a man, but they seldom practice it themselves, especially when driven by passion or self-interest. And they prize it in a man only as a guarantee that he'll always treat them well, even when they no longer deserve it.

"Francesco," I said at last, "if you keep your promise and say nothing about the letter, you'll greatly weaken your position when the time comes for you to face up to Vittoria."

"Face up to her!" he exclaimed, wide-eyed. "The expressions you use, Giulietta! I've never sought a quarrel with Vittoria."

"She'll seek one with you, and it will be a quarrel on the grand scale, you may be sure. That's all the reward you'll get for your silence."

I was right. It happened in my presence the following day, in Vittoria's bedroom, which we were both trying to make more habitable. Francesco knocked, entered, and said good day. Then, turning to Vittoria, he asked her with unusual clumsiness if she was comfortable in her new home.

"Comfortable, sir?" she deigned to reply, scornfully, fixing him with glittering eyes. "I am very *un*comfortable! Horribly uncomfortable! The walls are damp. The ceilings are moldy. The windows don't shut properly. They had to be forced open, and the wood has swollen so much since that they won't shut again. I ask for a fire and I'm told there isn't any wood left, it will have to be sent for, and that will take time. To crown all," she added, her voice rising, "to crown all, sir, one of my trunks was lost on the journey, and I haven't anything left to wear. But what does that matter? Why should I dress myself up, for whom? I don't see anyone. First you cloistered me in my palace in Rome and now you imprison me in a wilderness."

She was superb in her vehemence, superb in her aroused beauty. Unfortunately, she was also superb in the sense in which the word had been applied to her mother in Gubbio — in the sense of arrogant.

"Madam," said Francesco in a strangled voice, "I think you know who advised that these measures be taken, and why?"

I thought the "why" would stop Vittoria, or at least give her pause, but no. Her anger leaped neatly over it and attacked the "who" instead.

"Who, sir?" she cried. "Who? Who else but the Cardinal interferes in our marriage and usurps, with your consent, the rights of a husband? It's true you're not much of a husband, and even less of a father."

She'd been shutting her door to him for a month and a half, and here she was reproaching him for not being adequate as a husband! The cruelty, the unfairness, and — why shouldn't I say it, despite my affection for her?

— the meanness of this attack paralyzed Francesco. If he summoned up the courage to stay, it was not so much to defend himself, still less to counterattack, as to vindicate his father.

"Madam," he said shakily, "you know the Cardinal loves you like a daughter, and you must realize that if he advised the measures you complain of, he did so because he thought your honor was in peril."

"My honor, sir!" cried Vittoria. "Since when, and for what reason, has my honor been suspect? Do you think the best way to protect it is to incarcerate me and have me guarded by soldiers?"

At one and the same time I admired her and was annoyed by her insolence. She now had the effrontery to raise the very question she hadn't dared answer before. And in the process of diabolically confusing the issue she had uttered a veiled threat. She had hinted that her present imprisonment was not the best way to preserve her virtue.

I had only to look at Francesco's honest face to know what was going on inside him. He was shrewd enough to see that Vittoria's pose of injured innocence was disingenuous. But far from holding it against her, he was embarrassed for her. He looked down at the floor. Oh, Francesco, I thought angrily, now or never is the time to lose your temper, to voice your bitterness, to humble your wife's arrogance. Now's the time to speak out about the letter, which caused the agitation she admitted to her confessor. And why don't you just mention in passing that no one knows which of you is responsible for the fact that your marriage is childless?

My hope was vain. How could a perfect gentleman break his word to the most venerated of fathers? He stood there miserably, as if he were the guilty party.

"You are silent, sir," said Vittoria. "And I think you are right to be. I ask you, for the first and last time, to stop treating me like a criminal, when I am guiltless. I insist that you take me back to Rome tomorrow."

Francesco seemed to be angry at last, by her use of the word "guiltless." Over the years, she'd gained the upper hand so firmly, however, that he was incapable of voicing his grievance. When he broke his silence, he didn't even speak sharply; he merely said, with regret: "Madam, that is not possible." With an awkward bow, he left.

Vittoria had taken the offensive on every point, and, although she wouldn't have her way about returning to Rome, she'd won considerable moral advantage. She'd managed to assume the role of an innocent young martyr unjustly persecuted by a cruel husband. The alleged persecution would come in handy as a retrospective excuse for the liberties she'd taken with her marital duties, and would permit her to stifle any stirrings of remorse she might have.

As for the Cardinal, recently so dear to her, she now saw him as a tyrant, punishing her for no reason. It was certainly true that Montalto was imperious and liked to control other people's lives. As soon as I was twenty-five, he had tried to make me choose between two prisons: marriage or a nunnery. But as far as Vittoria was concerned, it was His Eminence's great love for her that had made him fear the worst, and with good reason. If Vittoria had an ounce of good faith, she couldn't believe he'd acted without cause.

But that's women for you, the wretched sex to which I belong — all carnality and passion. A minute's encounter with a handsome warrior, a letter read and burned, and everything is changed. The kind, affectionate, decent Francesco becomes a cruel husband; the Cardinal, a terrible tyrant. And I, her lifelong friend, am cast aside as useless because she suspects I might not give her my wholehearted approval.

I looked at her. How beautiful she was in her loose and simple morning gowns, followed everywhere by her long hair! When Francesco had gone, she paced up and down the room, and every time she turned, her golden mane moved with her, swirling around her shoulders like a cape. What a magnificent human animal! What harmony of form, proportions, and features! What energy in her movements!

I sat in a corner with my hands clasped in my lap, saying nothing. I had mixed feelings about her. In a way, I found her beauty oppressive — what woman wouldn't feel inferior to her? — but at the same time, like everyone else, I admired her with all my heart. I was also frightened of this new Vittoria, who had made a clean sweep of her former affections, who was so resolute and ruthless in their destruction.

She stopped in front of me, looked me up and down, and said, almost aggressively: "Well, you don't say anything! What do you think of all this? Why don't you speak?"

My turn now, I thought. She'd said nothing to me about the letter. She hadn't been frank with me, but she wanted me to be frank with her. And the tone in which she demanded it! She'd forgotten one thing though: I wasn't a man. I was moved by her beauty, not blinded by it. And I'm not a coward. I could use my claws as well as she could. "If I don't say anything, Vittoria," I answered mildly, "it's because no one has said anything to me.

I don't know what to think."

"Well, you can see how I'm treated!"

"Yes indeed. You're guarded as if you were in great danger. What that danger is, I don't know."

"It doesn't exist!" she cried.

"That's not what the Cardinal seems to think, or your husband."

"Has Francesco spoken to you about it?"

"No, he hasn't! He's like you: his lips are sealed on the subject. But . . ."

"But what?"

"I noticed he seemed angry just now when you said you were guiltless."

"But I *am* guiltless!" she cried in a fury.

"You should know," I answered coolly.

"You know too," she said, her eyes blazing. "You seem to know my thoughts better than I do myself."

"Oh, Vittoria," I said, "I make no such claim. If I did, and it were true, there'd be no point in this conversation."

She shrugged, put her hands suddenly to her temples, and said in exasperation: "This hair is too heavy! It give me terrible headaches. I've made up my mind: I'm going to cut it off."

"This is hardly the moment to sacrifice your crowning glory."

"What do you mean?"

"Just what I say. No more, no less."

She threw me a hostile glance and started to pace back and forth again. After a while she stopped in front of me again and said: "This conversation has tired me. Leave me, please, Giulietta. I want to be alone."

I withdrew, and in the afternoon she sent Caterina to me with a curt note:

Dearest Giulietta,
I would be glad if you would refrain from visiting me in my room while I am at Santa Maria. I would also be obliged if you would keep Francesco company at meals. I don't intend to join you.
Affectionately, Vittoria

"Dearest Giulietta" indeed! And I took the final "Affectionately" for what it was worth. There was a lump in my throat when I read this note, in which she so regally announced my fall from favor. But I did not cry. I'd already guessed what she'd do. I'd joined her uncle and her husband on the scrap heap.

## Caterina Acquaviva

I could tell by the foul temper she was in on

217

the journey that the signora was sad and angry at being snatched away from Rome. But she wasn't the only one! I was losing Marcello, because it was decided he should be left behind. He was, after all, Prince Orsini's secretary and La Sorghini's guest. He wasn't even told the date of our departure, at least not by Signor Peretti. It was I who told him the day and the hour and the destination, as soon as the signora told me. If you ask me, she had an ulterior motive: she knew the terms I was on with Marcello. I think Signor Peretti would have been well advised not to let his wife know in advance where we were going. But the poor signore's always too good and too naïve; he doesn't know the tricks even the best women are capable of. It's true men are sometimes very wicked too. Who'd have thought, after I'd been so nice to them, that Raimondo and Silla would ever threaten to "make lace of my innards"?

For the moment anyway, I'm reduced, like the signora, to dreaming. Except that I'm really worse off than she is, for I doubt she's ever known what love is.

My only consolation is the fact that Il Mancino is here too. Peretti brought him along to fence with, for my brother, who excels at everything except honesty, is very good with his blade, and the master, who's put on a little weight, is trying to lose it by exercise.

Here at Santa Maria, though, Il Mancino — even I often call him that — doesn't talk to me much. When he does, it's only in whispered monosyllables, away from everyone else, and usually just to give me orders. And the way he looks at me, I don't feel at all like disobeying.

On the morning of May 3, he found me in the woodshed. It's been restocked at last, and I go there to fetch fuel for the signora.

"Caterina, have you noticed the watchtower on the cliff above the inlet?"

"Yes, Domenico."

"I went and had a look at it the day after we got here. It was empty. But I have a feeling they've put a lookout there since then. We must check."

I made a face. "You know what'll happen if I go up to the tower and there's a soldier there."

"Does that frighten you?"

You see what people are like? Just because I like men, my own brother hints that I'm a whore. He should talk! He lives off women!

"Yes," I said, "if he stinks of wine and garlic."

"Caterina," he said severely, "your scented gentlemen have gone to your head. You're forgetting your duty toward your older brother."

"Is it my duty toward my older brother to get myself laid by just anybody?"

"No need for that. If you take him some wine, he might rather have the bottle than you."

"I wouldn't have to go right to the top. I could easily hear if there was someone up there."

"No. You must talk to him. I want to know if there's a lookout at night as well as in the daytime."

"It's important for you to find out?"

"It's important for the people you love."

"Don't you love them too?"

"I'm doing it for the money," he replied, trying to look superior.

"Your whores aren't enough for you, then," I said sourly.

His eyes flashed. He went to the door of the woodshed and looked around. When he came back, he gave me a couple of slaps, one on each cheek, but not very hard. It wasn't that he didn't want to hurt me; he just didn't want to make a noise or leave a mark.

"That'll teach you to respect your brother, you cow!" he said. "I don't eat with a fork, I can't read, and I don't fornicate with noble ladies. But I *am* your brother, and don't forget it."

"I'm sorry, Domenico," I said, blushing

with shame because I'd been rude to one of my elders and betters.

His glance softened at once. "So you'll do as I say?"

"Yes."

"You're a good girl, Caterina. But you must watch your tongue. It works faster than your brain." He put his arms around me and drew me close. He's not more than an inch or two taller than I am, and very lean — there's much more of me than there is of him. But he's so strong I seem to melt in his arms. He kissed me, as usual, behind my ear and on my neck. Il Mancino is the only one of my brothers and sisters who's ever shown me any affection. It was a sad day for me when my mother made me sleep with my sisters instead of him. When he had nothing better to do, he used to carve dolls for me out of scraps of wood. Later on, after he'd become a bandit — I admired him a lot for that — he used to lie low sometimes at Grottammare. And whenever he went away again, he'd slip a coin into my hand and say, "Here you are, little doll. Buy yourself something to eat." Yet in those days he was usually broke.

Being a bandit isn't all it's thought to be. Father Racasi says it's very wrong to live off women, and since he knows a lot I suppose he must be right. But it brings in much more money than being a bandit, and it's not so risky.

Father Racasi had to stay in Rome to take care of his parish, and the Cardinal had given us a Franciscan as a confessor in his place. His name is Barichelli. He's dark and young still. But he's got so much hair you can hardly see his forehead, and so many whiskers his beard comes nearly up to his eyes. I've already confessed to him once. I guessed why he was here. Before he gave me absolution, he told me to remember my body was "only a piece of mud," and that one day I'd return to dust. No doubt that's true, but to judge by the way men look at me, my little piece of mud must be very attractive. When Father Barichelli lowers his eyes, I can't help wondering whether it's so he can meditate or take a peek at my nipples. If it's the first, as I'd like to believe, why do his nostrils start to quiver?

The signora refuses to see Father Barichelli, on the grounds that she wasn't consulted about the change of confessor. But clearly that's only an excuse: back in Rome she wouldn't see Father Racasi after the palace was segregated, because she suspected he'd been involved.

During the afternoon of the day Il Mancino gave me my orders, I went to the watchtower twice: once by stealth, to make sure there was somebody there, and the second time, more boldly, to take the lookout some wine. He was a young soldier belonging to the papal army, and he wasn't either ugly or dirty, only very shy. He was so impressed by my airs and graces and my elegant Italian that he didn't dare touch anything but my bottle of wine. I was partly flattered and partly disappointed. I let him have a drink but didn't leave the bottle with him, and I made him promise not to say anything about my visit. By questioning him skillfully, I found out that the watch started at dawn and ended at nightfall. I also learned that the lookout was supposed to give the alarm if he saw a ship approach the coast and launch a boat.

When I told Il Mancino all this, he listened with no expression and made no comment. Two days later, he came and said good-bye: he was riding to Rome with a letter to the Cardinal from Signor Peretti. But on May 8 he was back again. And the next day, when I went to fetch some wood — it was still cold — he crept up behind me in the woodshed, put his hand over my mouth, and kissed me on the neck. It was by the kiss that I knew who it was.

"Caterina," he said, "I have two things to ask you. The first is this: on the edge of the castle grounds, by the steps down the cliff to the beach, there's a little house. The doors and windows are secure, the roof is sound, and it has two fireplaces, one at each end. The bishop used it to undress in before he went bathing in the creek, and also to get dry and dress again afterward — that's why it's so well heated. I want you to go and see it, and then get Vittoria to go and stay there. Don't ask me why," he said curtly, "because I won't tell you."

"I'll try to persuade her," I said, "but it my be difficult. She's not easily influenced, to put it mildly."

"Insist," he said in a curious tone. "Be a bit mysterious."

These words, and the voice in which he uttered them, sent a little shiver down my spine.

"If you succeed," he said, "you'll have to sleep there too, of course. There are two rooms — well, really one room, divided by a curtain. And there are two windows looking out on the sea. On the night of May 12, whatever the weather, you're to put as many lighted candles in the windows as you can. Leave the shutters open, of course."

"And what am I to say to the Signora to explain all this?"

Il Mancino drew himself up and looked at me coldly. "Tell her what you like," he said.

"From now on, this is your affair, not mine. I haven't said anything. Do you hear, Caterina? I haven't said a word to you about this. I leave again for Rome tomorrow."

"So soon?" I said, throwing myself into his arms. He hugged me to him, planted his usual little kiss on my neck, and slipped away without another word. As soon as he'd gone and I'd thought over what he'd said, I trembled with joy, hope, and fear. My life in Santa Maria was taking a decidedly new turn.

Luckily, I had a couple of days in which to induce Vittoria to go and live in the little house on the cliff. I began by asking the majordomo if I could visit it, and after I'd given him a few little smiles, he agreed. I liked the place, and, at my request, he had a fire lighted in the two fireplaces. They drew very well. As soon as the flames had taken hold, he sent away the servant he'd brought with him and started fondling me. I let him: from the look of him, I didn't think he'd be able to get very far. Sure enough, after a few moments and much gasping for breath, he stopped. But he seemed very pleased with himself, and thanked me for my kindness. When I asked him, he lent me the key to the house.

I didn't dare speak to Vittoria about it right away. She was in a very bad temper. She wouldn't speak a word and still refused to see Signor Peretti, Father Barichelli, or Giulietta.

I overheard her quarrel with Giulietta. Poor Giulietta! Why did she have to defend the Cardinal and Signor Peretti? She *will* always judge people! As I think I've said before, she criticizes me for showing off my bosom. Opportunity would be a fine thing for her. But she's a typical spinster. It's not that she's ugly, though she *is* a bit scraggy. It's that Vittoria is too beautiful. Giulietta grew up in the shade of a lovely plant that drank up all the sun and left her pale and weak in comparison. When she and her cousin are in the same room, who wants to look at her? If you ask me, a woman needs men to look at her from the very first minute she's born. She needs warmth to be able to grow properly.

Sometimes I'm seized with terror at the thought that one day I'll be old and won't have that warmth any more. Father Barichelli thinks he's clever when he threatens me with the torments of hell. One day I'll be in my own hell while I'm still alive. I'm in it already when I just say the words "One day I'll be old."

The watchtower, the little house on the edge of the cliff, the candles in the windows, the steps down to the beach — I wasn't a fool; I had a good idea of who was going to turn up on the night of May 12. All I hoped was that he wouldn't be alone.

But I hesitated to tell Vittoria what my brother had said. Since she hadn't received any more letters — I'd have known if she had — and had declared she was "guiltless," I didn't know how she'd take my revelation. My mother was right when she said noblewomen are very proud and feel they owe it to themselves to have airs and graces and virtue. Finally I decided not to tell her anything unless she positively refused to go and live in the little house. Dear God, the way things turn out! To think of me, and my great respect for Signor Peretti, helping his wife to be unfaithful to him! I'd never have done such a thing if it hadn't been for my brother and Marcello. Those two can make me do anything they like.

The signora put all the blame for the restrictions at the Rusticucci palace and the move to Santa Maria on Father Racasi. She hadn't the slightest suspicion about my reports to the Cardinal. And I was the only person she wasn't surly with. Ever since she'd refused to have her meals with Signor Peretti and Giulietta, she'd made me eat with her in her room. She also gave me presents of clothes and jewelry almost every day. I was really quite ashamed sometimes, she was so kind and generous. Well . . . kind? Yes and no. She was always kind to me. But how she treats her husband!

On May 10, very early in the morning, I asked the majordomo to have the house on the cliff thoroughly cleaned and to make a good fire. Then, while I was combing Vittoria's hair, I told her of my "discovery." She hadn't left her room for a week, and was dying of boredom in spite of Petrarch, so she was interested. But she made some objections. She didn't want to go through the grounds: the soldiers were camped there, and she didn't want to set eyes on her jailers.

"But, signora," I said, "they're not in that part of the grounds at all. And there's a path that goes around by the wall. That's the way I went, and I didn't see any soldiers."

I didn't mention that they'd certainly seen me. There was a covered way all around the parapet, with little turrets here and there that were bound to contain sentries.

Either my arguments or the desire to stretch her legs finally won her over. The sun was shining for the first time that rainy spring as I took her to see the little house. She fell in love with it at once, and started talking again. It didn't smell nearly as musty as the castle, she said. And it was so cheerful, the way the fireplaces faced each other. You were so near the sea you felt you were almost on it. What did she need with a castle, when it was only a prison to her? A little cottage was ample. She'd never been afraid of solitude, or, thank God, of poverty.

I agreed with everything she said, but thought about it later. Fancy talking of poverty with the sort of meals we were served! And calling it a "cottage!" — you could tell she'd never set foot in a house like the one I was born in. To me, the cottage on the cliff was a veritable palace.

I didn't even have to suggest that she move there. She decided on that herself, right away. She didn't consult Signor Peretti — she knew he wouldn't dare utter a word against it. She just sent for the majordomo and gave her orders there and then. He was to bring everything that was needed: carpets, hangings, her dressing table, her trunks and two beds. Now, at once! She reminds me of her mother when she orders people about like that.

She was happy and busy supervising all that day. The dressing table must be put there! No, there! The bed would be much better in this corner! Send someone to check that the cistern's full. It was. Stock the woodshed! We soon had enough wood for a whole winter. Clear the overgrown patch of land in front of the cottage. It was done. But don't touch the trees at the back — they hid the view of hated Santa Maria. I felt like saying the view wouldn't bother her anyway, because there weren't any windows on that side of the house. But I wasn't going to tell her, either, that, though it seemed a perfectly good place for the bishop to dress and undress in, and for having a light meal after a swim, it struck me as drafty, inelegant, and, despite the bright sunshine, rather sinister. It was only about ten feet from the edge of the cliff, which at that point fell in a sheer drop down to the sea. I wouldn't have done what Vittoria did for anything: she went and stood on a rocky spur hanging right over empty air and the waves breaking on the rocks far below. The tiny promontory was covered with long grass that I was sure must be slippery when it rained. Just to the right were the steps leading down to the beach.

The next day the sky was clear and the sun bright and hot. Vittoria, who'd recovered all her usual energy after our first night in the little house, decided to bathe in the sea. Naturally, I was supposed to go with her, to follow her down those horrible steps. I nearly died of fright! What did we find at the bottom? Just a tiny beach, about five feet by ten, with a little cave nearby.

"That shows the cliff is full of holes and

could collapse at any moment," I said.

"How stupid you are!" Vittoria said. "In two or three centuries, perhaps, at the very earliest."

But I soon got even. No sooner had she dipped one foot in the sea than she took it out again: the water was freezing! And because the little beach was in the shade in the morning, she was cold in nothing but her thin bathing shift. So we went back again. Although going up was not so bad as going down, I suffered almost as much. As soon as we were on the little promontory, I fell down with my face in the rough grass and wept.

"No one would think you were the daughter of a master fisherman," Vittoria said.

Cross about the unsuccessful trip to the beach, she was in a bad temper again. And the next day was even worse. When I opened the shutters, I couldn't see one bit of blue sky. Everything was gray; low, threatening clouds and a leaden sea covered with whitecaps. It was very chilly, and gusts of rain dashed every so often against the windows. As soon as I'd folded the shutters against the inside walls, I drew aside the red silk curtain that divided the room, stoked both fires, and made both beds. Vittoria, meanwhile, stood at the window, looking out at the sea. When I'd finished, she walked to and fro for a while, repressed a sigh, and sat down on a little chair by the fire. Then she plunged into her Petrarch.

I could see that the enthusiasm for the little house, and for the cheerful way the fireplaces faced each other, was over. The walls pressed in on her, and the nearness of the sea, so delightful yesterday, now got on her nerves. She wished she were back in the Rusticucci palace. Who knows if she didn't wish she were back in the castle at Santa Maria? But she'd never admit it. She was too proud. She relapsed into silence, and that meant I couldn't say anything either. This was disagreeable: partly because I'm talkative by nature and partly because I was anxious. That evening I was supposed to put the candles in the windows, "whatever the weather," Domenico had said.

It was the weather that was worrying me. I felt very gloomy as I stood brushing Vittoria's hair. It took a good hour and a light hand: her scalp was so sensitive, because of the weight of her hair. But in order not to be left with nothing to do, which I dreaded, I made the brushing last as long as possible. Unfortunately, Vittoria was obviously on edge too; she grew impatient and told me to stop. I put the brush away and, while I was there, tidied the dressing table. For the first time, I wished I did the washing and ironing —

that might have stopped the silly ideas I was fretting over. I have such a vivid imagination. I'd just had a vision of my poor Marcello, all white, his eyes shut, being washed up by a wave.

"Signora," I said, "with your permission —"

"Oh, Caterina," she cried, "you are a nuisance! Must you keep talking? You can see I'm trying to read."

Read or dream? I hadn't noticed her turning the pages very often. I'm not stupid. And I've got eyes.

"Forgive me, signora, but with your permission I'd like to clean your jewelry."

"I cleaned it myself not long ago."

"Gold can never shine too brightly, signora."

"All right, clean it then, clean it, if it'll keep you occupied!" she said, shrugging. "But for goodness' sake don't make a noise! And stop tearing around the room!"

"Yes, signora."

I put a small saucer of soapy water and another with a sponge on it on one of the broad wooden windowsills, took the jewels out of their casket and spread them on a red cloth. I'd have enjoyed myself if I hadn't been so worried. The windowsill came to my waist, a comfortable height for what I was doing. And I was looking straight out over the sea, which would have been very pleasant if it had been calmer.

When I'd finished cleaning one of the rings, I glanced at Vittoria — she wasn't turning the pages any more often than before — and slipped it on my little finger. That was the only one it would fit. Still, the ring looked just as good on mine as it did on her slender finger. So do the necklaces. I try them on when I'm alone in her room, so I can look at myself in the dressing-table mirror. The effect they make on my pretty bosom is enough to make anyone's mouth water! Especially the pearls: they show to great advantage on my smooth dark skin. I've got such a pretty neck, round and soft and without a wrinkle, that I don't know how any man worthy of the name could see my neck with a beautiful necklace around it and not want to cover it with kisses.

I was a little ashamed of forgetting my anxiety when there in front of me the sky was getting darker and darker and the sea rougher. I could hear the waves crashing like drums at the foot of the cliff, and the wrench of the shingle as they receded. It felt as if the cliff was trembling beneath me, but it probably wasn't. The truth is, I'd never set foot on a boat, and never bathed in salt water. At home in Grottammare, it's regarded as unhealthy.

When the majordomo and three or four of

his staff brought our midday meal, Vittoria was obliged to open her lips, if only to eat and to thank the majordomo for his trouble. When he'd gone, she glanced out the window and said idly: "I hope the weather improves."

"Oh, yes," I answered fervently. "I hope so too, with all my heart!"

She looked at me, surprised by my tone. But, afraid I'd said too much, I fell silent and looked down at my plate.

The afternoon was awful. The weather didn't improve. It got worse. Rain fell in torrents and the wind raged, throwing such violent gusts against the windows that water seeped in underneath. The sill on which I'd cleaned the jewelry was flooded. I mopped the water up with rags, which I then stuffed as best I could between the wood and the stone. It didn't keep the rain out altogether, but it helped.

It got much worse when the storm really broke. What with the noise of the waves and the peals of thunder, the din was deafening. I was sitting idle on a low chair by the fire, starting at each flash of lightning. How I wished Vittoria was frightened too, so we could cling together for comfort. In the Rusticucci palace, in the winter, she sometimes used to ask me to get into bed with her, because she was always cold and I was always warm. I loved that!

I glanced at her now and then. Did she jump when the lightning lit up the windows and the thunder growled as if it would never stop? Not at all. She sat there as calm as a Madonna, with her feet on a little stool and her golden hair hanging down behind her chair and carefully arranged by me on the carpet. I was the one who'd have to comb it out if it got tangled! And that was a devil of a job, I can tell you.

She was wearing a pale-blue house gown, very comfortable, for it didn't have hoops or petticoats underneath. She was beautiful, flawless. Even I, who've almost never been away from her for years, have never got used to her loveliness. Sometimes when I look at her I can't believe my eyes. I say to myself, it's impossible for a woman to be so beautiful!

Undisturbed by the roaring sea, the howling wind, the fall of thunderbolts, she was either reading or dreaming. Sometimes she'd let her book fall into her lap and sit staring into space, her lips moving. She might have been praying. But she wasn't. I knew what she was doing: she was learning one of those Petrarch sonnets by heart. In the Rusticucci palace she sometimes recited one aloud when everyone was bustling around washing her hair in a tub. The way she spoke it was very pretty, but I can't understand that kind of Italian.

Late in the afternoon, I heard a noise outside. Through a window, I saw Signor Peretti, rain streaming down his bare head and over his shoulders. Then there was a knock at the door. But when, at a sign from Vittoria, I opened it, it was the majordomo who entered. I had to use all my strength against the wind to shut the door behind him.

"Signora," said the majordomo, bowing low, "Signor Peretti earnestly requests you to spend tonight in the castle because of the storm."

"Thank him, majordomo," she answered loftily, "but this house is quite sound, and I feel as safe here as I do in the castle."

"Signora," said the majordomo awkwardly, "Signor Peretti told me to insist."

"Insisting will make no difference," said Vittoria with a scornful smile, "I've made up my mind. I shall stay here."

The majordomo bowed and withdrew. I opened the door to let him out, and through the crack I could see him shouting into Signor Peretti's ear, because of the hellish uproar of wind and waves. Signor Peretti, wondering, probably, whether he should speak to his wife himself, took a couple of steps toward the door. But then he turned and went away. I thought that was a mistake.

I was sure of it a few minutes later, when

Vittoria looked up from her book and said: "What a poor specimen of a husband I've got! Afraid of the rain and a few flashes of lightning. Instead of coming himself, he sends his majordomo."

"But, signora," I said, "Signor Peretti wasn't afraid. He was there, outside the door — I saw him. He was soaking wet. He just didn't like to come in because you've said you won't see him."

She looked at me, and suddenly her great blue eyes filled with tears. "What?" she said, her voice faint and plaintive. "You too, Caterina? So you're against me as well?"

I was shattered by her tone, by her tears, by the way she looked at me. I threw myself at her feet, seized her hands, and covered them with kisses. "Oh, no, signora!" I cried. "I'll always be on your side, whatever happens." I started weeping too. She took her hands away and stroked my hair. I felt so happy kneeling there with my face in the folds of her gown.

After a while she said gently: "There, there, it's all over. We've made up. You're a good girl, Caterina."

I went back to my seat by the fire. Yes, I was a good girl. Everyone said so. And perhaps they took advantage a little. But what I'd said was true too. I *had* seen Signor Peretti standing in the rain and looking miserable outside his wife's door, not daring to come in. I didn't see how it was betraying her and being "against" her to tell her so.

At about six o'clock the wretched major-domo, accompanied by four servants, came through the pelting rain to bring us our evening meal. I gave the old boy a smile on the sly, which pleased him. I noticed that Vittoria too, knowing how much trouble she was giving him, was very gracious once more. He went away drenched to the skin but enchanted. As he left I'd given him another smile. Amazing that I could still enjoy playing such tricks in the midst of all that nervousness and anxiety.

Night was falling, and it was time for me to follow Domenico's instructions and put as many candles as I could in the windows — without closing the shutters, of course. I did so with some apprehension, for it was a very strange thing to do, especially with the gale rattling the window panes.

"Have you gone crazy, Caterina?" said Vittoria, looking up from her book. "What are the candles for? You'd do better to close the shutters."

"Signora," I said gravely, "I'm thinking of the people at sea." I'd prepared this answer beforehand.

"But you're not at Grottammare now."

"We didn't have candles at Grottammare, signora. In the winter we had only the light of the fire. When we needed more light, we just put a few more twigs on."

"My dear Caterina, put out those candles! They might as well not be there, with the lightning flashing all the time."

"Excuse me, signora, but you've been reading and haven't noticed. The thunder stopped some time ago, and there isn't any more lightning."

"What does that matter?" she said. "Why must you keep arguing? Just do as I tell you!"

I looked at her. "Forgive me, signora, I want to ask you a question. I've been in your service for nine years. Have I been a devoted and affectionate maid to you?"

"Of course. But that's no reason why I should indulge all your whims and fancies."

"Oh, signora," I cried earnestly, "it's not a whim. It's a matter of life and death!"

My seriousness surprised her. She looked at me and hesitated. But the habit of command got the better of her, and she said curtly: "Now then, Caterina, no nonsense, please. Do as you're told! Put out the candles and close the shutters!"

I was cornered. I stared at her in terror, not knowing what to say or do. Our eyes met, and she sensed and was intrigued by the strength of my resistance.

"I can't make you out, Caterina," she said more mildly. "You're not usually so obstinate."

"Oh, signora, forgive me!" I cried. "But suppose your brother Marcello was at sea in such weather. Wouldn't you like him to see lights in the distance to guide him to you?"

She was astonished, so astonished that, in her place, I'd have asked a few questions. I thought for a minute she was going to. But that's just what she didn't do! She shrugged and said nonchalantly — or seemingly so: "Oh, well, do as you like. I'm tired of arguing. But remember, Caterina, I shan't overlook your waywardness another time."

I heaved a deep sigh. "No, signora. Thank you, signora. Forgive me, signora."

I was all repentance, gratitude, and humility. I could afford to let her bear off the honors now that she'd given in. She was soon deep in her book again, but I'm sure she wasn't reading a line of it. She was asking herself all the questions she'd have liked to ask me.

At least she had her book. I just sat on my little low chair with nothing to do, clasping and unclasping my hands in my lap, knowing I'd get up and move around had I been the mistress instead of the maid. When the signora's nerves got the better of her, she paced up and down, and no one said her nay. But if I did that I was "tearing around" and a nuisance.

Minutes went by, perhaps hours — who knows? Anyhow, it was late, very late. I watched the candles in the windows, their tall flames quivering in the draft. They'd already burned down by about a third, and the wicks were beginning to smoke. That gave me something to do: I got up and trimmed them. Then I blew up both fires with the bellows and threw more logs on. And that gave me away. At bedtime, even in winter, people don't put more logs on the fire; they cover the ones that are there with ashes. But Vittoria, though she'd been watching me, didn't ask any questions.

I sat down again and, to tell the truth, grew more terrified every minute. True, I'd never been on a boat, but I was a fisherman's daughter and had heard plenty of tales about storms and shipwrecks.

Vittoria turned toward me. "Why haven't you gone to bed yet, Caterina?"

I could have asked the same; I'd never known her to sit up so late.

"I'm not tired, signora."

Our eyes met. She looked away. She didn't say anything more, and neither did I. In this world, only men are allowed to tell the truth.

Women are taught hypocrisy in their cradles. So there we sat together, silent, though each of us knew full well why the other was trembling. I could tell she was frightened too. She had more self-command than I had, but her face was drawn, her eyes were anxious, and her book lay idle on her lap. She'd stopped pretending to read.

Suddenly someone banged on the door, and a voice shouted: "Open up! Open up! It's me — Marcello!"

I ran and opened it, and there was Marcello in the doorway. He was scarcely able to stand and soaking wet. His doublet was torn, and there was blood running down his cheek.

"Come and help me with the Prince," he gasped. "He fell just as we got to the top of the cliff."

"Is he dead?" cried Vittoria.

"No, no!" said Marcello.

Without stopping to throw on a cloak, Vittoria flew out of the room like a madwoman, right into a terrible wall of wind and rain. Marcello followed her, and I followed him. Even with all three of us, it was no easy matter to carry a man of the Prince's size back to the house. Finally, we laid him down in front of the fire, and with unspeakable relief I closed the door. Vittoria was already kneeling on the hearth rug, cradling Orsini's head on her bosom.

"He's only fainted," said Marcello. "He was coming up the steps in front of me, and tripped. He must have fallen on his bad leg, and the pain made him pass out.

We were all like drowned rats. I gazed in horror at Vittoria's blond locks, flattened and tangled by the rain.

"We must get his clothes off," said Marcello, "or he'll catch cold."

"But you're hurt too, signore," I said to him. "Your cheek is bleeding."

"It's nothing. A wave banged my head against a rock."

"A wave?" I said. "Didn't you come by boat?"

He managed to laugh. "It broke up when we hit the inlet."

"Stop chattering, Caterina, and help me!" Vittoria said impatiently.

I helped her undress the Prince. It wasn't easy, because he was so heavy. Then we rubbed him down with towels. He was a fine figure of a man, as well made and muscular as a statue. The wound in his thigh was bleeding, but the color soon came back into his face.

"Caterina," Vittoria ordered, "warm some wine and give him a drink."

She rose, drew the red silk curtain across

the room, and went behind it. I poured wine into a pewter tankard, added a lump of sugar, and put it in the embers.

"Blow the candles out, Caterina," said Marcello. "The Prince told the captain of the galley we'd put them out if we got safely ashore."

"I thought your boat broke up."

He laughed.

"Not the galley, silly. The little boat we tried to come ashore in."

"Let me wipe the blood off your cheek, signore."

"It'll dry by itself. Better go help Vittoria undress, and rub her down too. I'll give the Prince the wine."

I went to the other side of the curtain, where Vittoria was already as naked as the day she was born and drying herself with a towel. I twisted her hair up and wrapped it in another towel, holding it away from her back so she could dry it.

"How is he?"

"Better, signora. He's opened his eyes. As soon as he's had the wine, he'll be himself again."

"God be praised," she murmured.

I wouldn't have praised God for that, even in a whisper.

"Signora," I said, "you ought to sit by the

fire and let your hair dry properly."

"Sit," she said, "when he's braved death to reach me?"

She hastily threw on a simple gown that she got out of the trunk herself while I held her hair out behind her. I put another towel over her shoulders and let her hair fall free. The damp would soon go through both towel and gown, but what could I do?

The signora was unrecognizable. Who had ever said her eyes were cold? In that room, lit only by the glow from the fire, they looked as if they were shooting forth flames. As she went around to the other side of the curtain — where sin awaited her — she seemed to be dancing on air.

I shivered, and remembered that I too was drenched to the skin. Before I undressed, I put log after log on the fire, stoking up the flames till they reminded me of the hell that threatened all four of us, if I was to believe Father Racasi. But I only half believed him. It was bad enough to have to die one day; if we had to look forward to eternal torment as well, what price divine mercy?

Hell or no hell, as I was taking off my bodice and skirt I suddenly started to feel gloomy, despite the fact that Marcello was there on the other side of the curtain. It was man, not God, who frightened me. The very second the signora committed adultery, it would become Signor Peretti's duty to kill her. And me, too, as her accomplice. Worse still, if I didn't betray her guilt when I confessed to Father Racasi, it would be a bad confession and I'd be damned. This business would mean death for Marcello too: he wasn't a nobleman, and he had suborned his sister. Only the Prince would escape, because he was a prince. Dear God, was that justice?

My mood changed completely as soon as I was naked. I turned around and around in front of the fire, and as the warmth spread through me, so did intense joy. Why couldn't I just live happily without asking myself questions? Like a pretty little dog lying in front of the fire with her muzzle between her paws.

A hand raised a corner of the red silk curtain, and Marcello came to my side of it. I restrained my impulse to rush toward him; I could see at a glance that this wasn't the moment. For a man who'd just emerged from a brush with death, he didn't look upset or even tired. His face was expressionless. But I knew him. If I went near him now, he'd push me away. I knew what I had to do. I went and curled up by the fire, taking as little room as possible and not saying a word. I didn't even look at him.

Marcello undressed absentmindedly and in

silence, hanging his doublet and hose over the stools to dry. Then he warmed himself back and front by the fire, but apparently without experiencing the pleasure I'd felt. I glanced at him now and then, but only briefly. He's as sensitive as a woman and guesses everything. He was in a foul temper, and I began to be afraid he was going to let me crouch in front of the fire all night without touching me. Yet this was all his doing, right from the start! If it hadn't been for him, none of tonight's events would ever have happened. And there he was, silent, tense, and solemn. How complicated these people were! He and Vittoria were just the same. But she was a woman, so I could more or less figure her out. But him?

Suddenly he came over to me. Without a word, he grabbed me by the hair with one hand and put the other over my mouth, just like the first time. Then he pulled me to my feet, shoved me over to the bed, and roughly possessed me. He lay there with all his weight on me, looking at me with blazing eyes and whispering in my ear: "If you cry out at the end, as you usually do, I'll strangle you. Do you hear?" He clutched both my arms so hard I'd have groaned with the pain if I'd dared. At the same time, although his distorted face hung directly over me, he refused to kiss me.

He just gasped, as he came and went inside me, "You're just a little whore, and I hate you!" But suddenly he could have done and said anything he liked, as far as I was concerned, beat me black and blue, crush me to death, insult me. Everything changed to bliss.

When he'd finished, he withdrew and rolled to one side, overcome by fatigue. He just shut his eyes and slept like a babe. I propped myself on my elbow to look at him. The fire cast a red glow on his naked body. He was superb. And when he was asleep, he was mine, the fool! He'd had his little male triumph, but my pleasure still went on; I could feel its traces inside me. I wouldn't change places with you, Marcello, and it's your little whore who tells you so.

I laughed silently. That's what I was like now: I made love without crying out and I laughed without making a noise. That's how men like us to be. Even the signora fell into line, to judge by the silence reigning on the other side of the curtain. That must have been my last thought before I fell asleep. When I woke up in the morning, I was thinking the same thing.

# 6

## *Aziza the Wasp*

Paolo refused at first when I asked him to let me go with him on the galley taking him to the launching point off Santa Maria. Then he remembered I was a good sailor after being his servant so long at sea, and he gave in. He agreed, soon afterward, to let Lodovico go too, but reluctantly and, it seemed to me, less out of friendship than because of his superstitious respect for family bonds. I was proved right when, before transferring to the little boat to go ashore, he handed command of the galley, not to Lodovico, but to the mate. And he gave the mate his instructions privately, in a whisper.

The voyage from Naples to Santa Maria took three days. The nearer we got to our destination, the rougher the sea became, and the more worried I got about the danger of Paolo's venture. But knowing how set he was on it, I didn't say anything. I didn't even let him see how terrified I was, but stayed, up to the last minute, as cheerful, lively, and obedient as I'd always been, and as he liked me to be. He made love to me twice during the voyage, which astonished as well as delighted me. It also made me feel humiliated, in a way. For obviously there wasn't the slightest connection, for him, between what he was doing with me and his great love for Vittoria.

As we were approaching Santa Maria, Lodovico sent Folletto to ask Paolo if he could speak to him. Before agreeing, Paolo told me to lie on his bunk with the curtains drawn and listen carefully without being seen or heard. I did so, but through a gap in the curtains I kept an eye on Lodovico. Paolo asked him to sit down opposite him at the little table fixed to the floor, at which he took his meals. All I could see of Paolo was the back of his right shoulder, but I could guess what his expression was from the tone of his voice, which I knew so well. All the time they were talking, I lay clutching the edge of the bunk with both hands, because the galley was pitching and tossing, and every so often I could hear huge waves crashing against the hull, and the beams creaking and groaning.

"Paolo," said Lodovico, "you see what the weather's like! Don't tell me you still mean to launch a boat in the dark and go ashore with that intriguer. It would be madness."

"If Marcello was only an intriguer, would he be sharing in my folly?" said Paolo. "Intriguers aren't usually keen on risking their own skins. You ought to know that."

"Never mind about Marcello," said Lodovico. "You must see for yourself there's a raging sea, and you're bound to perish."

"We all have to die someday," said Paolo jokingly. "Come to think of it, what have I got to live for?"

"You have a duty to Virginio."

"He's amply provided for in my will. And because I was always away at sea, he was brought up by his uncles and is more of a Medici now than an Orsini."

"He's still your son."

"And you're my first cousin," said Paolo ironically. "And Medici's my brother-in-law. We're a very united family."

"Please, Paolo, be serious! I had a terrible dream the other night about this mad escapade. The boat was sinking on its way back to the galley, and Marcello, Vittoria, and you were all drowning."

"That would be very sad for us," said Paolo, still speaking lightly. "And for you too, Lodovico."

"Can you doubt it, Paolo?" said Lodovico, with what sounded to me a very hollow ring.

"No, not in the least. I know I've been a good kinsman to you, *carissimo* — open and generous. Though I fear Virginio wouldn't be the same, much as you've been taking his interests to heart lately."

"Why do you say that, Paolo?" asked Lodovico, uneasy.

"Because Virginio's a Medici now, as I said. And the Medicis, being bankers, keep a tight hold on their purse strings."

"You're being unfair to me and to them, Paolo. You don't like the Medicis."

"On the contrary. I like them very much. But I have a grudge against them for badgering me to kill their sister after she was unfaithful to me."

"You did it in the end," said Lodovico. "And for reasons that are perhaps less honorable."

"A great deal could be said, cousin, about the honor of the elder branch of the Orsinis. And about that of the younger branch too."

I sensed a cutting edge to the Prince's voice that meant there was a certain kind of smile on his face. Lodovico reacted to his tone too, and his face tensed for a moment. But he managed to control himself.

"You can't deny, Paolo," he went on coldly, "that you decided to kill Isabella only after you'd met Vittoria Peretti."

"The decision followed the meeting, but, contrary to what you and Raimondo may suppose, it wasn't a consequence of it. I'd made up my mind before I wrote to Vittoria, and before she gave me her ring to plight her troth. I'd already received reports from the major-domo at Bracciano that Isabella was giving herself to muleteers and scullions. The scandal had to stop."

This was a great surprise to me. Up till then, I'd thought the same as Lodovico. But knowing how truthful the Prince was, I couldn't doubt what he'd just said. Lodovico didn't believe him, though — that was obvious from the look on his face. It was a strange face. At first glance it was attractive, but in the long view its vulgarity made it seem ugly.

"I believe what you say, since it's you who say it," said Lodovico in a tone that hovered somewhere between insolence and suavity. "Let's leave Isabella out of it. Paolo, I appeal to your common sense! Look at the sea. You don't stand a chance in a hundred of getting ashore. How can you commit such folly?"

"Because I love Vittoria," said Paolo, still in the ironical tone he'd been using throughout this conversation.

"How can you love her when you've seen her for only a couple of minutes?"

"There," replied Paolo as before, "we're talking about one of the mysteries of the human heart."

He laughed and stood up. Then, putting his arm around Lodovico's shoulders with every appearance of the warmest affection, he led him to the door. As soon as his cousin was outside, he locked it behind him.

To my great surprise and delight, he came over, drew the curtain, and lay down beside me, slipping his arm around my neck and putting my little head on his strong shoulder.

"Well, Aziza, my wasp," he said with a smile, "what do you think of my fine cousins?"

"A couple of leeches, good-for-nothings. But they're not the same. Il Bruto, in spite of his nickname, isn't altogether heartless, and he does feel some affection for you. Lodovico, on the other hand, is just a snake. He's never been grateful for all you've done for him, and now that you've cut off supplies, he hates you."

"Why do you think he wanted so much to come with me?"

"To report to the Medicis and Virginio."

"Very shrewd, my wasp. Your black eyes aren't the only things that are sharp about you."

"Sharp she may be, but the wasp doesn't understand everything. For instance, knowing what you do, why did you let him come with you?"

"It's in my own interest to handle him carefully. If it ever comes to open war with the Pope, he and his brother and the rest of his family would represent a considerable amount of support. What's more, Lodovico has the ear of the people, and without their support no rebellion is possible."

I listened. He spoke calmly, even cheerfully. Yet at nightfall he was going to trust his life to a nutshell on a raging sea. "A chance in a hundred," Lodovico had said. What would become of me if he died? Would Virginio sell me to another master? By Almighty God, I couldn't bear it! I still had the little dagger Abensur gave me, from which I got my nickname. And there and then, with my head on my adored Prince's chest, I vowed to myself that I wouldn't survive him.

"Any other questions, my wasp?" said Paolo.

"Yes."

Oh, how I've come to regret that "yes"! What torture I'd have been spared if I'd never uttered it. What madness seized me, to want to fathom Paolo's feelings? If only I'd answered "no," I know well what would have happened. The roughness of the sea kept throwing us together on the narrow bunk. And the desire I could feel stirring within me, as well as the terrible risk he was about to run, would have excited him too.

Instead, I was as stupid as a real wasp banging itself against a windowpane. I asked the same absurd question Lodovico had already asked, and Paolo had evaded with a jest: How could he love Vittoria when he'd seen her for only a couple of minutes?

This time, unfortunately, Paolo didn't evade the question. He answered with a sincere and circumstantial account, uttered with fervor and enthusiasm and without an inkling of how much he was hurting me. For he really was a good master — fair, patient, and considerate.

"You know," he said, wedging his wounded leg against the side of the bunk, "when I met Vittoria at Montalto's house, that wasn't the first time I'd seen her. I first set eyes on her several years before, when she was still living in Gubbio. I was riding through the little town at the head of a large troop of soldiers. With some time to spare, I asked a well-dressed passerby what the finest sight was in the place. He was a very old man, but his black eyes sparkled when he answered.

" 'Some will tell you it's the ducal palace, but I say it's Vittoria Accoramboni. As it happens,' he added, 'I'm on my way to see her now. It's Tuesday, and every Tuesday and

257

Saturday afternoon Vittoria has her wonderful hair washed. When it's sunny, like today, she dries it on a balcony overlooking the street. It's a sight not to be missed, and, let me tell you, as long as my poor old legs will carry me *I* won't miss it! So if you want to see it too, signore, just come along with me.'

"I was very taken by this ancient: so close to his end and still going out of his way, quite disinterestedly, to contemplate feminine beauty. Delighted and amused, I dismounted and threw my reins to my squire. Then I walked along with the old man at his own slow and tottering pace. On the way, he told me his name was Pietro Muratore: he was a frame-maker, and said wryly that his frames were often more beautiful than the pictures they were intended for. Because of my buffalo-hide doublet, he took me for an ordinary captain and spoke to me quite familiarly. I didn't tell him who I really was for fear of embarrassing him.

"Vittoria Accoramboni was sitting on a low stool, her incredibly long fair hair spread out behind her on a kind of frame. A little Moorish slave girl kept the sun off her lovely face with a big white umbrella, which she shifted from one hand to another as she got tired. Her mistress wore a loose pale-blue gown with folds that fell freely about her like an Ionian tunic.

Her bare feet pointed up the resemblance to a Greek goddess: they were perfectly shaped, and plain for all to see on a little footrest outside the shade of the umbrella. No doubt she liked to feel the warmth of the sun on them, and didn't mind if they got brown.

"According to what Muratore had told me beforehand — he was now speechless in contemplation — Vittoria had just turned fifteen. But she was already a picture of womanly beauty. The slave girl didn't look more than ten. She too was very pretty, small and well formed, with a clear pale complexion, hair like a raven's wing, big black eyes, a small nose, and a large mouth."

"Like me!" I cried, with very mixed feelings.

"Yes, Aziza. And, as you'll see, the resemblance plays a part in the story. The little Moor struck me as an important element in the picture before us. It was as if a great artist had put her there, not only to prevent Vittoria's complexion being spoiled, but also to act as a foil to the pink of her skin, the blue of her eyes, and the splendid golden tresses spread out in the sun. As a matter of fact, I only guessed that Vittoria had blue eyes. I couldn't see them at first, because they were lowered. She was reading."

"But how could you see even as much as

that, Paolo? She was on the balcony and you were down in the street."

"There was a little church opposite the house with a raised porch level with the balcony. Vittoria's admirers — men and women of all ages — stood on the porch for a few minutes, lost in silent admiration. Even some of the parishioners coming out of the church, their thoughts still caught up in their prayers, lingered on the porch to join in the almost pagan worship of Vittoria's beauty.

" 'But we can't see her eyes!' I said to Muratore. I'd spoken in a reverential whisper, but the reproachful glances directed at me told me I'd disturbed the worshipers around me.

" 'Wait,' whispered Muratore, twitching my sleeve to remind me of the respect due to an idol.

"Sure enough, after a while Vittoria put her book down in her lap. With her left hand keeping the volume open at her place, she turned her head, looked at our little group with her great blue eyes, and gave us a slight nod. It was neither haughty nor familiar, but done with truly regal dignity and grace. A thrill ran through us all: the women bowed, and the men doffed their hats. I followed Muratore's example and did the same. Then he took me by the sleeve and indicated that it was time to go. A little way off, he pointed out that the porch was small, and it was only right to make way for others.

" 'Man lives as much by beauty as by bread,' he said."

There was a pause.

"He was a wise old man, Paolo," I said. "Do you know what became of him?"

"I inquired about him when I got back to Venice," answered the Prince. "He died soon after I met him in Gubbio. All that's left of him for me is his name and the memory of the bright little black eyes in his wizened face. Isn't it strange he should have played such an important role in my life? But how can I talk of this without casting aspersions on the Almighty and thus offending the Pope? Of course," he added mischievously, "there may be another God, called Chance."

"Oh, Paolo!" I said, with a smile — though the Madonna knows how little I felt like smiling — "you're not a good Roumi! You're not even a good Muslim! There's only one God!"

"But chance took a hand again during my first fight with the pirates," said Paolo. "When I captured Abensur's tartan and bought a little Moorish girl who looked just like Vittoria's."

I swallowed. "Was that why you bought me?" I asked in a strangled voice. I remembered how he'd stared at me as soon as he saw me.

"No, Aziza," he said, not noticing the emotion in my voice. "I'd have bought you anyhow. And since then," he added carelessly, "I've congratulated myself a hundred times over on my bargain. But it's true that in all the years we've sailed the seas together, I've never been able to look at you without seeing you holding a white umbrella over Vittoria's face."

"That wasn't me!" I cried.

"I know. I knew the very first day, after I'd asked you about yourself."

"So, then, I've acted as a reminder of the delightful picture you saw that afternoon in Gubbio."

"Yes. Exactly. Thanks to you, I can always conjure her up in my mind as alive and fresh and charming as when I actually saw her."

I said nothing. What was there to say? I'd had the answer to my question, but it was horribly painful. Of course I'd known from the beginning what my place was in his heart and in his life. Yet it was smaller than I'd thought. A brown hand holding a white umbrella over Vittoria's bright face. That was me.

# Prince Paolo Giordano Orsini, Duke of Bracciano

I used the three days of the voyage to get the carpenter to lay an extra deck fore and aft on the small boat I meant to use to go ashore. I ordered him to put underneath all the cork he could find, to make the craft as buoyant as possible and easily rightable if it capsized. For the same reason, I had the false bottom reinforced, so that if we keeled over, Marcello and I could brace ourselves against it and use our weight to get ourselves afloat again. This maneuver is easy in theory but difficult in practice: the boat must be light, and the two men must cooperate well. I'd often done the trick successfully in my youth, even in rough seas. As a further precaution, I had the oars lashed to the oarlocks with hemp cords so they wouldn't float away if we were swamped by a wave. I chose ropes rather than chains because they would stand the strain better.

I also made sure we were dressed as lightly as possible, without boots or swords, armed only with fighting daggers. The mate insisted on our wearing cork belts. I agreed, but without any illusions about how much use they'd be in that sea.

The great problem was launching the boat when the time came, getting ourselves down into it, and pulling away before the waves dashed us against the side of the galley. The whole operation was carried out in the lee of the ship, and I also had oil poured on the water. This surprised the landlubbers, but it's very efficient at calming waves over a small area. In this case, it prevented the boat from overturning when it reached the water. We got in as quickly as we could, because the galley was taking the wind on its beam in order to shelter us, and this exposed it to danger. As soon as we were clear and no longer in its lee, we were driven toward shore. The wind was so strong our oars served chiefly to keep us headed toward the tiny spots of light. When I turned my head, I could see them flickering up on the cliff, as Il Mancino had said they would be.

Although night had almost fallen, there was a greenish twilight over the sea. So whenever we sped along the crest of a wave, I could dimly make out the shape of the little cottage in which Vittoria Peretti was waiting for me. The thought made me wild with happiness, though my joy was tinged with incredulity. My idol had seemed completely inaccessible until this moment, when I was risking my life to be with her. If I'd had ten lives, I'd have staked them all for her.

I kept a cool head, however, and shouted brief orders to Marcello, on the thwart in front of me, telling him how to use his oars to keep us in line with the flow of the water. I knew the worst danger in a stormy sea was the shore — the risk of being smashed to pieces. When the lights on the cliff disappeared, I knew we were close. Our lives were going to depend on the next few seconds and whether we managed to find the inlet.

There was still just enough light to see the great fringe of foam where the waves broke against the foot of the cliffs with a savage roar. We were approaching so rapidly that the rocks seemed to be hurtling toward us. All I could do was act swiftly and trust to luck. I shouted an order and steered to the left. The wall of rock passed miraculously by on the right. To my immense relief, I'd somehow found the inlet.

My jubilation was short-lived. The sea rushed us into the inlet with such force we could no longer control the boat. I just had time to deduce, from the spray surrounding it, that we were heading for a rock, when a wave hurled us over it. I hoped for one wild moment that we might get past unscathed, but the bottom of the boat scraped on the rock, another wave washed us off the thwarts, and we found ourselves half swimming, half choking in the water. Then suddenly our feet touched a sandy bottom.

Strangely, just as we thought we were safe, we had another bad moment: the backwash was so strong that we were sucked again into the sea. I yelled to Marcello that we must dive into the next incoming wave, and when it landed us on the beach, clutch the sand deeply with both hands. But the undertow dragged us back three or four times, and we'd probably have lost the unequal struggle if there hadn't been a sudden lull that allowed us to reach the cave at the head of the inlet.

Luckily, the cave was at an angle to the face of the cliff, and we were protected from the pull of the receding waves. We could yield to our exhaustion and collapse on the sand, though we were still not out of the water. It was only about a foot high, however, and its gentle movement back and forth, faintly echoing the undertow, felt soothing and friendly after what we'd come through. But the wavelets that sometimes washed up to my neck struck me as much colder than the waves that had tossed us out in the inlet. The chill could do nothing, though, to detract from the sense of comfort and content.

I must have fallen asleep for a couple of minutes. All of a sudden, Marcello was shaking me and shouting into my ear that we must take advantage of a lull in the waves to climb up the steps in the cliff. By then, the thought of the house where Vittoria was waiting for me had become quite unreal. I felt a strong pang of regret at having to leave the womblike cave where I'd found refuge from a hostile world.

Emerging from our shelter was like plunging back into a nightmare. We were immediately buffeted again by the sea, which, even after we'd found the steps, seemed to be trying with malevolent persistence to pull us back. We could move only when the waves were receding; when they broke, the only thing we could do was cling like a starfish to any holds in the cliff. So our ascent was very slow. I remember feeling absurdly indignant with whoever had carved out the steps for not thinking to fix an iron handrail beside them. It didn't occur to me that they'd only been put there for people to use in summer.

Halfway up, we were beyond the reach of the waves, but the wind was gusting so fiercely we were in danger of being dashed off the face of the cliff. Even worse, drenched as we were, the wind that chilled us made our movements and our hold on the rocks less sure.

I had several attacks of vertigo and was tempted to let go. My mind was so numbed and divorced from all logic that I saw the resulting fall, not as a crash to my death, but as a respite that would enable me to survive. Still, I went on climbing automatically, blindly imitating Marcello, who, I was vaguely surprised to see, had outstripped me, his elder and leader.

What happened next was total confusion. I felt as if, instead of standing on rock, I was on something soft and slippery, like grass. When I lifted my foot to continue climbing, I seemed to step into a void. I pitched face forward to the ground. There was acute pain in my thigh.

Although I couldn't move, see, or speak I didn't quite lose consciousness. Without understanding what was said, I could hear voices around me and was aware of being carried and put down on a rug in front of a fire. But I seemed to be conscious intermittently. Sometimes I saw things and sometimes I didn't: there was an alternation of darkness and light.

I did feel my head being raised and my clothes being taken off, and in the surrounding hum of talk I made out two female voices, one high-pitched and the other low. I felt immensely relieved, though I wasn't thinking of Vittoria. I seemed to be back in my childhood, with my mother and her maids lifting me out of the bath and drying me in warm towels. Women I couldn't see, with sweet, musical voices, rubbed me down briskly and brought life and warmth back to my body. One of them dressed the wound in my thigh so carefully the pain was quite bearable. That did serve to bring me around a little, and I began to make out two faces leaning over me, one fair and one dark. I couldn't make out the color of their eyes, but I could see their expressions — gentle, anxious, friendly. I made an effort to smile, but found to my regret that my face muscles seemed to be frozen.

One of the women dried my hair and put a cushion under my head. Then they both disappeared, leaving me feeling abandoned. It didn't last long. Almost at once someone raised my head again, and a man's voice said, "Drink, my lord. It will do you good." My eyelids flickered, and this time I recognized Marcello quite clearly. I took several deep drafts, but then the receptacle was taken away. I was annoyed with Marcello, but soon the rim of the tankard was put to my lips again, and more of the warm, sweet, rough liquid poured down my throat. I kept my eyes shut until I'd drunk the last drop. Then I emerged at last from darkness, into a dazzling light. It was Vittoria.

The effect on me couldn't have been greater if I'd been a hermit praying in his cave and the Virgin Mary had suddenly appeared. Vittoria's face seemed to radiate all the beauty in the world. As I looked at her, with love changing into adoration, she leaned over me with a mild and motherly air and spoke. I could tell from the intonation that she was asking a question, though I couldn't understand a word. But the music of her voice was so soothing and consoling I felt myself melting with happiness.

With patience I found touching, she repeated her question, and this time I understood two words: "My lord." I shook my head and said "Paolo," to make her understand I wanted her to call me by my Christian name. The word cost me a great effort. She must have realized this. She smiled and replied: "Paolo."

She repeated her question, and this time I understood: Do you want something to eat and drink? I nodded. But this didn't satisfy her.

"Say yes, Paolo."

I made an effort: "Yes."

She bent over me: "Yes, Vittoria."

I made another effort, looking at her great blue eyes as they looked down at me, patient, indulgent, and sweet: "Yes, Vittoria."

She seemed satisfied, gave me a ravishing smile, and went and busied herself by the fire. I could see her body, until then concealed from me by the nearness of her face. It was clad in a loose gown, like the one she wore long ago on the balcony in Gubbio. I followed her every step, her every movement. I felt that she took the place of all existence, that I existed only through her.

She held a tankard out to me, but I didn't take it. I wanted to relive the moment when she raised my head and held it to my lips. This she did. And my strength and awareness revived at the warmth of her arm against my neck, the nearness of her face and bosom. My intense enjoyment must somehow have communicated itself to her, for her breath began to come faster.

I didn't take the bread she held out to me, either, though the sight of it made my mouth water: I hadn't eaten for some hours. So she crumbled it into the warm sweetened wine and fed it to me with a little spoon — rather anxiously at first, then more certainly as she saw how greedily I swallowed it.

She fed me two or three small flat loaves, and watched me eat them with delight. When I'd finished, she went and put the tankard down by the fire, then knelt by me and wiped my mouth with a napkin. I seized her hand

and kissed it adoringly.

"Oh, Paolo," she exclaimed joyfully, "you're moving at last! Your eyes are brighter. The color's coming back into your cheeks."

Bending over me, she put her lips lightly on mine. I kissed her, trembling lest she find my kiss too ardent and be shocked. But my arms settled the matter of their own accord. They quite involuntarily closed around her, and with indescribable relief I felt her body melt into mine.

## Caterina Acquaviva

When I woke up the next morning at dawn, I wondered what I was doing stretched out on the rug in front of the remains of the fire. Then it all came back to me. As soon as I'd seen Marcello fall asleep the previous night, I'd left him alone in the bed. It was too narrow for two.

I got up, my back hurting some from sleeping on the floor, and had a look at him. A cannonball wouldn't have wakened him.

I rekindled the fire. Not that it was really cold, but I wanted the room to be nice and cozy when he woke up. His doublet and hose, which he'd draped over the stools the night before, were dry, but because of the sea water they were stiff and covered with white streaks. They ought to be washed, or at least rinsed in fresh water. But I didn't dare do it unless he said so. He might need them in a hurry, to run away or hide.

I was glad to have him there, the brute, even with his sulking and foul temper. At the same time, I was frightened to death, and that's the truth. These two had thrown themselves right into the lion's jaws. It would be two of them, with a couple of daggers, against forty arquebusiers. It would end badly; I could feel it. What would my poor parents do when the priest in Grottammare announced from the pulpit that their daughter had been hanged for aiding and abetting adulterers? Would anyone in the village ever speak to them again?

Light began to creep through the shutters of the window, so I opened them a crack to see what the weather was like. The sky had cleared, and there were patches of blue between the clouds. The sun would soon be up.

Gingerly, so as not to wake Marcello, I opened the window for a breath of morning air. Hearing a sort of rustling in the grass, I leaned out, and to my amazement I saw Vittoria, a little cape over her indoor gown, walking up and down on the stretch of grass beside the cottage. She threw her head back

— which she ought not to have done, for it made her hair trail in the wet grass — and breathed deeply. How beautiful she was! A living statue of a goddess!

Perhaps she'd scold me, but I didn't care; I decided to join her. I pushed aside the red silk curtain and had a peep into the other part of the room. The Prince was asleep, naked, on Vittoria's bed. What shoulders he had! What a "morsel fit for a king!" as my mother would have said. I slipped out quietly. Vittoria saw me and, far from scolding, seemed happy too. She was happy anyway. Everything delighted her that morning.

"Caterina," she cried, her eyes sparkling, "see how lovely the world is! And how lovely it smells! Of damp grass, and earth, and wood smoke."

As she spoke she threw her arm around my shoulders and drew me close to her. It was the first time she'd ever done such a thing. I was quite overcome. But I knew which of us loved the other more. I'd always given more than I'd received.

"It smells of the sea too," I remarked, just for something to say.

"The sea that brought him to me," she whispered fervently.

To hear her, you'd have thought the sea had been created for that one purpose. I glanced at her out of the corner of my eye. My instinct told me she wasn't the same woman she'd been the day before. She looked like someone who'd gone to sleep in hell and awakened in heaven. I couldn't help feeling sad: what she'd experienced the previous night she'd have experienced long ago if she'd married someone other than Peretti. Poor Signor Peretti! Even in his own bed he'd had to obey the Cardinal. And now he'd lost his signora, forever.

She was silent. Even though he wasn't there, the Prince's arms were still around her and she was still clinging to his neck. As we walked up and down without a word, while our men still slept, we breathed in the air and the earth and I don't know what. The signora was radiant. But she was absolutely unaware of the real situation. If I'd told her all four of us might be killed within the hour, she wouldn't have believed me.

She linked her arm through mine, and I had to stand on my toes to be level with her. When I saw that she was making for the rocky spur, I snatched my arm away and said: "I'm sorry, signora. You won't get me over there, not for a king's ransom! That huge drop underneath! If you slip on the wet grass, you'll smash your head fathoms below."

"Don't be stupid, Caterina." She laughed.

"Why would I slip? And where's the grass? It's all rock. Come on!"

"No, no, signora. I can't! I'm sorry, but that spur looks so unsafe — sticking out like that! What if it gave under your weight?"

She laughed again. "It could hold a hundred like me. Come along, Caterina!"

"No, signora. It gives me a stomach ache just to watch you. Look, I'm trembling!"

"You really are trembling, silly thing. There isn't any danger."

"Not for you, perhaps," I said, retreating step by step toward the cottage. "But I've no head for heights — they draw me to them."

"It's just your imagination playing tricks, Caterina. There's no danger. Look!" she cried gaily.

As she spoke she walked out on the promontory, which at the end was no wider than the back of a stool. The farther she advanced, the farther I retreated. Finally I found myself with my back to the door of the cottage, trembling like a poplar leaf. She was certainly going to fall! I threw my skirt over my head — I didn't want to see her go, didn't want to hear the terrible scream when she felt the ground give way beneath her.

Even through my skirt, I could hear her saying, "Come on, come on, Caterina!" and her teasing laughter. Then, suddenly, nothing!

I uncovered my head.

She was standing on the very tip of the spur. Her long fair hair, gilded by the rising sun, floated out behind her in a little breeze that flattened her gown against her body. But she wasn't laughing now. She was pale and frowning, and her blue eyes were blazing, fixed haughtily on someone to the left of me. I turned and saw Signor Peretti, bareheaded and angry, advancing with drawn sword at the head of a dozen arquebusiers. He stopped, and the soldiers halted fifteen paces behind him.

"Madam," he said in a low, toneless voice, "the lookouts in the tower saw the wreckage of a boat in the inlet this morning. One of them went down to check, and on a piece of the prow he saw the name of the galley it belonged to. It's a galley of a nobleman I shall not name. I've come to make sure he's not hiding in your house."

He made for the door of the cottage. When he found me standing there, he looked bewildered, as if he'd never seen me before.

"My lord," said Vittoria, without raising her voice but pronouncing each word with emphasis, "I will not tolerate your entering my quarters without my permission, and, worse still, accompanied by soldiers. So listen carefully: if you touch that door, I will jump off the cliff."

"Jump off the cliff?" murmured Peretti, turning pale.

"You heard what I said."

What struck me about this exchange was that neither of them shouted or stormed. They spoke to one another quietly, almost as if they were trying not to wake the Prince. The truth was, as I realized later, they didn't want to be overheard by the soldiers, whose ears were flapping.

There was a long silence. The hand Signor Peretti had reached out toward the door fell back to his side. To say he was pale is to put it mildly; his face was drained of blood. I could tell what was going through his head. He knew his wife. He knew that if he opened the door, she'd do what she'd threatened to do. And of course he had no doubt by now about whom he'd find inside, at his mercy.

Holy Mother of God! He frowned. His hand moved forward again. He was going to push me aside and open the door.

But no! He didn't. He fell back a pace and sheathed his sword, though his hand shook so much he had difficulty with the scabbard. He made a low bow and said, with dignity, in a low, firm voice: "Vittoria, I've never been cruel to you, and I'm not going to start now, however much circumstances may try to force me to."

278

Turning on his heel, he left, followed by his men. Vittoria looked after him with an expression I'd never seen on her face before. She, who'd just been so bold, was trembling in every limb. Without a word, she stretched her arms out to me, as if she needed my help to get back to firm ground. And I went and got her! I who have such a bad head for heights!

Somehow, with one dragging the other, we were both safe at last outside our door. The signora took me in her arms, hugged me with her cheek against mine, and whispered in a strangled voice: "Oh, Caterina! How noble he was!"

## *Marcello Accoramboni*

It was Peretti's noble gesture that spoiled everything. It's true that if he hadn't made it, the Prince and I wouldn't be here to deplore his magnanimity. We'd both be dead, with a sword through our hearts — dead, as Father Racasi would say, "in the filth of our sins." Vittoria would be lying broken at the foot of the cliff. And Caterina, though surviving for a while, would have been handed over to the secular arm of the law and hanged soon afterward — the longest suffering for the one who least deserved it.

Peretti and his men had made little sound, and his conversation with Vittoria made even less. What woke me was the sound of my twin sobbing. Even when I was a child, I couldn't hear her crying without tears coming to my own eyes, whether or not I knew the cause of her grief.

In this case, her sobs were muffled twice, by her own efforts to stifle them and by the fact that they had to reach me through the door. But they were loud enough to rouse me and to wring my heart. I dressed in haste, and had just finished when Vittoria entered the cottage, followed by Caterina. She came around the red silk curtain, glanced at me, then without a word took off her informal gown and began to dress properly.

Whatever Tarquinia may say, there's never been any false modesty between us, from when we were young until now. Anyhow, La Superba has never understood our relationship. She's always thought it equally scandalous that I won't touch or kiss Vittoria and that my twin is quite prepared to undress in front of me. Tarquinia doesn't know that posturing between us is unnecessary.

When she was dressed, Vittoria went to the other side of the curtain and, waving aside

Caterina's help, sat down at her dressing table. I knew what she was going to do: she was going to cover the traces of her tears, not only out of vanity, but also because she was ashamed of having wept. Vittoria loves heroes, and sees herself as a heroic character. All the time she was attending to her face, she never once looked at the sleeping Prince. I found this surprising, not knowing what had happened out on the cliff.

When she'd finished, she beckoned Caterina to come and brush her hair, which she did without uttering a word. There were two reasons for this unusual silence: the Prince, who was still asleep, and the look on Vittoria's face. I poked at the fire and, when the flames had revived, sat in front of it on a low chair. From there, I could see Vittoria in *profil perdu,* as Raphael liked to draw his models: just the brow, the outline of the cheek and the upper part of the jaw, with the nose guessed at. Her face looked like marble. I wondered what this signified.

Caterina's brush made hardly a sound, so I didn't think it was that which woke Orsini, but, rather, the tensions among the three of us in the little room. When he woke, he immediately gave a start of joy at seeing Vittoria just a few feet from him. His eyes brightened, his whole face lit up with a smile, and he suddenly looked much younger. He said, in a clear, cheerful voice: "I wish you good morning, Vittoria."

Apparently the Prince's greeting struck a very wrong note for Vittoria. After a moment, she said in a distant, toneless voice, without looking at him: "It isn't a very good morning, my lord. It very nearly started with a massacre."

Caterina stopped brushing. Orsini sat up, pulling the sheet over his nakedness. Vittoria swung around on her stool to look at him.

"What?" he said. "What do you mean, Vittoria? Were we nearly discovered?"

"Nearly!" she exclaimed. In a voice devoid of any emotion, she told him what had happened on the cliff between Peretti and herself. I listened in astonishment, and I could see that Orsini heard it with growing uneasiness. It was plain to him that the hero of this story was not he, who'd risked his life to be with his lady, but Peretti, who had spared the guilty lovers when he had them at his mercy. I reflected that Peretti wouldn't have acted differently if he'd been the wiliest man on earth, for his clemency had completely reversed the situation in his favor. The strange thing was, though, and all three of us were conscious of it, that he hadn't acted out of calculation or guile, but simply on an impulse of the heart.

When Vittoria had finished her account, which she'd given with downcast eyes, she swung back to her mirror and signed to Caterina to continue her task. She said no more. We didn't speak either. All that was to be heard in the silence was the swish of the brush. All of us were crushed by Peretti's magnanimity. Law, custom, and honor bade him kill us. He had flouted them all to spare his wife, and therefore the rest of us.

I glanced at the Prince. His eyes were lowered, and his powerful chest was heaving as if he found it difficult to breathe. When he was confronting the sea, storms, dangerous rocks, or an unequal battle alone against forty other men, he was a hero. Yet when someone refrained from meting out his just deserts, he became a mere thief, who'd robbed a husband of his wife's affections. He must have felt diminished in Vittoria's eyes. And so he was. He had only to look at her sitting at her dressing table with that icy expression, and remember her addressing him ceremoniously as "my lord." Where were the sighs of the previous night?

Poor Orsini, who'd lost everything just as he thought he'd won it, realized he was clasping only a memory. He must have been beside himself with rage and despair. But fury is a poor counselor, and although he wasn't really lacking in subtlety, he set his teeth and said: "I don't accept Peretti's mercy. I shall go and challenge him, right away."

Vittoria's reply was devastating. "If I understand you correctly, my lord," she said with crushing scorn, not deigning to look at him, "you propose to go and ask Peretti, who just spared you, to lend you a sword to kill him with. What courage! What a glorious feat, for you, the finest swordsman in Italy, to kill a mere amateur in *fair* fight! And how delicate of you, by doing that, to proclaim *urbi et orbi* that I yielded to your advances!"

She turned around, looked at him fixedly, and added deliberately: "Since we're talking of my honor, my lord, don't you think yours requires you to do nothing henceforward that might directly or indirectly threaten Signor Peretti's life?"

The Prince, thank God, now recovered himself. To this question that sounded the knell of all his secret hopes, he made answer, in a voice that was firm enough: "I do think so, indeed."

"Do you promise?"

"I promise, since you require it."

He spoke coldly. He wasn't used to being treated in the way Vittoria had just treated him, and both his attitude and his tone indicated that he wasn't disposed to endure any more of it. Picking up his doublet and hose from where they'd been hung to dry, he went beyond the curtain.

After a moment, I got up and took the brush from Caterina. Her task required close attention and the use of both hands: one to take a big swathe of Vittoria's tresses, the other to handle the brush so as not to add to the weight and pull of her long mane of hair. I'd been doing it since I was a child, and I loved the job. It was the only real contact I'd ever had with Vittoria. And it seemed to exert some kind of magic: I felt as if through those gold threads I found my way more easily into the labyrinth of her thoughts. I looked at her in the glass. She was pale; her eyes lowered, her face still. But her hands kept clasping and unclasping in her lap.

"Haven't you been rather harsh?" I said quietly.

She glanced rapidly up and then down again, darting me a brief but very plain look in the mirror. No, it said, she wasn't harsh. She was only trying to teach herself to be. Her mind was made up, and she was suffering almost more than she could bear.

The Prince pulled aside the curtain, strode resolutely into our half of the room, and stood to the right of Vittoria. His face was pale but firm.

"Madam," he said, "the finest gift is spoiled when the giver stops loving us. Allow me to return the jewel you gave me."

He put the ring with the V down on the dressing table.

Vittoria raised her eyebrows and gave me a black look in the glass.

"I didn't give you anything, my lord," she said.

"That's what it pleases you to say now, madam. To my infinite regret."

He'd spoken in a subdued voice, and I saw Vittoria start. But I knew she wouldn't tell him how the ring had come into his possession. She did what she'd always done: she covered for me.

"How is it," she asked in a gentler tone, "that I didn't notice this ring on your finger earlier?"

"I've always worn it with the V turned inward. I thought it more discreet."

This exchange had taken place in quite friendly, even tones, but they knew it was only a lull, that the storm would soon break over them again.

"My lord," Vittoria went on with an effort, "there can be no sequel to last night. I cannot be your wife, because I am married. And I won't be your whore."

"Madam," replied Orsini indignantly, "I've

never thought of you in such terms."

"Your mistress, if you prefer."

"And you don't wish to be that?"

"No."

"Isn't it rather late to think of that?" he exclaimed in an outburst of fury. He regretted it at once. Clasping his hands behind his back so hard I saw his knuckles whiten, he went and stood by the fire, shoulders hunched and head bowed.

"It's never too late to mend," said Vittoria haughtily.

"That's a question of morality we won't discuss," Orsini answered in a voice shaking with anger. "When I left my galley yesterday evening, madam," he went on, "I told my mate that if I didn't return by dawn, it would be because my boat had been damaged. He was to wait until nightfall and, if he saw lights in your windows again, send another boat to fetch us. Until then, may it please you to grant me your hospitality? I shall try to inconvenience you as little as possible."

She didn't answer. He bowed stiffly and went to the other side of the curtain. I gave the brush back to Caterina and joined him. He was occupying the only chair, leaning his powerful shoulders against the back, his long legs stretched out before him, staring into the flames.

I sat on the bed and looked at the flames too. If I'd had the heart, I'd have admired them. They came from a clump of heather root, which produces smaller, steadier flames than other kinds of wood. The root was round and solid, like a skull, and out of the glow around its edges leapt little bluish, almost transparent wisps, not more than a couple of inches high. It isn't grand passion that crackles, flares and burns you, I thought. It's the low flame that can kill you, by inches. But for us, though we had nothing else to look at, there was no question of dying. We were all too abjectly alive, and, judging by the Prince's face, he felt humiliated in addition.

An hour later, there was a knock at the door. Orsini didn't move and neither did I. If Peretti had changed his mind, and the affair was going to be ended ingloriously here and now, so be it! I was weary of the frantic business of life. What did it all lead to, anyway?

But the knock heralded only a majordomo and some servants with a meal. Apparently he didn't suspect our presence, for he hung about chattering like a magpie.

When he'd gone, Caterina brought us a share of the food. As I took the tray from her, she stroked my hands. Did our ration come out of hers and her mistress's? Or had Peretti sent an extra amount? I could see that the Prince wanted to refuse the offer. After what had happened, wouldn't it be wrong to take food and drink from Peretti? But he must have decided it would be childish and self-defeating to refuse. Silently, he began to eat, and with a good appetite too. It was a long time since the bread and wine Vittoria had fed him last night.

Caterina, who hadn't shrunk from peeping through the curtain during the night, had told me of that poetic scene. Yes, Vittoria had fed the Prince with a spoon, like a baby! And now she'd cast him from her bosom as if he'd bitten her. It was hard to believe. What changes of fortune the unlucky Prince had gone through in a few hours! One after the other, he'd been a tenderly nursed casualty, a babe, a cherished lover, and this morning a rejected one. What a farce human affection was! All love began and ended in our heads. And they were as wild and empty as goat bells.

I thought that day would never end, and by the look of him the Prince felt the same. Yet there was no safe place to go. Why should he risk death now that Vittoria had dismissed him? True, if *I* lost my sister's love, I'd just as soon lose my life too. But Orsini didn't love Vittoria in the same way I did. Witness the fact that he'd hated her just now, when she treated him so cruelly. In front of her fire, he loved and hated her by turns. For a day at least, he was imprisoned in the worst of all jails — one shared with a woman who has stopped loving you, or so he thought.

In the middle of the afternoon he turned to me and broke his silence. "Marcello," he said, "I noticed there were some books here. Will you ask if I can borrow one?"

Such an impersonal way of putting it! I got up and went to the other side of the curtain. There, for some reason I don't understand, I delivered the message in a whisper. There weren't "some" books; there were three. Vittoria was holding one: the Petrarch. The others were on the mantelpiece. Vittoria stared at me as if I'd appeared from nowhere, and took an age to reply to my question. Caterina devoured me with her eyes meanwhile. She at least was a simple, straightforward creature: love certainly didn't begin and end in *her* head.

"Give him a book, Caterina," said Vittoria flatly.

"Which one, signora?" asked Caterina, no doubt to remind me that she could read.

"Whichever you like."

This wasn't very gracious to the Prince, and didn't give Caterina the chance to show off her learning. She picked one of the volumes at random and handed it to me. It was Ariosto's *Orlando Furioso*.

I didn't know what Orsini was going to think of this choice, but I thought it unfortunate. Vittoria had made me read the poem long ago, when she was trying to educate me. It tells how Orlando, a proud paladin in the service of Charlemagne, underwent incredible dangers to win the love of the beautiful Angelica, only to be steadily rejected by her and lose his reason. Not very cheering in present circumstances. Still, Orsini was a cultivated man and a lover of the arts. Perhaps he'd enjoy it for its style.

The hours crawled by. The Prince buried himself in his book. On the other side of the curtain, Vittoria was reading too. The irony of the situation amused me. If Peretti had come in then, he'd have been edified by the innocence of our pastimes.

I heaved a sigh of relief when it got dark and Caterina put a lot of lighted candles in the windows. An hour later, I suggested to the Prince that I go down to the beach and wait for the boat. He agreed. I said farewell to Vittoria, who responded coldly. She might have been angry with me about the ring. And I didn't blame her. But if I exceeded her intentions, I only translated her desires. Last night had proved it.

I'd only got as far as the grass outside when the door opened behind me and Caterina ran out with a handkerchief I'd left behind. I wouldn't be surprised if she'd stolen it as an excuse to see me alone. She threw herself into my arms and squirmed about trying to kiss me on the lips. She probably wouldn't have minded being laid there and then. She always knows exactly what she wants, and with her attractions she'll never have any trouble getting it. I disengaged myself from the little octopus's tentacles, but not roughly. Surprisingly, I was quite touched.

It was getting darker, but I climbed safely down to the beach and stood in front of the cave that had served us as a refuge. The sea, as fickle as all females, now scarcely washed up as far as my feet.

Visibility was poor, but by straining my ears I could hear a regular clicking noise, which I soon recognized as the sound of oars. The boat sent from the galley to pick us up had managed to avoid the rock we'd struck.

In the darkness the boat was upon me before I could make out its shape. A shadow jumped into the water to prevent its scraping on the sand. As I approached, the shadow drew back.

"It's me — Marcello." I thought I knew the voice that replied. "Geronimo?" I asked.

"Yes, signore."

It was only when our faces were almost

touching that I really knew him. He looked frightened.

"I'll go and get the Prince."

"For the love of God, be quick, signore!"

"Don't worry. There's no danger."

I groped my way back up the cliff. It was very strange. Although it was easier this second time, it still seemed terribly difficult — perhaps because it was linked in my mind to failure.

As soon as I got to the top, I dropped to my knees. There was a light in the watchtower overlooking the inlet, and I could see the lookout's head silhouetted against the glow. Perhaps I'd spoken too lightly when I told Geronimo there was no danger.

Not knowing if the rough grass could hide me from view in the candlelight, I crawled to the door, glad I was dressed in black. As I tapped on the oak panel I called: "Caterina, put out the candles and close the shutters. Then open the door."

She did as I said. The grass was plunged in darkness, and, luckily, the fires on the hearths had burned down. I went in.

"My lord," I said, "the boat's here. But the lookout is on the alert. It's time to go."

Vittoria was standing by the fire, Orsini facing her. Despite all his experience of the world and his princely self-assurance, I had the impression that he didn't know what to say or do. He leaned to kiss her hand, but it didn't come out to meet him.

"Madam," he said. He didn't go on. No words seemed suitable. He bowed, straightened with dignity, then turned abruptly on his heel.

When he reached the door, Vittoria, till then as still and impassive as marble, took a step and said in a subdued voice: "Good-bye, Paolo."

The good-bye sounded final enough, but she had called him by his Christian name, which she hadn't done since the scene with Peretti. Orsini turned his head and looked at her. Then he put an end to his hesitation by marching resolutely out of the cottage. To put it plainly, he didn't dare go and take her in his arms. If you ask me, he was wrong there, clever as he is. It's no use being a great captain if you can't fathom female ambiguity better than that.

# 7

## *Caterina Acquaviva*

After Marcello and the Prince went out, the
Signora insisted on seeing they got away safely.
The night was inky and very cool for the time
of year. We listened hard but couldn't hear
anything, and all we could see were some little
lights bobbing out at sea: Vittoria said they
must be on the Prince's galley, to guide him
back. There was still a light in the watchtower,
and we were careful not to let it fall on us.

Back in the cottage, I helped Vittoria undress, and she went right to bed. When I'd
nearly finished taking my own clothes off, on
the other side of the curtain, she said she was
cold, and asked me to come get in beside her.
I found that her hands and feet were like ice.
Mine were hot. This always surprises her,
though it's really quite natural, seeing that I
run around all day and she doesn't do anything, not even put on or take off her own
skirt by herself. It's odd when you think about
it: noblemen and noblewomen need a nurse-

maid to look after them from the cradle to the grave. They'd be lost without us.

As soon as I got into bed with her, Vittoria put her feet on mine, and I took her frozen hands and put them between my breasts. I didn't say anything though; I didn't want to annoy her with chitchat. She was quite capable of turning me out again as soon as she was warm. I preferred to stay. She was so beautiful and smelled so nice. What a pity she wasn't an ordinary girl like me; then we could have spent most of the night talking about our men.

Surprisingly, she did talk about them, though not in the way I would expect.

"Tell me, Caterina," she said. "Last night — did you sin with Marcello?"

I wondered whether I should lie. I was sure she hadn't heard anything. Still, I didn't think it wise not to tell her the truth. That's never really worked with her.

"Well," I said sanctimoniously, "You know what Signor Marcello's like, signora. When he wants something, it's impossible to resist him."

"And of course," she said ironically, "you put up a lot of resistance."

"No, signora, not much. Resistance makes such a noise. And I didn't want to disturb you while you were asleep," I added, sounding very innocent.

"Be quiet, you little witch," she said.

She didn't sound really annoyed. And I was glad to have shown I wasn't as stupid as she always made out. In bed we weren't a great lady and a maid, only two women, even if I did use a certain amount of politeness.

"Tell me, Caterina," she went on, "are you going to confess to Father Barichelli that you sinned last night?"

"Of course, signora. I'm a good Catholic."

"He'll want to know who you sinned with. What will you tell him?"

"The truth, of course, signora."

"Will you really, Caterina?" she said, sounding frightened. "Don't you know the truth will bring dishonor on me?"

"How is that, signora?"

"Come now, Caterina. Who's going to believe the Prince mounted an expedition and launched a boat in the middle of a storm just so Marcello could come and see you?"

I said nothing. So she was under no illusion about the links between Father Barichelli and the Cardinal, nor about the priest's discretion. This conversation was like walking in a swamp — I was going to have to step carefully if I didn't want to get sucked under.

"I didn't think of that, signora."

"Now that I've made you think of it, what are you going to do?"

"I don't know, signora."

"Oh, Caterina," she said crossly, "you must see you can't tell Barichelli who it was you sinned with."

"Who shall I say it was with, then?"

"Well, you could say it was a soldier. There are about forty of them around the grounds."

"What if he asks me his name?"

"The soldier didn't tell you."

I thought about it, and decided to be a bit awkward.

"Oh, signora!" I said. "What will I look like, not knowing the name of the man I granted my favors to?"

"Caterina, don't start giving yourself airs. Can you swear to me it's never happened before?"

"No, signora," I said firmly. "No. It never has happened to me before."

That was a lie. I lied first of all because I didn't like her accusing me of putting on airs, and second because even if she didn't believe me, she'd never be able to check.

But I knew she was anxious, and I didn't want her to worry too long. She was disappointed enough, by the way things had turned out. I resisted a little bit longer, however, so as not to give in too easily.

"I'm sorry, signora," I said, "but I don't like the idea of lying to my confessor."

"It's not serious. You won't be lying to him about the fact — only about the person."

She was right. Anyway, I'd never told the whole truth to my confessors, especially when they started going into details the way old Father Racasi did. Father Barichelli was more discreet, perhaps because he was younger. He almost seemed afraid of me. He was the one who blushed when I told about the naughty things I'd done.

"Very well, signora." I sighed. "I'll do as you say."

"Thank you, Caterina. You're a good girl. Go to your own bed now. I'm sleepy."

I was disappointed that she hadn't said anything about the Prince. But it had been naïve of me to think she would. She asked me for my secrets, but she didn't tell me hers. Her hands were warm now, and even her feet were beginning to thaw out against mine. I'd served my purpose. Thank you, Caterina. Go to bed now, Caterina. I felt like crying. If I cried now, though, all I'd get would be: "Don't be a nuisance, Caterina!"

"Good night, signora," I said in a strangled voice.

"Good night," she said.

As I sat up, she caught me by the arm, drew me to her, and kissed me on the cheek.

I quite melted. That's me all over! One little

kiss on the cheek and I melt.

Next morning, after dressing with the utmost care, Vittoria asked me to deliver a note to Signor Peretti. Unfortunately, I couldn't read it on the way, because it was sealed. I soon saw its effects, however, for at ten o'clock Signor Peretti turned up at the cottage, alone and unarmed.

"Caterina," Vittoria said. "go for a little walk. I want to be alone."

"With all those soldiers?"

"You needn't go far. Go on, Caterina, do as you're told!"

"Yes, signora."

On the pretext of going to fetch my cape, I went behind the curtain and quietly unlocked a little door at the back of the cottage that opened into the woodshed. Then I went out the front door, around the house, and into the woodshed. There I quietly lifted the latch of the little door, opened it an inch or two, and put my ear to the crack. I'd taken the signora at her word: I hadn't gone far.

At first I couldn't hear a word. Maybe they were embarrassed to be face to face after what had happened the day before. Finally, and not surprisingly, it was Vittoria who decided to speak.

"Signor," she said, "I have been guilty of a few small offenses against you, and I want

300

to tell you exactly what they amount to. In Rome, I received a letter from a great nobleman I'd met briefly at Cardinal Montalto's house. I read the letter. Far from answering it, I burned it immediately. But it was wrong of me to read it, and I ask you to forgive me."

"Vittoria," said Peretti quietly, "it's a pity you didn't admit this wrong to me the day after you committed it."

"I did admit it the day after — to my confessor," said Vittoria, with some suppressed anger. "The real pity is that you should have heard about it through his indiscretion, and that you didn't say anything about it to me."

"I didn't hear about it from Racasi!" cried Peretti — very tactlessly, if you ask me.

"From your father, then. What's the difference? What I say before God is repeated by the priest to the Cardinal and by the Cardinal to you. How despicable! And can you tell who it was who decided I should be confined, first in the Rusticucci palace and then in this wilderness, if it wasn't for your father?"

"He's your father too, madam," answered Peretti sorrowfully.

"No!" cried Vittoria. "A thousand times no! He's no longer my father, or my uncle, after the tyranny he's imposed on me through you."

"Yet, madam," said Peretti more firmly, "events have shown that our precautions had some justification. There's every reason to believe that the nobleman of whom we're speaking made a desperate attempt to join you here."

"Was that the reason you tried to rush on me, sword in hand, with a score of your henchmen?" cried Vittoria violently. "If so, let me tell you that if there was an attempt, I swear to God it was neither instigated nor agreed to by me."

When I heard that, I did admire the signora! She'd managed to lie and tell the truth at one and the same time. Who'd have thought, to hear her, that Orsini had ever set foot in our cottage?

"The wreck of a boat belonging to one of his galleys was found in the inlet below."

"What does that prove?" asked Vittoria vehemently. "Nothing! Not that there was a galley, not that he was in the boat, not that the boat succeeded in putting anyone ashore. The fact that it was smashed proves the opposite."

"You gave weight to my suspicions when you threatened to throw yourself off the cliff if I forced your door."

"Fie, sir," cried Vittoria scornfully. "How can you refer in my presence to the grotesque scene that so cruelly insulted me? The sudden raid, the naked sword with which you threatened me, the soldiers! Of all the outrages I've suffered at your hands in the last month, that was by far the worst! How can you blame me for saying something senseless? And it was all for a letter burned as soon as read. Read without thought of harm, out of feminine curiosity. You can't seriously suppose, Francesco," she went on in a gentler voice, addressing him for the first time by his Christian name, "that I'm in the least interested in that cripple, a man seen for only a minute at the Cardinal's."

Another silence. I admired the signora but I didn't envy her. She must have had difficulty getting that "cripple" out.

As for Peretti, could he tell her she was lying when he had no proof of it? The proof he needed today was inside the cottage yesterday. Now it was gone, and he'd never get it. All he had left was doubt.

How I'd have loved to be invisible in a corner of the room, to see them staring silently at each other! I knew how Vittoria must look: dignified and regal. But poor Francesco — I couldn't imagine him.

"Madam," he said at last, in a subdued voice, "you asked to see me urgently. Was it just to argue about this, or have you something else to say?"

"I want to say something more," she answered calmly. "As I've just admitted, I made a mistake, and that mistake has caused you to suspect me. If we return to Rome, and I'm set free again, I swear to you as I hope to be saved, Francesco, that you'll never again have cause to doubt me."

Silence again. My neck ached from stretching out to hear what came next.

"Vittoria," he said uncertainly, "I'll think about it."

He said no more. I heard the door shut behind him. So I scuttled as fast as I could out of the woodshed and around to the side by the cliff so as not to meet him. I sat and waited two or three minutes on the top step of the stairs down to the beach before going back inside.

Vittoria was sitting in the chair with her hands clasped in her lap and her eyes fixed on the hearth, though the fire wasn't lit. It wasn't nearly so cool this morning.

I didn't know what to do. I pretended to tidy the dressing table, and then I just rushed about, as the signora puts it. Finally, in order not to get on her nerves, I sat down on the little low chair.

After a moment she looked at me and said: "We're going back to Rome, Caterina."

"Is that what Signor Peretti's decided?"

"Not yet. But he will."

"Are you glad, signora?"

"Yes," she said. "I am."

And she went over to the window and

leaned on the sill, looking out at the sea.

"Leave me, Caterina," she said.

I went to the other side of the curtain and took the opportunity to lock the little door to the woodshed. Then I lay down on my bed. It was sure to be some time before she called me. I knew what she was doing there, with her elbows on the windowsill and her head in her hands. She was weeping.

## Marcello Accoramboni

In the boat going back to the galley, I asked the Prince to grant me an interview alone before he said anything to Lodovico. He agreed, and as soon as we were on board he told his cousin he had to change his clothes and would see him later. Then he took me to the quarterdeck and asked me to wait. Five minutes later, he came back and took me to his cabin, where I noticed at once that the curtains of his bunk were drawn. I deduced that his little Moorish slave girl was hiding behind them. The Prince had let me glimpse her once or twice, being somewhat Moorish in these matters himself. Because I knew, through Folletto, that she was fanatically devoted to him, her presence didn't stop me from saying what was on my mind.

"My lord," I said, "I suppose you intend to tell Lodovico your venture failed."

"What do you mean?" he asked, raising his eyebrows.

"That you found the lady less than pliable and she turned you down."

"Honor requires me to say that," replied Orsini at once, "if only to protect her reputation."

"There's something else I'd like you to do too, my lord."

"Something else?"

"Yes, my lord. I'd like you to terminate my duties as your secretary."

At that he looked at me with a mixture of surprise, sorrow, and anger. "What, you want to leave me, Marcello?"

"Only out of necessity, and with reluctance," I declared. "But it's absolutely necessary that I go. There are so many witnesses to this expedition here on the ship that, before long, the story's bound to leak out. There'll be all sorts of conjectures. If you dismiss me when we get back to Rome, it will strengthen your version of the affair — the one that says you failed. And that version's the one that will do the least harm to Vittoria's reputation."

"Then I wouldn't see you again," said the Prince sadly, looking away.

I knew what he valued in me most was my resemblance to Vittoria. Just the same, I was touched, and replied warmly: "I'll always be entirely at your service, and you'll only have to ask for me and I'll come. You know you can always reach me through Il Mancino."

He came over and took me in his arms. And so we parted.

Next day, as I was on the poop deck having some target practice with a pistol and a playing card, Lodovico approached and said loftily: "They say you're quite a good marksman, Accoramboni."

"Yes, Count. I'm not bad with swords either."

"I regret all the more that your low birth prevents me from crossing them with you."

"I don't know what you mean by low birth, Count. Birth is the same, whether it be low or high. So is death."

"Still," he said mockingly, "I don't see the point of being such an expert fencer if one's not a nobleman."

"Unfortunately, I have to be an expert: certain people dislike me."

"I take pride in being one of them," said Lodovico provocatively. "Would you like to know why?"

"Count, if you want to be unpleasant, go ahead. Haven't you just said your birth exempts you from having to bother about me?"

"Exactly. I'd be demeaning my sword if I crossed it with yours."

"You're quite safe, then. I'm listening."

I concentrated my attention on loading my pistol. Then I fixed another card as a target, and waited.

"First," he said, "I think you're an intriguer who's wormed his way into the Prince's good graces out of self-interest."

"So far, I've never accepted one piaster from him. Can you say the same, Count?"

"Second, I think you're a pimp, who lives at the expense of a rich widow."

"You've said that before, and I've given you my answer."

"Third, I consider you a vile seducer."

"Your third is the most interesting charge, Count. Can you be more precise?"

"You tried to corrupt your own sister in order to deliver her to the Prince."

"You're not subtle enough, Count. I helped the Prince gain access to Signora Peretti only so that he might see that her virtue is unassailable, and that there'd be no point in his having her abducted. After that I resigned from my post as his secretary."

"I already know that."

"Is that why you're trying to provoke me?"

"It's one reason, but not the main one."

"You haven't yet told me what that is."

"No."

"You whet my curiosity."

"The main reason is that I can't stand such incredible arrogance in one who was born, like you, in the mud of the common people."

"And what are you going to do about it?"

"Chastise you."

"I don't see how, if you won't accept my challenge."

"The streets of Rome are dangerous, and accidents will happen."

"What sort of accidents, Count?"

"I don't know — a tile falling off a roof, a stabbing by a crazy passerby. In short, Accoramboni, you might die from some quite fortuitous cause."

I turned the barrel of my pistol in the direction of his stomach and said with a gracious smile: "So might you."

He became extremely pale and fell back a pace, his hands in front of his belly with the palms toward me, as if to protect himself.

A voice said: "Marcello!"

I turned and saw the Prince's head just above the level of the deck.

"Lower your weapon, Marcello."

"Certainly, my lord. But the Count of Oppedo took fright for nothing. The cur wasn't armed."

The Prince climbed slowly up the ladder to the deck, looked coldly at Lodovico, and said: "You're behaving very recklessly, cousin. You refused to fight Marcello, then you insulted him and threatened him with an accident. Do you want to suffer the same fate as Recanati?"

"My lord," I said with a little bow, "I have no intention of killing the Count of Oppedo. Having been born, as he puts it, in the mud of the common people, I'm too low for his insults to reach me."

"You see, Paolo!" cried Lodovico. "The blackguard still defies me. And in front of you too."

"He's not defying you. He's making clever replies to your stupid insults. You should thank both of us. If you weren't my cousin, he'd have put a bullet in your stomach by now. Marcello, go down to my room, please. I want to talk to you."

"With your permission, my lord, I'd like to empty my gun first. Accidents do happen."

"Very well."

I cocked my pistol, noticing out of the corner of my eye that Lodovico had edged behind the Prince. My target was a playing card — a knave of spades, if I remember rightly — fixed in a cleft stick I'd wedged in the lid of a chest.

I aimed carefully and fired. I hit the knave of spades right in the middle.

"You're a remarkably good shot, Marcello," said the Prince. "Yet strangely enough your hand is shaking."

"Yes, but my eye is accurate. It makes up for my hand."

I bowed to him, nodded to Lodovico, who didn't respond, and went down the ladder. At the bottom, instead of going straight to the Prince's room, I stayed where I was and listened.

"Lodovico," said the Prince, "I don't understand you. All this is ridiculous. What are you up to? You have an insane hatred for Marcello. As soon as you set eyes on him, you started insulting him. What do you expect? Do you think he's going to go on all fours to you and lick your boots? You're a fool, cousin. You know the sort of man you're dealing with. Marcello sets no value on his own life, he's afraid of nothing, he's ready for anything. I tell you again: if you weren't my cousin, he'd already have put a bullet through you, just like this playing card. Here, take it, keep — it'll serve as a reminder. And if you're thinking of engineering an accident, forget it. I'd never forgive you."

I don't know how Lodovico answered this reprimand, for, hearing footsteps overhead, I hurried to the Prince's cabin. I knocked before I went in, not wanting to disturb the little Moorish girl, and it was a good minute before Folletto came and let me in. As soon as I was admitted to the holy of holies, I noticed that the bunk curtains were drawn. Since I was hungry, I also observed that the table was laid for two. I looked at Folletto, raising my eyebrows and pointing to my stomach. He nodded: Yes, the Prince had invited me to eat with him. I was amused to think how this would make Lodovico hate me more than ever.

The Prince came in and signed to Folletto to withdraw. Then, as always, he came straight to the point.

"Marcello," he said, "I heard the beginning of your conversation with my cousin, and I was very struck by something you said. You said, 'I helped the Prince gain access to Signora Peretti only so he might see that her virtue is unassailable.' Tell me, please, was that really your reason?"

"No. What I said was the truth as adapted for Lodovico."

"And what is the truth as adapted for Marcello?"

I looked him in the eye, thought for a moment, and said: "As far as I can make out, the truth is that I serve Vittoria's desires but wouldn't act against her will."

312

"What would you do if her desires got the better of her will?"

"If that was clear beyond all possible doubt, I'd serve her desires."

The Prince put his hands behind him and paced back and forth as well as he could in the confined space. Then he looked at me, but said nothing. I concluded he hadn't given Vittoria up. I can't say I was particularly surprised.

"Sit yourself down!" he said, suddenly cheerful, nodding me toward a chair and clapping his hands to summon Folletto.

"Marcello," he said, "one more question. If I hadn't interrupted when your pistol was aimed at Lodovico, would you have shot him?"

"No, but I wanted to. And at one point I nearly did."

"When?"

"When he started saying I'd corrupted my sister. If he'd said one more word against her, I'd have fired. But he's shrewd enough to know that. As a matter of fact, he's careful to keep all his taunts from going too far. He's really just a coward."

"That's what makes him dangerous," said the Prince. "Watch out for yourself in Rome, Marcello."

## Caterina Acquaviva

To say I was glad to be in Rome again was putting it mildly! I couldn't see myself spending months at Santa Maria, especially with all the bad weather there. It was as if blue skies and a hot sun had been waiting for us back in the courtyard at the Rusticucci palace. What's more, in Santa Maria I'd spent only one night with Marcello in two whole weeks, and in Rome I was almost certain to see him more often.

But if Vittoria was pleased to be back in Rome and free again, she didn't show much sign of it. She was neither cheerful nor sad. She didn't talk much. Most of the time she seemed to be dreaming. She did take her meals with the rest of the family, and she no longer shut the door of her room against Signor Peretti. But she kept me with her, and though she spoke to him nicely, she didn't encourage him to stay. I felt quite sorry for him, as he sat wretchedly in a corner, talking of this and that and not daring to claim his rights as a husband. If you want my opinion, I think he was too considerate. No man in Grottammare would behave like that with his wife. He'd better not try!

Sometimes Vittoria seemed rather embarrassed at the way she was treating her husband, but not to the point of opening her arms to him. She must have been put off him by the Prince's embrace, and was making him pay for forcing her to choose him instead of her hero. That's what we women are like when the devil gets us by the innards — too kind to the one and too cruel to the other.

We hadn't been in Rome a fortnight, when one day I was brushing her hair and in came Marcello, without knocking. Holy Madonna! My heart started to pound just at the sight of him! But do you think the wretch so much as brushed my hand or gave me a single glance? It was the same with his sister. Hardly a look at her in the mirror as he stood behind her fumbling in his doublet. He put a letter down on the jewel box without a word.

"Who is it from?" she asked without expression.

"Can't you guess?" he answered coldly. "Do I have to explain?"

She didn't hesitate an instant. She seized the letter, held it briefly in the flame of a candle, then set it in a saucer and watched it burn. Her guardian angel must have been pleased. Still, I'd have been a little worried in his shoes. She'd burned the letter, but she hadn't forbidden her brother to go on acting as intermediary between herself and the Prince. She'd have been afraid he might obey.

Marcello took leave of her at once, if you can call it that: he just nodded and went. He didn't look at me either. I went on brushing with a heavy heart, not knowing if I'd dare go to his room when I was free. I didn't have much time to wonder. After a few moments, Vittoria said in a subdued voice: "That will do, Caterina. Go to bed."

"But, signora, I'm only half finished!"

She glared at me. "Don't argue! Do as I tell you."

In spite of that, I did stay long enough to tidy the dressing table, though not long enough to make her angry. She sat looking at the ashes in the saucer as if by some magic that might turn them back into the letter she hadn't read. But only the devil could do that, and after what had happened at Santa Maria who could blame him for staying in the background for a while?

"Good night, signora."

That was mere formality; I'd be surprised if she did have a good night. She didn't answer; she hadn't heard me. As I was leaving, it struck me that she'd sent me away not because she wanted to be alone, but because she hoped I'd go and get Marcello to tell me what she hadn't dared ask. Because I have such a kind heart, I was only too glad to do this errand, not to mention that it gave me a good reason for going to see him.

He'd nearly finished undressing when I went in, without knocking. He's so handsome my throat went dry and my legs started to tremble with longing. But I got an icy welcome.

"What are *you* doing here?" he said with a scowl.

"With your permission, signore, I've come to see you."

"My permission? Did I ask you to come?"

"No, signore."

"Is this a public place, that you just march in without knocking?"

"I didn't like to knock, signore."

"Why not?"

"If I had, you would have asked who it was."

"Naturally. So?"

"I was afraid if I said who I was, you'd tell me to go away."

"Well, I'm telling you to go away now. What's the difference?"

"The difference is that I've seen you," I said humbly. At the same time, my eyes were boldly looking him up and down.

He laughed. It looked as if I'd won, but

I knew that with him everything could suddenly be lost at the last minute, so I persevered in my humility. There's not a slave girl in Rome more slavish than I can be.

"Take your clothes off," he said.

I had so many buttons to undo that my hands shook with impatience.

"Do you know what you are, Caterina?"

"No, signore."

"The most clinging octopus in creation."

"Yes, signore."

"Do you know what an octopus is?"

"Yes, signore. I caught a little one once at Grottammare. They cling to you with their tentacles. But if you twist their heads around, they let go."

"Unfortunately, I can't twist your head around."

Fat lot I cared what he said. What mattered was that he'd said it in a low, silky voice and looked at me with those eyes of his, like a tiger's. I waited with delight for him to leap on me, drag me into his lair by the scruff of the neck, and devour me.

Which he did. When it was over, instead of saying, "Go away now, Caterina; I'm tired," he seemed inclined to chat. He propped himself on an elbow and delivered a string of insults. But his voice was soft, and his eyes were kind. It was now or never.

"Signore, may I ask you some questions?"

"Fire."

"Are you still with the Prince?"

"No. I've left him. I'm not his secretary any more."

"So you have gone back to live with your old woman?"

His eyes darkened, and he boxed my ear. Hard, and richly deserved. "That'll teach you to be disrespectful about Signora Sorghini. And me."

"Sorry, signore."

"Anyhow, I never left her. The only difference now is that I don't go to Montegiordano."

"How did the Prince get the letter to you?"

He shrugged. "Can't you guess who was the go-between?"

"Yes."

"So why ask stupid questions? Do I ask you questions?"

"Signore," I said, rather vexed, "you might well ask me how I confessed the sin I committed at Santa Maria."

"But I don't. I presume you didn't mention my name."

"I'm not as stupid as that!"

He laughed, rolled me over on my back, and lay on top of me, gripping my wrists and holding my arms outspread. Then he knocked his forehead against mine, rubbed noses with me, and said through clenched teeth: "Yes, Caterina, you *are* stupid. And ugly too. Very ugly. The ugliest girl in all Italy! And your breasts are as shapeless as sacks of wheat on a donkey's back."

He looked at me with his tiger's eyes, and all I could think was, Rape me! It's delightful to be raped by a man you love! But then, of course, it's not really rape.

The following evening, I was brushing the signora's hair, as usual. At night I brush it before I plait it into braids, loose enough not to pull on her scalp, but tight enough to keep it from getting tangled in sleep. In the morning, I brush it again to undo the plaits and make them "melt into a single rippling mantle." That's how Signora Tarquinia describes it.

Suddenly, Marcello appeared, again without knocking — despite his reproaches to me — and without a word or a glance for anyone put a sealed letter down on the jewel box. Immediately, as if she'd been waiting all day for this moment, Vittoria picked it up, put it to the flame of one of the candles, and we all watched it burn.

Not a word from anyone. Vittoria didn't tell Marcello not to bring any more letters, and Marcello didn't say it was hardly worth his trouble to do so. He just nodded and left. Later, when I went and tried to talk to him, he told me roughly to be quiet.

The same silent scene was repeated the next night, and the next, each night for a week. I wondered what the Prince found to say. He must often have repeated himself.

On the eighth day — a Friday, I think — there was an important change. Marcello spoke. When the daily letter had duly been reduced to a heap of ashes, he glanced at his sister in the mirror and said dryly: "What a farce! Don't expect me to keep it up indefinitely."

The next day, Vittoria let the brushing go on and on in vain, instead of telling me to stop and braid her hair. Finally, at eleven o'clock, when my arms were nearly dropping off, I started to do the plaits of my own accord. Her face was impassive; I couldn't see the expression in her eyes, because she kept them lowered, but I could tell she was as unhappy as I was that Marcello didn't come. She must have been wondering whether it was because he'd had enough of watching her burn the letters, or if the Prince had got tired of writing.

For days, we waited, but no Marcello. It was a horrible time for both of us. Sometimes the signora was so agitated she got angry with me for nothing; sometimes she lay face down on the bed with her head buried in the pillow. She refused to go down to meals and closed her door again to Signor Peretti.

Finally, at eleven o'clock on Thursday, Marcello came in, nodded to Vittoria, and sat down on the bed with his legs apart and his hands clasped between them. He stayed like that for a good quarter of an hour, with his head bowed and not saying a word, while Vittoria fidgeted on her stool, biting her lips.

At last she could hold out no longer and asked in a quavering voice: "Haven't you brought anything?"

"What do you mean, 'anything'?"

"Don't pretend!" she cried angrily. "You know very well what I mean!"

"I know. But I'm surprised. I brought you a letter from the Prince every night for a week, and each time you burned it. Tonight I don't bring anything, and you ask me for a letter. What for? To burn it?"

"I don't care a rap if you're surprised or not. Tell me straight out: did the Prince give you a letter for me?"

"Yes."

"Well, what are you waiting for? Give it to me!"

"So you can burn it?"

"It's none of your business what I do with

it. You're supposed to give it to me, that's all!"

"Unfortunately, I can't," he said casually.

"What do you mean?"

"I burned it myself."

"You burned a letter addressed to me?" she cried, beside herself. "That's disgraceful!"

"Why? Isn't that what you'd have done with it yourself?"

"That doesn't matter. You had no right! It was *my* letter!"

"Not at all," said Marcello calmly. "Since you weren't going to read it, it wasn't anyone's letter. A letter's written to be read. If you burn it instead of reading it, it isn't a letter — it's just paper."

"But it was for me to decide whether to read it or not."

"What do you mean, 'decide'? Your decision was already made, no question about it. For a whole week, without hesitation, you've burned every letter I've brought you. And you know very well you'd have done the same today."

"But it's I who have done it!"

"Come, Vittoria," he said patiently, "this is childish. I was just as capable as you of reducing today's letter to ashes. And that's what I've done with them all."

"What do you mean?"

"The Prince has written to you every day since Friday. Six letters altogether. I thought I was obeying your wishes. I burned all six of them."

She stood up, pushed me aside, and faced him, her eyes blazing: "You're a thief!" she cried. "You had no right to do such a thing. You've betrayed the Prince's confidence."

"Write and tell him so!" he mocked. "I'll deliver the note."

"Get out!" she cried.

Snatching the brush from my hand, she threw it at him. He ducked, picked it up, put it carefully on the dressing table, and left without a backward glance.

As soon as he'd closed the door, she threw herself down on the bed, not bothering about her hair. I could see that all my brushing was wasted.

I was flabbergasted as well as annoyed. Close as Vittoria and Marcello were to one another, they often quarreled, but never before so violently. The poor signora was sobbing on her bed, her lovely face buried in the pillow. I didn't know what to do. Should I go and see Marcello or try to comfort her? I didn't really have much choice, since it was her right to dismiss me or not. We'd been up till eleven o'clock for six days. Each was a long day's work. It was true I didn't really have much to do, and it was certainly better to be a lady's maid in the Rusticucci palace than the wife of a master fisherman in Grottammare. I knew how *they* treated their women — more clips on the ears than kisses.

There was a knock at the door. Vittoria took her head out of the pillow and said: "Don't open. Ask who it is."

I did so.

"It's Signora Accoramboni," said an authoritative voice.

"I'm sorry, Mother. I can't see you," said Vittoria firmly. "I've got a bad headache."

"I don't really like talking to you through the door, but I want to ask you a favor. My maid's ill. I'd like you to lend me yours to undress me."

"I'm afraid that's impossible. I don't lend my maid."

"That's not very gracious of you, Vittoria."

"I am as you've made me. Get Giulietta to help you."

"She's asleep."

"Undress yourself then. You've got all your arms and legs."

"Vittoria! You treat your mother like the fifth wheel of a coach. You're a monster of rudeness."

"So you've often told me. Good night, Mother."

"Your night can only be a bad one after the way you've treated me."

"Don't worry, it will be. Good night, Mother."

I could hear La Superba crossing the anteroom where I slept when the signora really was unwell. She slammed the door angrily. I was glad she'd been put in her place.

"Caterina," Vittoria asked, "do you think Marcello really did burn those letters?"

"Perhaps not," I said. I hadn't any idea. I said "not" to please her, and "perhaps" to be on the safe side.

"You know what a tease he is."

"Yes, signora."

"Caterina, go to his room, please, and if he's there, bring him back to see me."

"Yes, signora."

I went toward the door, but just as I was about to turn the handle, it opened and Marcello burst through like a jack-in-the-box. After what had happened, I expected the signora to give him a cool reception. Not at all. She gazed at him anxiously. He took in everything: Vittoria lying on the bed, her lovely hair in tangles, her eyes red, a tear-drenched handkerchief in her hand. And he said to her wryly: "The 'fifth wheel' says you're a monster of rudeness. I regard Flaminio as a monster of devoutness and Giulietta as a monster of

326

chastity. And you regard me as a monster pure and simple. But don't think you're an exception, Vittoria. You're the most interesting specimen in the whole family: you're a monster of willful blindness. As soon as a fact is inconvenient, you tuck your head under your wing and pretend it doesn't exist."

"What does all that mean?" she asked, with much less resentment than I'd have expected.

She was obviously handling him with care, afraid of what he might say.

"Nothing unkind. I'm never cruel to you except to be kind. For instance, to stop you from lying to yourself, which in the long run could endanger your soul. I didn't burn your letters, Vittoria. I even numbered them so you could read them in chronological order. Here they are."

He took them out of the pocket in the armhole of his doublet and threw all six of them on the bed. Vittoria was overcome. You'd have thought those letters were a holy sacrament. She didn't dare touch them at first. When she finally made up her mind to, she didn't even try to conceal her eagerness. She seized the letter marked with a one, broke the seal with trembling fingers, and devoured it.

"You have plenty to keep you occupied," said Marcello, "so I'll leave you. I'll be back in an hour."

She didn't answer. She hadn't heard.

"Caterina," she said without looking up, "bring a candlestick closer."

I could tell this was going to take a long time, a very long time, because no doubt she'd read every letter more than once, so I moved a low table close to the bed and brought one of the candlesticks over from the dressing table.

Then I sat on a stool in a corner, leaned against the wall, and watched her. I envied her. When a man takes the trouble to write to you every day, it means he really adores you. I can't think of anyone who'd do that for me. Of course, I'm much more available. Can you see a pope and a cardinal mustering forty soldiers to guard *my* virtue?

The Prince would have gone wild if he could have seen her then, lying there in her nightgown with her arms and a good part of her bosom bare. I noticed that her breasts were as firm as mine, only not so big. I don't say that to criticize, just to do myself justice. The signora's a hundred times better-looking than I am; quite simply, she's a pearl of a woman. Especially like that: reading the letters over and over, wrapped in her long hair (two hours' brushing for me tomorrow), her lovely face flushed with emotion, her cheeks shaded by her long lashes, her bosom rising and falling.

Time passed. Fascinating as I found the sight, I couldn't help feeling sleepy. But I wasn't going to interrupt her to ask if I could go: she looked too absorbed. Or was I staying out of self-interest? Marcello had said he'd be back.

There's something diabolical about Marcello. I've only got to mention or even think of him and he appears. He pops up in the signora's room without knocking. It's true they're twins and don't mind if they see each other without any clothes on. The contrast with family modesty at Grottammare! There, everyone's shocked if you show an inch of bare skin. And the acrobatics to get out of your nightgown and into your day clothes without letting anyone see anything! I remember as if it was yesterday the slap and the scolding I got from Il Mancino one morning because I got out of the bed I shared with him and crossed the room naked. I was only ten years old, and thought he'd like to see the little body he caressed every day. Yes, but the caressing took place at night, and under the bedclothes, and while both of us pretended to be asleep.

So in came Marcello, and as Vittoria looked up inquiringly he said point-blank: "There's more than one way into Margherita Sorghini's house. In the days when she didn't want anyone to know about our liaison, I used to go in through a back way, off a little cul-de-sac only wide enough for one person. On the left, there's a small porch opening into a corridor, and the corridor leads to a little chapel that Signora Sorghini has turned over to some mendicant friars. She's very pious, and acts as their patron. The chapel's open to the public, but hardly anyone goes there. Farther down the corridor, there's another door. It's dark green, and here's the key to it."

He threw it adroitly into her lap.

"If you open that door, you'll find a staircase, and if you have the patience to go up three flights, you'll come out on a flat roof, where Signora Sorghini has put a tent up, with curtains to keep out the sun and the wind and prying eyes. It's a charming spot, surrounded by lots of red and white geraniums. If you go there tomorrow during Vespers, you can rest without being disturbed. Signora Sorghini won't be there, she and I leave tomorrow at dawn for her house at Amalfi, to enjoy a month's sea breezes."

He left without so much as a glance at me. Vittoria seized the key, and not between finger and thumb. She clasped it to her bosom with her whole left hand, and put her right hand around that to make doubly sure it was safe. Oh, that little key wasn't going to run away — it was so cozy there between her breasts.

"Signora, may I go now?"

"Good night, Caterina," she said absently, staring into space with a faint smile on her lips.

I went to Marcello's room. It was empty. The wretch hadn't even waited to say good-bye to me. I looked around. The place couldn't have been emptier. Worse still, it was going to be empty for a month, since he was leaving at dawn with his old woman. I said it aloud: "His old woman!"

If I'd been Vittoria, I'd have thrown myself on Marcello's bed and buried my face in the pillow. But that's not my way. I blew out the candle he'd left burning, went out to the gallery, and leaned my stomach against the balustrade. There was a fine moon, and down in the courtyard I could see our little white cat lying full length with her claws out. She was scratching at the ground and growling, with her eye on a male tabby hiding under a bush. Where had he sprung from? Where had she found him? She was growling, our little Moujoute, ready to either scratch the tom or accept him. When he'd taken her, he wouldn't get away without a good clout. And serve him right! The tears were streaming down my cheeks. I wiped them away. That's how it was with my mistress and me: when one laughed, the other wept.

## Lodovico Orsini, Count of Oppedo

I nearly fell for it. But not quite. I'd had my suspicions from the start, knowing Paolo and being pretty sure that, if necessary, the vile Marcello could give his master points in Machiavellian cunning. When I went and reported to Francesco de' Medici in Florence, he was skeptical too.

"Women being what they are," he said, "that is, virtuous only when they're forced to be, it's hard to believe Paolo found Vittoria intractable and only slept beside her like a brother. Especially since up till now he's never had a heart or body refused him in the whole of Italy! And he's a fine-looking fellow and the sort of hero the weaker sex dotes on. What's more, would Paolo have boasted about it if he really had failed?"

I too thought the whole thing looked like a plot, and that Marcello's dismissal was likely part of it. Paolo showed such affection for the creature, even inviting him to his cabin on the galley and leaving me, his own cousin, to eat with the mate!

Medici gave me ten thousand piasters for my trouble and to cover the expenses I'd incurred in going to see him. He asked me to keep a close eye on what happened, so that Virginio's inheritance wouldn't be threatened by his father's remarrying. I saw Virginio several times while I was in Florence, and, with an eye to the future, tried to make friends with him. In spite of his youth, I found him thoughtful, cool, and cautious, seeing much and saying little; in short, a Medici already, with none of the legendary Orsini rashness. He didn't give me one piaster. But perhaps he knew his uncle had already paid me. Not that I considered that the Medicis rewarded me adequately for my services. But since Paolo had made up his mind not to give me any more money, I had no choice. I wished I was still with him, though. I don't really like the Medicis. They smell too much of banks and trade.

Back in Rome, I put a spy on Paolo's tail, selecting him with care from among the outlaws I gave bed and board to in my palace, though this was against papal law. That I don't have the right of asylum is a great injustice.

The man I chose was a monk who'd had to renounce the cloth to escape being sent to ecclesiastical prison. I got him to wear his habit again to trail the Prince; Rome is full of monks, and nothing escapes notice so easily. Also, whereas a mask attracts attention, no one looks twice at a cowl modestly pulled down over the eyes to ward off worldly temptation.

Because Paolo often went out on horseback, I provided the monk with a mule. It couldn't have kept up with the Prince's horse on the highways outside Rome, but in the city's congested traffic, it managed very well. Since Vittoria Peretti had given up riding, or so I'd heard, I guessed that if the two of them met, it must be in some discreet spot in Rome itself.

More than a week went by without the monk's pursuit bringing any result whatever. But on the ninth evening, he asked to see me. His hands were shaking, his eyes staring, and his knees practically knocking together.

"Signor Count," he said, "I've found out what's going on. But I'd be obliged if you'd relieve me of my task. If I don't desist, I'm a dead man."

"What *is* going on, Giacomo, and where?"

"In the widow Sorghini's house."

"Good heavens! What a coincidence!"

"There's a cul-de-sac behind the house, and a porch that opens on a corridor. This leads to a little chapel that's unlocked and then to a green door that's locked. The signora has a key to the green door, and so has the Prince."

"Where's the danger to you?"

"It's a mortal danger, Count. When I saw the Prince go in, I waited a few minutes and then followed. He wasn't in the chapel, so I knew he must have gone through the green door. I'm very religious by nature, and I knelt down at the front of the chapel and started to pray —"

"Spare us your piety, Giacomo!"

"It didn't prevent me from watching the door to the chapel, Count."

"How could you see it, kneeling up front?"

"I made a hole in the back of my cowl so I could see if I turned my head."

"And what did you see?"

"A signora coming in, followed by her maid. Both wore masks and hoods and long cloaks down to their ankles, in spite of the heat. But when the signora knelt down and crossed herself, some of her hair showed, and I knew who it was."

"They were praying, I suppose."

"Fervently but briefly. When they got up and left the chapel, I followed. But before I got out, someone burst from a confessional, and a huge arm grabbed me by my cassock. He pinned me against the wall and stuck the point of a dagger under my chin. 'What are you doing here and where are you going?' he hissed. 'As you can see, signore,' I said humbly, 'I'm a monk and I often come here to pray. Signora Sorghini has put her chapel at our disposal.' 'Monk?' he said. 'We'll see about that!' And he tore off my cowl and felt my tonsure. Thank God I'd thought to go to the barber, so it was smooth as an egg. But that wasn't enough for him. He searched my pockets. He found a rosary and a few religious medals I'd put there on purpose, but he was still suspicious. He made me recite the Pater, the Ave, the Credo, and the Confiteor in Latin. I didn't make a single mistake. And, believe me, Count, it's a long time since I prayed so hard."

"Well, your prayers were answered: you're still here."

"This time he let me go — yes. But it would be folly to tempt fate again."

"Who do you think it was?"

"One of the Prince's men, there to protect the signora."

"How can you be so sure?"

"Count," said Giacomo proudly, "I may be afraid, but I'm not a coward. I waited for the wretch and trailed him later in the afternoon. When the signora came out, the man followed her back to the Rusticucci palace. Then he went on to Montegiordano. So he must be one of the Prince's soldiers. He's tall, wears a coat of mail and a sword, and has a dagger and a pistol in his belt. His nasty black eyes got a good look at me in the chapel, and I don't want him to see me again."

"Don't worry, Giacomo. Your part is over, and you won't have to appear again. For your own good, padlock your tongue forever and pocket these piasters."

I spent that night thinking about what to do. I considered two courses of action and the consequences of each. The first was to inform Signor Peretti anonymously of where and when the guilty lovers met. Unfortunately, everything I knew about him led me to suppose he wouldn't kill his wife, but only shut her up again in some place like Santa Maria. From which, I didn't doubt, the Prince would manage to free her and, if Peretti should happen to meet with a fatal accident, marry her. The very opposite of what I wanted.

The other course, more radical and more attractive from every point of view, was to have Vittoria killed by a hired assassin. But this would be difficult, and dangerous for me. She went out only in the daytime, and was protected by the wily and resolute armed giant Giacomo had come up against. You'd have to be wily to think of hiding in a confessional! Moreover, a hired assassin might be caught and speak under torture, implicating me. If that happened, I wouldn't give much for my chances: even if I escaped death from the papal court, Paolo would finish me off.

I could have written the Medicis about it

and let them decide what was to be done. But I knew they would be too circumspect to give me advice or to make any move until I'd got the chestnuts out of the fire myself. I'd be lucky if they let me have a few for myself when, thanks to my efforts, Virginio came into his full inheritance.

While I was still undecided about which course to take, I was surprised to get an invitation from Monsignor Cherubi, then visiting Rome. He was staying in a palace rented by the Patriarch of Venice, whose right arm he had become after he was dismissed by Montalto.

Cherubi was an amiable fellow: frivolous and imprudent but not a fool, inquisitive as a squirrel, and talkative as a magpie. He was unique in the Vatican, where there are so many clever men, because, contrary to logic and expectation, he'd made a nice career for himself in the church through an endless series of gaffes. The reason was that his clumsiness was soothing to the Machiavellian schemers who surrounded him. He amused everyone and harmed no one.

I was even more astonished when I saw that only Cherubi and I were to be present at the meal he'd invited me to. I concluded that the interview had been organized — perhaps at the instigation of Gregory, under whose protection Cherubi was — to worm information out of me about Paolo. I sat down highly tickled by the situation.

Most of the meal passed in the usual chat. Cherubi was a big, fat man, with a face the color of a Parma ham. He was a great trencherman and a heavy drinker, so the fare was excellent. But when we got to dessert, his appetite seemed to slacken, as did his talk, and I sensed we were approaching serious matters. They came sooner and more abruptly than I expected.

"Count," he said in a jovial, tipsy voice, "I'd like to ask you a question that was put to me by His Holiness but that I couldn't answer. In your opinion, has the inevitable happened between your cousin and Signora Peretti?"

I laughed, first because the word "inevitable" struck me as piquant coming from a prelate, and second because laughing gave me time to think before I answered.

"Monsignor," I said gaily, "your question has a virtue I greatly admire: it is frank. And I ask nothing better than to answer it, at least if you'll promise in return to satisfy my curiosity about the Holy Father's feelings on the subject."

"I'll tell you what I know," said Cherubi, apparently throwing Vatican diplomacy to the winds. "You know me," he added with a chuckle, putting his hands on his belly: "Round in speech and square in business."

I laughed too, beginning to see how Cherubi had done better with his gaffes than others with their wisdom. A gaffe is a diplomatic blunder. And a gaff is a long pole with a hook on the end to pull another boat toward you or push it away. Since Cherubi's gaff, in this case, was clearly designed to bring my little barque alongside his great galley, I decided not to offer any resistance.

"Yes, Monsignor," I said, "the inevitable has happened. I can't prove it, but I am certain of it."

"Oh, how unfortunate!" said Cherubi gravely. "The Holy Father will be very sorry to hear it, and, because he had the gift of tears, no doubt he'll shed a few."

He said this without a trace of irony, as if he shared the Pope's sorrow in advance.

"But what can he do?" I asked.

"That's just it — nothing. That's what's so galling. Telling the husband wouldn't do any good. He'd only lock the flighty creature up again, and sooner or later our hero would manage to set her free."

He was right, but there was something here that intrigued me. Adultery was a sin not rare in the papal state. Why then did the Pope find this example of it so distressing?

"I understand the Holy Father's apprehensions," I said. "No doubt he's afraid Peretti might meet with a fatal accident."

"The Holy Father," answered Cherubi, "has never expressed such a fear. But men being what they are, such an eventuality can't be excluded. What do you think?"

I said, very guardedly: "Monsignor, Paolo Orsini is my first cousin. Apart from his son, I'm his nearest relative. And I'm very fond of him."

"Exactly. Who knows him better than you do?"

"It's certainly true Paolo is very passionate," I went on. "And, like all passionate people, he's unpredictable. Moreover, his military fame has gone to his head. In my opinion, he wouldn't be restrained by the laws of the state. He thinks he's above them." As I was suavely delivering myself of this, while being richly entertained by a senior dignitary of the church, I suddenly remembered with amusement that at that very moment my two bandits were holding travelers for ransom in the Nora mountains and perhaps, being bloodthirsty by nature, even slaying them.

"So you don't rule out the idea," said Cherubi, "that Peretti might meet with an accident?"

"Unfortunately no. And now may I ask you a question?"

"By all means."

"If our hypothesis were to prove correct, would the Vatican dare arrest Paolo?"

"It would be better to deprive him of the fruits of his crime."

"You mean imprison Vittoria?"

"When you want to break a chain," said Cherubi sententiously, "you attack the weakest link."

At these words I felt a wave of satisfaction surge through me. But it didn't last long. I soon saw the flaw in this plan.

"Our hero would take up arms to free her."

"Probably," said Cherubi impassively.

"But we think we could get the better of him if —"

"If — Monsignor?"

"If you don't join forces with him."

Now we're getting to it, I thought. Here at last is the reason for this invitation, this openness, these frank answers. Not only would my men be useful support for Paolo, but because I had the ear of the lower orders, the revolt would become a popular uprising if I joined it. And that development would be highly dangerous for the Holy Father.

I was silent for a moment, not because I didn't know what I was going to say, but to lend more weight to it.

"Monsignor," I said at last, "you must know I have no sympathy for this caprice of my cousin's. And, despite my great affection for him, I'm too mindful of my duties to his Holiness to rule out my remaining aloof from any conflict that may arise out of Paolo's follies. But I must point out that my neutrality will have to be negotiated when the time comes."

"And so it will be," said Cherubi.

"Through you?"

"With my mediation."

He smiled as if he was pleased to have used a phrase that was different from mine. I smiled too. I was nicely replete after an excellent meal, and the prospect of "negotiating" my neutrality when the time came was very pleasant. The Vatican was rich, and my purse was empty — the Medicis' ten thousand ducats had bailed me out only temporarily.

"However," Cherubi continued, "that's only a hypothesis. It's highly unlikely a man of honor like our hero would go so far as to defy the law."

"Highly unlikely," I echoed, an octave lower.

The meal was over. I stood up and cut the leave-takings short. The future was beckoning me in the most seductive manner, and I was anxious to examine it more closely.

# 8

## *Gian Battista della Pace, Bargello*

At nine o'clock on the morning of July 6, I, as chief of the papal police, went to the Rusticucci palace with my assistant, my clerk, and a surgeon, to record the death by murder of Signor Francesco Peretti, adopted son of His Eminence Cardinal Montalto and third chamberlain to His Holiness Pope Gregory XIII.

The mother of the deceased, Signora Camilla Peretti, was watching over the body in the main hall, with his mother-in-law, Tarquinia Accoramboni, and two of the latter's children, Giulietta and Flaminio. According to her mother, Signora Vittoria Peretti was shut up in her room, "out of her mind with grief," and unable to talk to anyone.

I requested the family to withdraw and ordered the surgeon to examine the body. He observed a wound from an arquebus bullet in the right leg. The shot, which had been fired from behind, had broken the victim's femur and caused him to fall. Death was due to a stab wound in the heart, delivered by a dagger, probably when the victim was lying defenseless on the ground. According to my assistant, Signor Peretti's sword had been found unsheathed several yards from the body. This detail intrigued me, until it was explained by the testimony of Filippo, a footman, the only witness to the murder, whom I interviewed in the palace.

*Bargello:* Filippo, I'm told you were the last person to see Signor Peretti alive.

*Filippo:* I didn't have anything to do with it, Signor Bargello. Don't blame me for the murder, please. Dear God, I'm innocent.

*Bargello:* Come now, Filippo, don't be silly. And stop shaking like a leaf. Sit down on this stool. No one suspects you. Just answer my questions.

*Filippo:* Yes, Signor Bargello.

*Bargello:* Do you know why Signor Peretti ventured out alone at half past eleven at night?

*Filippo:* Well, first of all, Signor Bargello, he wasn't alone. I was with him. I went in front with a torch to light him along.

*Bargello:* You weren't armed?

*Filippo:* No, Signor Bargello. Anyhow I

couldn't have used a weapon, because I was carrying the torch.

*Bargello:* How was Signor Peretti armed?

*Filippo:* He only had a sword.

*Bargello:* Why do you say "only"?

*Filippo:* I was surprised he didn't take his pistols too. He was usually so careful.

*Bargello:* Where did he keep his pistols?

*Filippo:* On his bedside table. They were always kept loaded and primed, and no one was allowed to touch them, not even to dust them. As I said, he was very careful.

*Bargello:* It wasn't very careful of him to walk the streets of Rome at night so lightly armed and escorted.

*Filippo:* That's what I thought, Signor Bargello, when he told me to go in front with a torch. To tell you the truth, my heart was in my boots.

*Bargello:* Do you know the reason for this nocturnal errand?

*Filippo:* No, Signor Bargello. But I know where we were going. He told me.

*Bargello:* Where?

*Filippo:* To the Villa Sorghini.

*Bargello:* But it's been shut up for a week.

*Filippo:* I know. I was surprised.

*Bargello:* There were quite a number of things that surprised you about all this.

346

*Filippo:* Oh, yes, Signor Bargello. There were indeed. Lots of things.

*Bargello:* For example?

*Filippo:* For example, that Signor Peretti didn't take more people with him. There are half a dozen able-bodied men in the palace here, not counting the gatekeeper, who's an old soldier.

*Bargello:* What time was it when Signor Peretti decided to go out?

*Filippo:* I was about to go to bed. So, a little before eleven o'clock. Il Mancino had just brought him a note.

*Bargello:* Do you know what was in it?

*Filippo:* No, Signor Bargello.

*Bargello:* Signor Peretti received the note a little before eleven o'clock, but he didn't go out till half past. What happened in that half hour?

*Filippo:* All the family were there in the courtyard begging him not to go out.

*Bargello:* What do you mean by "all the family"?

*Filippo:* The old Signora Peretti, Signora Accoramboni, Signorina Giulietta, Signor Flaminio. They clung to Signor Peretti, begging him not to risk his life. Oh, Signor Bargello, you ought to have heard them. The crying and wailing.

*Bargello:* What about Signora Vittoria?

*Filippo:* The Signora's not one to cling to people. But she did speak to Signor Peretti afterward.

*Bargello:* After what?

*Filippo:* After he'd shaken off the others.

*Bargello:* Did you hear what she said to him?

*Filippo:* No. There was too much noise. But I could tell from the way she looked that she was trying to stop him from going out too.

*Bargello:* How did she look?

*Filippo:* Very frightened, very anxious. She was wringing her hands.

*Bargello:* How long did they talk?

*Filippo:* I don't know. A good ten minutes, I think, but in two parts.

*Bargello:* What do you mean?

*Filippo:* At one point the signora left Signor Peretti and went over and spoke to Il Mancino. Then she went back to Signor Peretti again and went on begging him.

*Bargello:* How do you know she was begging him if you couldn't hear what she was saying?

*Filippo:* I could tell by how she looked.

*Bargello:* You must have heard her, since you were lighting the scene with your torch.

*Filippo:* Signor Bargello, I'm not a liar. I'm telling you the truth. There was a terrible din all around me. And there were three torchbearers, and I wasn't the one nearest the signora.

*Bargello:* Then what happened?

*Filippo:* Signor Peretti sent Piero to fetch his sword.

*Bargello:* You heard that?

*Filippo:* No, I didn't, Signor Bargello. But I knew when I saw Piero come back with the sword. Please, Signor Bargello, don't keep calling me a liar.

*Bargello:* I'm not calling you a liar. What happened next?

*Filippo:* Piero came back with the sword in its scabbard and the belt to hang it on.

*Bargello:* And then?

*Filippo:* The master unsheathed the sword and threw the belt and the scabbard angrily on the ground.

*Bargello:* Angrily?

*Filippo:* Yes. He looked really furious. Then he barked at me to lead the way with my torch and rushed out like a madman. I'd never seen him in such a state. Out in the street, he told me we were going to the palace at Montecavallo, and shouted at me to go faster, faster.

*Bargello:* Then what happened?

*Filippo:* You know very well what happened. They killed him.

*Bargello:* Come, Filippo, don't cry. Men don't cry.

*Filippo:* Why not, if they're unhappy? And I'm unhappy twice over. First because Signor Peretti was a good master, and also because I don't know what will become of me now he's dead.

*Bargello:* Tell me how it happened.

*Filippo:* Signor Bargello, would I had never been born, to see such a thing. What a misfortune.

*Bargello:* Now, now, Filippo, get on with it, please.

*Filippo:* I'm sorry, Signor Bargello. I really don't know what I'm doing. Well, you know the street leading to the Montecavallo palace? It's very steep, and the master had to slow down. He was tired by then too. Halfway up the street, I heard a shot behind me. I turned around, and there was Signor Peretti lying on his back on the ground. His right thigh was bleeding. But he hadn't let go of his sword.

*Bargello:* What did you do?

*Filippo:* I threw down my torch and ran away.

*Bargello:* Instead of helping your master?

*Filippo:* Helping him? How? And with what? I didn't even have a knife. And the others had an arquebus. Now everyone here has it in for me. You ought to hear them. They say, "Filippo hasn't got the balls of a baby rabbit!" It's not fair. I'd like to have seen them there. How would they have fought the bandits? With their teeth?

*Bargello:* Calm down, Filippo. Calm down.

*Filippo:* I didn't just run away, Signor Bargello. When I saw the murderers weren't coming after me, and that they couldn't even see me, because the torch had rolled away down the hill, I crept back. I didn't make any noise, because I was wearing felt shoes. I hid in a doorway and listened. The bandits were lighted by the torch, a few yards below Signor Peretti's body. So I could see them as plain as I see you. They walked calmly up the hill to where he was lying. There were two of them.

*Bargello:* What were they like?

*Filippo:* Very polite.

*Bargello:* What do you mean?

*Filippo:* Signor Bargello, once again, I'm telling the truth. They spoke to Signor Peretti very politely.

*Bargello:* They spoke to him?

*Filippo:* Oh, yes. Quite a conversation. I couldn't believe my ears.

*Bargello:* What did they say?

*Filippo:* First, the master — he was still holding his sword threw them his purse with his left hand and said, "If that's what you want, take it." The taller one answered: "With respect, Signor Peretti, we'll get your purse anyway when you're dead. Our job is to murder you." "Who gave you the job?" my master asked. "A monk. He pointed you out to us and told us who you were last Sunday, when you went to Mass at Santa Maria della Corte with your lady wife." And my master asked, "Do you know why the monk wanted me to die?" "If you ask me, Signor Peretti, he was only an intermediary," the man said. "What made you think that?" my master asked, and the man said, "A remark he made." My master wanted to know what it was, so the man said, "I'm sorry, Signor Peretti, it was very nasty." "Tell me anyway," my master insisted. "He said Signor Peretti had too beautiful a wife to keep her to himself." Then the other bandit said to the tall one, "Barca, you shouldn't have repeated that. It's vulgar."

*Bargello:* Barca?

*Filippo:* Yes, Signor Bargello.

*Bargello:* Make sure you've got that name, clerk: Barca. What was he like?

*Filippo:* Tall, broad shoulders, a beard right up to his eyes.

*Bargello:* And the other one?

*Filippo:* Short, beardless, slim, with a soft voice. If you ask me, he was the other one's faggot.

*Bargello:* Faggot?

*Filippo:* From what I've been told, there are men who act as women to other men.

*Bargello:* Go on.

*Filippo:* After that —

*Bargello:* After what?

*Filippo:* After Barca had repeated the nasty remark, Signor Peretti said, very crossly: "Well, what are you waiting for? Why don't you finish the job?" "Signor," Barca said, "you have a sword but we haven't. We've got to wait till the arquebus is reloaded." "Here you are," said the little one, "it's ready." He handed it to Barca, who aimed it at Signor Peretti, but it didn't go off. "Use your daggers, then," my master ordered.

*Bargello:* Ordered?

*Filippo:* It's the truth. And that's still not the most amazing thing. When Signor Peretti told the two bandits to use their daggers, Barca said, "Signor Peretti, a dagger against a sword?" Then the master did something hard to believe. He drew back his arm and hurled his sword down the hill with all his might. It rattled down over the cobblestones. Oh, signore, I can still hear it.

*Bargello:* Come, Filippo, stop crying and pull yourself together.

*Filippo:* Holy Mother of God, why did he do it? Disarm himself with armed bandits around him.

*Bargello:* Perhaps he thought it was hopeless to struggle. There were two of them.

*Filippo:* But if he'd held them off, I'd have had time to go for help. I did go, but it was too late.

*Bargello:* What happened after Signor Peretti threw his sword away?

*Filippo:* The two murderers took their time. They leaned over and undid his doublet. When my master got impatient, Barca explained that he wanted the doublet and didn't want to spoil the fine buffalo hide by making a hole in it with his dagger. I ran like mad to the Rusticucci palace to raise the alarm. When I got back, with all the able-bodied men in the house, the master's body was still warm.

I later interviewed Domenico Acquaviva, known as Il Mancino. This too was recorded by my clerk in the Rusticucci palace.

*Bargello:* Acquaviva, I have some questions to ask you.

*Il Mancino:* Here, Signor Bargello? In this cellar? Surrounded by instruments of torture? Have you forgotten I'm no longer a bandit?

*Bargello:* Your present career is just as immoral.

*Il Mancino:* But it's no threat to law and order. And among the pleasures it's brought me, Signor Bargello, is that of doing you some small favors.

*Bargello:* It's a treat to talk to you, Acquaviva. You express yourself so well.

*Il Mancino:* It's a pleasure I can do without — except, as I said, when I can be of use to you.

*Bargello:* That's twice you've reminded me. But there's no need. I remember. However, my gratitude isn't endless. It'll depend on how you answer my questions.

*Il Mancino:* I'll tell the whole truth whatever you ask.

*Bargello:* Who? Where? When?

*Il Mancino:* I don't understand.

*Bargello:* I'll concentrate on the "who." The rest will follow. Who gave you the note you delivered yesterday, just before eleven o'clock, to Signor Peretti?

*Il Mancino:* A monk. At the Mount of Olives tavern. At ten o'clock in the evening.

*Bargello:* Did you know him?

*Il Mancino:* Didn't know him from Adam.

*Bargello:* What did he look like?

*Il Mancino:* Difficult to say. He kept his hood down over his eyes. You know how modest monks are in the company of ladies. And some of the ladies where we met were showing off their charms.

*Bargello:* What sort of height and figure?

*Il Mancino:* Short, slim, long thin hands, almost like a skeleton's. But he could guzzle enough for half a dozen. Scar on his left thumb.

*Bargello:* Good. Pity you're on the wrong side of the law. You'd have been very useful to me on the right side. What did the monk say?

*Il Mancino:* He asked me to deliver the note right away to Signor Peretti, said it was urgent. He gave me twenty piasters to do it.

*Bargello:* Didn't you think it a rather suspicious errand at that time of night?

*Il Mancino:* From just anyone, it would have been. But not from a monk. I'm a good Catholic.

*Bargello:* Was the note sealed or only folded?

*Il Mancino:* Folded.

*Bargello:* So what could be easier than to unfold it and read it before delivering it to Signor Peretti?

*Il Mancino:* Yes, for someone who could read.

*Bargello:* You can't?

*Il Mancino:* Alas, no, Signor Bargello. I can neither read nor write.

*Bargello:* You speak Italian remarkably well for an illiterate.

*Il Mancino:* So everyone says. Perhaps I was meant for better things.

*Bargello:* So you don't know what was in the note?

*Il Mancino:* As a matter of fact, I do. Signor Peretti read it aloud when I gave it to him.

*Bargello:* What did it say?

*Il Mancino:* You know that as well as I do, Signor Bargello.

*Bargello:* Never mind. Tell me.

*Il Mancino:* The note was supposed to be from Marcello Accoramboni, and asked Signor Peretti to come to his aid. He was

357

lying wounded on the steps of the Monte-cavallo palace.

*Bargello:* Why do you say "supposed to be"?

*Il Mancino:* Because Marcello Accoramboni couldn't have sent the message. He's been in Amalfi with Signora Sorghini for the last ten days.

*Bargello:* He could have come back to Rome yesterday.

*Il Mancino:* You'd have known if he had. Everyone has to go through the police and the customs to enter Rome.

*Bargello:* They never used to give *you* much trouble.

*Il Mancino:* That's different. I was a bandit. I knew the ropes.

*Bargello:* You could have told him.

*Il Mancino:* I don't give away information.

*Bargello:* So I've noticed. One day we must come back to these ropes of yours, Acqua-viva.

*Il Mancino:* If you like. But there isn't much point. When one door closes, another opens.

*Bargello:* Let's get back to the note. You don't think it was genuine, then?

*Il Mancino:* With all respect, Signor Bargello, neither do you. Why would Marcello Accoramboni put his name to a note that would send him straight to the gallows as soon as his brother-in-law's murder was discovered?

*Bargello:* He might have been counting on protection in high places.

*Il Mancino:* In Amalfi?

*Bargello:* Not in Amalfi, no. But perhaps in Montegiordano.

*Il Mancino:* From what I've heard, Marcello Accoramboni has no connection with Montegiordano now.

*Bargello:* Is that all you've heard, Acquaviva?

*Il Mancino:* Yes, Signor Bargello.

*Bargello:* Yet your sister is Signora Peretti's maid.

*Il Mancino:* True, Signor Bargello.

*Bargello:* Perhaps she'll be more willing than you are to consult her memory.

*Il Mancino:* My memory has nothing to reproach me with except my past. As for Caterina, she confessed regularly to Father Barichelli at Santa Maria. And in Rome she confesses to Father Racasi. She'll confess to you too, if you like. You'll find her as open as the day.

*Bargello:* We shall see.

*Il Mancino:* Signor Bargello, don't be too hard on my little sister.

*Bargello:* No harder than on you. I'm trying to find the truth.

*Il Mancino:* It may not be where you think.

*Bargello:* What do you mean?

*Il Mancino:* Whoever ordered this murder is trying to incriminate Marcello Accoramboni.

*Bargello:* Thank you for your valuable help with my inquiry.

*Il Mancino:* You're making fun of me, Signor Bargello.

*Bargello:* A little, perhaps. Let's go back to when you gave Signor Peretti the note. Did he ask you what you thought?

*Il Mancino:* Yes, Signor Bargello. And I strongly advised him not to venture out into the streets of Rome at night.

*Bargello:* You'd done that yourself to bring him the note.

*Il Mancino:* That's different. I'm known. Dog doesn't eat dog.

*Bargello:* Did Signor Peretti listen to you?

*Il Mancino:* No. He seemed determined to go to his brother-in-law's aid. So I went and saw Signora Tarquinia Accoramboni. She asked to see the note, and declared loud and clear that Marcello hadn't written it.

*Bargello:* And that's when all the family

came running, and all the screaming and crying started?

*Il Mancino:* That's right. There must soon have been about twenty people out in the courtyard, counting the servants. Even those who'd gone to bed got up and came out. They were running hither and thither in the torchlight, weeping and wailing and waving their arms around. Just like a play.

*Bargello:* It seems Signora Peretti asked to see you at one point. What did she say?

*Il Mancino:* She asked me if I thought it was safe to go, and if I would go with him.

*Bargello:* What did you say to that?

*Il Mancino:* I absolutely refused. Even if he took an escort of ten. I said that in my opinion the rendezvous was a trap, and the only thing to do with a trap was to stay well away from it.

*Bargello:* What did she do then?

*Il Mancino:* She went and told Signor Peretti what I'd said, and begged him not to go. She was very emphatic about it.

*Bargello:* She threw herself in her husband's arms?

*Il Mancino:* No. She's not like that. She's rather regal.

*Bargello:* How do you explain that?

*Il Mancino:* Everyone's worshiped her for her beauty ever since she was a child.

*Bargello:* Did you hear what she said to her husband?

*Il Mancino:* No. Not really. There was too much noise.

*Bargello:* Where was Caterina just then?

*Il Mancino:* With the signora. She follows her like a shadow.

*Bargello:* So she can tell me what husband and wife said to one another?

*Il Mancino:* Signor Bargello, please, don't be hard on her. She's very sensitive. One little slap and she sheds tears.

*Bargello:* One would think you loved women, to hear you talk. Yet you live off them.

*Il Mancino:* Signor Bargello, I've never asked my sister for money.

*Bargello:* Don't get excited. I wasn't talking about her. I meant the girls at the Mount of Olives.

*Il Mancino:* That's different. I may live off them, but they owe their lives to me. If I wasn't there they'd get themselves murdered by their customers.

# Caterina Acquaviva

When Filippo brought us the terrible news that Thursday night, I thought the signora would go out of her mind. She wept and scratched her cheeks and literally tore out her hair. And it was worse when the servants brought Signor Peretti's body back covered with blood. She threw herself on it, sobbing louder than ever and getting her nightgown and her hair stained with her husband's gore. She was shaken by violent spasms and sometimes let out heart-rending shrieks and sometimes groaned like a beast. But, thank God, she couldn't utter a word. I say "Thank God" because she'd lost all self-control, and I was half dead with fear that she might say more than she should in front of the family and the rest of the servants.

Fortunately, it became too much for her, and she fainted. With the help of Giulietta and two of the servants, I was able to get her up to her room.

As soon as she was on the bed, I sent the servants away. Unluckily, I couldn't do the same with Giulietta. She hadn't been allowed in Vittoria's room since their quarrel at Santa

Maria. So now she was trying to look important and pretending to be indispensable. I could tell from her prying eyes that she was preparing to stick her long old maid's nose into everything. She might even send me away on some errand, I thought, so that she could search the room or try to worm the signora's secrets out of her when she came to.

So I acted first. I pretended to search among the pots and phials on the dressing table, and said: "Signorina, I can't find the signora's smelling salts. Would you be kind enough to fetch yours?"

I could see she was dying to send me, but I knew she wouldn't. She has an obsession about tidiness and can't bear anyone else to touch her things. She hates anyone even to set foot in her room, and she stays there all the time her maid does the dusting. So she said, giving me a decidedly poisonous look: "I'll go and get them."

The look was because the silly fool is madly in love with Marcello, and by spying she'd found out about my relationship with him. She'd immediately complained to Signor Peretti, and also to the mothers of both men, several times. But why would they care about the son of a good family having an affair with a little lady's maid like me? They cared much less about it anyway, than about Marcello's

364

publicly living in sin with an old woman! And who'd dare confront Signora Vittoria and ask her to dismiss me?

As soon as Giulietta left, I locked the door and tried to revive Vittoria with little slaps on the cheek. Her eyelids were flickering, and she was getting some color back. I pitied her: sorrow was going to return with consciousness. But I kept my head, and as soon as I saw she was able to understand, I said: "Signora, I've locked the door. I thought you wouldn't want to see anyone."

"No," she said feebly. "No one."

When Giulietta came back and couldn't get in, she called to me from the gallery. I had some trouble finding the right tone of voice to say: "I'm sorry, signorina. The signora told me to lock the door. She doesn't want to see anyone."

"Who says so?" asked Giulietta crossly.

"The signora, of course, signorina."

"I don't believe you."

"Signora," said I, turning to my mistress, "Signorina Giulietta doesn't believe me."

"Giulietta," Vittoria said faintly but distinctly enough, "I want to be by myself."

"Very well! As you wish!" Giulietta said furiously. "I was only trying to help."

I almost wished I could see her face. I sighed. Holy Mother of God, it had been a narrow squeak. And I'd been right to be afraid: no sooner had I shut the door that led from the anteroom to the bedroom than Vittoria burst into a torrent of jumbled words, which would have been all too clear to Giulietta if she'd heard them.

"The wretch! He's killed him! He's broken his promise, his oath. Francesco spared him, and this is his reward: a despicable ambush, a cowardly murder, hired assassins! He didn't even have the courage to kill him with his own hand. Oh, how hateful! How hateful! I'll never forgive him. He, a hero? A fine hero! A Turk wouldn't have acted worse. But I'll avenge Francesco. I'll dishonor the coward publicly. I'll confess everything. Everyone shall know how he suborned me, lulled me with fine words, sullied me with his filthy love. Everyone shall know how nobly Francesco had mercy on him, and with what baseness he in return . . . Oh, I hate him, I hate him!"

I listened, amazed and terrified as the silence of the initial shock was succeeded by this flood of angry words, uttered, fortunately, in a low voice as she strode back and forth — tearless now but with flashing eyes and lips twisted with rage.

When at last she paused for breath, I said quietly but firmly: "Confess everything, signora? You're not serious! They'd put you on public trial for adultery. And because you married into the nobility, they'd do you the great favor of strangling you with a red silk cord."

"Well then," she cried, her eyes huge, "I'll die! I have so much to expiate! Wasn't it because of me that Francesco died?"

"You're right, signora," I answered coldly. "Being strangled with a red silk cord is nothing. It takes only a minute. A minute's soon over, even if the seconds seem long. When you don't belong to the nobility, they hang you with a rope, and Il Mancino says that takes twenty minutes."

"Why are you telling me that, Caterina?" she asked, taken aback.

"Because *I* don't belong to the nobility, signora. And if you confess, I'll be hanged as an accomplice."

"I hadn't thought of that," she said.

If she hadn't been my mistress, I'd have told her that didn't surprise me, that she didn't usually think much about other people. It's not that she's not generous. It's just that she's been worshiped too much. Back to those sessions on the balcony in Gubbio.

"Not to mention Marcello," I added. "He'll be hanged too."

"But he had nothing to do with this horrible murder," she cried. "He's in Amalfi, and the note wasn't in his handwriting."

"They'll say he came back to Rome secretly and disguised his handwriting. As for you, signora, if you reveal your liaison with Paolo, who's going to believe you didn't have a hand in your husband's murder?"

"Oh!" she cried. "That would be shameful! I couldn't bear such a suspicion. I'd kill myself."

"Then you'll be damned! But the fact that you're dead won't stop them from hanging Marcello and me. The sole survivor of this business will be the Prince. He'll get off free. Can you see the Pope daring to attack him in his fortress at Montegiordano? That'll be the only outcome of your revenge. Work it out! The Prince safe and sound in his fine palace, and, far below, four dead bodies: you, me, Marcello, and Signora Sorghini."

"Signora Sorghini?"

"Of course. She's an accomplice too. Didn't she lend you her house?"

"That's true," she said, and dropped to a chair, overwhelmed.

Reality was beginning to break through. She'd have to give up the heroic role of the adulteress making public confession and dying in the odor of sanctity.

"Of course," I added, "once you're dead, all the women in Rome will be wilder about the Prince than ever and throw themselves at his head."

"Caterina," she said, "don't speak to me of that abject creature!"

I'd probably been hurting her, but there it was — it was about time she suffered. Other people existed too. All through this conversation I'd been trembling, and cold shivers ran up my spine. I could almost feel the noose tightening around my neck.

"Signora," I said, after a moment, "where did you hide the key to the Sorghini house?"

"In my jewel box. Why?"

"I'm going to put it in Marcello's room. If they search his room, it will be quite natural for the key to be there. Whereas if they find it in your room . . ."

"You think they'll search my room?" she asked faintly.

"I'm sure of it."

"How can you be so sure?"

"Signora, I'm Il Mancino's little sister. I've been hearing about what the police do all my life."

"Do as you like," she said wearily.

I had no trouble finding the key to the garden of delights. Poor Vittoria, they'd been so brief. It looked quite dull amid the pearls, the precious stones, and the gold.

"Signora," I said, "be so good as to lock

the door after me, so no one can intrude on you while I'm gone, and then let me in again when I come back."

"Yes," she said. "Go."

I didn't meet a soul, either going or coming. Everyone was with the dead man in the main hall, lamenting his departure to a better world, or, in the case of the servants, lamenting their future and wondering who was going to pay them now that the third chamberlain to the Pope was no more.

When I got back I found the room bright. Vittoria had lit the candles on the dressing table and was burning the six letters Marcello had brought her. I didn't say anything. I was glad she'd started taking precautions at last. And while she watched icily as the letters she'd read with such love scarcely two weeks ago were reduced to ashes, I was thinking about what we ought to say to the Bargello so as not to contradict each other.

The next day, when I saw the Bargello shut himself up with Filippo, I thought it would soon be my turn, and I hoped I'd be interrogated before the signora. I'd advised her to say she'd be ready to answer questions near noon, so I might have time to prepare her.

I went into my little room to change into a bodice with a square low neck, the kind that suits me best. On reflection, I decided to leave nothing to chance, and undid the top two buttons, not so much to show more, as just to catch the eye. I also rehearsed my part. Though I was pretty sure of myself deep down, I couldn't help feeling nervous. I'd never seen this man before in my life, so I didn't know the sort of person I had to deal with. My heart turned right over when Piero came and told me the Bargello was waiting for me in Marcello's room. I didn't know if it was right, but I said a little prayer and asked God to let him be a man who likes women.

He opened the door to me himself, and when he locked it and turned around and looked at me, that one look was enough. I knew my prayer had been answered.

He proved to be a good-looking fellow: quite tall, broad-shouldered, slim-waisted, with curly brown hair. His aquiline nose and piercing black eyes made him look severe, but his mouth showed he was no cold fish. It didn't escape me that his clerk was not with him, as he had been for Filippo.

"Caterina," he said gravely, with his eye resting briefly on my neckline, "I have some questions to ask you about what took place at Santa Maria between the unfortunate Signor Peretti and the signora."

"Well, Signor Bargello, it's very simple — they quarreled. The signora was angry with the signore for shutting her up at the back of beyond just for reading a letter that she burned immediately afterward and never answered."

"Who delivered the letter?"

"Signor Marcello. At the time, he was secretary to —"

"No names, please!"

I looked at him. The Prince was lucky! Not only would *he* not be questioned in *his* palace, but his name wasn't even going to be mentioned in the inquiry.

"Was that all they quarreled about?" asked the Bargello, who'd understood my reaction perfectly and didn't look very comfortable himself. That made me feel well disposed toward him. He struck me as the sort of policeman who wouldn't hesitate to go and question the Prince in his palace if anyone ever had the courage to order him to.

"No, Signor Bargello. There was another bone of contention. The signora didn't like living in the Santa Maria castle. She preferred a little house on the cliff, and she went and stayed there. One night, there was a terrible storm, and the next morning the wreckage of a boat was found on a little beach at the foot of the cliff. Signor Peretti arrived in a fury, sword in hand, while the signora and I were walking quietly in front of the cottage, enjoying the morning sun. Signor Peretti rushed up to us, waving his sword and yelling that the boat must have belonged to the nobleman who'd written to the signora. I tried to protect my mistress, and Signor Peretti, without meaning to, wounded me slightly in the shoulder. Would you like to see the scar, Signor Bargello? . . . The signora was furious and heaped reproaches on him and he went away. But he came back two days later and apologized, and they were reconciled."

"How?"

I raised my eyebrows and said: "How do you think a husband and wife are reconciled, Signor Bargello?"

"I don't know," he said. "I'm a bachelor."

But he smiled. What a smile! And he had a little black mustache that went with it.

"Well," he said, growing serious again, "now let's turn to Thursday night. What explanation is there for the fact that Signor Peretti disregarded the pleas of his whole family and committed the unbelievable folly of going out in the streets of Rome, alone and at night, armed with only a sword? No one's been able to tell me why he did it."

The Bargello seemed to be dangling a bait of some importance in front of me, and I wondered if it was to the signora's advantage, or to mine, to bite. I decided it was. He must have been told I was with the signora all the time that night, and have heard what she and Signor Peretti said to one another. As a matter of fact, I'd discussed this point with her while she was burning the letters, and we'd agreed on our version of what had happened. It wasn't too far from the truth, though it wasn't close enough to compromise her. As I was thinking, I was also trying various wiles to distract the Bargello's penetrating glance from my face. I didn't know if I'd succeeded. Those black eyes might let themselves dally a little, but they soon came back to fix themselves on mine.

"I don't know," I said, but pretending to hesitate, "if the signora would really like me to tell you this. . . ."

"Come along, my beauty," he said. "Don't stand on ceremony. Speak! I'll be grateful if you do."

"Well, that Thursday there was a little dispute between them. The signora had had a bad headache all day, and in the evening, when Signor Peretti came and asked to spend the night in her room, she was reluctant . . ."

"Rather curt, perhaps?"

"Let's say she wasn't very amenable. The signore got cross, and you know what it's like when that happens."

"No, I don't. I'm not married."

"They both dug up old resentments. In particular, what had happened at Santa Maria."

"His turning up in front of the cottage, brandishing a naked sword?"

"Among other things."

"There were other things?"

"Yes. But if you ask me, they were trivial."

"Tell me about them."

"The day after the quarrel outside the cottage, there was a terrible storm. Signor Peretti sent the majordomo to tell the signora he feared for her safety and to ask her to return to the castle."

"And she blamed him for that? He was only trying to look after her."

"She blamed him for sending the majordomo instead of coming himself. She said he was afraid of the thunder and lightning."

"Just like a woman! And how did Signor Peretti take that?"

"Very badly. He said: 'You dare to tell me you think I'm a coward?' He was white and grinding his teeth; he could scarcely speak. But when he did, I heard him, for the first time, say disagreeable things to his wife."

"What?"

" 'You're a madwoman! Quite mad! You read too much, and your head's full of heroes out of books.' And he went out and slammed the door."

"And all this came up on the night of the murder? At what time?"

"Just before eleven. At least, I think so. My brother arrived just afterward with the terrible note. Unfortunately, he can't read. Otherwise he'd never have delivered it."

"Not even for twenty piasters?"

"Signor Bargello, my brother owes a great deal to Signor Peretti. It was thanks to him that his banishment from Rome was lifted."

"And thanks to me . . . I've been told the whole family gathered around Signor Peretti, shouting and weeping and begging him not to go."

"Yes."

"The signora didn't join them?"

"She's not one for clinging to people's necks or throwing herself at their feet. But when Signor Peretti got rid of the others, she spoke to him."

"What did she say?"

"That the note from Marcello was a forgery, and the rendezvous was a trap, and he mustn't fall into it. But he wouldn't listen. He was still angry after their quarrel, and whatever she said, he just answered, 'I'll show you if I'm a coward!' He kept saying that."

"What did the signora say?"

"That she hadn't meant he was a coward, it was a misunderstanding. She asked him to forgive her. But he wouldn't listen. He just kept repeating what he'd said before."

"I see," said the Bargello.

He put his hands behind his back and looked at me silently with his piercing black eyes. For the first time since he'd started questioning me, I felt afraid.

"That's all very fine, my beauty," he said.

He must have liked the sound of that, because he said it again. "That's all very fine, my beauty. I'm sure you're telling me the truth. Well, more or less . . ."

A pause, another piercing look. "You're a good girl, Caterina. You have a kind heart. You're fond of your mistress. You're fond of Il Mancino. And there's certainly someone else you're fond of, perhaps even in this room. But that's of no consequence. I'm not your confessor. Only . . ."

He looked at me, grimaced, and was silent, as if he expected me to ask a question. I didn't say anything. Perhaps that was a mistake. But I simply couldn't open my mouth. A little shiver ran up my spine.

"Only," he said, "there's one thing that surprises me. It seems to me that if the signora had *really* wanted to prevent Signor Peretti from going, she had a way of stopping him."

Again he waited for me to ask a question, and again I said nothing. This time I was sure it was a mistake. Although I was furious with myself, I still didn't speak. There was nothing I could do about it.

"You don't ask me what that way was."

"What was it?" I said feebly.

"Come now, Caterina," he said, "you know very well what it was. So why do you ask?"

"Signor Bargello," I said angrily. "First you tell me to ask you a question, and then when I do, you reproach me!"

He laughed, but wryly.

"What a sly little minx you are!" he said. "Come, Caterina, don't try to slide out of it. Tell me frankly, if you'd been in the signora's shoes, what would you have done to keep your husband at home? Especially when he'd just asked you to let him spend the night with you."

"Oh, Signor Bargello," I cried, "why ask me when you know the answer? But I'm not the signora. She's a queen! And once she's said no, it's not easy for her to go back on it."

"You mean it didn't occur to her?"

"Yes," I answered at once, "but too late. He'd already gone. And she bitterly regretted not having thought of it sooner."

Although I sounded genuine enough, what I said was both true and untrue. It was true she regretted it now. But it wasn't true she regretted it then. I'm sure that at the time the idea never entered her head.

As for the Bargello, I couldn't tell whether he believed me or not. His black eyes, fixed on mine, were impenetrable. All he did was shrug his shoulders, as if, after all, such speculation was beside the point. Then suddenly his expression changed, and he said, with an air of not caring but with a playful little curl of the lip: "Now let's see that scar on your right shoulder that Signor Peretti's supposed to have given you."

"Do you doubt it, Signor Bargello?"

"I will until I have seen it."

"As you please, Signor Bargello."

I started unbuttoning my bodice, slowly and enticingly, but without overdoing it. The Bargello's mouth now seemed more expressive than his eyes, for the simple reason that I couldn't see his eyes: he'd lowered them to follow my performance.

When he finally passed his hand over my scar, I was surprised to find his fingers so soft and his touch so delicate.

"To be frank," he said with a little laugh, "I couldn't say whether this scar is a year old or only a month, or if it was made by a sword or a thorn. Perhaps someone did hit you, but only with a rose. You're such a good girl. And not only do you have a good heart, Caterina, but what covers it isn't bad either."

He held my left breast in a swift, light caress that made me quiver from head to foot.

My God, I'd been so frightened, and now it was all right. I let him undress me and do as he liked with me. But, oh, the questions he'd asked: a lot of little traps with teeth ready to snap on me like twenty tigers if I fell in, and a rope at the end of it!

It was such a relief not to have to puzzle my brains any more about what I ought or ought not to say, and then say it fast enough to make it look natural. Now all I had to do was let myself go. It gave me a special thrill, deep down, to be made love to by a man who'd frightened me so. Now he was no longer asking me questions, with his eyes boring into mine. Now his eyes were down by my neck, and his mouth was there too, biting. No more words, thank God! Instead, panting and sighs. I was in my element now. And so was he, with his masculine pride.

But which of the two of us was being had, that's something I'd very much like to know.

## Gian Battista della Pace, Bargello

While I was out, my clerk received two letters,

one forwarded by His Excellency the Governor of Rome, the other handed to one of my men by a beggar, who ran away. The first was signed; the second was anonymous. Both were curious.

The letter forwarded by the Governor was signed by Cesare Pallantieri. I knew him well, having had him banished from Rome for his crimes. In the letter he said that with the help of Marcello Accoramboni he'd had Peretti murdered, because of a quarrel they'd had recently. He didn't say what the quarrel was about, nor where and when it took place. I assumed someone had paid him to write this. It seemed to have two purposes: to exculpate whoever really instigated the murder, and to incriminate Marcello Accoramboni.

Despite the fact that it was anonymous, I took the second letter more seriously. It said that while Signora Sorghini was out of Rome, Vittoria Peretti had secretly met with "a certain nobleman" in her house. She got in through a little door at the back to which she had a key.

I went there immediately, and found it just as described in the letter. A porch opened on a passage that led to a door, unlocked, which opened into a small chapel. Farther down the passage was another door. This was locked, but must have led into the palace, or at least to the roof.

Thanks to some obliging neighbors, I was able to look out on this roof from the window of their nearby house. There were masses of geraniums around the parapet and in the middle a large tent of white curtains. And white indeed must be the souls of those who dallied inside.

It was easy to imagine a closely masked woman going into the innocent ground-floor passage and kneeling for a moment in the chapel before going up to the roof through the little door. The gate may have been strait, but it certainly didn't lead to salvation.

After getting Governor Portici's approval, I had the Rusticucci palace searched. My men didn't find anything in the signora's room, but in Marcello Accoramboni's they discovered a key that fitted the little door in the Sorghini palace. That didn't prove anything against his sister: Marcello was known *urbi et orbi* to be the widow Sorghini's lover.

I talked to the neighbor again. "On the roof! La Sorghini, the shameless hussy!" she said. "And would you believe it, Signor Bargello, one day I saw that good-for-nothing Marcello outside the tent, basking naked in the sun in broad daylight!"

"Naked, signora? In broad daylight?"

"Well, I would have seen him naked," she said, blushing, "if it hadn't been for all the geraniums."

"What did you see after Signora Sorghini went away to Amalfi?"

"Nothing," she said regretfully. "The curtains were always closed."

So what might have been a crucial witness turned out to be worthless. Of course, imagination can always complement reality. Just as the lady next door could see Marcello naked even if the geraniums were in the way, so I could imagine Vittoria in the white tent, disporting her lovely body and long hair in the arms of "a certain nobleman." But what would that prove?

Governor Portici and I got a good hundred or more letters after the first two, all anonymous and all accusing and insulting Vittoria Peretti, her brother, her mother, her maid, and, indirectly, "a certain nobleman," though without naming him. Courage wasn't these correspondents' strong point, even though they wrote anonymously. Five or six of the letters addressed to the Governor criticized my inquiry and accused me of incompetence for not having yet brought it to a successful conclusion. We read and reread these in search of the slightest serious clue, but didn't find one. So we burned them.

A week later, Alfaro, my assistant, told me that on the Saturday following Peretti's murder, a former soldier had been arrested for stabbing a drinking companion in a tavern. The murder had been committed in front of witnesses, so there was no question about the man's guilt. It took the judge only ten minutes to sentence him to hang. The sentence was to be carried out in three days' time, and the prisoner was asking to see me. He had some confession to make.

"Confession?" I said. "He's already been found guilty."

"He says he committed another crime and wants to relieve his conscience before he dies."

"His conscience! Let him relieve it by confessing to the chaplain. I can't hang him twice."

My squire was holding my horse ready for me to mount and ride home, and I was hungry and eager to get my dinner. But when I was in the saddle, I turned and said to Alfaro, out of pure routine, I suppose: "What's this conscientious convict called?"

"Barca."

"Barca! Did you say 'Barca'? God in heaven, that changes everything. Bring him to me!"

"Now, Signor Bargello?"

"This minute!"

I dismounted, threw the reins to my squire,

and rushed back inside. "Hurry, Alfaro, hurry!"

When at last Barca appeared before me, his hands and feet in chains. I was no longer in any doubt. He was the man Filippo had described: tall, broad-shouldered, with a beard up to the eyes, and very polite. He looked like a brute and sounded like a lamb.

"You wanted to speak to me?"

"Yes, please, Signor Bargello."

"What for?"

"To confess to another murder and ask a favor."

"A favor? Would you prefer the galley to the gibbet?"

"Oh, no, Signor Bargello. I'm a soldier. If I have to go, I prefer to go quickly."

"Let's hear about this other murder."

Barca drew himself up, took a deep breath, and said solemnly: "It was I who killed Signor Peretti, Signor Bargello."

"By yourself?"

"No, Signor Bargello, my dear friend Alberto Machione was with me. But I was the one who shot Signor Peretti. And I was the one who finished him off with my dagger."

"You're going to a lot of trouble to clear your dear friend Alberto Machione. Where is he?"

"I killed him."

385

I stared at him. "You killed him?"

"Yes, Signor Bargello. He was the one in the tavern."

"So he wasn't really dear to you?"

"Oh, yes, he was!" he said, his eyes suddenly brimming with tears. "His death was a sort of accident."

"Tell me about it."

"Well, we went for a drink in the tavern after we'd done the job. And we quarreled about the loot. He wanted the dead man's doublet as well as half the money. And all he'd done was be there and reload the arquebus! We'd drunk a lot of wine, and things got hot, and I stabbed him."

"For a doublet?"

"It was a very fine doublet, Signor Bargello. Real buffalo hide. With pockets in the sleeves. The turnkey of the prison took it!" said Barca in despair, tears streaming down his cheeks now. "He had no right to do that, Signor Bargello! No, he had no right! I know the rules. My things belong to me until I'm executed. And when I'm dead, they're supposed to go to the hangman, not the turnkey. It's a disgrace, Signor Bargello. The turnkey's not only robbed me, but he's robbed the hangman too."

"We'll talk about that later," I said impassively. "Let's get back to the facts. Tell me about the murder of Peretti."

In his soft voice, Barca gave me an account that exactly coincided with Filippo's. When he'd finished, I asked, "Did you kill Signor Peretti to rob him?"

"Oh, no, Signor Bargello. I'm not a thief. I'm a soldier, even if I'm not in service at the moment. I kill only to order."

"And who ordered this murder?"

"A monk in a tavern."

"Did you know him?"

"No, Signor Bargello."

"Tell me what he looked like."

"It's difficult. I never saw him without his hood. He was small and thin. I don't know his name."

"Why did you do what he told you?"

"He paid me."

"How much?"

"A hundred piasters."

"You killed a man for a hundred piasters?"

"Signor Bargello, when I was a soldier, I killed men for much less than that. And, as I said, I was not in service, and I was broke. Everyone has to eat."

"Whom did you serve under when you were a soldier?"

"Prince Orsini. He sacked me a couple of months ago — and Machione."

"Why?"

"He suspected us of immorality."

"What sort of immorality?"

"You know, Signor Bargello."

"Was he right?"

"No."

"You don't sound very sure."

"Signor Bargello!" he said angrily. "What do you want? Isn't hanging enough? What would satisfy you? Would you like me to be burned as a sodomite?"

"No, no, of course not. Calm down, Barca. All this is between us. In your opinion, might your former master have ordered this murder, using the monk as an intermediary?"

"I did wonder about it, seeing how beautiful the widow is, and given the monk's dirty remark. But I don't think so."

"Why not?"

"The Prince wouldn't have chosen soldiers to commit a murder. He'd have used bandits. And there's no shortage of them at Montegiordano. The courtyard's full of them."

"Why bandits?"

"They do that sort of thing better than we do. It's their profession."

"You don't think you made a good job of it?"

"Terrible. The arquebus wasn't a good idea, Signor Bargello. If Signor Peretti had had some pistols, Machione and I would have been dead before we got near him."

He was right. The arquebus was a typical soldier's idea and not at all appropriate. It's noisy and unreliable, especially at night. Bandits would have hidden in a doorway and stabbed Peretti from behind, not forgetting to dispatch the only witness, the torch-bearer, too. Moreover, there are so many of them in Rome that if they'd been caught, it would have been impossible to work back to the person behind them. Using a soldier, or an ex-soldier, was tantamount to putting your signature to a murder. Could the Prince have been so stupid? Wasn't it more likely that the real instigator of the crime had chosen two of Orsini's former soldiers purposely, in order to incriminate him? There were too many fingers in this affair pointing at him and at Marcello. It was as if someone was trying to influence my judgment.

"Well, Barca," I said, "is that all?"

"No, Signor Bargello. I still want to ask you a favor."

"Tell me what it is."

"I'd like the turnkey to give me back my doublet."

"Forgive me for reminding you, Barca, but you'll be able to wear it for only three days."

"Never mind. I'd like to be decently dressed on the scaffold."

"You shall have it back."

"Thank you very much indeed, Signor Bargello," he cried.

He leaned to kiss my hands, but the guards wouldn't let him. At a sign from Alfaro, they led him away.

"Alfaro, go to the prison and make sure Barca gets his doublet back. And see that he's well treated and well fed until the end."

"Now, Signor Bargello?"

"Now. Why will you always procrastinate? And tell the hangman to strangle him quietly before he puts the rope around his neck."

"The hangman usually asks the condemned man ten piasters for that."

"Ten piasters isn't much for a buffalo doublet he wouldn't have got if Barca hadn't complained about it. If that consideration isn't enough, tell him it's an order."

I went home and ate and drank heartily as usual, then spent the afternoon writing my report. I went into the most circumstantial detail, with all the different testimonies, and concluded that, as things stood, it was impossible, first, to find out who had organized the murder; second, to say definitely that there had been a guilty relationship between Vittoria Peretti and "a certain nobleman," and third, still less to show that Vittoria Peretti, or anyone belonging to her entourage, had been an accomplice in the murder. I was forced to the reluctant conclusion that she had had nothing to do with it.

I handed my report to Governor Portici the same evening. The Pope had expressed a wish to see it, and Portici wanted to read it first. The next morning, he sent me a note saying that my report was "most excellent" and he was taking it to the Vatican that day.

A week later, Portici sent for me. I noticed his eyes as soon as I went in: they were evading mine. He looked simultaneously worried and embarrassed. After a long irrelevant preamble, he finally told me His Holiness had decided to incarcerate Vittoria Peretti and her maid in Castel Sant' Angelo.

I was struck dumb. When at last I could speak, I said: "As the case stands, there's not enough evidence to bring her to trial."

"The Vatican is aware of that. Therefore, it doesn't intend to try her. Only to imprison her."

My surprise was succeeded by stupefaction. "For how long?" I asked.

"Long enough for the Prince to stop thinking of marrying her."

"So the Vatican," I said with an effort, "believes there was a guilty relationship between her and the Prince?"

"Yes."

I gazed at Portici open-mouthed. "Your Excellency, were you able to find out what that belief is based on?"

"No. I came up against a wall."

After a moment, I went on. "If they did commit adultery, it seems very unlikely the signora would have admitted it to her confessor. Or the Prince to his."

"Very unlikely."

"I don't know if Cardinal Montalto is going to like seeing her imprisoned without trial."

"His Holiness has never sought to please Cardinal Montalto."

That was true, but it wasn't for the pleasure of upsetting Montalto that the Pope was incarcerating his son's wife. I was silent, overcome with resentment. If the Vatican had other police apart from the papal police, and followed their recommendations rather than mine, what purpose did I serve?

"Your Excellency," I said. Then I stopped and counted ten. The Pope is not only the head of Christendom; he's also my sovereign, and I owe him loyalty and obedience.

"Speak freely, della Pace," said Portici kindly. "Your words won't go beyond this office."

"Your Excellency, don't you think this imprisonment will be felt by all concerned as a crying injustice?"

"I'm afraid so. But among the Holy Father's entourage there are some who think . . ." He sighed, and went on with an effort: ". . . who think injustice is better than disorder."

"But injustice often engenders disorder," I said angrily.

"What are you thinking of, della Pace?"

"Of a rebellion by the great nobles. Or one of them."

"That possibility didn't escape me either," said Portici. "I mentioned it in the Vatican, but I was told there was no danger, that every precaution had been taken to prevent it."

# 9

## *Monsignor Rossellino*
## *(Il Bello Muto)*

Although His Eminence Cardinal Montalto goes to bed late and sometimes reads into the night, he invariably rises at half past five in the morning. He says for a monk to get up later than that only encourages sloth and lust. That's why — though it's only one of the reasons — the Franciscans in Venice, whose lax ways he tried to reform when he was still only a bishop, conceived a great hatred for him and intrigued to get the Senate to expel him from the republic.

However, His Eminence allows me to get up a quarter of an hour later than he does, since because of his infirmities it takes him longer to dress, and his valet has to help him. But it's understood that on the stroke of six I meet him in the palace dining room. This would be a pleasant place if only the Cardinal would allow a fire there in the winter. But in that, as in everything, he's inflexible: "We'd be tempted to linger over our meals if we weren't so cold," he says. But in the study we share, we do have a fire, though a small one, so his rheumatic hand can hold a pen. All this is due to austerity, not avarice. His Eminence owns some fine woodlands, and we have enough logs in store to keep us amply supplied through ten winters.

As for what we eat early in the morning, it's very frugal. When I think of the breakfasts I used to have at the Countess's, I'm ashamed of my greed, and happy I can no longer succumb to a sin bound to lead a man on to others even more serious.

As we enter the dining room, one after the other, on the stoke of six, Sister Maria Teresa, who's very old and fabulously wrinkled, brings us each a bowl of hot milk and a few slices of rye bread. That's all. On Sundays she adds a couple of little goat cheeses, except during Lent, when we observe a rigorous fast.

His Eminence doesn't open his lips during breakfast except to eat his bread, which he dips in the milk first because his teeth aren't very good. They laugh in the Vatican at this Spartan fare. "Montalto doesn't eat," they say. "He fills himself up like an ox for a day's plowing."

Although this is said in a far from charitable spirit, it has some truth in it. One day when

I asked His Eminence why he dined so lightly in the evening too, he said: "I don't need much. I don't work at night."

The Cardinal says a short prayer before he rises, and another, not very long, in his oratory after breakfast. I've heard him say to a young priest who was always stringing together paters and aves: "Don't think you have to say the same thing a hundred times over. God isn't slow-witted."

He prays standing up: he can't kneel because of his crutches. Then he goes into his study, where with my help and that of his valet he drops to the chair behind his desk. He then becomes entirely transformed, and sets about his day's work briskly and cheerfully.

I greatly admire this alacrity, and have only once seen it fail him. That was on the day Filippo brought the news that Francesco Peretti had been murdered.

In an instant, the Cardinal's firm countenance was ravaged by the most pitiful despair. For what seemed an interminable while, he sat slumped, so overcome with grief, virtually stupefied, that I turned my head away with a mixture of consternation and embarrassment. I was ashamed to witness this moment of weakness in a man whose fortitude I revered. I described this interval as "interminable" because it was so painful to me, but, thinking about it later, I don't suppose it lasted more than five minutes. Then the Cardinal turned to Filippo and said faintly: "Tell your mistress I'll come see her this morning." And to me: "Order my coach to be got ready and come and fetch me in an hour's time." Then he waved me away imperiously, and hid his terrible countenance in his great hands.

When I returned an hour later to tell him the coach was ready, I found him as I'd always known him: his eye commanding, his voice loud, his face impassive. This stoical calm didn't fail him even in the Rusticucci palace, when he saw the bloodstained body of his adopted son and prayed beside him, leaning on his crutches. But the prayer was brief, and, leaving the hall where the corpse lay without a backward glance, he summoned the family and the majordomo into another room. He spoke first to the majordomo, telling him to go at once and calm down the servants, who were in an uproar of tears and lamentation. "Tell everyone to go about their ordinary duties," he said, "and to do so in silence."

Alone with the family, he called for an account of the money available in the palace. It soon appeared that the only person who could answer this question was Giulietta Accoramboni, whom Francesco Peretti had greatly respected and who had acted as his steward. She went and got the papers in which she entered receipts and expenses, and read them out. Despite their grief, the family members were plunged into consternation by what emerged: without the emoluments the Vatican paid to the third chamberlain, the palace could be maintained for only about three more months.

Signora Accoramboni then announced that she would now take over the household finances. At which Vittoria said angrily and scornfully, "You!" The one word spoke volumes. Her mother opened her mouth to reply, but the Cardinal crushed her with a look and said in a voice that brooked no argument: "Giulietta was an excellent choice on Francesco's part. I shall stand by it."

He sent away everyone except Giulietta and discussed with her how to reduce expenses. The first thing, clearly, was to dismiss half the servants. The majordomo was called in to help draw up a list of those who were to go. Giulietta, pen in hand, tried to include Caterina's name among these, but the Cardinal said severely, "Do you want to drive Vittoria to despair?" and the signorina drew in her horns.

Later on, Giulietta expressed the hope that the Pope, of his indulgence, might bestow a small pension on his third chamberlain's widow.

"Don't count on it," said the Cardinal. "The Pope will shed plenty of tears over Francesco's death, but that's about all."

He spent a good hour with Giulietta examining Francesco's assets and deciding how they might be realized to support the family. He advised selling a couple of farms that brought in practically nothing and investing the proceeds with the Medicis in Florence. When Giulietta objected that the Medicis were known to practice usury, the Cardinal shrugged his powerful shoulders and said: "Do you want to be more Catholic than the Pope?" He was alluding to the fact that, although usury was forbidden by the church, Gregory had entrusted the Medicis with large sums of money, which were intended to yield a profit.

Finally, when Giulietta said she didn't know how she was going to pay for Francesco's funeral, this man, whom some people called a miser, replied: "There's no question of your paying anything. I'll see to it." And he drew his purse out of his cassock and gave it to her, saying: "Do what you think best, but no ostentation."

After that he didn't speak for some time. Giulietta, completely subdued by his authority, didn't dare breathe a word.

"Giulietta," he said at last, "you're the only

member of the family with an ounce of common sense. What frame of mind would you say Vittoria is in?"

"She's overwhelmed with grief."

"And remorse?" asked the Cardinal, with a piercing look.

"No," said Giulietta. "In my opinion, she hasn't any reason to feel remorse."

For a moment that must have seemed endless, the Cardinal gazed at her as if to plumb her very soul. But she didn't flinch.

Two days later, referring to this exchange, the Cardinal told me: "There are three possibilities. Either Vittoria is not guilty of adultery, and Giulietta is telling the truth. Or Vittoria is guilty, and Giulietta doesn't know. Or Vittoria is guilty, and Giulietta knows but is lying to protect her."

I looked at him inquiringly. He went on, with a sigh: "How is one to tell? Women are a complete enigma. They're taught to dissimulate from the cradle."

I asked him by means of signs whether he thought Vittoria had been an accomplice in the murder.

"No!" he answered emphatically. "A thousand times no! I'll never believe it."

To return to the day after the murder, when we arrived back at the palace after His Eminence's conversation with Giulietta, I asked him if he intended to go to the meeting of the consistory to be held that day.

"Of course," he said. "I must. It will be an ordeal, but it would be cowardly to avoid it."

Before the meeting of the consistory began, it was customary for the seventy cardinals to kneel at the Pope's feet and pay him homage. This ceremony took some time, because the Pope addressed a few words to each of them. What he said was amiable but unimportant, like the cardinals' replies; so they were in the habit of conducting private conversations at the same time. They did so in respectfully low voices, but so many people were bound to produce a loud buzz, which stopped only when the first chamberlain announced that the meeting was about to begin.

On this day, however, the hum of voices was interrupted long before the chamberlain's announcement, and more abruptly than usual. A profound silence fell as everyone saw His Eminence Cardinal Montalto going forward to salute the Holy Father.

The room in which the consistory was held was oblong, with the Pope's throne on one of the shorter sides and the prelates' stalls facing each other on the longer ones. As soon as His Eminence appeared in the central aisle, dragging himself along on his crutches, all heads on both sides of the room turned to watch his slow progress. All eyes were riveted on him; all ears strained to hear what he and the Pope would say to one another.

By that time none of them, and I daresay no one in Rome, was unaware of the murder, and no one could doubt the gravity of its implications for both men. It was a blow to the Cardinal's affections, and a blow to the Pope's authority. Though the crime had probably been committed for private reasons, the assassination of the third chamberlain was an insult and a challenge to the Pope himself.

His Eminence was exempted from kneeling to the Pope because of his infirmities, so a stool had been placed for him. The first and second chamberlains had to help him lower himself to it, and this seemed to heighten the drama.

There was certainly no handsomer old man than the Pope, either in Rome or in the whole of Italy, nor one healthier and more alert. His snow-white hair framed a face with regular, aristocratic features. His pink cheeks and blue eyes gave him a youthful look, at almost eighty, and his expression was full of sweetness and nobility. If I hadn't known the faults and weaknesses that lay behind that magnificent appearance, I'd have been the first to be won over by his lofty demeanor, melodious voice, and affable manners. What a sad figure my poor master cut in comparison, slumped on his stool with his shoulders hunched, hair and beard disheveled, to say nothing of his crooked nose, prognathous jaw, and bushy eyebrows. He might well have been compared with Socrates, whose roughness and ugliness shocked people at first, though it was only from the imperceptive that they concealed his virtue, wisdom, and fortitude.

The Pope, a consummate actor, was silent a few moments, thus lending weight to what he was about to say. When he finally spoke, in a voice both loud and musical, it was clear he was addressing the cardinals in general rather than the individual before him.

"My very dear son," he began, though how could he say otherwise in the circumstances, little though he loved Montalto? "We were deeply afflicted to learn of the cowardly murder of which our beloved son and chamberlain Francesco Peretti was the victim, and we wish to convey to you the indignation and sadness that overcame us when we heard the dreadful news."

At this point the Pope's eyes filled with tears, which continued to run down his cheeks for the rest of his speech, though without at all impairing the harmony or clarity of his diction. He went on: "We cannot but see the work of the devil in a base assault that bereaves us of the most worthy of our children. But how can we forget that a human hand collaborated with the Evil One in a crime that cries out to heaven for vengeance? May heaven hear our prayers and supplications and aid us in the search for the assassins and whoever armed them, that they may receive the wages of their iniquities here on earth before they are summoned to answer to the Divine Judge. . . ."

He went on in this vein, angry and vengeful, for a good ten minutes, expressing himself with such energy and forcefulness that I would have been impressed if I hadn't known how little of those qualities he'd shown in the exercise of his power.

The Holy Father's tears dried up at the same time as his eloquence, and he gave a courteous and condescending wave of the hand to invite the Cardinal to speak. The general attention redoubled, and the silence grew more profound, as all strained to hear what the Cardinal would say. The Pope, while retaining his usual haughty reserve toward him, wore a look of eager curiosity that to me seemed tinged with malevolence. God forgive me if I was mistaken!

His Eminence spoke in a faint, toneless voice, interrupted by coughing but devoid of any emotion. By contrast with the winged eloquence of the Pope, his answer was brief.

"Most Holy Father," he said, "I thank you for your kind interest in my family. Since I already have one foot in the grave, I regard this bereavement as just one more test sent by my Divine Master before He calls me home. That is why, far from asking that the murderers be found and punished, I forgive them with all my heart for the evil they have done me."

The Holy Father gave another wave of the hand, and the two chamberlains helped His Eminence back onto his crutches. After the Pope blessed him, he made his way to his stall. I could tell that the consistory was more astonished than edified by what he'd said. Although Christians consider the forgiveness of injuries the highest of virtues, it is one that is seldom practiced, even in the Vatican.

I learned what the Pope thought before the end of the consistory, when I unwittingly overheard a conversation between two prelates. The cardinals never hesitate to talk about my master in my presence: because I'm dumb, they think I'm deaf as well.

As soon as my master had, so painfully, turned his back on the Pope, the Holy Father bent over to one of his familiars and said: "He really is a typical monk!"

This was repeated from one to another and didn't take more than half an hour to reach me. What was meant was that this former Franciscan's speaking of the forgiveness of injuries was just a hypocritical sham: Cardinal Montalto's only concern was to become the next pope, and he was for letting Prince Orsini off lightly so that he wouldn't be his enemy when it came to the vote.

When we got back to the palace, I, as in duty bound, told His Eminence what the Holy Father had said. He shrugged his great shoulders, set his teeth, and replied: "And I might have been stupid enough to ask that fellow for justice. You'll see, Rossellino. Apart from weeping and talking, he won't do a thing."

A week later, "that fellow," as His Eminence hadn't shrunk from calling the Pope — the only strong language he ever used in that connection — sent him the Bargello's report. The Cardinal read and reread it. His face showed no reaction and he made no comment. But when he heard that Vittoria had been incarcerated, his impassiveness ended. "What an injustice!" he cried in a fury. "And what a mistake!"

A little while later, sensing he was still preoccupied by this affair, I ventured to ask him by signs why he considered Vittoria's arrest a mistake.

"It's doubly so," he said. "First, because there's nothing in the Bargello's report that points to her guilt. Second, and more important, it's a political error. If the Pope thought the Prince guilty, he should either have had the courage to confront him, or else done nothing at all. Imprisoning Vittoria was ridiculous. Pretending to act when you're not really acting only exposes the weakness you're trying to hide."

### Lodovico Orsini, Count of Oppedo

I didn't feel very comfortable when Paolo sent a messenger asking me to see him at Montegiordano. Even before the messenger arrived, I'd had various reasons to be worried. The two scoundrels operating for us in the Nora mountains, harassed up hill and down dale by the papal police, had had the stupid and dangerous idea of coming to Rome and taking refuge in my palace, though I had no right of asylum.

Raimondo, impulsive as ever, wanted to do away with the two idiots there and then. "If the police arrest them," he said, "they'll talk under torture and that'll be the end of us."

"Now, now, Bruto," I said. He scowled at

my use of his nickname, so I put my arm around his neck and kissed him on the cheek. "How can you kill them without all the men who camp in our courtyard knowing? And how much would they trust us after that?"

"What do we do if the Bargello and his henchmen turn up at our door?"

"Keep them talking long enough to hide the bandits in the cellar, and then let them in."

"Let them in?"

"Yes, if there are not too many of them."

Raimondo made a face and was about to speak, when Paolo's messenger arrived and gave me the note.

"I'll be at Montegiordano in an hour," I said, throwing the messenger a piaster.

I regretted it immediately; funds were low. Why, just because you're a nobleman, must you always do what the peasants expect of you? In a way, they're our masters! The trouble I've gone to for the mob outside! Including setting up a barrel of wine at holiday time. So they can guzzle for nothing!

"I don't like the sound of this," I said gloomily.

"Why not?" asked Raimondo. "Paolo's our cousin and head of the family. He may have stopped funding us, but he's still fond of us."

"To be frank, I think it will be dangerous for me to go to Montegiordano today."

"Dangerous?" he repeated, in amazement.

"Yes."

"Why?"

"It would take too long to explain."

"I know, I know. I'm a fool!"

"Come, *carissimo*, don't be cross. I have my reasons for not telling you. And it's safer for you to know nothing. Still, I'd feel safer if you'd come with me."

"Is it as bad as that?"

You couldn't call Raimondo handsome, but his big mug isn't entirely without expression, and I could see from the way he was looking at me that he was simultaneously annoyed by my secretiveness and anxious for my safety.

"Dear brother," I said, putting a hand on his shoulder, "forgive me for leaving you in the dark. Let's put it that I've been somewhat of a Machiavelli. I'll explain later."

"Who's Machiavelli?"

"I'll explain that later too. Meanwhile, arrange for us to have a large escort."

"Large?"

"About thirty men."

"Thirty?"

"Please, Raimondo, stop echoing everything I say. I want some noblemen too. Who's here today?"

"Silla Savelli" — he started with him because he was his bosom friend — "Pietro

Gaetano, Emilio Capizucchi, Ascanio di Ruggieri, and Ottavio di Rustici."

"All the best people! Why are there so many of them?"

"We had a party last night, with some girls, and they were all so drunk, they stayed the night."

"That's where all the money goes!"

"You're not so economical yourself."

"True. Anyway, Raimondo, will you please tell them to get ready? I want them all."

"You mean you need five of the noblest sons of Rome as well as me to help you face Paolo?"

"Yes."

"What have you done to make you so frightened of him?"

"Nothing but good. But he thinks it's harm."

"More mysteries," said Raimondo.

I left this escort in the courtyard at Montegiordano and, with my heart thumping and Raimondo following me like a shadow, I went up to meet Paolo in his favorite little room on the second floor. He was standing by the window, looking down.

"I see," he said dryly as he turned around, "that as part of your large escort you've brought the nobility with you. I see Savelli, Gaetano, Rustici. And also Ruggieri and Capizucchi. What are you thinking of, Raimondo? We can't leave all those young men to fret in their saddles till we've finished talking. Please go and tell my majordomo to get them some wine and food, then do the honors of my dining hall."

Graciously though it was framed, this was an order, and Raimondo, curious though he was to hear what we were going to say to one another, obeyed. So I was left alone with Paolo, after all.

"Well, here you are!" he said, his lips smiling but his eyes scathing. "Thank you for coming. I'm in a quandary, Lodovico. The Pope has insulted me."

I raised one eyebrow.

"He's incarcerated Vittoria," he said.

"The main thing," I said, "is that he hasn't arrested you."

"He hasn't arrested me because he knows very well I didn't have Peretti murdered. But by imprisoning Vittoria he makes everyone believe I'm the murderer. That's how the Pope has insulted me."

"How can you expect people not to think you're the murderer?" I asked. "Your expedition to Santa Maria has probably leaked out."

"Rumor isn't proof. I've managed to get hold of a copy of della Pace's report. He concludes that the murder was perpetrated in such

411

a way as to make everyone think Marcello and I did it; but he doesn't believe we did."

"Della Pace's a clever man," I said, trying not to smirk. "So you're cleared."

"Except that the Pope has designated me *urbi et orbi* as the guilty party."

"What are you going to do?"

"Take up arms and overthrow him."

"Paolo! You can't mean it! Attack the head of Christendom? He'll excommunicate you."

"And if I succeed in getting him off his throne, his successor will absolve me. Anyhow, it's not the Pope I'll be attacking; it's the ruler."

"I suppose you invited me here to ask my advice."

"Not at all. My mind is made up. It's your help I'm asking for. You have a good army and the ear of the people."

"My help in attacking the Pope?" I pretended to be taken aback. "But, Paolo, I'm a good Catholic!"

"So am I."

"The risks will be enormous. You're asking me to stake my property, my palace, and my life in a completely unpredictable contest."

"Isn't it the duty of all the Orsinis to take up arms when one of them is insulted?"

"Paolo," I said with a faint smile, "don't you think it would be better if we spoke

412

frankly? You want to attack the Pope not because you've been insulted, but to set Vittoria free. And that's why I refuse to help you. Vittoria's a widow. I have Virginio's interests very much at heart. So I don't want you to marry her."

"In short," he replied with a piercing look, "it suits you that she should be shut up in Castel Sant' Angelo?"

His tone and look made my blood run cold. I didn't know what to say.

"Would you like a drink, Lodovico?" he asked.

"No — no, thanks. I'm not thirsty."

"You must be. You've been swallowing all the time we've been talking. Besides, it's very hot. Come on, pour yourself a drink. Pour one for me too. And take whichever glass you like. Then you won't think I'm trying to poison you."

He laughed, and I, rather mirthlessly, joined in. When I'd filled the glasses, Paolo took the one I handed him, and seeing I wasn't touching mine, emptied his in one gulp. Though the wine was excellent, I had difficulty swallowing mine.

"Lodovico," he said conversationally, throwing himself on a chair, "I've just heard something strange. The Pope has sent a big sack of piasters from the Vatican to Cardinal de' Medici's palace in Rome, and *he's* sent it to the Patriarch of Venice's palace in Rome, where Cardinal Cherubi's staying. According to my information, that sack contains fifty thousand piasters."

"That's a lot of money."

"Indeed. Isn't it strange that such a large sum should be traveling from one palace in Rome to another? Who knows who Cherubi will pass it on to? Do you know Cherubi, Lodovico?"

"I met him once. I dined at his house."

"Really! What did you talk about?"

"This and that."

"Did you talk about me?"

"Among other things."

"What did he want to know?"

"Whether you were Vittoria's lover."

"What did you say?"

"I said I didn't know anything about it."

"Well," said Paolo icily, "that was a good answer. You're a good kinsman, Lodovico. And I wish you good day."

At that, he stood and looked at me with a terrifying expression. My knees turned to water, and I backed out of the room, afraid he might plant his dagger between my shoulder blades if I turned around.

Down in the courtyard I called Alfredo and told him to go get Raimondo and his noble friends. It took him a good ten minutes to drag them away. I could see that Raimondo had had too much to drink again. His face was red, he was shouting, and as he walked along he was slapping his sword, obviously looking for trouble.

"What's the matter with you, *carissimo?*" he bawled. "You look pale. If anyone's insulted my brother, I'll spit his liver on my sword!"

"No one's insulted me. But you're as red as a turkey cock. To horse! Help him, Alfredo."

"I don't need Alfredo," cried Raimondo, not even noticing that Alfredo was putting his foot in the stirrup and giving him a good boost into the saddle.

Once he had mounted, however, he sat straight as a ramrod. His horse started to buck, but he brought it under control at once and gave it a little tap with his riding crop.

"What, beating your horse, Raimondo?" cried Savelli.

"A woman, a mare, and a walnut tree . . ." began Raimondo, who'd never struck a woman in his life, being as soft and easy-going with the opposite sex as he was rough with his own.

"Shame on you, Raimondo!" said Gaetano, laughing. "My mare has nothing but caresses from me. I couldn't bear to hurt her."

"A crop never hurt a horse," said Ruggieri. "Their hide's too thick. It just annoys them, that's all."

This was debatable, and the discussion went on with much shouting and laughter as we rode through the courtyard. The outlaws and bandits who filled it made way for us grudgingly, looking askance at the handsome young men in their glistening doublets who didn't even deign to glance at them but jabbered at the tops of their voices, as if Montegiordano belonged to them. Turning in the saddle, I saw Paolo standing at the second-floor window, motionless as a statue, looking down at us. The sensation of having his eyes on me and the sight of the huge courtyard and all those men totally devoted to him felt like a weight on me. I spurred my horse and was the first through the gateway. Out in the street again, I felt better. Paolo had understood, or guessed, everything, and I'd got off lightly. It was almost too good to be true: his whore shut up in Sant' Angelo, Paolo paralyzed by my neutrality, and, later this evening, fifty thousand piasters falling into my money bags like rain. Alas, how little a man knows of his own future! A word, a gesture, and in a few seconds it all collapses.

We were about a hundred yards from our own palace, and I was already imagining the festivities with which I'd celebrate my success, when our troop was brought to a halt. A score or more of horsemen were riding toward us with arquebuses by their sides and della Pace at their head. He greeted us politely and, since the street was too narrow for us to pass, said that his party would go back a little way to let us through. I agreed, and he turned his men around. In the subsequent confusion, I saw — and my eyes nearly started out of my head — that our two bandits from the Nora were tied to one of the horses, the reins of which were held by a particularly gigantic man.

"Bargello," I yelled, "what's this? Have you broken into my house in my absence and abducted two of my men?"

Della Pace took off his hat and rode back toward me, closely followed by his men.

"Signor Count," he said politely, "I'm extremely sorry to have had to do it, but I was ordered to arrest these two bandits by His Excellency Governor Portici. I didn't break in. I rang and was let in. My men did the rest."

"You've violated the Orsinis' right of asylum!" yelled Raimondo.

"Forgive me, Signor Orsini," said della Pace, "but the right of asylum belongs to the elder and not to the younger branch of the family."

"Elder or younger, what do I care?" Raimondo answered. "Just you untie our men and give them back to us, you blackguard."

"Signore," della Pace said, putting his hat on again and speaking more stiffly, "you forget you are speaking to the Bargello."

"Don't you get mixed up in this, Raimondo," I said. "Let me talk to the Bargello."

"I'll get mixed up in it if I like!" Raimondo said. The wine had given him the courage to disobey me. "You heard me, Bargello, you scum. Untie those men and hand them over."

"Signore," said the Bargello, "you insult me, and that's unworthy of both of us. Have you forgotten I'm a nobleman too?"

"A lousy flea-ridden minor nobleman!" roared Raimondo.

"Be quiet, Raimondo, and let me speak," I said.

"Minor nobility, perhaps," said the Bargello grimly, "but none of my servants has ever gone robbing and murdering travelers in the Nora mountains."

"Blackguard!" shouted Raimondo. "You dare to cast aspersions on the Orsinis' honor? I'll make you eat your words."

"Come, come, Raimondo, you go too far," said Savelli, who was gentle and conciliatory by nature.

"Let me speak!" Raimondo was foaming at the mouth by now. "I'll flay this rascal and his stinking policemen alive. Meanwhile" — he raised his riding crop — "I'll give him a good hiding."

"Signore," said the Bargello, "I advise you not to use violence. The fuses of our guns are lit, and my men don't like being defied or insulted."

"We'll see!" Raimondo raised his crop still higher.

At this point, Savelli, who was on Raimondo's right, urged his horse closer and grabbed him by the wrist. But Raimondo shook himself free and brought the crop down as hard as he could on the Bargello's face.

There was a moment of stupefaction. I watched incredulously as blood welled up and started to run down the Bargello's cheek. He turned in his saddle. Contrary to what I said later, for the good of the cause, he did not give the order to fire. He just showed his men his bloody face. They fired immediately. The noise was deafening, and by the time the smoke had cleared from the narrow street, the police and their leader had ridden away. I dismounted. Five of our people were lying on the cobblestones: Raimondo, Silla, Pietro Gaetano, and two of the escort.

I sent at once for a barber-surgeon, who

gave me little hope for Raimondo and Silla. An hour later, they both died, before they could be given extreme unction. They'd been so close in life that they'd shared everything, even their mistresses. Now they'd breathed their last almost together.

The news of the fatal volley spread swiftly through Rome, and by one o'clock in the afternoon all the nobility of the city had gathered in my courtyard to file past the dead and injured in grief and anger. They shook their fists and swore vengeance on the Bargello and his men. And, already, ordinary people who loved the nobles as much as they hated the Pope, were besieging my door and demanding weapons, as well as torches "to go and smoke the old fox out of his lair in the Vatican."

Paolo arrived an hour later. There was a stir among the nobles when he appeared, for everyone knew his military talents and now hoped he'd be the leader of the rebellion.

He knelt and prayed for a long while by the two bodies, and when he stood up, Alfredo, who was beside him, told him in detail what had happened. Paolo walked past me, pretending not to see me. Then he changed his mind and came back. He put his arm around me, kissed me on the cheek, and whispered: "Now you *have* to be with me!"

## His Excellency Luigi Portici, Governor of Rome

In my opinion, nothing is worse for a country than secret diplomacy. If some of a ruler's officials agree with him on a policy the others know nothing about, the latter may in all good faith take contradictory measures that completely undermine the secret plan. A government may thus find itself in the dangerous and ridiculous position of a snake that, instead of biting the enemy, bites its own tail.

That's exactly what happened with Lodovico Orsini. I, Governor of Rome, was kept in ignorance from beginning to end of the Vatican's negotiations with him. These were designed to ensure, through Cardinal Cherubi, Lodovico's neutrality if Prince Orsini declared open war on the papacy.

The consequences of this secrecy have been extremely grave. I list the facts here for the edification of those who may wish to conduct their politics on sounder principles.

First: If I had known the Vatican intended to negotiate with Lodovico Orsini, I would have advised against having anything whatever to do with that vice-ridden, debt-riddled gentleman.

Second: I would have told the Vatican of the suspicions the papal police had concerning the two bandits who were robbing and murdering wayfarers in the Nora mountains, and how those suspicions had become certainties when the bandits in question took refuge in Lodovico Orsini's palace.

Third: Should the Vatican have disregarded my advice and treated with Lodovico Orsini, I would certainly not have ordered the Bargello to force an entry into his palace and arrest the two bandits. Knowing how proud Lodovico is, and how violent his younger brother, Raimondo, is, I would have felt that such an intrusion might end in bloodshed — as, alas, it did.

In the subsequent skirmish, two gentlemen who belonged to important families in Rome were killed. This sounded the knell for the Vatican's plans. It soon became evident that, because of Raimondo's death, Lodovico could not remain neutral. And the Roman nobility would not be indifferent to the death of Silla Savelli. More important, Prince Orsini would not let slip this opportunity to assume the leadership of a rebellion that might enable him to free Vittoria Peretti.

Though they did not choose it knowingly,

the conspirators could not have taken up arms at a more propitious moment. Popular discontent was at its height, for reasons I shall now explain.

As leader of Christendom and head of a sovereign state, the Pope exercised both spiritual and temporal power, which together gave him unlimited authority. Gregory XIII used this unwisely. He too often confused the papal tiara and the princely crown.

The year before the rebellion, being short of money, he had taken back from certain gentlemen the fiefs his predecessor had granted them. When some of these gentlemen complained too boldly about how they had been despoiled and ruined, the Pope promptly excommunicated them, thus adding injustice to expropriation.

There were many excommunications for nonreligious reasons during Gregory XIII's papacy, and these, in addition to dealing cruel blows to innocent people, also scandalized many of the faithful. Another example of how the spiritual power was made to serve the interests of the temporal was the Pope's use of a *precetto* against a political opponent — an irrevocable decree annulling his marriage. If the unfortunate victim refused to quit the marital home, he found himself living in concubinage, and thus in a state of mortal sin, with the woman he loved, who only the day before had been his lawful wife. This was an abuse that angered the Pope's least sophisticated subjects as well as theologians. The latter murmured, under their breath, that marriage was a sacrament in which the husband and wife were the ministers, and therefore no external authority had the power to set it aside.

Gregory used his temporal power arbitrarily too. Nepotism had always been a main weakness of the papacy, but Gregory's indolence and thoughtlessness allowed the nephews to whom he entrusted the main instruments of power to wield it without let or hindrance, according to their mood, their purse, or their mere likes and dislikes. They didn't hesitate to throw people into papal prisons without charge or trial, and for unlimited periods, and many of these were honest people whose only crime was to have displeased or opposed them.

I feel some qualms about mentioning one class of Gregory's enemies. They were not numerous, but their animosity was all the fiercer for having to remain secret. I refer to those Lutherans whom the Inquisition and fear of the stake had reconverted to the old religion. They still had strong hidden affection for their former opinions, and could not forgive the Pope for celebrating a Mass of thanksgiving on hearing of the massacre of Protestants in

Paris on St. Bartholomew's Day. Some Catholics too, even in Rome, were shocked by this, and by the public bonfires the Pope had had lighted on the same occasion.

Worse still, Gregory's government managed to be weak as well as tyrannical. Not daring to attack Prince Orsini after Peretti was murdered, the Pope imprisoned a woman, who appears not to have been involved in the crime. Then, having thus provoked Prince Orsini, he tried to paralyze him by purchasing the neutrality of a dubious character who might otherwise have been his ally. Since the Pope did not dream for a moment that this plan could fail, he had no alternative ready, and took no special precautions, such as reinforcing his Swiss Guard while there was time.

The uprising took him completely by surprise. And it was doubly threatening because the people soon joined the nobles. They did so partly because they hated the Pope's nephews and the papal police, and partly because they were attached to Lodovico and to other great households for the largesse they bestowed. This bounty cost the aristocracy little, for they were as harsh and extortionate toward their peasants as they were generous toward the lower orders in the towns. The reason was that the peasants were scattered throughout the countryside, so the nobles were not afraid of them, whereas they had to handle the townspeople carefully. Their number and concentration made them dangerous, but they could be turned without undue expense into a useful following.

I sent spies to all the nerve centers of the city as soon as della Pace, his face bloody, told me about the confrontation with the Orsini brothers, in which Raimondo Orsini and Silla Savelli lost their lives. The Bargello had not given the order to fire, contrary to what Lodovico Orsini said later. My spies brought back alarming news. The nobles were swiftly organizing under Prince Orsini, and were handing out knives to their followers but prudently keeping the arquebuses for themselves. The mob was already swarming through the streets, chasing the papal police, and killing more than one of them. This state of affairs brought all the robbers and cutthroats out of their holes, ready for looting, murder, and other villainies.

I informed the Pope's nephews that they should take refuge as quickly as possible in the Vatican — their servants were being molested already — and went there myself with della Pace. I readied the whole place for a state of siege, barricading the exits and training the cannon on the streets. The Vatican had already sent for help from the Spanish troops stationed in The Two Sicilies under the command of an Austrian general. But knowing how long it took Philip II to make a decision, and how long it took the Austrians to carry one out, I guessed that nothing would come from that quarter for at least three weeks. And the way things were going, it would be too late in three days. The mob running around outside the Vatican with torches was shouting that it was going to "smoke the old fox out."

At night, by a secret door I had left open, though strongly guarded, I sent out several emissaries. One had orders to try to get into Montegiordano, where the rebellion had set up its headquarters. There was so much activity there that he succeeded, and found the nobles both excited and embarrassed at finding victory so near. They were also worried that the mob might get out of hand. Although they alone had guns, they were afraid they would no longer be safe in their own palaces.

The emissary to Montegiordano was a monk, a man of courage and resource. Seeing how anxious the nobles were, he was bold enough to speak to Prince Orsini. He explained who he was and asked on what conditions the rebels would make peace with the Pope.

The Prince took him into a little room, locked the door, and said: "There are two conditions. First, a coach with my coat of arms on it, surrounded by a platoon of my soldiers, will be waiting at midnight outside the little door at the back of Castel Sant' Angelo. Two women prisoners unjustly detained there by the Pope will come out and get into the coach. If they have not appeared by one in the morning, my men will attack a gate of the Vatican with a battering ram."

"And the second condition, my lord?"

"It is one that the others insist on, though I find it repugnant. The nobles want della Pace's head."

"That is a horrible request, my lord!"

"Yes. But it's the price the Pope has to pay for peace."

"But, my lord, even if the Pope agrees to sacrifice the Bargello, it seems doubtful the people would be satisfied with that. They're crying out for him to abdicate."

"Don't worry. We have the troops and the guns. We'll cut the mob to pieces."

"What, my lord? Your allies?"

"What else can we do? Do you want this anarchy to go on? In the end, we will be the victims."

"My lord, I shall report your conditions faithfully."

"Remember that the two go together. If the first is not fulfilled, there will be no point in fulfilling the second."

"My lord, forgive me for speaking frankly. But what would happen if only the second condition were fulfilled, and the nobles were satisfied with that?"

"I'd continue the siege myself, and the people with me. Would you like to wager on whether I can capture the Vatican by tomorrow at noon?"

"You'll be excommunicated."

"Are you here to negotiate or to threaten?"

"My lord, pardon me for my straight speaking. May I go on, or shall I say no more?"

"Go on, please. I find your conversation instructive."

"What will happen if the Vatican fires its cannon on the besiegers?"

"I have cannon too. And instead of just tickling your main gate with a battering ram, I'll blow it to pieces. You know what will happen then. The mob will pour through the breach, and loot and kill all in its path!"

"You'd allow such carnage?"

"How could I stop it?"

"Oh, my lord! All this because of a woman!"

"I'm sorry, Father. That subject is outside your competence. Go back whence you came and report my conditions word for word."

When the monk, safely back within our walls, told me all this, I could scarcely believe my ears. The second condition — that della Pace's head be thrown to the mob — seemed utterly insulting to the person it was addressed to. Rather than repeat it to the Pope myself, I decided to take the monk with me and let him tell his tale.

I found the Holy Father with the captain of the Swiss Guard and a dozen or so senior Vatican dignitaries, in a state of great alarm. They were discussing whether to use our cannon. The captain of the Swiss Guard was very much against it, saying they would be ineffective in the city, where there were plenty of walls for the assailants to shelter behind. "It will only enrage them!" he declared in his heavy German accent.

The Holy Father had noticed me and, guessing that I brought news, beckoned me forward. After kneeling and kissing his slipper — a ceremony he did not curtail even in those circumstances — I told him about the monk and requested him to hear what he had to say.

While the monk was speaking, I watched the faces of the Pope and his advisers and was amazed to see them show immense relief. When the monk had finished, the Holy Father, instead of indulging in his usual eloquence, merely asked his counselors for their opinion. There was a long, embarrassed silence: none wanted to be the first to speak. The subject was extremely thorny, and they did not know, and could not guess, what the Pope's wishes were in the matter.

The silence must have irritated the Pope. He turned to one of the cardinals present and asked imperiously: "Cherubi?"

The choice was no accident: Cherubi was well known for his frankness and his gaffes.

"Most Holy Father," he trumpeted, "I think that if the proposals are accepted, we'd get off very lightly."

"Very lightly?" murmured another cardinal.

"I mean," Cherubi went on, not in the least put out by the interruption, "things might be much worse. For instance, if the nobles decided to unleash the mob. That's why we ought to treat with the nobles while there's still time."

"But the conditions are very harsh," said another cardinal, "especially the second."

He spoke very softly and hesitantly, not at all like Cherubi.

"No doubt the conditions are harsh," went on the latter, "especially the one concerning della Pace. All of us here are fond of the Bargello. We respect him. But it was through him the trouble started, so he'll have to put up with being the means of stopping it. The Holy

Father must be as courageous in sacrificing him as Abraham was in sacrificing Isaac."

Since the Pope heard this speech with some signs of approbation, no one else dared protest. But to compare the demands of a band of bloodthirsty nobles to a command from the Almighty . . . !

"My most dear sons," said the Pope, suddenly desperate to have the discussion done with, "which of you shares Cardinal Cherubi's opinion?"

It escaped no one that this way of putting the question dictated its own answer. All but two raised a hand.

I then did something extremely audacious. I threw myself at the Pope's feet and panted: "Most Holy Father, if anyone has to be sacrificed, let it be me! I was the one who ordered della Pace to arrest the two bandits. So I am really responsible for the fatal incident."

The Pope seemed taken aback. He gazed down at me with his big blue eyes as if he did not know what to say.

"My dear Portici," said Cherubi loudly, "unfortunately, it's not your head the rebels are after. If we gave it to them, it wouldn't satisfy them. So there's no point in going back on our vote. What I suggest," he went on, looking at the captain of the Swiss Guard, "is that the thing should be done discreetly and without warning, so that the person concerned hardly notices he's being killed. The head can be separated from the body afterward."

I looked at the Holy Father. He was nodding gently, but it was impossible to say whether this was a sign of approval or of senility. It suddenly struck me that he was exploiting his great age to appear weaker and less alert than he really was. As recently as the previous day, I'd seen him laughing, lively, and incisive, and holding his slim frame perfectly upright.

"Most Holy Father . . ." I started to make a last effort.

He immediately interrupted me. "My very dear son," he said, "believe me, I'm terribly grieved that the tyranny of circumstance has forced us into this painful decision. I am the first to deplore it. I should now like to be left alone to offer my suffering and affliction up to the Lord." His pink cheeks streamed with tears.

"My very dear son," he added, blessing me, "go in peace."

Despite his tears and his blessing, the Holy Father never forgave me for the embarrassment I had caused him. He took his revenge at leisure, a few months after peace was restored. While I was enjoying a summer holiday at my villa in Ostia, he wrote to tell me I need not come back: it was time for me to rest from the exertions of my office. The style of the letter was suave and flowery, but the result was: not only was I relieved of my duties as governor, but I was also banished from Rome.

### *Alfredo Colombani, Squire to Raimondo and Lodovico Orsini*

I don't have much to say; I haven't got the gift of gab. So I'll say it simply. Forgive me if I use the Venetian dialect. I can understand Italian, but I don't speak it well.

To start with, I was Lord Raimondo Orsini's squire. Then I was squire to his brother Count Lodovico too. I knew both of them well.

They used to call Raimondo Il Bruto, mostly because of his mug. Mine's not much better. In fact, it's worse. If I was judged on that alone, I'd go straight to the gallows.

But I'm not a bloodthirsty type. It's true I've stabbed about half a dozen people in my time, but always on orders from my masters — never on my own account. And to tell you the truth, I wouldn't have liked to be a bandit in the Nora mountains, like some I might name.

Well, Raimondo was only a brute when he'd

had too much to drink — and with him, "too much" was a lot. Then you had to watch out. But he was kindhearted. The trouble he went to in killing Duchess Isabella at Bracciano! And afterward he cried his eyes out, and never stopped praying. As bad as a priest! She *was* very beautiful. I've never seen such a fine figure of a woman. But she *had* betrayed Prince Paolo with just about everybody.

I have happy memories of that time in Bracciano. After the thing was done, and Raimondo had finally finished saying his prayers, we really enjoyed ourselves. Stuffing away food, boozing, wenching — a whole week of it. None of the maids escaped, whether they liked it or not. With the Duchess dead, we were the masters.

But the brutal side of Lord Raimondo was his undoing. If he'd let Count Lodovico do the talking that day, he wouldn't have been shot. But he would go and work himself up! Of course, he'd been drinking. Still, insults are one thing, but hitting the Bargello with his crop was going too far. Mind you, the Bargello didn't give the order to fire. He just turned in his saddle so his men could see the outrage he'd suffered. Too bad the fuses of their arquebuses were already lit. I found out afterward why, and I'll tell you.

When they had entered our courtyard to

capture the bandits, our men showed their teeth. There were a good many of them, so the police withdrew into the gate tower. There, the Bargello ordered them to light their fuses before renewing the attack. This time our bunch were less of a problem.

That's the explanation. It was simply because they had their fuses already lit that they fired. And also because they were very fond of him. If they hadn't been, they would have laughed at him for getting hit in the face. Not in front of him, of course! But the fact is, good masters are mourned; you wouldn't mind giving a shove to bad ones to help them into the next world.

The police didn't aim; they just fired at random. It's a miracle only two died. I was just behind Raimondo. The bullet that went through his chest grazed my arm. But what was most unfair was the death of poor Lord Savelli. You couldn't find a nicer, gentler young man, and very polite with ordinary people too. He tried to hold Raimondo's hand back when he lifted his riding crop, and all he got for this was a ball in the head.

I'm not ashamed to say it: I wept for Raimondo. The more so as I have one master now: Lodovico. I won't say anything about him one way or the other. It's not for me to judge. They say he has a special devotion to the Madonna and prays to her every day, morning and evening. But if you ask me, he's not the sort of person the Madonna would like very much — not if she knew him as well as I do.

Perhaps I didn't explain clearly about the arquebuses and the lighted fuses. What I mean is: if the fuses hadn't already been lit, the police wouldn't have fired. Why not? Because they wouldn't have lit them without being ordered to by the Bargello. You may say they *fired* without being ordered to. But that's not the same thing. It takes a second to fire. But it takes some time to light a fuse. You've got to get the flint out of your pocket, strike it, light the touch, blow on it to keep it burning, move it close to the fuse, and blow again: a whole rigmarole. So the Bargello would have had time to say: "What do you think you're doing? I haven't given you an order!" And on our side, even if he hadn't said anything, we'd have seen what they were up to and would've had time to drive them away with a few good thumps from the flat of our swords, without even having to kill them. Don't forget there were thirty of us, and only twenty of them.

You see what a small thing it revolved around: just those lighted fuses. But oh, the enormousness of the result! By the next day, the city was being put to fire and sword. All the nobility were mobilized, and all the people were out on the streets. *All* the people, good and bad. As it turned out, there wasn't much to choose between the two: respectable artisans took to murdering and looting along with the riffraff. The police were killed wherever they were found. The same with the servants of the Pope's nephews. The nephews would have met the same fate if they hadn't taken refuge in the Vatican. Anyway, their palaces were looted, and they weren't poor!

The Vatican was surrounded and besieged. People rushed around shouting "Abdicate! Abdicate! Death to della Pace!" and even "Death to the Pope!" Yes, you heard me: "Death to the Pope!" And all of them devout Catholics, God forgive them!

The nobles, on horses, held back. Their soldiers were armed with arquebuses. Some of these had wheels, though this newfangled kind isn't reliable. But you can be sure all the fuses were lit!

Back of the crowd and in front of the main body of nobles was Prince Paolo on his white mare. On his right was Marquis Giulio Savelli, poor Silla's father, and on his left was Count Lodovico. They were all quiet. Maybe afraid. Seeing the mob rampaging like that, they must have been afraid for their own palaces. What struck me most of all was that they weren't doing anything. Nothing at all! When I dared ask Count Lodovico what they were waiting for, he snapped, "For the moon to fall into our pockets!"

True, there was a moon, and it was almost as light as day. You could have read a book, if you knew how to read. Prince Paolo looked at his timepiece every so often; he said the time aloud. He was also able to read a note his squire trotted up with. Afterward he looked happy. We didn't know what was in it until later.

Suddenly he said, "Let's get it over with."

He ordered a musket salvo to be fired at the windows of the Vatican. Not much harm was done except to the glass. Just a little tickle. But it pleased the people, who applauded as if it were a show.

Prince Paolo advanced three cannon. They weren't very big. And the gunners on the other side were piling bags of sand to shelter them from our arquebuses. The horsemen tried to clear a way through the mob so the cannon could fire at the Vatican gate. It took two ranks of foot soldiers to hold back the idiots ready to be made into mincemeat just to get a better view.

I could see that the gunners inside were taking their time making their shelter, and so could the mob, which shouted, "Hurry up! Fire!" Prince Paolo sent a dozen or so soldiers forward with a battering ram. They began to attack the gate. But their efforts seemed half-hearted. When the mob saw no result, they yelled, "Harder! Harder!" The hotheads among them shouted, "Let us do it. Then you'll see!" The double row of soldiers had all they could do to hold them back.

Then, over the gate, a white flag appeared. There was an uproar! Soon a box was let down on a rope.

"Go see what it is, Alfredo!" Count Lodovico said, his eyes blazing.

I spurred my horse forward and told one of the soldiers to leave the battering ram and go open the box. He did. It contained della Pace's head, the neck still dripping with blood. I seized it by the hair and galloped back so that the mob couldn't snatch it away.

Prince Paolo was our general, so I offered the head to him. He declined it with disgust. So did Marquis Savelli. But don't think Count Lodovico was so sensitive. He grabbed the head by the hair and pranced in front of the mob, brandishing it at arm's length and shouting, "Della Pace! Della Pace! Victory! Victory!" When they all rushed toward him, he threw it to them.

I won't say what those scum of the earth

did with it. It makes me feel ill just to think of it.

The nobles were silent. If you ask me, they weren't feeling too happy. After all, della Pace was a nobleman too — of second rank, but honorable — and a good man, respected by everybody. They were probably revolted that the Pope had been such a coward as to sacrifice a loyal servant to save his throne. I was ashamed of him myself. And of the good Christians who kicked that poor bloodstained head around as if it were a ball.

Don't think that was enough to calm them down. They were beside themselves. Cries of "Abdicate! Abdicate!" and "Down with the tyrant!" and "Death to the Pope" started again. Some piled kindling against a small gate to the Vatican. Others got the battering ram away from the soldiers. Then ten or twenty began hitting the main gate, and this time it was serious.

Prince Paolo turned in his saddle and asked the nobles: "Shall we let them go on?"

What a question? They certainly weren't going to do anything of the kind. After the Pope, it would be their turn. The answer was unanimous. In the blink of an eye, they'd changed sides!

Prince Paolo ordered the cannon to be turned, and without warning he fired on the people. The crowd was so dense that the cannon balls caused havoc. Next, a volley of musket shots rang out. Men fell by the dozen, dead or wounded. The mob began to fall back. Another volley! There was no need to aim, there were so many of them. They fell like flies all over the place. It was a real massacre. As the rebels started to retreat faster, Prince Paolo turned to the nobles and ordered a charge. There was a hiss in the air as they unsheathed their double-edged swords. No messing around with the flat of them! Cut and thrust for anyone who didn't run fast enough!

As Count Lodovico, bloodthirsty as ever, was about to join in, Prince Paolo held him back, saying: "Cousin, go home now. And please stop trying to be a Machiavelli. If it hadn't been for you, none of this would have happened. And, believe me, all this bloodshed is pointless: the prisoner of Sant' Angelo is in my house and, God willing, I shall marry her tomorrow."

He rode off, leaving the Count white and grinding his teeth like a madman.

Work it out: he was one of the two cuckolds in this business. He'd lost his brother Raimondo and fifty thousand piasters, and the Prince was going to marry Vittoria! The other cuckold was the people. They'd helped the nobles, and the nobles, as soon as the demands of their vendetta were met, had hacked them to pieces.

The day after the massacre a Franciscan went through the streets of Rome saying he'd heard the devil laugh when the nobles turned their cannon on the populace. For a piaster he'd describe or even imitate the laugh, and by the end of the day he'd collected a small fortune. The following day, he vanished, and a good thing for him that he did, because his victims, ridiculed by their neighbors for believing him, were looking for him everywhere to beat him up.

I've heard many accounts of the argument between Raimondo and the Bargello from people who were there and from people who weren't. But I've never heard anyone repeat one threat Raimondo made: "If you don't hand our men over here and now, the biggest pieces that'll be left of you will be your ears."

I don't know where he picked that up, because he wasn't very bright. At least, no brighter than I am. But he was a good master. It's true I got more kicks than piasters, but when we went out for a good time together, he shared everything, wine and women alike.

Except Caterina Acquaviva. The only person he shared her with was Silla Savelli. He was so fond of him that some people in Rome said the handsome Savelli was his faggot. I don't believe it. But when you're drunk what's the difference?

I often think of them. They were so young, so brave, so full of life. And now they're dead. And they both died in a state of mortal sin. That's the worst of it. I don't often pray, but when I do it's to ask the Lord to let them into His heaven. I know it's for Him to judge, and He alone holds the balance in which souls are weighed. But an ounce of prayer on the right side can't do any harm.

# 10

## *Caterina Acquaviva*

We weren't badly treated in Castel Sant' Angelo, and the living conditions were passable. We had two quite spacious rooms with a door between, on the second floor. The only thing wrong with them was that the windows were on the small side, and barred. Our meals were brought to us by an elderly nun or a young novice who might have been about twenty. The old one lowered her eyes as soon as she came in, and looked up only to find her way out. She didn't answer when we said good morning or good night.

At first we thought she was deaf. But when I dropped the hairbrush on the floor one day, she jumped, so I knew it must be put on. No doubt she thought our sins might enter into her through her eyes or ears. We were lucky she didn't think of holding her nose.

The young one, who was quite pretty, didn't talk much but had a ready smile and was easily amused. It amazed me that a girl could still be cheerful after vowing never to let a man come near her. Since she seemed to like me, I began to show her out, and I took the opportunity to ask her a few questions, which she quite innocently answered. That's how I found out that our food would have been less good and less plentiful if His Eminence Cardinal Montalto hadn't paid the jailer. When I told the signora this, she cried, "Oh, he *is* still fond of me!" And she wept. But they were the sort of tears that did her good.

It was the novice who brought us our meal the evening the rebellion broke out. Hearing the shouting and tumult, I asked her what was happening. She either didn't know or didn't want to say. She looked frightened and advised me not to look out the window. As soon as she'd gone, I did look: there was a big moon, but all I could see was many horsemen galloping on the other side of the Tiber. The noise seemed to be coming from the direction of the Vatican, behind us, but our windows looked out on the river.

There was so much excitement it would have been impossible to sleep, and Vittoria wouldn't get undressed. She was right about that, as it turned out.

The thing that had bothered her most about her imprisonment was that as soon as she set foot inside Castel Sant' Angelo, the old nun had taken away her books, which della Pace had let her bring with her when he came for us. She wrote a petition to the Pope, in Latin, asking to be allowed to have them back, but she received no answer. I was surprised, but she smiled faintly and said: "Who knows? Perhaps the Holy Father can't read Latin."

She didn't speak much, and not once did she ever utter the Prince's name or mention his existence. Several times she did remember Signor Peretti and each time she spoke of him with affection. She seemed much fonder of him now he was dead.

She asked so often to have her books back that the nun finally lent her a New Testament. She read it continuously, and after a few days she almost knew it by heart and could recite whole passages. But sometimes she said things that surprised me.

One day, she looked up from her reading and said: "I don't understand why Saint Matthew went to all that trouble listing Joseph's genealogy. What's the point, since he wasn't Christ's father? He'd have done better to give Mary's family tree."

"Signora," I said, "if he didn't, it was because Mary was only a woman."

"You're probably right," she answered, looking at me as if she'd been struck by what I'd said.

Then she started to laugh. "You talk like a heretic, Caterina. How can you say Mary is only a woman when she's the Mother of God?"

I didn't know what to think. First she praised me and then she blamed me. Who was she making fun of — me or St. Matthew? She was the one who was a heretic! Or maybe she was taking it out on St. Matthew because she was angry with the nun for taking her books.

Anyhow, she never really complained. I admired her courage. I wasn't as strong as she was. I restrained myself during the day, so as not to annoy her, but at night in bed I cried my eyes out. I thought of my family in Grottammare, and what the parish priest would be saying about me from the pulpit. I thought about my sweethearts too, and went over them in my head. At first it did me good, but afterward it made me feel lonelier and more miserable on my straw mattress. What a disgrace that I had to sleep on a straw mattress! Vittoria had a proper bed.

When he took us to Sant' Angelo, della Pace, the nice man, managed to bring his mustache close to my ear and whisper: "You can both sleep easy. They won't put you on trial. They haven't got anything against you." I told Vittoria, but she refused to be reassured.

"We'll be here for years, then," she said,

with a sigh. "Until the Pope dies, at least. And he's very fit."

That night on my pallet I prayed with all my heart that the Lord would take the Holy Father to Himself as soon as possible. I had a few qualms about it afterward; I wasn't sure it was right for a Catholic to pray for the Pope to die.

I thought about della Pace too, and how I felt when his mustache tickled my ear. If only he could come to Sant' Angelo and interrogate me alone. But that dream disappeared when the novice told me he wasn't in charge at Sant' Angelo. It had its own governor.

As for Marcello, I refused to think about the scoundrel. I hoped he was enjoying himself with his old woman in Amalfi. At first I worried about his safety, but Vittoria said the Viceroy of Naples hated the Pope and would never hand Marcello over to him.

The night we heard all that noise near the Vatican, we didn't know what to think at first. Then we heard a volley of musket fire. After that there was noise inside Castel Sant' Angelo too, with people running up and down the stairs and muffled rumblings overhead.

To our surprise, the Governor appeared. Until then he hadn't deigned to visit us. He was a fat, pompous man with bulging eyes, who looked about as trustworthy as a lawyer.

"Signora," he said, making a courtly bow, "I have come to reassure you. The Castel Sant' Angelo is as solid as a rock. You are in absolutely no danger."

"Thank you, Governor," Vittoria said, smiling politely, "but I wasn't at all alarmed."

He seemed rather taken aback, and maybe also by her failure to ask any questions about the noises.

"Signora," he said, "it's going to be a long night. If you wish, I'll send you some refreshments."

I could see she was going to say no, so I signed to her behind the Governor's back to accept.

"Many thanks again," she said. "I'd like some herb tea."

The Governor bowed again, straightened up, and made for the door. He walked as if he expected the floor under his feet to be impressed by his importance.

As I'd hoped, it was the novice who brought the herb tea. She was pale, and her hands were shaking. As I saw her out, I asked what the rumblings upstairs were.

"They're moving the cannon."

"Who's attacking us?"

"I don't know. Wicked people, anyhow."

"Forgive me, Sister, but you're trembling.

Are you afraid for your life?"

"No," she said. "I'm afraid of the soldiers, if they capture Sant' Angelo."

I nearly said, "Come, come, it's not as bad as all that," but I restrained myself. She was a nice girl, and I didn't want to shock her. What a funny world it is! I thought. What some people long for, others dread.

Half an hour later she came back.

"Signora," she said, "on the Governor's orders I've come to help you pack. You're going to be moved. You'll be safer where you're going."

Vittoria didn't ask any questions, and neither did I, though I was dying to. I don't suppose the poor girl knew where we were going anyway.

In a quarter of an hour, we'd done our packing and were led downstairs by a man who carried our portable goods. There was no sign of the Governor.

We went out through a little door guarded on the inside by several men. The noise outside was deafening, but I didn't have time to see anything. A coach was waiting a few yards away. It looked golden and shiny in the moonlight. An officer, hat in hand, was holding its door open. Men on horseback blocked the view on both sides.

The man with us gave the luggage to one

of the soldiers and scuttled away for dear life, slamming the door behind him. the men in the escort started to laugh, but the officer silenced them with a gesture.

The coach was padded with red velvet trimmed wit gold braid; I thought it looked fit for a cardinal, and that it was going to take us to safety in another fortress belonging, like Santa Maria, to some prelate. But I didn't dare ask questions. Vittoria sat regally silent, and the officer opposite didn't speak either. The coach went very fast, and I couldn't see anything because the red velvet curtains over the windows were closed, and I was too overawed by the officer, who was wearing a black mask, to try to peek out.

To my great surprise, the coach slowed down very soon, turned a corner, and stopped. When the officer jumped out and opened the door for us, I glimpsed a big courtyard full of people, but I couldn't see much because a thick black cloud was passing over the moon. The officer led us up to the second floor and into a small room furnished with hangings and rugs. Then he took off his mask. I'd never seen his face before, and out of the corner of my eye I saw that Vittoria didn't recognize it either. I wondered why he'd gone to so much trouble to hide it. For a jailer, he was incredibly polite; he bowed almost down to the floor and said, with the greatest respect: "Signora, this small drawing room and the two adjoining bedrooms are at your disposal. I hope you will be comfortable here. I have been ordered to do everything I can to that end."

I could tell that Vittoria was surprised by this consideration, by the rooms and the fancy coach that had brought us here. As the officer was backing out of the room, his hat sweeping the floor, she asked eagerly: "Signore, I've never been here before. Can you tell us where we are?"

"In Montegiordano, of course, signora," he answered, raising his eyebrows in astonishment. When she said nothing more, he made another low bow and was gone.

"My God!" Vittoria cried, putting her hands to her throat.

She had turned so pale I was afraid she was going to faint, and I rushed over to her. But she thrust me roughly aside and started to pace to and fro in a rage, her fists pressed to her cheeks. I got out of her way and sat quietly in a corner. I knew her too well to think I could calm her down with words. You might as well try to still a tempest by catching hold of the lightning.

She turned from white to red, and every so often moved her hands from her cheeks to her throat, as if choking with indignation. She marched up and down for about ten minutes, and all she managed to say was: "How shameful! How degrading!" Though even with knitted brows and face tense, she managed to look beautiful.

At last she sat down — exhausted, I suppose, from emotion — but she sat rigid, with her lips clamped together and her jaw set, her arms folded over her chest. I understood all too well what was going on in her head, and was uneasy at the way she was taking the situation.

There was a knock at the door. Vittoria was silent, motionless, but after another she signed to me to open the door.

It was Prince Orsini. As I stood back, he strode into the room, his presence making it seem smaller. He really was a fine-looking man. What I liked most was the determined, triumphant, joyful expression on his face. Unfortunately, it vanished at once when he saw how Vittoria was looking at him. He gazed at her, apparently incapable of speech.

"My lord," she said cuttingly, "can you explain to me how and why I come to be in your palace?"

The Prince looked as if she'd struck him. When at last he spoke, it was in a strangled voice. "I didn't expect this sort of welcome, madam," he said. "I don't think I have deserved it. I've moved mountains to get you out of Castel Sant' Angelo! I've risen up against my sovereign, I've fomented a rebellion, I've staked my dukedom, my possessions, and my life for you! And the lives of others too, unfortunately. Many others. Blood has flowed in torrents for you tonight. And you ask for an explanation?"

"Yes, my lord," she said icily.

"Well," said the Prince, his amazement giving way to anger, "since you want an explanation, here it is: your liberty is the price the Pope has had to pay to save his throne."

"And who gave you authority to barter me for a throne? Did I agree to this bargain? Did you consult me?"

"Consult you? About trying to set you free?"

"Free? Do you call my being here freedom? Montegiordano is the worst possible prison to me. The very worst! Because it dishonors me."

"What?" cried the Prince, transported with anger. "Do you call it a dishonor to become my wife?"

"Oh," she cried, rising and looking at him with flashing eyes, "now we have it! You barter me like merchandise, and the merchandise is supposed to say yes to becoming

455

your property for life. If that's what all those intrigues and all that bloodshed were for, let me tell you, I'll never be the wife of a gentleman who has broken his word as cravenly as you have."

"Vittoria," exclaimed the Prince, "what are you saying? Why are you insulting me? You accuse me of breaking my word, of acting like a coward? You shall account to me for those words, here and now!"

"Account to you?" she said scornfully. "In a duel, perhaps? Take the quickest way and kill me. And if you haven't the courage to do that, follow your natural bent and hire an assassin. Or if, with a last spark of humanity, you spare my life, grant me one last favor and take me back to Castel Sant' Angelo."

"Take you back?" said the Prince, aghast.

"You've freed me, haven't you? If I'm free, here is my free decision: I do not wish to stay in your palace a moment longer."

"Vittoria, what you're saying is madness."

"On the contrary, it's very sane. I repeat: every minute I spend here dishonors me, and proclaims to the world that I am your mistress and your accomplice in my husband's murder."

"What?" cried the Prince. "*I* had nothing to do with the murder of Francesco Peretti. How could you think for a moment that I'd broken the vow I made to you at Santa Maria not to make any attempt on his life?"

"How am I to believe you?" she asked.

But I could see she was shaken by his vehemence. She went on more quietly. "Who else but you benefited from his death?"

"Vittoria," he said firmly, "I won't allow you to doubt my word. I repeat: I had nothing to do with the unfortunate man's death. I swear it, as I hope to be saved!"

Vittoria, impressed by the gravity of his oath, was silent — though only for a little while. When she spoke again, it was more in sorrow than in anger.

"Unfortunately, my lord, it makes no difference whether you are guilty or not. No one who learns I am here will believe in your innocence, or in mine. My presence here condemns both of us — you as Francesco's murderer, me as an adulteress and your accomplice. So my decision is irrevocable: I insist that you take me back at once to Castel Sant' Angelo."

"And I say again that you're out of your mind. Can't you see that if you go back voluntarily, it will be tantamount to admitting you're guilty and want to be punished? Listen," he went on, restraining his anger. "I can see I haven't convinced you, and you mean to stand by your insane decision. Just grant me a delay of one night. And think about it, I beg you. Think before you throw yourself into the prison of your worst enemy for the rest of your life. One night is all I ask. One night's reflection."

He turned on his heel and left. He was so blind with anger that, although he hit his left shoulder on the doorframe as he went out, I'm sure he didn't feel a thing.

Vittoria sat down on the chair she'd occupied before. Her body again rigid, her arms folded, and her eyes quite dry.

I was completely taken aback. I'd expected her to relax and burst into tears. But no — there she sat without a tear, her jaw set, and stiff as a ramrod. Suddenly that struck me as a bad sign for the future.

"Signora," I said, "with all due respect, do you really want to go back to prison?"

"Yes."

"For the rest of your life?"

"Yes."

"Even now that you know the Prince didn't kill Signor Peretti?"

"I don't know if I can believe him."

"Oh, yes, you do! You do believe him, signora!"

"Why do you ask, if you know what I think better than I do?"

"Because, signora, if the Prince didn't kill

Signor Peretti, there's no reason why you shouldn't marry him."

"Really?"

"If you ask me, it would be more sensible than going back to prison."

"I don't ask you."

"Forgive me, signora, but perhaps I have some right to an opinion, seeing that if you go back to prison, I go too."

"You don't have to go with me."

"I'll go with you because I love you. But also because I have no choice."

"What do you mean?"

"Can you see me living in the Rusticucci palace under Giulietta's thumb? Or, worse, in Grottammare, after all the priest will have said about me from the pulpit?"

"If I listened to you, I'd marry the Prince just to please *you*."

"And because you love him."

She sprang up and came at me, eyes blazing. For once, I stood my ground. I stayed where I was. I meant to have my say, and without mincing words.

"No, I don't love him, you foolish creature," she said. "At least, not any more."

"You might make him believe that, signora," I answered, "because he's a man. But I'm a woman, and you won't convince me. I know that all the time you were insulting

459

him, your one desire was to rush into his arms."

"Wretched girl, how dare you be so stupid?"

"It's no stupider than wanting to go back to prison after you've been let out."

"You go too far. You dare to say your mistress is stupid?"

"I never said that. But I do say my mistress takes too much account of what people think."

"Really!"

"Signora, forgive me, but it's the honest truth. You say you don't want to be dishonored, and you want to go back to prison so that people won't think you're an adulteress and accomplice in a murder. But what is this honor you're talking about? It's not what you've done; it's what people think about you. But let me tell you, you're too beautiful for them not to say nasty things about you. They'll make out you're guilty whether you marry the Prince or jump back into the clutches of the Pope. The difference is that in Sant' Angelo you'll be subject to snubs and insults all the time. But if you become Princess Orsini, people won't dare gossip. And that's the truth!"

"Dear God, you sound just like the Prince! You repeat everything he says, and even everything he doesn't say but just thinks. It's quite simple — you can't see a pair of trunk hose without falling in love with the man inside them. You adore the Prince. You're on his side in everything. And against me!"

"Not against you, signora. I agree with him because he's right."

"Well, my little moralist," she said, drawing herself up to her full height and glaring at me, "go and tell the Prince I've had enough of your insolence and chatter, and that I dismiss you from my service. Let him take you into his if he wants to. And let him make you his whore if he feels like it."

And she gave me two stinging slaps. She hit me so hard I lost my balance. The tears sprang to my eyes. But I didn't lower them. I kept on looking her straight in the face.

"Oh, signora!" I said. "How dreadful! Hitting me after all the years I've served and loved you! Me, the only friend you have left. Me, who would follow you to hell if necessary."

I was exaggerating there. And she might well have answered that if I wasn't keen to go back with her to Sant' Angelo . . . Holy Mother of God, the silly things you say when you're quarreling. But I really was utterly upset and humiliated. It was the first time she had hit me so hard. Like the clouts I got from Il Mancino, but they're not the same, because he's my elder brother.

As Vittoria looked at me, probably not very proud of what she'd done but too haughty to apologize, I went and picked up my little bundle from the heap of baggage in the corner of the room and headed for the door.

"Where do you think you're going, you little idiot?"

"I'm going to tell the Prince you're fed up with me and my insolence and my chatter, and that you've dismissed me and he's to take me into his service if he wants to and make me his whore if he feels like it."

"Caterina!"

"Wasn't that what you told me to say, signora, with two slaps to help me make up my mind?"

"Oh, you little witch!" she cried. "How can you be so irritating?"

But I could see she wasn't sure whether to rage or to laugh.

There wasn't time to see which she'd chosen. Suddenly she threw herself at me, hugged me so tight I could hardly breathe, and started planting little kisses on my forehead. So I flung both arms around her waist and buried my face in her neck. I was melting with love, and weeping.

Weeping for joy, fool that I am.

## Marcello Accoramboni

As soon as the news reached me in Amalfi that the uprising against the Pope had set Vittoria free, I borrowed Margherita Sorghini's swiftest horses and made for Rome. I took two footmen with me, all three of us armed to the teeth, and we rode as fast as consideration for our mounts would allow.

Although della Pace's report had cleared me of my brother-in-law's murder, I took the precaution of sending one of my men ahead to spy out the land before entering the city. He came back grinning. Rome was still plunged in such anarchy, he said, "it was a treat to behold, signore — the custom posts are deserted." The only police he'd seen were corpses rotting in the streets. There was no one to bury them. It was disgusting, but, still, pleasant for anyone who'd had anything to do with them.

The only trouble I had was getting into Montegiordano. Finally, after much shouting, the guard got hold of the majordomo, who recognized my face despite the dust from the road. I was overjoyed to hear that Vittoria was in the palace, but I decided to wait till morning to see her.

The advantage of being the master is that at the end of a day's journey the servants have to see to the horses, whereas I, in the room the majordomo had shown me to, could sit on the bed and take my boots off immediately. But before I had time to remove the second one I'd keeled over, asleep.

The first thing I noticed when I woke was that I was still wearing one boot. The next, which disturbed me considerably, was a monk sitting at my bedside with his cowl down over his eyes. Beside him was a candle, almost burned out. Am I dead? I thought.

"Signore," said the monk, "forgive this intrusion at night. I made the majordomo let me in. I must speak to you urgently."

He threw back his cowl. I blinked and began to see more clearly. It was Il Mancino.

"Domenico," I said, laughing, "what's the habit for? Are you going to exchange the tavern for the monastery?"

"I'm too young yet to repent," he said, "and, with your permission, signore, I'll take this thing off. It's a hot night and I'm stifling."

He emerged in trunk hose and shirt and as I'd always known him: small, lean, muscular, straight as a ramrod, bright-eyed, and quick-tongued.

"I didn't want to be seen entering the

Prince's palace," he said.

"Why not?" I asked. "The Prince is at the height of his power. What are you afraid of?"

"The reaction. There's always a reaction. The Prince's success is precarious. What he's done can't be done twice. He's made too many enemies, not to mention the Pope. He exploited the nobles' vendetta to free your sister, and cut the people to pieces after making use of them. If he's insulted by the Holy Father again, he won't be able to count on either the aristocracy or the mob."

"Domenico, you're wasted organizing your troop of whores. You ought to be governing the state."

"Governing the state is much the easier of the two," he said, seriously. "All you need is a few clear rules. The first is: never do things by halves. If I'd been the Prince, once I'd taken up arms against my sovereign, I'd have dethroned him, and killed him while I was at it. . . . But forgive me, signore, I'm wasting your time and mine. I really came to tell you what happened."

In the elegant and distinguished Italian that always astonishes me in one who can neither read nor write, though he must be a very good listener, he gave me a vivid account of everything that had occurred between the murder of Peretti and the rebellion.

"In a nutshell," he said, "whoever organized the murder was trying to incriminate the Prince, your sister, and you. And that's what della Pace thought, though he couldn't prove it. But, thank God, I have my own ways of finding things out. I noticed that the monk who gave me the note for Signor Peretti was a heavy drinker and had an eye for women, so I knew where to look for him. And, though his cowl had hidden his face, I'd seen that he was very thin and had a long scar on his left thumb. So I set what you kindly call my troop of whores to work, and one of them finally spotted him — with what bait you can easily guess — and lured him to the tavern. I shut him up in my cellar, put a dagger to his throat, and made him talk. Peretti was killed on the orders of Lodovico. The Prince knew nothing about it. . . . Signore, you don't look surprised."

"I suspected as much. But it's good to have proof of Lodovico's tortuous maneuvers."

"Too tortuous, signore. Much too tortuous. One should never overdo things. That's my second rule of government. Most machinations rebound on their perpetrators. That's what I call the law of reaction."

"What did you do with your monk?"

"Locked him in my cellar and started looking for della Pace, to hand this useful witness

466

over to him. Unfortunately, the rebellion caused by the death of Raimondo and Silla broke out, della Pace just had time to take refuge in the Vatican, and the next I saw of him was a bloody head being kicked around by the mob. I don't mind telling you I wept."

"You! Wept for a police chief?"

"Yes, signore. He was an open, straightforward man, loyal to his sovereign and abnormally honest. That was his undoing. Believe me, signore, a virtuous Bargello can't last long in a state that's corrupt."

"You could hand your monk over to della Pace's successor."

"Oh, signore, forgive me, but you haven't much of a head for politics. It's not in the Pope's interests, especially now, to proclaim the Prince's innocence. My witness wouldn't have time to open his mouth. He'd end up in a sack, and the sack would end up in the Tiber. As for me, I'd be banished again. You know I'm barely tolerated in Rome as it is. No, the only person I can negotiate with now is the Prince. On condition, of course, that he uses my witness carefully."

"How do you mean?"

"Just to convince Cardinal Montalto that he had nothing to do with his son's murder."

"Why Montalto?"

"Because he's the signora's uncle, and probably *papabile* when the present Pope dies."

"You amaze me! What makes you think he might succeed?"

"A very weighty reason: when Gregory XIII dies, the cardinals will want to elect a pope who's virtuous. The reaction, signore, the reaction. Would you like to bet?"

"God forbid! You're too deep for me. What do you want in exchange for your witness?"

"The Prince owns a large piece of land east of Rome. There's a little road that goes through it that he owns too. There's nothing on the land except a tavern, built there illegally. I'd like the Prince to let me buy the land for a modest sum."

"So that you can own the tavern?"

"Oh, no, signore! Our laws are more complicated than that. I could own the land without owning the tavern, even though it has no right to be there. But if I do own the land, I can block the road that leads to the tavern, ruin the owner, and thus force him to sell."

"For a modest sum."

"That goes without saying."

"I suppose your third rule, Domenico, is: use a nice simple, legal combination rather than a complicated intrigue. What do you want me to do?"

"Get me an interview with the Prince."

"All right, I will."

As soon as Il Mancino had gone, I went to find Vittoria. I knocked on the door and heard Caterina's slippers clattering hastily over the tiled floor at the sound of my voice. She opened the door, breathless, a candlestick in her hand, and clung to me without any shame, even in front of her mistress. I shoved her aside so roughly that she dropped the candlestick, and the candle went out. And the little octopus flung her arms around my neck and embraced me in the dark! I was annoyed by this second assault, but I'm so susceptible to female curves that it took me a few seconds to pull myself together. Then I struck my flint and relighted the candle.

Vittoria was propped up on an elbow. She fixed her blue eyes inquiringly on mine. Strangely, her face, familiar as it was, seemed to be wearing a new expression, at once more mature and sadder. No doubt this was a reflection of her captivity in Sant' Angelo, the unjust suspicions that had hung over her, and her doubts about the Prince's complicity in Peretti's murder.

I sat on the edge of the bed and told her about the evidence supplied by Il Mancino's prisoner. She listened wide-eyed, and as soon as I'd finished, she leaped out of bed and rushed to the door.

"Where are you going?" I asked.

"To see the Prince!"

"In the middle of the night?"

She wasn't listening. She was already out in the gallery. I just had time to snatch up the candlestick, then stride along to light her way, Caterina at our heels.

I'll never forget the look in the Prince's eyes when he saw Vittoria burst into his room, her long plaits hanging down. A child seeing his beloved mother arrive after he'd given up expecting her wouldn't have looked more intensely and naïvely happy. He started to rise, but she didn't give him time. She ran to the side of the bed, took his face in her hands, and kissed it wildly.

"Oh, Paolo!" she said in a low, breathless voice. "Forgive me! Forgive me! I was so unfair to you. I'll be your wife whenever you wish."

## *His Eminence Cardinal de' Medici*

When I heard the grievous news that Paolo Orsini had married Vittoria Peretti at Bracciano — in the very palace where my sister Isabella had perished — I immediately asked the Pope for an audience for myself and my brother Francesco, Grand Duke of Tuscany.

I made my request by word of mouth, for, as his secretary of state, I have the privilege of seeing him every day. The biggest problem was not obtaining the audience, but getting Francesco to come with me.

What bound him to Florence was not so much affairs of state, which he bothered with as little as possible, as his chemical experiments and Bianca. The throne of the grand duchy of Florence was occupied, alas, not by a prince alive to his duties, but by a chemist and a lover.

I am well aware that when, several years later, Francesco and Bianca died rather suddenly after dinner one day in their villa at Poggio, odious rumors were put about by my enemies accusing me of being a second Cain and having murdered them. This Spanish, or Jesuitical, slander — it is well known that there is an affinity between the two terms — rested on the fact that Francesco died without an heir, so I was obliged to abandon the purple and succeed him as grand duke. I treated the vile accusation with nothing but silence and contempt.

Having recalled these slanders only to deal with them as they deserve, I now return to my journey to Rome, and the trouble I had persuading Francesco to go with me. I knew how weak my elder brother was, and how every night Bianca would undo any resolution I had managed to instill in him during the day.

As a matter of fact, Bianca hated me, and, although as a churchman I may not entertain such an unevangelical sentiment, it is true I did not care much for her either. I raised my eyebrows when Francesco installed her as reigning mistress after our father's death, thus mortally offending his wife, the Grand Duchess Giovanna of Austria, instead of being satisfied with a few discreet affairs with girls whose lack of birth or brains would have made them harmless. My anxiety increased when the Grand Duchess died, and I hastened to suggest several good matches that would have brought Francesco substantial property, useful alliances, and princely connections. But he found excuses to reject them all, and secretly married Bianca, though he dreaded my wrath so much that he did not dare make it public for several months. I cannot described the grief and indignation I felt at seeing my brother fall into this carnal trap and betray his princely duties so unworthily.

Bianca opposed Francesco's going to Rome because she had a good idea of the object of our journey, and she did not want Francesco to do anything against Vittoria Peretti and her marriage to Prince Orsini.

She met the Prince only once, and had never seen Vittoria. Yet how could she fail to be struck by the likeness between their extraordinary careers? True, neither Vittoria nor Bianca was of really low birth, but their family connections, though respectable, placed them far below the ducal and grand-ducal unions to which they had had the audacity to aspire. Neither was without learning, wit, or love for the arts. But who would believe it was these qualities alone that had made illustrious princes wed them? The truth was that both had fleshly charms, and the princes, forgetting the lessons of Genesis, had yielded to the magic of appearance.

Alas, they share this weakness with the whole of Italy, perhaps with all the world. It fills me with rage when I see sensible, educated men in Rome and Florence making idols of women like Bianca and Vittoria, and, just because they are beautiful, paying them the homage due only to God. Such pagan worship is corrupting, and does incalculable harm.

I finally prevailed, however, and Francesco went with me, leaving Bianca in Florence, tearful, anxious, and full of resentment. She could only just bring herself to kneel and kiss my ring before we left. I raised her up kindly, but you should have seen the look she darted at me with her blazing eyes. She would have killed me if she could. I suppose it is as a joke that our good Italians call women "the gentle sex."

Naturally, I made the most of the opportunity afforded by the journey to lecture my brother on the subject of Vittoria and Paolo. But I only half convinced that weak spirit. All I could get from him was a promise to support, if only by his presence and his silence, what I was going to say to the Holy Father.

He scarcely kept us waiting at all. And as soon as we'd kissed his slipper and received his blessing, he looked at us with an expression that reflected both the loftiness of his position and some inner satisfaction.

"Well, my beloved sons," he said, without beating about the bush, "what do you want of me? I am listening."

I began by congratulating him on his flourishing health and eternal youth — an exceptional favor from heaven and blessing from the Almighty. He listened benignly, lapping it up like a kitten with a bowl of milk. Then he reminded me modestly that he was mortal like the rest of us, though it was obvious from the way he said it that he did not really believe it.

This preamble took a good quarter of an hour, and I did not hurry it, knowing how much store Gregory XIII set by such assurances of long, not to say eternal, life. It is true he astonished everyone in this respect. Almost eighty years old, he had a face as smooth as a baby's, with pink, delicately rounded cheeks, unwrinkled eyelids, and eyes of periwinkle blue that lent him a disingenuous look, about which it paid to be skeptical. In fact, he was jovial, selfish, unwilling to put himself out; a lover of luxury and ease, of jewelry and the arts, but disinclined to improve his capital city; authoritarian, but neglectful of the state and even of Christendom; affable and lively to those who approached him, but inwardly an unforgiving bearer of grudges. With his subjects, he was tyrannical in the extreme, not by nature but because of his situation and out of fear and caprice.

When I had delivered my compliments, I waited with an air of extreme respect, and only when he asked for the second time what I wanted of him did I come to the point.

"Most Holy Father," I said, "the Grand Duke of Tuscany and I heard with profound affliction of the marriage of our beloved brother-in-law and cousin Paolo Giordano Orsini to the widow Peretti. It seemed to us that the circumstances surrounding the death of the unfortunate Peretti would make this union an object of scandal in the state, in the church, and in Christendom as a whole."

"Alas, that is true, my beloved sons," said His Holiness with a sigh. "But what can I do? The inquiry carried out by the unfortunate Bargello" — and here two tears rolled down his pink cheeks, but only two, making me once again admire his unfailing self-command — "did not find any evidence that Signora Peretti committed adultery, nor that she was involved in that heinous crime. At the most, there were strong presumptions, in the sense of the Latin adage *Fecit cui prodest:* The one who did it is the one who profits by it. But presumption is not proof."

"Nevertheless, Most Holy Father," I answered humbly — I knew how he disliked being contradicted unless it indirectly served his purpose — "in people's minds, the Prince's subsequent marriage to the object of his desire has considerably strengthened the presumption."

"Indeed," said His Holiness, "the presumption is strong, very strong."

"Especially, Most Holy Father, because, before his marriage, the Prince went so far as to rebel against the head of Christendom. Is it not obvious that if he was so carried away by passion as to commit that abominable crime, he might easily have prefaced it by hatching a plot against His Holiness's third chamberlain? Whoever can do the greater can do the less."

"Well reasoned, my son," said the Pope. "The presumption is indeed extremely strong. . . . Many, including perhaps myself, might call it conclusive."

"Your moderation does you credit, Most Holy Father, and if Your Holiness will allow me to say so, I admire the exemplary magnanimity and evangelical leniency with which, when safely reestablished on your throne, you forgave the deadly insult of the insurrection. You did not even, as you might have done, punish its leader with excommunication."

At this, Francesco started and gave me a reproachful look, which I pretended not to notice. He had always been friendly with Paolo Giordano.

"By forgiving him," the Pope said, lowering his eyes, "I only did my duty as a Christian. Moreover," he added, glancing up and giving me a meaningful look, "it was not easy. If I had excommunicated the person you allude to, I would have had to excommunicate the Count of Oppedo, the Marquis Savelli, and many other Roman nobles. They were all involved in the uprising. And although the person you refer to was the leader of the revolt, he did not aim at my abdication and death. He treated with me. And when he had got what he wanted, he crushed the mob."

"What *did* he want, Most Holy Father?" I said indignantly. "A woman! The woman you had imprisoned precisely to prevent him from marrying her! He married her in deliberate violation of your wishes. A misalliance frowned upon by the whole of the Roman nobility."

"Presumably, at least," said Francesco suddenly. "We've been here only since yesterday evening, so we haven't had time to ask them."

My brother's interruption, which hardly pleased me, brought an almost imperceptible smile to the Pope's lips. He could easily guess how reluctantly Francesco was supporting me, especially on the subject of unsuitable marriages. I decided not to insist on this point, for fear of widening the rift that had just appeared between Francesco and me.

"Most Holy Father," I went on, "there are other, even weightier, reasons against this insane marriage. As you know, my sister Isabella had a son, Prince Virginio, from her marriage to Prince Orsini. Until now, he, of course, would inherit all his father's possessions. But in view of Paolo Giordano's blind passion for this intriguer, it is to be feared that he will make a new will that may seriously damage our nephew's interests."

The Pope was silent, looking from Francesco to me, and from me to Francesco.

"Does the Grand Duke agree," he asked gravely, "with what the Cardinal has just said?"

"I fully agree with *that* aspect of things," said Francesco, implying that he did not agree on the question of a misalliance.

But this nuance escaped the Pope, who smiled once again. The longer the audience lasted, the better his mood became. Bright-eyed, his lips parted eagerly, he seemed to be enjoying it.

"My beloved sons," he said finally, "what cure do you suggest for the ills you have so well described?"

"In order that crime should not profit the person who committed it," I declared, "and that an innocent son may not be harmed by the consequences of this scandalous union, I respectfully suggest that Your Holiness issue a *precetto* annulling it."

"Does the Grand Duke agree?" the Pope asked.

"Yes, Most Holy Father," said Francesco, more firmly than I expected.

It's true he was very fond of Virginio, and, being childless himself, treated him like a son.

"So," said the Pope, straightening up on his throne, "your joint request is this: you ask me for a *precetto* annulling the marriage of

Prince Paolo Giordano Orsini to the widow Peretti. Is that it?"

"Yes, Most Holy Father."

"Are Cardinal de' Medici and the Grand Duke of Tuscany ready to send me that request in writing?"

"Yes, Most Holy Father," I said.

"Yes, Most Holy Father," Francesco said, after a pause.

There was a gleam of triumph in the Pope's eyes. He swiftly bowed his head.

"In your request, my beloved sons," he said, "it would be best if you omitted your fears on the subject of Prince Virginio's material interests. They are hypothetical, and judgment in such a case may not take account of hypotheses. Nor should you stress the question of misalliance, if misalliance there be." He glanced briefly at Francesco. "That is too worldly a consideration, and therefore open to challenge. The only element that should be taken into account is the scandalous aspects of this marriage, at least as you see it."

"Most Holy Father," I said, "in drawing up our request I shall take care to follow your valuable advice with accuracy and respect."

"Even so, my dear sons," said the Pope firmly, "do not count on success. There are many thorns on this path and few roses. As you know, I have been much criticized in the past for issuing *precetti* to annul marriages. There has been much grumbling, especially on the part of the theologians, a dire and disputatious lot who think they know the divine will better than I do. I would not wish to expose myself afresh to such detractors, especially in the case of the leader of an insurrection, against whom ill-wishers might think I bear a personal grudge."

He lowered his eyes as he said this, then swiftly looked up to deliver some of his usual sprightly ecclesiastical pleasantries.

"I'll see, I'll see. Patience is the thing. Rome wasn't built in a day. And in Rome nothing is done in a day, especially in the Vatican. Go in peace, my most dear sons."

He gave us his blessing, and we backed out of the room, as etiquette requires. Neither of us opened our mouths so long as we were still inside the immense palace, where it's said that even the walls have ears.

I ushered the Grand Duke of Tuscany into my coach, sat down beside him, and ordered the officer in charge of my escort to take me back to my palace. He knew which one.

I have two palaces in Rome, but for reasons of economy I live in the smaller one and let the larger one out at a handsome rent. That makes my peers, the cardinals, laugh up their sleeves: "What's bred in the bone will come out in the flesh," they say. "Medici is the son and grandson of bankers." It's true. But then, *I* do not have to keep body and soul together by selling my vote in the conclave to Philip II.

As soon as I'd drawn the curtains of the coach, Francesco turned to me.

"Well, what do you think? Will the Pope issue the *precetto?* He seems very undecided."

"Ah, Francesco!" I smiled. "You were right to study the chemistry of matter; the chemistry of the soul is beyond you. If the Holy Father hesitated, it was before our visit. Now he is as pleased as can be. We've served Paolo Giordano's head up to him on a silver salver, if you'll forgive the metaphor, and he doesn't have to soil his own hands cutting it off. He can tell the Sacred Congregation we asked him to issue the *precetto.* And he can prove it by showing our written request."

There was a moment's silence.

"I said what I did for Virginio's sake," Francesco said. "But it grieves me, just the same. Poor Orsini! He raised a whole rebellion to set that woman free and make her his wife. And when the *precetto*'s issued she'll only be his whore."

# 11

## *Prince Paolo Giordano Orsini, Duke of Bracciano*

It was on July 28, 1584, that I received, by special messenger to Bracciano, the *precetto* annulling my marriage. It was handed to me by a courier at seven o'clock, as Vittoria and I were about to have dinner. When I broke the seal and read this monument of iniquity and hypocrisy, I could scarcely believe my eyes.

Nowhere did it actually say that I, with Vittoria's complicity, had had Peretti killed for the sole purpose of marrying her, but everywhere it suggested as much, with hints much worse than assertions, and wrapped in a style of ecclesiastical suavity.

The decree, it said, had been issued by the Holy Father and his counselors after much reflection and "a most painful moral debate," and at the express request of Cardinal de' Medici and the Grand Duke of Tuscany.

Trembling with rage, I handed the *precetto*

to Vittoria without a word. During the time I'd been trying to take it in, she had been looking at me with growing anxiety.

When she had read the decree, she paled and set her teeth, but did not weep. She read it twice, the second time more slowly, then folded up the parchment and handed it back to me in silence.

"Well, what do you think, Vittoria?"

She came and put her head on my shoulder.

"This decree hurts us," she said, "but not as much as it would like. We're alive, and we love one another."

"Nevertheless," I said, holding her close, "it's infamous. I should have let the mob invade the Vatican and tear the old fox to pieces."

"No, no, Paolo," she said earnestly, "you were right to do as you did. If a pope were slain on this throne, it would be a terrible scandal throughout Christendom."

"But the Pope," I said, "now takes a petty revenge on me for saving his life."

Unexpectedly she started to laugh.

"Well, you did begin by threatening his life, Paolo. You made him tremble inside his golden palace. That's what he can't forgive." Then she said pensively, "I don't see where Cardinal de' Medici and the Grand Duke of Tuscany come into it."

"They're defending, or think they're defending, or pretend they're defending, Virginio's interests. The Medicis are bankers. They see everything through a prism, and the prism is money."

Vittoria looked at me with raised eyebrows.

"They're afraid," I explained, "I might change my will in your favor. While I was fighting, they brought Virginio up at their court in Florence and made a Medici out of him. They've counted on everything I own coming to them by way of Virginio when I die."

"My God! A cardinal thinks like that?"

"This one was a Medici before he was a cardinal. He has another motive too: he hates women. The more beautiful a woman is, the more he hates her. There isn't any kind of snub he hasn't inflicted on poor Bianca."

"But he's never so much as seen me."

"He doesn't have to see you to hate you. Your reputation for beauty is enough. Worse still, your wit and love of the arts, far from finding grace in his eyes, only aggravate him the more."

"Oh, Paolo!" she exclaimed, putting her lovely bare arms around my waist, "how small and lonely I'd feel in this cruel world if I didn't have you!"

I was silent, feeling full of love and compassion, but also deeply concerned about the uncertainties of the future. And also about my unhealed wound. Of late it had gnawed at the roots of my newfound, unending, insatiable happiness at being able to see Vittoria all day long, and to feel her warm soft body, wrapped in her long hair, beside me at night.

When one's in love, there's a charm even in sadness. The night that followed the arrival of the *precetto* was, despite that terrible blow, or perhaps because of it, delicious as well as melancholy. We spent it in one another's arms as if we wanted to prove that the decree had no power to separate us. Asleep or awake it was the same: our embraces were never-ending. We used few words; those we did speak were added caresses.

It was only as the first rays of the sun appeared that we spoke again of the Pope's ordinance.

"I notice," said Vittoria, "that, not content with annulling our present marriage, he forbids us ever to marry again. Isn't that rather strange?"

"He may be afraid his successor will annul his decree. So he's trying to tie his hands in advance."

"What a Machiavelli! And what relentlessness! Is there any chance he might be brought to reverse his decision before he dies?"

"Only one," I said, "and it's a very small one. This is the first time a *precetto* has been aimed at one of the leading families. I shall appeal to the solidarity of the nobles. Tomorrow I'll leave for Rome."

"Without me?"

"Oh, Vittoria! How can I expose you to the gibes of the mob? I'll feel happier knowing you are inside the walls of Bracciano, guarded by your brother."

So I left for Rome next day, taking care to be accompanied by a strong escort. It was a good thing I did. The same crowds that before had so often acclaimed me when I appeared in the streets now greeted me with scowls: they bore me a deadly grudge for having suppressed the insurrection after inciting it. Wherever I went, I met with nothing but averted looks, clenched fists, muttered insults, or people spitting at my horses' hooves. Someone threw a stone that hit my squire on the ear and made it bleed. It was only with the greatest difficulty that I restrained my men from retaliating. I was not, however, going to give Gregory XIII the chance to say my presence in Rome caused disorder. I decided I would use a coach without my coat of arms on it, and my escort would not wear livery.

I dismounted painfully, for my wound hurt every time I made a sudden movement, and summoned my secretary. To him, I dictated a letter respectfully requesting an audience with the Pope. I sent it off at once. I received a polite but curt reply the next morning: the Pope apologized for not being able to see me; he was unwell and had to keep to his room.

The Pope's reputation for good health was such that I didn't know if this excuse was to be taken seriously. My brother-in-law Cardinal de' Medici could have enlightened me, but since he had inspired the *precetto*, I could not longer look on him as a friend. For the same reason, I did not feel I could go and see the Florentine ambassador. Although, personally, he had been close to me, I could not disregard the attitude the Grand Duke of Tuscany had adopted toward my marriage. As for Lodovico, I had tacitly excluded him from my affections since the revelations of the monk Il Mancino had brought to see me.

I was depressed. The feeling had a number of sources: Vittoria's absence, my wound, the Pope's refusal to see me, my unfriendly reception by the Roman people, the hostility of my in-laws, and Lodovico's betrayal. The world I'd always inhabited seemed to be collapsing around me, leaving me to stand alone.

I made an effort to pull myself together. I had many friends among the Roman nobility, the oldest and truest being the Marquis Giulio

Savelli, whose son Silla had been killed at the same time as Raimondo in the scuffle that had provoked the rebellion. I sent him a note asking him to see me. A few hours later, in the evening, I received the following reply:

My dear Paolo,

I am in bed and unable to see you. I only just have the strength to write you this note. I can guess the reasons for your visit. I was infuriated by the *precetto* that undid your marriage, and I did not conceal my opinion from those around me. But I am sorry to have to tell you that I was almost the only member of the Roman nobility to take this position. The rest blame you for what they call your "misalliance," and for that reason the *precetto* was not objected to. No doubt this is partly due to the aristocratic prejudice so rife among us; but another cause is probably jealousy, pure and simple, because your wife is so beautiful and so accomplished.

Since you are a great general, I do not suppose I need warn you to be extremely careful in circumstances where the balance of power has turned so much against you. If, at the moment, you were to attempt anything against the Holy Father, you would do so without the support of Lodovico, who is banished and hunted, and of the people, who hate you now as much as they loved you before, and of the nobles.

Bide your time, *carissimo*. The Pope is eighty-two years old and, despite his healthy appearance, he cannot live forever. The last time I saw him, I thought I detected a change: he was less glib and more tearful.

As for me, I am bound to die before he does. Silla was my favorite son, and his loss has been a terrible blow. My health fails more each day. I do not much care: I have lived long enough. And in vain, it seems to me now. I regret many of the things I've done, especially having brought about della Pace's death. It was unjust and cruel, and it did not give me back my son.

Please give the signora your wife my greetings and respects. Perhaps the present Pope's successor will be more favorably inclined to you both.

As for me, I shall remain, even in the jaws of death, your old and faithful friend,
Giulio Savelli

Comforting as the affection in this letter

was, it didn't escape me that it sounded the death knell of any hopes I might have invested in the solidarity of the nobility. The Pope had been extremely clever. If he had excommunicated me immediately after the rebellion, he would have incurred the opposition of all the nobles who had taken part; they would fear a similar fate. By merely annulling a marriage, of which they, in any case, disapproved, he set me apart from them and, at no danger to himself, turned me into a scapegoat.

Because I had certain doubts about the validity of the decree, I decided to consult a theologian. I sent a note to Father Luigi Palestrino, asking him to come and see me. He sent me his answer by word of mouth: I was to send a coach, without my coat of arms on it, to fetch him at nightfall, and I was not to repeat anything he said to me. If I disobeyed, he would publicly deny everything. This caution seemed only natural under the current tyranny, so I accepted the conditions.

Father Palestrino was so thin and attenuated that you wondered how his body managed to carry his enormous head. His head was also out of proportion: the brow was wide and monumental and full of bumps; the lower part of the face was insignificant, with a ridiculously small nose, hollow cheeks, a mere slit of a mouth, and a weak chin. His complexion was paler than his habit, so wan one wondered if it was really blood in his veins. But when, at my invitation, he sat down, occupying only about a quarter of the chair, and briefly waved away the wine I offered, he asked me what I wanted in a voice that surprised me by its strength and by its diction.

Without a word, I handed him the *precetto*, which he seized with the eagerness of a squirrel pouncing on a nut. Then he started to dissect the contents swiftly, with his inquisitive jet-black eyes: he had hardly started reading it when he seemed to have finished.

He shut his eyes and remained silent so long I grew impatient. At the very moment I was opening my mouth to ask what he thought of it, he opened his eyes, and, with the same rapid, peremptory gesture he'd made in refusing the wine, said in his strong, precisely articulated voice: "My lord, pray do not ask me any questions. There is no need. I shall answer without being asked, not only all the questions you can think of, but also those you can't."

"In that case, Father, speak. I am listening."

"The first thing you have to understand, my lord, is that marriage is a sacrament in which the ministers are the husband and wife, and that it is regarded by the church as indissoluble, especially since the Council of

Trent. However, one of the two spouses may ask the Pope for an annulment if he or she can argue that his or her consent to the marriage was obtained by deceit or violence, or that the union has not been consummated physically, or that it has been barren. This last point is very debatable, as Henry VIII found out when he asked Clement VII to release him from his marriage to Catherine of Aragon on the grounds that she had not given him a son. But she had given him six daughters. So she was not barren. Henry, seeing the weakness of this argument, put forward another. Catherine was a near relative, and this consideration, although weak enough, since their kinship did not come within the prohibited degrees, might at a stretch have received the Pope's approval if Catherine's nephew, the Emperor Charles V, had not opposed it with all the power at his command. In this he was wrong; without his opposition, the divorce would have been granted, and the schism that separated England from the Vatican and the rest of Christendom would never have happened. Small causes, great effects . . ."

"Father," I said, "this is all very interesting, but it does not have anything to do with my *precetto*."

"Oh, yes, it has, my lord — indirectly. The

object of my preamble was to establish the general rule: the annulment of a marriage is requested by one of the spouses. So it is very surprising that an annulment should be pronounced by the Pope without either of the spouses having asked for it, as in your case, and in that of many previous *precetti* issued by Gregory XIII in the course of his pontificate."

"So do you think, Father, that these *precetti* constitute a misuse of power?"

"I did not say that. I said that they are very surprising. And may I remind you, my lord, that it was agreed you would not ask me any questions?"

"Forgive me, Father. I'm not used to obeying. But I can be if I try."

The irony was lost on Luigi Palestrino. Or so I thought. He went on, with no expression.

"Since the two spouses are, as I said, the ministers of the sacrament of marriage, it is difficult to see how any authority external to the marriage, even the head of Christendom, could lawfully abolish that sacrament. Unless the said marriage is surrounded by circumstances that make it scandalous. And that, my lord, is what the *precetto* suggests in your case. The weakness of its argument resides in the fact that it suggests this in veiled and allusive terms: it does not state it clearly, and it does not establish, or even try to establish, your guilt."

"Because there isn't any proof of my guilt," I said. "And perhaps because there's no belief in it either. Father, is there nothing I can do?"

"No. You cannot appeal to the Pope against the Pope."

"Even if I prove my innocence?"

"Not even then."

"So there is no solution?"

"When Gregory dies, you can appeal to his successor. He might find it excessive that Gregory, not content with having annulled your marriage, forbade you to marry again, and free you from having to obey that clause. You might also take advantage of the interregnum between the death of Gregory and the election of his successor."

"How could I do that?"

"My lord, I will tell you, but only when the time comes. Now, I must take my leave."

He rose, and, to my great surprise, a smile appeared on his thin lips. It vanished almost at once, but it had undoubtedly been there.

"My lord, you have asked many questions. Despite all your good intentions, you have been an unruly client. But that is hardly surprising when one remembers that you used to fight against pirates in the Adriatic, and in so doing became, to a certain extent, one of them. Now, however, it is not a matter of rushing on the enemy, but of learning a virtue you lack: patience. But remember, my lord, your case is far from desperate."

Having made a low bow, he headed for the door.

"Father," I said, taking a purse from my doublet, "you're forgetting this."

Palestrino skipped back, snatched the purse with his squirrel-like swiftness, tucked it away somewhere, bowed again, and vanished through the door. He was so famous that people came to consult him from all over Christendom. From each he must receive some kind of largesse, which, as I'd just learned, he didn't ask for, but didn't refuse either. I wondered what he used the money for. He certainly didn't spend it on food.

That night, for the first time since I'd been in Rome, I saw a gleam of hope. Palestrino was right: I had always been too inclined to attack, even if the enemy galley was the Vatican. Now my grappling irons were no longer available, and I had to get used to the waiting, the procrastination, the stratagems and intrigues of peace.

## Domenico Acquaviva (Il Mancino)

I was in my room at the Mount of Olives, doing my accounts late one night. There weren't many customers, and such as there were belonged to the docile kind that let themselves be fleeced without a murmur. La Sorda came to tell me that four armed horsemen had just come in, and a fifth was minding their horses in the stable.

"How are they armed?"

"Swords, daggers, and pistols in their belts."

"Damnation! Are they robbers?"

"Not by the look of their horses."

"So you thought to take a look in the stables? There's something inside your pretty head then, my pet."

"There's something inside my pretty ass, too," she said, laughing.

Normally, I don't like my women to talk this way, but I let it pass.

"What did you do in the stable?"

"I stroked their fine horses. Their coats were quite dry. They haven't ridden far."

"So they're from Rome. What about the man looking after them?"

"From Calabria, but well turned out for a servant. A leather jerkin."

"So you made up to him to loosen his tongue?"

"I couldn't loosen anything — not his tongue, not his fly. The cold fish wouldn't have anything to do with me. Told me in that strange language that he was a married man and faithful to his wife."

"Let's get back to the four downstairs."

"That's what I did. They didn't want women either. Only wine — the most expensive. The tallest — he had his hat pulled down over his eyes — asked to see you."

"How is he dressed?"

"Buffalo doublet, the sort soldiers — captains — wear."

"His hat? Out of shape? Faded? Feathers bedraggled?"

"Not at all. The felt is quite new, and the feathers look fresh."

"Not a captain, then. Well, bring him up. But first post three of my men behind the curtains in the mezzanine window with their arquebuses. What does this so-called captain look like?"

"Tall, big shoulders. A manly mouth, wide and firm. That's all I could see, because of the hat. He speaks quietly, but like someone used to being obeyed."

"Wait a while before you show him up. And when he's here, sit on the stairs and warn my men if the other three try to come up. Send all the women straight to bed, except the ones who are occupied."

When I was alone again, I felt quite tense. I don't like the unexpected. And I'm not keen on having four men armed to the teeth burst in on me at one o'clock in the morning, even if their mounts do reek of the aristocracy. Some barons are brigands, and some counts are not much better, like the Count of Oppedo. And thinking of him, I remembered he wouldn't be very pleased if he knew what I'd done with his monk. I slipped a knife into my left boot, loaded a little lady's pistol, and put it in my doublet.

There was a knock at the door. I opened it, but stood right behind it with my hand in my armhole pocket.

"Acquaviva," cried a voice I thought I recognized, "is this any way to greet people?"

I peered around the door. The visitor saw me, smiled, and nonchalantly took off his hat.

"My lord!" I cried, bowing to the floor. "You here! You had only to say the word, and I'd have rushed to Montegiordano."

"It would have taken too long for a messenger to come and go," said the Prince, "and

I leave for Bracciano tomorrow at dawn. The pavements of Rome burn my feet. I wanted to see you first."

"I'm at your service, my lord. Pray be seated."

"Thank you."

He made a little grimace as he sat down.

"What happened with the monk? Did Cardinal Montalto agree to hear him?" he asked.

"He saw both of us, in great secrecy."

"What happened?"

"The Cardinal listened extremely closely. Especially to the monk."

"What did he say?"

"As far as the monk is concerned, there's what the Cardinal said and there's what the Cardinal thought. What he said wasn't very encouraging."

"I'm listening."

" 'One witness is no witness.' In Latin."

"Do you understand Latin?"

"I learned that kind of Latin from a little misunderstanding that arose once between myself and a law court."

"What was his reaction to *your* evidence?"

"Nothing. He lectured me about my 'unfortunate way of life.' I agree with him. Who knows? With a little education I might have climbed higher. They say the Cardinal himself used to mind the pigs when he was a boy."

"That's what they say. Let's get back to the monk."

"The Cardinal lectured him on renouncing his vows. He was so severe that the monk went down on his knees and wept."

"What makes you think the Cardinal took his evidence more seriously than he cared to admit?"

"His face, terrible as it is, couldn't quite hide how glad he was to hear it."

"Why do you think that was?"

"Because the monk's evidence cleared his niece."

The Prince was silent for a while, but then he seemed to rouse himself. He looked up and said brightly: "What's the situation with the tavern on that piece of land I sold you?"

"It's mine now. The work I had done on the road leading past it took so long the owner lost all his customers and handed it over to me. Unfortunately, I don't have enough money left to fix it up."

"There may be a remedy for that. Cardinal Cherubi would like to get hold of the little wood adjoining that land to enlarge the grounds of his villa. I'll sell it to you."

"Without my having to pay for it right away?"

"Without your having to pay for it ever. When it's yours, resell it to Cardinal Cherubi."

"I suspect there's a condition attached to that transaction."

"It's verbal and confidential. The Cardinal is to give you a daily account of the Pope's state of health."

"That would be a surprising condition, coming from a humble innkeeper like me."

"It won't surprise the Cardinal coming from a neighbor who kindly clears the undergrowth from the wood he's just sold him. Cherubi's a simple man. He talks to everyone he meets when he's out taking his constitutional."

"Perhaps he'll need your Venetian connections when the old Patriarch of Venice gives up the ghost."

"Perhaps. You're very well informed, Acquaviva. Where do you get your information?"

"From the women here, my lord. I blush to say it. And they don't mix only with the lower orders."

"Acquaviva, it's very important that I know as soon as possible when Gregory's end is near. You know that kind of thing is often hushed up in the Vatican. Sometimes they even delay the announcement of the Pope's death."

"My lord, when the time comes, I'll gallop to Bracciano with the news myself."

"It's a bargain. Come to Montegiordano tomorrow morning. I'll be gone, but my majordomo knows about this and he'll sign the deed of sale for me. Don't see me out. I know the way."

As he left, I noticed he was limping badly and had some difficulty negotiating the stairs. I shut the door behind him, though I was sure La Sorda would be in to find out what was going on.

I sat on the stool the Prince had just vacated, filled a clay pipe with good tobacco, struck my flint, and meditated for a while in a pleasant cloud of smoke. I was making money so fast that one day I'd have to quit my present "unfortunate way of life." But I'd miss it. I was fond of the women, in a way.

La Sorda burst in, hopping like a flea with excitement. She came and sat on my lap, and I told her about the Cardinal and the land, but not about the condition attached to the resale. She looked at me with eyes like saucers, full of admiration. When I'd finished, she started to caress me. What with the time of night and the pipe, she hadn't chosen a very good moment. But knowing it came from the heart, I didn't stop her.

# His Eminence Cardinal Cherubi

I am well aware that I have been greatly blamed, by, among others, the cardinals who were in the Vatican on the day of the insurrection, for suggesting to His Holiness that he should sacrifice della Pace. Certainly, that sacrifice, dictated though it was by the need to save the Pope's life, was in itself a horrible thing. But most of those present, including His Holiness, had already accepted it in their hearts when I was bold enough to express aloud what everyone else was thinking.

Once the danger was over, His Holiness might, like others, have looked at me askance. Instead, he was kind enough to say he was grateful for my courage and frankness.

I claim no credit for these qualities. My character is such that I say what I think quite spontaneously. Thus I have never made any secret of the fact that I would like to succeed the Patriarch of Venice when it pleases the Lord to call him home. I know it is not usual in the Vatican for people to reveal aspirations so ingenuously; they tend to hide them and then let them leak out at the most propitious moment. I do things differently. Having been born in Venice, I think I know the people there, and I consider myself especially suitable to represent the church in the Most Serene Republic. It is a perfectly legitimate ambition, so why should I hide it? And is it not best, when one aims at a particular office, to declare oneself as soon as possible, if only to cut the grass from under the feet of candidates less determined or slower at making up their minds?

According to the gossips, my frankness has made me the clumsiest prelate in the Vatican, and at the same time the one who has best overcome his gaffes. That strikes me as a contradiction. If my blunders have helped my advancement, were they really so maladroit?

Anyway, there can be no doubt that after the insurrection I became the Pope's most valued adviser. Some considered my influence excessive. True, it was considerable. But how could it be excessive when it was always exerted in the cause of moderation?

After the terrible evening when he had feared for both his throne and his life, the Pope did his best to make himself invulnerable by recruiting more Swiss Guards and buying cannon. But the stronger he grew from the military point of view, the weaker, rasher, and more irresolute he was himself. He never had had much resilience, and what spirit he did possess seemed broken by the strain he had gone through. He gave himself up to resentment.

As soon as he was reestablished on his throne, he wanted to excommunicate Prince Orsini and annul his marriage by means of a *precetto*. I was against both these measures; they looked too much like revenge. I said as much to the Holy Father, and he was angry. But when I pointed out that he could not excommunicate the Prince without excommunicating the whole of the Roman nobility too — a thing not only impossible, but also almost comically absurd — he fell back on the *precetto*. There was no dissuading him from that.

When the decree was promulgated, the Pope was very pleased with himself. As he was when, with some reason in this case, he banished the Count of Oppedo. And was also when, on the pretext of being unwell, he refused to see Prince Orsini in the Vatican. After that, he relapsed into apathy, and seemed to drift as if he had no further aim in life.

One day, seeing the Venetian Ambassador, Armando Veniero, emerge from a papal audience with a worried look on his face, I took him by the arm and asked him what was the matter.

"I'm afraid," he said, "the Pope isn't as fond of Venice as he used to be. I asked to speak to him about a problem currently troubling the republic. He saw me for five minutes and scarcely listened to what I said. You would have thought he wasn't in the least interested."

"Armando," I said, drawing him into a window recess and whispering in his ear, "don't worry. It's not Venice in particular. The Pope isn't interested in anything these days. He cuts his audiences as short as possible and doesn't pay much attention while they're going on. He can't even be bothered now with important affairs of state or of Christendom."

"Oh, so that's it!" said Armando. "I noticed he was rather weepy."

"He's always had the gift of tears," I replied. "The difference is that now they come to his eyes unbidden, and whether the context is suitable or not."

"How sad!" said Armando. He didn't look very sad to me. "The trouble is, I don't know what to say in Venice."

"What is the difficulty?" I asked. "You know how much I love the republic. And how much I hope one day it will love me . . ."

At this, Armando, who was not unaware of my ambitions, managed a smile, which was, at the same time, friendly yet full of diplomatic reserve.

"Venice would like to conclude an extradition treaty with Rome," he said. "The republic is full of Romans who have fled from the rigor of your laws. No doubt you have the same difficulty here in reverse."

"I'll talk to the Holy Father about it," I said, "and if I don't manage to engage his attention, I'll get a clerk to draw up a memorandum. Then at least there will be a written, dated record of your suggestion, which can be revived and dealt with more effectively under the next pope."

A few days later, I found the Holy Father deep in one of his melancholy moods. When I ventured to ask him the reason, he said, lugubriously: "Castel Sant' Angelo was struck by lightning last night. It destroyed the standard flying on top. That's a bad sign, my friend, a very bad sign."

He said no more. When he had withdrawn into his apartments, the first chamberlain, having noted my interest, whispered: "Because Your Eminence was born in Venice, you're not familiar with the superstitions current among the lower orders in Rome. When lightning strikes down the flag over Castel Sant' Angelo, it's supposed to mean that the Pope is going to die before the end of the year."

"Does His Holiness believe in this?"

"It looks like it. Which is surprising. Because the standard has been struck by lightning twice before, and this is the first time the Holy Father has taken any notice."

A little later, I happened to pass a certain prelate who shall be nameless on one of the Vatican staircases. He smiled at me and stopped. I smiled back and halted too. A landing between two flights of stairs is the best place in the Vatican for exchanging confidences. If you position yourself properly, you can see anyone coming up or down in time not to be overheard.

"My friend," he said, "you see the Holy Father every day. Haven't you noticed a change in him?"

This question and the raised eyebrows that went with it constituted an offer: You tell me what you know and I'll tell you what I know. I decided to accept, because this person was usually well informed. I did not mention what the Pope had said about the standard over Castel Sant' Angelo, though: I regarded that as confidential. But I did describe the much less significant impressions his brief audience with the Pope had made on Armando Veniero.

The prelate listened avidly and said, with a knowing smile: "Yes, that confirms it! Without going so far as to say he's failing, one might apply the famous phrase and say, 'Homer's nodding.' Yet he still looks very well. And he eats and sleeps well." This was questionable, I thought. "It's as if the inner man were falling asleep. I consider it significant that he's stopped insisting so much on the eminence of his position. Did you know that some evenings he has himself carried to his son Giacomo's house in a litter, and takes part in that useless young fellow's goings-on? Oh, nothing really depraved, apart perhaps from some dancing by scantily clad Moorish slave girls. But it would be disastrous if a thing like that became known."

Upon which, having greatly contributed to its getting out, he left me, a little twinkle in his eye belying his sanctimonious sighs.

To tell the truth, His Holiness was coming to rely on me more and more. He would send for me at any hour of the day, or even of the night, when he couldn't sleep. As soon as he saw me, he'd say, "Cherubi, I'm feeling low. Amuse me."

It wasn't very difficult. When he liked a story, you could tell it a hundred times over, and he would still enjoy it. So long as you repeated it exactly. He would even ask you to tell it again.

"Cherubi, tell me about having a meal at Montalto's."

"To start with, Your Holiness," I'd say, "the dining room was always freezing. His

Eminence wouldn't have a fire lighted."

"Why not?" asked the Pope, who'd asked the same question a dozen times before.

"Because people would be tempted to linger at the table if they weren't cold. And then, the nun who waited on us . . ."

"No, no, Cherubi. You're going too fast. Montalto used to make little jokes in French about eating."

"Quite right, Your Holiness. He'd say" — and I would imitate Montalto's deep voice — "that *chère* leads to *chair,* and after *panse* comes *danse.*"

"Excellent! Excellent! Go on!"

"The meal the nun brought us . . ."

"No, no!" the Pope would say. "You're still asleep, Cherubi. You're forgetting half of it. You haven't said what the nun was like."

"Well, Your Holiness, she was old and fabulously wrinkled. And so thin she looked like a skeleton, so bony she creaked as she walked. All she needed was a scythe."

"Excellent! Excellent! Go on, Cherubi!"

"Once, before the midday meal, she told us with horror there was a deficiency in her supplies, and all she had to give us was two eggs. 'That's all right,' said Montalto. 'Give the larger one to Cherubi — he's a big eater. Rossellino and I will share the little one.' "

"Excellent, Cherubi! Excellent!"

Although his recent memory was unreliable, he could remember perfectly what had happened several years before. Nor had he forgotten his various grudges, which sometimes gave rise to malicious remarks.

"Do you remember what Montalto said the first time he saw Vittoria? 'How could anyone see her and not love her? Hear her and not adore her?' "

He laughed, and added sourly, though under his breath: "Our saintly friend must be pretty peeved now to see his beloved niece living in sin with a pirate."

One day, he granted me a rare favor, and one that not many prelates in the Vatican could boast of: he showed me his collection. Unlike his predecessors and his illustrious successor, Gregory XIII did not go to much expense to beautify the Eternal City. On the other hand, he spent money like water to add to his collection of jewels. This was the work of a lifetime, for which he had a special room, with cases lined with mirrors, so that the gems were reflected to infinity. Tall windows lighted them by day, and Venetian chandeliers with countless candles illuminated them at night. My visit took place during one of His Holiness's bouts of insomnia, when he hadn't hesitated to send for me. An unfortunate footman was also routed out of bed, and had to spend half an hour lighting the candles in all the chandeliers. Then he could snooze against a doorframe for a couple of hours, until the inspection was over.

If I hadn't been so sleepy myself — I'm a person who needs plenty of sleep — I would have been dazzled. The Pope unlocked every case himself and took the marvelous specimens out one by one, exhibiting them to me and stroking them with his smooth hands, though he was too jealous of them to let me actually hold even one. There were precious and semiprecious stones from all over the world, though most were from the Indies, Brazil, Ceylon, and Siberia. Some of them were unknown to me, though I did not like to ask their names. They had sumptuous gold settings engraved by the greatest masters. The Pope told me he had had an expert come to value his treasures, but he thought the estimate too low and had sent for a famous artist from Lombardy to make another one.

While he was showing me his jewels, a distant smile hovered on his lips, and his somewhat vague glance seemed to lose itself in the glow of his stones and their reflections in the mirrors. Throughout our visit — and it seemed a very long one to me — he looked bright and fresh. As soon as it was finished, he was overcome with weariness. He dropped into the chair I pushed forward for him, rested his neck on the back, and closed his eyes. He would not leave until the footman had put out all the candles. He explained in a faint voice that he wanted to lock the room himself, with three keys he always carried. When, finally, the last candle was out, he got up and, leaning on my arm, but with a firm and unerring hand, he locked the door. It was very heavy and strongly reinforced with iron.

I escorted him back to his room, where a servant was waiting to undress him. As he passed from my arm to that of his chamberlain, he looked up at me and said, as if in surprise: "You here, Cherubi? Is it day already?"

At the same time, heaven knows why, great tears were coursing down his pink cheeks. Perhaps he was grieving because he would be unable to take his treasures with him when his time came.

In spite of all the signs of decay in his demeanor, memory, and intelligence, his health remained good. If I may so express it when talking about a pope, his animal being was still magnificent, considering his great age.

This thought occurred again to me, and to many others, on April 4, 1585. That day, on the stroke of noon, the Pope emerged from the Vatican to go to the Medici palace, to which the Cardinal had invited him for the midday meal. I can see him now, in St. Peter's Square, preparing to mount his white palfrey — straight as a ramrod, slim, smiling, his sky-blue eyes and rosy cheeks shining. He was wearing a red hat, a white cassock, and a red velvet hood that matched the harness of his magnificent mare. Two hundred officers and court dignitaries were there on horseback, waiting to escort him through the streets of Rome. He stood for a while in the midst of them, chatting with Cardinal de' Medici: he was a head taller than the Cardinal, and presented such a picture of elegance, dignity, and nobility that we were all impressed. When he took the reins from his squire, waved him aside, put his foot in the stirrup, and swung into the saddle with lightness and vigor, we were more so.

Unusual for the time of year, there had been a frost that morning, but the sun had melted the rime and dissipated the fog, and was now high overhead, pleasantly warming our shoulders. Care had been taken to station Swiss Guards all along the Pope's route, but the ordinary folk, though they didn't actually applaud, seemed admiring, rather than hostile, when they saw our splendid procession.

Many stupid things have been said about the Medicis, and they've often been taunted for dabbling in banking and commerce. But

I must say that the Cardinal's reception was worthy in every way of a great prince of the church; it combined splendor with the most exquisite taste. Although the Pope ate moderately, and was a gourmet rather than a gourmand, on this occasion he willingly lingered at the table, conversing cheerfully. When the meal was over, Cardinal de' Medici, who was also the owner of some valuable jewels, offered to show them to the Pope. He accepted gladly, saying to me, with a bright smile, "You come too, Cherubi, and tell me whether you think they're better than mine."

As a matter of fact, the Medici jewels were not as good as the Pope's, in either quantity or quality, with the exception of a large salt-cellar, a reproduction of the one Benvenuto Cellini made for King Francis I of France. It consisted of two naked figures, a man and a woman, one representing the sea and the other the land, sitting with their legs entwined, an allusion to the way bays and inlets relate to the continents. The land, a woman of ravishing grace and beauty, rested her hand on a charmingly carved little temple designed to hold pepper. The sea had a boat intended to hold salt.

The Pope gazed at this magnificent piece and stroked it with his plump hands as if he couldn't bear to leave it. Finally, as I had expected, he offered to buy it. The Cardinal, who must have been cursing himself for having shown it to him, was a picture of embarrassment. To sell his treasure was terrible to contemplate. But the Pope was so vindictive, it might be dangerous to refuse.

A Medici isn't easily caught, however, and the Cardinal did not hesitate for long.

"Sell it to you, Most Holy Father!" he exclaimed, throwing up his hands. "Certainly not! But it would give me great pleasure to make you a present of it, provided you'll leave it with me long enough to have a set of drawings made so that I can keep at least the memory of it."

So saying, he put it back in its place, locked the case, and escorted the Pope out of his palace with the utmost courtesy. He was using a typical commercial trick: he was gaining time.

Outside, we were disagreeably surprised by the temperature. The sun was hidden by big black clouds, and the air had grown quite cool. I noticed that after he had mounted his horse, His Holiness shivered, and when he dismounted in the courtyard at St. Peter's he shivered again. A severe attack of fever ensued, and the Pope took to his bed. When the remedies of the Vatican doctor proved of no avail, Andrea da Milano was sent for. He was a descendant of Giovanni da Milano, famous professor of the equally famous school of medicine in Salerno, which was unrivaled in Europe except for the one at Montpellier. The preeminence of both these schools, I'm told, derives from their incorporation of Jewish and Arab medicine, passed on to them by Jews expelled from Spain.

Andrea da Milano examined his patient, took his pulse, and uttered soothing words. Having seen me constantly at the Pope's bedside — His Holiness, who was quite lucid, insisted on my staying with him — he signaled to me to join him in the anteroom. When we were alone, he spoke quite differently. "Both lungs are infected, Your Eminence. But since His Holiness has an exceptionally sound constitution and a heart in excellent condition, he may recover."

By the next day, there was no change, and Andrea da Milano was much less hopeful. "Frankly, Your Eminence, illustrious as the patient is, I'm disappointed in him. He has no resilience. He's not putting up a fight. Instead of helping the doctor, he's helping the disease."

The following day he was franker still. "It is time to give him the last rites."

I sent for Cardinal San Sisto, one of the Pope's nephews, and he came running, weeping copiously, a talent no doubt inherited from his uncle. Because His Holiness was drowsing at the time, I took the liberty of leaving him for a while and going home. I ordered a light meal, after which I went out for a breath of air and to have a look at a little wood I had just added to the grounds of my villa. There I met the former owner, Domenico Acquaviva, busy clearing the undergrowth. As soon as he saw me, he threw himself at my feet and kissed my ring.

"Good work, Acquaviva," I said. "And many thanks for your kindness."

There was a silence. Then Acquaviva said: "Your Eminence, everyone's saying His Holiness is very ill. Has all hope been abandoned?"

I nodded. "Alas, yes, my son."

At that moment a footman ran up to tell me Cardinal de' Medici was waiting to see me. I went in at once and found him in the main hall, striding up and down.

"Cherubi," he said briefly, forgetting, for once, his courtly manner, "how is the Pope? I haven't seen him for three days."

I threw out my arms, then let them drop. "At this moment, San Sisto is giving him extreme unction."

"How very sad!" said Medici sanctimoniously, bowing his head.

But there was a faint smile on his lips, which disappeared as soon as he felt me looking at him. There was silence between us as we shared a secret joke: Medici had won. Now he wouldn't have to send his precious saltcellar to the Vatican.

# 12

## *Father Luigi Palestrino, Theologian*

It was on April 10, 1585, that Gregory XIII breathed his last. I prefer that expression to "rendered up his soul," which wrongly confuses the soul with a breath, whereas there is nothing material about it and no image or metaphor drawn from the terrestrial world can convey any idea of it.

I distrust the frivolous and reckless way people speak, and am particularly shocked when they talk, or even write, that a child's soul is created by its parents at the moment of conception. That is pure heresy. The son of Adam possesses no such privilege. God alone has the power to create a soul.

The point is irrevocable and beyond dispute. What is debatable, however, is the point at which the soul is breathed into the infant: whether at the moment of conception or at the moment of birth. Whichever alternative one chooses, there are difficulties. If you say the infant receives a soul only at birth, that means it did not possess a soul during its nine months in the uterus. If the infant receives a soul at the moment of conception, should it not be baptized while still in its mother's womb? For what would happen to that soul if the mother were delivered prematurely and the child was born dead?

The reason we theologians are always arguing with one another is because we are trying to deal with points in our holy religion that revelation left obscure, and because we cannot support our various theses with definite proof. I'll cite an example: ever since St. Thomas Aquinas, we have been discussing whether angels have any material being. Aquinas denied it. Despite his eminent authority, some of us are far from accepting that point of view.

Gregory XIII — who, permit me to observe, without acrimony, did not look with favor on theologians because of their strictures concerning his matrimonial *precetti* — died before he could receive extreme unction from Cardinal San Sisto. This caused great and painful anxiety about the fate of his soul, since his conduct had not always been edifying, not in life, or in his leadership of Christendom, or in his government of the state.

I was surprised, the day after the Pope's death, when Prince Orsini sent an anonymous coach to me with a note asking me to see him at Montegiordano at nightfall. I thought he was at Bracciano. And indeed he had been there the previous day. But having, apparently, maintained sources of intelligence close to the Holy Father, he had had warning of his imminent death and ridden in to Rome as fast as he could during the night.

This was not good for his injured leg, as I saw at once on entering the room where he was waiting for me. He was half lying in his chair, his left leg stretched out in front of him. He had both hands on his thigh, as if to curb the pain, and his lower lip was slightly twisted. This significant glimpse lasted only a second. As soon as he saw me, he stood with military swiftness and hastened forward to greet me, though with a pronounced limp. Holding both my hands, he made me sit down in the chair he had just left. I was touched by such affability, especially in one with so many sources of suffering, both physical and emotional.

"Father," he said, coming straight to the point, "the last time we met, you said it might be possible for me to take advantage of the interregnum between the death of Gregory and the election of the next pope. What is the situation now?"

"My lord," I said, "I would be obliged if you would refrain from asking questions in general, and from asking this one in particular. It is unnecessary, for I know well why I am here."

Far from being vexed, he smiled. And I felt I understood why he was much loved by women: there was something warm about him. Yet, without knowing why, I felt a kind of pity too. So great, I might almost say so exemplary a prince: brave, intelligent, well educated, enthusiastic friend of the arts, physically tall and broad and athletic — such a fine figure of a man — but made of flesh, and flesh so precarious, so ensnared in this fleeting world.

"My lord," I went on, "an interregnum is a very temporary state of society, but it allows great scope to those who, like you, have a wrong to set right. At the moment, the Papal States are without a ruler and Christendom without a guide."

"Am I then to conclude," he said, forgetting my prohibition, "that I may make use of the interregnum to declare my marriage valid?"

"My lord, that would be extremely unwise. You cannot treat the dead Pope's decree with such contempt without arousing the wrath of his successor. You must go about it more tactfully. For example, call the major theologians together and consult them. Then if, and only if, their verdict is favorable, you can remarry."

"Remarry?" he said, staring. "I'm married already!"

"Forgive me, my lord, but you are not. You are no longer married in the eyes of the church. And there is not a theologian in the world who can annul a papal *precetto*. All he can do is tell you that in his opinion you may remarry."

"But," he asked, "what's to stop the next pope, when he's elected, from issuing a *precetto* annulling my remarriage?"

"Nothing, my lord, absolutely nothing. It is a risk you have to take."

"My God!" he muttered, under his breath, clutching his head. "What tyranny!"

To this I made no reply. In the case that concerned us, I was not far from sharing his opinion. But my feelings did not change the principle I held to: *dura lex, sed lex;* it is a harsh law, but it is the law. I believe the benefits that Christendom derives from papal omnipotence are greater than the disadvantages arising from its misuse.

"If you mean to follow my advice, my lord," I said, "here is a list of seven of the most highly respected theologians. Call them together here and let them deliberate."

"Why seven, Father?" he asked, glancing at the list.

"To have a majority, even if only of one.

For we shall take a vote, a secret ballot."

"Why secret?"

"In order not to draw the new pope's anger down upon any one individual if he does not agree with our decision."

"Can these theologians be brought together by tomorrow?" he asked anxiously.

"I will do my best. But first I should like to have a private interview with the signora, your wife. Please don't question me about it: I will not answer. You may ask the signora afterward."

I could see from his frank and open countenance that he was pleased I had referred to Vittoria as his wife, though he must have guessed I did so purely out of courtesy.

"I'll call her," he said briskly, "and leave you alone together."

I stood and bowed. He came over to me with his limping stride and, as before, took both my hands in his: they were so large that mine almost disappeared in them. He looked at me silently for a moment, with an expression of friendship and gratitude. My head reached only to his chest. What a mountain of a man! I thought. What huge bones and enormous muscles. And, inside the giant body, what powerful organs there must be! When his hour comes, he will have difficulty leaving behind so much flesh, whereas with me the job is already almost done. There is so little matter about me that St. Thomas Aquinas might have taken me for an angel. God forgive my little joke. Life is only a long waiting for death, so it is as well to brighten the time occasionally as it passes.

I sat down again and waited some time for the signora. This did not surprise me: ladies have a reputation for never being ready. I do not know if this is justified. I know little about them. My mother died giving me birth, and the rest of my family was lost soon afterward in an earthquake. I was brought up by nuns who were silent, and I might never have learned to speak had it not been for the convent's old gardener, with whom I lodged and who became my mentor.

It was early in my twentieth year that I went out into the streets of Rome for the first time and saw some real women. I was shocked, and thought at first they belonged to a different species. The nuns had a kind of fusty smell about them, whereas the women I saw in the streets were enveloped in a peculiar perfume. I was not sure whether I liked it. Their eyes were bright and shining and never stopped turning to look at everything. They spoke in high clear voices that rang in my ears like music. These discoveries frightened rather than pleased me. It was not long before I got a more terrifying shock: one of the women in the street, probably by accident, looked at me. My nuns lived with their lids lowered; their eyes had never encountered mine. So when this woman looked at me as she passed, her glance, brief and accidental though it was, made me shake from head to foot. It was as if she sent out little pincers that got hold of you and turned you around for inspection. Ever since then I have been frightened of women.

This probably absurd feeling made me uneasy as I waited for the signora, though I was sure the interview was necessary to her and to the Prince's cause. My lips were dry; my throat felt paralyzed. I noticed my hands shaking, and hid them in my wide sleeves. What I was most afraid of was that she might see my panic — me a man old enough to be her father.

She came at last. I sprang up. With a gracious wave of the hand, she said in a low, sweet voice: "Father, I'm told you want to ask me some questions. I am at your service."

She was a head taller than I, and as she looked at me with her great blue eyes, their light was so dazzling I had to lower my own. Not so far, however, that I could not still see her. She seemed elegantly dressed, and I noticed that, instead of flattening and imprisoning her body like the habits of the nuns, her clothes followed her shape and seemed designed to show it off. Her fair curly hair was immensely long; it reached her heels and trailed behind her as she moved. Her face seemed excellently proportioned, the skin taut over the bones. Her complexion was pink and white, her teeth regular and gleaming white.

"Father," she repeated, as if surprised at my silence, "I am at your service."

Her voice shook a little, which made me think that, in spite of her self-possession, she dreaded this interview as much as I did. Then something curious happened: her fear largely dispelled mine.

"There is a slight difficulty, signora," I said, finding my voice again. "I want to speak to you alone, but I need to have a written record of your answers."

"If that's the difficulty," she said with a ready smile, "I think I can take care of it quite easily. I'll write my answers, and be both your witness and your clerk. Then you'll have my evidence not only in writing but in my own hand."

This was both witty and gracious. I signified that I accepted her offer, and she installed herself on a stool in front of a desk. This took some time; before she sat, she gathered her Absalom locks, then after she took her seat brought them around into her lap. This was probably so their weight would not trouble her as she wrote. As I watched, I pondered what feminine beauty should mean to a theologian. Some saw the hand of the devil in it, but that thesis did not stand up to scrutiny. The devil could intervene only where things were put to bad use. And there was no doubt that beauty, in itself, was a gift of God. But what for, since the function of women is procreation? All women, beautiful or ugly, can bear children, so I could not see the need to bring together so many excellences in one of them. If the purpose of theology was to explain religion, I had to admit that outside the bright circle of revelation all was darkness, even a detail as trivial as the one I was pondering. However it might be, I was sure not a leaf ever fell from a tree except by the will of Providence.

"Signora," I said, "the first question I have to ask is this: Was it at your own desire and by your own will, without threat, blackmail, or any other external pressure, that you married Prince Orsini?"

"Yes, it was of my own free will."

"Will you please write all that down, signora?"

"In our exact words?"

"Yes."

She wrote, and I waited until she lifted her quill from the paper.

"Signora, why did you marry Prince Orsini?"

"Because I loved him and wanted to be his wife."

"How many times had you met Prince Orsini before you were shut up in Castel Sant' Angelo?"

"Once. At the house of my uncle, His Eminence Cardinal Montalto."

"Did you have any communication with him, written or oral, after that meeting?"

"The Prince wrote to me, but I did not answer. Am I to write all this down, Father?"

"Just the answers. You can leave out the questions."

She continued accordingly.

"In your view, signora, why did the Pope incarcerate you in Castel Sant' Angelo?"

"Because he thought Prince Orsini had murdered my husband, and that I was his accomplice."

"Was that true?"

"No, it was not!" she said, flaring up. "Not only was it untrue, but also it was categorically denied in the Bargello's report. Della Pace told me that when he came to get me."

"Please go on writing, signora."

She did so, making the pen squeak angrily

on the paper. It was obvious she had not expected me to ask that question, and was offended.

As soon as she had finished, I said: "Signora, need I tell you I believe what you say? Would I be here if I thought you were guilty?"

"Thank you, Father," she said, evidently moved.

"Let us go on. When you met Prince Orsini at the palace of your uncle, Cardinal Montalto, did you speak to him?"

"No."

"How long did this meeting last?"

"About five minutes."

"And that was enough for you to love him?"

"Yes." Then she added, somewhat belligerently: "Does that strike you as improbable?"

"I don't know," I answered curtly. "I have no experience of human passions, even by hearsay. I'm a theologian, not a confessor."

She looked at me as if she was sorry to have spoken to me like that.

"Write, please, signora," I said gently.

After a while I went on. "Suppose His Holiness had not imprisoned you in Castel Sant' Angelo; would you have married Prince Orsini then?"

"I do not think so. I would have been afraid people would think I was guilty."

"Why did you marry him after you were

freed from Castel Sant' Angelo?"

"The harm was done. Because I had been imprisoned, no one believed I was innocent."

"Write it down, please."

I continued: "Signora, you know that as a result of Gregory XIII's *precetto* you are no longer married to Prince Orsini?"

"I know. It is iniquitous!" she cried passionately.

"I must ask you, signora, out of respect for the Holy See, to withdraw that comment. Otherwise you will have to record it, and it will make a bad impression."

"I withdraw it."

"Here is my last question: If, in the near future, it was possible for you to remarry Prince Orsini, would you do so?"

"Yes. With all my heart."

"Is that your considered and unalterable intention?"

"Certainly!"

"Write it down, please."

When she had finished, I asked her to date and sign what she had written. Although, for me, the interview had been something of an ordeal, though much less painful than I would have believed, I was pleased with the signora. She had answered my questions clearly, firmly, logically, and, I hoped, frankly. The only thing that bothered me, a little, was that she had fallen in love with the Prince after having seen him for only five minutes. If women could so rapidly forge a bond that was going to last a lifetime, they were greatly to be pitied.

The signora rose, handed me the document she had recorded, and took a most gracious leave. Setting aside her beauty, the purpose of which seemed to pose an insoluble theological problem, I concluded that she was a highly estimable human being. I sent up a brief prayer that she and her chosen companion might be restored to spiritual peace.

When the Prince returned, I handed him the signora's record, without comment. He read it through, apparently with some surprise.

"Father, one question, perhaps the last. Why do you put so much stress on the fact that the signora married me — and would, if the case arose, remarry me — of her own free will?"

"My lord, I have already told you: in the eyes of the church, the basis of the sacrament of marriage is the intention of the spouses to give themselves to one another. What I am trying to establish is the soundness and authenticity of the bond that the *precetto* untied."

"I understand that. But why don't you ask me the same questions?"

I could not help smiling at such naïveté. "My lord, your wish to marry the signora needs no further proof. It is public knowledge. You fomented an insurrection to free her from prison, and what you are doing now is moving heaven and earth to remain her husband."

Later, as the unmarked coach was taking me home, I thought about what I had said. "Moving heaven and earth" was a singularly inappropriate expression. Men, being made of such changeable stuff, may possibly move earth, but the decrees of heaven are immutable and eternal.

## His Eminence Cardinal Cherubi

Things started to move the minute Gregory XIII died, so great were the interests, personal and national, involved in the choice of his successor.

Because I had never been *papabile*, owing to my reputation for clumsiness, and because my only ambition was to become patriarch of Venice someday, I observed the various maneuvers and intrigues quite disinterestedly, taking care only that I would support a cardinal who would not oppose my plans if he became pope.

No one in the Vatican was so naïve as to imagine that the princes of this world would not try to influence the election. The most powerful of these was Philip II of Spain, whose possessions included Austria, the Low Countries, Portugal, and, in Italy, the duchy of Milan, the Kingdom of Naples, and Sicily, not to mention his huge empire in the Americas, source of the gold that maintained his armies and his influence.

Before the doors were locked upon the conclave, Philip's ambassador, Count de Olivares, took care to visit the cardinals in Rome and put pressure on them to elect a pope favorable to the interests of Spain. He spent quite a long time with me, supposing my influence on the conclave to be greater than it actually would be. He was not stupid, but he lacked finesse. No one ever had more of the arrogance universally attributed to his countrymen. He spoke to church dignitaries as if he were giving orders, and lost his temper at the least sign of opposition. Generous with promises, he was equally lavish with threats, which he scarcely took the trouble to veil. My opinion, after our meeting, was that he was trying too hard, and doing his master's cause more harm than good.

Henry III of France had little chance to influence the conclave: he had his hands full with the rebellious Holy League, which was hand in glove with Philip II. But he had some sympathizers among those who mistrusted Philip's power, and these included Cardinal d'Este, who had family connections with the King of France. The d'Estes were very powerful; they owned the duchies of Ferrara, Modena, Reggio, and Rovigo. Thus he was influential among us.

We went into conclave on April 21, after Mass, and spent the rest of that day taking possession of our cells and paying courtesy calls on one another, each using his long antennae to try to weigh the leading candidates' chances, in some cases his own.

It was rather amusing to leave our splendid palaces behind and become cloistered in modest cells. It made us feel young again, and the feeling was all the more pleasurable because we knew our discomfort would not last long. The conclave, of such great moment for Christendom, for the state, and for ourselves, thus began in a state of suppressed excitement and in a monastic atmosphere lightened by innocent high spirits.

The temptation to continue that mood was tempered by the necessity to be on guard. The most amiable words and the friendliest glances might hide calculation. Though my inveterate blundering was usually accepted indulgently by my colleagues, even I felt the need to tread carefully, and to be frank in appearance only.

None of the prelates raised his voice above a murmur. When we tapped on a door, we did so quietly. As the scarlet robes passed in the narrow gallery alongside the cells, the only sound was a smooth rustle; footsteps were silent. Gestures were slow and restrained. Eyes were often lowered. Despite the thickness of the walls, conversations were whispered. And the talk was all understatement. Smiles, shrugs, and glances said more than words, and sometimes contradicted them. No one spoke ill of anyone, except by omission or paralipsis. The silence, meditation, and piety on display at our services, morning and evening, would have edified the most skeptical observer.

On the second day, the conclave really got started, and the hopes of the cardinals aspiring to the papacy began to seethe. Almost all of them could aspire, even the most unassuming, for it had sometimes happened that an obscure cardinal was elected just to rule out another so talented as to be thought dangerous.

On the face of it, Alessandro Farnese looked the most likely candidate to me. He belonged to the famous princely family that ruled over the duchy of Parma and Piacenza. He was intelligent and able, a humanist and patron of the arts. Perhaps most important, his nephew and namesake Alessandro Farnese, who was half Austrian, through his mother, had been made governor of the Low Countries by Philip, and had won renown for restoring peace there. The virtues of the nephew added to those of the uncle, and the favor of Philip II toward both lent convincing weight and luster to Farnese's candidacy. He had not yet offered himself as a candidate, but his position made it inevitable that he should.

Everyone was therefore surprised when, on the second day of the conclave, Cardinal Altemps and Cardinal de' Medici put forward Cardinal Sirleto. He was a Neapolitan, and thus a subject of Philip II and a partisan in his cause.

The motives of the sponsors were very different. Altemps supported Sirleto because he was pro-Spanish and he really wanted him to succeed. Medici supported him because he wished to appear pro-Spanish, though he was not, and, above all, to block the candidacy of Farnese, who seemed to him much more of a threat. Moreover, he could expect some recompense from Sirleto: Medici had been secretary of state to both Pius IV and Gregory XIII; why not to Sirleto too?

This candidacy at once met with strong, though mixed, opposition. Many of the cardinals did not want Sirleto precisely because Medici might become secretary of state for the third time. Cardinal d'Este and Cardinal Farnese were against Sirleto for other reasons. The first, with the interests of France at heart, feared a pope who was a subject of the King of Spain. The second wanted the papal tiara for himself. The votes were counted. Sirleto was eliminated.

At this point, two things happened, both of which contained an element of comedy. One, which happened inside the conclave, seemed important at first, but in fact had little effect on the election. The second took place outside the conclave, and, what is worse, in the street, and ruined the chances of the most brilliant candidate.

Just before noon that day — Easter Monday — someone hammered on the trebly locked door of the conclave. It was Cardinal Andrea, who had just arrived in Rome and was demanding admission. He was not only a cardinal; he was also Archduke of Austria. When someone opened the judas hole and we were informed who it was, we were alarmed, especially because he was accompanied by the Spanish Ambassador. To admit the Archduke was tantamount to having his cousin Philip II in our midst during the election. But how were we to refuse, given that Gregory XIII had been weak enough to make him a cardinal?

With out whispered approval, Medici had

recourse to the method that had proved so successful in the matter of his precious salt-cellar: he played for time. "May it please Your Eminence to defer your entry. The members of the conclave are about to sit down to their morning meal. If you enter now, it will take a good two hours to read you the bulls establishing you as an elector, a great pity for those of us who are hungry and need to recruit our strength."

Though this was politely put, it was taken badly on the other side of the door.

"There can be no question," said Olivares haughtily, "of His Eminence the Cardinal Archduke waiting outside a locked door while his colleagues stuff themselves. If they elect a pope in the course of the meal, that would greatly infringe on the Cardinal Archduke's rights. So I hereby declare that if he is not admitted at once, the King, my master, will consider null and void any election in which he has not taken part."

This outrageous threat left us aghast: Philip II, through his arrogant Ambassador, was by anticipation calling in question the sovereignty of the conclave. All of us, even the most Hispanicized among us, were at a loss what to say or do.

Once again Medici came to the rescue. He went to the judas hole and said: "May it please

541

Your Eminence to wait a few minutes. We are about to confer among ourselves." And he firmly closed the judas.

Though he handled the Spanish power tactfully, he also feared it, as did his brother the Grand Duke of Tuscany, the Most Serene Republic, and Cardinal d'Este's brother the Duke of Ferrara. These three principalities, though famed and prosperous, were small, and were afraid of suffering the same fate as the duchy of Milan and the Kingdom of Naples. Philip II's greed for new territories was as vast as his empire was great.

Someone then remembered that the Archduke of Austria was only a deacon and had not received holy orders; his cardinal's title was merely a courtesy one. According to a bull promulgated by Pius IV, he needed to be ordained in order to enter the conclave and take part in the vote. At first, our gathering was delighted by this discovery; but then everyone drew back. Who was going to be bold enough to bell the tiger, Olivares, already banging impatiently on the door with an iron hand that had never known a velvet glove?

Medici declined the task, saying he had already braved Olivares's claws twice. They thought of me next, even politely insinuating that one more blunder on my part would not matter. I firmly refused. Finally, after hasty consultation around the table had resulted in nothing but negatives, Cardinal d'Este offered to be the martyr. He did not get much thanks for it: everyone knew he was pro-French, and had nothing more to lose to the Spanish faction.

Cardinal d'Este did not fail to note this ingratitude. Nevertheless, he marched stoutly over to the locked door, opened the judas, and said: "Your Eminence, the conclave regrets it cannot admit you. According to the bull *In Eligendis* of 1503, no one can participate in the conclave who is not in holy orders."

Once again Olivares spoke for the Cardinal Archduke, and very curtly too: "We foresaw that objection. Here is a document that does away with it. It is a bull issued by Gregory XIII exempting the Cardinal Archduke from having to take orders and giving him the right to vote in the conclave. Read it."

He passed the bull through the judas. Cardinal d'Este took it, unrolled it, and read it. Others crowded around to read the scandalous document over his shoulder.

"What do you think, Medici?" asked d'Este sourly. "Is it really Gregory XIII's signature? You were his secretary of state; you must have written the thing out."

"I don't remember anything about it," Medici answered.

This insolence brought him some unamiable looks. He did not seem to care. Drawing himself up — he wasn't very tall — he went and unlocked the door with his own hand.

Cardinal Andrea entered, and as soon as the door was locked behind him, we enveloped him in a great swirl of robes, vying with one another in civilities. We also looked at him with some curiosity, for he had been in Rome only once before, just long enough to receive his red hat from the hands of the Pope. He was a big fat man with pale-blue eyes and a polite but indifferent expression. He accepted our Italian compliments graciously, but as if he did not really understand them. Someone tried Latin. He still did not understand. French and Spanish were equally unsuccessful. Moreover, he did not know any of us, and was quite unfamiliar with our cliques and factions, the various interests at stake, large and small, and our numerous intrigues. Those who spoke German tried to draw him into their respective parties. He listened to them politely but without taking the least interest in their suggestions. He was clearly bored, even during Mass, and never opened his lips during the whole course of our discussions, except to yawn behind his glove.

Strangely, although the Cardinal Andrea's entrance into the conclave had little direct influence on the votes, it gave rise outside to an incident that had a considerable effect on the election. The trouble Olivares had caused over the locked door soon leaked out, and the people of Rome, by wishful thinking, assumed that the Spanish faction was going to win, and that Cardinal Farnese would soon be elected, if he had not been already. There was much rejoicing, and a mob rushed off to sack Farnese's palace. This was not out of spite: the populace adored the Cardinal. They were following a custom — I do not like to call it a tradition — that says that since a cardinal who succeeds to the tiara gains access to great wealth, he can afford to make the people a present of his personal possessions.

We were shocked beyond expression that the Romans should have dared to anticipate our decision — and perhaps even more to see that Farnese was so popular. If elected, he would rely partly on Spanish influence and partly on the favor of the people, and could afford to snap his fingers at our opposition. We sent guards to protect his magnificent palace, and took a vote. Farnese had only eleven supporters. So he saved his possessions but lost the tiara.

Then Cardinal San Sisto, who was very influential among the Roman cardinals because nearly all of them had got their red hats from his uncle, Gregory XIII, on his recommendation, put forward one of them, Cardinal Castagna, as a candidate. Most members of the conclave wanted a virtuous pope to succeed Gregory XIII, and Castagna was virtuous. But he did not have a strong character. Many were afraid San Sisto would be behind him, pulling the strings. So he too was rejected.

The next to be suggested was the Grand Inquisitor, Cardinal Savallo. He was a Roman too, but as soon as his name was put forward, all the other Roman cardinals opposed it. They were in a good position to know that Savallo was a fanatic who saw the devil's hand in everything, was suspicious of his own shadow, and dreamed of nothing but autos-da-fé and burnings at the stake. Even his colleagues did not feel safe from him. His candidacy was soon nipped in the bud.

Then Farnese suggested Santa Severina, probably thinking that because he was so young, he would be easy to handle. But his age was used against Santa Severina by those who did not want a Farnese protégé on the papal throne: "What," one said, "scarcely forty years old? Are we going to elect a *putto papa?*" Terror had eliminated the Grand Inquisitor; ridicule finished off Santa Severina.

At this point, we had been shut up for three long days. Everyone was anxious to bring the matter to an end. We were getting tired of all the maneuverings, and of our Spartan conditions. Farnese, still smarting from his failure, sensed this waning enthusiasm and decided to stir things up. He put forward the name of the Spanish Cardinal, Torres, due to arrive in Rome the following day.

I was in my cell, ruminating on this staggering piece of news, when Medici knocked at the door. He was pale, and his brow was streaming with perspiration.

"Cherubi," he said right away, dispensing with his usual diplomatic precautions, "what do you think of the Torres candidacy?"

"I'm aghast! A Spanish pope on the throne of St. Peter? Why not Olivares himself? It would amount to the same thing. If Torres is elected, Olivares and Farnese will rule for him. They will be our masters. And the leader of Christendom will be a mere chaplain to the King of Spain. What a disgrace!"

I fell silent, astonished at my sudden outburst of frankness. But there was no time now for concealment. Medici, Machiavellian though he was, knew this too.

"Since that's how you feel, Cherubi," he said hastily, "come and see me in my cell in ten minutes. There will be others there who think as you do."

Unusual for him, he shook my hand before

he left. His was quite damp. The poor fellow was terrified, and with reason. How could a Spanish pope defend the grand duchy of Tuscany against the voracity of Philip II?

Ten minutes later, in Medici's cell, I found Alessandrino, Santa Severina, Rusticucci, and d'Este, all of them tense.

"Farnese," said Medici, "is hatching a very skillful plot. He means to exploit the fact that when a cardinal is introduced into the conclave, we all crowd around to greet him. By the time Torres arrives, Farnese hopes to have convinced enough cardinals to elect him by acclamation, taking advantage of the confusion and the impossibility of counting, in the heat of the moment, who is for and who is against."

"Very clever," said d'Este, "but we can use the same trick. Let us be quick and choose a candidate of our own, campaign on his behalf, and elect him by acclamation before Torres arrives, when we're all together in the chapel."

"We must hurry, then," said Medici. "Let's pick a candidate at once. I eliminate myself right away."

"And arithmetic eliminates me," said d'Este. "I would get only the votes of the three French cardinals, and maybe not all of them. Pellevé's an ardent supporter of the Holy League."

"As for me," said Rusticucci, "my ambitions don't fly that high."

He meant that he would rather get from the next pope what he had never been able to get from Gregory XIII — an important state position.

"My ambitions do not fly at all," I said. "They sail in the direction of Venice."

"Mine neither fly nor sail," said Alessandrino soberly.

Since Santa Severina had already been eliminated, there was a pause. Finally, Rusticucci cleared his throat and said: "Should we consider Montalto?"

"He would make a change from Gregory," said Santa Severina. "He's virtuous, capable, and a hard worker."

"I respect him," d'Este said. "He refused a pension from the King of Spain."

"But he voted for Farnese," Alessandrino said.

"Mere *captatio benevolentiae,* a maneuver," said Medici. "He knew Farnese did not have a chance, after the insurrection."

"What do you think, Cherubi?" asked d'Este, raising his eyebrows.

Everyone turned to look at me, remembering the disagreement Montalto and I had in the past.

"I'm extremely grateful to Montalto," I said

with an air of mock seriousness, "for sending me 'back to my gondolas.' Otherwise I would never have become a cardinal. I will vote for Montalto."

They all smiled, and I thought I had been rather witty. If, as seemed likely now, Montalto's chances prospered, it would be an advantage to have been one of his main supporters. My Venetian ambitions needed the favor of the next pope.

"One good thing about Montalto, apart from his virtues," said Rusticucci, "is that, since the death of Peretti, all his nephews are too young to be given official positions. Gregory's nepotism was unbearable. By the time he'd provided for all his kinsmen, there were no important jobs left for those who really deserved them."

Everyone agreed, though with some amusement: in our friend's view, the first among "those who really deserved" high office was Rusticucci himself.

"Alessandrino?" Medici said.

"Oh, I agree," Alessandrino said in his usual lofty tone. "I see no reason to oppose the poor old man. We'll be the masters."

"Do you think so?" Medici asked.

# Prince Paolo Giordano Orsini, Duke of Bracciano

The theologians started their deliberations on the *precetto* on April 11, ten days before the conclave began. Twelve days later they still had not reached any conclusion.

Thanks to a clever arrangement that I owe to my grandfather and his architect, anyone speaking in the room I had assigned to the theologians could be heard in the room overhead. I'd intended by this means to follow their discussions, but they spoke Latin, so I couldn't understand a word. I called in Vittoria. She listened for a good hour, her brow furrowed with concentration, and then reported.

"They keep weighing the pros and cons, with endless quotations from Scripture and the Fathers of the church. They can always find a text to support whatever point of view is advanced. They can't agree about anything, not even on what Our Lord is supposed to have thought about the dissolving of the marriage bond. Some say He was for it and others say He was against it. They argue passionately, and get very impatient with one another."

"My love, you're as learned as you are beautiful! I'm full of admiration that you can understand these pedants. They may also be very crafty. I wouldn't be surprised if they kept us hanging indefinitely, until one fine morning the conclave gives us a new pope, and they still won't have reached a decision."

"That's what I'm afraid of too, Paolo. One thing struck me as I was listening to them: apart from Father Palestrino, who keeps trying to make them stick to the point, they hardly ever mention our *precetto!*"

"Our!" I said. "How strange that sounds! But you're right, Vittoria; it is ours, like a disease eating away at us or a leech clinging to our skin."

It was a mistake to talk about a disease eating away at us. A cloud passed over Vittoria's lovely face, and I could see she was thinking of the wound in my leg. She worried about it a great deal, however much I tried to hide the fact that it was getting worse.

"Vittoria," I went on, pretending not to understand why her expression had changed, "don't worry. I'll hurry them up. I'll tell Father Palestrino not to let the conclave steal a march on us."

I did so that very day.

"My lord," he said in the loud, clearly articulated voice that always surprised me, coming from that frail body, "the good fathers are not deliberately keeping you waiting. They are embarrassed, and afraid."

"Afraid?"

"My lord, like me, they belong to the church and must obey its laws. You treat them so well, they would like to make a decision that pleased you, but for them there is a danger involved. How do they know if the next pope will be your friend?"

"I understand. But what can we do to make them come to a decision?"

"Nag them."

"Nag them?" I said, surprised. "But how?"

"If you really want to do it, I'll tell you how, my lord, in the morning."

Thereupon he asked to be allowed to take his leave. Because I knew he would only shut up like a clam if I asked any questions, I let him go.

I told Vittoria about our conversation, and we spent a few hours, not exactly depressed — after all, we were together — but in a very disagreeable mixture of impatience and anxiety. Our marriage seemed to depend on everything except us: on the theologians, the conclave, the next pope, and heaven knew what else.

At the end of the evening, we decided to

set our somber mood aside and play dice. The stakes had to do with love, and we whispered them in one another's ear because Caterina was there, gently brushing her mistress's hair.

There came a discreet tap at the door. The majordomo came in, apologizing because it was so late, to tell me a monk insisted on seeing me. From his description, I knew it must be Il Mancino.

"Let him in! Let him in!" I said. "He's welcome here."

He might have been waiting outside the door, so swiftly did he appear, in his doublet, having shed his monkish garment in the anteroom. As soon as he entered, Caterina ran and threw her arms around his neck, covering him with kisses. He bore it with patient indulgence, like one used to being adored by women.

"Come, come, little sister," he said at last. "Have you forgotten where you are?"

He freed himself and swept Vittoria a low bow expressive of both respect and admiration, then honored me with one entirely of respect. As I had previously noticed, he was capable of fine distinctions.

He drew himself up proudly, reminding me of a little fighting cock, thin and wiry. Nor was he devoid of beak and claws, for he had a dagger in his belt, another, Italian-style, at his back, and a knife in his boot. It was late at night, of course.

"My lord," he said with dignity, "I wouldn't have ventured to disturb you at this hour if I did not have very important information to impart."

"I'm listening."

"His Eminence Cardinal Torres arrived in Genoa yesterday evening and will set out for Rome tomorrow. He's in a great hurry to get here. And Ambassador Olivares is eager to take him to the conclave as soon as he arrives."

He was silent long enough for me to ask why.

"Because of a plot he's hatched with Cardinal Farnese. When Torres enters the conclave, Farnese is to round up all the pro-Spanish prelates and have him elected by acclamation."

"A Spanish pope!" cried Vittoria. "How disgraceful!"

"And how dangerous for you and the Prince, signora!" said Il Mancino, with another of his gallant bows.

"Dangerous, Acquaviva?" Vittoria asked.

"I used to be a general in the service of Venice, my angel," I said. "That's enough to make Philip mistrust me."

"And your military talents, my lord," said

Il Mancino. "Philip hates good generals, signora, unless they're his, like Alessandro Farnese."

"Acquaviva," I said, "once again your political acumen amazes me. Where did you get the news about Torres?"

"One of my women," Il Mancino said, lowering his eyes. "They call her La Sorda, though she isn't deaf. She's reliable, faithful, and devoted, and she has plenty of brains."

"But a whore's a whore, after all," said Caterina sourly.

Il Mancino scowled at her, and Vittoria, half scolding and half protecting her, at once intervened.

"Caterina, come and sit by me on this stool. And hold your tongue."

As soon as Caterina had obeyed, Vittoria put a hand on her shoulder and said with a laugh: "And after all a lady's maid's a maid too."

Il Mancino looked swiftly at both. He was furious with Caterina, and at the same time grateful to Vittoria for protecting her.

"Well," I asked, "what did La Sorda do?"

"She made friends with Olivares's secretary."

"Friends!" said Caterina derisively.

"Be quiet, Caterina," said Vittoria, giving her a little tap on the cheek.

Caterina caught hold of her hand and kissed it.

"The secretary is Italian," said Il Mancino, "but he speaks Spanish very well and acts as Olivares's interpreter."

"And how did he come to confide in La Sorda?"

"Out of friendship, as I've said, but also because he was angry at the thought that there might be a Spanish pope."

"A thousand thanks, Acquaviva. Please take this purse for your pains. Would you like me to send you back by coach?"

"I thank you, my lord, but that won't be necessary," he said, with an excellent imitation of nonchalance. "My servant is waiting for me in the courtyard with our horses. But may it please your lordship, I'd like to have a word with my sister before I go."

"Of course."

By the time he had bowed to us and opened the door, she had bounded to it. He ushered her out in front of him, treating her to a stern look as he did so. I'd never seen a girl run so gleefully into a good clip on the ear.

"What are we going to do, Paolo?" Vittoria asked.

"Nag the theologians."

"How?"

"I'll know tomorrow morning."

I was up betimes next morning, and when Palestrino arrived, I took him aside and told him about Olivares's scheme.

"A Spanish pope!" he cried, crossing himself. "God save us from such an affliction! Those people would burn one half of Christendom to save the other half."

"Be that as it may, Father, the conclave is about to conclude. There isn't a minute to lose. What must I do to hurry those theologians?"

"To hurry us *all*, my lord. I mustn't be treated as an exception."

After signing to me to bend down, he spoke at length into my ear.

When I left him, I gave my majordomo some orders that surprised him. Then, after he told me all the theologians were now in their room, I went and addressed them in no uncertain terms.

"A word, if you please, Reverend Fathers. Since I don't know Latin, I shall speak to you in good plain Italian. Your discussions have been going on for twelve days now without result. This delay is very damaging to my cause, and I cannot allow it to continue. So I have decided to keep you here at Montegiordano until you have reached a conclusion. You won't die of hunger. You'll be provided with as much bread and wine as you want."

"What!" said Father Palestrino, pretending

to be indignant. "Are we your prisoners, my lord?"

"No doubt about it, Reverend Fathers."

"That's tyranny!" cried another of the priests, as if outraged.

There were various murmurs, and another said: "You're subjecting us to force."

"Reverend Fathers," I said firmly, "let us not argue, I beg you. I'm not dictating your decision; I'm only speeding it up."

With a brief nod, I left, locking the door behind me.

I went straight to Vittoria and told her about it. She listened wide-eyed. "They must be foaming at the mouth," she said.

"That's the impression they tried to give. But, really, they're delighted. It makes things so much easier for them. If their verdict about the precetto displeases the next pope, they can say I used force on them and they could not do otherwise."

I kept the theologians in as strict seclusion as the cardinals were in the conclave. I also sent the majordomo every hour to ask them how they were getting on.

The pressure produced results. On the stroke of six, the majordomo brought me a sealed scroll. I broke it open at once, but it was written in Latin and I had to wait for Vittoria to come and translate it for me.

Here is the result of the consultation, as far as I can remember, set down without any attempt to reproduce the ecclesiastical rhetoric of the original:

## FIRST POINT

We have diligently studied the *precetto* in which the Most Holy and Late Lamented Pope Gregory XIII annulled the matrimonial bond uniting Prince Paolo Giordano Orsini, Duke of Bracciano, and Signora Vittoria Accoramboni, widow of Signore Francesco Peretti. It seems to us, both because of the imperfect Latin in which it is written and because of the unsoundness of its arguments, that the *precetto* was drawn up not by the Holy Father himself but by a clerk.

## SECOND POINT

The reasons given for dissolving the bond are moral. It is suggested, though not clearly stated, that the said marriage was scandalous because Francesco Peretti was murdered on the orders of the Prince, with the signora as his tacit accomplice. However, not only is no proof offered to support this implicit accusation, but

Bargello della Pace's report, which is known to us, also fails to indicate the guilt of the two people concerned.

Moreover, when Signora Vittoria Accoramboni was imprisoned in Castel Sant' Angelo there was no question of bringing her to trial. Any presumptions against her must therefore have been too weak to be put before the judges.

### THIRD POINT

The *precetto* was issued at the request of two influential noblemen whose names for honorable reasons we shall not mention. Both gentlemen are related by marriage to Prince Orsini. The reasons for their request were moral, and identical with those examined above. We have therefore nothing to add to our previous analysis. It seems possible that the petitioners might have been moved by worldly considerations, since Prince Orsini's remarriage might have seemed to them to threaten the interests of his son by his first marriage.

### FIRST CONCLUSION

Despite the weaknesses, omissions, and inaccuracies in the arguments of the *pre-*

*cetto,* it cannot be regarded as null, because of the sacred character of its author, the Most Holy and Late Lamented Gregory XIII, deciding and judging ex cathedra under the inspiration of the Holy Spirit. Nor is it possible to maintain that the death of the Most Holy and Late Lamented Pope Gregory XIII renders the above-mentioned *precetto* null, unless it be expressly declared so by his successor.

### SECOND CONCLUSION

The prohibition in the *precetto* forbidding the parties concerned to contract another marriage cannot now be considered binding. Firstly, because the Most Holy and Late Lamented Gregory XIII, having been summoned by his Creator to enjoy eternal bliss, has left this vale of tears and is no longer in a position to punish the offenders. Secondly, because no one can prejudge the decision a future pope may make concerning them, since he cannot be bound by the decisions of his predecessor and possesses complete sovereignty over his own.

As soon as Vittoria had translated this document, I went to the theologians and said:

"Reverend Fathers, the report of your consultation is a masterpiece of wisdom, prudence, and moderation. I am completely satisfied with it, and shall always be infinitely grateful to you. Thanks to you, the signora and I will be able to live again as a Christian couple, in dignity and fidelity. Be good enough to wait here a little while longer, and my majordomo will summon you one by one to convey to each of you a more concrete token of my gratitude. Reverend Fathers, I ask all of you to pray that the bond you have just saved may never again be broken."

The theologians bowed and uttered friendly murmurs. I left the room, and the first person my majordomo summoned was Father Palestrino. I wanted to see him myself before he left Montegiordano. When I went up to him and clasped him affectionately in my arms, I was shocked to find I was embracing a skeleton.

"You're crushing me to death, my lord," he said, a faint tinge of pink appearing in his cheeks. But can I speak of cheeks? His withered skin was stretched so tightly over the bones there seemed no trace of flesh.

"I'm sorry, Father," I said. "But I owe everything to you."

"As a matter of fact," he answered, "neither I nor any of the others did very much. And

I don't know if we had the right to do what little we did. However, it's enough to enable you to remarry. Only remember that your second union will be precarious until the next pope has accepted it."

I knew this was true. Our waiting, our anxiety were still not over: we had negotiated only one step.

On the following day, April 25, 1585, in the chapel at Grottapinta, I married Vittoria for the second time.

# 13

## *His Eminence Cardinal de' Medici*

The original nucleus of Montalto's supporters consisted of myself, d'Este, Alessandrino, Santa Severina, Cherubi, and Rusticucci. Plenty of talent there, but it would take at least six times that number to get Montalto elected by acclamation. So as soon as we had agreed on him, we set about trying to increase our little party through a whispering campaign and all the other devices usual on such occasions.

Admittedly, the candidate we were trying to help had already done a lot to help himself. Since the beginning of the conclave, he had shown great prudence and skill. He had visited every cardinal in his cell, presenting himself quite humbly, and without mentioning that he wanted to be elected, but promising that if the opportunity arose he would do all he could for each one. For years he had been at pains to study his colleagues and find out all he could about them; now he knew how best to approach them.

He effected a reconciliation with Cherubi, whom he had treated harshly in the past, asking forgiveness for having sent him back to his gondolas, and adding wittily that perhaps one day it would turn out to be prophetic, and Cherubi would achieve his ambition of presiding over the church in Venice.

Montalto's discernment was so keen it amounted almost to divination. Whereas most of the cardinals wrongly supposed I wanted to be secretary of state again under the new pope, he realized I was tired of the job. Instead of promising it to me when I visited him in his cell, he spoke only of his attachment to the grand duchy of Tuscany and his desire that it should retain its independence "against all comers" — no doubt referring to Philip II. He was well aware that my elder brother, the Grand Duke, was childless, that one day I would be called upon to succeed him, and that that was now my only ambition.

He showed the same skill in steering a safe course between the Charybdis of the Spanish faction and the Scylla of the French. He promised Farnese his vote, and did in fact vote for him, though only when Farnese had no chance of being elected. He spoke to d'Este about the duchy of Ferrara as he had spoken to me about Tuscany. Moreover, he was affable though dignified with the Archduke of Austria: he was able to be useful to him because he spoke German.

Knowing how fond Cardinal Altemps was of his brother the Marquis, Montalto gave him to understand that the Marquis would make a very good governor of the Borgo, the quarter of Rome that includes the Vatican. To San Sisto he praised his brother Giacomo, expressing the hope that after the election he would be confirmed in his post as general of the papal army. He made no promises to Alessandrino, probably because the man was so overbearing; he merely flattered his inordinate pride with equally inordinate compliments. With Rusticucci, whom he considered both modest and able, he ventured a few subtle hints, having known for a long time that he aspired to become secretary of state.

His attentions were so skillfully measured out and his demeanor so modest and natural that the less perspicacious swallowed the bait without realizing it. The sharper ones among us, knowing he was a man of his word, stored his promises and admired his adroitness without necessarily being taken in. Before the conclave, we had regarded Montalto as a virtuous and able prelate, but the diplomatic talents he showed now made him rise considerably in our estimation. It must be admitted that when you see a man so cut out for success — as long as that success does not do you any harm — you feel like helping him and making a friend of him rather than an enemy.

I knew our little group could never rally enough people behind Montalto unless we managed to win Cardinal di San Sisto to our side. Undistinguished as he was in both heart and mind, he had much influence over the many cardinals created by his uncle, Gregory XIII, for the simple reason that he had engineered their nominations.

San Sisto was tall, pale, and spineless, like a candle. His character was much the same: he was weak, irresolute, and fickle. I do not want to push the metaphor too far and say he melted like a candle, but one day when I was talking to him, I grabbed his arm in the heat of the moment and could feel neither bone nor muscle. I wondered for a moment what on earth he *was* made of.

To win him over, we put our heads together and came up with a little ruse I do not like to describe as pious, though it did aim at the good of the state and of Christendom. Then we primed Cherubi, and sent him to see San Sisto.

Cherubi is talkative, kind, and exuberant, and, because he is a blunderer, people think he is straightforward and frank. He spoke to

San Sisto bluntly, if speciously.

"My lord, I want to give you a friendly warning. The matter is still very secret, but Montalto's candidacy is so popular that by all calculations he's the one most likely to be elected."

"What! What!" said San Sisto. "But he's keeping so quiet! I haven't seen him bustling around."

"He doesn't bustle, my lord, but he does make progress, and his election is almost certain now. If he hasn't approached Your Eminence, it may be because he thinks you're against him, as was your uncle, the Most Holy and Late Lamented Gregory XIII."

"No, no!" cried San Sisto in horror. "I'm not in the least against him! I think both his virtues and his talents make him eminently suitable."

"How is it then that he hasn't approached you?"

"Now I come to think of it, he has. He said very kind things to me about my brother. If I remember rightly, he even said he hoped that under the next pope he'd be confirmed in his post as general of the papal army."

"Well, that certainly was an opening, my lord. And if I were to give Your Eminence a word of advice, I'd say don't let that opening close again and leave you out."

"I'll think about it," said San Sisto, shaken. "And many thanks, Cherubi, for your kindness, and for speaking to me so frankly."

When Cherubi told us about this interview, we decided that San Sisto was so spineless and changeable we had better strike while the iron was hot. We sent Cardinals Riario and Gustavillanio to see him. They had just joined our cause, and they spoke to him in the same strain as had Cherubi. As a final touch, we sent Alessandrino to him.

This choice of messenger was mine, and I may say in all modesty it was very apt; it took into account the characters of both men.

Alessandrino was the most imposing of all of us, and that was why, for all his talent, he never had the slightest chance of being elected pope. He was tall, strong, still young, and intelligent; he was also imperious and arrogant. But the considerations that prevented him from ever being *papabile* also made him an influential voice in all the conclaves in which he took part.

He was much briefer and more abrupt with San Sisto than Cherubi had been, and did not bother addressing him as "my lord" or "Your Eminence." They were of equal rank, but he did not use such courtesies to an individual he regarded as his inferior.

"San Sisto," he said, drawing him aside in

an authoritative manner no one else in the conclave ever used, "I want a word with you, please. Do you respect Montalto?"

"Oh, very much, very much," San Sisto said hastily.

"A word of advice, then. Wake up and exert yourself in his favor. In any case, you'll only be in at the victory. His candidacy is so well sewn up, he's bound to be elected. But you don't want the next pope to have a grudge against you, do you? You don't want him to treat you as your uncle treated him?"

"What? What? Is his election as certain as that?"

"Consider it done, my dear fellow," said Alessandrino, fixing him with his black eyes. "It's up to you to decide whether to act. I'm only giving you some friendly advice."

"Decide? Act?" San Sisto said. "How can I decide to support him without consulting the cardinals my uncle created?"

"Do you mean to say," asked Alessandrino, "that you, their leader, are going to follow them? Shouldn't you do the opposite, and show them the way?"

"I ought to consult them, at least," said San Sisto, who seemed utterly confused. "What's the difference?"

"It lies in how you ask the question. For example, if you say, 'What do you think of

571

Montalto's candidacy?' you leave them free to decide for themselves. But if you say, 'I'm going to vote for Montalto. What do you think about it?' you'll be guiding their choice."

"That's a good way of putting it," said San Sisto. "I must remember that."

When Alessandrino told me about this, I remembered that the Cardinal Archduke of Austria, as well as being Philip II's cousin, was also one of the cardinals created by Gregory, at his nephew's instigation. So, summoning up the little German I knew, I went to his cell and began, prudently, to sound him out.

"My lord, some of us, including Cardinal di San Sisto and myself, are considering voting for Montalto, whom we regard as a very saintly and able man. What do you think?"

"Who? Who did you say?" exclaimed Cardinal Andrea.

"Montalto."

"Who's he?" Yawning behind his glove, the *Homo germanicus* looked down at me out of his big pale-blue eyes — as well he might, since my head came only to his stomach.

"Your Eminence must know Montalto! He's about sixty-five and uses . . ." I didn't know the German for "crutches," so I mimed Montalto using them.

"Oh, him!" Cardinal Andrea said. "Of

course I know him. A charming old man. He's been very useful to me. How could I forget that it's thanks to him I've been allowed to have an armchair in my cell? What did you say his name was?"

"Montalto."

"Oh, yes, Montalto. I must fix that in my memory. Montalto. Well, why not Montalto? He's a very amiable old fellow. And supported by San Sisto. He speaks German, too! A pope who speaks German — what an honor that would be for Austria."

Without much reason, he started to laugh, or chuckle, his big belly shaking. I laughed politely too. The Austrian Archduke clearly did not take our Italian affairs seriously.

"What I would like to know, Your Eminence," I insisted, "is whether Montalto's candidacy would be agreeable to Spain."

The Cardinal Archduke grew serious again. He took a folded piece of paper from the inside pocket of his robe.

"This," he said, unfolding it, "is a list of the cardinals my cousin absolutely does not want to have as pope."

I was staggered to hear him speak so undiplomatically, and more astonished still when he adjusted his spectacles and began to read the list of black sheep aloud. Aloud! I found it amusing, but not surprising, that my name was on the list, as well as d'Este's, the French cardinals', with the exception of Pellevés, and some others', which I, being discreet, prefer not to name.

"Well," he went on, "one thing is clear: my cousin doesn't regard Montalto as persona non grata. So, all right: Montalto will do."

"So, Your Eminence, may I tell my friend San Sisto that you're in favor of Montalto's candidacy?"

"Certainly."

"I thank you, Your Eminence."

After bowing low, I turned and was going through the door when he said: "May I ask what *your* name is, my friend?"

Without a second thought, I replied: "I am Cardinal San Gregorio, Your Eminence, entirely at your service."

May God forgive me for the joke that was also a lie. But how could I say I was the Medici written down on his list of rejected candidates? And what did it matter? Ever since he had arrived at the conclave, the Cardinal Archduke had been mixing up all our names. If he did happen to quote me, no one would dare tell him there was no such person as Cardinal San Gregorio.

On the evening of April 23, the original nucleus of Montalto's supporters met in my cell to consider how his candidacy was progressing. It seemed very promising. Alessandrino's cavalry charge had won over San Sisto, who had then carried out his promise to consult the cardinals created by his uncle, with excellent results. I reported on my conversation with the Cardinal Archduke, and how I had secured the support of the Spanish faction. D'Este had won over two of the French cardinals; he had not approached the third, an unregenerate supporter of the Holy League. Santa Severina, Il Putto Papa, as they called him now, had fluttered from group to group spreading the news that Montalto's chances were growing by the hour. The sound and solid Rusticucci had done even better: he had gone to Farnese and asked him straight out if he would vote for Montalto if his name was put forward.

Farnese's reaction had been both friendly and bitter.

"Eleven cardinals voted for me," he said. "Yes, you heard — only eleven! Isn't that disgraceful, for me? But Montalto was one of them. Tell him I'll remember that. At least, if Torres doesn't arrive meantime."

This made us decide to act the following day, April 24, although we could count on the votes of only slightly less than half of the conclave. A difficulty arose at the last minute: San Sisto came and said in his soft voice that he would vote for Montalto only if the latter would adopt his name if he became pope. I thought this extremely childish, but knowing how obstinate the weak-willed can be, I decided not to object. I sent Rusticucci to Montalto to ask him if, as pope, he would agree to be called Sisto, and if he had any objection to our proclaiming him pope the following day after Mass.

The answer was swift and resolute: "Sixtus I and Sixtus II were both saints and martyrs in ancient Rome: I would be very glad to bear their name. April 24 is a Wednesday, and Wednesday is a propitious day for me: it was on a Wednesday that I took religious orders and on a Wednesday that I became a cardinal."

Encouraged by this good omen, we decided to precipitate events the next day in chapel, after Mass.

Unluckily, just as it was ending, the arrival of two cardinals was announced. Our group was dismayed as the conclave flocked to the door to greet them. Would the Spanish faction take advantage of the confusion to proclaim Torres pope?

But as soon as we saw the new arrivals, we heaved a sigh of relief. True, Cardinal de' Vercelli was a member of that faction, in the flesh — and plenty of it — but the Spanish cardinal was Madruccio, not Torres. We scarcely knew him, so he probably never understood why we seemed so glad to see him that day.

We went back into the chapel, where, as was the custom, the master of ceremonies began to read out to the newcomers the bulls governing the election. Though not actually obliged to, many cardinals, out of politeness, attended this rather tedious ceremony.

That was the moment we chose to act. I nodded to Alessandrino. He went out, accompanied by San Sisto, who gave his group of cardinals a significant glance as he left. They joined him one by one. Then, as had been agreed, d'Este rose and left the chapel, alone, closely observed by the Spanish faction. At regular intervals after that, Cherubi, Santa Severina, Rusticucci, Riario, and Gustavillanio went out, each taking with him the cardinals he had convinced to join us.

The cardinals who were not in our group did not notice these departures. The conclave usually thinned out during the interminable reading of the bulls, which all of us had heard five or six times already.

We gathered in the royal hall, where the first thing we did was take a count. We had a pleasant surprise. Since the previous day, our numbers had increased. We had a majority — a small majority of two. And not all were determined: you had only to look at some faces to see anxiety and uncertainty.

San Sisto's changeable nature nearly spoiled everything again. Now, he said he would vote for Montalto only if the Cardinal Archduke told him in person that Montalto's election would not offend Spain.

I took Santa Severina and Alessandrino aside and asked them to go back into the chapel: the first, who spoke some German, to fetch Cardinal Andrea; the second, to ask Farnese to join us.

Farnese arrived first, and understood immediately what was going on. Since he was really neither for nor against, he decided to say nothing. He merely looked contemptuously at all the cardinals who had failed to vote for him and were now proposing to vote for a former keeper of pigs. On the other hand, great prince that he was, he thought it unworthy of his honor to refuse to support Montalto, when Montalto had supported him.

Santa Severina had great difficulty in rousing the Cardinal Archduke, who had fallen asleep listening to the bulls, and then in making him understand that we were waiting for him in the royal hall. At last he came, one hand on Santa Severina's shoulder. As soon as he saw us, he swiveled his pale, astonished eyes around the gathering, saw me — though, thank God, without remembering the name

I'd given him — and said to me: "What's this all about, Cardinal?"

Before I had time to answer, Alessandrino did. "Your Eminence, we want to elect Cardinal Montalto pope."

"Montalto!" said Andrea, wide awake at last and throwing up his hands. Then, in stentorian tones: "*Ja, Montalto!*"

Falling from Austrian lips, that was decisive. The last hesitations vanished, and it was with enthusiasm that we set off in procession to the chapel, led by the Cardinal Archduke, Farnese, San Sisto, and Alessandrino. I stayed in the third rank, not wanting my hand in the election to be seen too clearly before it had succeeded.

When we entered the chapel, the master of ceremonies interrupted his reading in surprise, and the cardinals who had stayed there and knew nothing of our machinations looked at us in petrified silence, some turning pale and others red. The four at our head advanced toward Montalto, and San Sisto said loudly: "Your Eminence, we have acclaimed you pope, and I myself ask you to take the name Sisto."

"I shall certainly do so," said Montalto.

He could not say more, for his voice was drowned by cries of *"Papa! Papa!"* from his supporters, who crowded around him to kiss him on the mouth, as is the custom.

Then Alessandrino turned to the cardinals who were still seated, gazed at them with his dark eyes, and said in a commanding, almost threatening voice: "Do you want to take part in a formal vote? Or will you join with us in electing him by acclamation?"

They stood up, some hastily, others more slowly, but in the end they all rose, cried, *"Papa! Papa!"* and went to join their colleagues surrounding Montalto and singing his praises.

When I saw this, I went over to the master of ceremonies, who was standing open-mouthed on his rostrum, his hands tangled in the bulls. I told him in a whisper what he had to say.

Though his mind was slow, his voice was strong, and he had no difficulty making himself heard above the cries of *"Papa! Papa!"* echoing through the chapel.

"Your Eminences, I see you have unanimously and by acclamation elected the Most Reverend and Illustrious Cardinal Montalto to be pope. As soon as His Holiness has chosen the name he wishes to be known by as pope, His Eminence Secretary of State Cardinal de' Medici will announce it to the people."

There was a sudden silence, and the new Pope said, firmly and clearly: "I take the name of Sisto Quinto, Sixtus V."

# His Excellency Armando Veniero, Venetian Ambassador

When the conclave was over, and the cardinals, freed from their incarceration, returned with a sigh of relief to their marble palaces, I was overcome by a kind of retrospective terror when I learned we had very nearly had a Spanish pope. I literally trembled like a leaf at the thought. How could a Spanish pope have stopped Philip II from seizing the rest of a peninsula of which he already owned more than half? Venice would have gone the way of the duchy of Milan, the Kingdom of Naples, and Sicily. And my own dear country would have lost its liberty, its merchant fleet, and its flourishing trade all over the world, and would instead have groaned like the Low Countries beneath the yoke of Spain and the Austrian generals.

The end of a conclave is the beginning of indiscretions. It was as if the cardinals, back among their creature comforts, felt they could relax and tell their secrets. So, I got to know of various things. Some were of great political interest, and I shall keep those to myself. Others shed an ironical light on men and manners, and of these none amused me more than Cardinal Alessandrino's comment when he decided to support Montalto's candidacy: "I see no reason to oppose the poor old man. We'll be the masters."

I wrote this to the Doge and senators of Venice, among other more serious matters, knowing how they like to amuse themselves sometimes at the expense of the Romans. They were so delighted with Alessandrino's remark that, throughout the whole five years of Sixtus V's reign, I couldn't appear in Venice — either to take the air by the lagoon or to deliver a personal report to the Doge — without meeting a senator who laughed and said, "Well, Armando, how's the poor old man?"

As a matter of fact, the "poor old man" was the master from the very first minute of his reign — a stern master too, who made evildoers tremble: the thief in his lair, the whore in the tavern, and the bandit in the mountains, not to mention venal judges, priests who bought and sold preferment, dealers in indulgences, shady bankers, absentee bishops, and nobles who gave outlaws asylum.

Even before he was crowned, he instituted the death penalty for anyone found bearing firearms in the streets of Rome, by day or by night. And when, out of bravado, two young brothers belonging to the nobility went out carrying small arquebuses, he had them thrown in jail and, despite the pleas of cardinals and important families, two gallows were put up on the Ponte Sant' Angelo and the culprits were hanged side by side.

The results of this inflexibility were not slow to appear; I could observe them from my window, which overlooked the Tiber. During the reign of Gregory XIII, not a day had gone by without my Venetian valet saying as he drew the curtains in the morning: "Another corpse floating down the river, Your Excellency! This city's a den of murderers!"

I don't know where the murderers went after the accession of Sixtus V, but the fact is that, although dead bodies didn't disappear from the Tiber altogether, they did become much rarer.

Soon after the advent of the new Pope, Cardinal de' Medici told me about something that struck him as symptomatic of the new reign. One day, riding along a street in an open coach, he saw two respectably dressed men engaged in a fierce fight. He stopped the coach, and, on inquiring the reason for the brawl, was told that two of Cardinal di San Sisto's servants had come to blows over some woman. Medici, who was such a misogynist he could hardly bear the sight of a woman, especially if she was beautiful, thought this

583

a ridiculous reason for such fighting. Taking advantage of a moment when the two men paused for breath and merely glared at each other, he offered them ten piasters each to be reconciled, or at least to stop fighting. His offer was rejected out of hand, and the fisticuffs began again.

Eventually, one downed the other. He pinned him to the ground with one knee, held him by the throat, and drew his stiletto. The crowd gasped and held its breath, but the man suddenly lowered his arm, sheathed his weapon, and said: "You can thank Pope Sixtus. If I weren't afraid of him, I'd have slit your throat."

"If you'd thought of that sooner," said Medici, in whom the banker was never far from the surface, "you'd be ten piasters better off."

But he stayed and listened to the comments of the people around him, which struck him as significant. They all agreed with the man who had spared his enemy's life. The Pope who'd had two young noblemen hanged for walking in the streets with guns was not only feared, but also respected. The people admired such swift and, above all, such even-handed justice.

Medici was one of the cardinals who had exerted himself to get Sixtus elected. But he was incapable of appreciating a man of such caliber, and was therefore amazed by the vigor and rigor with which this great Pope took things in hand and briskly reformed the evil ways that had characterized both church and state in the previous reign.

Medici was extremely witty and sharp, but his heart was arid and his senses inert. He loved nothing and no one. He was indifferent to good and evil, regarding them as equally unimportant to his purpose. And his only purpose was gaining power — or power in its other form: money. He was quite unable to understand a man like Sixtus, for whom the supreme throne was only an effective means of correcting abuse and iniquity. Sixtus, nearly sixty-five, was still the pure-hearted Franciscan who had taken the habit at twenty with the firm resolve of making good triumph over evil wherever Providence pleased to place him.

Less than a week after the new Pope's accession, a servant came to me from Montegiordano with a note from Prince Orsini asking me to see him. Having learned that it was difficult for him to walk, I sent word to say I would call on him the same day.

I was struck by the change in his appearance, and by how hard it was for him to move about.

After he had offered me something to drink

— it was the beginning of May and very hot — he said: "Armando, I'd like you to ask Sixtus to grant me an audience."

"But, Paolo," I replied, "you're a great prince, a great power in the state. Why don't you ask yourself?"

"I want you to be present, Armando, and to guarantee my safety the entire time I'm inside the Vatican."

"Why me particularly, Paolo?"

There was a shadow of a smile on his lips. "Dear friend, do you want me to ask Count de Olivares to go with me?"

"God forbid!" said I, smiling too. "To speak plainly, you want the backing and protection of the Venetian Ambassador. Are you afraid that if you go into the Vatican, you might not be able to get out again?"

"Yes," he said.

"I don't see why. Sixtus must have read della Pace's report, so how could he think you guilty of murdering his nephew?"

"That's not what I'm afraid of. I took up arms against his predecessor, and he has some reason to regard me as a rebel. Especially since, despite quite an ominous order from him, I still haven't sent away the outlaws who live in my courtyard."

"Forgive me, but isn't that somewhat rash?"

"I promised them my protection and am

586

therefore responsible for them."

"They don't all deserve it."

"No doubt. But how can I turn them out unless I get some assurance they won't be thrown straight into prison?"

"Have you asked the Pope for that assurance?"

"Yes, by letter. He hasn't answered. And he can't be very pleased by my having taken advantage of the interregnum to remarry Vittoria."

I thought for a while before I said: "I don't think your fears are really justified, Paolo. But if you want me to go with you —"

"I do."

"I'll have to refer it to Venice."

"That will take days!"

Suddenly there was something so tragic in his eyes and voice that I wondered if he thought his days were now numbered. I tried to conceal my sadness by burying my nose in my cup of wine.

"You're right," I said, after a pause. "It will take a long time to hear from Venice. And I suppose, in this heat, you must be anxious to leave Rome and enjoy the cool shade with your wife in Bracciano. All right, then, Paolo, I agree. I'll ask the Holy Father to give us an audience, and I'll do it this very day."

I made my request to the Vatican on the

morning of May 2. The same day, at five in the afternoon, a courier from the Vatican brought me the answer: the Holy Father would see me and Prince Paolo Giordano Orsini the following day, at ten in the morning.

I sent a footman to tell Paolo, and to say I would call for him in my coach at nine o'clock on the third. True, the streets were quiet now, and there was no longer need for the Prince to be afraid of stones. But who was going to stop the Romans, especially the women, from hurling insults, or even rotten apples, as he went by?

We went to the Vatican in my coach, with the windows shut and the curtains drawn. Paolo was pale. The slightest movement was painful for him, and he had to lean on my shoulder and that of his secretary to climb the stairs.

It wasn't a week since his coronation, but the new Pope's methods were already becoming established. Unlike his negligent predecessor, Sixtus V never put off a decision, and once it was made, he never went back on it. When someone asked for an audience, it was either granted or refused in forty-eight hours. If it was refused, there was no point in insisting. If it was granted, the audience began exactly on time. You were told by the chamberlain that it must not exceed the stated length.

The Prince began by offering the Pope his earnest and respectful felicitations on the "most lofty and august dignity" to which he had just acceded. Then he added: "I come, Most Holy Father, to the leader of Christendom and to my sovereign in order to swear loyalty and obedience and, as the humblest of his servants and vassals, to put at his disposal all my forces and possessions."

"Prince Orsini, that is more than I ask," Sixtus answered.

This interruption made the Prince uncomfortable. For a moment he was at a loss for words, and sweat showed on his brow.

"Go on," said the Pope.

"The links that bind the house of Orsini to the sovereign of Rome," the Prince said, as if reciting a lesson, "are too ancient and too well known to need rehearsing. I should just like to recall with gratitude that my lands at Bracciano were elevated into a duchy by your illustrious predecessor."

"And you demonstrated your gratitude," said the Pope caustically, "by fomenting an insurrection against him."

This blow was so sudden and direct that the Prince knew he must abandon formality and confront the Pope on the plane of fact.

"Most Holy Father," he said with some firmness, "I did not foment an insurrection. I joined in one that had been raised by the nobility in order to right a wrong. As soon as that wrong was righted, I put down the popular rising."

"True. But you had no authority to put right the injustice you refer to. You were not related to the person who had been imprisoned."

"There was a link between us," said the Prince bravely. "The same accusation hung over us both, and charged us with a crime we had not committed."

"We'll come to your innocence later," said the Pope. "For the moment, make your request, and let it be brief."

"It is this," said the Prince, invigorated by the verbal duel. "When Gregory XIII died, certain theologians held that the ban on my remarrying contained in his *precetto* was no longer valid. I therefore took Vittoria Accoramboni as my wife for the second time. I humbly ask Your Holiness to allow things to remain as they are."

"Here is my opinion on the matter," said Sixtus, giving the Prince a sharp look and speaking loudly and resolutely. "First, the theologians you refer to, some from conviction, some out of greed, gave an opinion they now try to slide out of by saying it was extorted under duress. That is a specious excuse. If they did not want to be constrained, they could have refused to go to Montegiordano in the first place, the purpose of their meeting being obvious. Second, they had no authority whatsoever to offer an opinion in this matter. I shall take no account of their deliberations."

I glanced at the Prince: he was swaying and so pale I thought he was going to swoon. Unluckily, I was too far away to prevent a fall that would be bound to do his leg great harm. I felt very sorry for him. The Pope's words seemed to sound the knell of all his hopes.

"As for the *precetto*," the Pope went on, "a distinction must be made between those who requested the dissolution of the marriage and those who agreed to it. The first were motivated by sordid considerations of inheritance, and the second harbored a grudge. I shall say no more on this point."

I thought he had said enough already! He had not named either of them, but he had rapped both Medici and Gregory over the knuckles. True, the latter was dead, and the former needed the Pope's help too badly to try to harm him. I certainly admired the Pope's character. He reminded me of my father, who, when he was doge of Venice — scarcely for a year, alas, before he died — skillfully alternated the subtlest diplomacy with the most brutal frankness, as the case required.

As for the Prince, the color came back into his face, and he was clearly encouraged by hearing his enemies so roughly categorized.

"As for the innocence you proclaim yet again," said the Pope, "it has two faces: one is light and the other dark."

"Dark, Your Holiness?" said the Prince indignantly.

"You shall tell me about all that in due course," interrupted Sixtus. "Meanwhile, I will concede one point: there is absolutely no proof that you were implicated in the murder of . . ." He was probably going to say "my son" or "my unfortunate son," but instead went on impassively: "Of Francesco Peretti. On that point, the police report drawn up by poor della Pace implicitly exonerated you. And the evidence of the unfrocked monk whom you sent to me, and who made a full confession, probably much fuller than you expected, showed that the murder was planned with Machiavellian cunning by one of your relatives — a real gallows bird — in order to harm my . . ."

Again he checked himself, and continued with an effort: "To harm Vittoria Peretti. That's the light side. Now let us consider the dark. It is, unfortunately, beyond all doubt that the ruffian I have just mentioned would never have plotted to murder Peretti if he had not known of your fatal passion for Peretti's wife. To quote the Ten Commandments, you coveted your neighbor's wife, you wooed her with numerous letters, you pursued her with ceaseless attentions, and finally you prevailed on her weakness to obtain various guilty encounters, one at Santa Maria and others at the Villa Sorghini in Rome."

Here Sixtus paused, his piercing eyes fixed on those of the Prince, as if to give him a chance to reply. But it was a good half-minute before the Prince spoke, and that is long for a silence, especially one that follows precise accusations. As he told me later, he realized then that the unfrocked monk had not only been Lodovico's go-between in the matter of Peretti's murder, but also, before that, he had spied on the Prince's meetings with Vittoria. His evidence, of which the Prince had known only a part, turned out to be double-edged: it cleared him of the murder, but it convicted him of adultery.

"I haven't much time," said the Pope. "So I will say this in conclusion. Prince Orsini, you are not guilty of Francesco Peretti's murder, but you are certainly indirectly responsible for it."

He left another pause for a reply, but the

Prince seemed stunned and incapable of uttering a sound. The theologians, Medici, and Gregory XIII had all been hauled over the coals, and now it was his turn. The rebuke was so severe that it might have worse consequences than the annulment of his second marriage.

"Prince Orsini," the Pope said loudly, enunciating every word, "I am not speaking to you as an enemy. I wish no harm to your property, your titles, or your liberty, still less to your life. Because both you and your spouse undoubtedly intend to give yourselves to one another, that constitutes the sacrament of marriage. I therefore shall not issue a *precetto* annulling your second marriage. But I do require that, to use your own words, you will be my loyal and obedient servant, and I shall see that you are. I have already ordered you to eject from Montegiordano those you sheltered there under the previous reign by a privilege I grant to no one. I repeat that order, and I require you to obey it within twenty-four hours."

"Most Holy Father," said the Prince, trying to speak firmly, "I have written to you on this subject. It seems to me incompatible with my honor to hand these men over to the Bargello."

"Prince," thundered the Pope, with a terrible look, "it would certainly be incompatible with your honor to disobey your sovereign! Besides, I am capable of distinguishing between bandits and those who have merely been banished. The exiles are mostly respectable folk who for various reasons were unlucky enough to displease my predecessor. I shall examine each of their cases, and most will be amnestied. As for the bandits, if their crimes are proved, they will take their last look at the sky through a noose."

"Most Holy Father," said the Prince, bowing his head in submission, "it shall be as you wish."

"When?"

"Tomorrow, before noon."

"One last word: I am told you are having trouble with your leg. I advise you to go and take the waters at Albano, near Padua. Padua belongs to Venice, and because of the glorious services you have rendered the Most Serene Republic in the past, you will be among friends there."

The Prince started. "Most Holy Father," he said, "how am I to understand what you say? As a banishment?"

"Not at all. As urgent advice that I expect to see followed. I do not hate you, Prince Orsini, but I do hate the disorder your passion has introduced into the state. I would like it to have time to fade from people's memories."

He straightened his powerful torso, placed his great hands flat on the arms of his chair, and raised his heavy head. Then, with a look that conveyed as clearly as his words that he wanted neither thanks, protestations of devotion, nor respectful farewells, he said: "Prince Orsini, our interview is at an end."

## *Giuseppe Giacobbe, Leader of the Roman Ghetto*

By 1585, and the accession of the present great and noble Pope — truly inspired by the spirit of Adonai, despite the fact that he professes the Christian heresy — our people had for a quarter of a century been subject to more and more persecution in the Papal States. In 1569, Pius V had gone so far as to expel all Jews from his possessions, except those who lived in Rome and Ancona. And by an incredible refinement of cruelty, he threatened them with fines, confiscation of property, and imprisonment if they did not leave within three months.

Such a bad example in high places awoke the age-old hostility against us. Not even in Rome and Ancona were we free from restrictions, insults, wrongs, and humiliations that have always been our lot among the Gentiles.

Those of us unfortunate enough to be only tenants in our houses found our rents doubled overnight. The land allowed us for our cemeteries was restricted. Our religious ceremonies were strictly forbidden. We had to wear yellow whenever we went outside the ghetto. Our taxes were increased. Jewish doctors — the best in Rome — could no longer enter Christian houses. All kinds of restrictions were imposed on our trade. In the special courts set up to hear our cases, we were certain to lose if our adversary was a Christian.

Vexation became our daily bread. Butchers either refused to serve us or gave us pork instead of the beef we asked for. If we refused it, they called the police. And there were the jokes. "What's the difference," they would ask in Rome, "between a Jewish dog and a Christian dog?" The answer was: "A Jewish dog is fatter, from eating all the pork his master is forced to buy."

Gregory XIII was no better disposed toward us than Pius V had been, but because he was indolent by nature, the special measures against us were less rigorously applied during his reign.

Then, in strange circumstances, I came to meet the new Pope.

It is typical that there are always some Jews

who want to be more Jewish than everyone else. Some of them, soon after the accession of Pope Sixtus, decided to print and circulate the Talmud. That was a perfectly worthy idea, but it needed permission from the Vatican.

I tried in vain to make them see how foolish and useless it would be to try to do this. How could the Vatican, which had forbidden the practice of our religion, authorize the publication of one of our holy books? When Montaigne came to Rome, his *Essays* had been seized and censored, and there was nothing heretical about them.

But the more I argued, the more excited and enthusiastic the zealots became. They almost accused me. "Be careful, Giacobbe!" they would say. "You're so cautious you're in danger of becoming craven and losing your Jewish faith!"

So, despite my protests and without my support, they made their absurd request to the Vatican. Young Cardinal Santa Severina, who received the petition, called it "an incredible piece of audacity," and asked the new Pope to hand the petitioners over to the Inquisition.

I was horror-struck, as was everyone in the ghetto. Stupid as the zealots had been, they were still our brothers. If they were burned at the stake, there might well be a new outburst of popular persecution. Experience had told us that for every Jew who was burned in public in the light of the flames, ten others were stabbed to death by fanatics in dark alleys.

The zealots were, of course, terrified, and came to me with their tails between their legs to ask me to intercede for them with the Pope. It was a good opportunity to scold them, and I took advantage of it.

"You poor fools, why did you have to take such risks when there was so little chance of success? We have twenty or so copies of the Talmud left, in the excellent Venice edition. And how many of us know enough Hebrew or Aramaic to read them? About ten rabbis and scholars! With your request to publish a new edition, you have given the Vatican the idea that we want to proselytize. We don't want anything of the sort! That's the only reason the Gentiles tolerate us. Otherwise, we'd have gone the same way as the Lutherans long ago."

Then came the tears and lamentations. "Giacobbe, Giacobbe! You're not going to abandon us to our fate, are you? You're our leader!"

"A leader you have called a coward," I replied. "What am I supposed to do now? Go and confront the Pope and offer myself as a scapegoat? Take on myself all the consequences of your stupidity? We know very well this Pope used to be the Grand Inquisitor in Venice, and he has been a member of the Holy Office all his life. How can you hope that he would be merciful?"

At this, the supplications burst forth louder than before. Everyone joined in: relatives, wives, children, cousins, neighbors, even babes at the breast. They moaned and groaned, tore their hair and beards, rent their garments — or at least pretended to — threw themselves at my feet, grabbed at my hands, and swore eternal gratitude.

So then I did what I'd decided to do anyway, and what they, deep down, always knew I would, because I was their leader and had never let them down: I asked the Pope for an audience.

It was granted within forty-eight hours, though I was told that, instead of receiving me in public, he would see me in private. I was to use a side entrance, which I did in fear and trembling, not knowing what fate awaited me inside this enemy fortress. Who was I, after all, lost in the labyrinth of this great palace, where the very walls were hostile to me and my faith? Nothing but a little old Jew in a long yellow robe, with a pepper-and-salt beard standing on end with fear and a skull seething with anxiety beneath its little cap.

Sixtus V received me in a small, simple room, where we were alone except for a monsignor, quite a handsome fellow but presumably dumb, since he communicated with the Pope by signs. His Holiness, as the Gentiles call him, was sitting, not on a throne, but on an ordinary chair, with the Monsignor standing by him.

"Sit on that stool, Giacobbe," said the Pope briskly, "and, for goodness' sake, stop trembling! I'm not a monster who's going to eat you. I'm a man just like you. I feel cold when it snows, I'm hot in the dog days, and if I put my hand in a flame it burns. I suffer from the same diseases as you do, and I'm just as mortal. So tell me your business quickly."

I told him about our zealots' request.

"Which Talmud?" he cried. "The Jerusalem or the Babylonian?"

"The Babylonian."

"If I'm not mistaken, that was published in 1520, by a Christian publisher in Venice."

"Yes, but that edition is out of print, Most Holy Father."

"Ask the publisher or his descendants to reprint it then. If the Venetian Republic allows you to do that, I have no objection. Only the ignorant think the Talmud contains passages that are anti-Christian. I go by the opinion of Reuchlin, a scholar who knew Hebrew and Aramaic and read both editions carefully. He never found anything in either that might offend the faith of a Christian."

"If only His Eminence Cardinal Santa Severina saw it as you do, Most Holy Father," I ventured to reply.

"It doesn't matter whether he does or not," the Pope replied, exchanging a smile with the Monsignor. "I have taken the matter out of his hands. And in order that the Grand Inquisitor doesn't take it up, I've requested the Talmud be examined by the Congregation of the Index. That is the same as saying I've asked a lot of blind men to read it, for not one of them knows Hebrew."

I was doubly delighted to hear this. Because it dispelled my fears of fresh persecution, and because the Pope's strategy of giving the book to a lot of blind men to read seemed to belong to Biblical tradition. From then on, I had high hopes of a sovereign who concealed so much wit and humanity beneath his rough appearance. So much learning too; unlike Santa Severina, he had read Reuchlin and was not taken in by the slanders about the Talmud invented by malice and spread by ignorance.

Nor were my hopes disappointed. Not long afterward, the Pope promulgated his bull *Christiana Pietas,* which greatly improved the

602

status of the Jewish community in the Papal States. We were given the right to live in all cities. More extraordinary still, the bull granted us liberty of worship and the right to build synagogues and open new cemeteries. Our legal cases were to be tried in ordinary courts, instead of special ones as hitherto. To our great relief, we no longer had to wear yellow robes. Before, when we'd had to do so at fairs and markets, they made us the target of ill usage at the hands of both competitors and customers. Jewish doctors — who had introduced into current medical teaching, based on Galen and Hippocrates, not only traditional Jewish medicine, but also the Arab medicine they'd learned in Andalusia — were given permission, long asked for but never before granted, to treat Christian patients.

This bull was supplemented by a decree, drawn up by Secretary of State Rusticucci but prompted by Sixtus, that forbade the Pope's subjects, on pain of fine, to insult, humiliate, strike, or spit on Jews. Two more provisions lifted a great burden: landlords were forbidden to double their rents when leasing houses to Jews, and butchers were forbidden to sell us any other meat than the kind we asked for. Those who tried to ignore this decree could be reported by us to the Bargello, and they would immediately be punished.

Since ghetto folk joke about everything, it became common, when someone asked how one was, to answer, "Well, you can see how thin my dog's getting!"

We rejoiced greatly at having our disabilities so much reduced, and the other leaders of the ghetto met with me to decide what kind of present we could give this enlightened Pope to show our gratitude.

Our race is good at arguing and holding forth, so the debate was both long and passionate. Finally it was concluded that the only gift the chief of the Christians could accept from us would be a richly decorated pectoral cross.

I had nothing to do with this decision, but as soon as it was arrived at, my colleagues asked me to make the cross, with all the care and skill I bring to my craft. Unlike many others, I not only sell but also design and make the jewelry I trade in. For a long time, to make them more eager, I wouldn't agree. When I finally did, I insisted, knowing how changeable my brethren can be, that the necessary money be got together before the work was started. Arguments began again. Each one wanted to contribute a share proportional to his income, but since that figure was always left vague, to help evade Roman taxes, it was a great struggle to establish who was really rich and who was as poor as he claimed to be. When, after endless difficulties, the collection was made, the result was paradoxical: stingy as the individual members of the ghetto were, or seemed to be, the community as a whole was very generous. We collected the enormous sum of a hundred thousand piasters.

To protect myself from suspicion and slander, I declined to keep the money at my house, or even to take charge of it. I arranged for five treasurers to be elected. They were to pay when necessary for the gold and precious stones I would use in the work. Even so, there was one person who had the impudence to say, in front of the whole council: "What about you, Giacobbe? Aren't you going to make a contribution?"

I glared at him. "I'm contributing my labor and my skill!"

Unlike many others, I don't want to blow my own trumpet, so I won't describe the cross I made with so much trouble. Suffice it to say that when I exhibited it in my shop window, everyone in the ghetto filed past to see it, fascinated by its beauty. So much so that old Rabbi Simone, who was with me in the back of the shop, shook his head and said: "Just like us Hebrews! Always ready to worship idols. Yesterday they made fun of the cross and called Christ 'the little gallows bird' " — a joke in doubtful taste, in my opinion — "and today they admire it open-mouthed just because it's made of gold and studded with diamonds, rubies, sapphires, and I don't know what. It wouldn't take much to make them worship it. To think I might have lived to see that, Giacobbe — a cross worshiped like an idol, in a ghetto!"

When, having asked for and been granted an audience, I took the cross and presented it to the Pope, he was at the same time admiring and embarrassed.

"It is wonderful," he said, turning it over and over in his hands, which were slender and shapely, unlike his rugged countenance. "I am glad to see there are artists in the Roman ghetto as good as any in Florence. And the cross is sanctified by the kind feelings that inspired you and your brethren to think of such a gift and make it. So I accept it with pleasure as a token of the loyalty and gratitude of my subjects in the ghetto. I mean to go on protecting them from the malice of fanatics: they are hardworking, inventive, peaceful, law-abiding citizens, and contribute greatly to the prosperity of Rome and the Papal States. However, although I do accept your gift, Giacobbe, I must make it clear to you and your brethren that the leader of Christendom cannot wear a cross presented to him by subjects not themselves Christians. But it will remain in my family, and I shall bequeath it to my descendants."

Then he engaged me in the friendliest and easiest conversation about the improvements he'd made in the status of the Jews. Referring to the wearing of the yellow robe, he said: "If I had not been afraid of shocking my Christian subjects and the Catholic hierarchy too much, I would have abolished it altogether."

"Most Holy Father," I said, "you have done a lot for us in exempting us from wearing it when traveling. That's a great relief; in the past, it meant that all over Italy everyone thought they could charge us what they liked in inns and at tollgates, and even molest and rob us."

"Do you travel much, Giacobbe?"

"Twice a year. At the beginning of the summer and at the end of the year, I go to Brescia, Padua, and Venice on business."

"Brescia? That's interesting!" He said no more.

I reported this conversation to the ghetto, and was surprised to find the most fanatical among us somewhat cooler toward the Pope than before. On reading the bull *Christiana Pietas* more closely, they'd discovered that three times a year they were to be summoned to church, where the word of the Christian

607

God would be preached to them. Some of the more excitable said we shouldn't go. I could scarcely believe my ears when I heard such mad talk.

"You are a pack of hopeless idiots," I said. "You suffer from the strange disease of never being satisfied. For twenty-five years you've had a terrible time under two bad popes, and now that you've got a good one, you want to defy him. What does it matter if you have to sit in a Christian church and hear some parish priest talk nonsense about Christ? Are your souls going to be in danger just because your backsides are on benches worn out by generations of Gentiles? Are your Jewish asses better than Christian buttocks? Or is your faith in the God of Israel so fragile it collapses as soon as someone talks to you about Christ? Are you going to start worshiping Mary and the saints after half an hour of it? Do you know, you are worthy descendants of those who clamored for the death of Christ. Don't you realize that if he had not been crucified, no one would ever mention that gentle crank now? And we would not be branded as deicides."

That caused a fine row. Some yelled that Christ deserved to be killed, because he'd attacked the law of Moses even though he claimed to be defending it. There was no end to their resentment: they were still railing at

Christ for his teaching fifteen hundred years after his death!

Fortunately, Rabbi Simone intervened. He agreed with me, and said that those who disobeyed the summons to church would put the Jewish community in Rome in grave danger. He spoke in a sweet, quavering voice, looked at them with black eyes still shining and youthful in a face more wrinkled than an old apple. When he'd finished, no one had anything more to say.

This fracas was still echoing in my ears a week later, when the Pope summoned me to the Vatican. I went through the same side door and found the Pope sitting in the same small room, a little table on his left and the mute and motionless Monsignor — I knew now that his name was Rossellino — standing on his right. As usual, Sixtus cut short the formal exchange of greetings.

"Giacobbe," he said in his quick clear voice, "when are you thinking of going to the north this year?"

"In a fortnight's time, Most Holy Father."

"If you put your journey forward by a week, I could give you an escort of ten of my Swiss Guards, who will be going home on their annual leave — and I could entrust you with an errand."

"Most Holy Father," I said with a bow, "I

609

would be glad of the escort and honored by the errand."

"It won't take you far out of your way. If I remember rightly, your business will be taking you to Brescia? I want you to take this box and a letter from me to the Duchess of Bracciano, who is at present staying on the shore of Lake Garda. And would it be possible for you to take along a Jewish doctor who is expert at treating wounds?"

"Arquebus wounds, Most Holy Father?"

"No. Wounds caused by arrows. I suppose they're not all that different. The Duke of Bracciano was hit by an arrow a long time ago, and I am told that the wound has been getting worse."

"My friend Doctor Isacco is very competent in that field. He studied at the medical school in Salerno, and has translated Ambroise Paré's book on wounds into Latin. His translation, with his own annotations, is used all over the world."

"Do you think you can get him to go with you?"

"I think so, Most Holy Father."

The Pope looked pleased, and made a sign to Rossellino. I had noticed that, although the Monsignor was dumb, not deaf, the Pope often spoke to him in signs. I've been told he invented this language himself, so that his attendant could make himself understood to him. Rossellino immediately fetched a little silver casket from a table and handed it to me, with a sealed letter addressed to the Duchess of Bracciano, Sforza palace, Barbarano, Lake Garda. When I was leaving through the little door, I could tell by feeling the letter that it must contain the key to the casket.

My sons, my nephews, and I — eight of us in all — laid out some money for clothes for the journey, since it was to be made in such worthy company and to the gates of so great a prince. I also hired some good horses, and we hid a few stout pistols under their saddles: for Jews to carry them on their persons would have been considered too provocative. We had to think of the return journey, when we'd be without the Swiss Guards. There were ten of them, and their sergeant presented me with a safe-conduct drawn up in my name in complimentary terms and stamped with the papal seal. I have kept this precious relic, thinking that if the persecution ever starts again, it might be useful.

The worthy Swiss were with us for a fortnight. They were much the same age as my sons, but they took up about twice the space. They were big boys, brought up in the fresh air and on the fresh milk of their Swiss mountains, with bodies used to hard work since childhood. Whereas we Jews grow up pale and packed together in urban ghettos, forbidden to live in the country, let alone to buy land there. But to be fair, I must point out that the placid countenances of the Swiss lacked the subtle spark to be seen in the shining eyes of my own boys.

When we got to Salò, we were disappointed not to be able to see the lake. The hostess at the inn where we took our midday meal told us there was no hope of its clearing. The mist was usual at this time of the year, she said, and might last a whole month.

From Salò to Barbarano, the space between the shore and the hills narrows: the slopes grow steeper and leave less space for the road. After thirty minutes' ride, we saw to our right a building that, from the hostess's description, we took to be the Sforza palace. To make sure, however, I knocked at the door of a monastery perched on the hill on the other side of the road. Only the judas window opened in reply to my knock, and a Capuchin looked at me suspiciously, as if sensing that I was some kind of outcast. But when I'd shown him my safe-conduct and the papal seal, he relented and told me the building opposite was indeed the Sforza palace. I slipped a small offering through the bars — not because I wanted to, but because he seemed to expect it, and because, like all our people, I am rather afraid of priests. By way of thanks, he was good enough to open his thin lips again — they were like the salt in a collecting box — to tell me Admiral Sforza had finished building the palace only eight years ago. I might have guessed as much: the stone was still quite white.

The safe-conduct and papal seal worked a miracle at the palace too, but we had to wait while the servant fetched the majordomo, the only person who could order the drawbridge to be lowered. You could tell the place had been built by an admiral. It looked more like a fortress, with its long bare façade relieved by only a few narrow, heavily barred windows and a big square tower at each end. It was surrounded by a broad moat fed by water from the lake.

As soon as we'd been let in, the majordomo told me I'd have to be patient: the Prince and his wife had gone off in one of their galleasses to visit their friends in the castle at Sirmione, and would not be back until late in the afternoon. Seeing my surprise that anyone was able to navigate in that mist, with visibility no more than a quarter of a mile, he explained that the sailors on the lake took their bearings from the sun, the faint outline of which could always be glimpsed through the haze.

It wasn't until I followed the majordomo into the courtyard that I understood the overall plan of the palace. Behind each of the towers, there was a wing, stretching as far as the lake, and, by a curious arrangement, in between and parallel to the wings was a third, which also reached from the main building down to the water, dividing the courtyard in two. This part of the palace was gabled and had a balcony running along the second floor. The balcony, with the two glass doors opening onto it and the three vaulted arcades supporting it at ground level, was the only really elegant and imposing section of what was otherwise a rather uncouth building.

The arcades opened onto a square expanse from which a short flight of steps led down to a little harbor. I could see a boat moored there, a little galleass of the same type as those that acquitted themselves so well against the Turks at Lepanto. It had a space for the oarsmen, but instead of being left open it was covered by a deck from which sails could be manipulated.

I asked the majordomo if the vessel had been built here or brought from Venice. His reply was so long and confused that, what with trying to listen to him, the fatigue of the journey, and the discomfort I felt from the mist and its musty smell, I felt quite faint. I sat down on the steps and almost swooned away.

I could feel that someone — I could tell it was Isacco from the smell of him — was loosening my ruff, patting me on the cheeks, and trying to make me drink sugared water. At first it was hard to swallow, but soon I was drinking it greedily. I blinked, but couldn't open my eyes, and I could hear Isacco saying in his fine bass voice, probably to one of my sons: "Don't worry. He's very strong. He'll live to be a hundred."

My vision was clearing, and the first thing I saw properly was a row of six magnolia trees growing by the water's edge, to my right. They looked more like huge round bouquets than trees; their white flowers were delicately tinged with pink. I must have seen them as I entered the courtyard, but I couldn't remember them. Now, however, in my weakness, with my mind almost as misty as the lake, my thoughts fixed upon them with a pleasure that I wished would last forever.

"What are you looking at, Giuseppe?" asked Isacco.

"The magnolias."

He looked surprised. "Yes, I see," he said. "They grow all around the lake."

But speaking was too tiring. How could I explain that two minutes ago I'd felt as if I were dying, and now, looking at these magnificent bouquets, I was being reborn?

"They are all the beauty in the world," I said, with an effort.

Isacco guffawed. "You're a poet, Giuseppe!" he said. Then he added, with a mixture of indulgence and affection: "But you have to be, to create such beautiful jewelry."

Meanwhile, some servants had come with trays of refreshments. The majordomo must have ordered them in the belief that I'd fainted from hunger.

I realized wryly that this was the first time a Gentile had ever been so *gentile,* so kind, to me. It needed only Rusticucci to put a Christian kind of name on my safe-conduct, and the Pope to allow Jews to travel in ordinary clothes, for everyone to be friendly to me. Yet what's in a name, or in a coat? Isn't it always the same man underneath those fleeting rags?

Out of politeness to the majordomo, I made a pretense of eating, but my sons and nephews and Isacco fell to as if their midday meal was a distant memory. Isacco in particular was a hearty eater: in everything, he showed an appetite for life that seemed to belie the unfailing, though cheerfully voiced, pessimism of his words.

"My lord and lady are approaching," said the majordomo.

Everyone turned toward the lake, but all we could see was the white mist that two hundred yards away shrouded the landscape.

"I can't see anything," I said.

"If you listen, signore, you'll hear the sound of the oars. The wind has dropped, and they've abandoned the sails. It's the rowers who are bringing her in."

Yes, I could hear the regular beat of oars, and, on the return stroke, the creak of the oarlocks. Then suddenly the galleass burst through the mist like a ghost ship. Someone rapped out an order. The galleass seemed almost to stop. Then it coasted gently forward for a moment and veered in majestic silence into the little harbor. The oars were shipped simultaneously, and it slid smoothly to its mooring alongside its twin.

The Duchess, followed by a maid, came lightly down the gangplank, but I saw that the Duke had to be helped ashore by two of his gentlemen. The Duchess waited for him, smiling, though her great blue eyes were full of anxiety. It was the first time I'd seen this celebrated beauty; although my mind had been prepared for it by many descriptions, I knew they all fell far short of the truth. Behind her — and, as I afterward noted, inseparable from her — was her maid. In contrast with the mistress's golden look, the maid was as dark as a daughter of Israel, with bold black eyes and an ample bosom that made me lower my gaze, for even at my age I am only too easily attracted by such charms.

The majordomo went to the Prince and spoke to him sotto voce at some length, no doubt explaining who we were. He showed him my safe-conduct too, while we stood deferentially some distance away.

"Welcome, my friends," said the Prince, coming toward us. We all made a low bow.

At a sign from the majordomo, two servants brought a chair and placed it in front of the arcades of the central building. The Duke seated himself with the aid of his two gentlemen, one of whom was very handsome, a dark replica of the Duchess. We knew he must be the famous twin brother, who one day in broad daylight stabbed Lord Recanati to death in an open coach in Rome. A chair was brought for the Duchess too, but she refused it and placed a little stool at the Prince's feet instead. Then she sat down gracefully, bringing her long mane of hair around into her lap. The maid sat on a step behind her, taking advantage of the fact that her mistress couldn't see her to dart bold looks at our party, not excluding me. Signor Marcello, noticing this, started up the steps and in passing dealt her a sly little kick on the thigh, which made her grimace but not cry out. He sat down nonchalantly a couple of steps higher up.

"Master jeweler," began the Duke. He apparently didn't want to call me by my real name, which he knew well from having commissioned jewelry from me for his first wife. Nor did he want to use the Christian appellation written on the safe-conduct. "I'm surprised to see you so far from Rome, and curious as to the errand with which the Holy Father charged you."

I told him about the letter and the casket, and explained Isacco's presence.

"Master jeweler," said the Prince, a shade of sadness falling over his face, "pray give us what the Holy Father has sent. Vittoria," he went on gently, "perhaps you will wish to retire to your apartments, the more easily to read the letter and examine the contents of the casket."

"As you wish, my lord," said the Duchess, rising.

Then I gave the Prince the casket and the letter, which he put into Vittoria's hands with a tender glance and a smile that vanished as soon as she had gone up the steps, through the arcades, and into the palace, followed by her maid. As soon as they and their shimmering finery were gone — for the maid was scarcely less well dressed than the mistress —

the courtyard seemed duller and colder.

"Doctor," the Prince said then, looking at Isacco gravely, "please don't be offended at what I'm going to say. But I'm mortally weary of doctors and medicine, and I fear the word 'mortally' is only too appropriate. Fourteen years ago, at the Battle of Lepanto, I was wounded in the thigh by an arrow. The wound has troubled me almost ever since. I've consulted dozens and dozens of doctors, each more eminent than the last, but, not only have I not been cured, but also the wound has gotten worse and worse. Quite recently, at the request of my wife, the Duchess, two famous scholars came from Venice to examine it. They began by wondering what to call it. If I understood them correctly, they thought it important that it be called by the right name. They discussed it for an hour and then agreed to call it *lupa*, which is Latin for a female wolf. When I asked them why, they said, 'Because it devours the flesh around it'! 'An ingenious name,' I said, 'but how does it help me? What treatment do you propose?'

"One of them said they'd have to bleed me morning and evening, and when I asked why, he answered, 'When the water in a well is murky, you draw water out of it until it becomes clear: and the same with your blood, my lord. By bleeding, we draw the bad blood out of your body, and your wound will stop devouring you.' "

The Prince gave a bitter smile. He waited for Isacco to make some comment, but when he said nothing, went on: "I agreed to be bled morning and evening, but after a week of this treatment I felt much weaker and my wound wasn't any better. I concluded that the bleedings couldn't distinguish good blood from bad and were taking away the first and not the second. So I paid that physician and sent him back to Venice.

"But the second one was still there, and he was pleased to see the first go. 'You're quite right, my lord,' he said. 'He's an ignoramus, not to say a quack. He just uses whatever cure is fashionable for every case. Whereas my own treatment is always adapted to the circumstances.'

" 'And what is your treatment in these circumstances?' I asked.

" 'Apply a compress of raw meat to the wound every day. Then the *lupa* will have something else to eat and stop eating your leg.' "

"Did you try it?" asked Isacco, staring.

"I did, and the result was that after a week I was much worse. I deduced that the female wolf preferred my flesh to all other kinds of meat however appetizing, and sent my Hippocrates packing. And you, doctor," he said, looking at Isacco with a mixture of mistrust and hope, "what remedy do you suggest?"

"My lord," answered Isacco, "I cannot say until I have examined the wound."

"Very well," said the Prince. "As soon as the Duchess has retired for the night, I will show it to you."

Isacco had been given a room in the palace next to mine, and as soon as I heard him enter it after his consultation, at about eleven o'clock, I went in and asked him about it. He seemed in a bad humor, and said sourly, keeping his deep and sonorous voice low: "The trouble is, the Prince has been dealing with ignoramuses whose medicine is merely a matter of words and based only on metaphors. Bad blood like the murky water in a well! A wound like a wolf devouring flesh!"

"But even in the ghetto there are doctors who argue like that —"

"I know, I know! Who better? But the poor man has undergone so many ludicrous treatments that now, when the right one is suggested to him, he won't agree to it."

"What is the right one?"

"To cut the leg off before it's too late."

"He won't agree?"

"He absolutely refuses," said Isacco angrily. "He says he'd rather die than live mutilated."

"Naturally," I said. "Such a fine figure of a man. A hero. A prince. And in love, too!"

"What's that got to do with it?" said Isacco, who refused on principle to understand what he understood very well. "Would you agree to die rather than lose a leg?"

"I'm not married to the most beautiful woman in Rome."

"And what good would it do you if you were?" said Isacco, who was proud of his own fecundity and gave his wife a child a year, as well as putting the maids in the family way.

There was a pause.

"What can be done for the Prince, then?" I asked.

"Apart from amputation?"

"Yes."

"Nothing."

"So the outcome is bound to be fatal?"

"Yes. The summer that's just beginning will be his last."

"Oh, Isacco," I said reproachfully, "what a dreadful thing to say!"

This was too much for him.

"Damn your mawkishness, Giuseppe!" he roared. "Do you think I'm going to shed tears over him? He was born in a silver cradle with a golden rattle. He's had everything all his life: titles, wealth, fame, love! And now he's suffering the fate we all suffer. Gentile or Jew, we all come to it. No, don't say anything. Leave me now, Giuseppe, please. I'm tired. And I can't wait till tomorrow, when I can go home. I don't like this lake. I don't like the smell of it. I don't like the mist here. They say this is a miniature paradise, and maybe it is — if you can see it. Nor do I like this palace. How can anyone sleep under a ceiling that high? These people want us to think they're five or six times taller than we are. I'll tell you, I'll be glad to be back in my ghetto. And, above all, above all, I can't bear a patient who turns up his nose at living! If he'd been through what we've been through in Rome since the days of Pius V, maybe he'd be more eager to stay alive. What use am I, I'd like to know, if the patient himself isn't determined to cling to life for all he's worth?"

# 14

## *Prince Paolo Giordano Orsini, Duke of Bracciano*

I haven't much longer to live. I hope I'll show some courage in the time I have left, though in such circumstances courage is only another kind of vanity and doesn't change anything.

All my life I've known that one day it would have to end; but I never really believed it. At least, I believed it only halfheartedly, or perhaps I should say half-mindedly. And my first reaction, when death became certain, was to say to myself: "What? Is it really happening to me too? So soon?"

It's easy to understand that sort of incredulity. How can a thinking being imagine his thinking will cease?

Thank God I'm neither a philosopher nor a theologian. But now that I can't walk, I have time to think. And it seems to me human beings go to a lot of trouble to believe in a life after death. Yet how can they either rejoice in heaven or suffer in hell if their bodies and

625

minds no longer exist? Suppose I were damned: what would there be of me to burn if I didn't have a body any more? How would I know I was burning if my skull was empty?

Nothingness makes more sense. We did not exist before we were born, so why should we exist after we die?

I'll take care not to say this to my chaplain. He's a good man, but rather silly. He's still repeating what he learned when he was ten, and he's sure it must be true because he's been saying it for sixty years.

I don't want to upset him. And I don't want him to refuse me absolution. I want to avoid worrying or scandalizing the people around me. It's mainly for the sake of the people around them that men try to die according to the rules.

As regards heaven, we're pretty well taken care of in the Sforza palace. Behind us there is a monastery full of Capuchins, and on the island facing us there's a monastery full of Franciscans. I've handed out the largesse they expected of me, and in return they've promised to pray for my recovery, or, if that fails, for my salvation. How can I doubt that their prayers will be answered?

That Jewish doctor was the first one to tell me the truth about my situation — a truth I knew but had managed to hide from myself.

He was also the first who seemed sincerely anxious for me to survive. He looked very disappointed when I refused to let my leg be amputated.

I've seen that sort of operation performed more than once at sea. It is horrible butchery. Few people survive it. Those who do are wrecks, dragging themselves around on crutches, in pain for the rest of their lives from a limb that's no longer there. How could I inflict the sight of such degradation on Vittoria?

This morning I told her I was going to die. Until now, we had pretended that my difficulty was nothing serious. We each did our best to keep that myth alive. She was better at it than I was, perhaps because she believed in it more.

When I told her, she turned pale. After a moment, tears rolled silently down her face. I was lying on the bed, and she came and lay down too, and took my hand. We lay there side by side like effigies on a tomb. Just as that thought occurred to me, she said: "We look like effigies on a tomb."

"That's what I was thinking."

"I wish it were true. I wish I could go with you."

"Even so," I said, "we'd be separated. How could we see each other without eyes? Touch each other without hands? Kiss each other without lips?"

"Our souls, at least, would stay together."

I didn't answer, not wishing to undermine that belief if it comforted her. After a while, I said: "Vittoria, what is your happiest memory? I mean since we've been together."

"Before that," she said gravely, "I have no happy memories. With you, everything has been so wonderful, I can't choose."

She was silent for a moment or two; then she pressed my hand. "Perhaps the Villa Sorghini. Though I suffered terrible remorse, because I was committing adultery. And because I couldn't confess. A single word, and I'd have been locked up. I wept every evening. But the next morning, when I thought about our coming meeting, the chains fell from my heart and I was happy and carefree, as if I were dancing on mountaintops."

"I often think of the Villa Sorghini too. That white tent on the roof, right in the middle of Rome, and yet so far away from everything. We could see the geraniums through the white curtains, and the shadows of the swifts passing above us. I can still hear their shrill cries mingled with our sighing."

Vittoria was silent, and when I turned my head to look at her, I saw she was weeping again. I held her hand more tightly and said in a different tone of voice: "Vittoria, when it's over, I'd like you to go live in Padua. I've rented the Cavalli palace for you."

"Why Padua?" she asked, turning toward me, her immense blue eyes still shining with repressed tears.

"The Podesta of Padua is a friend of mine. He will protect you."

"Will I be in danger?"

"Yes. From the Medicis."

"Why?" she asked in astonishment.

"What else could motivate the Medicis except money?"

"What money? What harm have I done them?"

"This afternoon, two learned lawyers are coming from Padua to draw up my will. I am leaving all my property to Virginio, and to you, Vittoria, I am bequeathing a large sum of money, enough for you to live in a suitable manner."

"If that legacy is going to make the Medicis hate me, Paolo, don't make it."

"Vittoria," I answered, "can I leave the Duchess of Bracciano in want? Your share, large though it is, is only a tenth of what I'm leaving Virginio. He's not being unfairly treated. It's only the Medicis' greed that will make him think so."

"Oh, don't leave me anything, Paolo!" she

cried. "I have the valuable cross the Pope has given me. I can sell it and go back to Rome. I can live in the Rusticucci palace with my mother and Giulietta, under my uncle's protection."

"My love, first of all, you will offend Sixtus very much if you sell his cross. And, second, it would be very unwise of you to make yourself dependent on him. It's true he's very fond of you, but he manages his personal affairs the same way he rules the state — with a rod of iron. Didn't you suffer enough at Santa Maria under his tyranny? That's not the kind of future I want for you. I want you to live in Padua. When the Podesta as proved my will, and you have possession of your legacy, you can live free and independent and respected. In Rome, under the Pope's thumb, you'd never by anything but Francesco Peretti's widow. In Padua, you'll be the widow of the Duke of Bracciano."

"Oh, Paolo," she cried, "don't use the word 'widow'! I can't bear it! And, please, don't worry on my account. Of course I'll do anything you want. My life without yours will be nothing to me."

That afternoon, in answer to my urgent message, the lawyers Panizoli and Menochio arrived from Padua. I closeted myself with these gentlemen, Marcello, and my majordomo, and dictated my last wishes for them to draw up in legal form. I left all my property, both at Bracciano and at Montegiordano, to my son, Virginio; and to my wife, Vittoria, Duchess of Bracciano, I left the sum of one hundred thousand piasters, the jewels I had given her, and the furniture, hangings, and carpets I brought with me to the Sforza palace.

When the will had been drawn up, it was signed and witnessed by the two lawyers, Marcello, and my majordomo. At my request, a copy was made by the same scribe and signed by the same witnesses. One copy was to be given by the two lawyers to the Podesta in Padua; I gave the second to Marcello, knowing it would be safe in his brotherly hands.

This cost me great effort, and I felt tired when the lawyers had gone, taking with them my thanks and a fee that surpassed their hopes. I needed to have a few words with Marcello.

"Dear friend," I said, "you must take good care of Vittoria, immediately after my death especially. She has said she would like to come with me."

"I heard her."

"Were you listening at the door?"

"I always listen at the door when Vittoria is concerned. The best way to be careful is to be well informed. And you, my lord, do you think you're taking good care of her by making that will?"

"I'm providing for her future."

"You could provide for her future in other ways. For example, by giving her, directly, your collection of jewelry."

"I do not have it any more. I pledged it, when I left Rome, to pay my debts."

"To whom, my lord?"

"Giuseppe Giacobbe."

"Who's he?"

"The jeweler you saw here with the doctor who wanted to take off my leg."

"Is he so rich?"

"Not he himself, but the ghetto is."

"Hence this unfortunate will."

"Why 'unfortunate'?"

"Because it's as if you were giving the Medicis a loaded pistol."

"It is a loaded pistol, but I'm giving it to Vittoria."

"She won't know how to use it. She's too good, too generous. The Medicis will shoot first."

"They wouldn't do such a thing! Not in Padua, a city that belongs to Venice."

"You're right, my lord. They won't do it. They'll get someone else to."

"Lodovico?"

"Who else? The Medicis themselves won't

say anything or write anything. They won't even see him. They'll stay in the background and pull the strings."

"Well, get in before them. Kill him!"

"I've thought about that, but it's not so easy. He's always surrounded by his band. Oh, my lord, what on earth possessed you — paying your debts!"

"An Orsini always pays his debts."

"Unless his name's Lodovico. My lord, I also don't think you've done the right thing in renting a palace for Vittoria in Padua. She'd be safer in Rome under her uncle's wing, I think. Everyone's afraid of his beak and his talons."

"In Padua she'll be protected by the Podesta."

"Not so closely. The Venetians are like the Medicis: they're merchants, men of compromise, who don't mind compromising their consciences too."

"Marcello, you do make me wonder if I've done right. But if Vittoria went to Rome, Sixtus would leave her almost no freedom. What am I to think? What am I to do? How can I see into the future when I have so little future myself?"

## Marcello Accoramboni

When the Jewish doctor left at the end of May, the Prince was sure he had only two or three weeks to live. But several months went by without any further change. I mean without any improvement or any appreciable deterioration. He had great reserves of strength, and although he was sometimes in great pain, he looked like someone withstanding a siege and determined never to surrender.

Strangely, although he alluded almost every day to his approaching end, his remarks seemed somehow propitiatory, as if he were trying to disarm death by talking about it. For that reason, and not wanting to seem to take his references to the fatal issue seriously, I didn't mention our disagreement over his will.

Moreover, my opinion on the matter had grown less clear-cut. On reflection, I thought the Padua decision might, after all, be better than my Roman alternative. The latter involved great risks for both Vittoria and me. For her, it might mean, at the worst, being sent to a convent to expiate her adultery. For me, it could mean the scaffold for having killed Recanati. True, Gregory had pardoned me for

the murder, but I'd heard that Sixtus was re-
viewing his predecessor's "pardons" and,
every day, sending people to the gallows
who'd forgotten all about their crimes.

Since the Prince's health remained stable,
the summer was not so bad as we'd feared,
especially because it was warm and sunny, and
almost without mist.

The Prince had made a little beach beside
the harbor by having cartloads of sand
dumped, half on the land and half in the
water. He'd had the area fenced in on three
sides so Vittoria could bathe there unseen. He
liked to be carried down to the beach to watch
her swimming, clad only in her mane of hair.
She was a good swimmer and went in the water
alone; Caterina, who thought cold water unhealthy, wouldn't so much as dip her toe in.
As for me, I splashed around in the lake in
the morning, not wanting to spoil the Prince's
pleasure by joining Vittoria in the afternoon.
I kept him company by the water's edge,
where we played checkers, though he spent
most of the time watching Vittoria's splendid
white body gleaming in the waves, her long
hair streaming out around her. Behind us,
where the Capuchins were, the sun would go
down. In front of us, to the northeast, when
the weather was clear, we could see the eternal
snows of Mount Baldo, hardly distinguishable

from the little white clouds that floated high in the sky and seemed so happy to be free. Looking up at them, I realized why lakes, however beautiful, are so melancholy: it's because the water is imprisoned.

In the morning, Paolo and Vittoria went for a sail in one of the galleasses. Although the Prince had to lie down, and there was a helmsman, he liked to give orders, as in the days when he scoured the Adriatic for Barbary pirates: it gave him an illusion of action. I don't know if Vittoria enjoyed these cruises as much as he did, but she was glad to see him interested and amused. Since he'd become unable to walk, she'd been more maternal toward him. While taking care not to overwhelm him with solicitude, she enveloped him in her affection.

I must say women are very good at coiling themselves around a man, either to stifle or to pamper him. They're like ivy; they've got little pads with which they cling to a person. Margherita Sorghini wrote to me every day after I left Rome, telling me how much she missed me. And, to tell the truth, despite the comforts Caterina supplied, I missed her too.

I liked her mature charms. For me, there was still nothing to compare with a beauty whose beauty was fading. Love had become an art and a religion to her. She was consumed by a passion to please, and that made her attractive. As soon as I wrote that I missed her, Margherita rushed north and rented a little house at Salò, on the shore of our lake. After the midday meal, when Vittoria and Paolo had gone to their room for a siesta, I had my horse saddled and galloped to Salo to spend an hour with Margherita.

One day I asked her: "What do you do with the rest of your day, my love?"

"I wait for you."

"Do you think I deserve so much? After all, as the Pope rightly said, when he was still only Montalto, there's not much to be said for me. I'm a liar, selfish, lazy, hard-hearted, and I exploit you ruthlessly."

"You're not hard-hearted. And I love you as you are."

"I've forbidden you to say you love me."

"All right — I don't love you," she said with a slow and ravishing smile.

I could feel the little ivy suckers sticking all over me. At first, it used to worry me, but finally I decided they weren't dangerous. I considered love to be an illusion born of desire and pleasure. Man, the only mammal with enough wit to make love whenever he chooses, couldn't help feeling some affection for the female concerned. And she, naturally, felt some affection too, because in most cases he

637

protected and provided for her. And that was all there was to it.

When I said this to Margherita, she objected strongly, despite her anxiety not to displease me. "It may be true of what you feel for me, but it's certainly not true of what I feel for you! I . . ."

She stopped herself in time, and, with the nimbleness I so much admire in women, skipped to safer ground. "For example, you adore Vittoria."

I shrugged. "That's different. Vittoria is the same as myself."

I brushed her lips with a kiss, but she insisted on coming with me to the stable where my mare was waiting. I vaulted into the saddle, and her eyes sent me a kiss, and another when she went to the gate to watch me ride away.

I'd be happy to see her again the next day, but I was happy to leave her now. Her kind of love is burdensome. I told myself yet again, as I rode home, that the best way to be happy with a woman is not to live with her.

Living under the same roof as Caterina, meanwhile, was becoming a problem. Of course she'd found out about Margherita's being at Salò, and made scenes that I didn't know how to deal with. If I scolded her, she just laughed. If I beat her, she complained that I didn't slap her nearly as hard or as often as Il Mancino did. She actually liked being beaten: she liked bursting into tears, repenting, throwing herself at my feet, and begging me with heaving bosom to "rape and kill" her. How can you control a woman who converts everything into pleasure, even her own chastisement?

Vittoria, though grieved by the thought of losing the love of her life, yet managed to be concerned about other people. One day she said to me: "Why don't you love anyone, Marcello?"

I didn't answer, so she went on: "And why don't you do anything? A man ought to have an aim in life."

I still didn't reply, but I thought: What sort of aim? Love? What a joke! Money? It only enslaves those who serve it. Fame? An empty echo! Ah, Vittoria, I wouldn't tell you so for anything in the world, but in ten years' time who will remember that the Prince fought so bravely at Lepanto? And in a hundred years' time, who will even remember Lepanto?

In November, everything took a turn for the worse. The mist came back over the lake, thicker than ever, and was dispelled only by a fierce east wind known in those parts as the vinessa. It brought cold and rain and storms. With incredible speed, the lake, which a minute before had been quite calm, was suddenly whipped into foaming waves that smashed down the fences around the little beach and covered its sand with silt. The moorings of the galleasses had to be strengthened and the smaller vessels moved into the moat; break-waters were built to protect the palace. There was no more bathing or sailing. Soon it was impossible even to stay on the balcony, because of the spray. At first, the Prince enjoyed the spectacle of the storm, which we watched from the arcades. But after the tempest had been raging for some days, he was tired of it, probably looking back with regret to the times he had stood on the deck of his galley braving the squalls of the Adriatic.

The sun vanished behind a ceiling of black and gray clouds. When the storm abated, rain took over, falling in slanting gusts. Everything grew depressing and damp and moldy. The waters of the lake, so clear in summer, grew murky, with yellow streaks here and there. It smelled musty, almost nauseating. The vinessa blew all day and made the windows rattle all night.

After we were forced to retreat inside the house and light the fires, and the Prince was deprived of his excursions on the lake and the pleasure of watching Vittoria bathe, his health rapidly declined. Curiously, his appetite wasn't affected. He ate and drank as usual — that is, copiously and fast. According to Caterina, his siestas were as active as ever. But his mood had changed. He was withdrawn, spoke little, and for long periods remained apathetic and languid. Sometimes his eyes were dull, and only brightened when they lighted on Vittoria.

Never before had he gazed at her so much or so intensely. It was as if her beauty had become the only thing that linked him to life. Yet even in his state of weakness and dependence, he was never selfish, and he insisted that she resume her daily rides alone, because the exercise did her good.

At her request, I kept the Prince company while she was out. Most of the time, at least when opium brought some respite to his suffering, he drowsed, or even slept, his head resting on his shoulder.

One day — it was November 12, if I remember rightly — he suddenly awoke with a loud cry.

"Aziza! Aziza!"

Then he saw me there, became fully conscious and said hoarsely, like someone speaking after a long silence: "Marcello, do you remember Aziza?"

"Your little Moorish slave girl? The one who wore a stiletto in her belt?"

"Do you know what happened to her?"

"No, my lord."

"The night I freed Vittoria from Sant' Angelo, Aziza plunged her stiletto into her own heart."

"Out of jealousy?"

"No. She left a note telling me she was going, not out of hatred or resentment, but because she was no longer of any use. That's what we all ought to do: go when we're no longer of any use."

I was inclined to agree with him, but I didn't say so. It was clear he had considered suicide. Otherwise, why did he keep a loaded pistol on the table by his bed? If he hadn't yet decided to use it, that was no doubt because he knew all too well that suspicion would fall on Vittoria.

He went on quietly, his eyes half closed. "I've just been dreaming about Aziza. I was alone at night in dense forest, absolutely lost. I was dragging my bad leg along. I was very thirsty and very worried. Then suddenly a path appeared through the trees, and along it came an open carriage drawn by four horses. Aziza was sitting in it in her best blue gown, wearing all her jewelry, just as she did on the day she killed herself.

" 'Come, get in!' she said. 'I'll give you a lift!'

"She helped me in. I could feel her hand on my arm. It was strong, with fingers like steel that sank into my flesh. I wondered if this could be the little Aziza who used to melt in my arms?

"The carriage swept us along at a furious pace. The road opened through the trees in front of us and then closed behind us, cutting off retreat. I could see Aziza only in fits and starts: her face was alternately lighted and in shadow as the moon was revealed or hidden by the trees. She turned to me and smiled. Her smile was sweet and affectionate when she was in the shade, menacing when she was in the light. But I felt reassured by the thud of the horses' hooves and the tinkling of the bells on their harness.

" 'Where are you taking me, Aziza?'

" 'Look at the coachman and you'll see.'

"But there was no coachman, and I could no longer hear the hooves or the bells. The carriage sped on as fast as ever, but I couldn't see anything, because we were enveloped in a thick mist. Then I guessed, from the sound of lapping waves, that we were now sailing over the lake, though there wasn't a breath of air to fill the sails, or any beating of oars. I was alone on the galleass with Aziza. She kept looking at me with an enigmatic smile.

"I asked again: 'Where are you taking me, Aziza?'

" 'Look at the helmsman and you'll see!'

"But there was no helmsman. The tiller was swinging idly back and forth. I made desperate efforts to get up and reach it, but I couldn't stand.

"Then I woke up. . . . Give me something to drink, Marcello."

He was pale and seemed exhausted from having talked for so long. At that moment, Vittoria came in from her ride, looking splendid, with tousled hair, bright eyes, and rosy cheeks. He made an effort and managed to smile, even to exchange a few words with her.

"My love, why don't you go to your room and dress for the evening meal? I'll sleep a little. When you're ready, don't hesitate to wake me to show me how beautiful you are."

He had strength enough to smile again, but as soon as she'd left the room, he lost consciousness. I called the majordomo, and we succeeded in getting a few drops of wine into him and reviving him. I had him carried upstairs and laid on his bed. There he summoned enough strength to forbid us to undress him: he didn't want to frighten Vittoria.

The wind and rain had stopped, so I went out on the balcony, pulling the door to behind me. I breathed deeply. The mist was back, but the air was warm and still. I liked the Prince's company, but the presence of death, an invisible third party, was beginning to depress me. I'd always thought my life wouldn't be a long one, and I wasn't much interested in it anyway. But I'd rather live what remained to me without that continual weight on my heart.

I stayed outside for a good half hour. I tried to remember a Petrarch sonnet that Vittoria had done her best to teach me when we were in our teens. I managed to conjure up a few lines and tried to fit them together. I got almost all of it and kept at it, pleased with what I'd done, vexed at what I couldn't do, and sure the missing parts were the best.

There wasn't a sound, not even, on the sunset-tinted lake, the beat of an oar. Then I heard a loud cry behind me. I turned and pushed open the door. Vittoria, in all her finery, was lying across the Prince's breast, shrieking like one who'd gone mad. One glance was enough. He was dead.

Though I loathe touching or being touched, I put my hand on Vittoria's shoulder. She shook me off fiercely. Then suddenly her piercing cries ceased. She rose to her full height, dry-eyed, seized the loaded pistol from the table, and put it to her temple. I was quick enough to grab her wrist and turn the barrel aside. The gun went off, and the bullet struck the ceiling, bringing down scraps of plaster that fell on the Prince's doublet, making white patches on the black velvet. Vittoria stood there, her eyes blank. I took the pistol out of her clenched hand. After a moment, she leaned her brow on my shoulder, put her arms around me, and wept. I was trembling from head to foot at the thought that I might not have been there, or might have acted a second too late. What would I have been without Vittoria? A creature half living, or half dead?

## Giordano Baldoni, Majordomo to Prince Orsini

The very morning after my master's death, the Duchess was good enough to say that if I had no other plans, she'd be glad to keep me on in her service. I at once agreed to stay, not mentioning that in fact I'd intended to retire to my native city, Genoa, and devote the rest of my life to my children. But seeing her so young and helpless and surrounded by dangers, with no family to defend her but her brother — the bravest of young men, certainly, but very inexperienced — I decided to remain in her employ at least until she entered into peaceful possession of her inheritance from the Prince.

Fearing she might not have enough money to pay and maintain all her late husband's soldiers, she wanted to dismiss most of them, but I prevailed on her to keep at least a score of the trustiest, most experienced, and most noble among them, as behooved the dignity of her household. And I arranged for us to move to the Cavalli palace in Padua with the least possible delay.

To tell the truth, we'd have been safer in the Sforza palace, with its drawbridge and moat and towers, than in an urban mansion lacking all such defenses. It was difficult to tell in advance whether this lack would be counterbalanced by the fact that we'd be near the Podesta and the city officers. When we got to Padua, and I checked the palace, I found that some of the ground-floor windows could easily be broken and used for entry. I decided at once to have bars put in them. But because it was near Christmas, which the good folk of Padua start preparing for a fortnight beforehand, the work couldn't be started immediately.

We hadn't been in Padua a week when the Duchess received a note from Lodovico Orsini, Count of Oppedo, asking to see her. Signor Marcello thought we should shut our door to him without even deigning to answer, but when I was consulted, I advised replying politely and saying there was no point in such a meeting. The Duchess decided otherwise. In his note, the Count had presented himself as the emissary of Prince Virginio, and she didn't want to offend the new Duke of Bracciano by refusing.

I must admit that Lodovico Orsini — bandit, murderer, and gallows bird that he was — proved to be very attractive. In face, figure, and gait, he bore some resemblance to the Prince, though the likeness was belied by the falseness of his expression. He was wearing an elegant doublet slashed with yellow, and had draped a corner of the skirt of his coat over his left arm, as gallants do in Rome. He made his way across the main hall in the Cavalli palace with his head held as high as is the Blessed Sacrament, and when he reached the Duchess, he swept her an apparently respectful bow. Then he began a funeral oration in praise of her late husband couched in terms designed to win her goodwill. And it succeeded in doing so, though to my mind his speech was pure hypocrisy. You could tell by the contradiction between the warmth of his words and the coldness of his eyes.

After purring and sheathing his claws for half an hour, he finally showed them.

"Madam," he said, "my cousin the late Duke of Bracciano had some silver plate that belongs to me, and I would like to have it back."

The Duchess looked at me inquiringly.

"That is so, my lady," I said, "but the plate was the pledge for a debt his lordship the Count contracted to the Prince that has never been repaid."

"Since the Prince is dead," said the Count, "it's obvious that the debt is canceled."

"It's not obvious at all," said Signor Marcello, entering the room. Then he went on, neither greeting nor looking at the Count: "The opposite is the case. Since the debt has never been paid, it counts as a claim outstanding in favor of the Prince's heirs — in other words, of Prince Virginio and of you, Vittoria."

"Precisely," said Lodovico. "Prince Virginio has commissioned me to come and defend his interests. Here's a letter to prove it."

He held it out to the Duchess, who read it and passed it to her brother. He read it and passed it to me. In fact, it was very vague, and didn't define at all clearly the powers delegated to the Count.

"Count Lodovico," said the Duchess, "this is what I have decided. I agree to give your silver plate back to you without your repaying the debt. I do this out of pure courtesy, and because of the family bonds between you and my late husband."

"Vittoria, you don't owe the Count anything," said Signor Marcello curtly.

His tone must have displeased the Duchess, for she said in a manner that brooked no reply: "My mind is made up."

"My lady," I said, "since the claim the plate represents pertains jointly to both you and Prince Virginio, if you hand it over to the Count, you must ask him for a receipt to cover you vis-à-vis Prince Virginio."

"A receipt!" cried the Count, turning crimson with anger. "You'd ask a gentleman for a receipt as if he were a merchant?"

"It strikes me as quite natural," said the Duchess calmly. "And the plate will only be given back to you on that condition."

"Madam," said the Count, through clenched teeth, "it's clear you grew up in a different world from mine. Otherwise you would not talk of receipts. My word of honor would be enough for you."

"Vittoria," Marcello said, with the utmost calm, "instead of being thanked for your excessive generosity, you are being scorned and insulted. You have only to say the word, and I'll put a couple of inches of steel in this boor's belly."

For the first time, I noticed that, before joining us, Marcello had taken care to buckle on his sword and dagger.

"*You* are insulting *me,* you wretch!" cried the Count. "And you think you can do it with impunity. You know very well you're too basely born for me to cross swords with you."

"You're quite right," Marcello drawled insolently. "I know. I know that rather than risk your own skin, you usually prefer to hire some henchman to murder a man in the street."

With this allusion to the murder of the Duchess's first husband, the Count turned from red to white, and, despite what he'd just said, his hand went to the hilt of his sword.

"I am mistress here," said the Duchess firmly, "and I order this quarrel to cease at once. Marcello, please be quiet. And you, sir, if you address another uncivil word to me, I shall order my servants to show you out."

"Madam," said the Count, managing to make his low bow show a touch of mockery, "I submit entirely to your wishes, and since you attach such importance to it, I'll sign a receipt."

The impertinence in his bow and the feigned respect in his voice must have vexed the Duchess. She said coldly: "Baldoni, please fetch the Count's plate."

Then, with the briefest of nods to the intruder, she began to walk toward the door.

"Madam," said the Count, the mockery scarcely concealed beneath the politeness, "I beg you won't deprive me so soon of your charming company. For, as Prince Virginio's proxy, I have other requests to make."

"Very well, sir. I will hear you," said the Duchess.

But she and Marcello retired to the other end of the room, leaving the Count the benefit of the bright fire burning in the fireplace that damp, cold December afternoon. With the pretext of warming his hands at the flames, he turned his back on his hostess. The only person he had with him was a secretary; I had requested him to leave his escort at the palace gate.

I left the room to carry out the Duchess's order, and used the opportunity to take a few precautions. Having noticed that the Count's escort was armed, I now armed our own soldiers and asked them to station themselves in a room adjoining the main hall. I returned to the latter with four sturdy footmen, whom I got to move a long table from beside the wall to the middle of the room. This was ostensibly for the plate, but my real intention was to divide the room, putting at least that obstacle between the potential adversaries. Then I had the plate brought in, and the footmen laid it out on the table. Though perhaps I ought not to say so, I was sorry the Duchess had so easily handed it over to a bandit who wasn't even grateful. The service was made up of beautiful pieces exquisitely chased, and it was worth a fortune.

"That's more like it, madam," said the Count.

This struck me as very meager thanks for such a large present.

"And here's the receipt, Count," I said, holding it out across the table. "All you have to do is sign."

He took it as if absentmindedly, ignoring the goose quill I was offering.

"Madam," he said, "Prince Virginio is very anxious that I should make an inventory of all the jewels that were in Prince Orsini's possession when he died."

"Have them brought, Baldoni," said the Duchess.

Despite its weight, I fetched the casket myself. I handed the Duchess the key, and she opened it. One by one, and not without emotion, she took out her dead husband's jewels and laid them on the marble table.

"What? Is this all?" said the Count, raising his eyebrows. "There aren't very many. I've seen my cousin's collection with my own eyes, and it used to be one of the finest in Rome, comparable to those of Gregory and Cardinal de' Medici!"

"The Prince," I said, "pledged his collection to pay his debts before he left Rome. What you see here are his personal jewels."

"He pledged his collection?" snarled the Count. "Strange that I should come to hear of it like this! Where's the proof?"

"Madam," I said, not looking at the Count, "the Prince's collection was pledged in the presence of the lawyer Frasconi, of Rome, and two witnesses. The transaction was recorded in writing and signed; the lawyer has kept a copy."

"You hear, sir?" said the Duchess.

"I hear, madam," said the Count, "but what I hear is very different from what I see. For instance, you are wearing a magnificent cross, which looks surprised to be on your bosom, for as a present to you from the Prince it ought to be on this table."

"It belongs to me personally!" cried the Duchess angrily. "It was a present from my uncle, Sixtus V."

"What's to prove it?"

"My word proves it. And if that doesn't satisfy you, the letter that came with the gift may."

"In any case," Marcello said, "all the jewels

the Prince gave to his wife while he was alive are part of his bequest to her. It's down in black and white in his will."

"So there's a will!" exclaimed the Count, and this time his disappointment wasn't feigned.

But it lasted only a moment. Then his face resumed the mask of polite insolence that had so exasperated the Duchess from the beginning.

"Madam," he said, "as Prince Virginio's proxy I must ask you to let me see the will."

"I don't think that is necessary," Marcello said, without looking at him. "A copy will be sent to Prince Virginio as soon as the will's been proved by the Podesta."

Again, rightly or wrongly — wrongly, in my opinion — the Duchess differed from her brother. It was probably because she wanted to show proper deference toward her late husband's son. But there I think she was being too scrupulous; whereas Prince Virginio, entrusting his interests to this unsavory blusterer, was not being scrupulous enough. It would have been a pleasure for me to put a couple of inches of steel in the impudent fellow's guts.

"Baldoni," she said, "please bring me the will."

Instead of leaving the room by the door on

the right, I went out by the one on the left, so I could tell the soldiers in the next room to burst in with drawn swords if they heard me clap my hands. Those of them who were gentlemen not only wore swords but also carried small arquebuses. Their eyes flashed when I told them the Count had been insolent and threatening toward the Duchess. She could certainly count on them. All her servants were very attached to her. They admired her for her beauty and loved her for the goodness of her heart. I shared these feelings, but with a slight difference. I say, with all possible respect, that I consider she had two small faults: she was naïve and obstinate. Because she was naïve she sometimes made unwise decisions, and because she was obstinate she stuck to them through thick and thin.

She provided a striking example of this when I returned with the will. As I handed it to her, I whispered: "Read it out yourself, madam. Do not let him get his hands on it."

Marcello heard this warning, and repeated it in her other ear. But in vain.

"If the Count wants to read the will, Baldoni," she said, "let him read it. We have nothing to hide."

So with heavy heart I had to hand the precious document to him across the table. Grabbing it and shamelessly sitting down, although the Duchess hadn't given him permission to, he started to read it. I guessed the scoundrel took Prince Virginio's interests so much to heart because he thought it in his own interest to defend them. The young Prince must have made promises to him, and the Count must also have hoped for the chance to exercise his natural talent for theft and plunder. Hadn't he already managed, by abusing the Duchess's generosity, to get her to hand over the silver plate he'd pledged to us a year ago for fifty thousand piasters?

"Madam," he said at last, standing up, "there's a legal term here I don't understand. Please allow me to consult one of my men, who's a clerk."

Immediately, without waiting for the permission he'd asked for, he whispered something to his secretary and sent him off. Soon I heard a great commotion, and a footman rushed in.

"Madam," he panted, "the Count's escort is forcing its way in!"

"Goodness," said the Count, with ironic calm. "Perhaps they think I'm in danger."

"And so you may be, now," said Marcello, drawing his sword.

I clapped my hands and unsheathed mine too. Our soldiers burst in, swords in hand, and lined up behind the table on which the plate and jewels lay. Those with arquebuses posted themselves between the ends of the table and the two side walls. All this took place in silence, but a few seconds later the Count's escort made a tumultuous appearance. When they saw the soldiers, they halted, realizing they were facing professionals and that it was no use making threats they couldn't carry out.

The Count stood and called loudly: "Madam, I am convinced this will is false — as false as your marriage, which Gregory XIII annulled! As false as the title you trick yourself out in!"

He whirled around and threw the will on the fire. Then, facing us again, he drew his sword and dagger. "Gentlemen," he said, turning toward his escort, "this plate and these jewels are mine. Take them away."

"My lady Duchess," said one of our gentlemen armed with an arquebus, "this fellow speaks too lightly. Will you allow me to put some lead in his brain?"

"No, sir," said the Duchess. "As for you, Count," she went on, "you may take the plate, since I was weak enough to give it to you. But you will not touch the jewels."

"Take no notice, gentlemen!" said the Count, laughing. "She's mad! She's only giving me what's mine. Pay no attention to her."

Two of the bandits put out their hands to

take the jewels. But they drew them back again quickly, covered with blood. Our men's swords made a formidable curtain over the jewels. They didn't attempt to defend the plate, so the bandits, as they fell back, took that with them.

"Count," said Marcello scathingly, "I propose a bargain. You and I will fight one another, and if you kill me, you take the jewels."

"You'll do nothing of the sort, Marcello," said the Duchess, taking him by the arm. "My orders alone are to be obeyed here. Count," she went on, "my majordomo has sent for the Bargello, and I advise you to leave before he arrives."

"If you don't want to escape the fate of your brother Raimondo," added one of our gentlemen.

"I'll make you pay for that," said the Count with a scowl.

"Now, if you like," replied the gentleman. But the Count and his bandits were already at the door, and he seemed in no hurry for a fair fight against an opponent as well born as he was.

As soon as the last bandit had left the room, I vaulted over the table, rushed to the fire, and tried to retrieve the will with the tongs. I did manage to get it out, but it was half burned, especially the part that contained the signatures. As the Duchess came up to me, gazing with horror at the shriveled, blackened pages, I told her not to despair; there was a copy. On the Prince's instructions, the lawyers who drew it up had taken this copy from the Sforza palace to the Podesta in Padua.

The Duchess and Lord Marcello retired to a smaller room and asked me to bring them some wine. A lively discussion followed, and I heard Marcello criticize the Duchess severely for the way she'd handled the affair. First of all, she should never have agreed to see Lodovico. Second, it was sheer folly to make him a present of the pledge we held. It would only encourage him to make further demands.

"There's no need for you to handle him so carefully, with all the things we know against him. Nor do you have to show Prince Virginio so much consideration, since he chooses an envoy like that to extort more than he has any right to."

It seemed to me that the Duchess knew Marcello was right, but she resented his criticism and wouldn't let him say more.

However, she did follow the advice he gave her immediately afterward.

When the Bargello of Padua arrived with his men, a good hour after I'd sent for them — a delay that showed he had no desire to confront the Count and his band — the

Duchess told him of her complaints against Lodovico. She also gave him a letter for the Podesta in which she'd written them down. She wrote and immediately sent off a similar letter to Sixtus V.

When the Podesta read the letter, he found himself in some difficulty: she'd presented a problem too big for him. Not knowing what to do, he passed it on to Venice, where they also procrastinated.

The Most Serene Republic knew all about Lodovico: the Pope had asked for his extradition on the first day of his reign. But behind Lodovico was Prince Virginio, and behind him the Medicis and the Grand Duchy of Tuscany. Venice didn't want to antagonize a power of that magnitude over a matter that didn't affect any of its own vital interests.

Instead of summoning Lodovico and ordering him and his band to leave Padua immediately, all the Venetian authorities did was to send courteous remonstrances through the Podesta. Lodovico listened politely and laughed up his sleeve. The Doge had made the same mistake as the Duchess, but he didn't have the excuse of naïveté.

Ten days later, Venice received a letter from the Pope complaining vehemently about the way Lodovico had treated his niece. The Doge and the Senate came up with a rough-and-ready solution. They placated the Pope by ratifying the will that the Duke of Bracciano had made in his wife's favor. The Podesta, therefore, didn't order Lodovico to leave Padua.

As to what happened after that, I'm not in a position to say. I had to go to Rome for my father's funeral, and didn't get back to Padua until after Christmas.

## Caterina Acquaviva

Everything that happened was my fault, all my fault, and it's my firm intention, as soon as I can, to go into a nunnery and spend the rest of my days in prayer and fasting to ask God's forgiveness. But I don't think prayer and fasting will do any good. Deep down in my heart, I'll always be tortured by remorse. The only thing I'm sure of is that it will only end with my life. When I think of what I used to be like — so cheerful and happy and pleased by men — and of what I'm like now — weeping day and night, or eating my heart out over my memories — I'm sure I won't suffer any more than I do now, even in hell being consumed by the flames I richly deserve.

In explaining how it all came about, I'll have

to stop every so often: whenever I think of the old days and how happy I was then, I can't hold back my tears.

Well, the treacherous way Lodovico burned the will and tried to get possession of the Prince's jewels by force made my mistress angry and alarmed Marcello. From that time on, the Cavalli palace was closely guarded day and night, and so was Vittoria. Whether she liked it or not, she was accompanied by a large armed escort whenever she left the house. She and her brother had arguments about this every day. She was too good and too innocent to believe Lodovico would kill her if he got the chance.

"What?" she'd say. "You don't mean he'd murder me just to save Prince Virginio a hundred thousand piasters, do you?"

"And for your jewels. You really ought not to wear them."

"I don't wear them out of vanity."

That's what it is to be a great lady. If I said a thing like that, who'd take it seriously? If I wore her uncle's cross, with Christ's feet almost touching the top of my nice soft bosom, I'd burst with pride. As a matter of fact, I actually tried it on one day when I was alone, in front of her mirror.

"I don't wear them out of vanity," she repeated, "but because each one brings back a memory."

Yes, but not always a happy one. That cross, for instance, could have reminded her only of the Prince's last days.

The arguments started again when the Podesta proved the will.

"Well," she said, "we've won! Lodovico can't do anything to me now."

"Not legally — no," Marcello said. "But on the practical level he still has daggers and guns. Your death would wipe out the will."

"Oh, Marcello," she cried, "you're being dramatic. Kill me here in Padua, a stone's throw from the Podesta, who's so well disposed toward me?"

"Not so well disposed as to banish Lodovico from the city."

"Suppose Lodovico did murder me," she said, laughing at such an idea, "wouldn't his obvious interest in my death point him out at once as the murderer?"

"Certainly! But it would have to be proved. And even if it was proved, and he was put to death, that wouldn't bring *you* back to life."

A week later, to her amazement, she received a letter from Lodovico asking her to see him. I was there when she read it out to Marcello.

Prince Virginio had complained that when his father left Rome, he'd taken the best horses from his estate with him. He now asked the signora to give back all or some of them. According to the will, the signora inherited all the furniture, but he didn't think horses counted as furniture.

"And he calls me signora!" she said angrily. "He doesn't even use my title. In his view, my marriage is null and void. Well, he won't get anything. Not one horse! Not even a mule!"

"Vittoria," said Marcello, "it's not at all certain the horses can be considered as furniture. It might be wise to give Lodovico at least a few of them to send to Prince Virginio."

"What?" she cried. "I can hardly believe my ears. Can it be you telling me this? You, who advised me not to give him his silver plate."

"This is a different matter altogether. The plate was undoubtedly yours. But it's not certain the horses are. Besides, it would be unwise to let Lodovico go away empty-handed. That would make him lose face with Virginio, and a man of his temperament won't put up with that."

"Let him lose his treacherous face!" she cried. "You've reproached me often enough for handling him carefully. Well, I've learned my lesson."

And she wrote an angry note to the Count,

in which she refused either to give him the horses or to see him. Marcello looked over her shoulder as she wrote.

" 'Our first meeting,' " he read out loud, " 'was not such as to make me wish to repeat the experience.' Vittoria, you're not going to send him this. It's insulting! It's like waving a red rag at a bull. He'll be furious. Let me write to him — more politely."

"Certainly not! I'm the one he's written to, and I'm the one who's going to reply."

I agreed wholeheartedly with Marcello, but I took care not to say so. Vittoria had always been rather quick-tempered, but after she was widowed she grew much worse. She flared up like tinder, and, once alight, was as difficult as tinder to put out. The fact was, the Prince's death had left a terrible void in her life. She missed him as a husband, as a companion, and also as a man. Poor Signor Peretti had a heart of gold, but that was about all. Vittoria had absolutely blossomed with the Prince. From the time of the Villa Sorghini on, she was a different woman. Radiant! If I'm to believe what I'm told, the Prince was an extraordinary lover almost to the day he died. I used to dream about him myself sometimes. Of course, every rose must have a thorn, and in the long run Vittoria would have realized that the thorn in this case was that she herself couldn't have a child. Poor Peretti — to think how she and I used to blame him.

But what's the use of talking about the future? It's been blotted out now. I don't like to say it, but Vittoria was losing her grip. She thought her beauty had declined and her life was over. And it affected her temper. Mine wasn't what it used to be either, since Marcello wouldn't have anything more to do with me. So Vittoria and I were both bundles of nerves. And, since she was the mistress, the air was thick with "idiot" and "impudent chit" and even, occasionally, slaps. And the reconciliations, the cuddles and kisses didn't come as quickly as they used to. The worst was the tears. She was always more or less on the brink of them, poor thing. And whose arms could she weep in but mine? You can't see anyone unburdening themselves on Tarquinia's or Giulietta's bosom! After the Prince died, they wrote and asked if they should come and stay with us in Padua. But Vittoria flatly refused. I think she was right!

It was my own fault about Marcello. I never stopped making scenes at the Sforza palace after I found out he was going to see Signora Sorghini at Salò every afternoon. It's the absolute truth that, when I found out about it, I was beside myself with rage, and if there'd been a dagger handy I'd have stabbed the wretch. As it was, he got more of my tongue than he'd bargained for.

"How disgraceful! How disgusting! The old leech! Following you here just to cling and suck your good red blood. And you let her! I must say you're not fussy. That old crone! Old enough to be your mother. All those wrinkles. Those varicose veins. Those sagging breasts."

"Her figure's perfect, you stupid slut," he would say, "and you can take this for not showing her more respect."

He'd throw himself on me, push me over, and beat me. I'd moan and groan, but it wasn't all suffering, because I managed to undo his aglet. So it wasn't too bad an arrangement: I'd insult his old woman, he'd beat me, and then he'd possess me. It was a habit that had its advantages. But in the end he got tired of it. That's men for you! You think you've worked out a little system with them, and they suddenly cut their moorings and sail away, leaving you high and dry.

It was because of the break with Marcello that the Alfredo business started. The wretch followed me in the streets of Padua and had the cheek to speak to me — me, a maid in a noble household! You can imagine how I'd have boxed his ears if I hadn't been feeling so humiliated and rejected. Especially since he wasn't much to look at, with his rugged face and tiny eyes. His only attraction was his strength, and that hit you right in the eye. Neck and shoulders like a bull's. In short, he was the sort of man who comes to seem good-looking if he gives you pleasure.

I did repulse him the first time he came up to me. And the second time. But he sensed that the second refusal was less inflexible, so he followed me to the church of the Eremites and leaned against a pillar while I was praying. Being in Padua, I might have prayed to St. Anthony and asked him to help me find my lost lover again, but I preferred to pray to the Virgin. She was more likely to understand a woman's sufferings. I asked her to touch Marcello's stony heart and soften it toward me.

All the time, behind my back, I could feel Alfredo's presence and the warmth it generated. When I'd finished praying, I let him speak to me.

He told me his name and said he was squire to a great nobleman, but he spoke very poor Italian; it was mixed with Venetian dialect. At first I found him ridiculous, but as he was speaking he got hold of my left wrist and squeezed it, and after that I forgot his faults. Later on, I won't say where, I let him do as he wished — and as I wished too. So that's what happened with Alfredo. It's not something to be proud of, and I'd rather cut both my legs off than do it again.

At the Cavalli palace, the soldiers still kept a close watch on the Duchess, indoors and out. Majordomo Baldoni saw to that. He'd been with the Prince longer than anyone else; everyone respected him, and when he gave an order, they jumped to it.

After his rebuff over the horses, Count Lodovico was expected to issue more threats and even offer more violence, but nothing happened. He bowed quite respectfully to my mistress once when he passed her at a distance in the street. Marcello was beginning to feel reassured. Then the majordomo left us to go to his father's funeral in Rome, and discipline grew slack among servants and soldiers, probably because it would soon be Christmas, and a festive atmosphere reigned in Padua.

There was great relief in the palace when, in the morning on December 24, the Bargello came and told us that Lodovico and his band of outlaws had left Padua in the early hours for Venice, to take part in the magnificent Christmas celebrations in the republic.

"Are you sure they've gone, Signor Bargello?" asked Marcello.

"Quite sure. Don't worry — it wasn't a false exit. I had them followed, and they really took the road to Venice. What's more, I've doubled the night guard at the Venice gate, so I'll be warned immediately if they come back during the night. You can rest easy, over the holidays at least."

After the Bargello had gone, the news spread among our soldiers, and the most senior man asked the Duchess if, in the circumstances, they could go to the Podesta's ball that evening. They were delighted when, ignoring Marcello's advice, she agreed; they'd led an austere life since they'd been in Padua. They were to be back in time to escort her to early Mass in the morning. She didn't want to attend midnight Mass, because it would be very crowded and probably noisy too, since wine would flow freely from nightfall on.

The men begged Marcello to go with them to the ball, but he refused, preferring to spend Christmas Eve with his sister. I was glad about this at first. Even though he wouldn't speak to me, I'd at least have the pleasure of seeing him. They sent for musicians, who played and sang Christmas songs for part of the evening. Since Marcello and Vittoria had dressed up just to spend the evening alone at the palace, I did the same. And Marcello deigned to pay me a little compliment on my gown, apparently forgetting he'd seen his sister wearing it a year ago. I was overjoyed, and, fool that

I am, my imagination immediately ran away with me, and I saw myself back in his arms again. Why not? That night, when Vittoria had gone to bed . . . But my happiness was shortlived. At about eleven o'clock a courier brought Marcello a note.

"It's from Margherita," he said. "She wasn't able to go to the Podesta's ball. She's not well, and she wants me to come and see her. I don't know though. My place this Christmas Eve is with you, Vittoria."

"Oh, no. Do go, Marcello," she said, without a moment's hesitation. "Margherita must feel very lonely here in a strange city amid all the rejoicing. Anyway, I'm rather tired and I won't sit up any longer."

The wretch didn't need telling twice. He buckled on sword and dagger, stuck a couple of pistols in his belt, and set off as fast as he could, accompanied by two servants, also armed. You'd have thought he couldn't wait to get to that bloodsucker's bedside. She was supposed to be ill, but no doubt she was waiting for him all painted and dressed up. Oh, I'd have stabbed the pair of them if some devil had been able to fly me there. The worst of it was I had to put a good face on it while I undressed Vittoria and brushed her interminable hair.

Then I went to my room, where I undressed

and put on my nightgown, trying not to cry. The fact that I wanted to made me angrier. The sight of my empty bed was unbearable, so I paced up and down with my fists clenched, grinding my teeth, and railing at the two wretches whose embraces I couldn't help imagining.

I was about to draw my curtains when a stone hit one of the windowpanes, though not hard enough to break it. Thinking it was some drunk, I opened the casement to tell him off. When I leaned out, I recognized Alfredo standing there in the bright moonlight, looking up at me.

"Let me in, Caterina," he said. "I've brought you a Christmas present."

"How can I let you in?" I said. "There's a porter on duty, and he'll never open the door, even if I beg him. He has strict orders not to."

"There's a little ground-floor window that's not barred. I can get in through there if you'll let me."

"Certainly not! What would the signora say if she knew?"

"She won't know. I'll only stay long enough to give you this pretty ring and a hug."

"Ring?" I cried. "What sort of ring?"

"A gold ring with a sapphire and some little diamonds. I spent all my savings on it."

I was touched by the ring and by his kind thought, not to mention his broad shoulders and bull-like neck. Holy Mother, I was going to be able to pay Marcello back! I was going to put another man in the bed where he had lorded it.

In my nightgown, I went down and opened the window. It was no easy matter. There was a heavy wooden shutter that I had to use both hands to unhook. Then I had to draw back the bolts, and that was difficult too: the window was in a little scullery, where nobody ever went, and they had rusted.

When I finally got it open, Alfredo was through in a flash, out of the moonlight into the dark.

"We can't stay here," I said.

"What?" he whispered. "Don't you want to see your present?"

"Come on, Alfredo! I can look at it in my room. There's a candle there."

"It shines so bright," he said with a laugh, "you won't need a candle."

Pretending to rummage in his doublet with his left hand, he gave me such a terrible blow on the back of the neck with his right that I fell to the floor at his feet.

It must have been some time before I came to. I had a gag in my mouth, and my hands were tied behind my back with a cord. Alfredo had hold of the end of it, and after a moment I could feel him pulling me to my feet.

"So far so good, my beauty!" he said. "I've stabbed the porter and opened the door, and my friends are all inside. Now march, you strumpet! The best part of the show is going to take place on the next floor, and I don't want to miss it."

He drove me up the stairs in front of him, jerking me by the cord now and then.

We were overtaken by two soldiers, one wearing a hood and the other a mask. Both were carrying bloody daggers.

"Why is this slut still alive?" asked the man in the mask. "We've killed the rest. You know our orders."

"This is my little sweetheart." Alfredo laughed. "She let me in, and she's going to stay alive a little longer than the others. I'm saving her for last."

The men laughed too and bounded up the stairs ahead of us, so fast they must have been very young. I wondered why they still had their daggers in their hands; from what they'd said, they didn't need them any more. Perhaps they wanted to show off to their friends.

I was still half stunned. My mind was so numb I wasn't afraid. I saw everything as if it didn't concern me.

Upstairs, about thirty masked soldiers were

trying to get into Vittoria's room. Alfredo, cursing and swearing, pushed me in front of him and forced a way through. "What's this slut doing alive?" several yelled. Others grabbed at my breasts. None of them pitied me. As far as they were concerned, I was as good as dead. They reeked of wine and sweat and leather. I could breathe better when Alfredo pushed me out in front of them, to a small circle, in the middle of which stood Vittoria in her sky-blue nightgown, her hair hanging down around her. She'd probably just risen from her prie-dieu, interrupted at her evening prayers. She held herself upright and dignified despite her scanty attire. Facing her was a tall man in a mask.

"Madam," he said, "I'm sorry to disturb you at your prayers, but, thanks to us, you're going to rise from this prie-dieu straight to heaven."

The taunt didn't ruffle her calm. Casting her great blue eyes over the thirty or so soldiers crowding around, some standing on her bed to get a better view, she said: "Do you really need so many men to kill a defenseless woman?"

The man made no reply. Either he couldn't think of one or he felt a pang of shame.

"You, sir, who are you?" she asked. "And what harm have I done you?"

"My name will mean nothing to you, madam," he said. "But because you won't be in a position to repeat it, I'll tell you I'm Count Paganello. It's not me you've wronged, but my friend Count Lodovico Orsini."

"I have not wronged the Count," she declared firmly. "I have merely defended my legitimate interests."

"Maybe, madam. But we've talked long enough," Paganello said. "The time has come to act."

He seized the neck of her nightgown and ripped it to the waist. As her breasts were revealed, the soldiers let out a gasp of satisfaction. Paganello stepped back to contemplate his handiwork. Vittoria clutched the torn material over her bosom with both hands, looked at him with flashing eyes, and said, almost in a tone of command: "Kill me if you must, but I will not die unclothed."

Her look and tone must have had some effect on Paganello. Instead of tearing off her nightgown, as he and the soldiers no doubt would have liked, he drew his dagger as if he was now in a hurry.

Vittoria saw this and demanded: "First, let me have a confessor."

"I'm the only confessor here," said a Franciscan friar, with his hood pulled over his face.

"Father!" she cried, starting toward him in a burst of hope.

But the Franciscan moved forward into the circle and pulled back his hood. It was Count Lodovico.

"You?" she cried in horror. "Well," she continued imperiously, "kill me, and spare me both your presence and your words."

"I could still spare your life, signora," said Lodovico. "On one condition."

"It's bound to be ignoble, coming from you," she said haughtily. "I do not wish to hear it."

"You will anyway. You have to choose between death and me."

"I would never choose you."

"Comrades," said Lodovico, turning to the soldiers, "you heard her. Of her own free will, she chooses death."

The soldiers remained silent. I think they were beginning to admire my mistress's courage. Lodovico must have sensed this too. He went up to her and grabbed her nightgown. She offered no resistance; she just looked at him with scorn. When she was naked, she pulled her long hair around in front of her body.

Lodovico drew his dagger.

"Help me, Paganello," he said hoarsely.

Paganello knew what was expected of him

and pulled her hair behind her back. Lodovico put his hand around her waist and grabbed her left arm. Drawing her close, he locked her right arm against his shoulder. Then he plunged his dagger below her left breast, but only halfway. He turned the blade back and forth in the wound and asked if he was giving her pleasure. Vittoria groaned; her eyes half closed. As her groans grew fainter, Lodovico drove the dagger in to the hilt and cried: "This time at least, madam, I touch your heart!"

My dear mistress turned her head toward him, opened her eyes wide, and murmured, before she died, *"Nel nome di Gesù, vi perdono!* In Jesus' name, I forgive you."

## Baldassare Tondini, Podesta of Padua

Shortly before midnight, on Christmas Eve of 1585, a girl in a nightdress covered with blood banged on the Bargello's door. She told him the Duchess of Bracciano had just been murdered, and all her household except her brother, Marcello Accoramboni, and two servants, who were at the house of Margherita Sorghini.

The girl said she was Caterina Acquaviva,

age twenty-nine, and she had been in the Duchess's service for more than ten years.

She was very agitated, weeping and expressing herself in a confused manner. She accused Count Lodovico Orsini of the murders, whereas we knew he had left that very morning, with all his doubtful friends, for Venice. The Bargello therefore thought she was deranged. But seeing that her gown was covered with blood and her wrists bore traces of having been bound, as she alleged, he decided to take a dozen or so men and go see what had happened.

He found that it was as Caterina Acquaviva had said, and sent word to me, discreetly, as I presided over the ball I give every Christmas Eve in the town hall. I went to the scene at once, and was appalled at the audacity of the massacre. It had been perpetrated only a gunshot away from my palace, and against a person of high rank — one, what's more, whom His Holiness Pope Sixtus V regarded as his niece. Without waiting to refer the matter to Venice, I ordered the Bargello to carry out an inquiry with the utmost speed, sparing no one.

On the second floor of the Cavalli palace, the Bargello identified the corpse of Alfredo Colombani, squire to Count Lodovico. Caterina Acquaviva declared that after forcing her to watch her mistress's murder, he took her to her own room, untied her hands, undressed her, and tried to rape her. She was able to unfasten the dagger he wore, Italian-fashion, behind his back, and drove it with all her might into his left shoulder blade. He let out a shriek and tried to strangle her, but she stuck her fingers in his eyes and managed to slip away from him. She plucked the dagger out of the wound and stabbed him again and again, all over his body — "like a fury," was her expression. She said she did it partly to avenge her mistress and partly because Alfredo had said he would stab her as soon as he had had his way with her.

According to her, he got into the palace through the window of a scullery on the ground floor, overpowered her, stabbed the porter, and let in the rest of the band.

Asked why the window was unlocked, she said she didn't know. The Bargello was unable to clear up the point. When she was asked why all the maids had been killed except her, she said Alfredo had probably taken a fancy to her; he had told the rest he was "saving her till last." This struck us as plausible, because the witness was a comely wench and, though rather common, might pass for pretty in certain circles.

After a systematic search of the house, it

became clear that the intruders had carried off all the jewelry, the late Prince's as well as that belonging to the Duchess, including a splendid gold pectoral cross set with precious stones that was given to her by her uncle, Pope Sixtus.

Various indications showed there had been a large number of intruders, and we guessed that Count Lodovico and his band might have returned to Padua during the night. We checked the city gates and found, to our surprise, that, whereas the guards at the Venice gate were awake and alert, those at the southern gate were still fast asleep, after drinking wine that had been tampered with. Examination of the ground around the southern gate, and in particular the road leading to Stra, showed that the verges had been trampled, suggesting that a considerable number of horses had been left there during the night.

The still-fresh hoof marks and the stupor of the guards spoke for themselves. The Bargello sent an experienced spy to look around Stra. He reported that Lodovico and his band had feasted in a well-known inn there the previous evening. It is only a few leagues from Stra to Padua: a good horse could cover the distance twice in a night.

It did not escape either the Bargello or me that, although the presumptions against

Lodovico were strong, the evidence was weak. It consisted solely of the word of one witness, which Lodovico could easily challenge by saying, "How could the crazy girl have seen us in Padua when we were feasting in Stra?"

We decided to let it be understood that our inquiry had come to no conclusion. Count Lodovico no doubt had friends with their ear to the ground in Padua. When they told him he was not under suspicion, he would probably return to the Contarini palace, which he had rented for three months.

We had to make sure neither Caterina Acquaviva nor Marcello Accoramboni gave the game away. The Bargello, who was a widower, was kind enough to take the girl into his service, and he impressed on her that she must hold her tongue. Marcello was in no state to talk. When he had seen his sister's corpse, he had tried to stab himself in the heart, but the leather doublet he was wearing deflected the blade, giving him only a deep gash. It was serious enough to keep him in bed at Signora Sorghini's villa with a high fever.

Our plan worked perfectly. Count Lodovico was back in Padua two days later, more arrogant than ever, and flaunting his Roman nobility. This did not impress the citizens of the Most Serene Republic, though, either in Venice or in Padua.

His palace and his comings and goings were kept under constant surveillance day and night. We thus discovered that he was short of money and owed rent; that he had had dealings with Giuseppe Giacobbe, a master jeweler who visited Padua two or three times a year. Before we had summoned him, Giacobbe asked the Bargello for a private interview. The Bargello told me this, and we decided he should come to the Bargello's house at ten o'clock at night. He turned up with three of his sons and three of his nephews, who seemed to hold him in great respect and waited for him, without saying a word, in the anteroom. If only my own children were as well behaved as those Jews!

Giacobbe began by showing me his Roman passport, signed by Cardinal Secretary of State Rusticucci. We realized from the Christian name attributed to him in this document that, despite his religion, he enjoyed the protection of the present Pope. What followed confirmed it. Giacobbe told us that to thank the Holy Father for the measures he had taken in favor of the Jewish community in Rome, the ghetto had commissioned him to make a valuable pectoral cross. The Pope had accepted the gift but said that, though he could not wear it himself, he would keep it in his family. A few weeks later, he had asked Giacobbe to take it to his niece, the Duchess of Bracciano, in the Sforza palace on Lake Garda. Now, to Giacobbe's surprise, Count Lodovico had, that very morning, given him the cross as a pledge for a loan of twenty thousand piasters. The Count did not know, of course, that he, Giacobbe, had made the cross and knew its history.

The jeweler brought out from among his robes the same cross that the Bargello and I had admired on the Duchess's bosom when she first came to Padua. He laid it carefully on the table, and we all gazed at it in silence. You would need to have a heart of stone not to marvel at its beauty, and at the same time not to be moved by the tragic end of the woman who had worn it. We sent someone to wake Caterina Acquaviva, to see if she recognized the cross and could testify that it really had belonged to her mistress. The maid appeared, only half awake and less than half dressed. As soon as she saw the cross, she cried, "My God! My God! My poor mistress!" and burst into sobs. The Bargello considered this proof enough, and kindly sent her back to bed. By the way he looked at her as she left the room, I concluded it was not just out of kindness that he had taken her in.

Giacobbe produced a document signed by Lodovico Orsini, Count of Oppedo, declaring that he had given a pectoral cross belonging to him — followed by a detailed description of the article — to Giuseppe Giacobbe, jeweler, as pledge for a loan of twenty thousand piasters. Giacobbe was prepared to give us this document in exchange for a written promise, signed by me, that the city of Padua would return the twenty thousand piasters to him should Count Lodovico be unable to do so. I wrote and signed the required paper and let Giacobbe go, promising, at his request, that I would not act against the Count until the jeweler left the city. He and his sons and nephews did at dawn the next day.

I then had all the city gates closed, and summoned Count Lodovico to appear in court. He came with all his band, and when our men tried to keep all of them out but him, they forced their way in. The forty or so, all armed, were separated from me and the other judges by only the dais and the long bench behind which we sat.

I whispered to the Bargello to get as many men as he could find and post them in the room behind me, but not to intervene unless I gave two strokes with my gavel. I did wonder, however, what kind of resistance our fellows could put up against such determined scoundrels. I decided that in the circumstances I would question the

Count as unprovocatively as possible.

He was extremely arrogant from the outset. Before I had opened my mouth, he declared it was outrageous for one of his rank to be subjected to interrogation. It was an intolerable affront, he said, to treat him as a suspect, almost as the accused, in a matter that was none of his affair.

"Signor Count," I said in the mildest of voices, "you are not appearing as the accused — only as a witness.

"Could you please tell me what your squire Alfredo Colombani was doing in the Cavalli palace at the time of the massacre?"

"From what I've heard, he was having an affair with a maid there. That's why he didn't go with us to Venice."

"Have you ever seen this maid, Count?"

"No."

"She claims to have seen you, and Count Paganello, in the Cavalli palace on the night of the massacre."

"She's crazy."

"Perhaps. I have been told that you and your friends, instead of going to Venice, stopped and feasted that night in an inn at Stra, not far from here."

"That's right. Is that a crime?"

"Not at all, Count. I have also been informed that the Duchess of Bracciano's pectoral cross has been seen in the hands of a Jewish jeweler. Do you know anything about it?"

"Absolutely nothing."

"That is a pity, because the jeweler has run away, and we are looking for him."

"I hope you find him."

"Thank you, Count. That is all. You and your friends are free to withdraw."

"Am I free to leave the city?"

"Not yet, Count. The gates have been shut on orders from Venice, and they cannot be opened without further instructions from there."

"Can I at least send a courier to take this letter to Prince Virginio Orsini in Florence?"

"Yes, Count. On condition that you tell me what it says."

"Here it is," he said scornfully, giving it to one of his men to pass to me.

I read it carefully. It was so completely innocuous it aroused my suspicions.

"Count," I said, "please write down the name of your courier, and I will give orders for him to be let through."

He complied. As soon as he had left, I sent the Bargello to give our men two precise orders: first, let the courier through; second, stop him a league outside the city and thoroughly search both him and his horse, not forgetting the saddle.

The search, which the Bargello supervised personally, produced the results I had hoped for. The letter I had read was found in the courier's doublet. In his right boot, there was another, briefer but not nearly so harmless.

To Lord Virginio Orsini:

Most illustrious lord, I have carried out that which we agreed upon. I have been under some suspicion, but have outwitted the Podesta and am now regarded as the cleverest gentleman in the world.

I did the job myself. Send me men and money. I am destitute.

Your devoted servant and cousin,

Lodovico Orsini

"I did the job myself." He was boasting about it, the wretch. The more I studied the letter, the more I was struck by Lodovico's baseness and stupidity. Why did he write it when he knew he was under suspicion? He had only reinforced that suspicion by saying he knew about Alfredo's affair with a maid in the palace. And the fool preened himself on having got the better of me!

Armed with this irrefutable evidence, I gave

orders for the militia to surround the Contarini palace and cover it with all the artillery we possessed. Then I sent a courier to Venice with a copy of the incriminating letter. At seven the next evening, the most illustrious Avogador Bragadina arrived from the republic with orders to capture all the miscreants, dead or alive.

When those besieged inside the palace refused to capitulate, we used the cannon, the walls collapsed, and Lodovico had to surrender.

He did so in his own peculiar way — in other words, like a bad actor striving for effect. He appeared alone in the doorway of the ruined palace, somberly dressed, with a dagger at his side and the skirt of his coat thrown elegantly over his arm.

He was taken to the town hall, and relieved of his dagger. I found him leaning nonchalantly against a pillar, trimming his nails with a small pair of scissors. When he saw me, he dropped this affected pose. He put the scissors away in his doublet, gave me the bow required by my importance, apologized politely for putting me to so much trouble, and asked me to have him put somewhere appropriate to his rank. He later declared himself dissatisfied with the cell he was given. Then he asked for writing materials, and wrote a long letter

690

to the Venetian Republic requesting, as a count, a prince, and an Orsini, that he be spared the indignity of public torture. His wish was granted. He was strangled in his cell in accordance with all the legal forms, and with a cord of red silk.

In his last moments, he acted with studied bravado. You would have thought he was wearing a mask and buskins and performing on a stage. I felt like tearing the mask off to see if there was anything behind it: probably a terrified boy afraid to die.

His air of haughty self-assurance wavered for only a second. I had asked Marcello Accoramboni if he wanted to be present at the execution of his sister's murderer, and, to my great surprise, ill though he was, he said he did. He arrived leaning on two servants and looking pale and wan, as Count Lodovico was condescendingly pretending to do whatever the executioner required.

"Is this right, sir? Am I in the right position for you?"

I asked Accoramboni if he wanted to say anything to the condemned man.

"Yes," he whispered.

Fixing his feverish eyes on the Count, he said in a weak but audible voice: "Signor Count, I regard you as the most odious vermin God ever allowed to crawl over the face of the earth. But because my sister forgave you, I forgive you too."

The Count turned pale and opened his mouth to speak, but changed his mind. Maybe he did not want to detract from the decorum of his end. He turned to the executioner and said, with an affable smile: "I am ready, sir."

The executioner put the red cord around his neck. As he was tightening it, Lodovico murmured, *"Gesù, Gesù, Gesù."* He had probably planned this beforehand, to lend some dignity to his exit, though he had been so evil a Christian his whole life long.

The cord broke, but he had already fainted, and the executioner was able to apply another one without his regaining consciousness. When the Bargello rebuked the executioner for having twisted the tourniquet too fast, the man said: "I'm sorry, Signor Bargello, but I wanted to get it over with. Him and his airs and graces!"

With three exceptions, Lodovico's thirty-four men were put to various kinds of torture. The judges decided on this, against my wishes, to satisfy the populace.

About half of the ruffians had already been dispatched when the executioner asked the Bargello for two days' rest.

"Rest?" asked the Bargello. "What for?"

"Forgive me if I offend you, Signor Bar-

692

gello," the man said, hanging his head, "but I'm tired of all the blood. So are the people. They booed me yesterday."

So the judges met and decided to make do with hanging the rest. But it took them a long time to make up their minds, and while they were still deliberating, one of the condemned men, the majordomo Filenfi, managed to prove that he could not have taken part in the massacre at the Cavalli palace, because he was in Venice that night on his master's business. His reprieve arrived as he was standing on the scaffold with the noose around his neck.

I would like to say a word about the two survivors: Marcello Accoramboni and Caterina Acquaviva.

Marcello was a changed man after he recovered from his wound. He renounced his aristocratic pretensions, gave up wearing sword and dagger, and married Margherita Sorghini. He performed his religious duties devoutly and regularly. And he worked — something he'd never done before. With a loan from his wife, he followed in his grandfather's footsteps and set up a majolica factory in Padua. Since there were no competitors, he prospered, and soon became one of our leading citizens. There is still something strange about him that makes him less popular than his virtues and perseverance deserve. He is very taciturn, his eyes are blank, and he never smiles.

As for Caterina Acquaviva, when she first went to live in the Bargello's house, she talked quite seriously of going into a convent. This surprised everyone, for she did not seem the right kind of person. The Bargello must have been very persuasive, however, because she remained in his service. Gossips predicted she would bring dishonor into his house, but they were wrong. She looked after the place well and was an exemplary mother to their children.

The cross that the Pope had given his niece was returned to him at his request. He paid Giuseppe Giacobbe, out of his own pocket, the twenty thousand piasters he had lent Count Lodovico. Some people in Rome said the Pope was being too honest, considering the lender in question was only a Jew. But others, including myself, think Sixtus was right. If the head of Christendom does not set a good example, who will?

Not only in Venice and Rome, but also throughout Italy, I was thought to have handled the inquiry into this unfortunate affair with skill and prudence. But in Padua, even in the council, some people criticized me for not having banished Lodovico after he burned the will. I soon reduced these troublemakers to silence by reading out a copy of the letter

I had sent to Venice the day after that incident, asking for Lodovico to be banished. I also read out the reply, in which Venice rejected my request, for perfectly valid reasons. When the same troublemakers then criticized Venice, I ordered them to hold their tongues, and my firmness on this occasion was universally applauded.

My term as chief magistrate of Padua expires in three months, but I do not think I will have any difficulty in being reelected. I do not know whether to be glad or sorry: much as I appreciate the esteem my fellow-citizens so loyally demonstrate, I do sometimes weary of the burdens of power.

The unfortunate affair we have been examining teaches some lessons that might be regarded as remarkable if they were not so remarkably ambiguous.

The legacy by which Prince Orsini meant to assure his young wife's future cost her her life. Count Lodovico, whose crime aimed at gaining favor and money from Prince Virginio, got only death for his pains, and that less than a week after slaying an innocent young woman whom he despised because she was not of noble birth. But what does the word "noble" mean when applied to a creature as base as the Count?

If "justice was done" as regards Lodovico,

one cannot help regretting that the same justice was so negligent when it came to Prince Virginio, who was shown by Lodovico's secret letter to be his accomplice and the instigator of the murder. Even if the Venetian Republic had taken the right decision and summoned the young Prince, then sixteen, to appear in its courts, would it have had the power to make him do so, given that he was living in another sovereign state and was the nephew of the Grand Duke of Tuscany?

What happened immediately after the Duchess's death is no less a matter for astonishment to a perspicacious observer.

When dawn broke after the massacre at the Cavalli palace, the Duchess's naked corpse was displayed on a table in the church of the Eremites, and the mob flocked to see it. Her youth and beauty, as well as her reputation for kindness and piety, called forth their tears. One witness said some of them gnashed their teeth. They cried out for vengeance. So many people came to see her that the Bargello had to send some of his men to organize lines. Then everyone could file past to contemplate, admire, and pity her — and to pity Padua too for having lost the most beautiful woman in Italy.

At about eleven o'clock, the priest in charge of the church, shocked by this pagan adoration, brought a black cloth embroidered with gold to cover the Duchess's nakedness. But the people snatched it from him, almost accusing him of sacrilege. The priest and the adepts of this new religion started to argue so heatedly the Bargello's men had to intervene and impose a compromise. The Duchess's body would not be covered, but for decency's sake it would be wrapped in her long golden hair. It was expressly forbidden for anyone to cut off a lock of it as they went by, as some had secretly managed to do earlier.

The fact that the Duchess, as she was dying, had forgiven her murderer became public. Thenceforward she was regarded as a saint. Instead of supplanting the worship of her beauty, this only supplemented it. One woman genuflected when she reached the body, then made the sign of the cross and kissed the dead feet. All those who came after did the same.

The priest was very upset. Not daring to confront so determined a crowd, he came to see me and, with tears running down his face, implored me to put a stop to this scandal.

I went to the church and saw that the Duchess had indeed become the object of a fervent half-pagan, half-Christain worship. It seemed obvious that it would cause great offense if anyone approached her without genuflecting and kissing her feet, so, not wishing either to acquiesce in the ritual or to arouse the hatred of the crowd, I kept well away. I decided the best thing to do was wait until dark and then have the body removed on he pretext of having it embalmed. After that, I lost no time in giving it decent burial.

A few days later, there were new developments. The victim's mother, Tarquinia Accoramboni, wrote me asking for permission to take her daughter's body back to Rome. Despite all my precautions to keep this letter secret, a rumor of it leaked out, and masses of people crowded the town hall declaring in the most vehement terms that the Duchess's grave must stay in Padua.

I reassured them, quaking inwardly lest Sixtus V add his demand to that of Signora Accoramboni. If he did, I would have to refer it to Venice, and the decision would be out of my hands. Fortunately, the Pope did not intervene, and, with the support of Marcello, who, once he had decided to go on living, wanted to settle in our city, I was able to refuse the mother's request.

So the people of Padua still have Signora Vittoria's grave, and faithfully every spring cover it with flowers. Perhaps their children will remember her tragic story. But their grandchildren? And their grandchildren's children? One day the grave will be forgotten. And another day will come when even the lovely Vittoria's name will have vanished from the stone that shelters her dust.

THORNDIKE PRESS hopes you have enjoyed this Large Print book. All our Large Print titles are designed for easy reading, and all our books are made to last. Other Thorndike Large Print books are available at your library, through selected bookstores, or directly from the publisher. For more information about current and upcoming titles, please call or mail your name and address to:

THORNDIKE PRESS
PO Box 159
Thorndike, Maine 04986
800/223-6121
207/948-2962